Translational Systems Sciences

Volume 38

Jeffrey Yi-Lin Forrest

Systemic Principles of Applied Economic Philosophies I

Producers, Consumers, and the Firm

Springer

Jeffrey Yi-Lin Forrest
Department of Accounting Economics Finance
Slippery Rock University
Slippery Rock, PA, USA

ISSN 2197-8832 ISSN 2197-8840 (electronic)
Translational Systems Sciences
ISBN 978-981-99-7272-2 ISBN 978-981-99-7273-9 (eBook)
https://doi.org/10.1007/978-981-99-7273-9

This Springer imprint is published by the registered company Springer Nature Singapore Pte Ltd.
The registered company address is: 152 Beach Road, #21-01/04 Gateway East, Singapore 189721, Singapore

Synopsis

The objective of this book is to answer, as an initial attempt and early steps, the loud calls, from front-line managers/entrepreneurs and scholarly researchers, to reconstruct the theories of economics and business so that the new theories will be more relevant to real life than the prevalent ones. To do so, this book proposes to develop elementary postulates at the level of the four natural endowments of a business firm or an individual—self-awareness, imagination, conscience, and free will—and then establish conclusions based on these postulates through logical reasoning. On this realistic footing, the book employs the concepts, methodology, and logic of reasoning of systems science to answer a full list of theoretically and practically important questions surrounding such hotly debated topics as rationality, meanings of optima and choices of optimization method, the relationship between micro- and macro phenomena, and consumption preferences and utility representations.

This book is composed of five parts, addresses various key issues, and meets important challenges related to the aforementioned objective. The first part introduces the basics of systems science and the logic of systemic reasoning necessary for the rest of this book. It develops a general theory on how a freely competitive market evolves in terms of prices, and how an individual's and a firm's natural endowments function in terms of decision making. The second part provides a list of systemic critiques about the known theories of economics and business and methodologies widely employed in the literature. The third part endeavors to reconstruct the prevalent producer theory on the basis that each firm has its own particular way to prioritize available decision choices, while avoiding necessary conditions when results are established.

Similarly, the fourth part pays a revisit to the prevalent consumer theory on the basis that (a) each individual consumer has a specific order relation of real numbers; (b) consumption preferences are generally reflexive without satisfying transitivity and completeness; and (c) utility representations do not have to be real-number valued. As the conclusion, the fifth part examines how a firm's system of values and beliefs is closely related to the form's efficiencies.

The target audience of this book includes particularly graduate students and scholarly researchers who look for opportunities to develop new territories in the world of economic and business knowledge. And, it aims at front-line decision-making managers and entrepreneurs who seek sounder theories than the commonly available ones to base their critical decision-making outcomes. By competently employing the systemic intuition—the yoyo model, graduate students, scholarly researchers, decision-making managers and entrepreneurs will be able to discover never-before-seen conclusions and gain insightful understandings of market signals without spending unnecessarily other resources of limited availability.

Preface

My professional career can be divided into two parts with the first one in mathematics and applications and the second in economics and business studies, where by business studies I mean all business-related investigations beyond economics, such as management, marketing, etc. It is truly a real-life confirmation of the wisdom that the right college to attend is the one where you find inspirational minds, as similarly stated by Malcolm Gladwell in his bestseller *Outliers: The Story of Success*, published by Little, Brown and Company, New York, in 2008.

The first portion of my career started at Northwest University in Xi'an (China) from 1978 to 1985. It was during my first year in the graduate school in 1982 when I was mandated to take a course entitled "Natural Dialectics." Out of pure luck, the course, offered by the philosophy department, was taught by an ambitious young assistant professor. The teaching was mainly on how the great minds in history won their victories against all odds. Although I did not like the course at the time with no obvious reasons, I have to say every time when I look back into my own past that my entire career up to today has followed exactly what I learned in that very class from that particular professor. (I owe him all my gratitude although I no longer remember his name.) Not only so, the initial light of my career breakthrough in scholarly publications also came from a classmate's comment in that philosophy class, when he sarcastically compared the lofty objective of the science of sciences—a new scientific research field that attempts to investigate all sciences as one science—to that of Russell's paradox that shows why the set of all sets cannot exist. That comment made me think about how to argue against such lofty effort of the science of sciences. Eventually, my thinking led to the publication of the following paper, "A Mathematical Proof of the Definition of Science of Science," jointly with Yonghao Ma in the prestigious journal *Kybernetes* (Vol. 20, No. 3, pp. 53–56) in 1991.

Along this line of efforts, my colleagues and I over the years developed a general systems theory based on the great works of Mihajlo D. Mesarovic and Yasuhiko Takahara using both naïve and axiomatic set theory. Simultaneously, we explored applications of our systems theory in as many areas of knowledge as possible, such as the emergence of centers (a topic in networks and complexity), laws of conservations (a topic in physics), a number field that can help with the modeling of layered structures (a topic of mathematics), Bellman's principle of optimality (a topic in operations research), unreasonable effectiveness of mathematics (a topic in philosophy of science), and others. All of these explorations were ultimately collected into the following monograph, *General Systems Theory: A Mathematical Approach*, published by Plenum and Kluwer Academic Publishers, New York, in 1999.

In the process of completing the aforementioned monograph, an obvious weakness of my theory of general systems emerged. Because the theory is mainly developed on the basis of the modern Zermelo-Fraenkel (ZFC) set theory, it is difficult to employ it to analyze information, especially when what is available is in the form of either numerical or categorical data. In other words, when a set of data is given, what insights can my new theory of general systems produce, although the theory can be and has been applied to resolve some age-old, unsettled problems beautifully?

To potentially address this difficulty or challenge, I gradually and consciously turned my attention of learning to other areas of knowledge beyond those I explored earlier, such as sociology, economics, finance, management, and marketing. From my active learning in the expanding range of areas and countless number of discussions with colleagues from all over the world, I realized the fundamental importance of the Cartesian coordinate system in the development of calculus-related and statistics-based knowledge, while such a tool of intuition is missing in systems science and social sciences. From this realization, I was led to the following four criteria regarding how a scientific theory can possess a glorious and long-lasting life:

1. The theory must be readable by as many people as possible.
2. The theory must coincide with people's intuition.
3. The theory must possess a certain kind of beauty, which can be easily felt.
4. The theory must be capable of producing meaningful results and insights that excite the population.

For example, plane geometry satisfies all these conditions with its beauty and intuition placed on an almost real-life-like, but fictitious plane, on which each geometric figure is drawn and proofs are developed. Calculus surely satisfies these four conditions, too, with its success of applications in a very wide-ranging area, where the Cartesian coordinate system plays the role of intuition and playground.

This new round of explorations led me to the creation of another monograph, *Systemic Yoyos: Some Impacts of the Second Dimension*, published by Auerbach Publications (an imprint of Taylor and Francis) in 2009. In this monograph, I collected various works either by me alone or jointly with colleagues. In particular, this publication displayed an array of new discoveries in a number of different topic areas by using concepts and methodology of systems science. Other than topics in natural science, mathematics, and weather forecast, this monograph also displayed various topics of household economics, child labor, interindustry wage differentials, dynamics of long- and short-term projects, and structure of human thoughts. In other words, this monograph signals my official foray into the area of economic and business studies.

Although this particular monograph appeared in 2009, the initial seeds for me to expand into these new areas were really planted during the years of my Ph.D. degree program from 1985 to 1988. When Dr. Scott W. Williams of SUNY at Buffalo visited Auburn University (Alabama) in the Fall semester of 1985, he shared various fun moments of learning with colleagues at Auburn. What I have remembered vividly since that occasion for all these past years until this day is his following comment regarding the popularized version of the "invisible hands" of economics (see Chap. 6 for more discussions):

> Genie likes to grant each of *A*, *B*, and *C* a wish for their honorable deeds. *A*'s wish is to live in a city with all the wealth he will ever need. Bang, in a fraction of second, *A* now lives in his wished life style. *B*'s wish is to live on a beach with many beautiful women around. Bang, as soon as he stated his wish, *B* is sunbathing on a beautiful beach in his wished-for conditions. Genie shows a difficult face when *C* states his wish: I like my friends *A* and *B* live with me in this mountainous area.

That was how the second part of my academic career got off the ground at around 2000 when I was equipped with the systemic yoyo model—the adopted intuition and playground for systems science. This model initially appeared as the artwork on the cover of my joint work with Yong Wu, entitled *Beyond Nonstructural Quantitative Analysis: Blown-Ups, Spinning Currents and the Modern Science*, published by World Scientific in 2002. And later, the model was more systematically investigated in the paper, entitled "Systemic yoyo model and applications in Newton's, Kepler's laws, etc.," Kybernetes, vol. 36, nos. 3–4 (2017), pp. 484–516. Since this publication appeared, a team of colleagues and I have been employing this model to the study of many economic and business topics, including, among others, how a nation could possibly suffer from a currency attack and how it could defend itself against a currency war, how market competition evolves, when to enter a new market, why once sustainable competitive advantages have become transient and how to ride the wave of transient competitive advantages, how a firm can become innovative, and how a nation could engineer a self-sustained momentum of growth, how values could be created and captured, and other topics in the business fields.

With colleagues, I systematically organized these new research findings into the following monographs, (a) *Managerial Decision Making: A Holistic Approach* and (b) *Value in Business—A Holistic, Systems-Based Approach to Creating and Capturing Value*, published by Springer respectively in 2020 and 2021. It was through such systematic organization of relevant contents, I came across various calls, from both front-line decision-making managers and entrepreneurs and research scholars, for reconstructing the prevalent theories of economics and business so that the new theories will be more practically applicable to real life than before.

Because the knowledge of economics is the foundation of all business theories, we then turned our attention to see how the practical applicability of business theories can be improved by making the basic theories of economics closer to real life than before. With this end in mind, several years ago, I, with colleagues, have revisited some of the basic assumptions, widely adopted by economists, and found that some of the key reasons for the lack of practical applicability of the prevalent theories of economics and business are that

(a) Condition 2 given above is not satisfied so that condition 3 is not met, either.
(b) Condition 4 is violated.
(c) Many of the most basic assumptions of economic theories are simply not true in real life.

In particular, regarding item (a) above, there is not any readily available intuition and playground for economic and business studies. As a matter of fact, most methods of reasoning and analysis employed in these studies are developed on the Cartesian coordinate system, which embraces linearity while problems considered in business tend to be nonlinear. Hence, the employed methods can readily produce incorrect conclusions due to the nonlinearity involved. The claim in item (b) is supported by the numerous calls from the field for reconstructing the prevalent theories of economics and business. By closely examining the issue listed in item (b), the observation in item (c) emerges.

With these discoveries, colleagues and I systematically examined a whole list of basic assumptions widely adopted in studies of economics and business. In particular, what's checked include, but not limited to, the following:

- Taste is used as the explanation for the basis of decision making, as suggested by George J. Stigler and Gary S. Becker in "De gustibus non est disputandum," American Economic Review, vol. 67, pp. 76–90.
- All decision makers have the same criteria to prioritize available alternatives.
- All decision makers use tools from the same set of optimization methods.
- Values and beliefs are not included in economic and business studies.
- An economist, as a superbeing, is assumed to exist to judge whose behavior is rational and who is not.
- Micro-foundations exist for the emergence of macro-level phenomena.
- Many mathematical conditions are inherited to derive relevant results of economics.
- Each consumer can completely order his set of all possible consumptions.

This book highlights the recent works related to the outcomes of our revisits to these basic assumptions. Other than showing various generations of some well-known results in the prevalent producer and consumer theories, this book also shows many conclusions not ever known before.

I hope you will enjoy reading and referencing to this book in your scholarly exploration and academic pursuit, while making the new theories of economics and business more real-life relevant. If you have any comments or suggestions, please let me hear from you by sending an email to: jeffrey.forrest@sru.edu.

Slippery Rock, PA, USA Jeffrey Yi-Lin Forrest
March 12, 2023

Acknowledgments

This book contains many research results previously published in various sources. We are grateful to the copyright owners for permitting us to use the material. They include:

Auburn University at Montgomery
Emerald Publishing Chaps. 3 and 18
IGI Global (Hershey, Pennsylvania)
Inderscience (Genèva, Switzerland)
International Institute for General Systems Studies, Inc. (Slippery Rock, Pennsylvania)
Meteorological Press (Beijing, China)
National Association of Business, Economics and Technology
New York State Economic Review
Northeast Business & Economics Association
Pennsylvania Association of Economics Chap. 4
Sciendo: Naše gospodarstvo/Our economy
Springer Nature
"Vasile Goldis" Western University of Arad
Taylor and Francis, Ltd.

Contents

About the Author

Jeffrey Yi-Lin Forrest, also known as Yi Lin, holds all his educational degrees in pure mathematics and had 1-year postdoctoral experience in statistics at Carnegie Mellon University. He had been a guest professor of economics, finance, mathematics, and systems science at several major universities in China, including Nanjing University of Aeronautics and Astronautics. And currently, he is a professor of mathematics and research coach for the School of Business at Slippery Rock University, Pennsylvania, and the president of the International Institute for General Systems Studies, Inc., Pennsylvania. He serves either currently or in the past on the editorial boards of 13 professional journals, including *Kybernetes: the International Journal of Systems, Cybernetics and Management Science*, *Journal of Systems Science and Complexity*, *International Journal of General Systems*, *The Journal of Grey Systems*, etc. Currently, Dr. Forrest serves as a co-editor-in-chief of the international journal *Advances in Systems Science and Application*, the editor- or co-editor-in-chief of four book series, "Series on Grey System (Springer, Singapore)," "Systems Evaluation, Prediction, and Decision-Making (CRC Press, New York)," "Communications in Cybernetics, Systems Science and Engineering (CRC Press, Balkema)," and "Communications in Cybernetics, Systems Science and Engineering—Proceedings (CRC Press, Balkema)."

Some of Dr. Forrest's research was funded by United Nations, State of Pennsylvania, National Science Foundation of China, and German National Research Center for Information Architecture and Software Technology.

As of the end of 2020, he has published well over 500 research works, including over 50 monographs and special topic volumes. Some of these monographs and volumes were published by such prestigious publishers as Springer, Taylor and Francis, World Scientific, Kluwer Academic, Academic Press, etc. Over the years, Dr. Forrest's scientific achievements have been recognized by various professional organizations and academic publishers. In 2001, he was inducted into the Honorary Fellowship of the World Organization of Systems and Cybernetics. His research interests are wide ranging, covering areas like data analytics, economics, finance, management, marketing, prediction, mathematics, systems research and applications, philosophy of science, etc.

Part I
The Overview

Chapter 1
Revisits to Some Fundamental Issues Facing Economic and Business Studies

Jeffrey Yi-Lin Forrest

Abstract This chapter introduces the reader to the exhilarating journey this book is about to embark on. It describes some of the very important issues that face the relevant knowledge of economics and business that this book will address and outlines how this volume contributes to the existent literature. Other than pointing out limitations of the methods widely employed in related studies, this chapter glances through the reasons why the concepts, methodology, and logic of reasoning of systems science are most appropriate for decision-making mangers, entrepreneurs, and scholars to use in their respective works. After having accomplished all these objectives, this chapter turns its attention to look at the differences between number-based concepts/methods and those that are system-based, and introduces the basics of holistic thinking, and what systems problem-solving entails.

The rest of this chapter is organized as follows. Section 1.1 outlines how some of the theoretical beginnings of the prevalent theories of economics and business have made these theories not very practically applicable. It consists of five subsections, focusing respectively on five fundamental aspects—tastes or natural endowments, rationality vs. bounded rationality vs. individually defined rationality, meaning of optima and method of optimization, micro-foundation of macro phenomena, consumption preferences, and utility representations. Section 1.2 introduces the basics of systems approach and systems problem-solving. This section consists of three subsections, which respectively examine such issues as how numbers and numerical variables are abstracted, why economic/business studies have to deal with reflexivity that makes systems science a necessary tool, and what the logic of systems thinking and systems problem-solving entails. Then, this chapter concludes with Sect.1.3 which outlines how the book is organized.

Keywords Decision-making · Economic and business theories · Logic of systems thinking · Natural endowments · Reflexivity · Systems problem-solving

J. Y.-L. Forrest, *Systemic Principles of Applied Economic Philosophies I*,
Translational Systems Sciences 38, https://doi.org/10.1007/978-981-99-7273-9_1

1.1 Theoretical Beginnings That Made Prevalent Theories Impracticable

As suggested by the title, this section examines some of the most fundamental beginnings of economic and business theories that have made these theories become invalid when faced with real-life applications. And, these examined beginnings represent what this book is about—modify or replace them so that the consequent theories will become more relevant to life.

This section consists of five subsections. The first subsection introduces natural endowments at both individual level and firm level as the bases for economic and business decision-making. The second subsection outlines how the long-debated assumption of rationality should be determined by individuals who or firms which are involved in the situation of concern. The third subsection briefly explains why the meaning of optimum and method of optimization are also indeed determined by the involved individual or firm. The fourth subsection shows the reader about how this book develops conclusions regarding the fact, among others, that not all holistic phenomena of a macro-level can be explained by behaviors and characteristics of the micro-level components. The fifth subsection elucidates how this book pays a revisit to the concept of consumption preferences and that of utility representations of consumption preferences.

1.1.1 Natural Endowments, on Which Economic/Business Theories Emerge

By examining a variety of counterexamples, it becomes clear that some key and necessary real-life factors have not been considered in theoretical studies of economics and business. That explains why the correspondingly established theories cannot be successfully applied to explain many real-life situations and to help productively counter a lot of practical difficulties, such as applying theories on Industrial Revolution for various nations from around the world to duplicate this significant success in different locations at different times (Forrest et al., 2018; Wen, 2016). For the purpose of making the prevalent economic and business theories more practically relevant, comparing the existent theories of economics and business with those of mathematics and physics leads to the following recognition: It is necessary to develop economic and business knowledge through using such a logical reasoning that is parallel to that employed in mathematics and to derive conclusions based on some clearly true elementary postulates (in the language of mathematics) or laws (in the language of Newtonian physics).

Other than the aforementioned realization, the literature also suggests that behaviors, growth, and aging of individuals and business enterprises are dictated either mentally or culturally or both by their underlying systemic structures, where each person and every firm is seen as a system. In particular, this end is well illustrated by

Lin and Forrest (2012) theoretically and confirmed practically by the categorization paradigm about how people receive and process information so that a host of consumer behaviors can be beneficially explained (Mandler, 1982; Sujan, 1985).

By looking carefully at the fundamental building components of the human mind as a system, this volume proposes to develop the imagined elementary postulates (or laws) at the level of the four natural endowments—self-awareness, imagination, conscience, and free will. This idea is different of that of standard economic models, which are developed on the assumption of a *homo economicus* who is rational and selfish, has computational capability, and never makes mistakes (Cartwright, 2014). By basing reasoning and analysis on these endowments, one is able to address the following very important question in economics and business: how does a person or a firm gather and comprehend information and then make his consumption decisions? To make our following communication convenient, each consumer, be it a person or a firm, will be seen as he/his/him. In particular, a person, as a consumer of final products, goods, and services, generally gathers relevant information about what he is interested in consuming in the product market. A firm, also as a consumer, examines what inputs, such as raw materials and/or specifically made parts for the next-step production of final products, goods, or services, should be considered to import.

To address this question, one has to first understand how consumers generally mobilize, either consciously or unconsciously, their individually different cognitive systems, which for a firm means its central decision-making unit. To make the consequent theory practically useful in real life, each consumer needs to be seen as an open system. By doing so, the consumptions of a consumer will be jointly determined by the underlying or systemic structure of the being of this consumer as a system and its ability to interact with the environment. In other words, consumers' consumption decisions are greatly affected by the composites of their cognitive systems or their natural endowments. To make this realization work in the development of the following theory in this volume, the conventional concepts of natural endowments of individuals will be generalized to those of business firms.

On top of such systemic logic of reasoning, the following chapters develop the necessary theory on how consumers collect and comprehend information, either about products, goods and services, or market calls for additional innovation and competition, and then consequently make their decisions of consumption or production. This objective is accomplished through systemically looking at the tiered structure of an individual consumer's mind or the decision-making unit and how the four natural endowments interact with each other.

Because decisions represent consequences of mind activities of either an individual or a firm's decision-making unit, this volume introduces the hierarchical structure of the individual's or the firm's collective mind. Moreover, because each mind activity is jointly affected by natural endowments, this volume establishes facts about these endowments and then consequent economic and business theories. Speaking differently, by knowing how the mind functions, it makes it easier for managers and entrepreneurs to understand behaviors and consumption decisions of consumers, for economists to comprehend how business entities, be they individuals or organizations, evolve and interact under different circumstances.

To accomplish what is intended to do, this volume applies such a logical reasoning, as realized earlier, that is similar to that widely employed in mathematics in general and plane geometry and set theory in particular and systemic logic of thinking as the preferred methodology. The reason why such specific tool of reasoning and analysis works is because the concept of wholeness appears within mind activities and how these activities interact with the environment. In particular, each thought, each mind activity, and every environment can be respectively seen as a system with its individually special structure. Hence, their interactions can be more effectively examined by using concepts of systems science (Forrest, 2018; Klir, 1985) than using structureless number-based empirical studies (Wu & Lin, 2002; Lin & OuYang, 2010). As for why there is a theoretical significance and practical need to go beyond the conventional methods, such as statistics-based approaches, anecdotal analyses, and calculus-based tools, see Forrest (2018, pp. 12–16) and Forrest and Liu (2021), or Chap. 10 in this volume.

Although what is proposed herein seems to be related to positive/normative economics, the two bear fundamental differences. Specifically, the latter aims to describe and address what various economic programs, scenarios, and environments are and should be (Caplin & Schotter, 2008); this work suggests a possibility to reshape the theoretical foundation of economic and business theories on a more manageable footing by starting all logical reasonings on the four natural endowments and relevant elementary facts. By accomplishing this objective, the consequently established theory will be able to avoid the difficulty, facing normative economics, of rigorously explaining problems and issues and the inevitable emphasis on empirical confirmations of the positive economics. The importance of avoiding the difficulty of normative economics is evident for both theoretical and practical purposes. Although empirical studies are inevitable in economic investigations, economists generally face the problem of erroneous thinking of the fallacy of composition when general recommendations need to be produced for decision-makers based on empirical discoveries (Finocchiaro, 2015).

Historically, this present book is also warranted, if one sees the parallelism between the current state of economic and business studies and that when Isaac Newton developed his laws of physics. In particular, presently in the world of business, deluges of data are collected and made available for analysis; and at the time when Newton was developing his laws of motion, large amounts of data were collected and various empirical formulas were proposed by different scholars (Lin, 2009). For more detailed discussions on this parallelism, see Forrest (2022).

As expected, this book attempts to push forward with the aforementioned proposal by revisiting some aspects of the prevalent theories of economics and business and seeing what improvements can be accordingly made. At the same time, if this proposal can be further carried out successfully in the years to come, one can expect to improve the following disconcerting situation of economic studies: Although a recognized business success is carefully analyzed, the established theory most likely cannot help reproduce the desired economic outcomes in another business setting at a different geographical location. One good example to illustrate this end is the Industrial Revolution of England. It has been widely investigated and theorized by many scholars over the years. However, when their theories were employed in practice by many developing countries, these countries experienced failures, because the applied theories, no matter which one was adopted, did not really work (Forrest et al., 2018, 2020; Wen, 2016).

1.1.2 Individually Determined Rationality

Traditionally, by rationality it means that when an economic agent, be it a person or a business firm, makes decision, the agent maximizes his advantage based on relevant cost-and-benefit analysis (e.g., Friedman, 1953; Wu, 2003, 2006). It is characterized by self-interested motives that lead the individual to the behavior of maximization of utility or production (Maialeh, 2019). Sen (1991) decomposes such neoclassical rationality into two parts: (1) the involved agent maximizes his self-interest and (2) the agent makes choices consistently. Such rationality, as widely assumed in studies of economics and business, represents one very important assumption developed to analyze economic and social behaviors (Gilboa, 2010; Gul & Pesendorfer, 2008). At the same time, it has also been widely criticized by behavioral economists; these scholars believe that the assumption rests on realistically untrue assumptions and is empirically confirmed with falsified evidence; and any behavior that deviates from maximizing self-interest is seen by neoclassical economics as irrational (Becker, 1962; Kahneman, 2011; Mullainathan & Thaler, 2000; Sen, 1991). So, how to understand and how to interpret this assumption of rationality have become an important issue in social science in general and economics and business in particular.

Later, Herbert A. Simon (Campitelli & Gobet, 2010) generalizes this assumption by introducing the concept of bounded rationality, as an alternative way to modeling decision-making; see Hudik (2019) for a systematic account of many very nice interpretations of rationality. Along this line of tradition and based on the aforementioned realization about the roles played by natural endowments, this work proposes that each decision-maker in general is rational in his own sense; and the decision-maker's sense of rationality is bounded by his value-belief system, as defined by the underlying natural endowments. When a person makes decision, he reasons simply by retrieving categorized values and beliefs and information in the memory (e.g., Chiou et al., 2018; Sahni, 2016) to quickly optimize the expected potential. Corresponding to their individually different systems of values and beliefs, decision-makers use their correspondingly varied methods to optimize utilities, profits, costs, risks, etc., although the stated objective functions might look the same from one economic agent to another.

More specifically, in studies of economic and business behaviors, a commonly employed approach is to first introduce an objective function, such as a utility function, a production function, a profit function, etc., and then based on some kind cost-and-benefit analysis of the underlying economic agent, this objective function is optimized (e.g., Friedman, 1953; Gilboa, 2010; Gul & Pesendorfer, 2008). As mentioned above, such approach has been unsympathetically criticized by behavioral economists. Hence, this work attempts to investigate the following question, among others, that arises naturally at the most fundamental level underneath all investigations of economic and business behaviors: Does an economic agent, be it an individual or a business firm, really go through such a general procedure when he decides on what to do in terms of making a consumption or production decision?

The importance of this question is well witnessed by the vast amount of related literature on rationality, where the aforementioned, commonly employed approach in studies of economic and business behaviors is widely known as the assumption of rationality.[1] Although such rationality has been criticized only in recent decades by behavioral economists, some degrees of inherent uncertainty this assumption implicitly embodies has been broadly felt and explored by a good number of leading scholars (Hudik, 2019). For example, all works related to this assumption consider its aim to be about the explanation, prediction, and/or understanding of choice behaviors. However, major differences exist in these scholarly understandings. For example, Herbert Simon (1986) maintains that the assumption of rationality is about accounting for the choice behaviors of individuals instead of differences and variability between groups. Frank Lovett (2006) argues that the assumption does not pinpoint those particular choices (or point predictions) but compares choices at different moments. By seeing each decision-making as a process, Ariel Rubinstein (1998) considers the assumption of rationality as a specific choice procedure, through which a decision-maker selects an element that is most preferred among all available alternatives in a given set of choices. Opposite to all these interpretations, Gary Becker (1962) believes that the assumption focuses on aggregated group decisions, because idiosyncratic individual behaviors are believed to dissipate and be averaged out at the aggregate level (Weyl, 2019), although this reasoning does not hold as recently shown (Gabaix, 2011; Wagner, 2012).

By closely comparing these sampled understandings of rationality, one can see at least the following pairs of inconsistencies and/or contradictions, among many others.

1. Individual choices vs. aggregated group decisions
2. Behaviors of choice vs. choices (or actions of choosing vs. what are actually chosen)
3. Procedures of choice vs. choices (or processes of making choices vs. what are actually chosen)
4. Differences between groups vs. choices at different moments

[1] This is the meaning of rationality addressed in this book, in Hudik (2012) and in Maialeh (2019), although a more recent definition concerns with such a consumer preference relation that is both complete and transitive (Mandler, 2001; McKenzie, 2010).

In other words, some people believe that the assumption is about actions or procedures of acts while others regarding specific choices; some involve the concept of time while others do not.

Although the effort to understand this assumption of rationality has been ongoing for decades, scholars are still currently debating on what this rationality really means (Hudik, 2019). This fact indirectly explains the reason why a compelling need for a meaningful reconstruction of economic theory has been called for by recent events, in particular, the 2008 financial crisis. For example, considering the inability for existing economic theories to describe, to predict, and to explain in a timely manner in the front of the recent financial turmoil, Paul Krugman commented as follows in *New York Times* (2009-09-02),

> The economic profession went astray because economists, as a group, mistook beauty, clad in impressive-looking mathematics, for truth … As memories of the Depression faded, economists fell back in love with the old, idealized vision of an economy in which rational individuals interact in perfect markets … Unfortunately, this romanticized and sanitized vision of the economy led most economists to ignore … things that can go wrong. They turned a blind eye to the limitations of human rationality that often leads to bubbles and burst; to the problem of institutions that run amok; to the imperfection of markets … that can cause the economy … to undergo sudden, unpredictable crashes; and to the dangers created when regulators don't believe in regulation.

while Paul De Grauwe wrote the following in *Financial Times* (2009-07-21):

> Mainstream (economic) models take the view that economic agents are superbly inform and understand the deep complexities of the world ... they have "rational expectations" … they all understand the same "truth", they all act the same way. Thus, modelling the behavior of just one agent (the "representative" consumer and the "representative" producer) is all one has to do to fully describe the intricacies of the world. Rarely has such a ludicrous idea been taken so seriously by so many academics.

This book aims at the objective of clearing up the existent inconsistencies of the literature, as listed above, and that of addressing the aforementioned question and other relevant ones of fundamental importance by basing the reasoning and analysis on decision-makers' four natural endowments. To accomplish these objectives, due to the novelty of the approach taken here, this work is able to establish a series of formal propositions. What is most important among these conclusions is the development of the following result:

> No matter whether it is at the micro individual level or the macro firm level, the assumption of rationality stands for an optimal fit of the decided choice within the underlying natural endowments (instead of self-interests) of the decision-maker.

In particular, the meaning of "optimal fit" is determined by the decision-maker instead of a superbeing, known as the economist. Moreover, no matter whether the decision-maker is an individual or a business firm, his (or its) natural endowments consists of the economic agent's self-awareness, imagination, conscience, and free will. See Branden (1969) and Lin and Forrest (2012) for discussions for the case of individuals.

In terms of literature, the concept of a man's natural endowments is different from that of Stigler and Becker's (1977) tastes. In particular, tastes represent a reason for people to act in different ways. Against the conventional view of tastes, which are seen as inscrutable and often capricious, Stigler and Becker (p. 76) believe that "tastes neither change capriciously nor differ importantly between people." In comparison, a man's natural endowments also dictate how an individual would act in specific ways and do not change easily (Lin & Forrest, 2012), similar to Stigler and Becker's interpretation of tastes. But, from one person to another, their underlying systems of values and beliefs, which are determined by their corresponding natural endowments, can change drastically, leading to, for example, different orderings of real numbers. See Chap. 8 for more related discussions.

And, what is derived in this book regarding rationality, as outlined above, enriches and generalizes what Mises (1949, p. 244) believed when he claimed that "the value judgements a man pronounces about another man's satisfaction do not assert anything about this other man's satisfaction. They only assert what condition of this other man better satisfies the man who pronounces the judgement." That is, in neoclassical economics, the rationality assumption means that the economist "asserts this other man's condition that better satisfies the economist," if what is concluded in this book is rephrased in the language of Mises. That is, in mathematical terms, although the starting point of optimization, such as an objective function, might be the same, the specifically employed criteria or methods of optimization can be different from one decision-maker to another.

1.1.3 Individually Determined Optima and Methods of Optimization

To confirm the last observation of the previous subsection, and to avoid the history of repeatedly falling back to treating impressive-looking beauty as truth, as noted by Paul Krugman, this work employs different approaches for the purpose of achieving the following goal: alter the devastating setup of the existent theories of economics and business at the most fundamental level so that all these theories can be rebuilt on a fresh start with the expectation that they will be more practically useful than before.

First, it pays a revisit to a network, initially seen in Hu (1982), that describes possible procedures of a particular production, while the manager wants to find the minimum path. By employing unlike decision criteria, it is found that different numerical answers can be produced. For more details, see Chap. 6.

Second, this book investigates such general utility of an individual as an explicit function in the dollar value of total consumption, the number of hours spent on waged work, and the person's particular system of values and beliefs. Because the third variable is categorical and mostly not known to others and maybe in many cases even not known to the person himself involved, the following values of this variable are examined individually one by one:

1. The system positively values the consumption of commodities while treating waged job negatively.

2. The system believes in minimal commodity consumption, under which the following two subcases are detailed:
   (a) The individual maximally enjoys providing his labor on the waged work.
   (b) The person likes to supply as little labor as possible to his waged work.
3. The system demands for a non-standard method of optimization of the established utility function, because the system defines an ordering of real numbers differently from the ordinary one.

By basing the reasoning and analysis on the novel ground of natural endowments, corresponding to these cases of the value-belief system, a series of formal propositions are established, revealing, among others, how an individual's marginal utility of commodity consumption and that of working on waged work vary respectively with (a) the income from non-waged sources, (b) the number of hours spent on waged work, (c) hourly wage rate, (d) additional savings, (e) unit commodity price, and (f) expense on leisure.

By comparing these results with each other, it indicates readily that within different systems of values and beliefs, the identified utility function behaves differently. Most importantly, such a comparison and several constructed examples collectively demonstrate that when an individual decides on how much commodity is to be consumed and how much labor output is to be supplied to his waged work by maximizing the corresponding utility subject to existing constraints, the individual's utility and his method of optimization are exclusively defined by his system of values and beliefs. In other words, conclusions in this book support Simon's (1986) claim that the widely adopted rationality is about the decision behaviors of individuals and Rubinstein's (1998) belief that the selected option is most preferred among available alternatives, where preference is defined by the individual's natural endowments. This end is majorly different from the well-adopted definition of rationality—maximize an individual's advantage based on a conventional version of cost-and-benefit analysis (e.g., Friedman, 1953).

Third, various examples are constructed throughout this book to demonstrate that irrational behaviors, as seen in the eyes of the standby economist who is mostly self-authorized to determine what is considered rational and what is not, and non-optimizers do exist in real life (Taylor, 1989). Moreover, various well-known results of the prevalent economic theories are shown to be not generally true, if the criteria of priority, as defined by the individual's underlying system of values and beliefs, do not agree with the ordinary order of real numbers.

Beyond what is described above, one important highlight of this book is its emphasis on that for each economic agent, be it a person or a business firm, there is an agent-specific order relation of real numbers and that of an agent-specific method of optimization. More specifically, each economic agent has his own particular means to prioritize the alternatives available in a decision-making situation and a very individual way to optimize its objective. This end is very different from the assumptions widely employed in the literature, where the ordering of real numbers and the method of optimization, although some of the particular details are different, are the same no matter whom the decision-maker is. In particular, the less than relation $3 < 10$, for example, is universally assumed in the literature, while it is not generally assumed in this book, because such a relation is solely determined by the economic agent of concern based on his system of values and beliefs. For example, when these figures stand for dollar values, then a good number of value-belief systems would order 10 as less than 3, if it is known to the people of concern that the particular $10 comes from an act of stealing, while the very $3 is the reward from helping a neighbor to clean off the snow on the driveway.

Because of the introduction of agent-specific order relations of real numbers and agent-specific methods of optimization, established conclusions in this volume are more general than the correspondingly similar ones in the present theories of microeconomics and are more real-life relevant. It is evident that in real life, these agent-specific order relations of real numbers and agent-specific methods of optimization do generally exist (Forrest et al., 2021; Hammerton, 2020; Van Fleet, 2021; Yang & Andersson, 2018). For example, there are firms that do not place profit maximization as their primary objective (e.g., Hussain, 2012; Jensen, 2001). Instead of maximizing profits for shareholders above all else, an increasing number of firms have also focused their operations on various other purposes, such as:

- Providing opportunities for citizens to succeed through hard work and creativity, while enjoying a life of meaning and dignity (https://s3.amazonaws.com/brt.org/BRT-StatementonthePurposeofaCorporationOctober2020.pdf, accessed on January 30, 2021)
- Taking corporate social responsibilities (e.g., Fahimnia et al., 2015)
- Protecting the environment through designing and producing green products (e.g., Hong & Guo, 2019)

In short, not all economic agents in real life are maximizers or minimizers, as defined conventionally in the literature. Hence, some of the established theoretical results of economics and business will most likely not be applicable to such agents (Taylor, 1989). In other words, an agent's system of values and beliefs directly affects how the agent prioritizes its decision choices and how it practically optimizes its objective function (Forrest et al., 2021). Correspondingly, this book studies how some of the well-known results of economics and business can be extended to the general case of no matter what a system of values and beliefs an economic agent may embrace, while how some other known results are only true under specific conditions. For example, due to such drastically different starting points from the ones widely adopted in the literature, this work is able to develop, among others, the following results:

- The firm's profit function in general is not homogeneous of degree one (Chap. 11).
- In Hotelling's lemma, a singleton optimal production correspondence is equivalent to the equation that the rate of change of the profit in the price of commodity h is equal to the amount of commodity h either inputted or outputted, for each commodity h (Chap. 11).

- In general, a firm's optimal production correspondence is generally not homogeneous of degree zero, unless the firm's order relation of real numbers satisfies the condition of positive multiplicativity (Chap. 12).
- In Shephard's lemma, the condition of a single conditional factor demand is equivalent to the equation that the rate of change of the cost in the price of commodity h is equal to the demand of commodity h, for each input commodity h (Chap. 12).
- Micro players' actions on their self-interests do not generally lead to unintended greater macro-level social benefits and public good (Chap. 13), as commonly believed and known as the "invisible hand" (Sen, 2010).

1.1.4 Micro Foundations of Holistic Phenomena of Macro-level

In the recent decade, scholars have once again realized that the currently available economic theories can neither predict the imminent arrival of a crisis nor help understand the mechanism behind the originating imbalances that led to the devastating consequences of the 2008 financial disaster on unemployment and the economy. To possibly overcome this recognized deficit in the relevant knowledge, the *Oxford Review of Economic Policy* developed a "Rebuilding Macroeconomic Theory Project" (Vines & Wills, 2018). The project examined a set of six broadly based questions related to the benchmark New Keynesian Dynamic Stochastic General Equilibrium (DSGE) model (Smets & Wouters, 2007). The participants focused on ways to improve or completely replace the benchmark model with another one; and they did not believe that a paradigm shift is needed other than enriching and improving the formulas of the model (Vines & Wills, 2018).

In contrast, a team of Italian scholars proposes to embrace a paradigm shift by employing the theory and methods of the complexity science (Delli Gatti et al., 2010). They suggest to apply the concept of complex networks and computer simulations instead of the current reductionist approach at the heart of the mainstream DSGE models. They demonstrate that computational techniques can vividly simulate the natural emergence of macro-level phenomena from unintended and uncoordinated behaviors of micro-level individuals, although these individuals follow some simple rules of action, such as financial contagion (Allen & Gale, 2001) and trade-credit relationships (Boissay, 2006; Battiston et al., 2007).

These two strings of efforts reveal a divergence of beliefs and logics of thinking in terms of how the community of economists should work in the coming years or even decades:

- Gradually enrich the benchmark New Keynesian DSGE model so that it can better predict forthcoming economic crises, provide more appropriate policy suggestions, etc.

- Radically adopt a revolutionary new approach so that the consequent theories will be mostly different from the ones currently available and the methods employed will be powerful and effective, both theoretically and practically.

Considering the fact that predicting natural disasters has been an unsettled world-class challenge to the entire world of natural science and mathematics (Lin & OuYang, 2010), the effort of simply modifying the current system of equations in the benchmark New Keynesian DSGE model to accurately forecast imminent economic crises (Vines & Wills, 2018) will be destined to be fruitless. In particular, most large-scale natural events play out through their processes without being disrupted by humans, no matter if their disastrous consequences had been predicted in advance or not. However, economic disasters are very different. They are reflexively influenced by human expectations; their courses of evolution are greatly and determinately affected by human participants' estimates and consequent actions (Soros, 2003). This end explains why the attempt of using a few simple DSGE equations (Smets & Wouters, 2007) to forecast disruptively different outcomes of reflexive human processes from any records of the past is practically impossible (Lin & OuYang, 2010). To this end, as a reference, it is necessary for the reader to note the following effort. For years, there was a well-funded research center for midterm weather forecasts in Europe. This center developed for its purpose of prediction a system of more than five million equations in over five million variables, while the actual forecasts of weathers had experienced uncertainties (Lorenz, 1993). For similar reason, the effort of providing more adequate scholarly supports for policymaking is destined to be unsuccessful if the focus is only on revising the current DSGE model, because adequate policymaking is essentially dependent on forecasts of the future (Forrest et al., 2020).

Based on what is discussed in the previous paragraph and the definition of a paradigm shift in an economic and business theory—drastic changes in both the content of the theory and the method employed to develop the theory (Vines & Wills, 2018, p. 5)—this book supports the Italian team's recognition of a forthcoming paradigm shift in economic and business theories (Delli Gatti et al., 2011). Specifically, in terms of contents, this book suggests to root each and every theoretical result of economic and business theories on some of the elementary facts of individual economic agents' systems of values and beliefs, as suggested by Forrest et al. (2020) and discussed briefly earlier in this chapter. Moreover, in terms of methods used to develop theoretical results, this book expands those of networks and computer simulations, as suggested by the Italian colleagues (Delli Gatti et al., 2010), to all methods of systems science established for studying organizations, evolutions, and interactions of organizations (Forrest et al., 2013).

Other than the holistic view described above, in comparison with the literature along the two lines given above, this book employs the concept of centralized systems to theoretically explain when macro-socioeconomic phenomena emerge out of unintended and uncoordinated actions and interactions of microeconomic agents. Such rigorously established conclusions are surely more general and more reliable than those observed from computer simulations, such as those respectively observed and recorded by Allen and Gale (2001), Boissay (2006), Battiston et al. (2007), and many others, because each computer simulation-based observation is constrained by particularly chosen models and specified parametric values. Second, other than converting simulation-based observations into theoretical conclusions, this work establishes conditions for when macro-level economic entities appear to answer market calls and how micro-level individuals with inconsistent or even conflicting interests can be organically congregated into operational business organizations. The importance of this end cannot be overemphasized in light of the current trend of developing macroeconomic results on micro-foundations, where macro-level conclusions need to be founded on micro-level components (Blanchard, 2018; Lucas, 1976).

Because of the novelty of the employed approach—systemic logic of reasoning—and methodology that is based on both set theory and game theory, this book is able to develop the following:

- A new way to interpret abstract conclusions of mathematics in terms of when some characteristics of micro-level individuals can give rise to macro-level phenomena of systemic wholes, as revealed by Delli Gatti et al. (2010, 2011) through using computer simulations
- How market sends out its invitations for new products and additional innovations and why new competition appears

And on top of these theoretical conclusions, this book is able to theoretically explain the following

- When some characteristics of micro-level individuals can give rise to macro-level phenomena of systemic wholes, as revealed by Delli Gatti et al. (2010, 2011) through using computer simulations
- How racial segregation in American cities appeared (Schelling, 1969) and how risk controls at local levels by individual lenders can collectively induce a large instability in prices and involuntarily create more systemic risk (Thurner et al., 2012)
- Why various macro firms are organized with microeconomic men and agents although these microcomponents have inconsistent or even conflicting interests. That is, not all macro-level phenomena can have direct micro-foundation or micro-founded explanations, as believed by economists since the 1970s (Blanchard, 2018; Lucas, 1976).

1.1.5 Consumption Preferences and Utility Representations

Many well-known conclusions about consumer preferences and utility representations of consumption preferences are developed on the assumption that when facing two possible consumptions, a consumer can always tell which one of the choices he prefers over the other. That is, the preference relation of any consumer is assumed to completely order the consumer's set of possible consumptions (e.g., Debreu, 1959; Levin & Milgrom, 2004; Mas-Collel et al., 1995). However, due to the reason that the physiological need of each human being is multidimensional, consumption choices from different dimensions generally cannot be compared by using preference relations. For example, a choice of shelter, an option of food, an offer of drink, and one type of medicine can be seen as possible consumptions from different dimensions. For basic survival, no person can really prefer one of these possible selections over others.

In terms of the literature, many researches have pointed to the same fact of the multidimensionality of human consumptions as what is outlined above. For example, Jacob et al. (2018) find that most US college students value living amenities, such as spending on student activities, sports, and dormitories, over academic quality that is only a concern of the small number of high-achieving students. By looking at cosmopolitan cultural consumption—consumer's openness for cultural products from foreign countries—Rössel and Schroedter (2015) maintain that cosmopolitan consumption is a class-based practice, determined by different forms of cultural capitals.

As for the issue of incompleteness in consumption preferences, several scholars had also noticed it, although not from the angle of dimensionality. For example, Aumann (1962) and Mandler (1999) find that due to wide range appearances of indecisiveness, consumer preferences tend to be intransitive, while Tversky (1969) reports that consumer preferences do not generally satisfy the condition of transitivity. Dubra and Ok (2002) introduce a risky-choice model in which an individual naturally possesses an incomplete preference relation. By using a new statistical technique and by revisiting the same gambles Tversky studied earlier, Birnbaum and Gutierrez (2007) conclude that there are indeed individual consumers who repeat intransitive preference patterns. For additional, relevant works, see, for example, Bosi and Herden (2012), Cettolin and Riedl (2019), Evren and Ok (2011), Hansson (1968), Nishimura and Ok (2016), and Ok (2002).

As one of the main issues this book attempts to address, the following chapters will look at what could happen when such an unrealistic assumption regarding consumption preference relations is removed. More specifically, this volume will examine the following questions:

- How can one alter the assumption that a consumer's set of consumption possibilities is completely ordered by his preferences (Dubra & Ok, 2002; Hervés-Beloso & Cruces, 2019) in order to reflect the fact that the opposite should be generally true?
- When a consumer's satisfaction from consumption is no longer measurable by the conventional concept of continuous utility functions (Estevez-Toranzo & Herves-Beloso, 1995; Ok, 2002), what can one do to reflect the levels of satisfactions?

These questions are important both theoretically and practically. As just discussed above, it can be expected that the consequent theories, developed from the efforts to address these two and other relevant questions, will be more relevant to real life than before.

Different from some of the known assumptions and/or conclusions in the literature, this book shows, among other results, that for an individual no matter how he prefers one consumption over another,

1. There are incomparable consumptions.
2. His consumption preferences may not be transitive.
3. His indifference relation of consumptions *in practice* may not be transitive.

The existing literature indicates that these results have been confirmed by different authors with varied settings. However, in comparison, the confirmations in this book are based purely on analytical representations and analysis without making use of any other auxiliary concepts and/or notations. More importantly, this work generalizes the classical conclusion of Debreu (1959) on when a continuous utility representation exists in a very different way from those published recently by Efe Ok and his colleagues. In particular, Ok (2002), Nishimura and Ok (2016), and Bosi and Herden (2012) consider the problem of how to represent an incomplete preference relation by means of a collection of real-number valued functions. Based on such a quickly expending literature, Alonso et al. (2010) present a web-based consensus support system that involves decision-makers with incomplete preference relations; Meng and Chen (2015) develop a group decision-making method to cope with incomplete preference information; and Cettolin and Riedl (2019) conduct experiments to test whether a preference is either complete or incomplete.

Although the assumption that consumer's preference can order all available consumption choices (Hervés-Beloso & Cruces, 2019) does not reflect the relevant reality, it does play the role of starting points of reasoning and analysis for countlessly many theoretical thoughts to blossom and for economic and business theories to find practical applications. Hence, to make relevant theories, developed consequently when the completeness assumption of consumption preferences is revised, practically relevant, it is important both theoretically and practically to address the previously posed problems so that adopted assumptions are closer to real life than the ones widely adopted currently.

Comparing to what has been established before regarding consumption preferences and utility representations, this work can be evaluated in both theoretical and practical perspectives. In the former way of evaluation, this work is the first in four different fronts.

1. It *analytically* shows the fact that for each consumer, there are possible consumptions that are not comparable in terms of his preferences.
2. It officially embraces the fact that each consumer or decision-maker orders real numbers differently based on his system of values and beliefs.
3. Due to measurement uncertainties in real life, a constructed example shows that for an economic and business theory to be practically useful, the theory has to allow some of the involved variables to assume interval values instead of exact numerical ones.

4. In terms of utility representations of a preference relation, this book takes a different approach from the one taken by Efe Ok and his colleagues. In comparison, the conclusion introduced here can be more easily fathomed behaviorally than the ones derived by Ok's team (e.g., Dubra & Ok, 2002; Evren & Ok, 2011; Nishimura & Ok, 2016; Ok, 2002; Ok & Masatlioglu, 2007).

1.2 The Systems Approach and Systems Problem-Solving

This section illustrates the reason why the logic of systems thinking and the methodology of systems science are appropriate for the development of the said theories of economics and business. In particular, the said theories will be constructed in a similar fashion as a scientific theory by using systemic yoyo model as the intuition and playground and a set of axioms and rigorously established game-theoretic results as the starting points. Here, such a logical reasoning as the one commonly used in mathematics and natural science will be used to derive generally true conclusions by relating each newly introduced concept to the starting points or previously established conclusions.

The rest of this section consists of three subsections. The first one reviews where numbers are from and how the concept of numerical variables is introduced. The second subsection examines the wide-range existence of reflexive relations that economic and business studies should pay attention to. That leads to the conclusion that the concepts, results, and methodology of systems science are needed for these studies. The third subsection details the logic of systems thinking and reasoning and the basic ideas behind systems problem-solving.

1.2.1 How Numbers and Numerical Variables Are Abstracted

Numbers initially emerged to satisfy the need for people to do various bookkeeping, such as the number of animals hunted and that of fish captured, where counting and recording were needed. Although the signs initially used to do counting had been different from one situation to another, such knots on a string or piles of sticks, uniformed symbols eventually were introduced and widely adopted. For example, out of 2 apples, 2 chairs, 2 people, and 2 families, the symbol and concept of number 2 appear. As numbers appeared in almost all human activities, Pythagoras of the ancient Greece treated numbers as the origin of everything. They believed that through numbers and their properties, the mankind could grasp all things under heaven. Such belief in the west led to the development of the traditional science as the religious foundation (Kenny, 2012). In roughly the same timeframe, Zhan Yin of ancient China, a scholar of the warring states time, realized that the use of numbers was limited, because there were things numbers just could not describe (Qu, 1985). Such distinct recognitions about numbers led to how later generations of Chinese people treated numbers and why they did not appreciate numbers as much as Westerners (Wu & Lin, 2002).

From the discussion above on how the concept of number 2 appears, it can be seen that when this 2 is successfully abstracted from an entire array of different situations, relevant relationships and organizations (or structures) are ignored. In particular, what is ignored includes the internal structures of and the mutual relationships between the apples, chairs, people, and families. If by a system, it means an organization (or structure) or relationship where components are related somehow to each other to form an organic whole, then the ignored structures and relationships above mean that when people successfully extracted the concept of numbers from the natural world, the concept of systems is unfortunately overlooked.

Additionally, this discussion indicates that numbers are limited in their power to describe things, such as organizations, events, and processes (Wu & Lin, 2002). Moreover, they cannot appear before existence, reflecting their original purpose—measurement and recording. This reality about numbers in fact demonstrates how well and useful numbers can be employed to predict the future and study the evolution and interaction of organizations, two key issues in the research of economic and business problems. In particular, since the time of Pythagoras of the ancient Greece, numbers have been identified as or modeled by points on the real-number line, which is an imaginary straight line, leading to the appearance of the concept of infinity ∞ and issues of nonlinearity. That explains why analysis and reasoning based on numbers or numerical variables must suffer from bounded validity, because there is no straight line of infinite length in real life and the natural world is curved so that one can never reach or even get close to this imaginary ∞ (Lin, 2009, pp. 21–22). This end implies that such a science and methodology that are appropriate for describing and studying organizations have to be introduced in order to deal with economic and business studies.

Because systems science—the totality of all studies of various general or particular systems—and related methodology are developed for the purpose of studying organizations, evolutions, and interactions of organizations (Klir, 2001; Lin, 1999), this science meets the aforementioned need. Therefore, it represents a great possibility to be adopted as the tool of reasoning and analysis and the logic of thinking for the planned theory of this book. For instance, to know how consumer preferences evolve and what is going to be favored next, producers that want to stay ahead of the coming curves have to consider the attributes and systemic structures of the forever changing market conditions and how these conditions interact with one another. However, the traditional science, which heavily uses quantities, variables, and inertial systems, requires a superbeing to provide the first push for the evolution of everything to begin, while systems science, which focuses on structures, organizations, and non-inertial systems, embraces movements of things as natural existence of the natural world (Lin & OuYang, 2010). That explains why in the language of natural science and mathematics, interactions of products, market forces, and organizations of component parts belong to the realm of non-inertial systems or the range of discourse of systems science.

For things either with or without internal structures, their evolutions and interactions generally reveal different characteristics. For example, when two objects without any internal structure crash into each other, the law of action and reaction applies. However, when the colliding objects possess their individually different internal structures, such as the situation when the cue ball hits another ball in a pool game, the movements of the objects after the collision can be very different. In other words, the third law of motion does not apply here. This end can be vividly confirmed when one observes how two weather systems collide in the sky. Moreover, it also explains why nations in real life need to have their own security systems to defend and preserve their peace and stability. In other words, the logics of reasoning and analysis and relevant methodologies needed to deal with these distinct evolutions and interactions of organizations or systems will have to be different from the traditional science.

As what physics has shown, methods of analysis, such as calculus, statistics/probability, and consequent theories, developed on the formality and generality of quantities, can be reasonably useful when applied to investigate evolution and interaction of things that have no internal structure. However, in terms of economic and business studies, where all economic agents involved, be they individuals or business firms, do possess internal structures, quantities and methodologies developed on quantities have experienced great difficulties, for details, see Chap. 10 in this book. To coordinate the methodological approaches—one provided by the traditional science and the other the systems science—one can associate them by using the concept of rotational stirring energies (Lin, 2009, Chap. 7) or the systemic yoyo model (Lin, 2009; Chap. 2 below). Doing so naturally leads to the overall system of a two-dimensional science with the first dimension focusing on the study of things without internal structure and the second dimension on matters involving internal organization (Klir, 2001). For relevant details, see Chap. 2 below.

By carefully examining the world systemically or through the lens of systems, one can readily see that the fundamental form of movement in the universe is rotation, no matter whether what is considered is physical, intellectual, or economic (Forrest & Liu, 2021; Forrest et al., 2020; Lin, 2009). To this end, it is Vilhelm Bjerknes (1898) who first recognized that the fundamental form of atmospheric or oceanic motion is rotation; then, it is Shoucheng OuYang (Wu & Lin, 2002) who generalized this result to solids. Based on this fundamental, rotational form of movement of fluids and solids, the concepts of stirring energy and second stir (Lin & OuYang, 2010), and the yoyo model (Lin, 2007, 2009) are introduced. For a quick introduction to the yoyo model, see Sect. 2.4 below.

In summary, the concepts and methodology of systems science are introduced and developed to investigate organizations and to deal with evolutions and interactions of organizations. The systemic yoyo model provides an intuition and playground to help the following:

- Managers and entrepreneurs quickly see how economic and business entities evolve and interact with each other.

- Scholarly researchers readily gain insightful intuitions about what general and particular conclusions might be true.

Hence, it can be expected that the methodology of systems science and the systemic yoyo model will jointly assist decision-makers to effectively process market information and make appropriate decisions and scholars to develop more reliable and practically useful theories (Forrest, 2018; Forrest et al., 2020).

1.2.2 Reflexivity in Economic/Business Studies and Need for Systems Science

To possibly address the issues posed in Sect. 1.1 and develop the correspondingly expected economic and business theories, one very important recognition is that all issues of economics and business really arise, either directly or indirectly, out of the universal human desire of living a better life and, consequently, out of the interactions of demands and supplies of products, goods, and/or services. In particular, the desire of living a better life inevitably increases the demand for more and better things, while the same desire simultaneously entices people with entrepreneurial spirits to find different ways to meet the demands. For more details, see Chap. 4 below. In other words, no matter which side a person is on—either the demand side or the supply side—he needs to appropriately understand the market information (see Chap. 4). For example, a consumer can dream freely about what living conditions he likes to live in and what commodities he wants to consume. However, without knowing what is possible in the marketplace, his dream will forever stay as a dream without any chance of materializing it. Moreover, a producer, at the same time, can also imagine extravagantly what life style he could successfully enjoy by meeting market demand(s). However, without innovatively and appropriately deciphering market signals, he may very well produce wrong products, leading to misery business failures and financial ruins. So, understanding market information appropriately and innovatively is extremely important. Then, what is information?

As a concept, it was Shannon (1949) who first officially defined what information is by using the concept of probability. Since then, this concept of information has been jointly investigated with those of various uncertainties (Liu et al., 2016) and greatly helped the debate between determinacy and indeterminacy within the world of learning (Lin & OuYang, 2010). When the school of determinacy imposes strong conditions, such as stability or continuity and differentiability, to smooth out noise in data and specifics that appear with each particular application, the school of indeterminacy removes small-probability events by focusing on stable time series. Hence, scholars reach the same destination of developing desirable generalities, although they take different approaches to eliminate either noises of data or specifics and complexities of the events and processes under consideration. For instance, to produce conclusions of desired generality, one widely used method in economic and business studies is to examine a representative consumer, a representative firm, or a representative family by smoothing out all specifics and complexities of individual consumers, firms, and families.

Such idea of smoothing, however, can produce and indeed has led to conclusions that are impossible to hold true in real life. One convenient example to demonstrate this end is the wide-range employment of expected values. In a lot of real-life cases of applications, expected values are guaranteed to be not reachable, ironically contradicting the meaning of expected values. For illustration, let us look at the following example of an elementary statistics course. The particular experiment is to flip a fair coin once, while assuming that the coin does not land on its edge. Define a random variable X below: $X = 1$, if the head shows up, and $X = 0$, if the tail is on the top. Then, the expected outcome of this experiment is $E(X) = 50\,\% \cdot 1 + 50\,\% \cdot 0 = 0.5$, an impossible value for X to take or the impossible situation that the coin is expected to land on its edge.

The key takeaway here is that to innovatively and appropriately understand market information, involved specifics need to be separated from noises of data; they cannot be ignored by decision-making managers and entrepreneurs and cannot be smoothed out by scholars in their research works due to the reason that quantitative methods cannot handle the specifics. At the same time, unique understandings of market cues lure managers and entrepreneurs to take their respectively different responses to potentially optimize their outcomes. Such responses in turn alter the meanings and significance of the original market cues. Hence, to make the newly developed theories practically useful, such reflexive nature between a piece of market information and innovative understandings of it needs to be dealt with by employing systems science and related methodologies. In other words, to echo the reflexive nature of economic and business events and processes, scholars and practitioners need to employ the systemic logic of reasoning and methodology of analysis to explore such economic and business issues as how to innovatively understand market information with relevant specifics and how to practically apply such understanding to make more reliable predictions and decisions.

From the angle of systems, it can be readily seen that an innovative understanding of market information is closely related to the evolution and interaction of various economic events, processes, and agents (Lin & OuYang, 2010). So, by purposely examining the product market from the angle of interacting economic events and agents, one will be able to discover business potentials in consumers' forever changing preferences. In other words, specifics of market information represent the dynamic mechanism of evolving structures of the underlying economic system. Their importance in terms of creating and capturing values goes beyond the formality of quantities. Innovatively understanding them relies directly on the attributes and properties of the systemic structure of the interacting economic entities and agents. The present-day effort devoted to big data uses the name of quantities to uncover hidden systemic structures. That signals the fact that human exploration of knowledge has gone beyond the limitations of numbers and numerical variables and into the era of wholistic and systems reasoning and analysis of economic and business events and processes.

In principle, specifics of market information reflect how underlying economic forces and policies change and how the interaction of demands and supplies evolves. Knowledge and technologies of big data provide new approaches to and capabilities for dealing with these changes and evolutions and for estimating what is coming up next. Such approaches and capabilities represent another methodology and technology different of those that are either calculus-based or statistics-based or a mix of the two. This development marks a new epistemological breakthrough in the knowing of the world through analyzing the underlying systems and their evolutions and interactions.

Because of the duality of action and reaction and that of spin directions, the appearance of each particular piece of market information indicates that some changes have already occurred in the market structure in an earlier time moment. So, the present era of transient competitive advantages (Forrest et al., 2020; McGrath, 2013) of the business world strongly suggests the necessity to introduce systems science and methodology into economic and business studies in order to generate innovative comprehensions of the market and to establish more practically useful conclusions. In this regard, the advantage of the systemic yoyo model, an intuitive logic of systemic thinking, is that the model can assist managers and entrepreneurs walk out of the realm of quantities and enter into that of interacting and evolving organizations and non-inertial systems (or systems science).

The presently available knowledge, developed on calculus- or statistics-based or a mix of these two, has not dependably helped managers and entrepreneurs to generate innovative understandings of market cues and researchers to derive sufficient number of practically useful conclusions regarding economic and business organizations, their evolutions, and interactions. No matter how this dilemma is examined, it truly represents a serious challenge facing the community of economists and business scholars. It needs to be addressed fully due to its theoretical and practical importance and the reason that once sustainable competitive advantages have become transient and short-lived (Forrest et al., 2020; McGrath, 2013).

To meet this difficult challenge, this book comes into being. It strives to investigate the issues raised in Sect. 1.1, while avoiding the erroneous logic of thinking of the Fallacy of Composition (see Chap. 10). To do so, this book employs concepts and methodology of systems science and considers the specific attributes of the scenarios in hands. The following chapters clearly demonstrate that systems are more adequate than quantities when managers, entrepreneurs, and researchers need to discover economic potentials and business opportunities. At the same time, this book demonstrates how the advantages of conventional methodologies can be taken by applying holistic thinking in terms of determining which such methodology can be used.

1.2.3 The Logic of Systems Thinking and Systems Problem-Solving

After having demonstrated in the previous two subsections the need for scholars, managers, and entrepreneurs in the area of economic and business studies to adopt the logic of systemic thinking and methodology, this subsection provides a quick glance of relevant basics of systems science.

By systems science, it means the totality of all studies about various specific systems along with those on general systems. Similarly, the methodology of systems science stands for the collections of all methods developed for the investigations of various systems. Both systems science and methodology jointly enable scholars, decision-making managers, and entrepreneurs to look at the world holistically by focusing on the investigation of systemhoods, including organizations (or structures), their evolutions, and interactions (Lin, 1999; Klir, 1985). Based on the discussions in the previous subsections and the fact that economic and business studies generally involve entities with respectively rich, yet different, internal structures, this book adopts systems science as its way of reasoning and intuition on which various significant and critical insights can be initially observed and then proved by using appropriate methods.

As is defined earlier, a system represents an organization or a structure whose component parts are associated to each other to form an organic whole. Due to the existence of associations between component parts, the systemic whole is generally greater than the sum of parts (Lin, 1999). From this definition, it can be seen that system is everywhere in the world, especially in investigations of economic and business issues. For example, other than being a complex biological system, each person is also a physical input and output economic system and a decision-making system that relies on the functionalities of his natural endowments (see Chap. 5 below). At the same time, each person is simultaneously a component member of many social systems or organizations, such as a family, a neighborhood, a community, and others. He interacts with humans (seen as systems); with various man-made systems, such as a car and an ATM machine; and with different social systems, such as the company of employment and sport clubs.

Historically, the concept of systems can be traced back to as far as the time when the written history of man started. Throughout time, it has been investigated either consciously or unconsciously by using various names in respectively different languages (von Bertalanffy, 1968). However, the current name was initially introduced by von Bertalanffy (1924) in the field of biology in the 1920s, when he recognized that the phenomenon of life is more than a pile of isolated cells. As for its usage in economic and business studies, an increasing number of scholars in our modern time have tried to employ the concept and relevant methods in their respectively works. See, for example, Forrest et al. (2020), Klir (1985), Lin (2009), Porter (1985), and Rostow (1960). Other than introducing a brand-new methodology into the relevant studies, these scholars have also demonstrated the power of the holistic, system-based thinking and relevant methodology and produced more theoretical insights and practically reliable and usable conclusions regarding business entities and how they interact with one another.

Beyond their common origin, numbers and systems represent two different aspects of the physical and intellectual world. For example, each business firm is studied as follows:

1. A collection of isolated component parts
2. As an organic whole within which the parts are somehow associated together so that the sense of a whole emerges.

It is for case (1) that the firm can be readily described with numbers and modeled by possible relationships between those numbers. For instance, the firm consists of $m$staff members, n office rooms, k printers, etc. Each of the employees shares n/m office rooms, while each printer carries on the average m/k portion of the total workload. As for case (2), beyond all above, the organic whole of the firm consists of all organizational aspects, such as the hierarchical ranks of the employees, composites of various work units that are connected by means of inputs and outputs, how the people with their respective ranks and the work units are threaded together by the flow of money within the firm and executions of commends, etc.

Basically, when the firm is investigated as a place where values, in the eyes of the employees, those of stakeholders, and those of consumers, are created, it becomes a system with its particular organizational structure and culture and an adopted system of values and beliefs. The success of such a firm generally depends on how well the component parts are mobilized through the strength of the organizational structure and culture and how the adopted system of values and beliefs is to be materialized (Forrest & Liu, 2021; McGrath, 2013). In such a process of achieving success, among others, different talents are coordinated, and operational routines are optimized. Such a firm exists as a whole, which, although invisible, makes the presence of the firm both physical and intellectual.

The firm, considered in the discussion above, can be readily replaced by an individual (seen as an economic agent whose behavior is dictated by his system of values and beliefs), a market, an industry, an economy, etc. That implies that behind each business entity, there is an abstract, theoretical system within which the relevant whole, component parts, and their interconnectedness are emphasized. Conversely, it is the whole and interconnected parts that make the totality known as an economic agent, or a firm, or a market, or an industry, or an economy. That is, other than specific circumstances where measurement or counting and consequently numbers play their roles, the business world is made up of dominantly systems (or organizational structures).

In comparison, numbers, if used in relationships, as just discussed above, describe small-scale and nonstructural phenomena (Wu & Lin, 2002), while systems portray large-scale and organizational structures. That is another reason why the concepts and methodology of systems science are more appropriate than all theories developed on numbers and numerical variables for the investigation of economic and business issues every time when the internal structures of involved economic entities cannot be ignored.

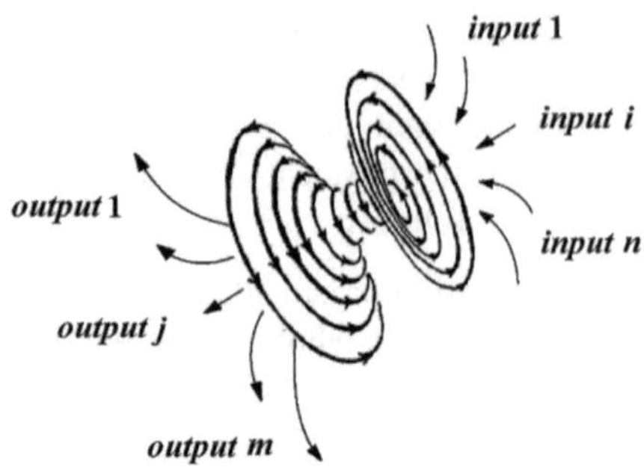

Fig. 1.1 General system's yoyo model in three-dimensional space

When the traditional science—the first dimension of knowledge, which investigates the thinghood—is complemented by systems science, an additional dimension of knowledge, which focuses on the studies of systemhood, human ability to learn gains additional strength; so, more problems that have been challenging the very survival of mankind since the beginning of time can be more adequately addressed than ever before. The materialization of such great expectation of systems science relies on the particular speaking language and intuition—the (systemic) yoyo model (Lin, 2007) (Fig. 1.1). That is similar to how the Cartesian coordinate system, consisting of several real-number lines crossing each other at a common point, plays its role in mathematics and the traditional science (Kline, 1972).

Specifically, any system of concern, be it physical or intellectual, tangible or intangible, a living being or an organization, and a culture or a civilization, can be intuitively treated as a spinning field structure, known as the (systemic) yoyo model of the system. When such structure is seen in the three-dimensional space we live in, the structure in Fig. 1.1 appears. If the system of concern continuously exists, then its yoyo structure remains in a relentless spin motion, where the spin models the internal organizational working of the system. Otherwise, the system will no longer exist as an identifiable entity, since the spin helps to hold all component parts together. For more in-depth discussions, see Chap. 2 below.

As indicated by the literature, this yoyo model of systems has successfully played the role of intuition and playground for scholars to investigate various problems and issues in different disciplines and to explore new knowledge and establish original conclusions holistically. The momentum of its success has been quite impressive, similar to what the Cartesian coordinate system did for the traditional science (Lin, 2009; Lin & Forrest, 2011; Forrest, 2013, 2014; Forrest & Tao, 2014; Ying & Forrest, 2015). In particular, this yoyo model of general systems has been successfully applied in the investigation of Newtonian physics of motion, the concept of energy, economics, finance, history, foundations of mathematics, small-probability disastrous weather forecasting, civilization, business organizations, and the mind, among others. Along this same line of thinking, this book employs this systemic intuition and related systems methodology to develop new theories of economics and business that generalize the corresponding conventional ones with insightful conclusions.

To solve a problem by using concepts and methods of the traditional science, the treasured idea of problem-solving is to establish equations or inequalities by ignoring minor or not closely related details (Kuhn, 1962). For examples of such approach of problem-solving, please go to Sect. 2.1 and/or Sect. 3.1.

On the other hand, to resolve problems or issues by employing concepts and methodology of systems science, the first step is to think and reason through using the logic of holistic thinking. As a cognitive skill, holistic thinking can be deployed successfully only through using the so-called holistic flexibility (Chowdhury, 2023). In particular, holistic flexibility stands for dynamic interplays between the mind of the researcher that absorbs the systemic complexity underneath and the state of the issue in hands (Chowdhury, 2019). When successfully applying the technology of holistic flexibility, one needs to possess five basic skills: thinking holistically, learning creatively, being flexible, deriving responsible outcomes, and producing realistic consequences.

Thinking holistically enables a person to rise above the conventional approach to problem-solving by considering problems contextually and in terms of evolution. Flexibility comes in three forms: cognitive, formulative, and substantive. The first form enables a person to think out of boxes; the second form makes a person readily examine various potential methodologies; and the third form motivates a person to evaluate resource alternatives. Learning creatively means continuously acquiring new information and knowledge and adapting to changing circumstances, expectations, and complexities. Deriving responsible outcomes means the aspiration to produce value additions in one's area of work. Moreover, producing realistic consequences stands for such a skill that can practically bring the above four skills together to produce tangible outcomes.

1.3 Organization of Contents in This Volume

Other than the introductory Chap. 1, this volume consists of five parts. The first part prepares the basic terminologies, necessary concepts, and conclusions for the rest of this volume in order to make the volume as self-contained as possible. The second part details the main systemic challenges that face several known economic and business theories and that encounter the methodologies commonly employed in the studies of economics and business scenarios. The third part pays several revisits to the prevalent producer theory by critically examining how firms may have their individually specific definitions and criteria for optimality and optimization. The fourth part looks at the problem of how to rewrite some of the main conclusions of the prevalent consumer theory. This objective is accomplished through recognizing that for basic survival of each and every consumer, be it a business firm or an individual, its set of possible consumptions can only be assumed to satisfy the condition of reflexivity without those of transitivity and completeness. The fifth part studies how differences between the system of values and beliefs of an employee and that of a firm that employs the individual can inevitably lead to various issues about the efficiencies of the firm. This end helps illustrate how the concept of consumers' natural endowments can open up new territories of knowledge beyond what has been created conventionally.

More specifically, the first part of this volume consists of Chaps. 2–5, where Chap. 2 introduces the concept of systems, its various formal definitions, and how this concept is specified for this volume. After acquainted with the systemic yoyo model of systems, the attention of the chapter turns to how different methodologies are employed systemically throughout this volume. Chapter 3 focuses on the concepts of open and closed systems due to the recognition that many important conclusions of the prevalent economic theory consider mostly closed systems. However, in real life, most economic agents and organizations are really open systems that participate in exchanges with the environment. Chapter 4 employs a simplified approach to study evolutions of an economic market from the angles of profits and market competition. From how primitive firms serve sporadically existent demands in an emerging market to that of the incumbent firms of a maturing market, this chapter establishes the conclusion that the forever evolving preferences of consumers help make market competition relentlessly intensify, while more firms are encouraged to enter the established oligopoly market. Chapter 5 introduces the concepts of natural endowments of individual persons and their generalizations to those of natural endowments of business firms. Moreover, it explains why this volume chooses these endowments as the bases for economic and business decision-making.

As for Part II, it consists of Chaps. 6–10, where Chap. 6 closely examines how some key and useful real-life variables are missing from theoretical studies of economics. It then explains what differences these missing variables can make if one or several of them are considered and included in relevant theories and consequent applications and why it is necessary for economists to identify elementary postulates (in the language of mathematics) and laws (in the language of Newtonian physics) at the level of the four human endowments (self-awareness, imagination, conscience, and free will) as the bases for developing the rest of the theory of economics. Continuing the previous chapter, Chap. 7 investigates how a consumer's utility and consequent optimization are determined by his/her natural endowments by focusing on such general utility that it is a function in the dollar value of consumption, the number of hours spent on waged work, and a particular value-belief system. For the third variable, which is categorical, the chapter examines the following three scenarios: (1) the system encourages the consumption of commodities and devalues waged job; (2) the system reinforces the practice of minimal commodity consumption; and (3) the system demands a non-standard optimization. Among others, the following important conclusion is derived: when an individual decides on how much commodity is to be consumed and how much labor output is to be supplied to waged work by maximizing his utility, the utility and method of optimization are exclusively defined by his value-belief system.

As for Chap. 8, it looks at the assumption of rationality from a different angle—natural endowments of individuals and business firms, respectively, in order to clear up inconsistencies and contradictions in the interpretation of this assumption, as shown in the vast amount of literature. To accomplish this goal, by employing systems logic of reasoning and analysis, this chapter develops the following main conclusion, along with others: At either the micro individual level or the macro firm level, the rationality stands for an optimal fit of the decided choice within the underlying natural endowments of the decision-maker. Corresponding to the following observation that computer simulations can reveal how characteristics of micro-level individuals give rise to macro-level phenomena of systemic wholes, Chap. 9 establishes this simulation-based observation as a theoretical result on a sound systems scientific foundation. In particular, it develops a sufficient condition for characteristics of micro-level agents to rise to the macro-level properties of a systemic whole, even though the former are heterogeneous and behave in an unintended and uncoordinated manner. Additionally, this chapter investigates how and why many macro-level entities appear to answer market calls through organically gathering micro-level agents into uniformly oriented operational wholes, even though these agents have inconsistent or even conflicting interests.

As the final component of Part II, Chap. 10 first looks at how the thinking logic of the well-known fallacy of composition has been widely and erroneously employed in economic and business studies. It then proposes systems science and methodology as an appropriate approach needed for investigating the organizations, evolutions, and interactions of business entities. To support this end both theoretically and practically, the centralizability theorem of general systems is restated here to confirm how unintended and uncoordinated micro-level individual desires can naturally lead to macro-level phenomena. In other words, although there are indeed many properties that emerge at the macro-level not directly out of the characteristics of micro-level individuals, these systemically emergent properties can indeed be explained by using systems logic. Additionally, this chapter proposes a possible way to rewrite statistically confirmed hypotheses into generally true conclusions by referencing to principle of mathematical induction.

Part III of this volume consists of Chaps. 11–13, where Chap. 11 looks at how an individual firm's system of values and beliefs, as reflected in the firm's mission statement, influences the firm's decision-making. Moreover, it derives conclusions on four axioms, used as the starting points of reasoning. By employing a set-theoretic model, concepts and properties of production and profit functions are investigated without using unnecessary assumptions, as those widely appearing in the prevalent microeconomic theory. Other than generalizing Hotelling's lemma and several other known results in producer theory, examples are constructed to show that these known results are not universally true when different systems of values and beliefs are considered. Based on the four axioms just introduced, above, Chap. 12 constructs counterexamples to demonstrate that the optimal production correspondence is not generally homogeneous of degree zero. At the same time, a few important conclusions of the producer theory, including Shephard's lemma, are improved to situation of much stronger versions. Many theoretically beautiful conclusions of the prevalent producer theory were derived by assuming that every firm attempts to maximize its profit and minimize its cost, while all firms employ the same methodology in their optimization efforts. By losing up these two behavioral assumptions, Chap. 13 reestablishes a few well-known results of the producer theory for the general case of not specifying what criteria of priority a firm holds. At the same time, this chapter shows by using counterexamples, among others, that generally, even when individuals act in their own best self-interests, they may not collectively produce unintended greater social benefits and public goods.

The fourth part of this volume consists of Chaps. 14–16, where Chap. 14 looks at what could happen when the following commonly adopted unrealistic assumption is removed: Possible consumptions of each and every consumer are completely ordered. As the consequence of this effort, this chapter shows, among other results, that for an individual no matter how he prefers one consumption over another, (1) there are incomparable consumptions, (2) his consumption preferences may not be transitive, and (3) his indifference relation of consumptions *in practice* may not be transitive. Although these results have been confirmed by different authors with varied settings, the confirmations given here are based purely on analytical analysis without making use of any auxiliary concepts. More importantly, this chapter generalizes the classical conclusion of Debreu (1959) on when a continuous utility representation exists in a very different way from those published recently by Efe Ok and his colleagues. Considering how important the concept of convexity is in the studies of economics in general and consumer theory in particular, Chap. 15 examines how the various concepts of convex preferences and relevant properties can be reestablished for the general system of values and beliefs. Among the series of formal propositions established and counterexamples constructed, this chapter shows (1) the weighted combination of two possible consumptions is not necessarily comparable with any of the possibilities; (2) not every convergent sequence of a consumer's preferable consumptions asymptotically preserves his preference preordering; (3) not all preferences satisfy either positive multiplicativity or additive conservation; and (4) all three types of preference convexities—weak convexity, convexity and, strong convexity—can be introduced to general convex spaces.

By clearly distinguishing three binary relations, the first one $\leqq$ defined on the Euclidean space $\mathbb{R}^\ell$, the second one $\precsim_i$ on a consumer's set of all possible consumptions, and the third one $\leq_i$ on real numbers, Chap. 16 pays a revisit to some of the elementary properties of budget sets, demand correspondences, and the relationship between an individual's preferences and his specific order $\leq_i$ of real numbers. It is found that these visited properties are not generally true without assuming that $\leq_i$ is equal to the conventional order $\leq$ of real numbers and/or without letting the preference relation $\precsim_i$ be complete, reflexive, and transitive on the set X_i of all consumption choices. Additionally, this chapter constructs four counterexamples to demonstrate that (1) when $\leq_i \neq \leq$, the continuity of the budget set is in doubt; (2) generally, an individual consumer's demand correspondence is not homogeneous of degree zero; (3) the preference relation $\precsim_i$ is generally not additively conservative or positively multiplicative; and (4) not every preference relation $\precsim_i$ is asymptotically preserving.

The fifth part of this volume contains only one chapter. As the last unit of this volume, Chap. 17 shows how the systemic yoyo model of general systems can indeed lead to insightful systemic conclusions regarding aspects of internal structures of a business organization. In particular, this chapter introduces the never-perfect value theorem, the selfish employee theorem, and two important principles of efficiency. One principle is on business management and the other on the structure of employees' efforts and devotion towards realizing the mission of their organization. These conclusions suggest that managers and entrepreneurs can simply devote more time and effort on continuously improving their firms' organizational cultures, codes of conduct, and flexibility in terms of management styles and focusing on the big picture of the corporation and its supply-chain ecosystem instead of dwelling on how to improve employees' efficiencies.

Acknowledgment Various specialists, scholars, colleagues, and friends had contributed more or less to the composition of the chapters in this book. I like to use this opportunity to send them my heartfelt thanks for various opportunities for me to collaborate with these highly inspirational professionals over the past years. The following are the details on how these collaborators contributed to each of the chapters of this volume.

Chapter 1 Jeffrey Yi-Lin Forrest (Slippery Rock University).

Chapter 2 Jeffrey Yi-Lin Forrest (Slippery Rock University).

Chapter 3 Jeffrey Yi-Lin Forrest (Slippery Rock University), Qiang Bu (Pennsylvania State University Hersey).

Chapter 4 Jeffrey Yi-Lin Forrest (Slippery Rock University), Joachim Wagner (Leuphana University, Germany), Melanie Anderson (Slippery Rock University), John Lipinski (Indiana University), Yong Liu (Jiangnan University, China), Xiaoguang Tian (Purdue University Fort Wayne).

Chapter 5 Jeffrey Yi-Lin Forrest, Lawrence Shao, Theresa A. Wajda (Slippery Rock University), Bailey C. Forrest (Google), Yong Liu (Jiangnan University, China), Michael Y. Hu (Kent State University), Dale Shao (Marshall University), Jun Liu (Nanjing University of Information Science & Technology), Zhen Li (Texas Woman's University), Brian W. Sloboda (University of Phoenix).

Chapter 6 Jeffrey Yi-Lin Forrest (Slippery Rock University), Kangping Wu (Tsinghua University), Baek-kyoo Joo (Slippery Rock University), Li Yan (Université du Québec en Outaouais, Canada), Kosin **Isariyawongse** (Edinboro University).

Chapter 7 Jeffrey Yi-Lin Forrest (Slippery Rock University), Ashkan Hafezalkotob (Islamic Azad University, Iran), Louie Ren (University of Houston – Victoria), Yong Liu (Jiangnan University), Pavani Tallapally (Slippery Rock University).

Chapter 8 Jeffrey Yi-Lin Forrest (Slippery Rock University), Lawrence Shao (Slippery Rock University), Jun Liu (Nanjing University of Information Science & Technology), Brian W. Sloboda (University of Phoenix), Dale Shao (Marshall University).

Chapter 9 Jeffrey Yi-Lin Forrest (Slippery Rock University), Zaiwu Gong (Nanjing University of Information Science and Technology), Erkan Köse (Nuh Naci Yazgan University, Turkey), Diane D. Galbraith (Slippery Rock University),Oğuzhan A. Arık (Nuh Naci Yazgan University, Turkey).

Chapter 10 Jeffrey Yi-Lin Forrest (Slippery Rock University), Joachim Wagner (Leuphana University, Germany), Jennifer Nightingale (Slippery Rock University), Huan Guo (Jianghan University, China), Jennifer Roy (Waynesburg University).

Chapter 11 Jeffrey Yi-Lin Forrest (Slippery Rock University), Davood Darvishi (Payame Noor University, Iran), Abdou K. Jallow (Slippery Rock University), Zhen Li (Texas Woman's University).

Chapter 12 Jeffrey Yi-Lin Forrest (Slippery Rock University), Kurt Schimmel (Slippery Rock University), Fen Wang (Central Washington University), Ashkan Hafezalkotob (Islamic Azad University, Iran), Jian Liu (Nanjing University of Science and Technology).

Chapter 13 Jeffrey Yi-Lin Forrest (Slippery Rock University), Zaiwu Gong (Nanjing University of Information Science and Technology), Rhonda S. Clark (Slippery Rock University), Reneta Barneva (The State University of New York at Fredonia).

Chapter 14 Jeffrey Yi-Lin Forrest (Slippery Rock University), Davood Darvishi (Payame Noor University, Iran), Rhonda S. Clark (Slippery Rock University), Mojtaba Seyedian (The State University of New York at Fredonia), Jun Liu (Nanjing University of Information Science & Technology).

Chapter 14 Appendix Jeffrey Yi-Lin Forrest (Slippery Rock University), Lawrence Shao (Slippery Rock University), Shynara Sarkambayeva (Jumadilova) (Satbayev University), Dale Shao (Marshall University), Sunita Mondal (Slippery Rock University).

Chapter 15 Jeffrey Yi-Lin Forrest (Slippery Rock University), Tufan Tiglioglu (Alvernia University),Yong Liu (Jiangnan University), Donald Mong (Slippery Rock University), Marta Cardin (Ca' Foscari University of Venice, Italy).

Chapter 16 Jeffrey Yi-Lin Forrest (Slippery Rock University), Zaiwu Gong (Nanjing University of Information Science and Technology), Zhen Li (Texas Woman's University), Shynara Sarkambayeva (Jumadilova) (Satbayev University, Kazakhstan), John Golden (Slippery Rock University).

Chapter 17 Jeffrey Yi-Lin Forrest (Slippery Rock University), Dillon Z. Forrest (Steady, LLC), Bruce Orvis (Slippery Rock University).

References

Allen, F., & Gale, D. (2001). Financial contagion. *Journal of Political Economy, 108*, 1–33.

Alonso, S., Herrera-Viedma, E., Chiclana, F., & Herrera, F. (2010). A web-based consensus support system for group decision making problems and incomplete preferences. *Information Science, 180*(23), 4477–4495.

Aumann, R. (1962). Utility theory without the completeness axiom. *Econometrica, 30*, 445–462.

Battiston, S., Delli Gatti, D., Gallegati, M., Greenwald, B., & Stiglitz, J. (2007). Credit chains and bankruptcies avalanches in supply networks. *Journal of Economic Dynamics and Control, 31*, 2061–2084.

Becker, G. S. (1962). Irrational behavior and economic theory. *The Journal of Political Economy, 70*(1), 1–13.

Birnbaum, M. H., & Gutierrez, R. J. (2007). Testing for intransitivity of preferences predicted by a lexicographic semi-order. *Organizational Behavior and Human Decision Process, 104*, 96–112. https://doi.org/10.1016/j.obhdp.2007.02.001

Bjerknes, V. (1898). Uber einen hydrodynamischen Fundamentalsatz und seine Anwendung besonders auf die Mechanik der Atmosphare und des Weltmeeres. *Kongliga Svenska Vetenskaps-Academiens Nya Handlingar, 31*, 1–35.

Blanchard, O. (2018). On the future of macroeconomic models. *Oxford Review of Economic Policy, 34*(1–2), 43–54.

Boissay, F. (2006). *Credit chains and the propagation of financial distress* (European Central Bank, Working Paper No. 573).

Bosi, G., & Herden, G. (2012). Continuous multi-utility representations of preorders. *Journal of Mathematical Economics, 48*, 212–218.

Branden, N. (1969). *The psychology of self-esteem*. Nash Publishing Corporation.

Campitelli, G., & Gobet, F. (2010). Herbert Simon's decision-making approach: Investigation of cognitive processes in experts. *Review of General Psychology, 14*(4), 354–364.

Caplin, A., & Schotter, A. (Eds.). (2008). *The foundations of positive and normative economics: A handbook*. Oxford University Press.
Cartwright, E. (2014). *Behavioral economics* (2nd ed.). Routledge.
Cettolin, E., & Riedl, A. (2019). Revealed preferences under uncertainty: Incomplete preferences and preferences for randomization. *Journal of Economic Theory, 181*, 547–585.
Chiou, J. S., Hsiao, C. C., & Chiu, T. Y. (2018). The credibility and attribution of online reviews: Differences between high and low product knowledge consumers. *Online Information Review, 42*(5), 630–646.
Chowdhury, R. (2019). Systems thinking. In R. Chowdhury (Ed.), *Systems thinking for management consultants: Introducing holistic flexibility* (pp. 3–28). Springer. https://doi.org/10.1007/978-981-13-8530-8_1
Chowdhury, R. (2023). Holistic flexibility for the application of systems thinking as a cognitive skill. *Systemic Practice and Action Research, 36*, 803.
Debreu, G. (1959). *Theory of value: An axiomatic analysis of economic equilibrium*. Yale University Press.
Delli Gatti, D., Gaffeo, E., & Gallegati, M. (2010). Complex agent-based macroeconomics: A manifesto for a new paradigm. *Journal of Economic Interaction and Coordination, 5*, 111–135.
Delli Gatti, D., Desiderio, S., Gaffeo, E., Cirillo, P., & Gallegati, M. (2011). *Macroeconomics from the bottom-up*. Springer.
Dubra, J., & Ok, E. A. (2002). A model of procedural decision making in the presence of risk. *International Economic Review, 43*(4), 1053–1080.
Estevez-Toranzo, M., & Herves-Beloso, C. (1995). On the existence of continuous preference orderings without utility representations. *Journal of Mathematical Economics, 24*(4), 305–309.
Evren, O., & Ok, E. A. (2011). On the multi-utility representation of preference relations. *Journal of Mathematical Economics, 47*, 554–563.
Fahimnia, B., Sarkis, J., & Eshragh, A. (2015). A tradeoff model for green supply chain planning: A leanness-versus-greenness analysis. *Omega, 54*(1), 173–190.
Finocchiaro, M. A. (2015). The fallacy of composition: Guiding concepts, historical cases, and research problems. *Journal of Applied Logic, 13*(2, Part B), 24–43.
Forrest, J. Y. L. (2013). *A systemic perspective on cognition and mathematics*. CRC Press.
Forrest, J. Y. L. (2014). *A systems perspective on financial systems*. CRC Press.
Forrest, J. Y. L. (2018). *General systems theory: Foundation, intuition and applications in business decision making*. Springer.
Forrest, J. Y. L. (2022). Reestablishing the producer theory on the basis of firms' natural endowments. *Pure Mathematics and Applied Mathematics, 38*(3), 322–343.
Forrest, J. Y. L., & Liu, Y. (2021). *Value in business—A holistic, systems-based approach to creating and capturing value*. Springer.
Forrest, J. Y. L., & Tao, L. X. (2014). *Investment and employment opportunities in China*. CRC Press.
Forrest, J. Y.-L., Duan, X. J., Zhao, C. L., & Xu, L. D. (2013). *Systems science: Methodological approaches*. CRC Press.
Forrest, J. Y. L., Zhao, H. C., & Shao, L. (2018). Engineering rapid industrial revolutions for impoverished agrarian nations. *Theoretical Economics Letters, 8*, 2594–2640.
Forrest, J. Y. L., Nicholls, J., Schimmel, K., & Liu, S. F. (2020). *Managerial decision making: A holistic approach*. Springer.
Forrest, J. Y. L., Hafezalkotob, A., Ren, L., Liu, Y., & Tallapally, P. (2021). Utility and optimization's dependence on decision-makers' underlying value-belief systems. *Review of Economic and Business Studies, 14*(2), 125–149. https://doi.org/10.47743/rebs-2021-2-0007
Friedman, M. (1953). *Essays in positive economics*. University of Chicago Press.
Gabaix, X. (2011). The granular origins of aggregate fluctuations. *Econometrica, 79*, 733–772.
Gilboa, I. (2010). *Rational choice*. The MIT Press.

Gul, F., & Pesendorfer, W. (2008). The case for mindless economics. In A. Caplin & A. Schotter (Eds.), *The foundations of positive and normative economics: A handbook*. Oxford University Press.
Hammerton, M. (2020). Deontic constraints are maximizing rules. *Journal of Value Inquiry, 54*(4), 571–588. https://doi.org/10.1007/s10790-020-09731-8
Hansson, B. (1968). Choice structures and preference relations. *Synthese, 18*, 443–458.
Hervés-Beloso, C., & Cruces, H. V. (2019). Continuous preference orderings representable by utility functions. *Journal of Economic Surveys, 33*(1), 179–194.
Hong, Z. F., & Guo, X. L. (2019). Green product supply chain contracts considering environmental responsibilities. *Omega, 83*(1), 155–166.
Hu, T. C. (1982). *Combinatorial algorithms*. Addison-Wesley.
Hudik, M. (2012). Transitivity: A comment on Block and Barnett. *The Quarterly Journal of Austrian Economics, 15*(4), 456–462.
Hudik, M. (2019). Two interpretations of the rational choice theory and the relevance of behavioral critique. *Rationality and Society, 31*(4), 464–489.
Hussain, W. (2012). Corporations, profit maximization and the personal sphere. *Economics and Philosophy, 28*(3), 311–331.
Jacob, B., McCall, B., & Stange, K. (2018). College as country club: Do colleges cater to students' preferences for consumption? *Journal of Labor Economics, 36*(2), 309–348.
Jensen, M. C. (2001). Value maximization, stakeholder theory, and the corporate objective function. *European Financial Management, 7*(3), 297–317.
Kahneman, D. (2011). *Thinking, fast and slow*. Farrar, Straus and Giroux.
Kenny, A. (2012). *A new history of Western philosophy*. Oxford University Press.
Kline, M. (1972). *Mathematical thought from ancient to modern times*. Oxford University Press.
Klir, G. (1985). *Architecture of systems problem solving*. Plenum Press.
Klir, G. (2001). *Facets of systems science*. Springer.
Kuhn, T. (1962). *The structure of scientific revolutions*. University of Chicago Press.
Levin, J., & Milgrom, P. (2004). *Producer theory*. Retrieved November 5, 2021, from https://web.stanford.edu/~jdlevin/Econ%20202/Producer%20Theory.pdf
Lin, Y. (1999). *General systems theory: A mathematical approach*. Plenum and Kluwer Academic Publishers.
Lin, Y. (2007). Systemic yoyo model and applications in Newton's, Kepler's laws, etc. *Kybernetes, 36*(3–4), 484–516.
Lin, Y. (2009). *Systemic yoyos: Some impacts of the second dimension*. Auerbach Publications.
Lin, Y., & Forrest, B. (2011). *Systemic structure behind human organizations: From civilizations to individuals*. Springer.
Lin, Y., & Forrest, B. C. (2012). *Systemic structure behind human organizations: From civilizations to individuals*. Springer.
Lin, Y., & OuYang, S. C. (2010). *Irregularities and prediction of major disasters*. CRC Press.
Liu, S. F., Yang, Y. J., & Forrest, J. Y. L. (2016). *Grey data analysis: Methods, models and applications*. Springer.
Lorenz, E. N. (1993). *The essence of chaos*. Washington University Press.
Lovett, F. (2006). Rational choice theory and explanation. *Rationality and Society, 18*(2), 237–272.
Lucas, R. (1976). Econometric policy evaluation: A critique. *Carnegie-Rochester Conference Series on Public Policy, 1*, 19–46.
Maialeh, R. (2019). Generalization of results and neoclassical rationality: Unresolved controversies of behavioural economics methodology. *Quality & Quantity, 53*, 1743–1761.
Mandler, G. (1982). The integration and elaboration of memory structures. In F. Klix, J. Hoffman, & E. van der Meer (Eds.), *Cognitive research in psychology* (pp. 33–40). North-Holland.
Mandler, M. (1999). *Incomplete preferences and rational intransitivity of choice. Mimeo*. Harvard University.

Mandler, M. (2001). A difficult choice in preference theory: Rationality implies completeness or transitivity but not both. In E. Milgram (Ed.), *Varieties of practical reasoning* (pp. 373–402). MIT Press.
Mas-Collel, A., Whinston, M. D., & Green, J. R. (1995). *Microeconomic theory*. Oxford University Press.
McGrath, R. G. (2013). *The end of competitive advantage: How to keep your strategy moving as fast as your business*. Harvard Business Review Press.
McKenzie, R. (2010). Predictably rational? In *Search of defenses for rational behavior in economics*. Springer.
Meng, F. Y., & Chen, X. H. (2015). A new method for group decision making with incomplete fuzzy preference relations. *Knowledge-Based Systems, 73*, 111–123.
Mullainathan, S., & Thaler, R. H. (2000, October). *Behavioral economics* (NBER Working Paper No. 7948). National Bureau of Economic Research.
Nishimura, H., & Ok, E. A. (2016). Utility representation of an incomplete and nontransitive preference relation. *Journal of Economic Theory, 166*, 164–185.
Ok, E. A. (2002). Utility representation of an incomplete preference relation. *Journal of Economic Theory, 104*(2), 429–449.
Ok, E. A., & Masatlioglu, Y. (2007). A theory of (relative) discounting. *Journal of Economic Theory, 137*, 214–245.
Porter, M. E. (1985). *Competitive advantage: Creating and sustaining superior performance*. Free Press.
Qu, Y. (1985). The songs of the south: An anthology of ancient Chinese poems by Qu Yuan and other poets (D. Haykes, trans). Penguin Classics.
Rössel, J., & Schroedter, J. H. (2015). Cosmopolitan cultural consumption: Preferences and practices in a heterogenous, urban population in Switzerland. *Poetics, 50*, 80–95.
Rostow, W. W. (1960). *The stages of economic growth: A non-communist manifesto*. Cambridge University Press.
Rubinstein, A. (1998). *Modeling bounded rationality*. The MIT Press.
Sahni, N. S. (2016). Advertising spillovers: Evidence from online field experiments and implications for returns on advertising. *Journal of Marketing Research, 53*(4), 459–478.
Schelling, T. C. (1969). Models of segregation. *American Economic Review, 59*(2), 488–493.
Sen, A. (1991). *On ethics and economics*. Wiley.
Sen, A. (2010). Introduction. In: Adam Smith (1790): The Theory of Moral Sentiments (6th ed.). New York: Penguin, vii–xxix.
Shannon, C. E. (1949). *The mathematical theory of communication*. Illinois University Press.
Simon, H. A. (1986). Rationality in psychology and economics. *The Journal of Business, 59*(4), S209–S224.
Smets, F., & Wouters, R. (2007). Shocks and frictions in US business cycles: A Bayesian DSGE approach. *American Economic Review, 97*(3), 586–606.
Soros, G. (2003). *The Alchemy of Finance*. Wiley.
Stigler, G. J., & Becker, G. S. (1977). De gustibus non est disputandum. *American Economic Review, 67*, 76–90.
Sujan, M. (1985). Consumer knowledge effects on evaluation strategies mediating consumer judgments. *Journal of Consumer Research, 12*, 31–46.
Taylor, C. (1989). *Sources of the self: The making of the modern identity*. Harvard University Press.
Thurner, S., Farmer, D., & Geanakoplos, J. (2012). Leverage causes fat tails and clustered volatility. *Quantitative Finance, 12*(5), 695–707.
Tversky, A. (1969). Intransitivity of preferences. *Psychological Review, 76*(1), 31–48.
Van Fleet, D. D. (2021). Utility, maximizing, and the satisficing concept: A historical approach at reconciliation. *Journal of Behavioral and Applied Management, 21*(2). https://doi.org/10.21818/001c.29691
Vines, D., & Wills, S. (2018). The rebuilding macroeconomic theory project: An analytical assessment. *Oxford Review of Economic Policy, 34*(1–2), 1–42.

von Bertalanffy, L. (1924). *Einfuhrung in Spengler's werk*. Literaturblatt Kolnische Zeitung.

von Bertalanffy, L. (1968). *General systems theory*. George Braziller.

von Mises, L. (1949). *Human action: A treatise in economics*. Yale University Press.

Wagner, J. (2012). The German manufacturing sector is a granular economy. *Applied Economics Letters, 19*, 1663–1665.

Wen, Y. (2016). *The making of an economic superpower: Unlocking China's secret of rapid industrialization*. World Scientific.

Weyl, G. E. (2019). Price theory. *Journal of Economic Literature, 57*(2), 329–384.

Wu, K. P. (2003). *Advanced microeconomics*. Tsinghua University Press.

Wu, K. P. (2006). *Advanced macroeconomics*. Tsinghua University Press.

Wu, Y., & Lin, Y. (2002). *Beyond nonstructural quantitative analysis: Blown-ups, spinning currents and the modern science*. World Scientific.

Yang, X., & Andersson, D. E. (2018). Spatial aspects of entrepreneurship and innovation. *The Annals of Regional Science, 61*, 457–462. https://doi.org/10.1007/s00168-018-0888-z

Ying, Y. R., & Forrest, J. Y. L. (2015). *Capital account liberation: Methods and applications*. CRC Press.

Part II
Preparation

Chapter 2
Systems Science and the Logic of Systemic Reasoning

Jeffrey Yi-Lin Forrest

Abstract To make this book as self-contained as possible, this chapter reviews the basic concepts and results of systems science and systemic reasoning that are related to this volume. When the logic of such reasoning is employed in either theoretical or applied works, the decision-maker, be it a scholarly researcher or a business manager, will be treating the scenario of concern as a system instead of a pile of some isolated components. The former holistically associates components into an organic whole, while the latter treats each component independently with the hope that the collection of the independent understandings of individual parts would naturally rise into a holistic understanding of the entire scenario.

For readers who are not mathematically inclined, the following sections that are heavy with mathematical symbols, notations, and terminologies can be skipped without causing much difficulty with the reading of the rest of this book.

This chapter is organized as follows. Section 2.1 quickly glances through the issue of how the concept of systems has been mostly ignored as a viable methodology when problems and issues of the business world are concerned with. Section 2.2 examines how difficult it is to define the concept of systems. Section 2.3 details the definitions of systems that are to be used in this book and some related elementary theorems. Section 2.4 introduces the systemic yoyo model and provides a few samples of how the logic of systems thinking and methodology can help produce insightful conclusions. Section 2.5 critically analyzes common methods used in the literature of economic and business studies and outlines how various methods are holistically employed in this volume. This chapter concludes in Sect. 2.6.

Keywords Cartesian coordinate system · Internal structure · Object · Relation · Systems thinking · Systemic yoyo model

J. Y.-L. Forrest, *Systemic Principles of Applied Economic Philosophies I*,
Translational Systems Sciences 38, https://doi.org/10.1007/978-981-99-7273-9_2

2.1 Systems: A Concept Mostly Ignored by Conventional Methodologies

The term "system" represents an organic whole within which components are so associated to each other that certain holistic properties of the whole emerge (Lin, 1999). Hence, systems are everywhere, especially in investigations of economic issues and business decision-making. For instance, each individual person is a biological system that is composed of numerous smaller systems, such as internal organs, body parts, etc. Moreover, individuals are also members of various social and economic systems (e.g., families, neighborhoods, communities, occupational groups) that compose their social identities. Beyond social identity, people regularly interact with different systems (e.g., vehicles, smart devices, retail stores, and organizations). Because of the existence of such individuals that are part of various systems simultaneously, systems are constantly interacting with one another. This end shows that when conducting scholarly studies, other than using numbers and variables to investigate problems and issues of business and economics, which is what is mostly done in the literature, there is a need to employ the concept of systems and relevant methods to study economic phenomena in order to obtain new understandings and innovative conclusions that are closer to the real-life situations than those obtained through employing numbers and variables only.

Although the concept of systems can be traced back to the very start of the recorded history, it was von Bertalanffy (1924) who formally introduced it in biology in the late 1920s through observing that "because the fundamental character of living things is their organization, the customary investigation of individual parts and processes cannot provide a complete explanation of the phenomenon of life." Following the lead of von Bertalanffy, approaches of systems analysis and theories of systems have been developed a great deal. In particular, starting in the early 1960s, the work to establish a theory of general systems has begun in order to lay down the theoretical foundation for all discipline-specific approaches of systems analysis. Led by some of the most powerful minds of our modern time, a systems movement of the global scale has been ongoing since over half a century ago. Within this movement, many scholars have tried to define the concept of general systems and then apply the concept and consequent theory to solving problems in various research areas. However, technical difficulties of introducing an ideal definition of general systems appeared; and notably unsuccessful applications of general systems theory identified [for details, see, e.g., Berlinski (1976), Lilienfeld (1978)]. Some of the main lessons learned include the following:

1. There might not exist an ideal definition for general systems, upon which a general systems theory could be developed so that this theory would serve as the theoretical foundation for all discipline-specific approaches of systems analysis.

2. Without an ideal definition of general systems in place, the ideal of developing a "general systems theory" becomes meaningless. For such circumstances, the main focus is placed in the name of systems analysis.
3. Based on historical experience and the "unreasonable effectiveness" of mathematics (Wigner, 1960), several fruitful definitions of general systems have been introduced since the early 1960s, although each such definition can only capture the concept of systems partially.

Although the idealized general systems theory cannot be developed without an adequate definition of general systems, each particular attempt of defining general systems has indeed led to a specific theory of general systems (Lin et al., 1997). Each of such specific theories reflects one or several aspects of the imagined, idealized theory of general systems by demonstrating that innovative conclusions can be obtained by using the particular definitions of systems and consequent theories.

With nearly 100 years of rapid development, systems science and methodologies have been widely accepted and employed by scientists, scholars, and practitioners in all disciplines (Blauberg et al., 1977; Klir, 2001), including business-related studies. For example, Rostow (1960) in economics wrote when he investigated the Industrial Revolution:

> The classical theory of production is formulated under essentially static assumptions ... to merge classical production theory with Keynesian income analysis ... introduced the dynamic variables: population, technology, entrepreneurship, etc. But ... do so in forms so rigid and general that their models cannot grip the essential phenomena of growth ... We require a dynamic theory ... which isolates not only the distribution of income between consumption, savings, and investment (and the balance of production between consumers and capital goods) but which focuses directly and in some detail on the composition of investment and on developments within particular sectors of the economy.

And many others, cf., Forrest (2018), Klir (1985), Lin (2009), and Porter (1985), also demonstrate how powerful systemic thinking and relevant methodologies can be in terms of producing conclusions that were unknown before regarding organizations. Beyond that, these conclusions are realistically more reliable and practically usable than those obtained without using the concept of systems.

One reason why these conclusions that were unknown before can be produced by using systemic thinking and methodologies is because there is an existing methodological gap in the literature of business and economics studies. In particular, all the methods of analysis and epistemological tools widely employed in social science cannot effectively describe and investigate interactions of business entities of different magnitudes, economies of various scales, and markets of whatever kinds unless one brings systems research and systemic reasoning into relevant works. As for evidence that supports the aforementioned lack of adequate methods and tools, one can simply examine recent issues of the journal, named "Organizational Research Methods," although the description of the journal says (https://journals.sagepub.com/home/orm, accessed on February 21, 2023) that "(it) brings relevant methodological developments to a wide range of researchers in organizational and management studies." As for the evidence that systems research and systemic reasoning have brought forward important conclusions in economic and business studies, here are a few recent publications: Forrest and Liu (2022), Forrest et al. (2020), Lin and Forrest (2012), and Porter (1985). Since the 1920s, a systemic and holistic view of nature, organizations, and social events has permeated the entire spectrum of knowledge. See, for example, Lin (2009) and references found there for details on how specific areas of learning have benefitted from systems science and related research.

Out of the physical world, two important concepts—numbers and systems—can be abstracted. However, these concepts are fundamentally different. Specifically, the concept of numbers is notionally extracted when the internal structure of the matter of concern is ignored or seen as a collection of not well related objects. For example, the concept of number 2 is extracted from such scenarios as 2 apples, 2 people, 2 companies, two states, etc., with the internal structures of the apples, people, companies, and states and possible associations between the apples, people, companies, and states ignored. Moreover, when a business firm is seen as a bundle of employees, investments, capital assets, products, and any other related stuffs, the whole of the organization is divided into pieces, while the underlying relationships among and between the components and factors of that organization are mostly ignored. To illustrate what is meant here, let us look at the following simple, however, typical example of middle-school algebra on how organizational structures are purposefully ignored in order to employ the concept of numbers and that of variables.

> If painter A can do a job in twelve hours and painter B can do it in eight hours, how much of the job can they do *per hour* if they work together?
>
> Solution: Based on the given condition, painter A can do 1/12 of the job per hour, while painter B can do 1/8 of the job per hour. So, when A and B work together, they can do 5/24 (=1/12 + 1/8) of the job per hour.
>
> Comment: The solution of this typical middle-school algebra problem ignores the structure of the job and that of the interacting people A and B. That is, the solution obtained above is only a mathematical estimate; it is most likely far from the actual number of hours needed to complete the job.

By using the concept of systems and the systemic thinking, each business firm is investigated as a holistic entity that has an internal structure and participates in exchanges with the environment. The focus is both the components that make up the firm and their associations, where exchanges with the outside world are studied by the concept of subsystems and open systems. In particular, each firm, as a system, is a subsystem of a larger system, known as the environment. For example, no matter which business organization is concerned with, it is surely a subsystem of a larger environment, such as the supply-chain ecosystem of the organization.

By comparing what is discussed above, it can be seen that when one limits himself to the concept of numbers and consequent methods, he has to suffer from the emerging difficulties of studying interactions of organizations. In other words, to understand how an organization, as an organic whole composed of component parts, operates and how it interacts with other organizations, its internal operational connections of the parts must be considered. Or, speaking differently, when an organization is seen holistically, as it should be in order to understand how the business world actually functions, the concept of systems needs to be employed, where such elements as employees, capital, and properties form an organic whole through various relationships. Without such relationships, the organization simply does not exist, although the component parts are still around. That is, studies in business-related disciplines are essentially about relationships of systems, be they firms, markets, industries, or economies.

In short, the concepts of numbers and systems are majorly different as follows:

1. The former is a small-scale local concept, while the latter a large-scale organizational concept (Lin, 1988, 1999).
2. Numbers appear only post existence, while systems emerge at the same time when a physical or an intellectual existence comes into being (Lin, 2009).

Item (2) above is the reason why systems methodology stands for a more appropriate tool than theories developed on numbers and variables for investigating economic entities and business activities when their internal structures should not be ignored. Moreover, that is also the reason why market participants still cannot successfully make advanced predictions for imminent economic disasters (for more in-depth explanation, see Lin & OuYang, 2010).

2.2 The Definition of General Systems

The so-called systems science is simply the totality of different studies of general systems and various specific kinds of systems. To potentially make this science practically useful, scholars from different disciplines within the last century have established many valuable approaches of systems analysis. Of course, as with any scientific theory, each of these approaches has to start from how a system is technically defined, leading to different areas and branches of systems science. To establish a theoretical foundation for all these approaches of systems analysis, Mesarovic, in the early 1960s, introduced the mathematical definition of (general) systems, based on Cantor's set theory, as follows (Mesarovic & Takahara, 1975): A (general) system S is a relation on nonempty sets V_i, $i \in I$:

$$S \subseteq \prod \{V_i : i \in I\}, \tag{2.1}$$

where I is an index set.

This structural definition of general systems reflects the unification of "isolated" objects, such as the elements in the sets V_i, $i \in I$, a relation, denoted by S, between the objects, and the structure of layers. Specifically, elements in the nonempty sets V_i, $i \in I$, are the objects of the system of concern, Srepresents the relation of interest between objects, and elements of the sets V_i, $i \in I$, can themselves be systems again. By using this technical definition of systems, a set of related theories of systems are established. For related details, see Mesarovic and Takahara (1975, 1989, 2003), Mesarovic et al. (1970), Kijima et al. (2022a, b), and references listed in these works.

To make this definition of systems more symbolically operational for the purpose of developing a practically useful systems theory, Lin (1987) generalizes the previous concept of general systems to the following:

> S is a (general) system, provided that S is equal to an ordered pair(M, R) of sets, written as $S = (M, R)$, where M consists of all elements of the system, and R is a set of some relations defined on the set M.

Each element in M is called an object of the system S, and M and R are called the object set and the relation set of S, respectively.

For the convenience of studying the interrelationship between the systems of concern and some of their environments, Bunge (1979) considered a model of systems as follows:

> For nonempty set T, the ordered triple $W = (C, E, S)$ is a system over T if and only if C and E are disjoint subsets of T and S is a nonempty set of relations on $C \cup E$; C and E are called the composition and an environment of the system W, respectively.

Different from the few technical definitions of general systems, Klir (1985) introduced a philosophical concept of general systems as follows:

> A system is what is distinguished as a system.

Theorctically, Klir's definition contains the most general meaning of the concept of systems originally posed by von Bertalanffy. In comparison, although the previously mentioned definitions do not explicitly mention the existence of a moderator who distinguishes what is considered as a system, such a moderator exists implicitly. In particular, the existence of the sets, such as V_i, $i \in I$, in the case of Mesarovic and Takahara, M and R in the case of Lin, and C, E, S and T in the case of Bunge, means that someone has to define these sets.

Starting in 1976, Xuemou Wu and his followers have studied many different theories, covered by the overarching title of pansystems analysis under the name "pansystems." This pansystems analysis is a new research of multilevels across all disciplines. The theory deals with general systems, relations, symmetry, transformation, generalized calculus, and *shengke* (means survival and vanquishing), called the emphases of pansystems. Based on the research of these emphases, the theory blends philosophical reasoning, mathematical logic, and mechanical structures into one solid body of knowledge (Wu, 1990).

The discussion here gives rise naturally to the following question: Why was the concept of systems not studied more in-depth until the recent century? One answer is that the development of modern technology, e.g., communication technology, designs of satellites, climate control of giant buildings, etc., reveals one fact: History is presently in a special moment, where the accumulation of knowledge has reached such a level that each discovery of a relation between different areas of knowledge will materially produce a useful or consumable product. That is the reason behind the claim (Forrest, 2018) that the next scientific revolution will be system based.

Closely related to the concept of systems are the following questions:

1. What is the meaning of a system with contradictory relations, e.g., $\{x > y, x \leq y\}$ as part of the relation set?
2. How can one know whether there exist contradictory or inconsistent relations in a given realistic system?

Klir's definition of systems, which is one of the definitions with the widest meaning among all definitions of systems, implies that generally these two questions cannot be answered. Concerning this end, a theorem of Gödel shows that it is impossible to show whether the systems representation of mathematics, developed on the ZFC axiom, is consistent. For a detailed discussion of the systems representation of mathematics, see Lin (1989). This fact implies that there are such systems, for example, the system of set theory on ZFC, that one does not know if propositions with contradictory meanings exist or not within the systems. This means that maybe not every system is consistent or that not every system contains no contradictory relations. This end is quite easy to understand in terms of business organizations, because conflicts or inconsistencies of various kinds always co-exist in business decision-making and consequent implementations.

Magnificent successes of the conventional science, for the most part, are achieved on the bases of the works of Descartes and Galileo. They systematically formulated the needed methods of reasoning and administration. Specifically, Descartes suggested to divide the problem under consideration into as many small parts as possible and study each isolated part (Kline, 1972), and Galileo recommended to simplify the complicated phenomenon of concern into basic parts and processes (Kuhn, 1962). In the history of science and technology, these methods of reasoning and administration have been very successfully applied, leading to great victories one by one (von Bertalanffy, 1972). Beyond so, these methods are still currently widely employed in research activities of natural and social sciences.[1]

The current world is witnessing the availability of increasing deluges of data and rising levels of complexity. Accordingly, scholars and managerial decision-makers are forced to study problems and issues with many cause-effect chains (i.e., systems) and non-negligible internal organizations and structures. So, relevantly adequate logics of reasoning and epistemological methodologies need to be introduced in order to successfully deal with such problems that heavily involve systems, organizations, and structures. Speaking differently, in the study of such problems, Descartes' and Galileo's methods have to be modified and improved, because these methods emphasize on separating the whole of concern into parts and isolated processes instead of being a whole. However, according to systemic thinking and real-life practice of economic and business decision-making (e.g., Porter, 1979, 1985), one needs to recognize that other than a pile of innumerable isolated "parts," each business decision is more about how these parts work together organically as a whole. One basic characteristic of economic and business decisions is about organization(s), interactions between internal components and processes, and

[1] In fact, such methods and approaches are also widely employed in economic and business studies, see, for example, Fiske and Pavelchak (1986), Forrest and Liu (2022), and Pavelchak (1989).

exchanges with and among external organizations. Therefore, the basic theories of economics and business need to be about systemically knowing individual companies, markets, economies, and the world that is filled with a myriad of interacting wholes.

2.3 The Concept of Systems Adopted for This Book

As suggested by the title, this section details the definitions of systems that will be employed in this book. It consists of two subsections with the first one looking at several related concepts needed to produce a systematic theory. Moreover, the second subsection dives into the study of the structures of general systems.

2.3.1 Comparisons of Systemic Structures

For the purpose of developing theoretically significant and practically useful results, this volume adopts the definition of a system respectively given by Klir (1985) and by Lin (1987, 1999): A system is what is distinguished as a system; and a system can be written as an ordered pair of sets

$$S = (M, R), \tag{2.2}$$

where M is the set of all objects of the system S and R a set of relations defined on M.

Before moving forward any further, let us note that this ordered-pair representation of the general system $S = (M, R)$ is of a very wide range of methodological coverage. For example, relations in the relation set R can be systems of algebraic equations, inequalities, differential equations, statistics-based expressions, etc. For related details, see Forrest (2018). At the same time, relations in R do not have to be numerical or quantitative. For example, it will not be appropriate to express the relationship that two people x and y are siblings quantitatively (Liu & Lin, 2010), unless one only likes to capture this relationship partially.

Theorem 2.1 Given two systems $S_1 = (M_1, R_1)$ and $S_2 = (M_2, R_2)$, $S_1 = S_2$ if and only if $M_1 = M_2$ and $R_1 = R_2$.

Proof By the definition of ordered pairs, we have

$$S_i = \{\{M_i\}, \{M_i, R_i\}\}, \quad i = 1, 2. \tag{2.3}$$

So, the sufficiency of this result is clear.

To prove the necessity, suppose that $S_1 = S_2$ or, equivalently, $(M_1, R_1) = (M_2, R_2)$. So, it follows that

$$\{M_2\} \in (M_1, R_1) \quad \text{and} \quad \{M_2, R_2\} \in (M_1, R_1).$$

That is,

$$(1)\{M_2\} = \{M_1\} \quad \text{or} \quad (2)\ \{M_2\} = \{M_1, R_1\}$$

and

$$(3)\{M_2, R_2\} = \{M_1\} \quad \text{or} \quad (4)\{M_2, R_2\} = \{M_1, R_1\}.$$

If equation (2) holds true, then $M_1 = M_2 = R_1$. That contradicts the definition of R_1. So, equation (2) cannot be true, while equation (1) has to be true. That is, $M_2 = M_1$. Similarly, equation (3) cannot hold true so that equation (4) has to hold. Since $M_i \neq R_i$, equation (4) implies due to $M_2 = M_1$ that $R_2 = R_1$.

To produce practically useful results, the sets M and R in the definition of a system $S = (M, R)$ in Eq. (2.2) are given the following interpretations: the object set M represents how the system S is made up the isolated component parts, while the relation set R describes how objects in M are associated with each other so that the whole of the system S emerges. For example, each business firm is composed of a set of specific employees, properties, equipment, assets, etc. This set is collectively known as that of objects of the organizational system of the firm. More importantly, these objects are associated with each other through a set of particular relations. It is these particular relations that the whole, known as the firm, emerges both physically and intellectually and is acknowledged by others as a functional firm. Symbolically, for each relation $r \in R$, there is an ordinal number $n = n(r)$ such that

$$r \subseteq M^n = \{(m_1, m_2, \ldots, m_\gamma, \ldots) : m_\gamma \in M \text{ and} \gamma \in n(r)\}, \tag{2.4}$$

where M^n stands for the Cartesian product of n copies of set M, and each ordinal number n is seen as the set of all ordinal numbers less than itself (Kuratowski & Mostowski, 1976).

For theoretical completeness and for the purpose of making Klir's definition practically operational in terms of developing useful theories, a system $S = (M, R)$ is said to be discrete if it satisfies

$$R = \varnothing \quad \text{or} \quad R = \{\varnothing\} \quad \text{and} \quad M \neq \varnothing, \tag{2.5}$$

where $\varnothing$ stands for the empty set. In other words, a system S is discrete when it consists of isolated objects only.

A system $S = (M, R)$ is said to be trivial, if $M = \varnothing$. Similar to the concept of zero in mathematics, both discrete and trivial systems are needed for making the consequent theory of general systems theoretically complete and practically usable.

For a given system $S = (M, R)$, another system $S_1 = (M_1, R_1)$ is said to be a subsystem of S, if M_1 is a subset of M and R_1 is a subset of R. Moreover, the system

$S_1 = (M_1, R_1)$ is said to be a partial system of S, if M_1 is a subset of M and for any relation $r_1 \in R_1$ there is relation $r \in R$ such that

$$r_1 = r \mid M_1. \tag{2.6}$$

That is, the relation r_1 of the system S_1 is the restriction of a relation r in the system S. In other words, for each relation r_1 in the subsystem S_1, there is a relation r in R of the original system S such that r_1 consists of all relationship descriptions in r that involves only objects contained in M_1. For convenience and without causing confusion, the subsystem S_1 is written as $S \mid M_1$ and the relation set R_1 as $R \mid M_1$, consisting of relations in R but restricted on M_1.

Let $S_i = (M_i, R_i)$, $i = 1, 2$, be systems and h: $M_1 \to M_2$ a mapping from the object set $M_1$to the other object set M_2. For each relation $r \in R_1$ and any object sequence $(x_1, x_2, x_3, \ldots) \in r$, let

$$h(x_1, x_2, x_3, \ldots) = (h(x_1), h(x_2), h(x_3), \ldots) \tag{2.7}$$

and

$$h(r) = \{h(x_1, x_2, x_3, \ldots) : (x_1, x_2, x_3, \ldots) \in r\}. \tag{2.8}$$

Without confusion, write h: $S_1 \to S_2$. Notice that h: $S_1 \to S_2$ does not imply that for any $r \in R_1$,$h(r) \in R_2$. A mapping h: $S_1 \to S_2$ is said to be partial, if for some object $x \in M_1$, $h(x)$ is not defined. The identity mapping id : $S_1 \to S_1$ is defined as

$$\mathrm{id}(x) = x, \quad \text{for } x \in M_1. \tag{2.9}$$

For two systems $S_i = (M_i, R_i)$, $i = 1, 2$, a mapping h: $S_1 \to S_2$ is said to be one-to-one if $h(M_1) = M_2$, and for any x, $y \in M_1$, $x \neq y$ implies $h(x) \neq h(y)$. The systems S_1 and S_2 are said to be similar, if there is a one-to-one mapping h: $S_1 \to S_2$ such that $h(M_1) = M_2$ and $h(R_1) = R_2$. In this case, the mapping h is known as a similarity mapping from system S_1 to system S_2.

Theorem 2.2 If h: $S_1 \to S_2$ is similarity mapping from system S_1 to system S_2, then the inverse function h^{-1}: $S_2 \to S_1$ is also a similarity mapping but from system S_2 to system S_1.

Proof Because h: $S_1 \to S_2$ is similarity mapping, it follows that h is one-to-one and $h(M_1) = M_2$. So, for any $y \in M_2$, there is a unique $x \in M_1$ such that $h(x) = y$. Therefore, the inverse mapping h^{-1}: $S_2 \to S_1$ is a well-defined one-to-one mapping defined by $h^{-1}(y) = x$. From $h(R_1) = R_2$, it follows that for any relation $s \in R$, there is a relation $r \in R_1$ such that

$$
\begin{aligned}
h^{-1}(s) &= \{h^{-1}(y) : y = (y_1, y_2, y_3, \ldots) \in s\} \\
&= \{(h^{-1}(y_1), h^{-1}(y_2), h^{-1}(y_3), \ldots) : y_1, y_2, y_3, \ldots \in M_2\} \\
&= \{(x_1, x_2, x_3, \ldots) : x_1, x_2, x_3, \ldots \in M_1\} = r \in R_1
\end{aligned}
\tag{2.10}
$$

Therefore, the inverse mapping h^{-1} is a similarity mapping from S_2 to S_1.

2.3.2 Structures of General Systems

Let $\{S_i = (M_i, R_i) : i \in I\}$ be a set of systems, where I is an index set. If for any two systems S_i and S_j, $i \neq j \in I$, their objects sets are disjoint, then the free sum of this collection of systems, denoted $\bigoplus\{S_i : i \in I\}$ or $S_1 \bigoplus S_2 \bigoplus \ldots \bigoplus S_n$, if $I = \{1, 2, \ldots, n\}$ is finite, is simply defined as the system whose object set is equal to the totality of the objects in the given systems and whose relation set that of all the relations in the individual systems. That is,

$$\bigoplus\{S_i : i \in I\} = S_1 \bigoplus S_2 \bigoplus \ldots \bigoplus S_n = (\cup_{i \in I} M_i, \cup_{i \in I} R_i). \tag{2.11}$$

Assume that $S = \{S_i = (M_i, R_i) : i \in I\}$ is a set of systems without assuming that the set $\{M_i : i \in I\}$ of all object sets is pairwise disjoint, where I is an index set. Define another set of systems $S' = \{S'_i = (M'_i, R'_i) : i \in I\}$ as follows:

$$M'_i = M_i \times \{i\}, \tag{2.12}$$

for any relation $r \in R_i$

$$r' = \{((x_1, i), (x_2, i), (x_3, i), \ldots) : (x_1, x_2, x_3, \ldots) \in r\}, \tag{2.13}$$

and $R'_i = \{r' : r \in R\}$. In this general case, the free sum $\bigoplus\{S_i : i \in I\}$ of the systems in S is defined as $\bigoplus\{S'_i : i \in I\}$.

Theorem 2.3 For each set of systems, its free sum exists uniquely up to a similarity. In other words, for any set of systems, although there are many different free sums, they are all similar to each other.

Proof This result follows directly from the fact that for a set of systems $S = \{S_i : i \in I\}$, any two free sums of these systems only differ by different index sets used to label the individual systems in the given set. If two free sums $\oplus_1 S$ and $\oplus_2 S$ of the set S involve respectively two index sets I and J, then there must be a one-to-one mapping $h : I \to J$ satisfying $h(I) = J$. This mapping h can help induce a similarity mapping from $\oplus_1 S$ to $\oplus_2 S$ as follows: For any object (x, i) in $\oplus_1 S$,

$$h(x,i) = (x, h(i)), \quad \text{for any } i \in I. \tag{2.14}$$

A system $S = (M, R)$ is connected if the system satisfies the following condition: for any m_1 and $m_2 \in M$, there are a sequence of objects $n_1, n_2, \ldots, n_k \in M$, and a sequence of relations $r_1, r_2, \ldots, r_{k+1} \in R$, for some natural number k, satisfying that r_1 relates m_1 and n_1, r_2 relates n_1 and $n_2, \ldots, r_k$ relates n_{k-1} and n_k, and r_{k+1} relates n_k and m_k. In other words, a system is connected if any two objects in the system are related through a finite number of relations of the system. Otherwise, the system S is known as a disconnected system, meaning that the system is really equal to the free sum of two or more subsystems, defined on pairwise disjoint object sets.

Theorem 2.4 A system $S = (M, R)$ is connected, if and only if for any two objects $x, y \in M$, there exist a natural number $n > 0$ and n relations $r_i \in R$ such that $x \in \text{Supp}(r_1)$and $y \in \text{Supp}(r_n)$ and $\text{Supp}(r_i) \cap \text{Supp}(r_{i+1}) \neq \varnothing$, for each $i = 1, 2, \ldots, n-1$, where for any $r \in R$,

$$\text{Supp}(r) = \{m \in M : m \text{ appears in the relation } r\}. \tag{2.15}$$

Proof ($\Rightarrow$) By contradiction, assume that the system S is connected and there exist two objects x and $y \in M$ such that there do not exist relations $r_i \in R$, $i = 1, 2, \ldots, n$, for any natural number $n \geq 1$, such that $x \in \text{Supp}(r_1)$and $y \in \text{Supp}(r_n)$ and $\text{Supp}(r_i) \cap \text{Supp}(r_{i+1}) \neq \varnothing$, for each $i = 1, 2, \ldots, n-1$. Hence, there must be relations $r_1, s_1 \in R$ such that $x \in \text{Supp}(r_1)$, $y \in \text{Supp}(s_1)$, and $\text{Supp}(r_1) \cap \text{Supp}(s_1) = \varnothing$. Let $U_0 = \text{Supp}(r_1)$ and $V_0 = \text{Supp}(s_1)$ and for any natural number $n$define

$$U_n = \cup \{\text{Supp}(r) : r \in R \& \text{Supp}(r) \cap U_{n-1} \neq \varnothing\}$$

and

$$V_n = \bigcup \{\text{Supp}(s) : s \in R \& \text{Supp}(s) \cap V_{n-1} \neq \varnothing\}.$$

Then two subsystems $S_i = (M_i, R_i)$, $i = 1, 2$, of S emerge such that $M_1 = \bigcup_{n=0}^{\infty} U_n$, $M_2 = M - M_1$, $R_1 = \{r \in R : \text{Supp}(r) \cap M_1 \neq \varnothing\}$, and $R_2 = \{r \in R : \text{Supp}(r) \subseteq M_2\}$. It can be readily shown that $S = (M, R) = (M_1 \cup M_2, R_1 \cup R_2) = S_1 \bigoplus S_2$. This end contradicts the fact that S is a connected system.

($\Leftarrow$) Again by contradiction, assume that S is disconnected. Then S is equal to the free sum $S_1 \bigoplus S_2$ of two nontrivial subsystems $S_1 = (M_1, R_1)$ and $S_2 = (M_2, R_2)$. Pick an object $m_i \in M_i$, $i = 1, 2$. Then there are no relations $r_j \in R$, $j = 1, 2, \ldots, n$, for any fixed $n \in \mathbb{N}$, such that $m_1 \in \text{Supp}(r_1)$ and $m_2 \in \text{Supp}(r_n)$ and $\text{Supp}(r_j) \cap \text{Supp}(r_{j+1}) \neq \varnothing$, for each $j = 1, 2, \ldots, n-1$, a contradiction.

A system $S_0 = (M_0, R_0)$ is multileveled, if there is at least one object $S_1 \in M_0$ such that $S_1 = (M_1, R_1)$ is a system, and there is at least one object $S_2 \in M_1$ such that

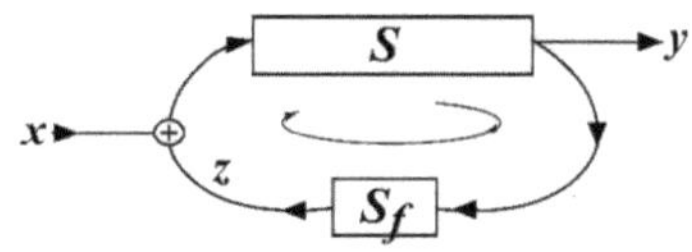

Fig. 2.1 The structure of a feedback system

$S_2 = (M_2, R_2)$ is a system, . . ., where S_1 is known as a first-level object system of S_0, S_2 a second-level object system of S_0, ...

Theorem 2.5 (ZFC). Each chain $S_1 = (M_1, R_1)$, $S_2 = (M_2, R_2)$, $S_3 = (M_3, R_3)$, . . . of object systems must be finite, where $S_{i+1} \in M_i$, for $i = 1, 2, 3, \ldots$.

Proof By contradiction, assume that there is an infinite chain of object systems $S_i = (M_i, R_i)$ such that $S_{i+1} \in M_i$, i is a natural number. Define

$$X = \{M_i : i = 1, 2, 3, \ldots\} \cup \{S_i : i = 1, 2, 3, \ldots\} \cup \{\{M_i\} : i = 1, 2, 3, \ldots\}.$$

From the Axiom of Regularity (Kuratowski & Mostowski, 1976), it follows that there exists $Y \in X$ such that $Y \cap X = \varnothing$. There now exist three possibilities: (1) $Y = M_i$for some i; (2) $Y = S_i$ for some i; and (3) $Y = \{M_i\}$ for some i.

If possibility (1) holds true, then we have $S_{i+1} \in Y \cap X$.Therefore, $Y \cap X \neq \varnothing$, a contradiction. If (2) holds true, then we have $Y = S_i = (M_i, R_i) = \{\{M_i\}, \{M_i, R_i\}\}$ and $\{M_i\} \in Y \cap X \neq \varnothing$, a contradiction. If (3) holds true, then we have $M_i \in Y \cap X \neq \varnothing$, a contradiction. These contradictions show that no chain of object systems is infinite.

Let X and Y be two linear spaces over the same field $\mathcal{A}$ and $S : X \to Y$ and $S_f : Y \to X$linear functions. Then the feedback system of S with a feedback component S_f is defined as the input-output system $S' \subseteq X \times Y$ such that

$$(x, y) \in S' \leftrightarrow (\exists z \in X)((x + z, y) \in S \text{ and } (y, z) \in S_f). \qquad (2.16)$$

A flow-chart depiction of the concept of feedback systems is given in Fig. 2.1, where the feedback component system S_f plays its role in the feedback loop. To help understand this concept in the figurative form, one can imagine that the input x is a particular government policy and y the output produced by implementing the policy. In real life, the output y is really a combined effect of the policy x and market reaction $S_f(S(x))$ to the policy, where $S(x)$ stands for the expected output of the market by the policymakers. This is similar to Soros' (2003)idea of reflexivity.

Theorem 2.6 Suppose that $S \subset X \times Y$ is a linear system and $S_f : Y \to X$ a linear functional system. Then a subset $S' \subset X \times Y$ is the feedback system of S with feedback component S_f, if and only if $S' = \{(x - S_f(y), y) : (x, y) \in S\}$.

Proof ($\Rightarrow$). Suppose that S' is the feedback system of S with feedback component S_f. Then, by the definition of feedback systems, for each $(x, y) \in S'$, $(x + S_f(y), y) \in S$.

This implies that $(x, y) \in \{(z - S_f(y), y): (z, y) \in S\}$. Again, Eq. (2.16) implies that for each element $(x, y) \in S$, $(x - S_f(y), y) \in S'$. That is, $\{(z - S_f(y), y) : (z, y) \in S\} \subset S'$.

($\Leftarrow$). It is clear because the assumed $S' = \{(x - S_f(y), y) : (x, y) \in S\}$implies Eq. (2.16).

To conclude this section, let us emphasize the theoretical and practical significance of applying the concept of systems and relevant methodology, such as the one just presented above, in economic and business studies. Specifically, if the business world and scenarios of business decision-making are studied by employing approaches of system problem-solving (Klir, 1985), then the following observation can be readily confirmed:

> Seemingly unrelated economic and business decisions are actually related to each other in one way or another. Different areas of the business landscape – macro or micro, large or small, global or regional – evolve and develop in concert.

As repeatedly confirmed by the stock market, when the state of affairs of a market segment changes, as the consequence of new decisions made within that particular segment, the states of affairs of many other seemingly unrelated market segments also change accordingly, although maybe only slightly (Soros, 2003). That confirms the fact that evolutions in the business world need to be seen as a whole; and the whole evolution of each and every business phenomenon need to be considered if one wants to understand how business entities or processes affect each other and evolve systemically as wholes and how they associate with each other.

At this junction, what needs to be emphasized is that beyond adding additional explanatory power to the existing knowledge on economics and business, applying logic systems analysis and methodology enables the discovery of new conclusions and provides general and practically applicable recommendations. Unmistakably, such outcomes stand for an academic endeavor that is worthy of further pursuing, within which the true power of systems methodology lies (Forrest et al., 2020).

2.4 Systemic Yoyo: An Intuitive Structure Behind Every System

As both mathematics and natural science demonstrate, it is important to have a playground available for researchers to intuitively see facts and possible facts before they can be proved or disproved. As far back as the recorded history of mathematics goes, general concepts of mathematics are always studied alongside with relevant intuitions (Kline, 1972). The following is list of several good examples of supporting evidence:

- Plane geometry, where each theorem is shown based on a line drawing
- Numbers, each of which is intuitively seen as a point on the real number line or a point in a high-dimensional Euclidean space

- Quantitative variables, each of which is treated as a moving point on the real-number line or in the Euclidean space
- Sets, each of which can be illustrated by using a Venn diagram

In comparison, instead of the continued employment of the Cartesian product coordinate, a widely used intuition and playground of mathematics, business, and economic studies do not have their own specific intuition and playground, although these studies tend to involve many factors (or variables). That is, such studies tend to deal with great masses of moving points in a Euclidean space, the playground of these scholarly explorations, which does not have any capability to help with the understanding of how organizations or systems evolve and interact with each other. This realization of such an important deficit experienced by scholars in areas of economics and business studies leads to the following systemic yoyo model of general systems.

2.4.1 The Systemic Yoyo Model of General Systems

Developing a playground, such as the Cartesian product system or Euclidean space in the conventional science and mathematics, that can assist researchers to intuitively see potential facts is extremely important. For example, to find what determines the innovativeness of a firm, scholars identified over 60 internal and external factors (Becheikh et al., 2006). As a totality, such studies do not have much theoretical or practical significance or implications. In particular, if Cartesian coordinate systems are used as our playground and intuition, such studies collectively mean that to understand the innovativeness of a firm, one needs to deal with over 60 moving points. The difficulty here is that these points move individually with their respectively different directions and speeds, while they also mutually affect each other. That is simply an impossible scientific project. As a matter of fact, as of this writing, natural science and mathematics still do not know how to deal with the mutual interaction of three factors, the well-known three-body problem (Lin, 2009), letting alone over 60 variables (or bodies). In terms of practical applications, do we expect that a frontline manager is able to simultaneously promote and monitor over 60 different economic forces and their interactions? Once again, this is an impossible task in real life.

Other than demonstrating the need to introduce methodological approaches beyond those prevalent currently, the discussion above also shows the necessity for investigators of business and economic problems to employ unconventional methods and approaches, such as systems science and methodology, in their works in order to avoid scientific impossibilities. Corresponding to systems science and methodology, one, of course, needs to have a playground within which he is able to intuitively observe facts and foresee potential realities regarding organizations, their evolutions, and interactions. To this end, the following question naturally arises: Can the conventional Euclidean spaces be still employed as the desired systemic playground and intuition?

The answer to this question is NO. Other than the issues, as just discussed above, of having to deal with masses of moving points, an impossible scientific problem, and many recent and age-old challenges, such as nonlinearity, chaos, etc., facing the traditional science is really consequences of how Euclidean spaces are composed of. In particular, each Euclidean space is composed of real-number lines that cross over each other at a common point, known as the origin. Hence, these axes represent linear measures, from which nonlinear phenomena, of course, emerge naturally. In other word, conventional academic studies, including all calculus- and statistics-based ones in business and economics, attempt to investigate "curvatures" using tools developed linearly in fictitious spaces (for more in-depth discussion, see Lin & OuYang, 2010).

By summarizing what is discussed above, it can be seen that systems science can be seen as the second dimension of science; it focuses on studies of systemhood. Moreover, the traditional science can be correspondingly seen as the first dimension of science; it studies thinghood. For more details, see Klir (1985). This end explains why the difficulty one faces when dealing with open, complex, giant systems, such as many business and economic situations, looks as a challenge that is seemingly impossible to overcome is because the researcher limits himself within the first dimension of science. Therefore, the desired playground and intuition in the second dimension should be more manageable than the intuitive situation in the first dimension where both theorists and frontline managers have to deal with masses of moving points in order to carry out large-scale tasks of entrepreneurial decision-making.

Based on various approaches of systems thinking and systems analysis developed in the past 90 some years, the needed playground and systemic intuition are the systemic yoyo model or simply the yoyo model (Lin, 2007) in Fig. 2.2. It is figuratively shown in the three-dimensional Euclidean space in which we live. Specifically, on the basis of the blown-up theory (Wu & Lin, 2002), a general theory of development and evolution, and the discussion on whether or not the world can be seen from the viewpoint of systems (Lin, 1988; Lin et al., 1990), the concepts of inputs, outputs, and converging and diverging eddy motions are joined together in the model shown in Fig. 2.2 for each system imaginable. In other words, each system can be imagined as an abstract multidimensional entity that spins about its axis. When such a spinning entity is fathomed in our three-dimensional space, such a systemic structure, as artistically shown in Fig. 2.2a, appears. The input side pulls in *things* (e.g., materials, information, investment, and human talents). After funneling through the body, things are spit out in the form of outputs. Some of the outputs do not return to the other side and some will, Fig. 2.2b. Due to its general shape, such a structure is referred to as a *yoyo*.

This systemic model indicates that each entity in the universe, be it physical or intellectual and be it a tangible or intangible object, a living being, an organization, a market, or an economy, can be intuitively seen as a realization of a certain multidimensional spinning yoyo. around which there an eddy field and a meridian

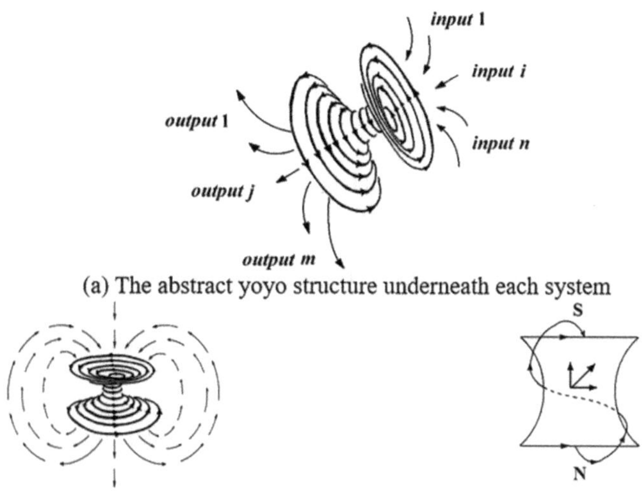

(b) The meridian field shown in dotted curves (c) Typical trajectory of how matters return

Fig. 2.2 The yoyo model of the general system. (**a**) The abstract yoyo structure underneath each system. (**b**) The meridian field shown in dotted curves. (**c**) Typical trajectory of how matters return

field. This systemic structure stays in a spinning motion as depicted in Fig. 2.2a. If it stops its spin, it will no longer exist as an identifiable system. What Fig. 2.2c shows is that due to the interaction between the eddy field, which spins perpendicularly to the axis of spin, of the model, and of the meridian field, which rotates parallel to the axis of spin, things that are either new to the yoyo body or returning to the input side travel along a spiral trajectory.

Comparing to the construction of Euclidean spaces (or Cartesian coordinate systems), one can tell that this yoyo model is more widely existing in the universe than the fictitious crossings of real-number lines. In particular, the phenomena of spin exist in all levels of the physical existence, in business interactions, and in political struggles. And to comprehend geometrically why this systemic intuition might help with investigations of business and economic scenarios, let us imagine a two-dimensional city surrounded by a circular steady wall (or an enclosed bounded area in the two-dimensional Cartesian coordinate plane). If the wall has no gap in the plane, then it will be difficult or impossible for any army to break into the city from within the two-dimensional space. Now, by going beyond the accustomed thinking logic, assume that one smart engineer designs an air-strike by making use of a third dimension and then the forces of his or her side can easily parachute into the city along the third dimension. That is, difficulties one faces when making decisions in economic and business situations are partially and mainly due to the reason that he keeps himself within the traditional way of thinking or the first dimension of science without truly taking advantage of systems science, the newly found second dimension of science.

This yoyo model of general systems includes the following key components: input, output, spin, and axis of spin. The first two components—input and output—

are easy to understand, because each viable business entity has to take in things, such as investments, information, materials for production, etc., and give off things, such as products, after-sale service, etc. Next, let us spend a little time and effort to comprehend the key terms—spin and axis of spin—by thinking about a business firm.

First, each business organization, such as a firm, is an objectively existing system that is made up of such objects as people and some physical elements, where some specific relations between the objects help the collection of the objects emerge into an organic whole or system or a firm. For example, without the specific setup of organizational whole (relationships), a university of higher education will not exist even though the people, the buildings, the equipment, etc. are all around. Second, there are many ways to see why each business organization spins about an invisible axis. In particular, as is well-known in management science, each firm has its own particular organizational culture; differences in organizational cultures lead to varied levels of productivity (Forrest et al., 2020). Now, the basic components of an organizational culture change over time. These changes constitute the evolution of the firm and are caused by the need for the firm to survive and to succeed through inventing and importing ideas from other organizations and consequently modifying or eliminating some of the existing ones.

The concept of spin beneath the systemic yoyo structure of the firm comes from what ideas to invent, which external ideas to import, and which existing ones to eliminate. If idea A will likely make the firm more prosperous with a higher level of productivity, while idea B will likely make the firm stay as it has been, then these ideas will form a spin in the organizational culture. Specifically, some members of the firm might like additional productivity so that their personal goals can be materialized in the process of creating the additional productivity, while some other members might like to keep things as they have been so that what they have occupied, such as income, prestige, social status, etc., will not be adversely affected. These two groups of employees will fight against each other to push for their agendas so that theoretically, ideas A and B actually "spin" around each other. For one moment, A is ahead; for the next moment, B is leading. And at yet another moment, no side is ahead when the power struggle might very well reach a state that is similar to the initial state of affairs. In this particular incidence, the abstract axis of spin is invisible because no one is willing to openly admit his underlying purpose for pushing for a specific idea (either A or B or other ones).

By shifting attention and focus from a firm of the micro-level to an industry, a market, etc., of the macro-level, each economy, no matter what scale it is on, can now be seen as such an ocean that is filled with countlessly many yoyo fields or eddy pools of different sizes, varied spinning strengths, and input-output orientations. The centers or spinning axes of the pools are either readily identifiable or not clearly visible.

2.4.2 A Sample of Successful Applications

To demonstrate how the concept of systems, the methodology of systems science, and the systemic yoyo model can bring forward successes, this section provides quick glances of several important advances presented later throughout this volume.

Scenario 2.1 Adam Smith's (1776) "invisible hand" originally describes merely how individuals' actions, in terms of production of goods, employment of capital, and domestic industries, that are self-centered without involving any public goods can lead to unintended social benefits. However, such initial description with a well-defined scope has been interpreted over the years in various ways by many different authors in different contexts. For example, according to Paul Samuelson's (1998), a 1970 Nobel laureate in economics, writing in 1948, this mystical principle—the existence of the invisible hand—means that when individuals pursue their respective selfish good, they collectively achieve the best good for all. However, the example below shows that this interpretation of Smith's "invisible hand" is not correct in general. In fact, it implies that respective maximizations of individuals' utilities can and do produce collective misery. For more relevant discussions, see Chap. 6.

Genie likes to grant each of three friends A, B, and C, a wish for their honorable deeds. Taking on the opportunity, A wishes he could live in the middle of a prosperous city with all the wealth he will ever need. In a blink of the eye, A now lives in what he wished for. Then, B says: "I love to live on a beach day after day with many beautiful women around me." Bang, as soon as having stated his wishes, B is now sunbathing on a beautiful beach, sipping his favorite drinks while served by many gorgeous women.

Turning to C, Genie questions: "What is the wish you like me to grant you?"

"I really like this mountainous area. The air is always fresh, water is clean, and everything around me is green. So, my wish is my friends A and B can live with me right here and immerse ourselves in nature," answered C without thinking much.

If Genie keeps his promise, what happens next will be either both A and B not happy or C not happy, because their individual wishes are not consistent and cannot be compromised with each other.

By using the terminology of utilities, this fictitious scenario can be modeled as follows: Assume that the friends' utility functions are U_{i}, i = A, B, C, such that

$$U_{\text{A}} = U_{\text{A}}(X_{\text{A}}, X_{\text{B}}, X_{\text{C}}), \quad U_{\text{B}} = U_{\text{B}}(X_{\text{B}}, X_{\text{A}}, X_{\text{C}}), \quad U_{\text{C}} = U_{C}(X_{\text{C}}, X_{\text{A}}, X_{\text{B}}, U_{\text{A}}, U_{\text{B}})$$

where X_{i}, i = A, B, C, represent respectively the consumptions of these people. Assume that U_{A}, U_{B}, and U_{C} are increasing functions in X_{A}, X_{B}, and X_{C}, while U_{C} is also a convex function in U_{A} and U_{B}, respectively. So, U_{C} is an increasing function in U_{A} until a given upper bound B_{A} and in U_{B} until a given upper bound B_{B}; then U_{C} becomes a decreasing function in U_{A} and U_{B}, respectively.

In this model expression, the friendship of these three people is reflected in the appearance of individual consumptions in each utility function; and both A and B are self-centered, because their utility functions do not contain the utility of C except their own consumptions. At the same time, C treats both A and B as his friends up to a point. Specifically, after A or B or both of A and B reach certain levels of "success" in life, C starts to feel bad and then worse. In other words, the maximization of C's utility can only be reached when the utilities of friends A and B are not more than their respective upper bounds B_A and B_B, while his diminishing utility cannot be offset by any amount of increasing consumption of goods.

Although the previous example is fictitious, it does depict a huge collection of commonly existing social phenomena in real life: some people enjoy their respectively increasing utilities through belittling others.

In terms of the literature, the most typical description of Smith's "invisible hand" seems to read more or less as follows: although individuals are selfish, their self-interest centered actions collectively produce unintended greater social benefits and public goods (Sen, 2010). Moreover, based on Greenwald and Stiglitz (1986), Joseph E. Stiglitz (Altman, 2006), a 2001 Nobel laureate in economics, believes that the invisible hand is often not there. In comparison, this volume presents a detailed analytic argument by using systemic thinking that Stiglitz's belief is correct. In particular, thinking holistically leads naturally to the following question: what does the word "greater" mean? According to the discussion in Chap. 13, a community of selfish individuals mostly likely does not have any order of real numbers that is consistent with that of every individual. In other words, there is not any unanimously acknowledged method to decipher the meaning of "greater social benefits and public good." It is because in any economy of more than two economic agents there are different systems of values and beliefs (Forrest, 2018), and these differences define an inconsistent economy-wide order of real numbers. For more details, see Chap. 13 in this volume.

Scenario 2.2 By using systemic logic of reasoning and the yoyo model of systems, Chap. 5 generalizes natural endowments of individuals to those of business firms as follows:

- By a firm's self-awareness, it means the firm's awareness that it exists as a business entity separate from other entities, such as people, firms, and things, with its business secrets, such as adopted customer value propositions, operational strategies, protected product designs, etc.
- By a firm's imagination, it describes the firm's ability to learn and to acquire new knowledge; to innovatively imagine what might be the right offer, such as a newly designed product, or an improved product or new (or improved) service; to satisfy the deciphered market demand; and to develop the necessary process of materially introducing the imagined offer.
- By a firm's conscience, it represents the ability for the firm to judge which business effort is more beneficial than other efforts.
- By a firm's free will, it means the capability for the firm to keep the promises, how to keep, and to what degree to keep these promises, as reflected in its contracts with the partners within its supply-chain ecosystem.

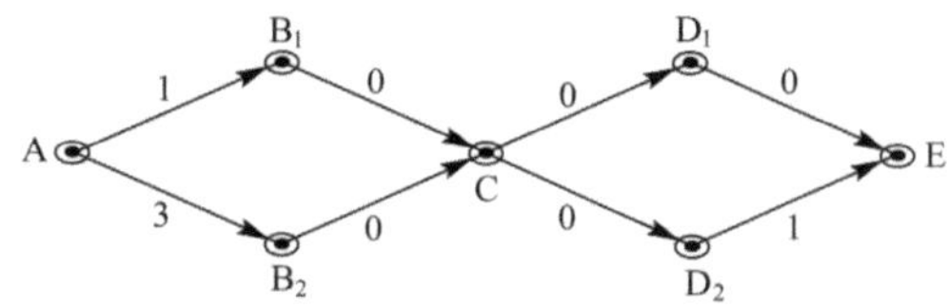

Fig. 2.3 The concept of minimum is defined differently

Based on these natural endowments of firms, which are parallel to those of individual persons, Chap. 8 of this volume establishes the following results through exploring the true meaning of the assumption of rationality (e.g., Friedman, 1953; Gilboa, 2010; Hudik, 2019):

1. The goal of each firm's effort is to materialize, at least partially or remotely, the firm's clearly stated mission.
2. At the macro firm level, the assumption of rationality stands for finding an optimal choice among all available alternatives with the criteria of optimality determined by the focal firm's management based on the firm's natural endowments.
3. Each firm has its unique and dissimilar system of values and beliefs.
4. When a firm faces a decision-making situation, it optimizes the potential subject to a set of given constraints by using its particular criteria of optimality, as formulated consistently with its system of values and beliefs.

The following example, rephrased from Hu (1982) and Lin (1999, p. 136) and detailed in Chap. 6, confirms the importance of these systemic conclusions.

Assume that the directed and weighted network in Fig. 2.3 represents a production routine of a business operation. The manager likes to find the minimum path that connect node A, representing the start of the production, with node E, the end of the production. If in his calculation the manager orders the real-number weights the same way as how real numbers are conventionally ordered, then the path $A \rightarrow B_1 \rightarrow C \rightarrow D_1 \rightarrow E$ is what the manager is looking for. The weight of this path is equal to 1. In comparison, other possible paths from node A to node E have weights 2, 3, and 4, respectively.

However, if in the manager's set of decision criteria there is a mod 4 function, that is, in his set of criteria, for any two real numbers x and y, $x < y$ if and only if $x(\text{mod } 4) < y(\text{mod } 4)$, then the path with the minimum weight is $A \rightarrow B_2 \rightarrow C \rightarrow D_2 \rightarrow E$. In particular, the weight of this particular path is $3 + 0 + 0 + 1 = 4\ (\text{mod } 4) = 0$, while other paths respectively have weights $1, 2$, or 3.

For in-depth explanation of all related terms used in this example, please go to Chap. 6.

Scenario 2.3 Consider a focal firm F and a selfish employee E of the firm. The interactions between the organizational yoyo of the firm and that of the employee can be depicted in Fig. 2.4. Specifically, because the firm transfers financial and other

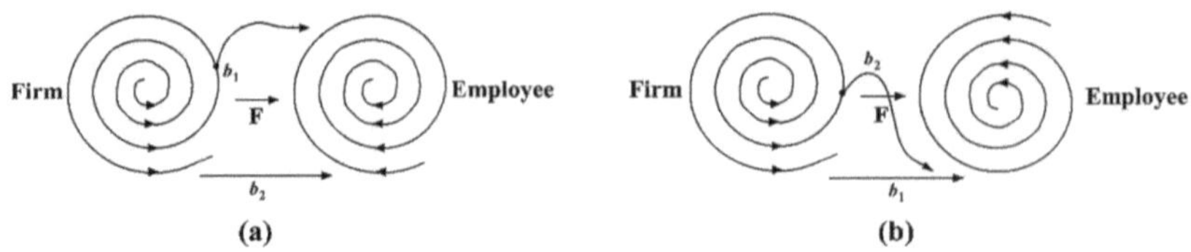

Fig. 2.4 Interactions between the focal firm and a selfish employee

benefits to the employee, the firm is represented as a divergent whirlpool, while the selfishness of the employee as a convergent whirlpool.

If both transfers b_1 and b_2 stand for contractual and/or voluntary monetary and benefit transfers from F, the spin field of employee E in Fig. 2.4 will accept b_1 happily and the transfer b_2 unwillingly (Fig. 2.4b) or even likely reject such a transfer (Fig. 2.4a). Here, b_1 is transferred to the selfish employee E without violating his preference of consumption, while b_2 is forced on E against his will or personal consumption preferences. In particular, although unwillingly, the employee accepts transfer b_2 (Fig. 2.4b). However, for the situation in Fig. 2.4a, transfer b_2 is rejected by the employee. Hence, the theorem of never-perfect value system (Lin & Forrest, 2008), established for the family (Becker, 1991), can be generalized to the case of a business firm as follows, where the same name for the theorem is used.

Theorem 2.7 (The Theorem of Never-Perfect Value System)
In a firm of at least two employees, one of them, named *h*, is the manager who evaluates each employee's performance against the system of values and beliefs of the firm. If a selfish employee measures up well against the value-belief system, the manager *h* will positively award the employee. Unfortunately, the more effort an employee E puts in to measure up to the value system, the more he or she will be punished by the award system.

In this theorem, the setting of a firm and its employees suggests that monetary and benefit transfers stand for a periodic, ongoing process without a definite end in sight. The role the firm's system of values and beliefs plays is that the manager confirms with the employees at some time moment(s) along the timeline that starting at a certain pay period, each employee's behavior and performance will affect how much he/she will receive from the company at the end of that period. And the manager will design his responses to employees' behaviors and levels of performance in such a way as to maximize his own utility (or measure of performance). Speaking differently, Theorem 2.7 portraits a progressive behavioral change and reflection over time between the manager and the employees of the firm.

The earlier understanding of Fig. 2.4 is that the firm makes transfers of b_1 and/or b_2 to employee E. However, in a real-life situation, as often seen in various work places, Fig. 2.4 can also suggest the possibility that the spin field of the selfish employee E may very well take its initiative and proactively grab as much of the potential total amount of the fund from the firm, although the exact amount might not be known until a future date, allocated for awarding employees for their hard works. Such possibilities have been well described in studies of the Samaritan dilemma (Buchanan, 1975; Lagerlof, 2004). To this end, the following result can be established.

Theorem 2.8 (Selfish Employee Theorem)
If the manager of the focal firm cares about all employees of the firm so that he distributes the funds of the firm, allocated for awarding employees for their good performance, to them as long as they need to satisfy their own desires of consumption, then the selfish employees will devote as little effort to their works as possible, while maximizing their amounts of transfers from the firm.

For more related discussions and illustrations, please go to Chap. 17 of this volume.

2.5 Methodologies Systemically Employed in This Volume

The great variety of different methods employed in studies of economic and business problems can be roughly classified into the following groups, while other methods can be seen as a combination of some of these listed (Forrest & Liu, 2022): ordinary language based, calculus based, microeconomics based, data or anecdote based, and systems science based. However, each and every of these methods suffers from their individually different sets of limitations and can easily produce generally untrue conclusions. For example, when ordinary language-based analysis and reason are applied, the advantage is that they tend to be most accessible by scholars and practitioners. However, no matter how logical and precise these analyses and reasonings may be, the derived conclusions are often inconclusive because of the linearity involved in the logic of thinking. Such linear way of thinking makes it difficult to control for the simultaneous effect of several arguments in combination. One illustrative case to this end is the studies on industrial revolutions (Forrest et al., 2018b; Rostow, 1960; Wen, 2016). More specifically, regarding the Industrial Revolution of England, scholars take their individually different angles and perspectives to draw inconsistent and even contradictory conclusions on what actually caused the appearance of that particular success. Due to the limitations of the language-based method, both primary and secondary determinants are seen as fundamental causes (Forrest et al., 2018b; Wen, 2016), although the latter naturally appear when the former are in place.

As for calculus-based methods of analysis and reasoning, they encounter difficulties in the stage of describing and modeling the phenomenon of concern, before any conclusion, useful or not, can be derived. These methods are valid only under the assumption of fundamental conditions, such as (1) all variables of concern need to take values on some sorts of continuums at least to a certain degree; (2) relationships between variables need to be expressible in functional form, be it implicit or explicit;

and (3) all functional expressions of associations between variables need to be continuous and differentiable on most parts of their domains.

In applications, condition (1) is often violated. For example, when studying a population, its size is often assumed to be continuous in order to take advantage of the methods and results of calculus. At the same time, both conditions (2) and (3) are simply assumed to be true without any supporting evidence. For example, before developing a dynamic industry model to study the impact of trade on intra-industry reallocations and aggregate industry productivity, Melitz's (2003) first introduced several key assumptions, including, among others, (a) the collection of all goods (indexed by ω) considered by a representative consumer is a continuum and (b) there is a continuum of firms, each of which produces a different variety ω of product. For the consequent conclusions to be relevant to real life, one has to acknowledge that the total number of goods a consumer considers has to be a natural number; and the same is true for the number of firms that produce the products a consumer is interested in consuming. Of course, the only reason for Melitz to introduce these assumptions is to modify the situation of his concern to fit the underlying requirements for calculus-based methodology to be valid.

In terms of microeconomics-based methods of analysis and reasoning, such as those using demand/supply curves, Edgewood boxes, and utility functions, they have provided means for scholars to develop very important conclusions. However, when a specific scenario is concerned with, some of the most powerful tools of microeconomics become limited in their use values. For example, based on the analysis of a particular business success, Ye et al. (2012) conjectured the following general conclusion:

> A demand-side synergy, where the willingness for a consumer to pay for a product or service is increased, can be produced by either the simultaneous consumer utility effect or the two-sided market effect.

To establish this conjecture as a generally true conclusion, Ye and colleagues looked at the following microeconomics model regarding a representative consumer

$$\begin{aligned} &\max_{q_1, q_2, \dots, q_n} U(q_1, q_2, \dots, q_n; \delta) \\ &\text{s.t.} \sum_{i=1}^{n} p_i q_i \leq Y \end{aligned} \tag{2.17}$$

where q_i is the consumed amount of good i at unit price p_i, Y the consumer's total financial ability, and δ all other consumption-related parameters.

If each consumed amount $q_i = D_i(p_1, p_2, \ldots, p_n; \delta)$ can be obtained from the previous maximization problem, then retailer i maximizes its profit

$$\max_{p_1, p_2, \dots, p_n} \pi_i = (p_i - c_i) D_i(p_1, p_2, \dots, p_n; \delta), \tag{2.18}$$

where c_i stands for the unit cost of retailer i. Therefore, the Nash equilibrium price

$p^*_{(\delta)} = \left(p^*_{1(\delta)}, p^*_{2(\delta)}, \ldots, p^*_{n(\delta)}\right)$ emerges. From

$$\frac{\partial p^*_{(\delta)}}{\partial \delta} = \left(\frac{\partial p^*_{1(\delta)}}{\partial \delta}, \frac{\partial p^*_{2(\delta)}}{\partial \delta}, \ldots, \frac{\partial p^*_{n(\delta)}}{\partial \delta}\right) = 0, \tag{2.19}$$

one is able to reveal the effect of δ on prices. In particular, if δ means shopping time spent on consuming goods 1, 2, . . .,n, then what is produced is how shopping time affects prices.

Now, the analysis basic stops at this particular point, because generally, without knowing more about the relevant details, such as the specifics of the costs, utilities, etc., almost nothing can further be done. In other words, although many microeconomics methods can be fruitfully employed to develop insightful conclusions for general cases, they become useless when used to confirm specific situations due to the problem of mathematical insolvability.

For anecdote-based analysis and reasoning, inferences, followed then by managerial suggestions, are generated by investigating one or several events or processes. Many publications in the area of business and economics are anecdote based. For instance, Rostow's (1960) work provides an example of how conjectures are derived in terms of what causes the appearance of one industrial revolution in one location based on a few success stories. This study is followed by Wen (2016), who outlines how modern China went through its three rounds of industrial revolutions. By using a similar approach, McGrath (2013) identifies characteristics most successful companies share and provides suggestions for other companies and individual persons to achieve magnificent performance in the business world or professional careers.

Such anecdote-based studies tend to be ordinary language based and provide easy accessibility and friendly readability to a large audience. So, they naturally compel frontline managers to implement the highlighted and identified best practices (e.g., Gliva-McConvey et al., 2020; White, 2017). However, for these practices to bring forward with desired successes, there must be relevant constraints within which they can potentially play their roles, as pointed out by Forrest et al. (2020, Chaps. 8 and 9).

Closely related to anecdote-based analysis and reasoning is data-based methods. These methods suffer from various issues and challenges, such as, among others, (1) sampling error, (2) availability of data, (3) subjectivity to different interpretations. and (4) conditional validity of econometric tools.

Specifically, by sampling error, it means the difference between estimates obtained from a sample and the corresponding parameters. Due to various reasons and constraints, an obtained sample can hardly be representative of the population of interest. This situation can be well illustrated by the proverb of "the blind men and an elephant" (Goldstein, 2010, p. 492). This proverb describes how a group of blind men attempt to conceptualize what an elephant is like by physically touching the elephant. It assumes that each of the blind men can only feel a different but a designated part of the elephant's body. So, these men produce inconsistent images of an elephant: the man who is on the animal's back conceptualizes the elephant as a small-scale mountain ridge; the man who feels the animal's tail suggests that the elephant is like a hairy rope; the man who checks on one of the animal's legs concludes that the elephant is a large, soft pole; . . . That is, although none of the men is incorrect, the group did collectively acquire the *holistic* and the *right* view of the elephant.

When a researcher attempts to examine a past event, he will most likely experience the issue that no data is available. For example, conclusions in studies of market entry and entry timing are derived without sufficient amount of data on failed attempts available (Zachary et al., 2015). In their attempt to fill a gap in the literature on accounting practices of the firms that existed during the Industrial Revolution, Fleischman and Parker (2017) find it challenging to collect reliable data. So, when causal relationships are derived in such studies, the validity of the conclusions are very questionable, because Spirtes et al. (2011) find such scenarios when new data becomes available, the previously established causation A → B is reversed.

As for the issue of different interpretations, it means out of the same data different inferences can be produced based on differences in the backgrounds and knowledge structures of the researchers. For example, many empirically confirmed conclusions on firms' innovativeness are universally stated. However, the very concept of innovation used in the confirmations means very dissimilar things (Becheikh et al., 2006). Therefore, in terms of economic and business studies, both theorists and practitioners need to question how much they can trust the validity of generally stated conclusions that are actually derived empirically.

As for systemic thinking and methodology, the relevant number of studies in areas of economic and business has been steadily increasing in recent decades. For example, Hassmiller Lich et al. (2017) present an overview on how methodologies of systems thinking have found their way into the field of program planning and evaluation. Kamitake (2009) develops the elementary terminology of meta-economics and economic systems theory, while emphasizing the significance of the "observation of observations." By considering the orthodox economic knowledge as a prisoner of the mechanical paradigm, Vasile (2012) creates his economic living logical system for the purpose of increasing the understanding of economic forces. In comparison, a more ambitious project is being carried out by a team from Italy. These scholars propose to embrace a paradigm shift by employing the theory and methods of the complexity science (Delli Gatti et al., 2010). Specifically, they suggest to apply the concept of complex networks and computer simulations instead of the current reductionist approach at the heart of the mainstream DSGE (dynamic stochastic general equilibrium) models. They demonstrate that computational techniques can vividly simulate the natural emergence of macro-level phenomena from unintended and uncoordinated behaviors of micro-level individuals when they follow some simple rules of action, such as financial contagion (Allen & Gale, 2001) and trade-credit relationships (Boissay, 2006; Battiston et al., 2007). Taking a completely different approach, Forrest and his team recently revisit a large array of different topics in economics and business and generalize some of the previously well-known concepts and results to much wider territories of practical applications.

To this end, see, for example, Forrest (2014, 2018), Forrest and Liu (2022), Forrest et al. (2018a, 2020), Liu et al. (2016), and references found in these publications.

Continuing what has been started by Forrest and his team, the methodology adopted in this volume is a holistic one in order to overcome the limitations of individual methodologies, as critically analyzed above. In particular, the basic playground or intuition applied in this volume is the (systemic) yoyo model. Although all other available methodological approaches suffer from various limitations, as discussed above, they are employed systemically when seen as appropriate. In other words, no particular method is given priority over others. And, based on what is available, a convenient methodological tool or tools will be selected to address issues in hands. When no misleading consequences are expected, language-based, calculus-based, and/or set-theoretic methodologies are utilized to produce most general conclusions.

2.6 A Few Final Words

As a preparation for the rest of this book, after introducing the reader to the concept of systems, this chapter demonstrates how generally true theorems can be established by using the language of naïve set theory, a restriction of which on the ℓ-dimensional Euclidean space $\mathbb{R}^\ell$ will also be the major approach. And after having described the composition of the systemic yoyo model for general systems, we look at three examples of how the concept of systems, the logic of reasoning of systems science, and the yoyo model can be actually employed to produce tangible results.

What needs to be noted at this junction is that this chapter attempts to quickly demonstrate each and every one of the methods commonly employed in studies of economic and business problems is limited in one way or another and why systems science and methodology are appropriate for studying organizations, their evolutions, and their interactions. Because this adopted methodology is not constrained by data or anecdotes, developed results are universally true unless some of the given if-conditions are violated.

As is well-known, although a figure is worth thousands of words, it can also easily lead to misconceptions and incorrect conclusions; for details, see Forrest and Liu (2022, Afterword). That is why in this volume we attempt to employ intuitions and analytical analyses jointly to avoid difficulties and to produce generally true results.

References

Allen, F., & Gale, D. (2001). Financial contagion. *Journal of Political Economy, 108*, 1–33.
Altman, D. (2006). Managing globalization. In Q & A with Joseph E. Stiglitz, Columbia University and *The International Herald Tribune*, October 11, 2006, 05:03AM. Retrieved February

3, 2022, from https://web.archive.org/web/20090122214457/http://blogs.iht.com/tribtalk/business/globalization/?p=177
Battiston, S., Delli Gatti, D., Gallegati, M., Greenwald, B., & Stiglitz, J. (2007). Credit chains and bankruptcies avalanches in supply networks. *Journal of Economic Dynamics and Control, 31*, 2061–2084.
Becheikh, N., Landry, R., & Amara, N. (2006). Lessons from innovation empirical studies in the manufacturing sector: A systematic review of the literature from 1993 to 2003. *Technovation, 26*(5), 644–664.
Becker, G. S. (1991). *A treatise of the family*. Harvard University Press.
Berlinski, D. (1976). *On systems analysis*. MIT Press.
Blauberg, I. V., Sadovsky, V. N., & Yudin, E. G. (1977). *Systems theory, philosophical and methodological problems*. Progress Publishers, Moscow.
Boissay, F. (2006). *Credit chains and the propagation of financial distress* (European Central Bank, Working Paper No. 573).
Buchanan, J. (1975). The Samaritan's dilemma. In E. S. Phelps (Ed.), *Altruism, morality and economic theory* (pp. 71–85). Russel Sage Foundation.
Bunge, B. (1979). *Treatise on basic philosophy* (Vol. 4). A World of Systems.
Delli Gatti, D., Gaffeo, E., & Gallegati, M. (2010). Complex agent-based macroeconomics: A manifesto for a new paradigm. *Journal of Economic Interaction and Coordination, 5*, 111–135.
Fiske, S. T., & Pavelchak, M. A. (1986). Category-based versus piecemeal-based affective responses: Developments in schema-triggered affect. In R. M. Sorrentino & E. T. Higgins (Eds.), *Handbook of motivation and cognition: Foundations of social behavior* (pp. 167–203). Guilford Press.
Fleischman, R. K., & Parker, L. D. (2017). *What is past is prologue: Costing accounting in the British industrial revolution, 1760–1850*. Routledge.
Forrest, J. Y. L. (2014). *A systems perspective on financial systems*. CRC Press.
Forrest, J. Y. L. (2018). *General systems theory: Foundation, intuition and applications in business decision making*. Springer.
Forrest, J. Y. L., & Liu, Y. (2022). *Value in business: A holistic, systems-based approach to creating and achieving value*. Springer.
Forrest, J. Y. L., Ying, Y. R., & Gong, Z. W. (2018a). *Currency wars: Offense and defense through systemic thinking*. Springer.
Forrest, J. Y. L., Zhao, H. C., & Shao, L. (2018b). Engineering rapid industrial revolutions for impoverished agrarian nations. *Theoretical Economics Letters, 8*, 2594–2640.
Forrest, J. Y. L., Nicholls, J., Schimmel, K., & Liu, S. F. (2020). *Managerial decision making: A holistic approach*. Springer.
Friedman, M. (1953). *Essays in positive economics*. University of Chicago Press.
Gilboa, I. (2010). *Rational choice*. The MIT Press.
Gliva-McConvey, G., Nicholas, C. F., & Clark, L. (Eds.). (2020). *Comprehensive healthcare simulation: Implementing best practices in standardized patient methodology*. Springer.
Goldstein, E. B. (2010). *Encyclopedia of perception*. SAGE Publications.
Greenwald, B. C., & Stiglitz, J. E. (1986). Externalities in economies with imperfect information and incomplete markets. *Quarterly Journal of Economics, 101*(2), 229–264.
Hassmiller Lich, K., Urban, J. B., Frerichs, L., & Dave, G. (2017). Extending systems thinking in planning and evaluation using group concept mapping and system dynamics to tackle complex problems. *Evaluation and Program Planning, 60*(C), 254–264.
Hu, T. C. (1982). *Combinatorial algorithms*. Addison-Wesley.
Hudik, M. (2019). Two interpretations of the rational choice theory and the relevance of behavioral critique. *Rationality and Society, 31*(4), 464–489.
Kamitake, Y. (2009). Fundamental concepts for economic systems theory. *Hitotsubashi Journal of Economics, 50*(2), 75–86.
Kijima, K., Iijima, J., Sato, R., Deguchi, H., & Nakano, B. (Eds.). (2022a). *Systems research I: Essays in honor of Yasuhiko Takahara on systems theory and modeling*. Springer.

Kijima, K., Iijima, J., Sato, R., Deguchi, H., & Nakano, B. (Eds.). (2022b). *Systems research II: Essays in honor of Yasuhiko Takahara on systems management theory and practice*. Springer.
Kline, M. (1972). *Mathematical thought from ancient to modern times*. Oxford University Press.
Klir, G. (1985). *Architecture of systems problem solving*. Plenum Press.
Klir, G. (2001). *Facets of systems science*. Springer.
Kuhn, T. (1962). *The structure of scientific revolutions*. University of Chicago Press.
Kuratowski, K., & Mostowski, A. (1976). *Set theory: With an introduction to descriptive set theory*. North-Holland.
Lagerlof, J. (2004). Efficiency-enhancing signalling in the Samaritan's dilemma. *The Economic Journal, 114*(492), 55–68.
Lilienfeld, D. (1978). *The rise of systems theory*. Wiley.
Lin, Y. (1987). A model of general systems. *Mathematical Modelling, 9*(2), 95–104.
Lin, Y. (1988). Can the world be studied in the viewpoint of systems?? *Mathematical and Computer Modelling, 11*, 738–742.
Lin, Y. (1989). A multi-relation approach of general systems and tests of applications. *Synthese, 79*, 473–488.
Lin, Y. (1999). *General systems theory: A mathematical approach*. Kluwer Academic and Plenum.
Lin, Y. (2007). Systemic yoyo model and applications in Newton's, Kepler's laws, etc. *Kybernetes, 36*(3–4), 484–516.
Lin, Y. (2009). *Systemic yoyos: Some impacts of the second dimension*. Auerbach Publication.
Lin, Y., & Forrest, D. (2008). Economic yoyos and never-perfect value system. *Kybernetes, 37*(1), 149–165.
Lin, Y., & Forrest, B. C. (2012). *Systemic structure behind human organizations: From civilizations to individuals*. Springer.
Lin, Y., & OuYang, S. C. (2010). *Irregularities and prediction of major disasters*. CRC Press.
Lin, Y., Ma, Y., & Port, R. (1990). Several epistemological problems related to the concept of systems. *Mathematical and Computer Modelling, 14*, 52–57.
Lin, Y., Hu, Q. P., & Li, D. (1997). Some unsolved problems in general systems theory (I) & II. *Cybernetics and Systems, 28*, 287–303; 591–605.
Liu, S. F., & Lin, Y. (2010). *Grey systems: Theory and applications*. Springer.
Liu, S. F., Yang, Y. J., & Forrest, J. Y. L. (2016). *Grey data analysis: Methods, models and applications*. Springer.
McGrath, R. G. (2013). *The end of competitive advantage: How to keep your strategy moving as fast as your business*. Harvard Business Review Press.
Melitz, M. J. (2003). The impact of trade on intra-industry reallocations and aggregate industry productivity. *Econometrica, 71*(6), 1695–1725.
Mesarovic, M. D., & Takahara, Y. (1975). *General systems theory: Mathematical foundations*. Academic Press.
Mesarovic, M. D., & Takahara, Y. (1989). *Abstract systems theory*. Springer.
Mesarovic, M. D., & Takahara, Y. (2003). *Organization structure: Cybernetic systems foundation*. Kluwer, Academic Publishers.
Mesarovic, M. D., Macko, D., & Takahara, Y. (1970). *Theory of multi-level hierarchical systems*. Academic Press.
Pavelchak, M. A. (1989). Piecemeal and category-based evaluation: An idiographic analysis. *Journal of Personality and Social Psychology, 56*(3), 354–363.
Porter, M. E. (1979). How competitive forces shape strategy. *Harvard Business Review, 57*(2), 137–145.
Porter, M. E. (1985). *Competitive advantage: Creating and sustaining superior performance*. Free Press.
Rostow, W. W. (1960). *The stages of economic growth: A non-communist manifesto*. Cambridge University Press.

Samuelson, P. A. (1948). Consumption theory in terms of revealed preference. *Economica, 15*(60), 243–253.
Samuelson, P. A. (1998). *Economics: The original1948 edition*. McGraw-Hill.
Sen, A. (2010). Introduction. In A. Smith (Ed.), *The theory of moral sentiments* (6th ed., pp. vii–xxix). Penguin. (Original work published 1790).
Smith, A. (1776). *The wealth of nations*, books IV, (1986 printing). Penguin Books.
Soros, G. (2003). *The Alchemy of finance*. Wiley.
Spirtes, P., Glymour, C., & Scheines, R. (2011). *Causation, prediction, and search*. MIT Press.
Vasile, B. (2012). The living logical system paradigm: The economic concept and the concept of living logical system—Necessary and sufficient predicates. *Studies in Business and Economics, 7*(1), 17–27.
von Bertalanffy, L. (1924). *Einfuhrung in Spengler's werk*. Literaturblatt Kolnische Zeitung.
von Bertalanffy, L. (1972). The history and status of general systems theory. In G. Klir (Ed.), *Trends in generalsystems theory* (Vol. 15, pp. 21–41).
Wen, Y. (2016). *The making of an economic superpower: Unlocking China's secret of rapid industrialization*. World Scientific.
White, M. (2017). Keep calm and simulate on: Faculty experiences and insights into implementing best practices in simulation. *Teaching and Learning in Nursing, 12*(1), 43–49.
Wigner, E. P. (1960). The unreasonable effectiveness of mathematics in the natural sciences. *Communications in Pure and Applied Mathematics, 13*, 1–14.
Wu, X. M. (1990). *The Pansystems view of the world*. People's University of China Press.
Wu, Y., & Lin, Y. (2002). *Beyond nonstructural quantitative analysis: Blown-ups, spinning currents and modern science*. World Scientific.
Ye, G. L., Priem, R. L., & Alshwer, A. A. (2012). Achieving demand-side synergy from strategic diversification: How combining mundane assets can leverage consumer utilities. *Organization Science, 23*(1), 207–224.
Zachary, M. A., Gianiodis, P. T., Payne, G. T., & Markman, G. D. (2015). Entry timing: Enduring lessons and future directions. *Journal of Management, 41*(5), 1388–1415.

Chapter 3
Closed and Open Systems: Seen with Examples

Jeffrey Yi-Lin Forrest and Qiang Bu

Abstract As the title of this chapter suggests, the following sections will introduce the concepts of closed and open systems, first intuitively and then symbolically using the set-theoretical language seen earlier in the previous chapter. After these concepts are adequately explained, the attention of learning turns to examine the practical importance of these new concepts by looking at three examples.

The first example is a simple problem of the middle school algebra. It illustrates how conventionally a business scenario of concern is described and resolved by treating an open system as a closed one. When doing so, a lot of organizational connections of the system with its environment are ignored or simply cut off. That inevitably leads to conclusions that are realistically unreliable. The second example considers the well-known law of one price and shows that the conventional argument for the law's truthfulness is flawed. The root problem underneath such an argument is once again the same as what is pointed out in the first example—a realistically open system is artificially and mistakenly treated as a closed one. That is, this law can at most be true within a closed economic system.

The third example demonstrates that when the researcher is able to think holistically and systemically, he is able to readily discover new facts and practically useful conclusions. This example provides researchers who are inclined more towards empirical investigations a chance to see how abstract concepts of systems science can be easily employed in their data-based works. Specifically, demonstrated here is an attempt to address the problem of whether direct and indirect sentiment measures are similar in terms of explaining the performance of a mutual fund by identifying direct sentiment as an open system, while indirect sentiment as a closed system. Doing so naturally leads to many practically useful conclusions. For example, to explain the performance of a mutual fund, the measures of both direct and indirect sentiment need to be considered as integral parts of each selected benchmark model. The direct sentiment index can play a robustly explanatory role when used

---

Jeffrey Yi-Lin Forrest (Department of Accounting Economics Finance, Slippery Rock University, Slippery Rock, PA, USA; Email: Jeffrey.forrest@sru.edu) and Qiang Bu (School of Business Administration, Pennsylvania State University-Harrisburg, Middletown, PA, USA; Email: qxb1@psu.edu) are equally contributed to this chapter.

J. Y.-L. Forrest, *Systemic Principles of Applied Economic Philosophies I*,
Translational Systems Sciences 38, https://doi.org/10.1007/978-981-99-7273-9_3

either independently or collectively; and measures of indirect sentiment can only provide explanatory power when employed jointly with other market factors.

In the concluding section, a discussion on the systems thinking and holistic flexibility is given. It shows that such thinking and flexibility can be employed, as a cognitive skill, without actually utilizing any particular method of systems science to produce important conclusions.

Keywords Explanatory power · Fund performance · Law of one price · Sentiment measures · Structural analysis · Structural method of prediction

3.1 The Concepts of Closed and Open Systems

Depending on what one studies, the system of concern in this volume is either closed or open. In particular, a system is said to be closed (Klir, 2001), provided that it can be studied without referencing to any element or factor from outside of the system. That is, the system is completely free from the influence of its environment. Symbolically, a system $S = (M, R)$ is closed if for every relation $r \in R$, there is an ordinal number $n = n(r)$ such that $r \subseteq M^n$. That is, each relation $r \in R$ describes a relationship of some elements from the set of objects or elements of the system S. This concept of closed systems has been widely employed either consciously or unconsciously in the conventional (both natural or social) sciences, where minor or unimportant variables are ignored in order to develop a manageable mathematical model.

To illustrate the statement above, let us look at an example from the middle-school algebra. Three people, named A, B and C, are look at a particular job. Assume that A and B can complete the job together in 2 h, A and C in 4 h, and B and C in 8 h. Question: If all three of them work together on the job, how many hours do they need to finish the job? One typical approach to solving this problem, as taught in middle school, without considering

- How these three people could affect each other
- How external factors might influence the progress of the job
- How the parts of the job is structured

can be outlined below. Assume that A, B, and C can individually complete the job in x, y, z hours. Then, we can establish the following model to describe the given scenario:

$$\begin{cases} \dfrac{1}{x} + \dfrac{1}{y} = \dfrac{1}{2} \\ \dfrac{1}{x} + \dfrac{1}{z} = \dfrac{1}{4} \\ \dfrac{1}{y} + \dfrac{1}{z} = \dfrac{1}{8} \end{cases}$$

So, in 1 h, A, B, and C can jointly complete $\left(\frac{1}{2}+\frac{1}{4}+\frac{1}{8}\right)/2$ portion of the job. So, they need 4/7 h to complete the job, if they work together.

Although this example is from the middle-school algebra, it illustrates very well how conventionally when we investigate a business scenario, some inconvenient interactions are simplified or unimportant variables or factors are ignored in the model development. That is, the underlying systemic structures are more or less filtered out of consideration. For example, in the illustration above, the time needed for each possible pair of these people to complete the job is given, while it is not assumed that when an additionally person is added to work on the job, he/she does not adversely affect the progress of the job. Such adverse effect in real life represents a very possible scenario. At the same time, the previous approach automatically assumes that these three people can individually work on different parts of the job simultaneously without adversely affecting each other. Again, in real life, this end might not be the case due to various reasons, such as the availability of necessary supplies, which would make a closed system under the influence of the outside world. That is, in this case, a possibly close system might not be closed at all.

Another example is the well-known law of one price, which explains why the prices of commodities, assets, and securities remain the same across markets regardless of the exchange rate. The commonly accepted reasoning for the correctness of this law goes as follows. If an asset is priced lower in one market, then investors will dive in and buy the asset in that market while selling it in a more expensive market to net a profit. Because of such arbitrage behaviors, the supply and demand will eventually level out the prices across markets.

Similar to the analysis of the previous example, this argument for the law of one price holds true only if what is considered is a closed system. However, in real life, markets tend to be located at different locations with varying degrees of availability, transportation costs, taxes, and tariffs. Speaking differently, when external factors are involved, the previous argument for the law of one price no longer holds true.

The analyses of these examples naturally lead to the concept of open systems. In particular, a system is said to be open if some of its component parts or relationships of the component parts are affected by elements or factors external to the system. If we see elements or factors outside the system as from the environment of the system, then the concept of open systems can be intuitively described as follows. A system is an open system if some of its component parts or relationships of component parts are influenced by elements or factors, such as information, how-to knowledge, capital, of the environment. Symbolically, $S = (M, R)$ is said to be an open system, provided that there are one relation $r \in R$ and a set $E_r = E(r)$, which is dependent of r, such that

$$M \subsetneq E_r, \quad r \subsetneq M^{n(r)} \quad \text{and} \quad r \subsetneq E_r^{n(r)}. \tag{3.1}$$

That is, each element of S that is involved in the relationship r and the relationship r are influenced by elements or factors from the environment $E_r - M$. Speaking differently, the system $S_E = (E, R)$ is an environment of $S = (M, R)$, which, strictly speaking, is not a system as defined in the previous chapter. But from now on, it will be referred to as an open system, where

$$E = \bigcup_{r \in R} E_r. \tag{3.2}$$

From the definition of open systems, it can be readily seen that most, if not all, business scenarios, considered in the literature of business and economics, should involve open systems, unless studied as special cases. In other words, for the convenience of reasoning of one kind or another, special cases are established by identifying external relationships or interactions as not significant and then ignoring them all together, as demonstrated in the two examples analyzed above.

By summarizing what has been discussed above, it follows that a closed system exists in the business world through one of the following two possible means: (1) the organization of concern is artificially cut off from its environment either physically or conceptually and (2) the entity of concern is universally encompassing beyond which nothing exists. For case (1), conclusions established can be at the best approximations and at the worst random guesses of the true states of affairs. For case (2), established result will be of little practical use in particular business situations.

In the following, we will look at more detailed applications of the concept of open systems. As for how the concept of closed systems has been employed, we only need to look into the pages of a textbook in the business field.

3.2 Measures of Direct and Indirect Sentiment on Mutual Fund Performance

This section, which is based on Bu and Forrest (2020), demonstrates how direct and indirect sentiment measures play a role on mutual fund performance in two circumstances: (1) a sentiment measure is included in market models and (2) a measure is used independently.

3.2.1 Some Background Information

Although the efficient market hypothesis assumes that information is readily available to the public and market participants are rational, most investors are emotional and irrational in their decision-making. Hence, it is important for us to measure investor sentiment and incorporate such measures in security valuations.

Since the capital asset pricing model (CAPM) was initially employed to study mutual fund performance (Jensen, 1968), various additional factors have been added to the model to understand abnormal returns. For example, CAPM and the arbitrage pricing theory jointly reveal that conventional measures of abnormal fund performance are sensitive to the selected benchmark (Lehmann & Modest, 1987). Adding size and style factors to CAPM enables people to explain the alphas of most funds (Fama & French, 1993). By further adding a momentum factor, the Fama–French three-factor model becomes the well-known Carhart four-factor model (Carhart, 1997) and then the Fama–French five-factor model (Fama & French, 2015). However, all these identified factors still cannot explain regularly documented abnormal returns. That motivates scholars to consider investor sentiment.

Since the time when investors were noted to overreact to unexpected news events (De Bondt & Thaler, 1985), scholars have examined investor sentiment from different angles. For example, it is found that VIX contains market expectations (Bekaert & Hoerova, 2013; Fleming et al., 1995; Malz, 2000); VIX is negatively correlated with aggregate net equity fund flows; there is a clear relationship between investor sentiment, stock characteristics, and returns (Statman, 2011); technical indicators of stocks perform better when sentiment is high than when the sentiment is low (Feng et al., 2017); the quality of institutional investors clearly matters when sentiment is high while market signals are noisy (Dong & Doukas, 2018).

As investor sentiment is brought into picture, scholars have used it to investigate fund performance. For example, investor behavior can be used to explain cross-sectional regressions on daily asset returns (Goetzmann et al., 2000); the sentiment indicators of the American Association of Individual Investors (AAII) do seem to affect net aggregate equity fund flows (Indro, 2004); for securities with highly subjective valuations and difficulty to arbitrage, investor sentiment has substantial effects (Baker & Wurgler, 2006); investor sentiment and market volatility are found to be significantly correlated (Beaumont et al., 2008); an index of financial and economic attitudes is constructed based on daily Internet search volume from millions of households (Da et al., 2015) or Twitter feeds (Bollen et al., 2011) as a measure of sentiment.

As for measures of investor sentiments, additional to the ones mentioned above, there are also other different kinds, such as Barron's sentiment index, the Commitment of Traders report, CNN's *Fear and Greed* indexes, the NYSE 200-day moving average, the NYSE high/low indicator, the University of Michigan Consumer Sentiment Index, the US consumer confidence index, and others. These measures of investor sentiments can be classified into two groups. One group contains direct measures by using surveys that collect individuals' feelings regarding stock markets and related economic conditions. Included in this group are, for example, the AAII indexes and the University of Michigan Consumer Sentiment Index. The other group includes indirect measures, which are calculated by using financial and economic variables, such as the VIX and the Baker and Wurgler (2006) index. As for how these sentiment measures affect stock returns, it is found (Brown & Cliff, 2004) that these measures have different effects.

For a measure of investor sentiment to function effectively, it needs to be a behavioral variable not related to other systematic risks already considered in various versions of CAPM models. Only in such a case, this measure can independently explain mutual fund performance. Hence, indirect sentiment measures should be out of our consideration, because they are derived from market variables, and what they can reflect have already exhibited by economic indicators. To this end, in the rest of this section, we will see how a systems model can be used to explain the difference between direct and indirect sentiment measures and their effects on mutual fund performance. Then, an empirical confirmation is employed to support the conclusions of this model.

3.2.2 Systemic Modeling

The basic idea of our systemic model is that to understand a phenomenon or a process more appropriately than before, we need to treat the phenomenon (or process) as a system and examine it holistically. In other words, we need to consider all relevant variables, factors, and their interactive associations. By doing so, we naturally treat the phenomenon (or process) in such a way that its internal organization or structure is emphasized. This end is fundamentally different from the cases of the two examples analyzed in the previous section. Specifically, the first example of three workers ignored almost all interactions and influences of various factors, while the reasoning of the law of one price holds true only for close systems.

To possibly accomplish what is needed to, it is noticed (Forrest & Liu, 2022) that symbolic and statistical models suffer from major limitations, such as assumed distributions, the functional form of the dependent variable in independent variables, and specific representations of variable values. However, most of these limitations stem from such problems as (Wu & Lin, 2002) that data generally become available only post event, many theoretically important variables are not practically definable, etc. In terms of the issue to be addressed in this section, humans, appearing as investors, are part of the process; they attempt to predict the future development of the economy and the stock market. In such a process, the involved human participants make things difficult or impossible to deal with (Lin & OuYang, 2010; Soros, 2003), because no matter whether a prediction is accurate or not, the human participants alter the path of development from the predicted one through adjusting their behaviors. That makes the early prediction mostly inaccurate. With such background discussion in place, this section addresses the following question. Why should not a person independently employ any indirect sentiment index to explain the performance of a mutual fund?

One explanation for the NO answer to this question is that fund managers generally do not invest their available funds purely based on economic indicators. Instead of doing so, they most likely employ some other nontechnical methods to support their decision-making. At the same time, the measurement of each indirect sentiment, by definition, is theoretically derived on a set of economic variables or indicators and practically calculated by using specific values of economic variables or indicators. Although these involved variables or indicators could have been identified as either leading or lagging gauges of the economy, to calculate the measurement of a specific indirect sentiment, certain observed values of the economic variables or indicators used in the definition of the indirect sentiment have to be first taken. That means that the events or processes of concern have occurred already; otherwise, no data values can be observed and collected. Or, past values of the events or processes are employed to predict the present and/or the future, meaning that the past patterns are assumed to continue into the future. No matter which situation is the case, it makes it difficult or impossible to determine whether or not a prediction, derived in one of these two possibilities, is accurate (Lin & OuYang, 2010). Symbolically, the measurement of each indirect sentiment can be written in the following functional form:

$$P = Q(e_1, e_2, \ldots, e_n), \tag{3.3}$$

where P represents the output of or the prediction made by using the index, while the symbols e_i, $i = 1, 2, \ldots, n$, stand for the economic variables or indicators used in definition of the index, and n the number of variables and indicators considered by the index.

To produce a particular prediction, we need to know either the value of P or the trend of development of P. For the former case, particular values of the variables e_i, $i = 1, 2, \ldots, n$, have to be known. Moreover, for the latter case, the development trends of these variables still need to be known. To this end, no matter whether it is for the case of particular values of P or the development trends of the variables e_i, $i = 1, 2, \ldots, n$, the needed information can only be observed and collected after the occurrence of related events and processes. Hence, each prediction, produced out of the measurement of such an indirect sentiment, will not be practically accurate, because the basic idea underneath the effort of making such predictions is to extrapolate in one way or another the past trends or the present pattern into the present moment or the future.

When we specify our attention to financial markets, it can be seen that corresponding to each predicted P-value or trend, made out of one index or a combination of several indices, investors and managerial business decision-makers will position themselves accordingly, either in favor or against the predicted P-value or trend. Consequently, the relevant economic development will be affected and/or altered. This analysis means that, instead of Eq. (3.3), a potentially useful model for financial market prediction should be reflexive (Soros, 2003) and written as follows:

$$P = Q(P, e_1, e_2, \ldots, e_n). \tag{3.4}$$

That is, the dependent variable P is a function not only in e_i, $i = 1, 2, \ldots, n$, but also in itself P.

For practical purposes, Eq. (3.4) represents several challenges. For example, first, the structure of this functional Q is not readily known in order to calculate the value of or study the development trend of the dependent variable P. In the literature, the functional Q in Eq. (3.3) is often assumed to be linear, such as in the studies that employ the method of various regressions. As for the general case in Eq. (3.4), the structure of Q remains unknown (Soros, 2003). Second, because the properties of this functional Q, such as continuity, differentiability, etc., are unknown, solving Eq. (3.4) is practically impossible. Third, many aspects of the economy cannot be captured by the concept of variables and described by the concept of functionals (Lin, 1999). These reasons, together with others, lead to the conclusion that structural analysis is more accurate in terms of making predictions (Lin & OuYang, 2010).

The previous paragraph provides an explanation for why measures of direct sentiment would work better in conjunction with the benchmark models than without such measures. More specifically, when individual investors spell out their opinions and beliefs about the development of the economy and about the direction of the stock market, they more often than not include some sorts of structural analyses of the economy. They do so either consciously or unconsciously for the purpose of making as beneficial decisions as possible. That is, changes in economic structures, such as domestic and international news, policy adoptions, and economic environments, are employed in individual investors' decision-making.

To help better understand what is discussed here, let us use A to represent a market shock and B an investor. Assume that A repeatedly knocks on B without a clear pattern in terms of time interval and strength. To predict when the next knock of A will come with what level of strength, if B is scientifically trained, then he would conventionally maintain a record of several related variables, such as when each past knock occurred, at what level of strength each knock was measured, etc. That is, over time, B would have collected a set of time-series data $X_i = \{X_i(1), X_i(2), \ldots, X_i(n)\}$, for $i = 1, 2, \ldots, k$. By using this set of data, B would then construct a symbolic model, as given in Eq. (3.5), to foretell when the next knock would come and at what level of magnitude the next knock would be:

$$X_i(n+\ell) = f_i(X_1, X_2, \ldots, X_k), \quad \text{for integer } \ell = 1, 2, .. \tag{3.5}$$

where $i = 1, 2, \ldots, k$.

Although the forms of the functionals f_i, $i = 1, 2, \ldots, k$, vary greatly depending on the particular mathematical theory employed, predictions, produced out of such an approach, are not generally relevant to what is under consideration due to several key reasons (Lin & OuYang, 2010). First, each applied mathematical modeling requires the association of selected variables to comply with a set of specified rules; otherwise, no meaningful conclusions could be produced. To satisfy such a requirement, some aspects of the interactions of the selected variables in real life have to be purposefully ignored. Second, the values and development trends of the selected variables can only be observed and recorded after the event and process of concern have already occurred or well on the way. Third, the idea of extrapolating the past into the present and/or the future as predictions can only possibly capture states of affairs that are similar to what the past represents. This end explains why the approaches, described above, generally cannot predict the imminent arrival of a major disastrous event (Lin & OuYang, 2010).

Methodologically different of the aforementioned approach of modeling, a structural method of prediction can be depicted as follows: B looks at the structure of the surrounding environment. That is, B adopts the concept of open systems so that the performance of a mutual fund is a joint effect of closely related economic variables and some important environmental forces. In particular, each time when A knocks, the structure of the environment changes first. For example, shock A has to first take shape in one way or another and then strikes when the formation of the shock reaches a certain level. This discussion shows that a measurement of investor sentiment, including both direct and indirect sentiment elements, should work better than without the former ones, because they reflect the joint effect of many market-related and environmental forces.

The previous discussion in this section indicates that when the concept of variables is employed to describe a phenomenon, such as the performance of a mutual fund, some important aspects of the phenomenon are lost. In other words, when a business phenomenon is investigated as a closed system, the derived conclusions may very well be irrelevant to the phenomenon of concern. The reason for this realization is that some aspects of the phenomenon may interact with certain elements of the environment. Particular to the question this section attempts to address, when an index does not adequately describe the underlying firm and its business or the economy, produced predictions will not be reliable. In the rest of this section, empirical tests will be used to compare the measures of direct and indirect sentiments so that we can statistically confirm whether the measures of direct sentiment are better than those of indirect sentiment in terms of explaining the performance of a mutual fund.

3.2.3 Empirical Confirmation

For this empirical endorsement, the time span covered is the 10-year period from January 2009 to December 2018, while the CRSP Survivor-Bias-Free US Mutual Fund Database is used to develop the sample of mutual funds. Although all US equity funds appear in the database, the sample contains only 1466 funds with complete monthly return records during the selected time period.

As for the proxy of indirect sentiment index and that of direct sentiment index, we use respectively the Baker and Wurgler (2006) (BW) index and the AAIIsentiment indexes. Specifically, the former is popular in academia and was initially proposed by Baker and Wurgler based on the first principal component of standardized sentiment proxies using six macroeconomic indicators. Moreover, the latter are developed by AAII through using weekly surveys to measure the percentage of individual investors who are bullish, bearish, or neutral on the stock market for the forthcoming 6 months. These three AAII sentiment indexes add up to 100%.

The data of the BW index were downloaded from the website of Jeffrey Wurgler at New York University. Moreover, the data of the AAII sentiment indexes from the AAII website, consisting of the bullish, bearish, and neutral indexes. The bullish-bear spread is also used in the tests below.

Corresponding to the benchmark models used, including the CAPM, the Fama-French three-factor model, the Carhart four-factor model, and the Fama-French five-factor model, the relevant data were downloaded from the data library on the website of Kenneth French at https://mba.tuck.dartmouth.edu/pages/faculty/ken.french/data_library.html. Moreover, the risk-free rate in the benchmark model data is the 1-month treasury bill rate, as the treasury bills were commonly employed as the proxy for the investment with zero risk.

3.2.3.1 Probability of Outperformance and Probability of Underperformance

To evaluate if a fund would perform either better or worse than the market, the fund's alpha was estimated by using the selected models over the entire time span of the sample. The model setup is given in Eq. (3.6).

$$R_{p,t} = \alpha_p + \sum \beta_p \cdot r_{p,t} + \varepsilon_p, \tag{3.6}$$

where β_p's are such market factors as the monthly market excess return, size, style, and momentum. In terms of the Fama–French five-factor model, the market excess return, size, style, profitability, and investment are the involved market factors. The intercept term α_p measures a fund's alpha or abnormal return. If $\alpha_p > 0$ is statistically significant at 5%, the fund is seen as a winner fund and performs better than (or outperforms) the market. If $\alpha_p < 0$ is statistically significant at 5%, the fund is seen as a loser fund and performs worse than (or underperforms) the market.

Additionally, the time span of the sample was divided into two 5-year subperiods—the earlier subperiod and the later one—for the purpose of controlling the effect of market state on fund abnormal returns. The estimated probabilities for a sampled fund to outperform the market based on the four selected models are given in Table 3.1, where monthly return data were used.

Table 3.1 Outperformance and underperformance probabilities (Bu & Forrest, 2020)

	CAPM (%)	F–F three-factor model (%)	Carhart four-factor model (%)	F–F five-factor model (%)
Panel A: outperforming probability				
Whole sample period	4.71	4.37	4.71	6.14
1/2009 to 12/2013	1.43	1.71	1.71	3.07
1/2014 to 12/2018	2.39	2.80	2.66	3.21
Panel B: underperforming probability				
Whole sample period	0.82	0.61	0.75	0.61
1/2009 to 12/2013	8.33	11.54	13.59	10.72
1/2014 to 12/2018	0.55	0.34	0.34	0.41

It can be seen readily that for the entire sample period, the probability for a fund to outperform the market ranges from 4.37% to 6.14%, while that for a fund to underperform spans from 0.61% to 0.82%. This result implies that only a small number of mutual funds performed better than the market, while a much smaller number of the funds did worse than the market. For such a phenomenon to occur, it could be either the case that the selected models missed certain market factors, or that some fund managers possess such skills that happened to work effectively with the market condition of the specific time period, or both. Because it is known that in a booming market of low volatility, the number of outperforming funds is greater than that of underperforming ones, the previously observed deviations between the probabilities of outperformance and underperformance might be a natural consequence of the bullish market in the sample period.

As for the first sample subperiod that covers the time span from January 2009 to December 2013, the probability for a fund to outperform the market dropped to the range from 1.43% to 1.71%, while the probability for a fund to underperform rose to the range from 8.33% to 13.59%. To understand what was going on, it is noticed that this time period was characterized by high market volatilities; this was especially true for the first 3 years during which the Chicago Board Options Exchange (CBOE) volatility index fluctuated dramatically. Therefore, one could see that the low probability for outperformance and high probability for underperformance during this time period could well be caused by the high levels of volatility. As for the second subperiod January 2014 to December 2018, the market rose steadily with low volatility, except for the market correction in late 2018. The corresponding probability of outperformance ranged from 2.39% to 3.21%, while the probability of underperformance from 0.34% to 0.55%.

What is discussed in the previous paragraphs seems to suggest that the probabilities of outperformance and underperformance are respectively related to both market return and market volatility. Because market volatility, investor sentiment, and investment decisions are related, there is a need to study how investor sentiment might affect the performance of mutual funds.

3.2.3.2 Correlations Between Sentiment Measures

Table 3.1 suggests that a small number of mutual funds earn statistically significant alpha, be it either positive or negative, and that the probability for a fund to either outperform or underperform varies from one market condition to another. Because investor sentiment plays an important role in stock valuations, it is natural to include it in the evaluation of mutual fund performance. Following this idea, the next natural question is: should one use measures of direct sentiment or those of indirect sentiment in his explanation of mutual fund performance? To this end, Table 3.2 reports the Pearson correlations between the AAII indexes and the BW index, as well as the bullish-bearish spread, where the former are typical measures of direct sentiment and the latter a well-established measure of indirect sentiment. All figures

Table 3.2 Correlations between sentiment measures (Bu & Forrest, 2020)

	BW	Bullish	Neutral	Bearish	BB spread
BW	1.000				
Bullish	0.0806(0.381)	1.000			
Neutral	0.3644(<0.01)***	−0.4098 (0.0001)***	1.000		
Bearish	−0.3999 (<0.01)***	−0.5877(<0.01)***	−0.4972 (<0.01)***	1.000	
BB spread	0.2742(<0.01)***	0.8851(<0.01)***	0.0618(0.503)	−0.8967 (<0.01)***	1.000

*** indicates statistical significance at 1% level, ** at 5% level, and * at 10% level

are calculated by using monthly data January 2009–December 2019. The figures in parentheses are the relevant *P*-value.

Table 3.2 indicates that the BW index is significantly correlated with the AAII bearish and neutral indexes and the bullish-bearish spread with respective correlation coefficients being 0.3644, −0.3999, and 0.2742. Moreover, no statistically significant correlation exists between the BW index and the AAII bullish index. All these observations suggest that the selected measures of sentiment are not the same so that it is important to investigate how these measures affect fund returns.

3.2.3.3 Effect of Investor Sentiment on the Probability of Funds' Outperformance

To accomplish the task that is described in the title of this subsection, both the BW index and the AAII indexes will be added to each of the models as selected earlier. By doing so, a comparison between one original model and the same model with an investor sentiment index incorporated can be made in order to check if the sentiment index matters. The following Eq. (3.7) represents the model setup:

$$R_{p,t} = \alpha_p + \sum \beta_p \cdot r_{p,t} + \mathrm{SF}_t + \varepsilon_p, \tag{3.7}$$

where $R_{p,\ t}$ represents the excess return of portfolio p in month t with equally weighted winners or losers and SF_t month t's the sentiment factor that is the BW index or one of the AAII indexes. All other variables are the same as those in Eq. (3.5).

The probabilities for a fund to outperform, as estimated by each of the selected models adjusted by the BW index, are reported in Table 3.3. As before, the entire time period from January 2009 to December 2018 was divided into earlier and later subperiods, and all results were produced based on monthly return data.

Table 3.3 shows that for the entire time period of the sample data, the probability for a fund to outperform the market ranges from 1.30% to 2.46%, when the selected

Table 3.3 Probabilities of outperformance as estimated by the BW-adjusted models (Bu & Forrest, 2020)

Period	CAPM + BW (%)	FF three-factor + BW (%)	Carhart four-factor + BW (%)	FF five-factor + BW (%)
Whole sample period	1.78	1.71	1.30	2.46
1/2009 to 12/2013	0	0.89	1.09	0.89
1/2014 to 12/2018	0.21	0	0	0

Table 3.4 Probabilities of outperformance as estimated by AAII index-adjusted models (Bu & Forrest, 2020)

	AAII indexes	1/2009 to12/2018 (%)	1/2009 to12/2013 (%)	1/2014 to12/2018 (%)
CAPM	Bullish	0.34	1.23	0.00
	Bearish	1.16	5.32	0.00
	Neutral	6.08	6.01	2.05
Fama-French three-factor model	Bullish	0.68	3.28	0.07
	Bearish	0.68	2.73	0
	Neutral	10.44	10.38	2.73
Carhart four-factor model	Bullish	0.68	2.59	0.14
	Bearish	0.21	1.84	0.00
	Neutral	3.41	1.37	2.87
Fama-French five-factor model	Bullish	0.82	2.94	0.14
	Bearish	0.96	3.69	1.98
	Neutral	15.09	3.62	7.37

models are adjusted with the BW index. This range is much lower than that obtained out of the original models in Table 3.1. For the earlier subperiod from January 2009 to December 2013, the probability of outperformance dropped from the range 1.43–3.07% in Table 3.1 to 0–1.09% in Table 3.3. Moreover, for the later period from January 2014 to December 2018, the probability of outperformance dropped from the range 2.39–3.21% in Table 3.1 to 0–0.21% in Table 3.3 when the models are adjusted with the BW index of investor sentiment.

A comparison of the test results shown in Tables 3.1 and 3.3 indicates how important investor sentiment is in terms of explaining the occurrence of fund alpha. In particular, it shows that the BW index, a measure of indirect sentiment, plays a significant role in the probability for a fund to outperform the market.

To investigate the effect of direct sentiment measures on fund performance using the AAII indexes, the selected benchmark models were once again used. The results are shown in Table 3.4, where the probabilities for a fund to outperform the market were estimated by using the models that were adjusted with the AAII sentiment indexes.

Table 3.4 demonstrates that when the benchmark models are adjusted with the bullish index, the estimated probabilities of outperformance drop more significantly than the cases when the models are adjusted with the BW index. For the entire time period of the sample, the probability of outperformance ranges from 0.34% to 0.82% when the bullish index is used to make adjustment, representing a huge difference when compared to the range from 4.37% to 6.14% produced out of the original benchmark models. This drop in the estimated probabilities means that investor optimism plays an important role in a fund' outperformance. If the subperiods of early and later 5 years are used in the tests, Table 3.4 shows that the sentiment-adjusted probability of outperformance is also comparatively lower. For example, for the early subperiod from January 2009 to December 2013, the probability ranges from 1.23% to 3.28%, while for the later subperiod from January 2014 to December 2018, the probability ranges as low as from 0.00% to 0.14%.

As for the case when the AAII bearish index is considered, Table 3.4 also shows a significant drop in the probability for a fund to outperform the market. For example, for the entire time period sampled, the probability of outperformance ranges from 0.21% to 1.16%. For the subperiod of the earlier 5 years, the bearish sentiment-adjusted probability of outperformance ranges from 1.84% to 5.32%, which is higher than that produced out of the original benchmark models. As for the subperiod of the later 5 years, the range of the outperformance probability, based on the four sentiment-adjusted models, is overly lower, equaling 0.00–1.98%.

When the AAII neutral index is concerned with, the range of outperformance probability is significantly higher than that of the original benchmark models, as shown in Table 3.4. This pattern exists for all the time periods considered. This end implies that the AAII neutral index does not play any role in the estimation of the probability for a fund to outperform the market. On the other hand, if this index is forced into the benchmark models, the consequent results might very well be distorted due to the noise introduced.

In summary, this subsection confirms that both the BW index, a measure of indirect sentiment, and the AAII indexes, measures of direct sentiment, do play their respective roles in fund performance. Additionally, abnormal sentiments are more closely related to the outperformance of a fund.

3.2.3.4 Probabilities of Underperformance Based on Sentiment-Adjusted Models

Different from the previous discussion on outperformance probabilities, this subsection examines the impact of the BW and the AAII indexes on the probability for a fund to underperform the market. Table 3.5 reports the results on how the BW index impacts the underperformance probability.

As what is shown in Table 3.5, it can be seen that when the BW index is incorporated, the probability of underperformance, as estimated by the four benchmark models, ranges from 1.64% to 3.28%. That is higher than that from 0.61% to0.82% when the BW index is not incorporated. Similar results are observed for the

Table 3.5 Underperformance probabilities based on BW-adjusted models (Bu & Forrest, 2020)

Period	CAPM + BW (%)	FF three-factor + BW (%)	Carhart four-factor + BW (%)	FF five-factor + BW (%)
Whole sample period	3.28	2.46	1.64	1.78
1/2009 to 12/2013	9.28	12.42	12.56	10.65
1/2014 to 12/2018	1.02	1.23	0.89	1.23

Table 3.6 Underperformance probabilities based on AAII index-adjusted models (Bu & Forrest, 2020)

	AAII indexes	Whole sample period (%)	1/2009 to12/2013 (%)	1/2014 to12/2018 (%)
CAPM	Bullish	1.16	1.09	0.21
	Bearish	1.57	14.54	1.71
	Neutral	0.14	5.80	0.00
Fama-French three-factor model	Bullish	0.55	1.78	0.07
	Bearish	10.99	15.02	1.91
	Neutral	0.27	7.37	0.00
Carhart four-factor model	Bullish	0.55	1.64	0.07
	Bearish	2.39	4.03	1.50
	Neutral	0.00	5.46	0.00
Fama-French five-factor model	Bullish	0.89	2.18	0.14
	Bearish	10.65	13.65	0.00
	Neutral	0.21	3.07	0.07

two subperiods; that is, the probability for a fund to underperform the market is higher when the BW index is factored in. Speaking differently, Table 3.5 confirms that measures of indirect sentiment, such as the BW index, is likely irrelevant to the underperformance of a mutual fund.

Similarly, each of the AAII sentiment indexes is incorporated into the four benchmark models to test the effect of these measures of sentiment. Table 3.6 reports the estimated probability for a fund to underperform the market.

It can be seen from Table 3.1 that the probability of underperformance ranges from 0.61% to 0.82% according to the original benchmark models, while Table 3.6 shows that the AAII neutral index impacts on the estimated probability of underperformance the most. For the entire time period as sampled, with the neutral index incorporated, the probability of underperformance drops to the range from 0.00% to 0.27%, while the effect of the bullish and bearish indexes is limited. As for the early subperiod from January 2009 to December 2013, the bullish index carries the most impact. In particular, the probability of underperformance, as estimated by the bullish index-adjusted benchmark models, drops to the range 1.09–2.18% from

8.33% to 13.59%, as produced by four original benchmark models. The other two AAII indexes display an effect of varying degrees on the probability of funds' underperformance. As for the later subperiod, a similar pattern can be observed.

In short, Tables 3.5 and 3.6 jointly confirm that the BW index is irrelevant to fund underperformance, while the AAII indexes more or less impact the underperformance of funds. Therefore, it can be inferred that direct sentiment seems to better explain the underperformance of funds than indirect sentiment.

3.2.3.5 Sentiments' Explanatory Power on the Performance of Funds

This subsection examines if measures of direct and indirect sentiments possess different explanatory powers on the performance of mutual funds. For this purpose, a fund's monthly excess return $R_{p,\,t}$ is dependent on a sentiment factor SM_t as the explanatory variable, as given in Eq. (3.8)

$$R_{p,t} = \alpha_p + \mathrm{SM}_t + \varepsilon_p, \tag{3.8}$$

where SM_t represents the measure of a direct or an indirect sentiment in month t.

The BW index and the AAII indexes are respectively used as proxies for the direct and the indirect sentiment measures. Moreover, for each model, its adjusted R-square is used to quantify the model's explanatory power. Shown in Table 3.7 are the means, median values of adjusted R-squares, and standard deviations (S.D.) of the sentiment indexes on the returns of the fund sample.

Table 3.7 demonstrates that no matter whether we look at the entire time period of concern or the two subperiods, the BW index's power of explaining funds' performance is minimal. In terms of the mean and median of the adjusted R-squares, they are respectively 0.81% and 0.57% with a standard deviation of 1.10 for the entire time period. However, the adjusted R-squares become negative for the two subperiods, which indicates that the explanatory power of the BW index on fund

Table 3.7 Explanatory power of investor sentiment indexes on fund performance (Bu & Forrest, 2020)

		BW (%)	AAII bullish (%)	AAII bearish (%)	AAII neutral (%)
Whole sample period	Mean	0.81	17.39	11.71	−0.38
	Median	0.57	17.68	12.01	−0.51
	S.D.	1.10	2.54	2.89	0.47
1/2009 to 12/2013	Mean	−0.16	28.87	18.84	−1.31
	Median	−0.40	29.42	19.02	−1.51
	S.D.	1.21	3.49	4.39	0.63
1/2014 to 12/2018	Mean	−0.86	4.62	14.08	−1.15
	Median	−1.29	4.52	14.05	−1.34
	S.D.	1.22	2.24	3.84	0.61

performance is insignificant. That is, statistically the BW index by itself has little explanatory power on the performance of a mutual fund.

By focusing on the AAII indexes, Table 3.7 shows that when used as the explanatory variable, the neutral index leads to negative adjusted *R*-squares so that the effect of this index on fund return is negligible. As for the bullish index when used as the explanatory variable, the adjusted *R*-squares upsurge expressively with the mean, median, and standard deviation of adjusted *R*-square being 17.39%, 17.68%, and 2.54%, respectively. Such observations for the entire time period are similarly seen for the two subperiods. For example, for the earlier and later subperiods, these values are, respectively, 28.87%, 29.42%, and 3.49% and 4.62%, 4.52%, and 2.24%.

When the bearish index is utilized as the explanatory variable, the mean, median, and standard deviation of the adjusted *R*-squares are also high. For example, these values for the entire time period are respectively equal to 11.71%, 12.01%, and 2.89%; for the earlier subperiod 18.84%, 19.02%, and 4.39%; and for the later period 14.08%, 14.05%, and 3.84%. That is, Table 3.7 confirms that the bearish index is also significant in terms of explaining the performance of a mutual fund.

By examining the BW index, Table 3.7 indicates that this index's explanatory power is minimal. As for the AAII indexes, both the bullish and bearish ones provide significant adjusted *R*-squares. That implies their effect on the performance of mutual funds and that the effect is significant both individually and collectively if used jointly with other market variables. This end once again demonstrates a serious difference between the measures of direct and indirect sentiments. Because the neutral index is negligible in terms of explaining fund performance, it implies that only when sentiments are abnormal, they become effective in terms of their power of explaining the performance of a fund.

3.2.3.6 Sentiments Usable to Explain Winner and Loser Funds

To examine how investor sentiment explains the performance of winner and loser funds, this subsection continues to employ the BW index and the AAII indexes as proxies for the measures of direct and indirect sentiments. The dependent variable represents the monthly excess return of either a winner or a loser fund portfolio, where a fund is a winner (or loser) if it earns a statistically significant positive (or negative) alpha at 5% based on the CAPM; and each winner (or a loser) fund portfolio is assumed to be equally weighted portfolio of winner (or loser) funds.

The time period used in this subsection is the same as before that is from January 2009 to December 2018. Moreover, among the 1466 funds in the previous sample, there are 70 winner funds and 14 loser funds. Table 3.8 reports respectively the means, medians, and standard deviations (S.D.) of the adjusted *R*-squares of the sentiment indexes on the returns of these winner and loser funds.

From Table 3.8 Panel A, it follows that when the performance of a winner fund is explained by using the BW index, the adjusted *R*-squares are respectively well below 1% and negative for the entire sample period and the two subperiods. That is, this

Table 3.8 Explanatory power of investor sentiment on winner fund performance (Bu & Forrest, 2020)

		BW (%)	AAII bullish (%)	AAII bearish (%)	AAII neutral (%)
Panel A: winner funds					
Whole sample period	Mean	0.42	16.79	11.12	−0.42
	Median	0.33	16.75	11.15	−0.50
	S.D.	0.76	2.46	2.23	0.28
1/2009 to 12/2013	Mean	−0.44	28.49	18.07	−1.36
	Median	−0.67	29.08	18.31	−1.48
	S.D.	0.99	3.56	3.69	0.36
1/2014 to 12/2018	Mean	−0.98	4.33	11.93	−1.43
	Median	−1.58	3.98	12.20	−1.57
	S.D.	1.51	1.87	3.48	0.34
Panel B: loser funds					
Whole sample period	Mean	0.47	17.01	12.18	−0.47
	Median	0.38	17.86	12.84	−0.54
	S.D.	0.86	4.21	3.28	0.35
1/2009 to 12/2013	Mean	−0.64	29.42	20.74	−1.52
	Median	−0.60	29.92	21.93	−1.70
	S.D.	0.74	2.68	2.91	0.33
1/2014 to 12/2018	Mean	−1.28	4.43	13.66	−0.97
	Median	−1.26	4.03	15.06	−1.28
	S.D.	0.38	2.66	5.89	0.75

observation confirms that the BW index by itself does not have any power to explain the performance of a winner fund. The bullish AAII index behaves similarly on the entire fund sample with the mean and the median of the adjusted *R*-squares being 16.79% and 16.75%, respectively. For the early subperiod from January 2009 to December 2013, this bullish index has respectively the mean and median adjusted *R*-squares 28.48% and 29.08%. The lowest adjusted *R*-squares are reached in the later subperiod from January 2014 to December 2018, over which the mean and median adjusted *R*-squares are respectively equal to 4.33% and 3.98%.

As for the AAII bearish index, it also displays significant effects on the performance of a winner fund with the mean and median adjusted *R*-squares falling in the range 11.12–11.15% in the entire sample period, 18.07–18.31% in the earlier subperiod, and 11.93–12.20% in the later subperiod.

Figures in Table 3.8 demonstrate that for the entire sample period and for the earlier subperiod, the AAII bullish index explains winner fund performance better than the bearish index. Moreover, for the later subperiod, the bearish index explains much better than the bullish index. These observed changes in adjusted *R*-squares between the bullish and bearish indexes suggest that the implication of direct sentiment about the performance of a winner fund is dynamic and varies with changes in market conditions. As for the AAII neutral index, when it is used as the explanatory variable, the adjusted *R*-squares all become negative.

From the comparison between the BW index and the AAII indexes in Table 3.8 Panel B, a similar pattern as in Panel A can be seen. In particular, neither the BW index nor the AAII neutral index carries no ability to explain the performance of a loser fund, if they are used individually. On the other hand, both the bullish and bearish indexes individually display their significant explanatory power with the former having a higher adjusted *R*-square than the latter over the entire time period of the sample.

In short, what is shown in this subsection is that measures of indirect sentiment by themselves do not have any explanatory power over the performance of a fund and that measures of direct sentiment do have significant explanatory power when used either individually or jointly with other market factors. That is, direct sentiment contains certain essential information investors actually use in their decision-making, while such information is missing in indirect sentiment.

3.2.3.7 Sentiment Factors in the Context of a Sentiment-Adjusted Model

This subsection examines whether or not adding sentiment can improve the explanatory power of a benchmark model. Table 3.9 reports the average coefficients of the added sentiment factor and the adjusted *R*-squares based on the four benchmark models, adjusted respectively with the BW index and the three AAII sentiment indexes. The sample includes 1,466 US equity funds covering the time span from January 2009 to December 2018. All results are obtained with monthly return data, as described earlier in this chapter.

From Table 3.9 Panel A, it can be seen that in all the four selected models, the average coefficients of the BW, and the AAII neutral index are less than zero. In

Table 3.9 Coefficients and statistical significance on sentiment factors (Bu & Forrest, 2020)

Sentiment indexes	CAPM	Fama–French three-factor model	Carhart four-factor model	Fama–French five-factor model
Panel A: average coefficient				
BW	−0.6022	−0.4316	−0.3105	−0.4649
Bullish	0.8240	0.0083	0.1305	0.3836
Bearish	0.6067	1.3939	0.8965	1.3335
Neutral	−1.3990	−1.4789	−1.0449	−1.8176
Panel B: average adjusted R-squared				
Model without SF	0.8246	0.8715	0.8762	0.8751
BW	0.8264	0.8730	0.8765	0.8768
Bullish	0.8243	0.8710	0.8757	0.8748
Bearish	0.8254	0.8726	0.8762	0.8762
Neutral	0.8247	0.8720	0.8760	0.8761

particular, the coefficient of the BW index falls in the range from -0.6022 to -0.3105; that of the AAII neutral index in the range from -1.8176 to -1.0449. In the contrary, in the models considered, the coefficients of the AAII bullish and bearish indexes are positive with the coefficient of the latter index being overly greater than that of the former index.

From the reported adjusted R-squares in Table 3.9 Panel B, it can be seen that these values range from 0.8246 to 0.8762 when no sentiment factor is incorporated. On the other hand, no matter which sentiment index is added, the consequent adjusted R-squares remain almost the same. This observation suggests that incorporating a sentiment variable does not improve any of the models with its explanatory power, although doing so could potentially reduce the possibility for a fund abnormal return to appear. The reason for this observation might be that each investor sentiment, be it direct or indirect, depends largely on market returns; that explains why the impact of investor sentiment on fund performance becomes significant mainly in times of high sentiment. Therefore, incorporating a sentiment variable can no longer improve the explanatory power of any of the selected benchmark model.

3.3 A Few Final Words

The purpose of this chapter is to introduce the concepts of closed and open systems and to demonstrate how abstract systemic concepts can lead to practically useful conclusions. First, a simple algebra problem and the conventional reasoning for why the law of one price holds true are employed to show the essential difference between closed and open systems in studies of business and economic problems. Second, we look at a detailed study from the angle of close and open systems on how differently measures of direct and indirect investor sentiment can affect the performance of a mutual fund. In particular, we start this detailed exploration first by proposing a systems theory to explain why measures of direct sentiment contain more information than those of indirect sentiment, and then by empirically developing the conclusion, among other practically useful results, that measures of direct sentiment can better explain the performance of a mutual fund than those of indirect sentiment.

A quick glance through the overall organization of this chapter reveals the following fact: although the overall thinking behind the three case studies is developed on two basic concepts of systems, no particular systems methodology is used directly. Instead, the logic behind the entire chapter flows forward smoothly by following the so-called systems thinking, which, as a cognitive skill, is deployed through using holistic flexibility (Chowdhury, 2023). In particular, holistic flexibility stands for dynamic interplays between the mind of the researcher and/or the reader that absorbs the systemic complexity underneath and the state of the issue in hands (Chowdhury, 2019). When successfully applying the technology of holistic flexibility, one needs to possess five basic skills: thinking holistically, being flexible, learning creatively, deriving responsible outcomes, and producing realistic consequences.

Thinking holistically enables a person to rise above the conventional approach to problems by considering them contextually and in terms of evolution. Flexibility comes in three forms: cognitive, formulative, and substantive. The first form enables a person to think out of boxes; the second form makes a person readily examine various potential methodologies; and the third form motivates a person to evaluate resource alternatives. Learning creatively means continuously acquiring new information and knowledge and adapting to changing circumstances, expectations, and complexities. Deriving responsible outcomes means the aspiration to produce value additions in one's area of work. Moreover, producing realistic consequences stands for such a skill that can practically bring the above four skills together to produce tangible outcomes.

Systems thinking has led to many great successes not only in theory but also in practice. For references of theoretical successes, one can consult with, for example, Kijima et al. (2022) and Klir (2001); and for practical successes, a good starting point will be Forrest and Liu (2022) and then references given there. A close-to-life success story is that of Dr. Luis Sambo (Jackson & Sambo, 2020). In particular, systems thinking helped Dr. Sambo steer through the on-ground complexities of the Ebola epidemic in West Africa and launch his leadership position in the WHO without using any systems methodology.

References

Baker, M., & Wurgler, J. (2006). Investor sentiment and the cross-section of stock returns. *Journal of Finance, 61*(4), 1645–1680.

Beaumont, R., van Daele, M., Frijns, B., Lehnert, T., & Muller, A. (2008). Investor sentiment, mutual fund flows and its impact on returns and volatility. *Managerial Finance, 34*(11), 772–785.

Bekaert, G., & Hoerova, M. (2013). *The VIX, the variance premium and stock market volatility* (NBER Working Paper No. 18995).

Bollen, J., Mao, H. N., & Zeng, X. J. (2011). Twitter mood predicts the stock market. *Journal of Computational Science, 2*(1), 1–8.

Brown, G. W., & Cliff, M. T. (2004). Investor sentiment and the near-term stock market. *Journal of Empirical Finance, 11*(1), 1–27.

Bu, Q., & Forrest, J. Y. L. (2020). Comparing sentiment measures in mutual fund performance. *International Journal of Managerial Finance, 17*(3), 478–493. https://doi.org/10.1108/IJMF-02-2020-0092

Carhart, M. M. (1997). On persistence in mutual fund performance. *Journal of Finance, 52*(1), 57–82.

Chowdhury, R. (2019). Systems thinking. In R. Chowdhury (Ed.), *Systems thinking for management consultants: Introducing holistic flexibility* (pp. 3–28). Springer. https://doi.org/10.1007/978-981-13-8530-8_1

Chowdhury, R. (2023). Holistic flexibility for the application of systems thinking as a cognitive skill. *Systemic Practice and Action Research, 36*, 803.

Da, Z., Engelberg, J., & Gao, P. J. (2015). The sum of all fears investor sentiment and asset prices. *Review of Financial Studies, 28*(1), 1–32.
De Bondt, F. M., & Thaler, R. (1985). Does the stock market overreact? *Journal of Finance, 40*(3), 793–805.
Dong, F., & Doukas, J. (2018). Fund management skill and noise trading. *Journal of Portfolio Management, 44*(5), 113–124.
Fama, E. F., & French, K. R. (1993). Common risk factors in the returns on stocks and bonds. *Journal of Financial Economics, 33*(1), 3–56.
Fama, E. F., & French, K. R. (2015). A five-factor asset pricing model. *Journal of Financial Economics, 116*(1), 1–22.
Feng, S., Wang, N., & Zychowicz, E. J. (2017). Sentiment and the performance of technical indicators. *Journal of Portfolio Management, 43*(3), 112–125.
Fleming, J., Ostdiek, B., & Whaley, R. (1995). Predicting stock market volatility: A new measure. *Journal of Futures Markets, 15*(3), 265–302.
Forrest, J. Y. L., & Liu, Y. (2022). *Value in business: A holistic, systems-based approach to creating and achieving value*. Springer.
Goetzmann, W. N., Massa, M., & Rouwenhorst, K. G. (2000). *Behavioral factors in mutual fund flows* (Yale Working Paper).
Indro, D. (2004). Does mutual fund flow reflect investor sentiment? *Journal of Behavioral Finance, 5*(2), 105–115.
Jackson, M. C., & Sambo, L. G. (2020). *Systems thinking*. OR 62. Retrieved from https://www.youtube.com/watch?v=oUwij18dirg&list=PLo52A9r56pbuRx4dM8P1x4iSDab8wT8mj&index=2
Jensen, M. C. (1968). The performance of mutual funds in the period 1945-1964. *Journal of Finance, 23*(2), 389–416.
Kijima, K., Sato, R., & Nakano, B. (Eds.). (2022). *Systems research I & II: Essays in honor of Yasuhiko Takahara on systems theory and modeling*. Springer.
Klir, G. (2001). *Facets of systems science*. Springer.
Lehmann, B. N., & Modest, D. M. (1987). Mutual fund performance evaluation: A comparison of benchmarks and benchmark comparisons. *Journal of Finance, 42*(2), 233–265.
Lin, Y. (1999). *General systems theory: A mathematical approach*. Plenum and Kluwer Academic Publishers.
Lin, Y., & OuYang, S. C. (2010). *Irregularities and prediction of major disasters*. CRC Press.
Malz, A. M. (2000). *Do implied volatilities provide early warning of market stress?* (Working Paper).
Soros, G. (2003). *The Alchemy of Finance*. Wiley.
Statman, M. (2011). Investor sentiment, stock characteristics, and returns. *Journal of Portfolio Management, 37*(3), 54–61.
Wu, Y., & Lin, Y. (2002). *Beyond nonstructural quantitative analysis: Blown-ups, spinning currents and modern science*. World Scientific.

Chapter 4
The Evolution of Freely Competitive Markets

Jeffrey Yi-Lin Forrest, Joachim Wagner, Melanie Anderson, John Lipinski, Yong Liu, and Xiaoguang Tian

Abstract This chapter, which is mainly based on Forrest et al. (Pennsyl Econ Rev 29(1):92–115, 2022), provides a simplified approach to the study of evolutions of an economic market from the angles of profits and market competition. It first looks at the profit landscape of the primitive firms that serve sporadically existent demands in an emerging market, followed by that of the incumbent firms of a maturing market. By doing so, this chapter is able to establish the conclusion that the forever evolving preferences of consumers help make market competition relentlessly intensify, while more firms are encouraged to enter the established oligopoly market.

Before we see how such a simplified approach will play an important role in the development of natural endowments for business firms, the appendix of this chapter shows how conclusions on the evolution of economic markets can be beautifully employed to further the understanding of the Gabaix's (Econometrica 79:733–772, 2011) granular hypothesis. Specifically, among other results, the appendix develops precise conditions for the phenomenon of Gabaix's granular hypothesis either to appear or not to appear. As a confirmation of these theoretically important conclusions, empirical case analyses are given, while several important unanswered questions are posted for future research.

Keywords Consumer surplus · Industry · Market competition · Sales · Technology · Top performing · Firm

---

Jeffrey Yi-Lin Forrest (Department of Accounting Economics Finance, Slippery Rock University, Slippery Rock, PA, USA; Email: Jeffrey.forrest@sru.edu), Joachim Wagner (Institute of Economics, Leuphana University, Lueneburg, Germany; Email: wagner@leuphana.de), Melanie Anderson (Department of Accounting Economics Finance, Slippery Rock University, Slippery Rock, PA, USA; Email: melanie.anderson@sru.edu), John Lipinski (Department of Management, Indiana University, Indiana, PA, USA; Email: lipinski@iup.edu), Yong Liu (School of Business, Jiangnan University, Wuxi, Jiangsu, China; Email: clly1985528@163.com), and Xiaoguang Tian (Department of Management and Marketing, Purdue University Fort Wayne, Fort Wayne, IN, USA; Email: tianx@pfw.edu) are equally contributed to this chapter.

J. Y.-L. Forrest, *Systemic Principles of Applied Economic Philosophies I*,
Translational Systems Sciences 38, https://doi.org/10.1007/978-981-99-7273-9_4

4.1 Introduction

The goal of the next chapter is to develop the natural endowments for business firms, similar to the case of individual persons. To prepare for such an end, this chapter examines the emergence and development of an industry or a regional or national economy and paints a general picture for such economic evolutions in light of profits and competition. Other than helping to materialize such a goal, a literature search reveals the fact that this adopted approach turns out to be novel and can indeed help fill some gaps that exist in the relevant studies.[1]

In areas of research on the emergence and development of an industry, the literature consists roughly of particular case studies and general explorations of conditions on which an industry emerges. In comparison, this chapter constructs the evolutionary picture for the emergence, growth, and maturing of an industry by investigating how the landscape of profits initially appears and then evolves. The motivation for adopting this approach is that positive cash flows represent the fundamental factor behind most business ventures and efforts. In terms of market competitions, although the literature is huge, what is missing is a general theory on why and how competitions emerge in the marketplace. To fill this gap, the following

[1] Because most parts of developmental economics are established on prima facie starts or statistically confirmed conclusions of limited validity, that explains why that particular area of economic studies tends to contain obvious inconsistencies or conflicting beliefs. For example, studies on industrial revolutions (Rostow, 1960; Wen, 2016) have led to inconsistent and even contradictory conclusions on what caused the appearance of that particular first Industrial Revolution. Another example is the studies on whether or not economic policies work in practice. These works have been parts of many rounds of debates between yes and no conclusions (Reinert, 1995) that appeared one after another without any end in sight. Since each argument in these related areas is based on theories of limited validity (Andreoni & Chang, 2019), claims have never been as lawful as conclusions established in natural science, leading to the phenomenon that a yes conclusion ends a debate and then later reversed to a no conclusion in the next round of debate. The superficial reasons for this phenomenon have been identified to be the forever existing, while not isolatable, interacting factors that affect the outcomes of analyses (Hanzel, 2010; Mäki, 1992; Rosenberg, 1995). To remedy this unfortunate situation, commonly encountered in social science, this work takes a completely different approach in order to produce generally useful and more lawful conclusions by identifying what is most fundamental underneath each and every decision-making effort. That is, a truly useful theory needs to be started on such starting points that are plainly and generally true and then conclusions need to be derived by following some kind of logical reasoning, as what is done in mathematics and natural science.

The importance of such effort can be well confirmed theoretically through reviewing the literature and practically by checking how much economic theories are expected to actually work in real life in order to save lives and reduce economic losses. For example, in the theoretical front, since the time of Marshall (1890), studies of economics have strived to establish its conclusions as those seen in natural science (Maialeh, 2019), although not much success is achieved. And in the practical front, every time when an economic crisis occurred, people asked why studies of economics did not help provide warnings or explanations about what led to the crisis, see, for example, the comments by Paul Krugman (*New York Times*, 2009-09-02) and Paul De Grauwe (*Financial Times*, 2009-07-21) regarding the 2018 financial crisis.

sections explore how market signals the potential of profits and encourages market competition.

The rest of this chapter is organized as follows. Section 4.2 provides a literature review while showing where and how this work makes its contribution. Section 4.3 presents a simplified approach to how the market whose appearance accompanies the emergence of an industry evolves from the angle of profits. It consists of two subsections with the first one looking at the emergence and growth of the market and the second on how competition plays out as the market matures. The chapter concludes in Sect. 4.4 with some relevant remarks.

4.2 Literature Review

The work presented in this chapter touches on two different while related literatures: emergence and development of industries and market competitions.

In terms of the emergence and development of an industry, the literature can be roughly divided into two categories—one on the analysis of particular cases of industry emergence and the other on general conditions that are underneath the emergence of an industry. For example, for the first case, Zhao et al. (2012) identify and analyze the growth path and the characteristics of the solar photovoltaic power industry by employing a multifaceted approach, including literature survey, statistical data investigation, law review, and regulation and policy. By using data on publications, patents, and firms combined with business history, Sanderson and Simons (2014) analyze how the solid-state lighting industry emerged out of light emitting diode technologies, which had advanced in the prior half a century, involving many researchers in universities, national laboratories, and firms from around the world. Maine et al. (2014) analyze the emergence and development of the global nanobiotechnology industry by identifying, classifying, and tracking firms with capabilities in both biotechnology and nanotechnology over time. Martin and Coenen (2015) try to understand the emergence of the biogas industry in the region of Scania in Southern Sweden by considering the interplay between technology, industry dynamics, and institutions based on in-depth interviews with key stakeholders and firms.

For the second case, Ruan et al. (2014) examine through a case study how government can shape the development of a disruptive innovation through employing both promotional and restrictive policies and how the distinctive nature of such innovations influences the strategies of individual firms with relevant industry and institutional environment co-evolving. Foray and Raffo (2014) look at two issues—the general conditions and procedures involved in the emergence of a tool industry and the other whether or not a tool industry is currently emerging in the area of education. These authors build a heuristic framework regarding the main conditions for the emergence of tool industries by using works on historical cases and describe an emerging population of firms specialized in educational tools and instructional technologies. Matti and Consoli (2017) study to what extent instruments at different levels of policy domains can be coordinated as part of the process of developing an industrial sector by using the case of Spanish wind energy sector. They confirm that with international commitments, governments of different levels deliver market signals and provide financial support and mechanisms to lucid actors and respective capacities. That is, governments of different levels jointly play a key role in the sector development. By surveying the literature on the emergence of industries, Gustafsson et al. (2016) show that industry emergence is a three-stage process: the initial stage, the co-evolutionary stage, and the growth stage that leads to the birth of a new industry. In the initial stage, a disruption to the existing industrial order appears, triggering the co-evolution of technology, markets, and activity networks, leading to the identity of a new industry (or birth of a new industry).

Different from the literature on individual cases of success and the stages, transitions between these stages that exist in the emergence, and development of an industry, our current work attempts to construct a more general picture by looking at the evolution of profits. It is because positive cash flow represents the fundamental factor behind the appearance of any industry.

Regarding market competitions, the literature can be roughly divided into the following tracks: management-related issues, matters of innovation, and topics related to finance. Regarding issues of management, Schmidt (1997) shows that an intensifying competition increases the probability of liquidation, a positive effect on managerial effort, and reduces a firm's profits, a negative effect on efforts. Empirically, Flammer (2015) finds that domestic companies respond to tariff reductions by increasing their engagement in corporate social responsibility (CSR). This finding supports the view that CSR can be used as a differentiating strategy that separates companies from their foreign rivals. Gu (2016) shows a strong positive correlation between the investment in research and development (R&D) and product market competition. In particular, R&D-intensive firms are generally riskier and earn higher expected returns than R&D-weak firms. Dhaliwal et al. (2014) find that accounting conservatism is greater when there is a higher threat of new entrants as well as stiff existing competition. That is, strategic considerations shape the degree of how product market competition influences conditional conservatism. Castellucci and Podolny (2017) propose, with supporting anecdotes, that other than being content with exchange partners, high-status positions help their occupants enter into new exchange relationships with partners of higher quality, while the positions undercut the firms' development of capabilities, leaving the firms less able with the resources provided by existing exchange relationships. Symeonidis (2017) maintains that both the number of strikes and the number of lost working days, as a result of strikes, increased significantly when competition intensified after the abolition of cartels in the UK in late 1950s. Chalioti and Serfes (2017) specify when higher risk reduces incentives for firms to invest in cost-reducing R&D and compete in the product market and examine when some firms will strengthen while other firms will weaken incentives provided to their agents. Spiegler (2016) reviews the theoretical literature of the choice complexity in competitive markets by addressing what determines the amount of choice complexity in market equilibrium, what relation exists between choice complexity and aspects of payoff of the market outcome, and what role consumer protection measures play.

In terms of innovation, Hartley et al. (2013) compare three major public innovation strategies by showing that both private and public sectors have a number of drivers of as well as barriers to innovation. Wu (2012) proposes that the impact of technological collaboration on product innovation is contingent on market competition and sectoral technology characteristics by referencing to the literature of strategic alliances and innovation. Then the author uses data from 944 Chinese firms across five manufacturing sectors to confirm the conjecture. Harmancioglu et al. (2019) empirically look at the question of how a firm can achieve ambidexterity and find that the answer lies in the adoption of two important organizational cultures—willingness to cannibalize and willingness to combine existing knowledge. These cultures allow a firm to attain superior performance through the implementation of both radical *and* incremental (i.e., ambidextrous) innovations. Based on product descriptions from firm 10-K statements, Kim et al. (2016) find that firms in competitive markets invest more heavily in R&D and corporate venture capital (CVC), and with increasing competition, a shift away from internal R&D spending and into CVC occurs, where CVC is a way of exploiting external knowledge for the IT-producing industry. By exploring the relationship among market competition, technology innovation, and firms' rise to a higher generation of production technology, Qian and Wang (2017) find empirically how concurrent market and technology competition lead a firm to defer advancement, although these competitions drive technology advancement.

In terms of topics related to finance, by comparing noncompetitive and competitive industries, Giroud and Mueller (2011) find that only in the former case firms with weak governance have lower equity returns, worse operating performance, and lower firm value; these firms suffer from lower labor productivity and higher input costs and make more value-destroying acquisitions and tend to be targets of activist hedge funds. Peress (2010) demonstrates that under monopolistic competition with shares traded in perfectly competitive markets, firms insulate their profits by using their monopoly power to pass on shocks to customers. That stimulates stock trading, capitalization of private information, and improvement in capital allocation. Cheng et al. (2013) uncover a positive relation between product market competition and earnings quality and one between such competition and the precision of public and private information held by investors and analysts. Bustamante and Donangelo (2017) suggest that competition wears away markups, exposing firms to more system risks, that the potential of increasing competition lowers incumbent firms' exposure to system risks, and that aggregate industry risk stands for a barrier to entry so that riskier industries become less competitive. By using retrospective cohort study and prescription claims from commercial health plans between 2008 and 2013, Dave et al. (2017) determine confirmatively the association between levels of market competition and changes in generic drug prices in the United States. By developing a two-stage Bayesian game for the market competition of differentiated products and empirical tests, Stoughton et al. (2017) study the impact of competition on information production and investment efficiency. They find that with a fixed market structure competition makes firms less efficient to a first-best case because the firms acquire less information and investments.

Although the literature on market competition is huge, what is missing is the mechanism that underlies the emergence of such competition. To fill this gap, this chapter establishes a conclusion on how market signals the potential of profits and encourages market competition.

4.3 Market Evolution: A Simplified Approach

This section provides a simplified theoretical picture on how an industry appears, grows, and matures over stages in terms of sales and market competition. The first subsection focuses on appearance and growth, while the second subsection looks at maturity and aging.

4.3.1 Emergence/Development of an Industry: Seen from the View of Profits

The emergence of a new industry (or a regional or national economy) represents a three-stage process: the initial stage, the co-evolutionary stage, and the growth stage that leads to the birth of a new industry (Gustafsson et al., 2016). In the initial stage, one or a few disruptive innovations first appear, suspending the existing equilibrium among existing industries. At this stage, the disruptive innovations, as a matter of any innovation, be it disruptive or incremental, on either the producer side or the demand side are generally brought forward by particular talents who suddenly and randomly hit on some bright ideas (Ridley, 2016). For example, Ye et al. (2012) analyze a case of how a firm innovatively created simultaneous consumer utilities by offering a collocated assortment of products and/or services to consumers. Specifically, a state university in northern United States has a student body of over 29,000. These students are mostly in their undergraduate programs, unmarried, and live on tight budgets. Considering the characteristics of young people, both physically and mentally active and always busy with different kinds of activities, such as their school assignments and part-time works, most of the rental properties, aiming at the students, do not offer laundry facilities due to various reasons such as that specific labor force is needed to maintain the fragile equipment. So, some other local business people serve the students by providing self-servicing coin-operated laundromats, located near the campus. Additionally, because of long and cold winters of the region, mostly college female students are attracted to indoor tanning salons, another successful college-town business in northern United States.

With associative thinking, two entrepreneurs offer simultaneously a coin-operated self-service laundry facility and an indoor tanning service at a convenient single location. These businessmen first fashion in thoughts and then produce in practice consumer synergies by combining these two commonly available assets. In this case, the overhead costs remain roughly the same as if they operated the operations separately, because these services require different sets of equipment, and so do the labor costs, because the combined laundry and tanning services require different skills for production and customer service. However, these joined business service operations generate magnificent amount of demand-side synergies because of the following two reasons:

1. Such activities as washing clothes and tanning skin can be carried out simultaneously, saving the otherwise unproductive and costly waiting time (beyond completing their homework, the students have to work to make their tight budgets sufficient for all of their living and school expenses.
2. A nice location and convenient opportunity are provided and created for students to establish relationships. The single location attracts females to the tanning service while enjoying the convenience of simultaneous clothes washing; and the good amount of appearances of single females attracts a large number of males to use the laundry facility.

In this business scenario, because of the created consumer or demand-side synergies, the business owners are able to collect higher fees from the laundry service than other single-purpose stores, while maintaining competitive pricings for the tanning service, the demand of which in turn grows substantially due to heavy flows of male users of the laundry facility. In other words, the pooled services for the student consumers generate a greater value, which is also handsomely netted by business owners because of the innovatively created consumer synergies from product-and-service diversification.

Based on how historically innovations appear (Ridley, 2016), how collaborations lead to innovations (Hartley et al., 2013; Wu, 2012), the previous example, and many other similar anecdotes, the following fact can be seen readily. When one or a few entrepreneurs are able to spot a business opportunity through their intimate knowledge of particular resources, business models, and/or circumstances involved (Ye et al., 2012), these capable people foresee the possibility of introducing a brand-new kind of product, practically produce or have the imagined product produced, and then consequently offer the product to the market. When a market particular to the product and related substitutes gradually forms with an increasing number of customers and rising consumer spending, the quality of the particular group of products improves with widening acceptance and usage of the product. At the same time, the technology employed to make the products becomes standardized, which helps lower the production cost (Forrest et al., 2018).

Assume that during this stage of development, the gradually appearing market is served by m firms, named Firm i $(= 1, 2, \ldots, m)$. These firms provide customers with mutually substitutable products. Because of the novelty and freshness of the products, no customer is loyal to any particular firm. On the other hand, the firms have to apply adjustable prices to attract customers who make purchase decisions based on whose price is more competitive. In the rest of this chapter, such customers will be referred to as switchers. Let β be the magnitude of the market segment of all switchers, which is in this stage of market development equal to the sum of all customers and potential customers. To make our analytical reasoning possible, assume that these firms produce horizontally differentiated products at constant marginal costs, which are set to zero without loss of generality. Assume additionally that to serve the emerging and growing market well, the managements of these firms share their pricing strategies with each other so that they individually establish their best responses by playing the Nash equilibrium through pure self-analyses. Specifically, for a non-cooperative game, the so-called Nash equilibrium stands for the most common solution, involving two or more players, so that each player knows the equilibrium strategies of the other players and cannot gain anything by changing his own strategy (Osborne & Rubinstein, 1994).

Because the product market is in a certain sense still emerging, one can treat each of the m firms as an entrant into a brand-new and unoccupied market, where the firms will be considered doing well as long as they make profits. Practically speaking, this end implies that each of these firms uniformly randomizes its selling price P over the interval $[C, R]$ as long as the firm could make profits on the average, where $C = 0$ stands for the normalized cost of production and R the reservation price customers are willing to pay for the product. Without loss of generality (for details, see Forrest et al., 2021), R can be normalized to 1. That is, each firm uniformly randomizes its selling price P over the interval [0,1] as long as the firm could make profits on the average.

If there is only one firm serving the emerging market, that is, $m = 1$, then the profit the firm makes is

$$\text{market occupency} \times \text{price} = \beta P = \beta(1-P)^0 P = \beta P(1-P)^{m-1}.$$

If there are two firms, $m = 1, 2$, that serve the market, then each firm's profit is

$$\text{each firm's market occupency} \times \text{price} = \beta(1-P)^1 \times P = \beta P(1-P)^{m-1},$$

where the reason why these firms set their selling price P the same is because if not, customers will make their purchases from the firm of lower price, say Firm 1. So, the demand for Firm 1's product increases and that for Firm 2 decreases, forcing Firm 2 to lower its price. Eventually, the prices charged by these firms have to be equal to each other if they want to stay in business.

Continuing the reasoning above produces that if there are three firms, $m = 1, 2, 3$, that serve the market, then each firm's profit is

$$\text{each firm's market occupency} \times \text{price} = \beta(1-P)^2 \times P = \beta P(1-P)^{m-1}.$$

So, by using mathematical induction, the general result follows:

Proposition 4.1 In the afore-described emerging market, if there are m firms that serve the market, $m = 1, 2, 3, \ldots$, then each firm's profit Π is equal to

$$\Pi = \beta P(1 - P)^{m-1}. \tag{4.1}$$

In the next stage of development and the emergence of a new industry, as triggered by the initial stage of disruption to the existing industrial order, relevant technologies, markets, and activity and organizational networks develop simultaneously along with increasing severity of competition among firms (Gustafsson et al., 2016). So, some firms thrive, some barely survive, and most others fail (Markman & Waldron, 2014). Except those firms that have failed, some of the m firms, as discussed above, become established so that each of them enjoys a base of loyal customers; see the next chapter on the formation of bases of loyal customers. Without loss of generality, assume that all these m firms survive the previous stage of development. Let α stand for the normalized magnitude of the established Firm i's base of loyal customers. So, $\beta = 1 - m\alpha$ is the magnitude of the market segment of switchers, known as consumer surplus, where it is assumed that both β and α have been normalized so that $\alpha, \beta \in [0, 1]$ and $m\alpha + \beta = 1$. Analyzing similarly as above leads to the following result:

Proposition 4.2 In the afore-described developing and stabilizing market, if $F_i(P)$ represents the price distribution of incumbent Firm i, $i = 1, 2, \ldots, m$, then Firm j's profit Π_j is equal to

$$\Pi_j = \alpha P + \beta P \prod_{\substack{i=1 \\ i \neq j}}^{m} [1 - F_i(P)]. \tag{4.2}$$

In fact, if $m = 1$, the profit of Firm 1 is the sum of its profit αP from the loyal customers and that from the consumer surplus βP. Symbolically, the following holds

$$\text{Profit of Firm } 1 = \Pi_1 = \alpha P + \beta P.$$

If $m = 2$, the profit Π_i of Firm i is equal to the sum of its profit αP from the loyal customers and that from the consumer surplus $\beta P(1 - F_j(P))$, for $i, j = 1, 2$, $i \neq j$. That is, the expression below follows

$$\alpha P + \beta P \prod_{\substack{j=1 \\ j \neq i}}^{2} [1 - F_j(P)].$$

So, Eq. (4.2) follows by using mathematical induction for every Firm j.

In the previous discussion, although each firm's cost C of production is normalized to 0 and the reservation price R customers are willing to pay for their products to 1, the normalization in practice means that Firm i charges price P_i for its product equal to or above its cost of production. That is, in the previous theoretical reasoning, although the selling price P is treated as the same, it is practically different from one firm to another in real life, where the applied normalization does not exist. In other words, the sales price P_i of Firm i is different of P_j of Firm j; but proportionally, these prices are the same in terms of their relevant cost C_k and reservation price R_k, for $k = i, j$. Symbolically, there are parameters $\alpha_k \in [0, 1]$ satisfying that

$$P_k = C_k + \alpha_k(R_k - C_k), \quad k = 1, 2.$$

So, the normalization of the prices means that identify P_k with α_k; and the same selling price means that the individual firms' prices satisfy the following condition: $(P_i - C_i)/(R_i - C_i) = (P_j - C_j)/(R_j - C_j)$. For more discussion regarding this normalization, see the following subsection.

With the initial stage of disruption to the existing industrial order in the past, the relevant technologies and markets developed, and organizational networks established, the emergence of a new industry enters into its third stage—birth of the industry, where the industry acquires its identity (Gustafsson et al., 2016). Other than studying the emergence and development of a new industry from different angles, such as conditions for an industry to appear (Foray & Raffo, 2014); identification, classification, and tracking firms' capabilities (Maine et al., 2014); policies (Matti & Consoli, 2017); business history (Sanderson & Simons, 2014); interplay of technology, industry dynamics, and institutions (Martin & Coenen, 2015); roles of governments (Ruan et al., 2014); growth path and characteristics (Zhao et al., 2012); etc., this subsection focuses on profits, the driving force behind individual firms' devotion of time, efforts, and resources.

4.3.2 Market Competition

Because preferences and tastes of customers evolve constantly, it is inevitable for new switchers to emerge either out of the loyal customers or new customers in the afore-described product market, especially if the incumbent firms become risk avert and comfortable with their market positions and levels of profits they are making, as suggested by Podolny (1993) when the market is seen as a hierarchy of status orders. So, the following natural question arises: Do evolving preferences and tastes of customers mean that new competition will appear in the product market? To this end, the result below follows:

Proposition 4.3 In Nash equilibrium, if the consumer surplus satisfies $\beta = 1 - m\alpha > 0$, then at least one new firm will enter the afore-described market as a competitor of the incumbent firms, while the expected total profit of all entrants is directly proportional to β.

Proof For the part of showing that at least one new firm will enter into the afore-described market as a competitor of the incumbent firms, see the technical proof of

Theorem 1 in Forrest et al. (2019b)). For the rest of this proof, the focus is on showing that the combined profit of all entrants is directly proportional to β.

To this end, assume that there is only one entrant that uniformly randomizes its price P over the interval [0,1] as long as the firm could make profits on the average. Here, 0 stands for the normalized constant marginal costs of the entrant and all incumbents and 1 those of the reservation prices individual customers loyal to their respective incumbent firms are willing to pay to buy their firms' products. Let $F_j(P)$ be the price distribution of incumbent Firm j. Then, the expected profit of the entrant is given by

$$E(\Pi) = = \int_0^{\alpha/\beta} \beta P dP + \int_{\alpha/\beta}^{+\infty} \beta P \prod_{i=1}^{m} [1 - F_i(P)] dP, \tag{4.3}$$

where the first term in the right-hand side of Eq. (4.3) stands for the expected profit of the entrant when it charges the lowest price in the marketplace and captures the entire segment of the switchers and the second term is the entrant's expected profit when it is in direct competition with the m incumbent firms. Therefore, the following holds true:

$$\begin{aligned} E(\Pi) &= \beta \left\{ \int_0^{\alpha/\beta} P dP + \int_{\alpha/\beta}^{+\infty} P \prod_{i=1}^{m} [1 - F_i(P)] dP \right\} \\ &= \beta \left\{ \frac{\alpha^2}{2\beta^2} + \int_{\alpha/\beta}^{+\infty} P \prod_{i=1}^{m} [1 - F_i(P)] dP \right\}. \end{aligned} \tag{4.4}$$

Now, in Nash equilibrium, there is only a symmetric pricing strategy for the incumbent firms (Forrest et al., 2019b) such that

$$F_i(P) = F(P) = 1 - \left(\frac{\alpha}{\beta P}\right)^{\frac{1}{m-1}}. \tag{4.5}$$

So, the second term in the braces of Eq. (4.4) can be rewritten as follows:

$$\int_{\alpha/\beta}^{+\infty} P \prod_{i=1}^{m} [1 - F_i(P)] dP = \int_{\alpha/\beta}^{1} P [1 - F(P)]^m dP + \left(\frac{\alpha}{\beta}\right)^{\frac{m}{m-1}}, \tag{4.6}$$

because $\lim_{P \to 1^-} F(P) = 1 - (\alpha/\beta)^{\frac{1}{m-1}} < F(1) = 1$, meaning that the cumulative distribution function $F(P)$ has a jump discontinuity at the reservation value $P = 1$, where the amount of jump is $(\alpha/\beta)^{\frac{1}{m-1}}$. That is, $F(P)$ has a mass point of size $(\alpha/\beta)^{\frac{1}{m-1}}$ at the reservation value $P = 1$.

Because $0 \leq P[1 - F(P)]^m \leq 1$, the first term on the right-hand side of Eq. (4.6) is a positive real number. So, the term in the braces in Eq. (4.4) is a positive real number. That implies that the expected profit of the entrant is directly proportional to the magnitude β of the consumer surplus. This ends the proof of Proposition 4.3.

Summarizing the proof and the statement of Proposition 4.3 leads to that from observing the development and growth of the newly emerging, while stabilizing, market, other business players want to share some of the visible and potentially increasing magnitude of profits. This conclusion holds true even if the industry that serves the market is risky, which is opposite to what was suggested by Bustamante and Donangelo (2017). On the other hand, increasing competition helps reduce the price of the product, benefiting consumers (Dave et al., 2017). That is, when the market competition increases, it forces the management of the incumbent firms to devote more of their effort and intelligence into their companies' governance (Schmidt, 1997) and designs of new strategies, such as applying greater accounting conservatism (Dhaliwal et al., 2014), embracing social responsibilities (Flammer, 2015), and investing more in research and development (Gu, 2016), in order to strengthen their competitive advantage in the product market through improved efficiency of governance (Giroud & Mueller, 2011) and their companies' behaviors in the equity market (Peress, 2010).

An important note at this junction is the normalization of the constant marginal costs of all firms considered above to 0 and the conservation price of loyal customers to 1. It practically means that each competing firm sells its product at such a price that is between its marginal cost and a profit. Because in real life the marginal cost varies from one firm to another, the selling prices for their products of competing firms are not really the same (for details on this, see the relevant discussion in the previous subsection). This understanding leads to the following conclusion based on Proposition 4.3: When a firm introduces a product with advanced features, the actual selling price can be literally higher than any of the other prices in the marketplace. In this case, market switchers judge whose price is "lower" by considering the product features comprehensively. For example, an old-fashioned walkie-talkie can be on sale at a very low price compared to that of an iPhone. However, market switchers most likely purchase iPhones of versatile functionalities instead of old-fashioned walkie-talkies made for a single, monotonic purpose, because the much higher absolute price of iPhones is practically considered "low" in terms of the functionalities involved when compared to that of walkie-talkies. This end both theoretically and practically implies that firms, either incumbent or not, need to address the question of how to achieve ambidexterity in their innovations—attain superior performance through the implementation of both radical and incremental (i.e., ambidextrous) innovations (Harmancioglu et al., 2019). To accomplish this end, an important first step is surely about how to understand market information, as indicated by an increasing consumer surplus (Forrest et al., 2019a), how to invest efficiently (Stoughton et al., 2017), and how to make use of venture capitals (Kim et al., 2016). Due to differences in cognitive abilities, out of the same piece of market information, such as increasing consumer surplus, entrepreneurs tend to introduce different products to satisfy the same demand, creating the so-called choice complexity (Spiegler, 2016). With increasing choice complexity in the marketplace, competing firms are encouraged to adopt production technologies of higher generations (Qian & Wang, 2017).

Assume that the m incumbent and established firms are named, respectively, m_1, m_2, m_3, … and that each of them enjoys a base of loyal customers of magnitude α, while other n firms, as new entrants, named n_1, n_2, n_3, …, still operate as the firms described in the beginning development stage of the market. These n firms compete over the market surplus with each other and with the incumbent firms. Now, similar arguments to those of Propositions 4.1–4.3 lead to the following result:

Proposition 4.4 For each of the n new entrants, its profit is equal to

$$\beta P(1-P)^{n-1}\prod_{i=1}^{m}[1-F_i(P)]. \tag{4.7}$$

And for incumbent Firm m_j, its profit is equal to

$$\alpha P+\beta P(1-P)^{n}\prod_{\substack{i=1\\ i\neq j}}^{m}[1-F_i(P)]. \tag{4.8}$$

When the market evolves into the stage of maturity, incumbent firms will generally have well established their status positions in the marketplace, a state known as mutual forbearance in the literature. That is when the incumbent firms alleviate the intensity of their competition by partitioning their market into sectors proportional to the firms' individual strengths (Bernheim & Whinston, 1990). Consequently, each firm surrenders its struggle to stronger ones in those sectors where it is less capable (Li & Greenwood, 2004). So, these incumbent firms become inter-reliant in their controlling of the market. Such equilibrium state of market competition stimulates the firms to detain their oppositions (Yu & Cannella Jr., 2012), leading to decreased number of entries into and exits from the market (Fuentelsaz & Gómez, 2006), while interfirm hostility lessens (Haveman & Nonnemaker, 2000). The reduced intensity of market competition also helps boost employees' satisfaction so that the number of strikes could be potentially reduced (Symeonidis, 2017). Moreover, decreased number of entries into the market stimulates firms to invest in cost-reducing R&Ds (Chalioti & Serfes, 2017).

Other than being content with their upstream-downstream partners, these firms' status positions help them to enter into new relationships with partners of higher quality, while the firms' status positions undercut the firms' development of capabilities within their boundaries. That leaves the firms less able to mobilize existing internal resources and those provided by partners (Castellucci & Podolny, 2017).

The growing incapability gradually pushes the firms and their industry into old age, which is characterized by disappearing or stabilizing consumer surplus (Proposition 4.3). So, according to Proposition 4.3, no more new business players want to enter the market as suppliers, while each incumbent firm makes its profits in the amount of αP, where the value of α also dwindles over time due to decreasing market competition and deteriorating earnings (Cheng et al., 2013).

4.4 A Few Final Words

To prepare for the rest of this book, this chapter first looks at the profit pictures of firms in an emerging and a maturing industry, respectively. By employing the established results on firms' profits, it then examines how competition appears in the market place due to constantly existing consumer surplus as caused by forever evolving consumer preferences and tastes. Under the condition of existing market competition, this chapter develops the profit pictures for new entrants and incumbent firms, respectively.

As for the contribution, this work is different from the literature on emergence and development of an industry. Instead of looking at individual cases of success stories and the stages and transitions between these stages that exist in the emergence and development of an industry as the literature commonly shown (for details, see the section on Literature Review in Appendix), this chapter presents a general picture by looking at the evolution of profits. Traditionally, it is positive cash flow that stands for the determining factor behind the appearance of any industry. To fill a gap that exists in the huge literature on market competition—what is the mechanism underlying the emergence of market competition—this chapter establishes how profits and potential of profits encourage market entries and innovations.

As for the limitation of this chapter, the conclusions established herein are developed by using the logical reasoning based on the following implicit assumption: All firms considered in our logical reasoning exist for the purpose of creating positive cash flows from the marketplace by selling their products, services, or goods. Traditionally, this assumption is generally true for most business enterprises (Sobel, 1999). However, in recent years, it is no longer the case because some of the important business firms nowadays can successfully generate positive cash flows year after year by producing great future promises, such as some of the major e-commerce firms, where the great promises come from the fact that they place their efforts on occupying larger and larger market territories (Li & Ma, 2015). This end leads to the following important theoretical and practical problems for future research: (1) If some of the firms considered in the reasonings of the previous sections are the latter kind, as described above, how would the established propositions in this chapter be? And (2) there is a need to investigate the scenario as described in (1) with all firms of the latter kind.

Appendix

This appendix to Chap. 4 shows how conclusions on the evolution of economic markets, as developed above, can be beautifully employed to further the understanding of the Gabaix's granular hypothesis. Specifically, among other results, the appendix develops precise conditions for the phenomenon of Gabaix's granular hypothesis either to appear or not to appear. As a confirmation of these theoretically important conclusions, empirical case analyses are given, while several important unanswered questions are posted for future research.

Introduction

In both natural and social sciences, inductive arguments have been used to draw overarching conclusions. For example, many theorems in mathematics, stated in affirmative tones, are shown by using a version of the known mathematical induction (Forrest, 2013); in macroeconomics, a standard reasoning, which helps actualize leaps from firm-level phenomena to those of the economy, generally leads to practically discarding the possibility for idiosyncratic micro-shocks of individual firms to cause aggregate fluctuations at the macro economy (Lucas, 1977). Against this backdrop, Gabaix (2011) proposes his granular hypothesis, suggesting that idiosyncratic firm-level shocks can indeed explain an important part of aggregate economic movements. Such hypothesis empirically confirms the existence of micro-foundations of macro-shocks.

Following Gabaix's (2011) work, the granular nature of economies has been examined from different angles. For example, by using econometric approaches, Wagner (2012), Hottman et al. (2016), and Atalay (2017) empirically confirm the existence of such phenomenon of granularity. By utilizing game theory, Acemoglu et al. (2015) examine how network interactions can function as a mechanism for the propagation and amplification of micro-shocks. Foerster et al. (2011) employ structural factor analysis to conclude that nearly all variabilities in industrial productivity are associated with common factors. On the bases of networks of either business or production, it is found (Acemoglu et al., 2012; Carvalho, 2014; Barrot & Sauvagnat, 2016; Boehm et al., 2019) that only when a significant asymmetry exists in the roles sectors play as suppliers to others, sectoral idiosyncratic shocks can lead to sizable aggregate volatility. It is confirmed (Giovanni et al., 2014) by using methods of decomposition that firm-specific components can substantially contribute to the volatility of aggregate sales volumes. Moreover, how sectoral shocks can possibly affect changes in the GDP is stochastically simulated by Roson and Sartori (2016).

In comparison, this appendix fills a gap in the literature by examining those "incompressible" firms that dominate the economy. It investigates when Gabaix's granular hypothesis holds true in general and when it fails in the perspective of profits, trades, and market competition. Based on this novel approach, established in this appendix is a series of generally true conclusions that are not subject to any constraints of data analysis.

The rest of this appendix is organized as follows. Section "Literature Review" reviews the relevant literature and outlines the contribution this appendix makes. Section "Granularity of an Industry or Economy" establishes conditions under which Gabaix's (2011) granular hypothesis either holds true in general or does not hold true at all. In section "The Granularity of German Economy: Numerical Case Study", a set of newly available data is employed to confirm the conditions established in section "Granularity of an Industry or Economy". This appendix concludes in section "Discussion", where some unsettled problems, which are both practically and theoretically important, are given for future research.

Literature Review

It is the work of Xavier Gabaix (2011) that started this exciting area of scholarly exploration on the granularity of economies. Since the publication of this influential paper on the now well-known granular hypothesis, over one thousand papers as of this writing have been published on related topics and issues. This part of the literature can be roughly classified into two groups: empirical confirmations of the hypothesis and theoretical examinations on why the commonly employed macroeconomic reasoning of averaging out microeconomic shocks does not work in this particular scenario.

Regarding empirical confirmations, Miranda-Pinto and Shen (2019) find that idiosyncratic firm-level shocks are important drivers of the Australian business cycle, where labor productivity shocks to the largest non-financial firms account for about 20–40% of the variation in Australian GDP growth during 2000–2018. Lucio et al. (2017) show that a small group of firms dominate exports in Spain. By using a data base covering the universe of French firms for the period 1990–2007, Giovanni et al. (2014) study how individual firms play their roles in generating aggregate fluctuations. Barrot and Sauvagnat (2016) find that negatively affected suppliers levy on their customers substantial output losses, which translate into significant market value losses that in turn spill over to other suppliers. By using data of the 50 largest economies in the world, Giovanni and Levchenko (2012) find that idiosyncratic shocks to large firms have an impact on aggregate volatility with small countries experiencing higher volatility and that with increasing importance within the globalizing economy, large firms raise macroeconomic volatility and can increase the aggregate volatility of some small open economies by 15–20%. Carvalho (2014) discusses by using examples how the propagation of sectoral shocks—and hence aggregate volatility—depends on the underlying production network and develops empirically properties of production networks. Hottman et al. (2016) empirically show that the imperfect substitutability of products within firms and large numbers of products offered by large firms imply that standard productivity measures depend highly on implicit demand system assumptions and dramatically understate the relative productivity of the largest firms. Amiti and Weinstein (2018) show that supply-side financial shocks have a large impact on firms' investment by using Japan's data for the period 1990–2010. Cravino and Levchenko (2017) show empirically that for a typical country the impact of foreign shocks cannot be ignored due to the combined effect of foreign multinationals and that the most integrated countries are significantly more affected by foreign shocks than others.

In terms of theoretical examinations, based on stochastic simulations, Roson and Sartori (2016) find that changes in the GDP, induced by sectoral shocks, are mostly determined by the degree of industrial concentration and the degree of centrality in inter-industrial connectivity is correlated with the industrial concentration index. Acemoglu et al. (2012) argue that intersectoral input–output linkages help facilitate the lift of microeconomic idiosyncratic shocks to aggregate fluctuations. This chapter highlights that sectoral idiosyncratic shocks lead to sizable aggregate volatility only when there exists significant asymmetry in the roles sectors play as suppliers to others.

Foerster et al. (2011) characterize the Great Moderation as a fall in the importance of aggregate shocks with the volatility of sectoral shocks mostly unchanged. By looking at the hypothesis that macroeconomic fluctuations are primitively the results of many microeconomic shocks, Carvalho and Gabaix (2013) reveal that the initial great moderation is due to a decreasing share of manufacturing between 1975 and 1985 and the recent rise of macroeconomic volatility due to the growth of the financial sector. By quantifying the contribution of sectoral shocks to business cycle fluctuations in aggregate output, Atalay (2017) develop a multi-industry general equilibrium model in which each industry employs the material and capital goods produced by other sectors. Acemoglu et al. (2015) develop a unified framework for the study of how network interactions can function as a mechanism for the propagation and amplification of microeconomic shocks. Veldkamp and Wolfers (2007) explore complementarity in information acquisition instead of that of production, suggesting that sectoral sharing makes information markets amplify business cycle co-movement. By offering a nonlinear characterization of the macroeconomic impact of microeconomic productivity shocks, Baqaee and Farhi (2019) demonstrate that in a business cycle calibration with sectoral shocks, nonlinearities amplify negative shocks and weaken positive shocks. By developing a quantitative theory of aggregate fluctuations caused by firm-level disturbances alone, Carvalho and Grassi (2019) explore the role of large firm dynamics in shaping aggregate fluctuations.

What is missing in this literature is the consideration of the evolutionary fact that large firms tend to stay large in their markets for at least a (either short or long) period of time. By combining this fact and the thinking logic of trades (that underlie revenues and profits of firms or industries), this chapter establishes results on when the granular hypothesis holds true in general and when it fails definitely.

Granularity of an Industry or Economy

Opposite to the previous sections, where our focus is on firm-level performances in terms of profits, this section considers how firm-level activities can affect phenomena of much larger scale economies, such as an industry, than the scales of individual firms. Conventionally, various scholars have reasoned that distinctive micro-level shocks to individual economic agents do not lead to aggregate oscillations of the much larger economic structure, such as industry or economy, of the agents, because firm-level shocks tend to happen in different forms and varied strengths; when these micro firm-level shocks are aggregated, their opposing and/or complementing forms and strengths will cancel each other and get averaged out at the much larger industry and economy level (Lucas, 1977; Wagner, 2012). For example, the literature of temporary equilibrium emphasizes on the existence of compatibility beliefs among individual agents for a much large-scale equilibria to exist, because differences in individual beliefs are smoothed out (Green, 1973; Hart, 1974). And in economics, a powerful paradigm is developed on that individual preferences are homogeneous across economic agents with individual differences assumed away (e.g., Lee & Sato, 1993; Stigler & Becker, 1977). This paradigm has helped explain many economic and social phenomena. However, our results analytically established in this section show that such conventional logic of reasoning is not generally true.

To this end, let $S(t)$ be the total sales of an industry that serves the product market discussed previously at a freezing moment of time t. Let $X(t)$ stand for the sales of one or a set of top-performing firms within the industry and $Y(t)$ the sales of the rest of the firms within the industry. That is,

$$S(t) = X(t) + Y(t). \tag{4.9}$$

If the ratio of the sales of the particular firm or the set of top-performing firms within the industry is equal to $r(t)$, that is, $X(t)/(X(t) + Y(t)) = r(t)$, then

$$S(t) = \frac{X(t)}{r(t)}. \tag{4.10}$$

So, the rate of change in $S(t)$ over time is given by

$$\frac{dS}{dt} = \frac{r \cdot \frac{dX}{dt} - X \cdot \frac{dr}{dt}}{r^2}. \tag{4.11}$$

Proposition 4.5 If the ratio $r(t)$ of the sales $X(t)$ of a particular firm or a particular set of top-performing firms over the sales $S(t)$ of the entire industry is a constant or experiences little change over a time period, then within this time period changes in $X(t)$ influence directly those in $S(t)$.

In fact, if $r(t)$ is equal to a constant or experiences little change over a time period, then $dr(t)/dt = or \approx 0$ holds true for this time period. So, Eq. (4.11) implies $dS(t)/dt = or \approx \frac{1}{r} dX(t)/dt$, where r is equal to a constant or roughly equal to a constant. That is, changes in $S(t)$ are directly proportional to changes in $X(t)$ over the said time period.

What Proposition 4.5 says is that idiosyncratic firm-level shocks, experienced by one or several good performing firms, either individually or collectively, that play an important role in an industry can explain an important part of aggregate economic movements of the industry and provide a micro-foundation for aggregate shocks. What is theoretically extremely significant about this result is that it is contrary to the well-accepted macroeconomic reasoning that idiosyncratic microeconomic shocks to individual firms do not lead to large aggregate fluctuations of the industry for the reason that these firm-level shocks cancel each other and get averaged out at the macroeconomic level (Lucas, 1977; Wagner, 2012).

Empirically, Gabaix (2011) is the first person who proposes that idiosyncratic firm-level shocks can indeed affect aggregate economic phenomena in the case of the United States, where the idiosyncratic movements of the largest 100 firms can explain about one-third of variations in the national output growth. Based on this discovery, Gabaix believes that many macroeconomic phenomena are caused by or attributable to the firm-level activities of the incompressible grains, the large firms. He then names this belief as the granular hypothesis. Following this research by Gabaix (2011) and Wagner (2012) looks at the German manufacturing sector by studying the data for enterprises from 23 manufacturing industries for the time period 2005–2008 and by considering the role of the 10 largest firms in each industry. His results are supportive of the granular hypothesis, leading to the conclusion that the German manufacturing sector is a granular economy. Lucio et al. (2017) confirm the granularity characteristics of Spanish economy by showing that in 2015 the top 200 firms were responsible for half of Spanish exports, while such concentration had been roughly maintained over the 1997–2015 period, and these firms explained around one-third of the growth in Spanish exports. Similarly, Miranda-Pinto and Shen (2019) confirm that labor productivity shocks to the largest non-financial firms in Australia account for a large percentage of the variation in Australian GDP growth over the period 2000–2018, while firms in the energy, construction, transportation, and consumer services sectors also seem to be drivers of GDP growth.

Next, let us look at the case when $r(t)$ is not equal to a constant over any time period. For this case, consider three scenarios separately:

(i) $dS(t)/dt = 0$.
(ii) $dS(t)/dt > 0$.
(iii) $dS(t)/dt < 0$.

For case (i), it follows that $r(t) \times dX(t)/dt = X(t) \times dr(t)/dt$. Solving this separable differential equation produces $X(t) = Cr(t)$, where C is a constant. That is, the following general result holds true, which describes when the general averaging argument for why discarded is the possibility that idiosyncratic microeconomic shocks to individual firms may lead to large aggregate fluctuations of all firms within an industry (Lucas, 1977).

Proposition 4.6 If the sales $X(t)$ of a particular firm or a particular set of top-performing firms is directly proportional to the ratio $r(t)$ of $X(t)$ over the sales $S(t)$ of the entire industry, then no firm-level shocks to these particular firms will bear any direct effect on macro-movements of the industry.

For case (ii), it follows that $r(t) \times dX(t)/dt > X(t) \times dr(t)/dt$. The situation can be divided into two cases: (a) $dr(t)/dt < 0$ and (b) $dr(t)/dt > 0$. If case (a) holds true, then the following practical conclusion holds true:

Proposition 4.7 If (1) each individual firm's performance improves, or stays stable, or does not drop much and (2) its weight in the entire industry shrinks, then the total sales of the industry increase, where the first if condition means

$$dX(t)/dt > -|[X(t)/r(t)] \times dr(t)/dt|. \tag{4.12}$$

The theoretical and practical significance of this result is the following implication: When an economy operates within its norm (or not in a crisis), market competition is beneficial to the growth of the industry, where competition reduces individual firm's influences on the entire industry.

On the other hand, for case (ii) and (b) when $dr(t)/dt > 0$, meaning that jointly some firms weigh increasingly more than before within the industry they belong to, the sales of these firms have to grow tremendously in order to maintain a positive growth of the industry. Summarizing this analysis leads to

Proposition 4.8 If some firms' joint influence within their industry increases, then these firms have to grow in large scales (or $dX(t)/dt > +[X(t)/r(t)] \times dr(t)/dt$) in order to help propel a positive growth for the industry.

Indirectly, this result implies that when the proportion of the sales of one or a few firms increases within the total sales of their industry, continued positive growth in the sales of the industry will become difficult to maintain.

For case (iii) where $dS(t)/dt < 0$, it follows that $r(t) \times dX(t)/dt < X(t) \times dr(t)/dt$ with shrinking sales of the industry. If $dX(t)/dt \geq 0$, then $dr(t)/dt \geq 0$. That means that top-performing firms are gaining further dominance in the declining industry. Proposition 4.3 indirectly indicates that the industry is losing its attraction to customers.

If $dX(t)/dt < 0$, there are two cases: (a) $dr(t)/dt \geq 0$ and (b) $dr(t)/dt < 0$. Here, case (a) means that along with the declining sales of the industry, the top-performing firms also experience dwindling sales, although the weight of the firm or the set of firms within the industry still either stays the same or even increases. Moreover, case (b) implies that within the industry of declining sales, the top-performing firms are not doing as well as before in terms of their sales and dominance in their industry. Once again, Proposition 4.3 indicates that the economy is aging quickly.

Summarizing the discussion in the previous paragraphs leads to

Proposition 4.9 If the sales of an industry decline, assuming that all other conditions stay unchanging, then the industry is either losing attraction to customers temporarily or aging quickly.

Although Propositions 4.5–4.9 are phrased in terms of industries, the term "industry" can be readily replaced by "economy."

The significance of the results established in this section can be highlighted by glancing through the scholarly efforts devoted by many authors since 2011 when Gabaix (2011) initially introduced his granular hypothesis. For example, Hottman et al. (2016) and Atalay (2017) use econometric approaches to confirm the phenomenon of economic granularity. Acemoglu et al. (2015) employ classes of games to examine how network interactions can function as a mechanism for propagation and amplification of microeconomic shocks. Foerster et al. (2011) apply structural factor analysis to discover that nearly all variabilities in industrial productivity are associated with common factors. Acemoglu et al. (2012), Carvalho (2014), Barrot and Sauvagnat (2016), and Boehm et al. (2019) utilize the concept of either business or production networks to find that sectoral idiosyncratic shocks lead to sizable aggregate volatility only when there exists significant asymmetry in the roles sectors play as suppliers to others. Giovanni et al. (2014) use methods of decomposition to confirm that firm-specific component contributes substantially to aggregate sales volatility. Roson and Sartori (2016) employ stochastic simulations to analyze how sectoral shocks affect changes in the GDP. In comparison, our results in this section show directly when the granular hypothesis holds true by focusing on sales of individual firms and their industries.

The Granularity of German Economy: Numerical Case Study

The basic setup for Gabaix's granular hypothesis is the existence of "incompressible grains" in an industry or economic sector. So, one of the first questions that is both practically and theoretically important to empirically confirm is the following: Is there such an economy or economic sector or industry within which no firm and no set of top-performing firms stay on the top for long? Theoretically, Propositions 4.1 and 4.3 jointly indicate that if such an economic scenario exists, the economy or economic sector or industry of concern has to be at the emerging and quickly expanding stage of development. Unfortunately, the data set available to us for this chapter reflects only certain aspects of the well-developed German economy. So, this chapter will not check on this question empirically. Instead, it will focus on empirically confirming the granularity of German economy by using conclusions developed earlier in this chapter.

Discretization of Two Established Conclusions

To numerically employ what is established above, let us first discretize Eq. (4.11) as follows:

$$S(t+1) - S(t) \cong \frac{r(t)[X(t+1) - X(t)] - X(t)[r(t+1) - r(t)]}{r^2(t)} \cong \frac{[X(t+1) - X(t)]}{r(t)}$$

if $X(t)[r(t+1) - r(t)] \cong 0$. So, Proposition 4.5 implies the following two results:

Proposition 4.10 When

$$S(t+1) - S(t) \cong \frac{[X(t+1) - X(t)]}{r(t)}, \tag{4.13}$$

Gabaix's granular hypothesis holds true, where t stands for a time moment and $(t + 1)$ the following time moment.

In other words, what this proposition says is that when the growth in the sales $S(t)$ of an industry from time moment t to the next moment $(t + 1)$ is roughly proportional to the growth $X(t)$ of one top-performing firm or a set of top-performing firms within the industry for the same time period, then Gabaix's granular hypothesis holds true. To empirically confirm this end, the roughly constant proportionality needs to be confirmed over several time periods, say from t to $t + k$, for $k = 2, 3, 4, \ldots$.

Proposition 4.11 When $X(t)[r(t + 1) - r(t)] \cong 0$, Gabaix's granular hypothesis holds true.

To empirically verify this conclusion, let the when-condition be identified as follows: If the magnitude of $S(t + 1) - S(t)$ is in 10^n, while that of $X(t)[r(t + 1) - r(t)]$ is in 10^{n-4}, then treat $X(t)[r(t + 1) - r(t)]$ as roughly equal to 0. For instance, the dollar value $\$900.00 = \$9.00 \times 10^2$ is in the magnitude of 10^2; and the dollar value $\$0.09 = \$9.00 \times 10^{-2}$ can be seen as roughly \$0.00 when compared to the original value of \$900.00.

As for when Gabaix's granular hypothesis is definitely false, Proposition 4.6 implies.

Proposition 4.12 If $X(t) = C \cdot r(t)$, for some constant C, then Gabaix's granular hypothesis does not hold true.

Speaking differently, what Proposition 4.12 says is that no firm-level shocks to these particular firms involved in the computation of $X(t)$ will bear any direct effect on the macro-movement $S(t)$ of the industry. To empirically confirm this conclusion, one needs to find such constant C that satisfies $X(t) = C \cdot r(t)$, for at least a few consecutive time periods. If such an industry and a time frame can be located, then Gabaix's granular hypothesis does not hold true for this industry and the time frame.

The Data

The following empirical exercise uses new and yet unreleased data on the top 100 companies in Germany that are prepared by the German Monopolies Commission. These are official data and can be regarded as high quality. For a detailed description of the data, see Buchwald et al. (2020).

Because the data do not contain any information of sales of individual companies, as discussed in the previous sections, instead this chapter will use the information on the number of employees in each company for every other year from 1976 to 2016 and on the total number of employees in the German economy as a whole. This substitution is both empirically and theoretically confirmed as reasonable by various scholars (e.g., Camison-Zornoza et al., 2004; Forrest et al., 2019b; Stock et al., 2002), because the number of employees tends to be highly, positively correlated with sales and values added at the firm level. So, symbolically, this chapter employs the following corresponding substitutions: $S(t)$ is the total number of employees in German economy in year t; $X(t)$ the total number of employees in the top 100 companies in Germany in year t; and

$$Y(t) = S(t) – X(t) \text{ and } r(t) = X(t)/(X(t) + (Y(t)).$$

The Calculations

Tables 4.1 and 4.2 display all the calculations of the symbolic components in Propositions 4.10–4.12, where if needed, the natural log function is applied (say, Table 4.2).

Proposition 4.10 says that Gabaix's granular hypothesis holds true if in Table 4.1, the column of $S(t + 1) – S(t)$ is about equal to the column of $[X(t + 1) – X(t)]/r(t)$. However, this is not the case. Moreover, Proposition 4.11 says that Gabaix's granular hypothesis holds true if the column of $X(t)[r(t + 1) – r(t)]$ is about equal to 0. Once again, Table 4.1 indicates that this is not the case. On the other hand, Proposition 4.12 says that Gabaix's granular hypothesis does not hold if C is constant over some consecutive time periods. To this end, Table 4.3 shows that this is the case, say, for example, the time periods 1976–1988 and 1994–2002. Hence, summarizing this discussion leads to the conclusion that Tables 4.1 and 4.2 display evidence that the German economy is not a granular economy, because Propositions 4.10 and 4.11 do not hold while Proposition 4.12 holds over some periods.

Table 4.1 Computations related to Propositions 4.10 and 4.11

$t + 1$	t	$S(t + 1) - S(t)$	$[X(t + 1) - X(t)]/r(t)$	$X(t)[r(t + 1) - r(t)]$
1978	1976	1,830,780	1,349,422	−13,898.66
1980	1978	474,600	323,152.9	−4477.422
1982	1980	−743,792	−545,848.3	6136.589
1984	1982	−1712	−585,526.9	−17,782.91
1986	1984	514,612	639,962.1	68,582.42
1988	1986	470,204	−99,590.44	−3616.084
1990	1988	1,373,004	1,481,618	−71,355.58
1992	1990	436,116	1,171,648	20,291.19
1994	1992	4,014,008	2,993,220	−25,926.66
1996	1994	−811,924	−2,026,183	−34,794.52
1998	1996	−36,316	−697,481	−16,628.88
2000	1998	468,904	−316,699.2	−18,350.22
2002	2000	−404,928	−1,371,957	−21,960.66
2004	2002	−1,175,988	−769,930.5	8799.194
2006	2004	268,050	−814,386.6	−22,863.14
2008	2006	922,004	−247,389.1	−21,939.72
2010	2008	305,646	−715,182.9	−17,849.54
2012	2010	1,053,540	703,638.5	−5474.085
2014	2012	952,324	2,737,397	27,338.05
2016	2014	1,330,068	390,130.7	−16,143.92

Table 4.2 Computations related to Proposition 4.12

t	1976	1978	1980	1982	1984	1986	1988
$C(t) = X(t) - r(t)$	1.74e +07	1.92e +07	1.97e +07	1.89e +07	1.89e +07	1.74e +07	1.74e +07
t	1990	1992	1994	1996	1998	2000	2002
$C(t) = X(t) - r(t)$	2.13e +07	2.17e +07	2.57e +07	2.49e +07	2.49e +07	2.54e +07	2.50e +07
t	2004	2006	2008	2010	2012	2014	2016
$C(t) = X(t) - r(t)$	2.38e +07	2.41e +07	2.50e.07	2.53e +07	2.63e +07	2.73e +07	2.86e +07

A Robustness Test

To confirm the conclusion of the previous subsection, use the approach suggested by Gabaix (2011) by using employment figures instead of those of productivity as the test variable. Based on equations (29), (30), and (33) in Gabaix (2011), compute the granular residuals, including those of one-period lag and two-period lag, and regress the growth rate of the economy on the granular residual. The results are reported in Table 4.3.

Table 4.3 Explanatory power of the granular residual for growth in total employment (Germany, 1978–2016) with growth rate of total employment as independent variable

Granular residual	0.4304 (0.875)	0.7259 (0.776)	1.447 (0.626)
Granular residual (lag 1 period)		−1.4540 (0.531)	−2.8506 (0.267)
Granular residual (lag two periods)			2.5061 (0.380)
Constant	0.0249 (0.038)	0.01726 (0.135)	0.0228 (0.070)
Number of 2-year periods	19	18	17
R^2	0.0009	0.0087	0.0312

Note: The numbers on the top are the estimated regression coefficient from an OLS regression and those in parentheses the probability values

From Table 4.3, it can be seen that the regression coefficient of the granular residual is never statistically different from zero, and the R^2-values are tiny. Therefore, there is no evidence for granularity.

In short, the regression approach, as suggested by Gabaix (2011), and the new non-parametric test, as established in this chapter, lead to the same conclusion: the German economy is not a granular economy at least for the time period from 1976 to 2016.

Discussion

Inspired by Gabaix's (2011) influential work and comparing what is missing in the literature, based on the evolutionary picture of profits, this appendix takes competition as the perspective to investigate the problem of when Gabaix's granular hypothesis holds true in general and when it fails definitely. Because of the novel approach taken here, this appendix is able to pinpoint out when Gabaix's granular hypothesis holds true assuredly and when it does not hold true definitely without suffering from any of the data- and anecdote-related constraints.

In terms of important problems for future research, one of the issues Gabaix's (2011) granular hypothesis reveals is that macroeconomic conclusions should not be drawn by simply "averaging out" observations from individual micro-level cases. Doing so involves major leaps in reasoning from micro-level cases to macro-level abstractions and may lead to completely incorrect macroeconomic assumptions or conclusions. For example, from the existence of a few seemingly indifferent minds, it should not be inductively assumed that all economic agents are homogenous; from behaviors of several forward-looking thinkers, one should not inductively adopt the assumption that every decision-maker thinks rationally by optimizing his/her decisions; and from the observation of a handful stably developing economies, one should not inductively believe that each economy is equilibrating. This situation of necessary avoidance in scholarly abstraction is well illustrated in mathematics by Forrest (2013), where one version of mathematical induction is shown to produce possibly contradictory conclusions, a similar scenario as what is revealed by Gabaix's granularity.

Realizing such a challenge in inductive reasoning widely used in macroeconomics, Haldane and Turrell (2018) attempt to develop an interdisciplinary approach to macroeconomic modeling by employing techniques from other areas of learning in order to address macroeconomic questions, where the concept of wholeness, such as complexity, heterogeneity, networks, and heuristics, plays an important role. Based on the discussion in the previous paragraph, the attempt of Haldane and Turrell needs to be more general and wider reaching than it is now. In other words, there is a need to scrutinize carefully all basic assumptions and conclusions in macroeconomics that are derived by employing such a reasoning that involves a leap from micro-level cases to macro-level abstractions.

Another open question that is worthy of our attention is to develop a theoretical mechanism for the general counting of granular firms within an economy. To this end, the empirical work based on Spanish data by Blanco-Arroyo et al. (2018) proposes a method to calibrate the granular size of the economy, i.e., the number of granular firms. On the other hand, if one models an economy by using the systemic yoyo model (Forrest, 2019), developing such a desirable mechanism of counting might be different, if not impossible. No matter which case it will turn out to be, this is an important question to address.

References

Acemoglu, D., Carvalho, V. M., Ozdaglar, A., & Tahbaz-Salehi, A. (2012). The network origins of aggregate fluctuations. *Econometrica, 80*(5), 1977–2016.

Acemoglu, D., Ozdaglar, A., & Tahbaz-Salehi, A. (2015). Networks, shocks, and systemic risk. *NBER Working Paper No. 20931*.

Amiti, M., & Weinstein, D. E. (2018). How much do idiosyncratic bank shocks affect investment? Evidence from matched bank-firm loan data. *Journal of Political Economy, 126*(2), 525–587. https://doi.org/10.1086/696272

Andreoni, A., & Chang, H. J. (2019). The political economy of industrial policy: Structural interdependencies, policy alignment and conflict management. *Structural Change and Economic Dynamics, 48*(March), 136–150.

Atalay, E. (2017). How important are sectoral shocks? *American Economic Journal: Macroeconomics, 9*(4), 254–280.

Baqaee, D. R., & Farhi, E. (2019). The macroeconomic impact of microeconomic shocks: Beyond Hulten's theorem. *Econometrica, 87*(4), 1155–1203.

Barrot, J. N., & Sauvagnat, J. (2016). Input specificity and the propagation of idiosyncratic shocks in production networks. *The Quarterly Journal of Economics, 131*(3), 1543–1592.

Bernheim, B. D., & Whinston, M. D. (1990). Multimarket contact and collusive behavior. *RAND Journal of Economics, 21*(1), 1–26.

Blanco-Arroyo, O., Ruiz-Buforn, A., Vidal-Tomás, D., & Alfarano, A. (2018). On the determination of the granular size of the economy. *Economics Letters, 173*(December), 35–38.

Boehm, C. E., Flaaen, A., & Pandalai-Nayar, N. (2019). Input linkages and the transmission of shocks: Firm-level evidence from the 2011 Tōhoku earthquake. *Review of Economics and Statistics, 101*(1), 60–75.

Buchwald, A., Hotten, R., Rothbauer, J., & Weche, J. P. (2020). The top 100 companies panel database. Five decades of aggregate concentration surveys in Germany. *Journal of Economics and Statistics, 241*, 787–800.

Bustamante, M. C., & Donangelo, A. (2017). Product market competition and industry returns. *The Review of Financial Studies, 30*(12), 4216–4266. https://doi.org/10.1093/rfs/hhx033

Camison-Zornoza, C., Lapiedra-Alcami, R., Segarra-Cipres, M., & Boronat-Navarro, M. (2004). A meta-analysis of innovation and organizational size. *Organization Studies, 25*(3), 331–361.

Carvalho, V. M. (2014). From micro to macro via production networks. *Journal of Economic Perspectives, 28*(4), 23–48.

Carvalho, V., & Gabaix, X. (2013). The great diversification and its undoing. *American Economic Review, 103*(5), 1697–1727.

Carvalho, V. M., & Grassi, B. (2019). Large firm dynamics and the business cycle. *American Economic Review, 109*(4), 1375–1425. https://doi.org/10.1257/aer.20151317

Castellucci, F., & Podolny, J. M. (2017). The dynamics of position, capability, and market competition. *Industrial and Corporate Change, 26*(1), 21–39.

Chalioti, E., & Serfes, K. (2017). Strategic incentives for innovations and market competition. *International Journal of Industrial Organization, 52*(May), 427–449.

Cheng, P., Man, P., & Yi, C. H. (2013). The impact of product market competition on earnings quality. *Accounting and Finance, 53*(1), 137–162.

Cravino, J., & Levchenko, A. A. (2017). Multinational firms and international business cycle transmission. *The Quarterly Journal of Economics, 132*(2), 921–962. https://doi.org/10.1093/qje/qjw043

Dave, C. V., Kesselheim, A. S., Fox, E. R., Qiu, P. H., & Hartzema, A. (2017). High generic drug prices and market competition: A retrospective cohort study. *Annals of Internal Medicine, 167*(3), 145–151. https://doi.org/10.7326/M16-1432

Dhaliwal, D., Huang, S., Khurana, I. K., & Pereira, R. (2014). Product market competition and conditional conservatism. *Review of Accounting Studies, 19*(4), 1309–1345.

Flammer, C. (2015). Does product market competition foster corporate social responsibility? Evidence from trade liberalization. *Strategic Management Journal, 36*(10), 1469–1485. https://doi.org/10.1002/smj.2307

Foerster, A. T., Sarte, P. G., & Watson, M. W. (2011). Sectoral versus aggregate shocks: A structural factor analysis of industrial production. *Journal of Political Economy, 119*(1), 1–38.

Foray, D., & Raffo, J. (2014). The emergence of an educational tool industry: Opportunities and challenges for innovation in education. *Research Policy, 43*(10), 1707–1715. https://doi.org/10.1016/j.respol.2014.07.010

Forrest, J. Y. L. (2013). *A systemic perspective on cognition and mathematics*. CRC Press, an Imprint of Taylor and Francis.

Forrest, J. Y. L. (2019). *General systems theory: Foundation, intuition and applications in business decision making*. Springer Nature.

Forrest, J. Y. L., Zhao, H. C., & Shao, L. (2018). Engineering rapid industrial revolutions for impoverished agrarian nations. *Theoretical Economics Letters, 8*, 2594–2640.

Forrest, J. Y. L., Nicholls, J., Schimmel, K., & Liu, S. F. (2019a). *Managerial decision making: A holistic approach*. Springer.

Forrest, J. Y. L., Trebing, M. E., Chatterjee, A., & Wagner, J. (2019b). Domestic firms, exporters and importers: A systemic perspective. *Theoretical Economics Letters, 9*, 649–674. https://doi.org/10.4236/tel.2019.94044

Forrest, J. Y., Gong, Z., Köse, E., Galbraith, D. D., & Arık, O. A. (2021). An economy's emergent properties and how micro agents with inconsistent or conflicting interests are holistically organized into macro entities. *Naše gospodarstvo/Our economy – Journal of Contemporary Issues in Economics and Business, 63*(3), 53–66. https://doi.org/10.2478/ngoe-2021-0017

Fuentelsaz, L., & Gómez, J. (2006). Multipoint competition, strategic similarity and entry into geographic markets. *Strategic Management Journal, 27*(5), 477–499.
Gabaix, X. (2011). The granular origins of aggregate fluctuations. *Econometrica, 79*, 733–772.
Giovanni, J. D., & Levchenko, A. A. (2012). Country size, international trade, and aggregate fluctuations in granular economies. *Journal of Political Economy, 120*(6), 1083–1132.
Giovanni, J. D., Levchenko, A. A., & Mejean, I. (2014). Firms, destinations and aggregate fluctuations. *Econometrica, 82*(4), 1303–1340.
Giroud, X., & Mueller, H. M. (2011). Corporate governance, product market competition, and equity prices. *The Journal of Finance, 66*(2), 563–600.
Green, J. (1973). Temporary general equilibrium in a sequential trading model with spot and futures transactions. *Econometrica, 41*, 1103–1123.
Gu, L. F. (2016). Product market competition, R&D investment, and stock returns. *Journal of Financial Economics, 119*(2), 441–455. https://doi.org/10.1016/j.jfineco.2015.09.008
Gustafsson, R., Jaaskelainen, M., Maula, M., & Uotila, J. (2016). Emergence of industries: A review and future directions. *International Journal of Management Reviews, 18*(1), 28–50. https://doi.org/10.1111/ijmr.12057
Haldane, A. G., & Turrell, A. E. (2018). An interdisciplinary model for macroeconomics. *Oxford Review of Economic Policy, 34*(1–2), 219–251. https://doi.org/10.1093/oxrep/grx051
Hanzel, I. (2010). *Studies in the methodology of natural and social sciences.* Peter Lang.
Harmancioglu, N., Sääksjärvi, M., & Hultink, E. J. (2019). Cannibalize and combine? The impact of ambidextrous innovation on organizational outcomes under market competition. *Industrial Marketing Management, 85*, 44–57. https://doi.org/10.1016/j.indmarman.2019.07.005
Hart, O. (1974). On the existence of equilibrium in a securities model. *Journal of Economic Theory, 9*, 293–311.
Hartley, J., Sørensen, E., & Torfing, J. (2013). Collaborative innovation: A viable alternative to market competition and organizational entrepreneurship. *Public Administration Review, 73*(6), 821–830. https://doi.org/10.1111/puar.12136
Haveman, H. A., & Nonnemaker, L. (2000). Competition in multiple geographic markets: The impact on growth and market entry. *Administrative Science Quarterly, 45*(2), 232–267.
Hottman, C. J., Redding, S. J., Weinstein, D. E., & D.E. (2016). Quantifying the sources of firm heterogeneity. *The Quarterly Journal of Economics, 131*(3), 1291–1364.
Kim, K., Gopal, A., & Hoberg, G. (2016). Does product market competition drive CVC investment? Evidence from the U.S. IT industry. *Information Systems Research, 27*(2), iii–vi, 219-470. https://doi.org/10.1287/isre.2016.0620
Lee, M. H., & Sato, K. (1993). Homogeneous preferences and heterogeneous growth performance: International differences in saving and investment behavior. *Kyklos, 46*, 203–223.
Li, S. X., & Greenwood, R. (2004). The effect of within industry diversification on firm performance: Synergy creation, multi-market contact and market structuration. *Strategic Management Journal, 25*(12), 1131–1153.
Li, T., & Ma, J. H. (2015). Complexity analysis of dual-channel game model with different managers' business objectives. *Communications in Nonlinear Science and Numerical Simulation, 20*, 199–208.
Lucas, R. E. (1977). Understanding business cycles. *Carnegie-Rochester Conference Series on Public Policy, 5*, 7–29.
Lucio, J. D., Mínguez, R., Minondo, A., & Requena, F. (2017). The granularity of Spanish exports. *Journal of the Spanish Economic Association, 8*(3), 225–259.
Maialeh, R. (2019). Generalization of results and neoclassical rationality: unresolved controversies of behavioural economics methodology. *Quality & quantity: An International of Methodology, 53*, 1743–1761.
Maine, E., Thomas, V. J., Bliemel, M., Murira, A., & Utterback, J. (2014). The emergence of the nanobiotechnology industry. *Nature Nanotechnology, 9*, 2–5.

Mäki, U. (1992). On the method of isolation in economics. In C. Dilworth (Ed.), *Poznan studies in the philosophy of the sciences and the humanities (special issue idealization IV: Intelligibility in science)* (Vol. 26, pp. 319–354).

Markman, G. D., & Waldron, T. L. (2014). Small entrants and large incumbents: A framework of micro entry. *Academy of Management Perspectives, 28*, 179–197.

Marshall, A. (1890 [2013]). *Principles of economics*. Palgrave Macmillan.

Martin, H., & Coenen, L. (2015). Institutional context and cluster emergence: The biogas industry in southern Sweden. *European Planning Studies, 23*(10), 2009–2027. https://doi.org/10.1080/09654313.2014.960181

Matti, C., & Consoli, D. (2017). Multi level policy mixes and industry emergence: The case of wind energy in Spain. *Environment and Planning C: Politics and Spaces, 35*(4), 661–683. https://doi.org/10.1177/0263774X16663933

Miranda-Pinto, J., & Shen, Y. T. (2019). A granular view of the Australian business cycle. *The Economic Record, 95*, 407. https://doi.org/10.1111/1475-4932.12495

Osborne, M. J., & Rubinstein, A. (1994). *A course in game theory*. MIT Press.

Peress, J. (2010). Product market competition, insider trading, and stock market efficiency. *The Journal of Finance, 65*(1), 1–43. https://doi.org/10.1111/j.1540-6261.2009.01522.x

Podolny, J. M. (1993). A status-based model of market competition. *American Journal of Sociology, 98*(4), 829–872. https://doi.org/10.1086/230091

Qian, L. H., & Wang, I. K. (2017). Competition and innovation: The tango of the market and technology in the competitive landscape. *Managerial and Decision Economics, 38*(8), 1237–1247. https://doi.org/10.1002/mde.2861

Reinert, E. (1995). Competitiveness and its predecessors: A 500-year cross-national perspective. *Structural Change and Economic Dynamics, 6*(1), 23–42.

Ridley, M. (2016). *The evolution of everything: How new ideas emerge*. Harper Perennial.

Rosenberg, A. (1995). Laws, damn laws, and ceteris paribus clauses. *The Southern Journal of Philosophy, 34*(1), 183–204.

Roson, R., & Sartori, M. (2016). Input–output linkages and the propagation of domestic productivity shocks: Assessing alternative theories with stochastic simulation. *Economic Systems Research, 28*(1), 38–54. https://doi.org/10.1080/09535314.2015.1132194

Rostow, W. W. (1960). *The Stages of economic growth: A non-communist manifesto*. Cambridge University Press.

Ruan, Y., Hang, C. C., & Wang, Y. M. (2014). Government's role in disruptive innovation and industry emergence: The case of the electric bike in China. *Technovation, 34*(12), 785–796. https://doi.org/10.1016/j.technovation.2014.09.003

Sanderson, S. W., & Simons, K. L. (2014). Light emitting diodes and the lighting revolution: The emergence of a solid-state lighting industry. *Research Policy, 43*(10), 1730–1746. https://doi.org/10.1016/j.respol.2014.07.011

Schmidt, K. M. (1997). Managerial incentives and product market competition. *The Review of Economic Studies, 64*(2), 191–213. https://doi.org/10.2307/2971709

Sobel, R. (1999). *When giants stumble: Classic business blunders and how to avoid them.* Prentice Hall.

Spiegler, R. (2016). Choice complexity and market competition. *Annual Review of Economics, 8*, 1–25.

Stigler, G. J., & Becker, G. S. (1977). De gustibus non estdisputandum. *American Economic Review, 67*, 76–90.

Stock, G. N., Greis, N. P., & Fischer, W. A. (2002). Firm size and dynamic technological innovation. *Technovation, 22*, 537–549.

Stoughton, N. M., Wong, K. P., & Yi, L. (2017). Investment efficiency and product market competition. *Journal of Financial and Quantitative Analysis, 52*(6), 2611–2642. https://doi.org/10.1017/S0022109017000746

Symeonidis, G. (2017). Does product market competition increase strike activity? Evidence from the UK. *European Economic Review, 97*(August), 42–56.

Veldkamp, L., & Wolfers, J. (2007). Aggregate shocks or aggregate information? Costly information and business cycle comovement. *Journal of Monetary Economics, 54*(Supplement, September), 37–55.
Wagner, J. (2012). The German manufacturing sector is a granular economy. *Applied Economics Letters, 19*, 1663–1665.
Wen, Y. (2016). *The making of an economic superpower: Unlocking China's secret of rapid industrialization*. World Scientific.
Wu, J. (2012). Technological collaboration in product innovation: The role of market competition and sectoral technological intensity. *Research Policy, 41*(2), 489–496.
Ye, G. L., Priem, R. L., & Alshwer, A. A. (2012). Achieving demand-side synergy from strategic diversification: How combining mundane assets can leverage consumer utilities. *Organization Science, 23*(1), 207–224.
Yu, T., & Cannella, A. A., Jr. (2012). A comprehensive review of multimarket competition research. *Journal of Management, 39*, 76–109.
Zhao, Z. Y., Zhang, S. Y., Hubbard, B., & Yao, X. (2012). The emergence of the solar photovoltaic power industry in China. *Renewable and Sustainable Energy Reviews, 21*(May), 229–236. https://doi.org/10.1016/j.rser.2012.12.066

Chapter 5
Consumer's Natural Endowments

Jeffrey Yi-Lin Forrest, Lawrence Shao, Yong Liu, Bailey C. Forrest, Theresa A. Wajda, Jun Liu, Michael Y. Hu, Dale Shao, Zhen Li, and Brian W. Sloboda

Abstract To support one of the key cornerstones of the current theory that will be systematically developed in the following parts of the book, this chapter presents a general theory on how each consumer, be it an individual person or a business firm, is a goal-oriented system. It reveals the systemic mechanism that underlies the operation of the four endowments of people and human organizations—self-awareness, imagination, conscience, and free will. For related discussions, see Forrest and Liu (2021, Chap. 10), Forrest et al. (Pennsyl Econ Rev, 2023), and Lin and Forrest (Systemic structure behind human organizations: From civilizations to individuals, Springer, New York, 2012, Part IV).

The motivation behind this line of thinking is that behaviors, growth and aging of individuals, and business enterprises are dictated by their underlying systemic structures either mentally or culturally. That is well illustrated by Lin and Forrest (Systemic structure behind human organizations: From civilizations to individuals, Springer, New York, 2012) theoretically and confirmed practically by the categorization paradigm about how people receive and process information so that a host of consumer behaviors can be beneficially explained (Mandler, Cognitive research in psychology, North-Holland, Amsterdam, 33–40, 1982; Sujan, J Consumer Res 12 (June):31–46, 1985).

Jeffrey Yi-Lin Forrest (Department of Accounting Economics Finance, Slippery Rock University, Slippery Rock, PA, USA; Email: Jeffrey.forrest@sru.edu), Lawrence Shao (College of Business, Slippery Rock University, Slippery Rock, PA, USA; Email: Lawrence.shao@sru.edu), Yong Liu (School of Business, Jiangnan University, Wuxi, Jiangsu, China; Email: clly1985528@163.com), Bailey C. Forrest (Software Engineer at Google, San Francisco, CA, USA), Theresa A. Wajda (Department of Accounting Economics Finance, Slippery Rock University, Slippery Rock, PA, USA; Email: Theresa.wajda@sru.edu), Jun Liu (School of Digital Economics and Management, Wuxi University, Wuxi, China; Email: liujun@nuist.edu.cn), Michael Y. Hu (Department of Marketing, Kent State University, Kent, OH, USA; Email: mhu@kent.edu), Dale Shao (Lewis College of Business, Marshall University, Huntington, WV, USA; Email: shaod@marshall.edu), Zhen Li (College of Business, Texas Woman's University, Denton, TX, USA; Email: zli@twu.edu), and Brian W. Sloboda (University of Phoenix, Phoenix, AZ, USA; Email: bsloboda@email.phoenix.edu) are equally contributed to this chapter.

J. Y.-L. Forrest, *Systemic Principles of Applied Economic Philosophies I*, Translational Systems Sciences 38, https://doi.org/10.1007/978-981-99-7273-9_5

Keywords Cognition · Creative power · Goal-oriented system · Happiness · Hierarchical network · Mind

5.1 Introduction

One very important question in business is how a consumer gathers and comprehends information and then how he makes his consumption decisions. To address this question, one has to first understand how consumers generally mobilize, either consciously or unconsciously, their individually different cognitive systems. If each consumer is seen as an open system, then his consumptions will be determined by the underlying structure of this system and its ability to interact with the environment. In other words, consumers' consumption decisions are greatly affected by the composites of their cognitive systems or their natural endowments—self-awareness, imagination, conscience, and free will.

On top of systemic reasoning, this chapter develops the necessary theory on how people collect and comprehend information and then consequently make their decisions of consumption. It accomplishes this objective by systemically looking at the tiered structure of an individual's mind and how the four human endowments interact with each other. And then the concept of human natural endowments is generalized to that of business firms.

Because decisions represent consequences of mind activities, this chapter focuses on the investigation of the hierarchical structure of the mind. Moreover, because each mind activity is jointly affected by self-awareness, imagination, conscience, and free will, this chapter establishes facts about these four endowments. Speaking differently, by knowing how the mind functions, it makes it easier for managers and entrepreneurs to understand the behaviors and decisions of consumers under different circumstances.

To accomplish what is intended to do, this chapter applies logical reasoning and systems thinking as the preferred methodology, because the concept of wholeness appears within mind activities and how these activities interact with the environment. Each thought, mind activity, and environment can be seen as a system with its individually special structure. Hence, their interactions can be more effectively examined by using concepts of systems science (Forrest, 2018; Klir, 1985) than using structureless number-based empirical studies (Wu & Lin, 2002; Lin & OuYang, 2010). As for why there is a theoretical significance and practical need to go beyond the conventional methods, such as statistics-based approaches, anecdotal analyses, and calculus-based tools, see Forrest (2018, p. 12–16) and Forrest and Liu (2021).

Because of the adopted unconventional methodology, this chapter accomplishes its goal successfully by developing the following main theoretical results of the mind, among others:

- Each person is a system that is oriented towards the goal of being happy.
- The endowment of self-awareness is not location specific; it helps a person examine his thoughts and respond to whatever circumstances given.
- Imagination and formation of mental images and concepts are achieved by matching what is presented with what has been experienced and learned before by mobilizing self-awareness.
- The endowment of conscience is genetically determined, although conscience is a learned two-valued ±function that is partially defined on imagination.
- The endowment of free will takes one of the following forms: promises are kept, occurrence is opposite to promised, and promises lead to no predictable outcome.
- A person's cognitive system demonstrates a clear systemic yoyo structure, consisting of hierarchical networks of his mind and environment.
- Within any taxonomy of things, events, and thoughts, no category of the highest level of abstraction can exist.

The rest of this chapter is organized as follows. Section 5.2 provides a review of the relevant literature and illustrates how this chapter contributes to the literature. Section 5.3 shows how each human being is a goal-oriented system towards happiness. Section 5.4 looks at the non-positional characteristic of self-awareness. Section 5.5 explores the structure and functionality of imagination. Section 5.6 examines the composition of conscience. Section 5.7 investigates free will and how it takes one of three possible forms. Section 5.8 combines what are established in the previous sections and demonstrates the formation of the systemic field of human cognition. Based on the discussions of previous sections, Sect. 5.9 establishes the natural endowments of a business firm. Then this chapter concludes in Sect. 5.10.

Note: Sects. 5.2–5.8 are mainly based on Forrest and Liu (2021, Chap. 10). Moreover, Sect. 5.9 is based on Forrest et al. (2023).

5.2 Literature Review

The related literature is enormously huge; it can be traced back many hundreds of years. However, for our purpose of this chapter, let us only survey some relevant studies regarding happiness, the mind, and the four human endowments.

By looking at sustainable happiness, as a pursuit of happiness without exploiting other people, the environment, or future generations, O'Brien (2008) links sustainability and happiness together and discusses livable communities, child-friendly planning, and education. Uchida et al. (2004) examine cultural variations in terms of the meaning, motivation, and predictors of happiness by looking at recent evidence on happiness and well-being. Shin et al. (2018) investigate words that are closely associated with happiness and find that individuals who use the crucial words frequently are much happier with their lives than others. Walsh et al. (2018) consider the association between happiness and career success. They empirically find that although these variables are correlated, happiness often precedes career success and positive emotions improve workplace performance.

Enriching this part of the literature, current chapter establishes the following result: Each person is a goal-oriented system, aiming either consciously or unconsciously at attaining happiness. Moreover, it provides a potential method for an individual to attain his desired happiness—constantly look for conquering further challenges and believe (either correctly or incorrectly) in his capability of attaining success.

As for the mind, by viewing it as a dynamic system and by examining commonalities between this and other systems, Moran (2018) attempts to understand complex mental processes. By introducing a dynamic framework for how the mind wanders and how the mind relates to large-scale brain networks, Christoff et al. (2016) maintain that as a spontaneous-thought phenomenon, mind wanders with creative thinking and dreaming. By investigating how the mind processes and organizes information and how it makes decisions, De Bono (2015) proposes the reason for why the mind works only in certain ways by singly or jointly utilizing natural, logical, mathematical and lateral thinking. By treating the mind as an intersubjective blender, Cavell (1998) believes that it is indispensable for humans to envision a shared external world in order for an individual to know his own thoughts as a subjective perspective on the world. Contributing to this line of the literature, this chapter establishes the systemic mechanism on which the mind functions.

In terms of the four human endowments, by empirically examining how self-awareness influences the perspective-taking and egocentrism of an adult, Abbate et al. (2016) are able to conceptually extend previous findings. Through designing a self-development curriculum based on Bloom's Taxonomy, Ugur et al. (2015) suggest that to unswervingly express selected values and characteristics, one needs to first internalize chosen items as guides for living, and then behave consistently, followed with a sense of well-being and personal growth. Yazdanparast and Spears (2018) look at how comparisons of the self to fashion models lead to body dissatisfaction and what can be used to potentially remedy harmful outcomes of such evaluations. They find that objective awareness can be potentially manipulated.

By referencing recent studies on how cognitive functions engross the anterior hippocampus, Zeidman and Maguire (2016) link the former to the structure of the latter. To examine how imagination creates reliable experiences, Derbaix and Gombault (2016) find that with support of immaterial dimensions, the material dimensions can facilitate consumers' imagination. That is, by making use of imagination, invisibles can help create reliability and authenticity. McFarland et al. (2017) hypothesize that depression is often connected with over-general memory and imagination, coupled with problem-solving deficits, while finding that brief interviews can temporarily enhance problem-solving capability of individuals with depression.

Based on the assumption that conscious experiences arise from one area in the brain, LeDoux and Brown (2017) derive the belief that emotional and non-emotional states are separated by the kinds of processed inputs of a general cortical network of cognition. Among others, these scholars believe that non-conscious inputs, provided by subcortical circuits, coalesce with other kinds of neural signals existing in conscious emotional experiences. Aronfreed (1968) provides a valuable survey on the literature of how behaviors and conscience interact with each other. Moreover, Langston (2001) presents a historical account on the development of the concept of conscience throughout time.

Libet (1999) experimentally addresses whether or not free will actually exists and finds that although volitional courses of taking easily voluntary acts are initiated unconsciously, conscience still controls the result. That is, free will indeed appears, even though it might not help initiate a voluntary act. Dennett (2015) argues that instead of being threatened by advances in science, variations of free will, which endorse moral and artistic responsibilities, are distinguished, explained, and justified in further details by these advances. Kane (2005) provides a good source of information on free will for scholars who do not have much background in the subject with an extensive survey of latest views on this central area of philosophy.

By employing systems science, systems methodology, and logical reasoning, this chapter carries relevant knowledge to a much higher level by showing the following theoretical results, among others, which can be practically applied in real-life settings:

- The endowment of self-awareness is innate and non-positional; it assists a person to examine his thoughts and to choose appropriate courses of actions.
- The endowment of imagination helps a person find parallels between what is presented and what is known from before and from his philosophical system of values and beliefs.
- Conscience is a genetically determined capability and represents a learned partial, two-valued function, defined on the reservoir of imagination. The two possible output values are + and −.
- An individual's free will takes one of the following three possible forms—promises kept, actual occurrence is opposite to promise, and no definite connection between promise and outcome.
- Each business firm, as an organization that involves people, also possesses and is tightly influenced by its natural endowments.

In short, as a consequence of the particular methodology employed, established hereafter are theoretically general and practically applicable conclusions. They provide universally applicable recommendations for managers and entrepreneurs unless stated antecedents are violated.

5.3 The Mental Orientation of Humans

In this chapter, each person is modeled as a yoyo field, which evolves with the yoyo fields of many other people, things, events, thoughts, etc. As is imaginable, these fields spin differently in terms of rotational speed, direction, and strength, as well as divergence and convergence, orientation, and occupied territories of varying scales. This systemic modeling of people and their surroundings suggests that each person lives within a rough sea of thousands of thousands of spinning fields that interact with each other. Therefore, the mind of a person also interacts with other minds, be they like or dislike, where two minds are said to be alike, if they hold similar views of life and the world and similar values; in other words, their yoyo fields spin in the same fashion in terms of the listed characteristics above. Accordingly, two minds are said to be different or dislike, if one of these characteristics of their yoyo fields is different of each other. The interactions of spinning fields in the rough sea jointly make a person suffer from self-doubt (or skepticism) about the suitability and potential of his desires in life.

By happiness, it means a state of mind (or feeling), such as contentment, satisfaction, pleasure, or joy (Cambridge Advanced Learner's Dictionary, 2008). A happy person is always such person who dreams of heights of some future achievement(s) (Hill, 1928, p. 153); and there are principles that govern enduring happiness and success (Covey, 1989, p. 23).

Proposition 5.1 The fundamental objective of all human efforts is to become a happy person. Sustaining the hope of future achievement is the only way to maintain the state of happiness. The feeling of happiness lies with the present and/or the past, while sustaining the feeling depends on the future.

To show this conclusion, let us model the concept of happiness (Lin & Forrest, 2012) as follows. At a particular moment of time, a person is happy, if and only if the yoyo field of the person just achieved an upper hand in its interaction with at least one field flow in its environment. This systemic understanding of happiness agrees with Aristotle's description of the concept, as given in his Nicomachean Ethics (Aristotle, 2016)—happiness (equivalently being well and doing well) is the only thing that humans desire for their own sake. As a direct consequence of this systemic modeling of happiness, the conclusions in Proposition 5.1 follow. In particular, the constant achievement of conquering greater and more challenging difficulties over time one after another keeps a person content and continuously excited with his state of affairs and set of circumstances. Moreover, no matter what was accomplished in the past, the yoyo field of a person is always presently interacting with other fields and experiencing challenges and difficulties. Hence, the only way to maintain the state of happiness is to sustain the hope of future achievement; and the feeling of happiness lies with the present and/or the past, while sustaining the feeling depends on the future.

In terms of the literature, Jeremy Bentham (1789), John Stuart Mill (1863), and other moral philosophers believed that happiness (or pleasure) was the only thing humans do and long for for their own sake; that happiness is the only intrinsic good such that the more happiness the better; and that the goal of the ethical life is to maximize happiness.[1] Then, these scholars claim that happiness can be measured

[1] This is the so-called "principle of utility" or "the greatest-happiness principle."

numerically with such a measurement that is named "utility." By assuming that the set of all possible consumptions is completely ordered by preferences, Debreu (1959) shows that such claimed utility indeed exists. By building on this important conclusion, the term "utility" has been widely employed in neoclassical economics (e.g. Mas-Collel et al., 1995). In comparison, Proposition 5.1 is concerned with "happiness" itself instead of any possible measure of it. Because the discussion in Chap. 8 will show that the set of all possible consumptions cannot be completely ordered in general, a need to revise the concepts of utility and utility functions arises.

The same analysis as in the argument of Proposition 5.1 in fact also indicates the following result:

Proposition 5.2 For a person to possibly achieve enduring happiness, the person needs to focus on constantly conquering additional difficulties in the indefinite future and have the confidence either correctly or incorrectly that he has the ability to do so.

The discussion above also directly leads to the following result:

Proposition 5.3 No matter whether it is conscious or unconscious, each person represents a goal-oriented system.

As a goal-oriented system (Mesarovic & Takahara, 1975), each person engrosses information and knowledge in a way like a magnet from all sources in the environment through automatic use of his four human endowments: self-awareness (or self-consciousness), imagination, conscience, and free will. If we model thoughts as the input side of the person's yoyo body while his actions as the other side, then we can conclude that the person's endeavors are carried out at their individually specific moments in manners aligned with the dominating thoughts of the person's mind of the respective moments (Lin & Forrest, 2012). Therefore, if a person, for example, desires to achieve a clear goal in life and possesses the necessary determination to materially realize it, then he can intentionally fasten and embrace the goal in his mind. As time passes, the fastened and embraced goal will sooner or later infuse the self-consciousness of the mind, which will urge the person's physical body to take actions towards the ultimate realization of the goal. There are many real-life manifestations of this theoretical fact. The magnificent life of Thomas Edison demonstrated how a news butcher was eventually transformed into a leading inventor of the world.

5.4 Self-Awareness' Non-Positionality and Examinations of Thoughts and Actions

By self-awareness it stands for a person's awareness that he exists as an individual and an entity that is different and separate from other people and objects with private thoughts and individual rights (Cooke, 1974, p. 106). The concept also implicitly indicates a person's realization that other people are similarly self-aware. It is because of self-awareness that people are considerate of their own attitudes and temperaments (Branden, 1969, p. 41).

Proposition 5.4 Self-awareness, as a natural existence, is not attached to any specific location. That is, the existence of self-awareness is non-positional.

This result is a natural consequence of the underlying systemic yoyo structure of any person of concern. In particular, the said yoyo field takes in and gives out things constantly, where the things that are being taken in and given out can assume any form, such as physical, intellectual, tangible, intangible, or epistemological. Things go in and out surely from the input and output sides, as well as in all horizontal directions and elevations along the axis of spin. The situation can be vividly imagined as that of a tornado in real life. Hence, different systems constantly push against or pull towards each other. Such pushing effects between people and between people of other things make each person sense the separation of himself from other people and things, and the pulling effect creates the sense of individual rights and entitlements.

These forever existing pushing and pulling effects collectively make all involved systems or individuals aware of their own existence, the existence of others, their private thoughts, etc. Because these pushing and pulling effects universally exist no matter where a person is and guarantee the appearance of self-awareness, that explains the reason why self-awareness is not attached to any specific location.

In terms of literature, as a French existentialist philosopher and one leading figure in the twentieth century French philosophy, Jean-Paul Sartre (June 21, 1905–April 15, 1980) is the first person who conjectured the result in Proposition 5.4 (Gerassi, 1989).

Proposition 5.5 Each person relies on his self-awareness to examine his thoughts and decide on how to respond appropriately and adequately to the circumstances he is currently in, where the examination is conducted by associating the circumstances with what have been learned before.

The truthfulness of this result can be seen as follows by continuing the systemic modeling and discussion in the previous paragraphs: for any chosen person, his self-awareness emerges from the interactions of his systemic yoyo field with those of all other beings and things existing within the environment. As the person grows with increasing maturity, he experiences various dealings with others, compares his varied approaches, and remembers those most satisfactory approaches that produced desirable or optimal outcomes.

When a unique and never-seen-before situation is presented to the person, he has two options to consider: (1) experience anxiety or (2) associate the new situation with one or a set of previously seen scenarios, each of which resembles at least slightly the current situation. No matter whether the person takes option (1) or (2) he has to eventually organize his thoughts in order to be able to formulate a reasonable course of actions by jointly employing other human endowments: imagination, conscience, and free will. Specifically, when the person is presented with a particular circumstance, he will have to find a way to jump into option (2) no matter whether or not he first experiences an initial shock of anxiety if he, somehow, has to deal with the situation, where running away from the situation is surely one possible action to take. Now, the person studies related actions taken before to deal with those previously seen scenarios, each of which resembles at least slightly the current situation to come up with a possibly appropriate reaction to the current situation that might potentially lead to desirable outcomes.

Speaking differently, through various interactions with the yoyo fields of different people, events, thoughts, concepts, etc., the person has acquired an increasingly improved understanding of himself and other people, events, and things. Hence, the person amasses over time a large deposit (or reservoir) of knowledge and experiences and has advanced a capability for him to freely and frequently mobilize the elements in the reservoir in his decision-making.

5.5 Formation of Mental Images and Abstract Concepts

By imagination, it means (Norman, 2000; Egan, 1992) the capability and the action (or process) of the mind to form mental images and concepts no matter what is presented in front of the biological senses, including the case that nothing is presented; with such aptitude, a person derives meaning out of each experience encountered and understanding to whatever knowledge learned. Imagination helps each person meet and experience things throughout life. Every time when a person physically touches an object, optically sees a scene, and acoustically hears a sound, he coalesces his senses into a mental picture via imagination. Such capability to imagine is innate through which a person forms his view of life, belief of how the world operates, and philosophical system of values within the mind based on how his yoyo field interacts with the yoyo fields of other elements within the shared world, both physical and intellectual (Harris, 2000). Speaking differently, the endowment of imagination can be virtuously seen as a workplace located within the mind. In this workplace, learned concepts and established facts are innovatively associated with each other in various ways to produce new and better solutions to problems. These innovative associations are known as the creative power of the soul (Hill, 1928).

Proposition 5.6 By match making with elements in the imagination's reservoir of experience and knowledge through using self-awareness, imagination helps a person imagine and form mental images and concepts out of what is presented either implicitly or explicitly to his sense organs.

In order to see why this result holds true, let us model imagination by going along with the systemic yoyo model of self-awareness in such a way that the human endowment of imagination becomes another natural consequence of a person's yoyo structure. With such a systemic modeling, a person's biological sense organs are simply the body parts of the three-dimensional realization of the person's yoyo field, although the underlying multidimensional spinning field of the person is very complex. Therefore, there are a great deal of the yoyo field structures and yoyo field interactions of elements in the world human sense organs cannot really detect. Speaking different, human sense organs can only collect a small portion of the extremely rich collection of experience and knowledge gained by a person through his constant interactions with the yoyo fields of other entities of the physical and intellectual world, when his yoyo field fights against others and attempts to snatch up things of common interests. In other words, a person's experience and knowledge, acquired from his interactions with others, are much richer than what his sense organs can materialistically collect.

This model of a person's imagination indicates that the endowment "imagination" can be identified with or is equal to the reservoir of all interactions between the person's underlying yoyo field and the fields of other people and things in the environment. More specifically, the reservoir contains both conscious and unconscious records of interactions, where the former records are collected by the person's sense organs, and the latter records are unknown to the person's conscious mind.

When a need arises for a person to develop images or concepts in his pursuing of happiness (Propositions 5.1 and 5.2), the person utilizes his self-awareness to reach into this reservoir. The degree of how well he can mobilize his self-awareness governs how deeply and widely (or individually and collectively) he can reach into this reservoir. This degree of utilization of his self-awareness in turn governs how thought provoking his consequently established concepts and images will be. The common systemic structure, shared by elements of the material and intellectual world and human thoughts (Lin, 2008), implicitly implies that when called to act, imagination simply plays the role of a match-maker. It matches the situation or issue of concern with related elements within the reservoir of imagination. If a nearly perfect match can be found, then an ideal image and concept are quickly formulated, and consequent course of actions is determined naturally. If not good or no match is found at all, the reservoir of imagination will then be expanded with new elements, consisting of unprecedent experiences and/or knowledge. This end explains why training, either formal or informal, is necessary for a person to go through. It is because with adequate training on how to commend over self-consciousness, a person will be able to mobilize a lot of information from the reservoir of his imagination. That reservoir is composed of conscious experience and knowledge learned through sense organs and those collected unconsciously without going through these sense organs.

Proposition 5.7 A person employs his imagination to form his individually specific view of life, belief of how the world operates, and philosophical system of values by associating different experiences and pieces of knowledge.

To establish this generally true result, imagine the birth of a representative person. For a period of time since this very moment of birth, this person lives within the constraints of many limiting conditions and has to acquiescently submit to what is available from the caretaker and the limited environment. These early exchanges with people and the world assist the newborn to develop its elementary beliefs, basic values, and fundamental philosophical assumptions. For example, the newborn quickly learns that "you must care for me by meeting my needs," "If not, you will have to suffer from the consequence – my crying," etc. By unconsciously using this set of elementary beliefs, values, and assumptions, the new born commands the caretaker and the sounding world to satisfy its wants and needs. As the new born grows, it starts to gradually use the expanding set of beliefs, values, and assumptions to explain whatever unfathomable, construct tactics to conquer adversities and creates ways to manage his own dealings and concerns.

With increasingly more mature mental capacity over time, the person gains more control over his self-awareness. That naturally assists the person to obtain more efficient tools and advanced knowledge from more diversified sources in the environment of an enlarging scale. Hence, his imagination's reservoir of experience and knowledge simultaneously grows with new elements constantly added, acquired either consciously and unconsciously, while the members of the reservoir start to associate with each other to form intellectual understandings of rising levels. Associations of these experience and knowledge become more and more fortified within his self-consciousness. As soon as the strength of these associations reaches and goes beyond a threshold value, Bjerknes's (1898) Circulation Theorem, for more details, see Chap. 3, assures that abstract, multidimensional eddy motions will appear within the self-awareness and reservoir of imagination of that person. That is exactly how imagination assists a person from his view of life, belief on how the world operates, and philosophical system of values within his minds.

Proposition 5.8 Different persons possess their individually different sets of views of life, beliefs on how the world operates, and philosophical systems of values. For short, each such set will be referred to as a (philosophical) system of values and beliefs.

The truthfulness of this result naturally follows from the fact that people are born into very different families, which are located within quite varied environments. Therefore, their underlying systemic yoyo fields interact with people and environments differently within their correspondingly diverse environments. These differences existing in families, environments, and interactions help lead to correspondingly different philosophical systems of values and beliefs.

5.6 Integration of Innate and Acquired Capabilities

By conscience, it represents such an ability for a person to know the principles that judge whether or not his behaviors are acceptable and to sense the degree to which his thoughts are in accord with the principles. In other words, each person employs his conscience to tell if his actions are either right or wrong (Tinbergen, 1951; Pfaff, 2007; Buss, 2004).In particular, when a person acts in a way that is not in agreement with his underlying principles (or known as moral values), his conscience will tell his that a wrong has been committed, making him feel remorse. On the other hand, when a person acts in alignment with his moral values, his conscience will make him feel morality or truthfulness.

For two sets X and Y of objects, f is a partial function from X to Y, provided that there is a subset D of X, written $D \subseteq X$, such that f is a well-defined function from D to Y. It means that for any element x in D, there is an element y in Y such that f clearly rules that y is associated with x. In this case, x can be seen as an input of f and y an output of f, written as $y = f(x)$. Speaking differently, f specifies a rule that assigns each element in D with an element in Y. The set Y is known as the range of the partial function f.

Proposition 5.9 Each person is genetically endowed with his capability of conscience, while his conscience represents an acquired partial function defined on the reservoir of his imagination such that $Y = \{+, -\}$ is the range of this partial function. In other words, for any element x in the person's reservoir of imagination, the person either has a moral value assigned to x or does not have any. For the former case, the assigned moral value to x is either + or −.

To see the truthfulness of this proposition, let us build our argument on the previous systemic yoyo modeling of self-awareness and imagination. Specifically, in this modeling elements in the reservoir imagination are spin patterns of various yoyo fields and interactions of these patterns. The value of + is assigned to some of the field flow patterns and interactions, which are seen to the person as being right, acceptable, or moral; the value of - is assigned to some other field flows and interactions, which are seen as being wrong, not acceptable or immoral.

The reason why this function is only partially defined on the reservoir of the person's imagination is because there are still plenty of other field flow patterns and interactions in the reservoir that are not assigned with either + or −. For convenience of communication, let us refer this partial function to as a ± function, which is defined on the domain that consists of all the elements in the reservoir with an assigned value of either + or −.

When a person grows more consciously over time towards the orientation of having a happy life (Propositions 5.1 and 5.2), his assignment of + or − to certain elements in the reservoir of his imagination starts gradually since the time when the person is still an infant; and then he continues this task throughout his entire life. In particular, in the beginning at birth, the domain of this ± function is the empty set. Along with the growth of the person, the domain of his ± function expands with his self-awareness and reinforcements of various environmental factors. If the person experiences something dramatic in his lifetime, certain elements in the domain of his ± function may switch their originally assigned values from + to − or vice versa.

For example, assume that early + values are assigned to field patterns that flow in the same direction and − values to currents flowing in opposite directions (Fig. 5.1). One explanation for such +/− sign assignments is that same directional flows help form sub-eddy pools, while other kinds of currents are not beneficial to the formation of sub-eddy pools. In the language of elementary education, initial + values (or adult approvals) are assigned to behaviors that help strength the well-being of all kids involved and − values (or adult disapprovals) to those behaviors that might lead to opposite effect. For instance, most likely encouraged is the behavior of sharing, which is assigned a + value. On the other hand, violence is disapproved with an assigned − value.

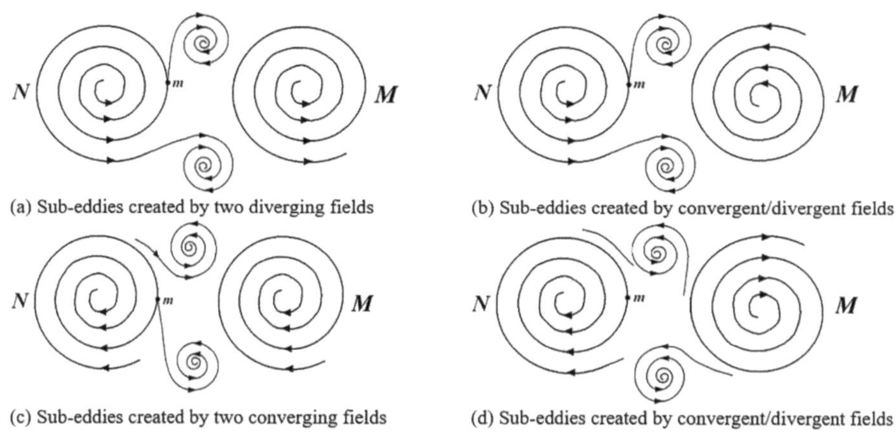

Fig. 5.1 Two adjacent fields *N* and *M* jointly produce sub-eddies in areas of their control, where *m* is a random particle in the spin field of *N*. (**a**) Sub-eddies created by two diverging fields; (**b**) sub-eddies created by convergent/divergent fields; (**c**) sub-eddies created by two converging fields; (**d**) sub-eddies created by convergent/divergent fields

As a person grows with increasing maturity, he will have his ± function well engrained in his mind so that every time when he intends to take an action or comes up with a thought, he automatically and unconsciously compares the action or thought with relevant elements in the domain of his ± function. If the intended action or the thought in his mind has an assigned + value, the person will feel justified and moral. If the assigned value is −, emerging is a sense of remorse. Moreover, if the intended action and the thought forming in the mind does not have any + or − assignment, the person will have to examine its potential + or − value. Doing so expands the domain of his ± function.

This analysis and discussion demonstrate that each person's capacity for conscience is genetically determined, where conscience resides totally on top of imagination, while imagination develops on top of the person's self-awareness, as innate capability of the person. At the same time, the specific contents of the person's conscience, the ± function, and assignments of the +/− values are learned throughout life, where some particular +/− assignments are switched back and forth several times throughout the person's life.

5.7 Three Different Possible Consequences of Promises

By free will, it means a person's capability to keep his promises that he makes to himself and others. That is, free will is a capability each person possesses that assists a person to make estimates for at least the near term regarding what he can do and cannot do and what choices or courses of actions are optimal for the state of affairs involved (Lin & Forrest, 2012). In other words, free will is such a human capability that helps make decisions, choices, and consequent follow-through actions that materialize those choices and decisions.

Proposition 5.10 A person's free will assumes one of the following three possible scenarios:

1. Promises are held.
2. Promises lead to opposite outcomes.
3. Promises do not lead to any predictable outcome.

To see why this proposition is true, let us continue the discussions in the previous paragraphs based on the particular systemic yoyo modeling established earlier. Developing on his self-awareness, an innate human capability, a person's reservoir of imagination expands constantly; and the domain of his ± function of moral values enlarges with each occasion of learning and interaction with others. There are three possibilities for the specific "self," which he becomes aware of sooner or later through his increasingly awaking self-awareness in relation to the domain of his ± function.

A. The "self" is in the domain of the ± function with an assigned + value.
B. The "self" is in the domain of the ± function with an assigned – value.
C. The "self" is not in the domain of the ± function.

If possibility A is the case, then the person is obligated to carefully investigate the situation of concern and estimate as accurately as possible what he can accomplish and what he cannot accomplish in order to actualize his promises. If he cannot assuredly foretell what he can accomplish for a presented situation, then he will promise to do his best without providing any assurance of producing the desired outcome. Therefore, in either case for possibility A, the person keeps his promises.

If possibility B is the case, then the person once again feels obligated to foretell as scrupulously and as precisely as possible about what he can achieve and what he cannot achieve. However, different from the possibility above, in this case, the person will most likely make promises that are opposite to what he is expectedly able to achieve, based on his imagination and ± function. By doing so, the negatively valued "self" will lead to an outcome of a positive value in terms of the ± function. That will make the person feel moral and truthful. That is, for possibility B, what is promised is opposite to what will actually happen.

If possibility C is the case, then the person's "self" is not in the domain of his ± function. That means that the childhood of the person has been badly spoiled so that he does not really know or care whether his "self" stands for something good or evil. In this case, no matter what the person faces, he simply makes random promises (or sounds) as long as they are pleasant to the ear without even further thinking about correspondingly taking necessary actions. As for why the person behaves this way, it is because whatever happens next, be it a promise kept or not, does not bear any conscientious impact on the person.

5.8 The Systemic Structure of Human Cognition

The discussions in the previous sections jointly imply the following conclusion:

Proposition 5.11 The reservoir of a person's imagination is of the structure of a hierarchical network that extends open-endedly on the first layer of human physiological needs and the second layer of specific values of the person's philosophical system (Fig. 5.2).

This hierarchical network in Fig. 5.2 displays the general structure of the mind. The first P level stands for all physiological needs of a representative person, including such basics of life as breathing, food, water, sex, sleep, homeostasis, and excretion (Maslow, 1943, 1954). The second V level is made up of specific values of a person's philosophical system on what life means, how the world actually functions, and how he needs to behave in order to comply with his codes of morality. On top of these two basic levels, the person's mind network contains interacting blocks of various knowledge and experiences about people; things, be they physical, intellectual, conceptual, etc.; events; and their associations with each other.

Proposition 5.12 The seemingly endless environment of a person can be both visually and conceptually seen as a hierarchical network, within which the elements of his family and relationships among these elements constitute the bottom layer (Fig. 5.3), where by family it represents the immediate environment in which the person grows up.

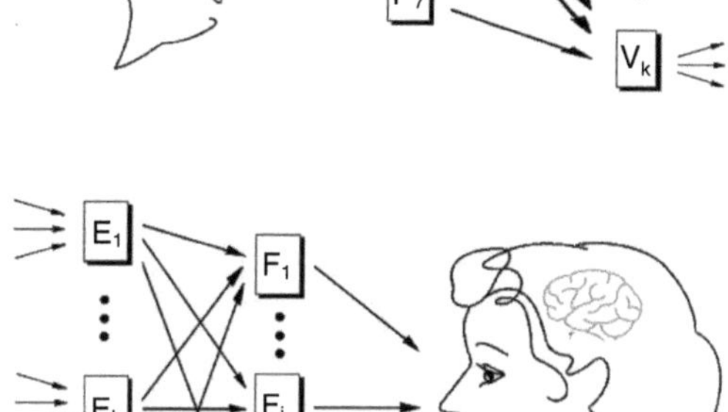

Fig. 5.2 The hierarchical structure of the networked mind

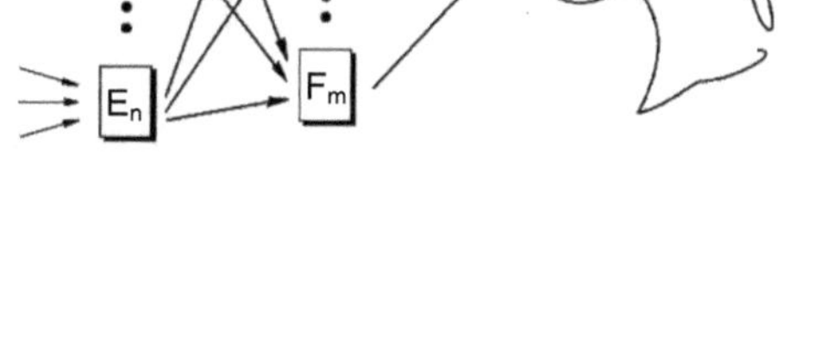

Fig. 5.3 The hierarchical network of a person's environment

This proposition illustrates that a person is initially limited to the family setting F within which his life starts. Then he ventures into an increasingly larger environment E with time and as he gains growing maturity. That is, as a person grows older and wiser, he simultaneously observes more finer details and increasingly larger wholes from the environment. He internalizes more information, more experience, and more advanced knowledge from the environment. As his vision multiplies further outward, the hierarchical network structure of his mind becomes further extended and enriched with scope and depth. Such extensions in all reaches of vision and in the complexity of the hierarchical network structure of his mind strengthen each other; and the further outwards his vision reaches, the wealthier his mind structure becomes. The wealthier mind structure in turn helps him see even further outwards than before. Such a reciprocating cycle of augmentation lingers until when the person is no longer exploring his sounding environment. From this discussion, the conclusion below follows:

Proposition 5.13 The hierarchically networked structure of a person's mind and that of his environment jointly form the person's cognitive system, whose systemic yoyo structure is shown in Fig. 5.4. In this figurative representation, each level, such as E, F, P and V, is in a circular movement, which is used to model the fact that elements within each level are in fact more or less associated with each other.

This proposition illustrates the layer structure of the cognitive system within the mind pictured in both Figs. 5.2 and 5.3. Conceptually, as one moves away to the right from the shown P and V levels, units of information, experience, and knowledge become either categories (i.e., the taxonomic organization of things and events), or schemas (i.e., spatially/temporally organized structures) (Stayman et al., 1992), or product-category schemas (Meyers-Levy & Tybout, 1989). More specifically, a product category (or schema) is such a structure of knowledge residing in a person's cognitive system that encompasses a myriad of details, including complete information about the attributes of each product, values of various attributes in terms of optimizing goal-achievement, the correlation of product attributes with one another, as well as the relationship between the stated product category and other categories (Stayman et al., 1992). When processing the information of a new

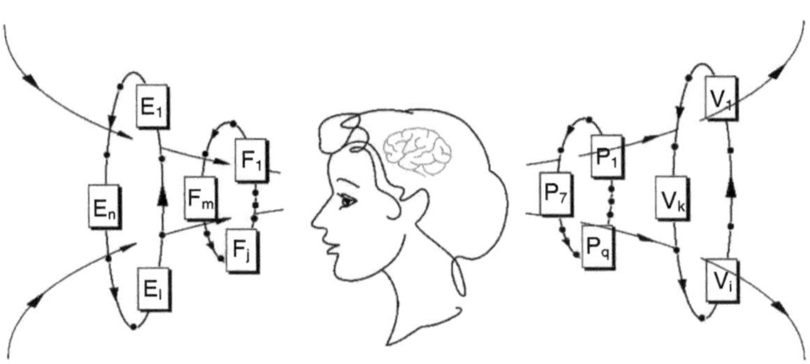

Fig. 5.4 The systemic yoyo structure of human cognitive system

product, the essence is how well the new information matches a product category stored in a person's cognitive system (Proposition 5.6). A product-category schema holds characteristics of a taxonomic category and can also be perceived as a schema to the extent that the use context of a product has been specified. For convenience of communication, the terms "category" and "schema" are used interchangeably in this chapter. In the rest of this chapter, by the cognitive system of a person, without causing confusion it means the conceptual, hierarchically networked structure in Fig. 5.2.

For the current purpose of study, let us employ Rosch's (Rosch, 1978) taxonomy. That is such a system that allows one category to relate to another category by means of class inclusion, denoted $\subseteq$. In particular, for two classes X and Y, $X \subseteq Y$ means that X is a sub-class of Y. That is, the more members a category accommodates (i.e., is more inclusive), the higher level of abstraction the category is of.

Proposition 5.14 For any chosen taxonomy of things, events, and thoughts, it is always a part of another category of a higher level of abstraction.

The argument for this result is set theoretic based on Lin (1999) and Kuratowski and Mostowski (1976). In particular, let X be an arbitrarily chosen category. There then is a condition $\varphi(x)$ that describes what this chosen category is. That is, the condition $\varphi(x)$ specifies what entity x is a member in X and what entity x is not a member in X. Assume that y is such a thing or an event or a thought that does not satisfy the condition $\varphi(x)$ and that Y is a category that contains y as a member and X as a sub-class. Then, Y is a category of a higher abstraction level than X. For example, the existence of such a category Y can be readily seen as follows: let y be the chosen category X and Y be a category constructed based on this particular y and elements in X. In this construction, y is simply the thought of seeing X as an intellectual existence.

Proposition 5.15 No category of the highest level of abstraction can ever exist, no matter which particular taxonomy of things, events, and thoughts is considered.

The argument for this proposition is similar to the one for the previous result. In particular, assume that there is such a category X that is of the highest level of abstraction. Then each category that contains all elements of X and the thought of X, as an existing entity represents a category of a higher level of abstraction than that of X. This end contradicts the assumption about X, as the category of the highest level of abstraction. This contradiction indicates that Proposition 5.15 holds true.

Although Proposition 5.15 holds true in theory, in practice we can still think about categories of the highest level of abstraction, because for any given practical situation, the boundary of consideration is always limited within a defined range, such as the categories of a particular group of furniture. Simultaneously, this proposition points out the fact that the clearly layered hierarchical structure of human cognitive system, as shown in Figs. 5.2 and 5.4, in theory is not quite evidently the case. In fact, the opposite is true: the reservoir of a person's imagination needs to be seen as a continuous field that does not have clearly defined hierarchies and layers that isolate one level of experience, information, and knowledge from another.

Proposition 5.16 No matter when, at least one area in the continuous field of the reservoir of a person's imagination experiences an active circulation of information, experience, and knowledge.

To see why this conclusion is true, we see from Propositions 5.1–5.3 that for the chosen person, he realistically and theoretically is a system that angles itself towards a goal, such as happiness, no matter how the person defines his happiness. Therefore, at any particular moment of time, the person can find himself focusing attention on something, such as a specific consumption or the nurturing of a particular relationship, that is more or less related to his orientation goal. This end implies that in the continuous field of the reservoir of his imagination, certain units of related experience, information, and knowledge are being connected in a special fashion, as stimulated by the puts from the current situation, in order to generate certain desired outcome. The desired outcome can be a moment of suddenly spiked utility or striking excitement. Hence, Bjerknes' Circulation Theorem (see Chap. 4 for more details) guarantees that these associated units of experience, information, and knowledge constitute an active circulation, composed of some newly or recently acquired information.

5.9 A Business Firm's Natural Endowments

To formulate the natural endowments for a business firm, the discussions of this section, which is mainly based on Forrest et al. (2023), are derived by employing the greatly simplified theory on how a regional or national economy evolves from its very humble beginning developed in Chap. 4.

In particular, the land and people, living on the land, are initially served by poorly equipped family-based workshops that provide the needs of their respective families with little or no trade exchanges with the outside world. As the production of crops is increased due to advances in agriculture-related knowledge and technology, needs for new tools appear, and consequently, more and more farm laborers are freed from the land and enter the construction of production tools and the production of consumer goods. Accordingly, a market of scale starts to emerge. That is when economic policies are introduced for various economic purposes, and the development of appropriate technologies beyond the purpose of agriculture starts to accelerate. As more people enter the production of commercial goods and services, the depth and width of market exchanges improve. That, in turn, requires more advanced and more massive manufacturing of new products and services of an expanding range.

At an early stage of economic development, assume that the gradually emerging product market is served by m firms, respectively named Firm i $(= 1, 2, \ldots, m)$, that provide customers with mutually substitutable products. For convenience, assume that each of these firms produces only one product. Because the market is emerging, assume that consumers are not yet conscious about making such purchases that will have positive social, economic, and/or environmental impacts (for conscious consumerism, see, e.g., Kautish and Sharma (2019). That is, consumers' individual systems of values and beliefs do not play a role in their purchase decisions regarding from where they buy their desired products. That is, consumers are not loyal to any particular firm and only make purchases based on whose price is most competitive. Such consumers are known as switchers. Let the magnitude of all switchers be β, which equals the total of all consumers and potential consumers.

On the other side, since the market is fledgling and still emerging from the earlier state of nonexistence, the firms produce their products without paying any attention to corporate social responsibilities (for a description of this concept, see, e.g., Fahimnia et al., 2015). That is, the marginal costs of production of the firms are different from one firm to another. However, without loss of generality, these different costs can be normalized and set to zero (Forrest et al., 2021). Considering how readily information and knowledge are available due to the rapid development of information and communication technology, assume that the employed pricing strategies used are known to these firms' managements so that the firms respectively establish their best responses by playing the Nash equilibrium through pure self-analysis.

Since these firms serve the market, assume that they are making profits; otherwise, they will be out of business. In other words, each of these firms more or less uniformly randomizes its selling price P over the interval $[C, R]$ as long as the firm could make profits on the average, where $C = 0$ is the normalized production cost and R the reservation price consumers are willing to pay for the product. Evidently, different consumers have different reservation prices due to their individually varied circumstances and their different systems of values and beliefs. As how the marginal costs of production are normalized above, similarly, these varied reservation prices can be normalized to $R = 1$ (for details, see Forrest et al., 2021). That is, each firm uniformly randomizes its selling price P over the interval [0,1] in such a way that it can make profits on average. Comparing this discussion with that in Chap. 4, the profit of each firm in this emerging market is equal to $\Pi = \beta P(1 - P)^{m-1}$ (Proposition 4.1).

In the next stage of development, industries emerge due to the introduction of new technologies, expansions of product market, and the formation of various organizational networks. Correspondingly, firm competitions intensify (Gustafsson et al., 2016) with some firms surviving while most others failing (Markman & Waldron, 2014). Assume that m firms, satisfying all conditions above, successfully survive and become established so that each of them has a base of loyal consumers. At this freezing moment in time, these bases of loyal consumers are materialistically formed as a consequence of how individual consumers' systems of values and beliefs play their roles and how the firms promote their respective consumer value propositions (CVPs) (for details on the concept of CVPs, see, e.g., Payne et al., 2017).

As discussed in Chap. 4, let α be the normalized magnitude of Firm *i*'s base of loyal customers (Forrest et al., 2021) and $\beta = 1 - m\alpha$ the magnitude of switchers, known as consumer surplus, so that $\alpha, \beta \in [0, 1]$. As analyzed above, switchers exist due to various reasons, one of which is that these people's systems of values and beliefs do not really agree with the promoted CVPs, but somehow the product is needed in life. Then, Proposition 4.2 says that Firm *j*'s profit Π_j is equal to

$$\Pi_j = \alpha P + \beta P \prod_{\substack{i=1 \\ i \neq j}}^{m} [1 - F_i(P)]. \tag{4.2}$$

where $F_i(P)$ is assumed to be the price distribution of Firm i, $i = 1, 2, \ldots, m$.

As consumers try out the products they purchased from the marketplace, they find out whether or not these products actually meet their expectations and satisfy their real-life needs. During this trail period, their systems of values and beliefs naturally come into place in making their eventual judgments. This end explains why consumer preferences change relentlessly, creating new switchers; and it is more so if the incumbent firms had become risk avert and comfortable with their market positions (Podolny, 1993). Of course, whether or not this situation actually happens to an incumbent firm really depends on whether or not the management of the firm has a "long-term, unwavering public commitment to the ambition of becoming world class, the best of the world; and such ambition is embraced, endorsed, and sought after by the leadership of the firm" (Forrest et al., 2020, p. 112). In other words, it depends on the natural endowments of the firm; for details, see the discussion behind Proposition 4.3, which shows the relationship between the magnitude of switchers and the intensity of market competition. In particular, this proposition states that if no firm, incumbent to the market, can gain anything by changing its own price and adjusting its customer value propositions (CVP), then the existence of switchers provides an opportunity for new competitor(s) to enter the market. As for whether or not there is actually a firm to enter the market, it depends on the number of the switchers. Specifically, a potential entrant has to come up with an innovative CVP that fits the systems of values and beliefs of a good number of switchers.

With Propositions 4.1–4.3 established as the needed preparation, the natural endowments of a business firm can be readily phrased. Specifically,

> By a firm's self-awareness, it means the firm's awareness that it exists as a business entity separate from other entities, such as people, firms and things, with its business secrets, such as adopted customer value propositions, operational strategies, protected product designs, etc.

This formulation of a firm's self-awareness is supported by Proposition 4.3. For a firm, no matter whether it is an incumbent or a new entrant of the market, it has to know its surroundings for it to first survive and then thrive. The so-called surroundings include who are the targeted consumers, their changing preferences and tastes, business strategies and tactics implemented by competitors, the customer value propositions adopted by others, newly emerging technologies, formations of organizational networks, strategic inter-firm blocks, etc. Therefore, a business firm's self-awareness represents the firm's self-conscious state within which its attention is focused on his own well-being. It is such self-awareness that a firm is potentially able to decipher market signals based on the firm's history, available resources, and human talents.

> By a firm's imagination, it describes the firm's ability to learn and to acquire new knowledge, to innovatively imagine what might be the right offer, such as a newly designed product, or an improved product or new (or improved) service, to satisfy the deciphered market demand, and to develop the necessary process of materially introducing the imagined offer.

This endowment—imagination—enables a firm to crystallize the deciphered market signal into the formulation of an appropriate customer value proposition, a reevaluation of the firm's strengths and weaknesses, the concrete design of its innovative market offer, and consequent production and marketing. The so-called market signal can be detected by estimating either the existence of a sizable market segment of switchers (Proposition 4.3) or the number of incumbent companies that crowd a specific market area.

> By a firm's conscience, it represents the ability for the firm to judge which business effort is more beneficial than other efforts.

This endowment provides a firm with a set of criteria that oversee the firm's operations and the degree to which a business decision and consequent actions are in harmony with the criteria. When a firm decides to pursue an opportunity, its conscience provides the management of the firm with an assessment on whether or not the action will be beneficial or not. Hence, the firm's conscience can inform the firm about its managerial judgment before it takes any action.

> By a firm's free will, it means the capability for the firm to keep the promises, how to keep and to what degree to keep these promises, as reflected in its contracts with the partners within its supply-chain ecosystem.

This capability enables a firm to make decisions and to carry out consequent managerial acts. In terms of a market signal, there are naturally many different ways for a firm to decipher. Among all foreseeable ways, it is free will that helps a firm take whatever judged most preferred. In terms of product design, there are similarly various approaches for a firm to take. And in terms of pushing the final product onto the market, there are different strategies to use. So, this endowment—free will—is very important regarding a firm's success.

As is well-known from real-world experiences (McGrath, 2013), although each firm naturally possesses these four natural endowments, how well a firm can mobilize these endowments is different from one firm to another. That explains why some firms do well in certain aspects of business while not as well in other aspects. Real-life examples that confirm this end are plentiful. For instance, in any economic sector, there are a few companies that dominate the market while others do not seem prominent or matter at all.

5.10 A Few Final Words

To possibly address the question raised in the beginning of this chapter on how a consumer gathers and comprehends information and then how he makes his consumption decisions, a systemic theory of human cognition is established here. As suggested by the literature (e.g., Forrest & Liu, 2021; Forrest et al., 2020), if economic reasonings can be started with such a theory of cognition as basis and starting point, a good number of thought-provoking, while practically more useful, conclusions can be derived. To see how this end plays out, please move on to the following chapters.

References

Abbate, C. S., Boca, S., & Gendolla, G. H. E. (2016). Self-awareness, perspective-taking, and egocentrism. *Self and Identity, 15*(4), 371–380.

Aristotle. (2016). *Nicomachean ethics* (translated by W. D. Ross with an Introduction by R. W. Browne). Digireads.com.

Aronfreed, J. (1968). *Conduct and conscience: The socialization of internalized control over behavior*. Academic Press.

Bentham, J. (1789). *An introduction to the principles of morals and legislation*. T. Payne and Son.

Bjerknes, V. (1898). Uber einenhydrodynamischenFundamentalsatz und seine Anwendungbesonders auf die Mechanik der Atmosphare und des Weltmeeres. *Kongl Svenska Vetenskaps Akademiens Handlingar, 31*, 1–35.

Branden, N. (1969). *The psychology of self-esteem*. Nash Publishing Corp.

Buss, D. (2004). *Evolutionary psychology: The new science of the mind*. Pearson Education.

Cavell, M. (1998). Triangulation, one's own mind and objectivity. *The International Journal of Psycho-Analysis, 79*(pt3), 449–467.

Christoff, K., Irving, Z. C., Fox, K. C. R., Spreng, R. N., & Andrews-Hanna, J. R. (2016). Mind-wandering as spontaneous thought: A dynamic framework. *Nature Reviews Neuroscience, 17*, 718–731.

Cooke, E. F. (1974). *A detailed analysis of the constitution*. Littlefield Adams.

Covey, S. R. (1989). *The 7 habits of highly effective people: Powerful lessons in personal change*. Free Press.

De Bono, E. (2015). *The mechanism of mind: Understanding how your mind works to maximize memory and creative potential*. Penguin Random House.

Debreu, G. (1959). *Theory of value: An axiomatic analysis of economic equilibrium*. Yale University Press.

Dennett, D. C. (2015). *Elbow room: The varieties of free will worth wanting. A Bradford Book*. MIT Press.

Derbaix, M., & Gombault, A. (2016). Selling the invisible to create an authentic experience: Imagination at work at Cézanne's studio. *Journal of Marketing Management, 32*(15–16), 1458–1477.

Egan, K. (1992). *Imagination in teaching and learning*. University of Chicago Press.

Fahimnia, B., Sarkis, J., & Eshragh, A. (2015). A tradeoff model for green supply chain planning: A leanness-versus-greenness analysis. *Omega, 54*(1), 173–190.
Forrest, J. Y. L. (2018). *General systems theory: Foundation, intuition and applications in business decision making*. Springer.
Forrest, J. Y. L., & Liu, Y. (2021). *Value in business—a holistic, systems-based approach to creating and capturing value*. Springer.
Forrest, J. Y. L., Nicholls, N., Schimmel, K., & Liu, S. F. (2020). *Managerial decision making: A holistic approach*. Springer.
Forrest, J. Y. L., Gong, Z. W., Köse, E., Galbraith, D. D., & Arık, O. A. (2021). An economy's emergent properties and how micro agents with inconsistent or conflicting interests are holistically organized into macro entities. *Našegospodarstvo/Our Economy—Journal of Contemporary Issues in Economics and Business, 63*(3), 53–66.
Forrest, J. Y. L., Shao, L., Liu, J., Sloboda, B. W., & Shao, D. (2023). The meaning of optimum and chosen method of optimization are individually defined. *Pennsylvania Economic Review*. Accepted for publication.
Gerassi, J. (1989). *Jean-Paul Sartre: Hated conscience of his century: Vol. 1. Protestant or protester?* University of Chicago Press.
Gustafsson, R., Jaaskelainen, M., Maula, M., & Uotila, J. (2016). Emergence of industries: A review and future directions. *International Journal of Management Reviews, 18*(1), 28–50. https://doi.org/10.1111/ijmr.12057
Harris, P. (2000). *The work of the imagination*. Wiley-Blackwell.
Hill, N. (1928). *The law of success: In sixteen lessons (reprint of 2007)*. BN Publishing, www.bnpublishing.com.
Kane, R. (2005). *A contemporary introduction to free will*. Oxford University Press.
Kautish, P., & Sharma, S. (2019). Determinants of pro-environmental behavior and environmentally conscious consumer behavior: An empirical investigation from emerging market. *Business Strategy and Development, 3*(1), 112–127.
Klir, G. (1985). *Architecture of systems problem solving*. Plenum Press.
Kuratowski, K., & Mostowski, A. (1976). *Set theory: With an introduction to descriptive set theory*. North-Holland.
Langston, D. C. (2001). *Conscience and other virtues: From Bonaventure to MacIntyre*. Penn State University Press.
LeDoux, J. E., & Brown, R. (2017). A higher-order theory of emotional consciousness. *Proceedings of the National Academy of Sciences of the United States of America, 114*(10), E2016–E2025.
Libet, B. (1999). Do we have free will? *Journal of Consciousness Studies, 6*(8–9), 47–57.
Lin, Y. (1999). *General systems theory: A mathematical approach*. Springer.
Lin, Y. (2008). Systematic studies: The infinity problem in modern mathematics. *Kybernetes: The International Journal of Cybernetics, Systems and Management Sciences, 37*(3–4), 385–542.
Lin, Y., & Forrest, B. (2012). *Systemic structure behind human organizations: From civilizations to individuals*. Springer.
Lin, Y., & OuYang, S. C. (2010). *Irregularities and prediction of major disasters*. Auerbach Publications, An Imprint of Taylor and Francis.
Mandler, G. (1982). The integration and elaboration of memory structures. In F. Klix, J. Hoffman, & E. van der Meer (Eds.), *Cognitive research in psychology* (pp. 33–40). North-Holland.
Markman, G. D., & Waldron, T. L. (2014). Small entrants and large incumbents: A framework of micro entry. *Academy of Management Perspectives, 28*(2), 179–197.
Mas-Collel, A., Whinston, M. D., & Green, J. R. (1995). *Microeconomic theory*. Oxford University Press.
Maslow, A. H. (1943). A theory of human motivation. *Psychological Review, 50*(4), 370–396.
Maslow, A. H. (1954). *Motivation and personality*. Harper.
McFarland, C. P., Primosch, M., Maxson, C. M., & Stewart, B. T. (2017). Enhancing memory and imagination improves problem solving among individuals with depression. *Memory & Cognition, 45*(6), 932–939.

McGrath, R.G. (2013). The End of Competitive Advantage: How to Keep Your Strategy Moving as Fast as Your Business. Boston: Harvard Business Review Press.

Mesarovic, M. D., & Takahara, Y. (1975). *General systems theory: Mathematical foundations*. Academic Press.

Meyers-Levy, J., & Tybout, A. M. (1989). Schema congruity as a basis for product evaluation. *Journal of Consumer Research, 16*(1), 39–54.

Mill, J. S. (1863). *Utilitarianism* (1st ed.). Parker, Son & Bourn, West Strand.

Moran, G. (2018). Chaos theory and psychoanalysis: The fluidic nature of the mind. *Zeitschrift für PsychosomatischeMedizin und Psychoanalyse, 40*(4), 384–403.

Norman, R. (2000). Cultivating imagination in adult education. In *Proceedings of the 41st annual adult education research*.

O'Brien, C. (2008). Sustainable happiness: How happiness studies can contribute to a more sustainable future. *Canadian Psychology, 49*(4), 289–295.

Payne, A., Frow, P., & Eggert, A. (2017). The customer value proposition: Evolution, development, and application in marketing. *Journal of the Academy of Marketing Science, 45*, 467–489.

Pfaff, D. W. (2007). *The neuroscience of fair play: Why we (usually) follow the Golden rule*. Dana Press, The Dana Foundation.

Podolny, J. (1993). A status-based model of market competition. *American Journal of Sociology, 98*, 829–872.

Rosch, E. (1978). Principles of categorization. In E. Rosch & B. B. Lioyd (Eds.), *Cognition and categorization* (pp. 27–48). Lawrence Erlbaum.

Shin, J. E., Suh, E. M., Eom, K., & Kim, H. S. (2018). What does "happiness" prompt in your mind? Culture, word choice, and experienced happiness. *Journal of Happiness Studies, 19*(3), 649–662.

Stayman, D. M., Alden, D. L., & Smith, K. H. (1992). Some effects of schematic processing on consumer expectations and disconfirmation judgments. *Journal of Consumer Research, 19*(2), 240–255. https://doi.org/10.1086/209299

Sujan, M. (1985). Consumer knowledge effects on evaluation strategies mediating consumer judgments. *Journal of Consumer Research, 12*(June), 31–46.

Tinbergen, N. (1951). *The study of instinct*. Oxford University Press.

Uchida, Y., Norasakkunkit, V., & Kitayama, S. (2004). Cultural constructions of happiness: Theory and empirical evidence. *Journal of Happiness Studies, 5*(3), 223–239.

Ugur, H., Constantinescu, P. M., & Stevens, M. J. (2015). Self-awareness and personal growth: Theory and application of Bloom's taxonomy. *Eurasian Journal of Educational Research, 60*, 89–110.

Walsh, L. C., Boehm, J. K., & Lyubomirsky, S. (2018). Does happiness promote career success? Revisiting the evidence. *Journal of Career Assessment, 26*(2), 199–219.

Wu, Y., & Lin, Y. (2002). *Beyond nonstructural quantitative analysis: Blown-ups, spinning currents and the modern science*. World Scientific.

Yazdanparast, A., & Spears, N. (2018). The new me or the me I'm proud of: Impact of objective self-awareness and standards on acceptance of cosmetic procedures. *European Journal of Marketing, 52*(1–2), 279–301.

Zeidman, P., & Maguire, E. A. (2016). Anterior hippocampus: The anatomy of perception, imagination and episodic memory. *Nature Reviews Neuroscience, 17*, 173–182.

Part III
Several Systemic Critiques of Known Theories and Methodologies

Chapter 6
The Need to Include Real-Life Factors in Economic Studies

Jeffrey Yi-Lin Forrest, Kangping Wu, Baek-kyoo Joo, Li Yan, and Kosin Isariyawongse

Abstract By using examples, this chapter, which is mainly based on Forrest et al. (J Bus Econ Technol 25(1):56–67, 2022), demonstrates how some key and useful real-life variables are missing from theoretical studies of economics. It then explains what differences these missing variables can make if one or several of them are considered and included in relevant theories and consequent applications. A comparison with the development of mathematics and physics suggests why it is necessary for economists to identify elementary postulates (in the language of mathematics) and laws (in the language of Newtonian physics) at the level of the four human endowments (self-awareness, imagination, conscience, and free will) as the bases for developing the rest of the theory of economics. To illustrate the potential of this proposal, this chapter uses a theorem with a straightforward argument to demonstrate when a firm experiences organizational inefficiency. Comparing with the literature, the contribution of this chapter is how it considers the general process of decision-making based on the most fundamental systems of values and beliefs of economic agents. By doing so, it will potentially help realize the goals of behavioral economics at the height of analytical analysis with greatly enhanced practical applicability.

Keywords Criteria of priority · Firm's mission · Invisible hand · Measurements of optimization · Organizational inefficiency · Rationality

---

Jeffrey Yi-Lin Forrest (Department of Accounting Economics Finance, Slippery Rock University, Slippery Rock, PA, USA; Email: Jeffrey.forrest@sru.edu), Kangping Wu (Department of Economics, Tsinghua University, Beijing, China; Email: wukp@sem.tsinghua.edu.cn), Baek-kyoo Joo (Department of Management and Marketing, Slippery Rock University, Slippery Rock, PA, USA; Email: baek.joo@sru.edu), Li Yan (Département des Sciences Administratives, Université du Québec en Outaouais, Quebec, Canada; Email: Li.Yan@uqo.ca), and Kosin Isariyawongse (Department of Business and Economics, Edinboro University, Edinboro, PA, USA; Email: kisariyawongse@edinboro.edu) are equally contributed to this chapter.

J. Y.-L. Forrest, *Systemic Principles of Applied Economic Philosophies I*,
Translational Systems Sciences 38, https://doi.org/10.1007/978-981-99-7273-9_6

6.1 Introduction

As the title suggests, this chapter employs a few examples to illustrate how some key and useful real-life factors are not considered in theoretical studies of economics. And by comparing researches of economics with those of mathematics and physics, it points to the necessity of developing economic knowledge through using logical reasoning, which is parallel to that employed in mathematics, and through originating each analysis on some elementary postulates (in the language of mathematics) and/or laws (in the language of Newtonian physics). To this end, this chapter proposes to develop these elementary postulates and/or laws at the level of the four human endowments—self-awareness, imagination, conscience, and free will. This idea is different of that of standard economic models, which are developed on the assumption of a *homo economicus* who is rational and selfish, has computational capability, and never makes mistakes (Cartwright, 2014).

Although what is proposed herein seems to be related to positive/normative economics, the two bear fundamental differences. Specifically, the latter aims to describe and address what various economic programs, scenarios, and environments are and should be (Caplin & Schotter, 2008); this chapter suggests a possibility to reshape the theoretical foundation of economic theories on a more manageable footing by starting all logical reasonings on the four human endowments and relevant elementary facts. By accomplishing this goal, the consequently established theory will be able to avoid the difficulty, facing normative economics, of rigorously explaining problems and issues and the inevitable emphasis on empirical confirmations of the positive economics. The importance of avoiding the difficulty of normative economics is evident for both theoretical and practical purposes. At the same time, although empirical studies are inevitable in economic investigations, economists face the problem of erroneous thinking of the fallacy of composition when general recommendations need to be produced for decision-makers based on empirical discoveries (Finocchiaro, 2015). Historically, this present work is also warranted, if we see the parallelism between the current state of economic and business studies and that when Isaac Newton developed his laws of physics. In particular, presently in the world of business, deluges of data are collected and made available for analysis; and at the time when Newton was developing his laws of motion, large amounts of data were collected and various empirical formulas were proposed by different scholars (Lin, 2009). For more detailed discussions on this parallelism, see Forrest (2022).

If this proposal can be carried out successfully in the years to come, one can expect to improve a current situation of economic studies. In particular, the current situation can be described as follows: although a recognized business success is carefully analyzed, the established theory most likely cannot help reproduce the desired economic outcomes in another business setting at a different geographical location. One good example to illustrate this end is the Industrial Revolution of England. It has been widely investigated and theorized by many scholars over the years. However, when their theories were employed in practice by many developing countries, these countries experienced failures, because the applied theories, no matter which one was adopted, did not really work (Forrest et al., 2018; Wen, 2016).

Specifically, although many human characteristics, such as personal charms and abilities, are not within the purview of economics (Pancs, 2018, p. 5), this chapter uses a fictitious example to illustrate a commonly existing social phenomenon and show that when individuals' wishes are involved, some conclusions in neoclassical economics will be different. The given example demonstrates that when human desires and wishes are involved, the mainstream economics can be further enriched by logical reasonings that start on individuals' systems of values and beliefs.

In terms of the concept of rationality, it is traditionally treated as that of optimization constrained by given conditions (Wu, 2003, 2006). It is later generalized by Herbert A. Simon (Campitelli & Gobet, 2010) when he introduces the concept of bounded rationality as an alternative approach to modeling decision-making; see Hudik (2019) for very nice interpretations of rationality. Along this line of tradition, this chapter proposes that each person in general is rational in his own sense, as defined or bounded by his underlying values and beliefs. When a person makes decision, he reasons simply by retrieving categorized values and beliefs and information in the memory (e.g., Chiou et al., 2018; Sahni, 2016) to quickly optimize the expected potential. Corresponding to their different value-belief systems, individuals use their correspondingly varied methods to optimize utilities, profits, costs, risks, etc., although the stated objective functions might look the same from one economic agent to another.

This chapter points out what issues exist with the analysis of the well-known prisoners' dilemma from the angle of individuals' value-belief systems in general and moral codes in particular. And to demonstrate how our proposed approach will work, this chapter develops a theorem regarding when a firm experiences organizational inefficiency.

In terms of the contribution this study makes to the literature, it can be readily seen that by considering decision-making on the basis of economic agents' most fundamental systems of values and beliefs, the goals of behavioral economics (Zeiler & Teitelbaum, 2018) are naturally carried many steps forward. The agents considered here can be either individuals or firms; and for the latter case, the value-belief systems take the form of organizational cultures that are crystalized as companies' missions (Forrest et al., 2020; McGrath, 2013). In particular, psychological, cognitive, emotional, cultural, and social factors can all be related to the natural human endowments—self-awareness, imagination, conscience ,and free will, on which individuals establish their systems of values and beliefs (Lin & Forrest, 2012).

The rest of this chapter is organized as follows: Sect. 6.2 looks at an example that vividly demonstrates the fact that when individuals pursue their respective selfish good, they do not necessarily achieve the collective best good for all. Section 6.3 uses a directed, weighted network to show that even when economic agents are rational, their rationalities tend to be different from one agent to another so that consequent optimizations used in their decision-making follow different sets of criteria. Section 6.4 pays a revisit to the well-known prisoners' dilemma and shows that this dilemma does not exist if prisoners' systems of values and beliefs are introduced in the analysis of the game. Based on the discussions in the previous sections, Sect. 6.5 proposes to rebuild theories of economics on the basis of the four human endowments—self-awareness, imagination, conscience, and free will—as some of the most basic building blocks. Section 6.6 concludes the presentation of this research.

6.2 Inconsistencies Among Individual Optima

To see such a situation that respective maximizations of individuals' utilities can and do produce collective misery, let us first paraphrase a fictitious scenario constructed initially by Dr. Scott W. Williams of SUNY at Buffalo over 30 years ago when he visited Auburn University, Alabama.

Three friends, named A, B, and C, did some honorable deeds. So, Genie likes to grant each of them a wish. Jumping on the opportunity, A demands that instead of the current location in a remote mountainous area, he wishes he could be living in the middle of a prosperous city center with all the wealth he will ever need in life. Bang, in a fraction of second, A now lives in the condition he wishes for.

Turning to B, Genie asks: "What wish do you like to materialize?" Looking at Genie. B answers: "I don't like to spend any additional single day of my life in this boring country out of nowhere. What I truly love is to live on a beach day after day with many beautiful women around me." Bang, as soon as having finished stating his wishes, B is now sunbathing on a beautiful beach, sipping his favorite drinks while served by many gorgeous women.

Facing C, Genie questions: "What is the wish you like me to grant you?" Without thinking much, C answers, "I really like this mountainous area. The air is always fresh, water is clean, and everything around me is green. So, my wish is that my friends A and B can live with me right here and immerse ourselves in the nature."

What happens next will be either that both A and B will be not happy or C be not happy, because their individual wishes are not consistent and cannot be compromised with each other.

If we use the terminology of utilities, we can model this fictitious scenario in terms of the utility functions U_{i}, i = A, B, C, as follows, where X_{i}, i = A, B, C, represent respectively the consumptions of these people:

$$U_{\mathrm{A}} = U_{\mathrm{A}}(X_{\mathrm{A}}, X_{\mathrm{B}}, X_{\mathrm{C}}), \quad U_{\mathrm{B}} = U_{\mathrm{B}}(X_{\mathrm{B}}, X_{\mathrm{A}}, X_{\mathrm{C}}), \quad U_{\mathrm{C}} = U_{\mathrm{C}}(X_{\mathrm{C}}, X_{\mathrm{A}}, X_{\mathrm{B}}, U_{\mathrm{A}}, U_{\mathrm{B}})$$

satisfying that U_{A}, U_{B}, and U_{C} are increasing functions in X_{A}, X_{B}, and X_{C}, while U_{C} is also a convex function in U_{A} and U_{B}, respectively, so that U_{C} is an increasing function in U_{A} until a given upper bound B_{A} and in U_{B} until a given upper bound B_{B} and then U_{C} becomes a decreasing function in U_{A} and U_{B}, respectively. In this expression, the friendship is reflected in the appearance of individual consumptions in each utility function.

In this modeling, both A and B are self-centered, because their utility functions do not contain the utility of C except their own consumptions. At the same time, C treats both A and B as his friends up to a point. Specifically, after A or B or both of A and B reach certain levels of "success" in life, C starts to feel bad and then worse. In other words, the maximization of C's utility can only be reached when the utilities of friends A and B are not more than their respective upper bounds B_A and B_B, while his diminishing utility cannot be offset by any amount of increasing consumption of goods.

Although the previous example is fictitious, it does depict a huge collection of commonly existing social phenomena in real life, where some people enjoy their respectively increasing utilities through belittling others. Beyond the existence of such people, another fundamental issue not within the purview of economics is individual differences in terms of personal charms, abilities, and other human characteristics (Pancs, 2018, p. 5), most of which are dictated by people's deeply rooted systems of values; and these value systems control what is considered moral or right or wrong in life (Lin & Forrest, 2012). In mathematical terms, this end means that even with the assumption that people do make consumption decisions by maximizing their utilities, the specifically employed criteria of maximization can be totally different from one person to another.

In discussions of economics, the famous "invisible hand" of Adam Smith (1776) originally describes merely how individuals' actions, in terms of production of goods, employment of capital, and domestic industries, that are self-centered without involving any public goods can lead to unintended social benefits. However, such initial description with a well-defined scope has been interpreted over the years in various ways by many different authors in different contexts (too many works to be listed here, so they are all omitted). For example, according to Paul Samuelson's (1998), a 1970 Nobel laureate in economics, writing in 1948, this mystical principle—the existence of the invisible hand—means that when individuals pursue their respective selfish good, they collectively achieve the best good for all. The example we just discussed above clearly and undoubtedly points out the fact that this interpretation of Smith's "invisible hand" is not correct in general. This end is exactly as what Basu (2010) states: Popularizers of economics often misrepresent conditionally-true conclusions of economics in general terms with the underlying conditions ignored. Especially, what is discussed above indicates that when human desires beyond living necessities are involved, the mainstream economics can be further enriched by starting logical reasonings from the basic properties of the human systems of values and beliefs.

6.3 Individually Defined Rationalities

To support the previous claim that even if people make consumption decisions by maximizing their utilities, the specifically employed definitions of maximization can be totally different from one person to another, let us look at the following example, constructed based on Hu (1982) and Lin (1999, p. 136).

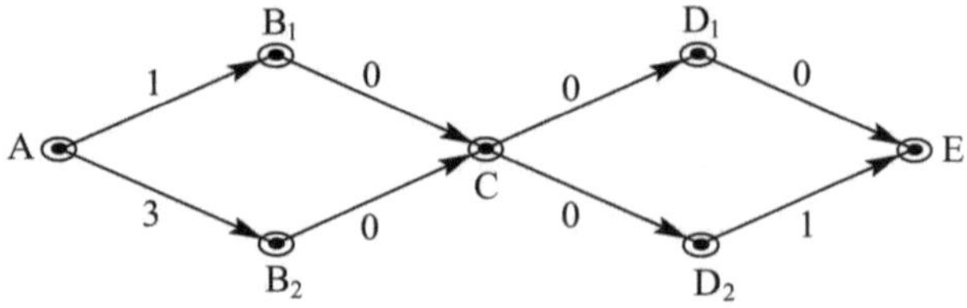

Fig. 6.1 The concept of minimum is defined differently

Assume that the directed and weighted network in Fig. 6.1 represents a production routine of a business operation. The manager likes to find the minimum path that connect node A, representing the start of the production, with node E, the end of the production. If in his calculation the manager orders the real-number weights the same way as how real numbers are conventionally ordered, then the path $A \to B_1 \to C \to D_1 \to E$ is what the manager is looking for. The weight of this path is equal to 1. In comparison, other possible paths from node A to node E have weights 2, 3, and 4, respectively.

However, if in the manager's set of decision criteria there is a mod 4 function, that is, in his set of criteria, for any two real numbers x and y, $x < y$ if and only if $x(\text{mod } 4) < y(\text{mod } 4)$, then the path with the minimum weight is $A \to B_2 \to C \to D_2 \to E$. In particular, the weight of this particular path is $3 + 0 + 0 + 1 = 4\ (\text{mod } 4) = 0$, while other paths respectively have weights 1, 2, or 3.

Speaking differently, what this example demonstrates is that when the criteria of priority are different from one person or business situation to another, the same profit (respectively, cost) function can have totally different maximum (respectively, minimum) values due to the fact that the measurements of optimization are different. Such differences in the measurement of optimization reflect the differences in individuals' systems of value and beliefs.

When looking at a real-life economic process, the mod 4 function in this example can be considered as periodicity 4, where the underlying process repeats itself periodically with period 4. In particular, if we apply this modular function on the time variable underneath an economic process, then the specific period 4 can be replaced by any positive real number r. In this case, it simply means that the economic process starts at time moment 0 and finishes at moment r, from which the process starts all over again to repeat itself. In terms of the consumption of foods, it is not true that the more the better. Instead, the opposite is generally true in real life. In particular, each one-time consumption of any food has to be generally restricted in terms of the amount of intake. Otherwise, the consumer will try to avoid the food completely in the future, although the food used to be his favorite.

With this understanding of the mod(r) function, the timeline (or the real number line) becomes a circle of circumference r on which a point travels one loop after another starting at the origin without end in sight (Fig. 6.2).

To illustrate the concept involved in the previous discussion, let us look at school semesters of an education system. Assume that the student evaluation of every course contains a question on student learning and the effectiveness of professor's

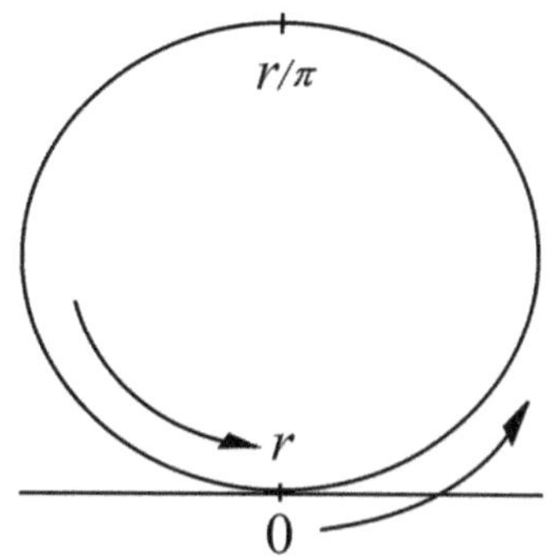

Fig. 6.2 How mod r function is modeled by a point on the circle of radius $r/2\pi$

teaching. Due to differences in the value-belief systems of individual professors, each professor generally employs his unique approach to maximize students' learning. In other words, although each chosen optimum approach comes out of the same objective function, different personal systems of value and beliefs lead to different optimal outcomes. In this example, the length of one school semester is the period, over which professors seek for their individually unique ways to deliver their effective teaching and produce the maximal student learning.

To summarize, instead of assuming that every economic agent is rational in a universally accepted sense and makes decisions by optimizing his expected outcomes through using tools from a defined set of approaches (Campus, 1987), the more realistic situation is the following:

> Each person has his own specific system of value and beliefs (Lin & Forrest, 2012). When a person makes decision, he optimizes the given situation by using his underlying individually specific criteria rooted in the person's system of value and beliefs.

To this end, one might challenge by asking: How can you explain impulsive purchase decisions, which later turn out to be against some of the underlying values or beliefs of the purchaser? Such purchases generally end up in one of two possibilities: the purchased good is returned or it is not used for the originally expected purpose. In either case, the violated values and beliefs are corrected.

More specifically, the aforementioned assumption of universally accepted rational agents implicitly means the existence of an external system of measurement, which judges whether a particular behavior is rational or the procedure of optimization is gone through universally no matter who is conducting the optimization. In the contrary, the realistic situation, as given above, assumes away any external measurement system and allows economic agents to optimize their objective functions by using their individually different sets of criteria; and these criteria are developed out of these individuals' underlying systems of value and beliefs. Because of this reason, to deal with a situation of concern, different economic agents take their individually different optimization approaches. These differences in approaches then lead to drastically different outcomes due to diversely dissimilar courses of actions taken. In short, what is considered optimal is different from one economic agent to another; and instead of being universal, the used methods of optimization are in fact also different from one decision-maker to another.

In terms of the literature, the concept of rationality has been studied in many fields of knowledge, including, but not limited to, economics (e.g., Krugman & Wells, 2017), game theory (e.g., Osborne & Rubinstein, 2001), decision science (e.g., Parmigiani & Inoue, 2009), artificial intelligence (e.g., Russell & Norvig, 2003), cognitive science (e.g., Varela et al., 1991), ethics (e.g., Ferrell et al., 2018), and philosophy (e.g., Bourdieu, 1998). In particular, in the context of economics, a customer is considered rational, if he has clear preferences, handles uncertainties by using functions of variables, and takes actions to optimize expected outcomes for him from among all feasible possibilities. When such a concept of rationality is employed to develop a scholarly body of knowledge as one of the fundamental building blocks, one can readily see that the knowledge will not be adequate enough to capture a major part of the reality. It is because in real life many decisions are made under the dominating influence of psychological, cognitive, emotional, cultural, and social factors. The realization of such challenge has led to the development of behavioral economics (Teitelbaum & Zeiler, 2019) in order to study the effects of psychological, cognitive, emotional, cultural, and social factors on the decisions of individuals and institutions and how such decisions vary from those implied by classical economic theory (Zeiler & Teitelbaum, 2018).

Since psychological, cognitive, emotional, cultural, and social factors are associated with the content in the value-belief system of a decision-maker for these factors to be part of decision-making (Lin & Forrest, 2012), we propose that each person in general is rational in his own sense as defined by his underlying values and beliefs. When a person makes decision, he reasons by retrieving categorized values and beliefs and information in the memory to quickly optimize the expected potential. This end has been confirmed repeatedly by scholars in the area of the categorization paradigm of the marketing research (e.g., Chiou et al., 2018; Mandler, 1982; Moss, 2009; Nedungadi,1990; Sahni, 2016; Sujan, 1985) and by studies of politics and the science of mind (Lakoff & Wehling, 2016). Because individuals have their own different systems of values and beliefs, the methods individuals use to optimize utilities, profits, costs, risks, etc. have to be different from one another although the stated objective function might look the same, as demonstrated by the previous example. That explains why a perfect logical reasoning in one person's standard, such as Donald Trump's handling of national and international affairs during his presidency from 2017 to 2021, can be seen as irrational in many other people's eyes.

6.4 A Critical Revisit to Prisoners' Dilemma

Before we present our suggestion on using human systems of values and beliefs as a fundamental building block of economic theories, let us first look at issues with the prisoners' dilemma (Poundstone, 1993). To make our points cross more easily, let us first outline the related details.

Two members of a gang are arrested and placed in solitary detention so that they cannot communicate with each other. Without adequate evidence to convict them on the principal charge other than a lesser charge, the prosecutors offer each gang member a bargain opportunity: betray the other by testifying the other's committing the crime, or remain silent. The associated payoffs are given below, where each negative number standards for the number of years in prison.

		B's choice	
		Stay silent	Betray
A's choice	Stay silent	−1, −1	−3, 0
	Betray	0, −3	−2, −2

The conventional study of this game assumes that the prisoners will not be rewarded or punished in any other way than what is given here. So, if the prisoners are rational, betraying the other is the only optimal choice. As a consequence, both of these prisoners serve 2 years in prison. That is worse outcome than that if they both stay silent cooperatively.

With the given assumptions, the analysis of this game is perfect. However, the very problem with this dilemma that disagrees with what often happens in real life appears with the assumptions, because in real life people make decisions by using their systems of values and beliefs instead of merely considering self-centered payoffs based on the so-called rationality. In other words, people generally do not make decisions that are against their moral codes rooted in their systems of values and beliefs even when offered with rewards. That explains why in real life, people tend to be biased towards behaving cooperatively instead of individually maximizing their own utilities without considering consequences others have to bear (Fehr & Fischbacher, 2003). Besides from the bias toward behaving cooperatively, there is also a part of conscience that could play a role in decision-making because betraying a close associate is generally regarded as a selfish or immoral act. On top of that, there may be a fear for revenge when the other gang member is released from the prison, which is also part of the imagination (Lin & Forrest, 2012).

Beyond what is presented above in terms of how some key real-life factors are not considered in theoretical studies of economics and business, another interesting observation is that scholars in economics commonly use such words as "believe," "should," "would," and "might." That is very different from how scientists speak in affirmative tones when they talk about their derived conclusions and established results. By comparing mathematics/physics and economics, one can readily see some major differences between the two. For example, for the former case, scholars traditionally investigate totally abstract concepts or lifeless objects, the associations among the concepts, and the operational laws underneath the evolution of physical things. They develop the consequent bodies of knowledge based on some basic postulates and the laws through logical reasoning. The magnificent success of this approach has been well confirmed by the recent scientific history and rapid development of technology of the past several hundred years. On the other hand, studies of economics do not evolve in the same way as that of mathematics and physics, as described above, due to the reason that as of this writing, those very elementary laws or postulates that are underneath mostly seen economic activities have not been identified and established.

The aforementioned differences between mathematics/physics and economics lead to quite varied practical consequences. For example, when a mathematical theorem is established, different mathematicians will be able to reestablish the result without knowing exactly how the theorem was initially proved, even though these mathematicians might experience some great difficulties to accomplish this end. Similarly, when a physical gadget is produced, other people will be able to develop gadgets with almost identical functionalities although these people do not know exactly how the initial gadget was designed and produced. On the other hand, for applications of economics theories, the situation is completely different. For example, by carefully analyzing business successes and by theorizing the reasons behind a business success, people most likely cannot reproduce the desired economic outcomes in another business setting at a different geographical location. To this end, one good example is the Industrial Revolution of England. It has been widely investigated and theorized by many scholars over the years. However, when their theories were employed in practice by many developing countries, these countries experienced failures, because the applied theories did not really work (Forrest et al., 2018; Wen, 2016).

6.5 Choice of Human Natural Endowments as Potential Starts of Theories

Following the discussions in the previous sections, this section demonstrates how individuals' systems of values and beliefs can be theoretically employed to establish new insights of economics. It attempts to show that what we propose here will go beyond what Cartwright (2014) states about behavioral economics—it analyzes the psychological underpinnings of human economic behaviors; it will improve economics on its own term. Related to this claim, in the fields of management and organizational behaviors, the fit between person and organization (PO fit) has been widely recognized since late 1980s and early 1990s. It is defined as the similarity between the characteristics of people and corresponding characteristics of organizations (Kristof, 1996). More specific, this concept refers to the alignment or congruence between characteristics of employees (i.e., personality, preferences, attributes, and perceptions) and those of organizations (i.e., business strategy, values, culture, and leadership) (Chatman, 1989; Joo, 2020; Kristof, 1996).

Before we can present related details, let us look at two concepts—a firm's mission and organizational inefficiency. First, for each firm, its mission clearly spells out the firm's purpose (including its values and beliefs), what it does, and what the targeted market segment it serves (McGrath, 2013). The goal of the firm is to maximize the realization of its business objective, as given in the mission statement, which might be making as much profit as possible, contributing to the wellbeing of the society as much as possible or others. Because different people have different underlying systems of values and beliefs (Lin & Forrest, 2012), each firm that desires to succeed in the marketplace needs to have a mission (statement) to unify these individually different systems of values and beliefs (Forrest, 2018; Forrest & Orvis, 2016). Second, by organizational efficiency, it is defined (Forrest & Orvis, 2016) as such a state of a firm that all employees help their firm reach the objectives stated in the firm's mission. So, a firm is said to be (organizationally) efficient, if all employees help the firm approach or actualize the firm's mission in one way or another. Otherwise, the firm is said to be inefficient. The following theorem confirms the existence of organizational inefficiency, assuming that the criteria a focal firm employs to maximize its business objective, as clearly spelled in its mission, follow the conventional ordering of real numbers. For more in-depth discussion along this line, please consult with Chap. 17 in this volume.

Theorem 6.1 If the value-belief system of a full-time employee is not in total agreement with his firm's mission, then the firm naturally experiences organizational inefficiency.

Proof By contradiction, assume the opposite is true. That is, there is such a firm within which the value-belief system of its full-time employee k is not in total agreement with the firm's mission. Hence, there is a variable Y that measures one aspect of k's personal values and beliefs such that the utility of k increases with Y while the work efficiency of k in terms of helping realize the mission of his firm decreases with Y. In real life, although it is very possible that this variable Y cannot be explicitly measured or even defined, its existence is definitely unquestionable. For example, when an employee goes through his annual performance evaluation, written comments generally reflect the totality of those underlying implicit measures of the evaluator.

Symbolically, what are assumed here can be written as follows:

$$U_k = U_k(X_k, Y),\ \text{satisfying}\ \frac{\partial U_k}{\partial X_k} > 0\ \text{and}\ \frac{\partial U_k}{\partial Y} > 0, \tag{6.1}$$

where U_k is k's utility function andX_k stands for k's total consumption. Moreover, the objective function Obj of the firm can be respectively written as follows:

$$\text{Obj} = \text{Obj}(X_c, U_k, U_1, U_2, \ldots),\ \text{satisfying}\ \frac{\partial \text{Obj}}{\partial X_c} > 0,\ \frac{\partial \text{Obj}}{\partial U_i} > 0,\ i = k, 1, 2, \ldots, \tag{6.2}$$

where X_c stands for the aggregated expenditure of the firm, including the monetary expenses on all employees except k, and U_1, U_2, …represent all other employees' utilities. Because this objective function is an increasing function in every employee's utility, the firm keeps its employees' well-being as part of its business objectives.

The monetary bonus that measures the work efficiency of k is written as follows:

$$B_k = B_k(Y), \quad \text{satisfying } \frac{dB_k}{dY} < 0. \tag{6.3}$$

Once again, the existence of the variable Y might only exist implicitly and cannot be measured readily in real life. However, its negative effect on the work quality and efficiency generally can be clearly seen by other people of the firm. Hence, for this symbolic proof, without loss of generality we assume that Y can be measured and used in determining the amount of employee k's monetary bonus.

The firm distributes its monetary resources to its employees by maximizing its objective function Obj in Eq. (6.2) subject to the budgetary constraint below:

$$X_c + X_k = X_c + (I_k + B_k), \tag{6.4}$$

where I_k stands for k's base salary from the firm. By maximizing the firm' objective function, Eq. (6.2), subject to the budgetary constraint, Eq. (6.4), the following appear

$$\frac{\partial X_k}{\partial Y} > 0 \quad \text{and} \quad \frac{\partial X_k}{\partial Y} = \frac{\partial B_k}{\partial Y} < 0, \tag{6.5}$$

a contradiction. This end implies that the firm that satisfies the given conditions is organizationally efficient is incorrect.

According to Lin and Forrest (2012), for each person, his system of values and beliefs is systemically developed over time on the four human endowments—self-awareness, imagination, conscience, and free will. Hence, all the discussions above points to that it will be adequate to employ human endowments as the starting postulates for us to develop theories of economics.

Note: In the proof of Theorem 6.1, we maximized the focal firm's objective function. Corresponding to this optimization, in economics, there is such a long-standing convention that firms' objective is to maximize their profits (Wu, 2006). In reality, however, are business firms truly place profit maximization as its primary objective? There has been a substantial debate on this issue (e.g., Hussain, 2012; Jensen, 2001). Recently, a group of powerful US chief executives abandoned the idea that companies must maximize profits for shareholders above all else (https://opportunity.businessroundtable.org/ourcommitment/, accessed on January 30, 2021). "Americans deserve an economy that allows each person to succeed through hard work and creativity and to lead to a life of meaning and dignity" and "we commit to deliver value to all of them, for the future success of our companies, our communities, and our country," said the statement from the organization (https://s3.amazonaws.com/brt.org/BRT-StatementonthePurposeofaCorporationOctober2020.pdf, accessed on January 30, 2021), chaired by JP Morgan Chase CEO Jamie Dimon.

The reason why many managers and executives do not put profit maximization as the number 1 priority can be explained by the four human endowments—self-awareness, imagination, conscience, and free will. In particular, the conscience of these decision-makers makes them want to contribute more to their respective communities, such as donations and offering various kinds of necessary supports to their communities. This end also supports the notion that how an individual behaves is dictated by his value-belief system.

6.6 A Few Final Words

This chapter examines examples on how the mainstream economics can be enriched if (1) personal wishes are considered as one of the decision-making criteria, or (2) rationality is seen as respectively bounded by individuals' value-belief systems, or (3) moral codes are treated as the foundation behind decision-making and the taking of particular actions. By summarizing the analyses of these examples, this chapter proposes that each person in general is rational in his own sense, as defined and bounded by his underlying values and beliefs. When a person makes decision, he reasons simply by retrieving categorized values, beliefs, and information in the memory (e.g., Chiou et al., 2018; Sahni, 2016) to quickly determine the optimal expected potential. What is particularly important is that corresponding to their different value-belief systems, individuals use their correspondingly varied methods to optimize utilities, profits, costs, risks, etc., although the stated objective functions might look the same from one economic agent to another. Speaking differently, the mainstream economics implicitly assumes the existence of an external reference frame, which dictates what is considered rational and how optimization is carried out. Contrary to this assumption, this chapter suggests that the real-life situation is the following: instead of the existence of such an external reference frame, each decision-making entity is its own reference frame that determines the meanings of rationality and optimality and the consequent method of optimization.

Because each person's system of values and beliefs is determined by the contents of his particular endowments—self-awareness, imagination, conscience, and free will (Lin & Forrest, 2012)—this chapter proposes to identify elementary postulates (if speaking in the language of mathematics) and/or laws (if speaking in the language of Newtonian physics) of economics at the level of these endowments. On the bases of these postulates and laws, the entire edifice of economics will be constructed in such a way that each time when a new concept is introduced, relevant results and knowledge will be established by logical reasoning that traces back to some of the postulates and laws. By doing so, many of the inconsistent results, developed by different scholars over time, such as those in the studies of the Industrial Revolution (e.g., Rostow, 1960), and many endless and emotional debates, where debaters generally base their arguments on some empirical conclusions (e.g., Andreoni & Chang, 2019), can be affirmatively settled.

As for potential future works along the line developed in this chapter, one can first identify the aforementioned postulates and laws. And then, similarly to how Theorem 6.1 is established, all other known theorems of economics can be reformulated on the bases of the identified postulates and laws. Doing so will inevitably help uncover new results. By referencing to the magnificent successes of mathematics and physics, one can expect that the economics knowledge established in the fashion just described here will possess a much wider range of practical applications.

References

Andreoni, A., & Chang, H. J. (2019). The political economy of industrial policy: Structural interdependencies, policy alignment and conflict management. *Structural Change and Economic Dynamics, 48*, 136–150.

Basu, K. (2010). *Beyond the invisible hand: Groundwork for a new economics*. Princeton University Press.

Bourdieu, P. (1998). Practical reason: On the theory of action (R. Johnson, Trans.). Stanford University Press.

Campitelli, G., & Gobet, F. (2010). Herbert Simon's decision-making approach: Investigation of cognitive processes in experts. *Review of General Psychology, 14*(4), 354–364.

Campus, A. (1987). Marginal economics. *The New Palgrave: A Dictionary of Economics, 3*, 323.

Caplin, A., & Schotter, A. (Eds.). (2008). *The foundations of positive and normative economics: A handbook*. Oxford University Press.

Cartwright, E. (2014). *Behavioral economics* (2nd ed.). Routledge.

Chatman, J. A. (1989). Improving interactional organizational research: A model of person-organization fit. *Academy of Management Review, 14*, 333–349.

Chiou, J. S., Hsiao, C. C., & Chiu, T. Y. (2018). The credibility and attribution of online reviews: Differences between high and low product knowledge consumers. *Online Information Review, 42*(5), 630–646.

Fehr, E., & Fischbacher, U. (2003). The nature of human altruism. *Nature, 425*(6960), 785–791.

Ferrell, O. C., Fraedrich, J., & Ferrel, L. (2018). *Business ethics: Ethical decision making and cases* (12th ed.). Cengage Learning.

Finocchiaro, M. A. (2015). The fallacy of composition: Guiding concepts, historical cases, and research problems. *Journal of Applied Logic, 13*(2, Part B), 24–43.

Forrest, J. Y. L. (2018). *General systems theory; foundation, intuition and applications in business decision making*. Springer.

Forrest, J. Y. L. (2022). Reestablishing the producer theory on the basis of firms' natural endowments. *Pure Mathematics and Applied Mathematics, 38*(3), 322–343.

Forrest, J. Y. L., & Orvis, B. (2016). Principles of management efficiency and organizational inefficiency. *Kybernetes, 45*(8), 1308–1322.

Forrest, J. Y. L., Zhao, H. C., & Shao, L. (2018). Engineering rapid industrial revolutions for impoverished agrarian nations. *Theoretical Economics Letters, 8*, 2594–2640. https://doi.org/10.4236/tel.2018.811166

Forrest, J. Y. L., Nicholls, N., Schimmel, K., & Liu, S. F. (2020). *Managerial decision making: A holistic approach*. Springer.

Forrest, J. Y. L., Wu, K. P., Joo, B. K., Yan, L., & Kosin Isariyawongse, K. (2022). Scenarios not adequately addressed by economic theories. *Journal of Business, Economics and Technology, 25*(1), 56–67.

Hu, T. C. (1982). *Combinatorial algorithms*. Addison-Wesley.

Hudik, M. (2019). Two interpretations of the rational choice theory and the relevance of behavioral critique. *Rationality and Society, 31*(4), 464–489.

Hussain, W. (2012). Corporations, profit maximization and the personal sphere. *Economics and Philosophy, 28*(3), 311–331.

Jensen, M. (2001). Value maximization, stakeholder theory, and the corporate objective function. *European Financial Management, 7*(3), 297–317.

Joo, B.-K. (2020). Positive organizational behavior: What's in it for HRD in South Korea? In D. H. Lim, S. W. Yoon, & D. Cho (Eds.), *Human resource development in South Korea* (pp. 197–217). Palgrave Macmillan.

Kristof, A. L. (1996). Person-organization fit: An integrative review of its conceptualization, measurement, and implications. *Personnel Psychology, 49*, 1–49.

Krugman, P., & Wells, R. (2017). *Economics* (5th ed.). Worth Publishers.

Lakoff, G., &Wehling, E. (2016). *Your Brian's politics: How the science of mind explains the political divide*. Societas essays in political &cultural criticism, imprint-academic.com.

Lin, Y. (1999). *General systems theory: A mathematical approach*. Kluwer Academic/Plenum Publishers.

Lin, Y. (2009). *Systemic yoyos: Some impacts of the second dimension*. CRC Press.

Lin, Y., & Forrest, B. (2012). *Systemic structure behind human organizations: From civilizations to individuals*. Springer.

Mandler, G. (1982). The integration and elaboration of memory structures. In F. Klix, J. Hoffman, & E. van der Meer (Eds.), *Cognitive research in psychology* (pp. 33–40). North-Holland.

McGrath, R. G. (2013). *The end of competitive advantage: How to keep your strategy moving as fast as your business*. Harvard Business Review Press.

Moss, G. (2009). *Gender, design and marketing: How gender drives our perception of design and marketing*. Routledge.

Nedungadi, P. (1990). Recall and consumer consideration sets: Influencing choice without altering brand evaluations. *Journal of Consumer Research, 17*(3), 263–276.

Osborne, M., & Rubinstein, A. (2001). *A course in game theory*. MIT Press.

Pancs, R. (2018). *Lectures on microeconomics: The big questions approach*. The MIT Press.

Parmigiani, G., & Inoue, L. (2009). *Decision theory: Principles and approaches*. Wiley.

Poundstone, W. (1993). *Prisoner's dilemma* (1st Anchor Books ed.). Anchor.

Rostow, W. W. (1960). *The stages of economic growth: A non-communist manifesto*. Cambridge University Press.

Russell, S. J., & Norvig, P. (2003). *Artificial intelligence: A modern approach* (2nd ed.). Prentice Hall.

Sahni, N. S. (2016). Advertising spillovers: Evidence from online field experiments and implications for returns on advertising. *Journal of Marketing Research, 53*(4), 459–478.

Samuelson, P. A. (1998). *Economics: The original1948 Edition*. McGraw-Hill.

Smith, A. (1776). *The wealth of nations*, books IV (1986 printing). Penguin Books.

Sujan, M. (1985). Consumer knowledge effects on evaluation strategies mediating consumer judgments. *Journal of Consumer Research, 12*, 31–46.

Teitelbaum, J. C., & Zeiler, K. (2019). *Research handbook on behavioral law and economics*. Edward Elgar Publishing.

Varela, F. J., Thompson, E., & Rosch, E. (1991). *The embodied mind: Cognitive science and human experience*. MIT Press.

Wen, Y. (2016). *The making of an economic superpower: Unlocking China's secret of rapid industrialization*. World Scientific.

Wu, K. P. (2003). *Advanced microeconomics*. Tsinghua University Press.

Wu, K. P. (2006). *Advanced macroeconomics*. Tsinghua University Press.

Zeiler, K., & Teitelbaum, J. (2018). *Research handbook on behavioral law and economics*. Edward Elgar Publishing.

Chapter 7
Each Customer Defines What Is Optimal and How to Optimize

Jeffrey Yi-Lin Forrest, Ashkan Hafezalkotob, Louie Ren, Yong Liu, and Pavani Tallapally

Abstract This chapter, which is mainly based on Forrest et al. (Rev Econ Bus Stud 14(2):125–149, 2021), investigates how a consumer's utility and consequent optimization are determined by his natural endowments—self-awareness, imagination, conscience, and free will. It focuses on such general utility that is a function in the dollar value of consumption, the number of hours spent on waged work, and a particular value-belief system. For the third variable, we examine that it encourages the consumption of commodities and devalues waged job; it reinforces the practice of minimal commodity consumption; and it demands a nonstandard optimization. This chapter uncovers how an individual's marginal utility from commodity consumption or waged work varies respectively with different variables, such as non-waged incomes, expense of leisure, hours spent on waged work, etc. At the same time, it demonstrates that when an individual decides on how much commodity is to be consumed and how much labor output is to be supplied to waged work by maximizing the corresponding utility, the person's utility and his method of optimization are exclusively defined by his value-belief system.

Keywords Consumption decision · Cost-and-benefit analysis · Leisure · Minimalist · Method of optimization · Optimal course of action

Jeffrey Yi-Lin Forrest (Department of Accounting Economics Finance, Slippery Rock University, Slippery Rock, PA, USA; Email: Jeffrey.forrest@sru.edu), Ashkan Hafezalkotob (Department of Management and Human Resources, La Trobe University, Melbourne, VIC, Australia; Email: A.HafezAlkotob@latrobe.edu.au), Louie Ren (School of Business Administration, University of Houston—Victoria, Victoria, TX, USA; Email: ren800us@yahoo.com), Yong Liu (School of Business, Jiangnan University, Wuxi, Jiangsu, China; Email: clly1985528@163.com), and Pavani Tallapally (Department of Accounting Economics Finance, Slippery Rock University, Slippery Rock, PA, USA; Email: Pavani.tallapally@sru.edu) are equally contributed to this chapter.

J. Y.-L. Forrest, *Systemic Principles of Applied Economic Philosophies I*, Translational Systems Sciences 38, https://doi.org/10.1007/978-981-99-7273-9_7

7.1 Introduction

In studies of economic and social behaviors, a commonly employed approach is to first introduce an objective function, such as a utility function, a production function, a profit function, etc., and then based on some kind cost-and-benefit analysis of the underlying economic agent, this objective function is optimized (e.g., Friedman, 1953; Gilboa, 2010; Gul & Pesendorfer, 2008). However, such an approach does not capture real-life scenarios, although it has been repeatedly confirmed with falsified empirical evidence, as so criticized by behavioral economists (e.g., Mullainathan & Thaler, 2000; Kahneman, 2011). Hence, the following question arises naturally at the most fundamental level underneath all investigations of economic and social behaviors, if one focuses only on the micro-level of individuals: Does an economic man really go through such a general procedure when he decides on what to do in terms of making a consumption decision?

The importance of this question is well witnessed by the vast amount of related literature in the name of rationality, where the aforementioned, commonly employed approach in studies of economic and social behaviors is widely known as the assumption of rationality.[1] Although such rationality has been criticized only in recent decades by behavioral economists, some degrees of an inherent uncertainty this assumption implicitly embodies has been broadly felt and explored by a good number of leading scholars (Hudik, 2019), including, among numerous others, Gary Becker (1962), Frank Lovett (2006), Fritz Machlup (1946), Ariel Rubinstein (1998), Paul Samuelson (1948), Herbert Simon (1986), Thurstone (1931), Max Weber (1949), and Glen Weyl (2019). In summary, after using this approach for so many decades, scholars are still debating on what the assumption of rationality really means (Hudik, 2019). This end indirectly explains the reason why a compelling need for a meaningful reconstruction of economic theory has been called for by recent events, in particular, the 2008 financial crisis. For example, considering the inability for existing economic theories to describe, to predict, and to explain in a timely manner in the front of the recent financial turmoil, Paul Krugman commented as follows in *New York Times* (2009-09-02):

> The economic profession went astray because economists, as a group, mistook beauty, clad in impressive-looking mathematics, for truth ... As memories of the Depression faded, economists fell back in love with the old, idealized vision of an economy in which rational individuals interact in perfect markets ... Unfortunately, this romanticized and sanitized vision of the economy led most economists to ignore ... things that can go wrong. They turned a blind eye to the limitations of human rationality that often leads to bubbles and

[1] This is the meaning of rationality addressed in this chapter, in Hudik (2012) and in Maialeh (2019), although a more recent definition concerns with such a consumer preference relation that is both complete and transitive (Mandler, 2001; McKenzie, 2010). Evidently, this newer version of rationality cannot hold true in real life, because each consumer is also a biological being; his physiological needs are multidimensional, where possible consumptions from different dimensions cannot be directly compared in terms of consumption preferences. For a related but different argument about why consumption preferences cannot be complete, see Ok (2002).

> burst; to the problem of institutions that run amok; to the imperfection of markets . . . that can cause the economy . . . to undergo sudden, unpredictable crashes; and to the dangers created when regulators don't believe in regulation.

while Paul De Grauwe wrote the following in *Financial Times* (2009-07-21):

> Mainstream (economic) models take the view that economic agents are superbly inform and understand the deep complexities of the world ... they have "rational expectations" . . . they all understand the same "truth", they all act the same way. Thus modelling the behavior of just one agent (the "representative" consumer and the "representative" producer) is all one has to do to fully describe the intricacies of the world. Rarely has such a ludicrous idea been taken so seriously by so many academics.

This chapter aims at addressing the aforementioned question of fundamental importance by basing our reasoning and analysis on the four natural endowments of human beings: self-awareness, imagination, conscience, and free will. To do this, we focus on the study of such general utility of an individual as an explicit function in the dollar value of total consumption, the number of hours spent on waged work, and the person's particular system of values and beliefs. More specifically, the third variable is categorical and mostly not known to others and maybe in many cases even not known to the person himself involved. We examine the following values of this variable individually one by one:

1. The system positively values the consumption of commodities while treating waged work negatively.
2. The system believes in minimal commodity consumption, under which the following two subcases are detailed: (a) the individual maximally enjoys providing his labor on the waged work and (b) the person likes to supply as little labor as possible to his waged work.
3. The system demands for a nonstandard method of optimization of the established utility function.

By basing our reasoning and analysis on the novel ground of natural human endowments, this chapter establishes a series of formal propositions, some of which, among others, reveal how an individual's marginal utility of commodity consumption and that of working on waged work vary respectively with (a) the income from non-waged sources, (b) the number of hours spent on waged work, (c) hourly wage rate, (d) additional savings, (e) unit commodity price, and (f) expense on leisure. By comparing these results with each other, it can be readily seen that within different systems of values and beliefs, the identified utility function behaves differently. Most importantly, such comparison and several constructed examples collectively demonstrate that when an individual decides on how much commodity is to be consumed and how much labor output is to be supplied to his waged work by maximizing the corresponding utility subject to existing constraints, the individual's utility and his method of optimization are exclusively defined by his value-belief system. In other words, this chapter contributes to the literature through supporting Simon's (1986) claim that the widely adopted rationality is about the decision behaviors of individuals and Rubinstein's (1998) belief that the selected option is most preferred among available alternatives, where preference is defined by the individual's natural endowments. This end differs majorly from the well-adopted definition of rationality—maximize an individual's advantage based on cost-and-benefit analysis (e.g., Friedman, 1953).

The rest of this chapter is organized as follows. Section 7.2 examines how and why each individual has his own unique system of values and beliefs regarding how the world functions, what are considered either right or wrong and to what degree, and where the person is positioned in the myriad of things in the world. Section 7.3 looks at such a situation that a person's value-belief system positively values the consumption of commodities while seeing waged job negatively. Section 7.4 considers the scenario that an individual's value-belief system believes in minimal commodity consumption. Section 7.5 investigates scenarios involving nonstandard optimizations of utilities that lead to the conclusion that both utility and method of optimization are exclusively determined by the value-belief system of the individual involved. Section 7.6 concludes this chapter while pointing to potential future problems for research.

7.2 Different Individuals Have Different Value-Belief Systems

As suggested by the title, this section argues for that each person has his individually specific system of values and beliefs.

Proposition 7.1 Through employing self-awareness, a person scrutinizes his feelings, judgments, and thoughts; and then he decides on how to properly answer the challenge in hands by reference to what have been learned before.

To see why this conclusion is true, let us first recognize that a person's self-awareness comes into being from constant interactions of the systemic yoyo structure of his mind with those of all other people and things in the environment. In particular, the yoyo field of a focal person's mind constantly takes part in exchanges with other fields in the environment. It absorbs and simultaneously gives off things that can take physical, intellectual, tangible, intangible, or epistemological forms. Hence, between and among the yoyo fields of different systems, there are constantly thrusts against each other and pulls that attract various yoyo fields towards each other. The thrusts make the focal person feel that he is a separate entity from other people and things, and the pulls create for the person the sensation of individual rights and privileges.

With age, the focal person acquires the necessary knowledge about how to satisfactorily handle various elements of the environment to yield desirable outcomes. When facing an unprecedented situation, the person can take one of the following two possible approaches:

1. He experiences anxiety and then receives help from others either proactively or passively.
2. He associates the present issue with some previously seen scenarios that are more or less related to the current situation.

No matter which approach is taken, the person organizes his feelings, judgments, and thoughts to settle on a reasonable course of actions by jointly applying other endowments: imagination, conscience, and free will.

To summarize, it is through various interactions with the yoyo fields of different people, events, thoughts, etc. that the focal person gains an understanding of himself, other people, and various situations and challenges. That is, with age, the person develops a reservoir of increasing magnitude, consisting of information, experience, and knowledge. One can refer to these elements as freely and as many times as needed, and what action is considered proper is judged by the person's philosophical system of values and beliefs.

At this mental stage, the endowment "imagination" comes into play. It helps the person acquire a good command over the elements within the reservoir so that he can associate the reservoir's elements in various ways imaginable. In other words, imagination can be systemically seen as the studio of mind. In this studio, information, images, experiences, concepts, and facts are associated with each other in different ways, constituting a dynamically living whole. When needed, these elements of the reservoir are innovatively reconvened and placed into new uses. As Hill (1928) phrases, this systemic whole is referred to as the creative power of the soul.

Similar to Proposition 5.6, we have

Proposition 7.2 When a person faces a situation, he mobilizes the natural endowment of self-awareness to match the situation of concern with elements in the imagination's studio so that an appropriate resolution can be potentially produced.

To argue for the correctness of this result, let us continue the aforementioned systemic yoyo model of self-awareness in the analysis of Proposition 7.1. Doing so will demonstrate that imagination is another natural consequence of the yoyo structure of mind. Specifically, the yoyo structure of a person's mind is a complex spinning field, involving many different dimensions. That is, this systemic structure involves a great number of different variables, which jointly contribute to the complexity of the systemic structure. Additionally, this structure of mind is made much more complex than it appears, where a great deal of the yoyo field structures and systemic interactions that exist in the world cannot be readily detected by human biological sense organs. Speaking differently, the construction of a yoyo field indicates that when systemic yoyos interact with each other, the forces of both thrusts and pulls coexist. Hence, relentless interactions between the yoyo field of a person's mind and those of other entities of the physical and intellectual world provide an enormous amount of experiences and knowledge that is way beyond what the person's sense organs can collect. Hence, this systemic analysis implies that imagination is such an organized system whose component parts include all the conscious and unconscious records of the interactions between the underlying yoyo

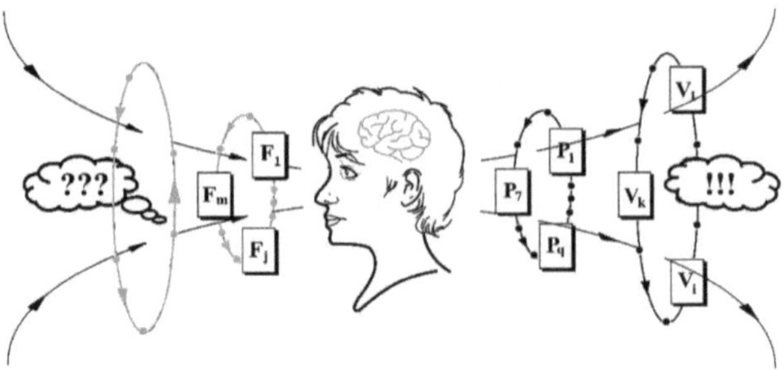

Fig. 7.1 The reflective nature of the mind

field and others. A record is considered conscious, if it is collected through human sense organs; otherwise it is an unconscious record.

When a situation arises in a person's pursuit of happiness (Proposition 5.1), he maps the situation onto elements in the structured reservoir of imagination by mobilizing the faculty of self-awareness. The level of how well the person can mobilize this faculty governs how deeply and widely he can reach into and establish associations within this reservoir, demonstrating the importance of education. That consequently leads to the provocative quality of established concepts and images. A graphic representation of this mapping from the physical and intellectual nature onto a person's cognitive system is given in Fig. 7.1. In particular, the seemingly infinite and boundless environment is both visually and conceptually seen as a hierarchical network with the family setting as the bottom layer. Moreover, the systemic structure of the mind correspondingly consists of such layers as those labeled by P, V, etc. In particular, P stands for the physiological needs of the person, consisting of such basics of life as breathing, food, water, sex, sleep, homeostasis, and excretion, as summarized by Maslow (1943, 1954). The V layer includes specific philosophical principles of value on how the world actually functions and how a person should behave in order not to violate his codes of morality. In this systemically structured mind, there are interacting blocks of knowledge, experiences, and information of various kinds, be they physical, intellectual, or conceptual. In this figurative representation, the question-marked cloud denotes a challenging situation the person faces, while the exclamation-marked cloud stands for a potential resolution of the challenge.

As shown by Lin (2009) and indicated in Fig. 7.1, human feelings, judgments, and thoughts possess the same systemic structure as the physical and intellectual world, while the former systemically reflects the latter. Hence, when the endowment "imagination" is needed for the potential of actions, this endowment simply matches what is under consideration with some relevant elements from the reservoir of imagination for possible suggestions. If a good match is found, then a quality resolution, appropriate for the issue in hand, is quickly formulated. On the other hand, if no good match is found, then the structured reservoir of imagination is expanded with new experience and/or knowledge. With suitable control of self-consciousness, a person can mobilize a lot of elements out of the reservoir and related associations between the elements. What can be drawn from the reservoir appears in two forms: such elements and their associations acquired through human sense organs and those attained not through these organs.

Proposition 7.3 Different people have respectively dissimilar reservoirs of imagination and unlike systems of philosophical values and beliefs.

To see why this proposition holds, let us first look at the concept of systems of philosophical values and beliefs. For each person, his system of philosophical values and beliefs consists of such beliefs about how the world functions and the moral codes with which the person is known with his particular identity and integrity. Now, the systemic yoyo model of systems implies that as a living system, each human being lives in a vast ocean of spinning fields of other people, physical objects, abstract thoughts, and a myriad of other things and matters.

As soon as a person is born, he starts to interact with the outside world, which expands in magnitude over time. It is through these interactions with people, physical objects, abstract thoughts, and the myriad of other things and matters that the person's philosophical values and beliefs start to germinate and are gradually formulated and solidified. This process is similar to how a civilization frames its system of values, beliefs, and codes of conduct (Lin & Forrest, 2012).

Evidently, from one person to another, the environment within which a person grows up and matures is different. For example, the caretakers are different from one family to another, letting alone other aspects of life, such as habits, daily routines, and the way of how these caretakers interact with themselves and with the particular person. Because of such differences in the environments and between the interactions with the environments experienced by one person from those by another person, each person has his own set of very specific system of philosophical values and beliefs. This system dictates the behaviors and decision-making of the person for the rest of his life. When compared to the magnificent scale of the entire ocean of spin fields of the world, the differences might very well be considered "subtle." However, they generally and majorly affect the individuals involved, causing important differences in these people's systems of philosophical values and beliefs. This end explains why people who grow up in the same household generally have different personalities, characteristics, and thinking processes.

To further prepare for the development of our new economic theory, the rest of this chapter looks at an individual who spends h hours working on a waged work or employment in the labor market. Assume that this individual's utility function U is real-valued and differentiable and is given as follows:

$$U = U(x, h, A), \tag{7.1}$$

where x stands for the individual's consumption of aggregate commodity and A his personal system of values and beliefs. As in real life, A is a categorical variable and is not definitively known to other people. To show that values of A really make difference, this chapter considers such A value as

- A positively values the consumption of commodities, while seeing waged work negatively.
- A believes minimal commodity consumption.
- A determines how uniquely the utility function of concern is optimized according to the value-belief system of the individual involved.

If w represents the constant hourly wage and y the income independent of the waged work, then the individual's total income is given below:

$$\text{total income} = wh + y. \tag{7.2}$$

That is, the individual faces the optimization problem of maximizing his utility function in Eq. (7.1) subject to the budget constraint in Eq. (7.2) by choosing $x > 0$ and $h \geq 0$.

7.3 More Consumption and Less Waged Work

This section looks at such a system A of values and beliefs that the consumption of commodities is valued positively so that the more commodities are consumed, the better, while working on a waged job is seen negatively such that the less time is spent on the waged job, the better. This scenario is the one typically considered in the literature (e.g., Pencavel, 1986; Prescott, 2004). To reflect this scenario, let us impose the following conditions on the individual's utility function in Eq. (7.1):

$$\frac{\partial U}{\partial x} > 0, \quad \frac{\partial U}{\partial h} < 0, \quad \frac{\partial^2 U}{\partial x^2} < 0, \quad \frac{\partial^2 \mathrm{U}}{\partial h^2} < 0, \tag{7.3}$$

where the conditions on the second-order partial derivatives are employed to guarantee the necessary concavity of the utility function.

7.3.1 Marginal Utility's Evolution

In this case, let p represent the fixed unit price of the aggregate commodity. Then the individual maximizes his utility function subject to the following budget constraint, assuming that no decision on saving is involved.

$$px = wh + y. \tag{7.4}$$

Using the method of Lagrange multipliers, the first-order condition of this constrained optimization problem is

$$\begin{bmatrix} \frac{\partial U}{\partial x} \\ \frac{\partial U}{\partial h} \end{bmatrix} = \lambda \begin{bmatrix} p \\ -w \end{bmatrix}, \tag{7.5}$$

where λ is the Lagrange multiplier.

Proposition 7.4 This individual's Lagrange multiplier λ is a positive function of income y that is independent from the waged work, the commodity price p, wage rate w, the consumption x of aggregate commodity, and the labor supply h, satisfying that

$$\frac{\partial \lambda}{\partial y} < 0, \quad \frac{\partial \lambda}{\partial w} \leq 0, \quad \frac{\partial \lambda}{\partial h} < 0 \quad \text{and} \quad \frac{\partial \lambda}{\partial p} \lesseqgtr 0. \tag{7.6}$$

Because λ is determined jointly by Eqs. (7.2) and (7.5), it follows that λ is a function of all the variables mentioned in the proposition. Moreover, from $\partial U/\partial x > 0$, as given in Eq. (7.3), and $\partial U/\partial x = \lambda p$, as indicated in Eq. (7.5), we know that λ takes positive values only. By solving Eq. (7.2) for x, we produce $x = (wh + y)/p$ and then the following:

$$\frac{\partial x}{\partial y} = \frac{1}{p} > 0, \quad \frac{\partial x}{\partial w} = \frac{h}{p} \geq 0, \quad \frac{\partial x}{\partial h} = \frac{w}{p} > 0, \quad \frac{\partial x}{\partial p} = \frac{-(wh + y)}{p^2} < 0.$$

And by equating the first cells on both sides of Eq. (7.5), it follows that $\lambda = p^{-1} \cdot (\partial U/\partial x)$. So, from Eq. (7.1) we have

$$\frac{\partial \lambda}{\partial y} = \frac{1}{p} \cdot \frac{\partial^2 U}{\partial x^2} \cdot \frac{\partial x}{\partial y} = \frac{1}{p^2} \cdot \frac{\partial^2 U}{\partial x_t^2} < 0,$$

$$\frac{\partial \lambda}{\partial w} = \frac{1}{p} \cdot \frac{\partial^2 U}{\partial x^2} \cdot \frac{\partial x}{\partial w} = \frac{h}{p^2} \cdot \frac{\partial^2 U}{\partial x_t^2} \leq 0,$$

$$\frac{\partial \lambda}{\partial h} = \frac{1}{p} \cdot \frac{\partial^2 U}{\partial x^2} \cdot \frac{\partial x}{\partial h} = \frac{w}{p^2} \cdot \frac{\partial^2 U}{\partial x^2} < 0$$

and

$$\frac{\partial \lambda}{\partial p} = \frac{-1}{p^2} \cdot \frac{\partial U}{\partial x} + \frac{1}{p} \cdot \frac{\partial^2 U_t}{\partial x^2} \cdot \frac{\partial x}{\partial p} = \frac{-1}{p^2} \cdot \frac{\partial U}{\partial x} - \frac{wh + y}{p^3} \cdot \frac{\partial^2 U_t}{\partial x^2} \lesseqgtr 0$$

Hence, all inequalities in Eq. (7.6) are shown.

Proposition 7.5 The following hold true in general:

1. The individual's marginal utility of commodity consumption decreases along with increasing income y that is independent from waged work.
2. The individual's marginal utility from working extra hours on the waged work increases with increasing income y.

To see the first part of this statement, let y_1 and y_2 be two different values of y such that $y_1 < y_2$. Then, Eq. (7.6) implies that $\lambda|_{y=y_1} > \lambda|_{y=y_2}$. So, Eq. (7.5) indicates the following inequality, which shows the first part of statement (1) above:

$$\left.\frac{\partial U}{\partial x}\right|_{y=y_1} = \lambda|_{y=y_1} p > \left.\frac{\partial U}{\partial x}\right|_{y=y_2} = \lambda|_{y=y_2} p.$$

To see the second part of this statement, let y_1 and y_2 be two distinct amounts of income that are independent from the waged work, satisfying $y_1 < y_2$. Then, Eq. (7.6) implies that $\lambda|_{y=y_1} > \lambda|_{y=y_2}$. So, Eq. (7.5) indicates the following, which confirms the second part of statement (7.1) above:

$$\left.\frac{\partial U}{\partial h}\right|_{y=y_1} = -\lambda|_{y=y_1} w < \left.\frac{\partial U}{\partial h}\right|_{y=y_2} = -\lambda|_{y=y_2} w.$$

Proposition 7.6 If the individual supplies a positive amount of labor on the waged work, then the following hold true:

1. The individual's marginal utility of commodity consumption drops along with increasing hourly rate of the waged work.
2. The individual's marginal utility from working extra hours on the waged work increases along with increasing hourly rate of the waged work.

The argument for this conclusion is similar to that of Proposition 7.5. All details are omitted.

7.3.2 *Reservation Hourly Wage and Unit Commodity Price*

Dividing the second equation in Eq. (7.5), as obtained by equating corresponding cells from both sides of Eq. (7.5), by the first one produces

$$\frac{w}{p} = \text{real wage} = -\frac{\partial U/\partial h}{\partial U/\partial x} = -m(x, h, A), \tag{7.7}$$

where $-m(x, h, A)$ is the marginal rate of substitution of the working hours for the consumption of commodities. By solving Eqs. (7.2) and (7.7) jointly for x and h, we obtain the functions of the optimizing demand x for commodities and the optimizing work-hour supply h as follows, if $h > 0$:

$$\begin{cases} x^{\max} = x^{\max}(p, w, y, A) \\ h^{\max} = h^{\max}(p, w, y, A) \end{cases} \tag{7.8}$$

The special hourly wage rate w^*, satisfying $w^*/p = -m(x, 0, A, \varepsilon)$, represents the implicit value of the individual's time at the given commodity price p and the personal system A of values and beliefs. This wage rate w^* is known as the individual's reservation wage (Prescott, 2004) for the given p and A. That is, only when $-m(x, h, A) = w/p > -m(x, 0, A) = w^*/p$, the individual will participate in the labor market. Hence, we have

$$\forall w \in \mathbb{R}^+ \ni (w > w^* \rightarrow h > 0) \wedge (w \leq w^* \rightarrow h = 0), \tag{7.9}$$

where $\mathbb{R}^+$ stands for the set of all positive real numbers. In other words, the reservation hourly wage rate w^* determines whether or not the individual will be prepared to supply his labor to the market.

If by leisure we mean any activity that is not any part of the waged employment, then the previous analysis shows the following conclusion:

Proposition 7.7 Assume that an individual has an endowed block of available time that is split between either participating in waged work or enjoying leisure and that he also receives income from at least one other source that is independent of his labor supply in the market, then the following hold true:

1. For any given unit price p of the aggregate commodity and personal system A of values and beliefs, there is a reservation hourly wage rate w^* so that when the market hourly wage rate w of a job is greater than w^*, the individual will participate in the labor market; otherwise, he will not enter the labor market.
2. For any chosen level of participation in the labor market and personal system A of values and beliefs, there is a reservation unit price p^* so that when the unit price p of the aggregate commodity is less than p^*, the individual's demand for the aggregate commodity is positive; otherwise, her demand will be non-existent.

Proposition 7.8 Let

$$V = U(x, h, A)|_{x = x^{\max}, h = h^{\max}} = V(p, w, y, A) \tag{7.10}$$

be the maximized utility of the individual. Then the maximum demand $x^{\max}$ for commodities and the maximum labor supply $h^{\max}$ are analytically given by the following formulas:

$$\begin{cases} x^{\max}(p, w, y, A) = -\dfrac{\partial V/\partial p}{\partial V/\partial y} \\ h^{\max}(p, w, y, A) = -\dfrac{\partial V/\partial w}{\partial V/\partial y} \end{cases} \tag{7.11}$$

In fact, applying the method of Lagrange multipliers to Eq. (7.10) and the budget constraint $xp = wh + y$ leads to

$$\begin{bmatrix} \dfrac{\partial V}{\partial p} \\ \dfrac{\partial V}{\partial w} \\ \dfrac{\partial V}{\partial y} \end{bmatrix} = \lambda \begin{bmatrix} -x \\ h \\ 1 \end{bmatrix},$$

where λ is the Lagrange multiplier, which, according to the third equation of above matrix expression, is equal to the marginal utility of the non-waged income y when the utility function is evaluated at its maximum. Through respectively dividing the first and the second equation by the third in the previous expression, we obtain Eq. (7.11).

Example 7.1 In this case, we use a specific utility function to confirm scenario (7.1) listed above. In particular, let the individual's utility function be

$$U = 2x^{\frac{1}{2}} - \frac{1}{3}h^3. \tag{7.12}$$

Then, this utility function satisfies the inequalities in Eq. (7.3). Let $p = 1$, $w = 1$, and $y = 0$, Eq. (7.4) becomes $x = h$. So, the method of Lagrange multipliers implies $x^{-1/2} = h^2$. So, $x = h = 1$, and

$$U_{\max} = \frac{5}{3} \approx 1.6667 \quad \text{and} \quad \left.\frac{\partial U}{\partial x}\right|_{y=0} = 1. \tag{7.13}$$

Similarly, for $p = 1$, $w = 1$, and $y = 1$, Eq. (7.4) becomes $x = h + 1$. Equation $x^{-\frac{1}{2}} = h^2$ implies that $h^4(h + 1) = 1$ so that $h \approx 0.8566$ and $x \approx 1.8566$. Correspondingly, we have

$$U_{\max} \approx 2.5156 \quad \text{and} \quad \left.\frac{\partial U}{\partial x}\right|_{y=1} \approx 0.7339. \tag{7.14}$$

The marginal utility function values for $y = 0$ and $y = 1$, respectively, in Eqs. (7.13) and (7.14) confirm the conclusion in Proposition 7.5(1).

Similarly, for $p = w = 1$, we can obtain

$$\left.\frac{\partial U}{\partial h}\right|_{y=0} = -1, \quad \left.\frac{\partial U}{\partial h}\right|_{y=1} \approx -0.7338,$$

where confirms the conclusion in Proposition 7.5(2).

Let $p = w = 1$, $y = 0$, and respective, $p = 1$, $w = 2$, $y = 0$, we obtain

$$\left.\frac{\partial U}{\partial x}\right|_{w=1} = 1; \quad \left.\frac{\partial U}{\partial x}\right|_{w=2} \approx 0.6600; \quad \left.\frac{\partial U}{\partial h}\right|_{w=1} \approx -1.7411, \quad \left.\frac{\partial U}{\partial h}\right|_{w=2} \approx -1.3195,$$

which confirm the conclusions in Proposition 7.6.

According to Eq. (7.7), the marginal rate of substitution of the working hours for the commodity consumption is given by

$$-m(x,h,A)=\frac{w}{p}=h^2x^{-1/2}.$$

So, the reservation hourly wage $w^* = 0$ and the reservation unit commodity price $p^* = +\infty$. In other words, as indicated by Proposition 7.7, if the individual values commodity consumption and devalues labor output in the waged work, then

1. For any given unit-commodity price p, as long as the hourly wage rate is positive, the individual will participate in the labor market.
2. The individual's demand for commodity consumption is positive.

For the special case of $y = 0$, we produce

$$\begin{cases} x^{\max}(p,w,y,A)=\left(\frac{w}{p}\right)^{6/5} \\ h^{\max}(p,w,y,A)=\left(\frac{w}{p}\right)^{1/5} \end{cases}$$

7.4 Two Cases of Minimalists

This section looks at such an individual that as dictated by his value-belief system A the person keeps his commodity consumption to the minimum level of basic survival. Under this condition, we study two scenarios respectively:

1. The individual maximally enjoys providing his labor on the waged work.
2. The person likes to supply as little labor as possible to his waged work.

7.4.1 When a Minimalist Enjoys His Waged Work

To reflect Scenario (1), which describes the situation of a workaholic (van Beek et al., 2011), let us consider the following utility function along with the imposed conditions, where s stands for savings:

$$U=U(x,h,s,A),\quad \text{satisfying } \frac{\partial U}{\partial x}<0,\quad \frac{\partial U}{\partial h}>0,\quad \frac{\partial^2 U}{\partial x^2}<0,\quad \frac{\partial^2 U}{\partial h^2}<0. \tag{7.15}$$

The reason why we include savings in this utility function is because when the individual enjoys working while is not motivated to spend extra on commodities, he has to have a place to park the additional earnings. And as before, the conditions on the second-order partial derivatives in Eq. (7.15) are employed to guarantee the needed concavity of the utility function. At the same time, the fact that no condition in Eq. (7.15) is imposed on the variable s reflects that earning additional money does not play a role on the person's utility. In this case, the budget constraint can be rewritten as

$$px + s = wh + y. \tag{7.16}$$

And the first order condition of this optimization problem is

$$\begin{bmatrix} \frac{\partial U}{\partial x} \\ \frac{\partial U}{\partial h} \\ \frac{\partial U}{\partial s} \end{bmatrix} = \lambda \begin{bmatrix} p \\ -w \\ 1 \end{bmatrix}, \tag{7.17}$$

where λ is the Lagrange multiplier.

Proposition 7.9 The following hold true:

1. The individual's marginal utility of commodity consumption decreases along with increasing hourly wage rate w of the waged work.
2. The individual's marginal utility from working extra hours on the waged work increases along with increasing hourly wage rate w of the waged work.
3. The individual's marginal utility from additional savings decreases along with increasing hourly wage rate w of the waged work.

To see the first part of this statement, the expression $\partial U/\partial x = \lambda p$ in Eq. (7.17) implies that $\lambda < 0$ due to Eq. (7.15). From Eq. (7.16), we have $\partial x/\partial w = hp^{-1} > 0$; and from Eqs. (7.15) to (7.17), we obtain

$$\frac{\partial \lambda}{\partial w} = \frac{1}{p} \cdot \frac{\partial^2 u}{\partial x^2} \cdot \frac{\partial x}{\partial w} = \frac{h}{p^2} \cdot \frac{\partial^2 u}{\partial x^2} < 0.$$

That is, λ is a decreasing function in w. So, for $w_1, w_2 > 0$, condition $w_1 < w_2$ implies $\lambda|_{w=w_1} > \lambda|_{w=w_2}$. So, from Eq. (7.17), it follows that

$$\left.\frac{\partial U}{\partial x}\right|_{w=w_1} = \lambda|_{w=w_1} p > \left.\frac{\partial U}{\partial x}\right|_{w=w_2} = \lambda|_{w=w} p,$$

which shows the first part of this proposition.

To see the second part of this statement, the previous argument indicates that λ is a decreasing function in w. So, for $w_1, w_2 > 0$, satisfying $w_1 < w_2$, we have $\lambda|_{w=w_1} > \lambda|_{w=w_2}$. So, from Eq. (7.17), it follows that

$$\left.\frac{\partial U}{\partial h}\right|_{w=w_1} = -\lambda|_{w=w_1} w < \left.\frac{\partial U}{\partial h}\right|_{w=w_2} = -\lambda|_{w=w_2} w,$$

which shows the second part of this proposition.

To confirm the third part of this statement, the previous argument implies that λ is a decreasing function in w. So, for w_1, $w_2 > 0$, satisfying $w_1 < w_2$, we have $\lambda|_{w=w_1} > \lambda|_{w=w_2}$. So, from Eq. (7.17), it follows that

$$\left.\frac{\partial U}{\partial s}\right|_{w=w_1} = \lambda|_{w=w_1} > \left.\frac{\partial U}{\partial s}\right|_{w=w_2} = \lambda|_{w=w_2},$$

which shows the third part of this proposition.

Proposition 7.10 The following hold true:

1. The individual's marginal utility of commodity consumption drops along with increasing income y that is independent from the waged work.
2. The individual's marginal utility from working extra hours on the waged work increases long with increasing income y.
3. The individual's marginal utility from additional saving decreases long with increasing income y.

To see the first part of this statement, from Eq. (7.16), it follows that $\partial x/\partial y = p^{-1} > 0$. Equations (7.15)–(7.17) imply that

$$\frac{\partial \lambda}{\partial y} = \frac{1}{p} \cdot \frac{\partial^2 u}{\partial x^2} \cdot \frac{\partial x}{\partial y} = \frac{1}{p^2} \cdot \frac{\partial^2 u}{\partial x^2} < 0.$$

Hence, λ is a decreasing function in y. So, for y_1, $y_2 > 0$, satisfying $y_1 < y_2$, we have $\lambda|_{y=y_1} > \lambda|_{y=y_2}$. So, from Eq. (7.17), it follows that

$$\left.\frac{\partial U}{\partial x}\right|_{y=y_1} = \lambda|_{y=y_1} p > \left.\frac{\partial U}{\partial x}\right|_{y=y_2} = \lambda|_{y=y_2} p,$$

which confirms the first conclusion of this proposition.

To see the second part of this statement, let y_1, $y_2 > 0$, satisfying $y_1 < y_2$, we have $\lambda|_{y=y_1} > \lambda|_{y=y_2}$. So, from Eq. (7.17), it follows that

$$\left.\frac{\partial U}{\partial h}\right|_{y=y_1} = -\lambda|_{y=y_1} w < \left.\frac{\partial U}{\partial h}\right|_{y=y_2} = -\lambda|_{y=y_2} w,$$

which shows the second part of this proposition. The third part of this statement follows the same argument as the one in the argument of the previous proposition.

From Eq. (7.17), it follows that

$$\frac{\partial U}{\partial x}\Big/\frac{\partial U}{\partial s}=p,\qquad \frac{\partial U}{\partial h}\Big/\frac{\partial U}{\partial s}=-w. \tag{7.18}$$

Solving the system of Eqs. (7.16) and (7.18) for x, y, and s produces

$$\begin{cases} x^{\text{opt}}=x^{\text{opt}}(p,w,y,A) \\ h^{\text{opt}}=h^{\text{opt}}(p,w,y,A) \\ s^{\text{opt}}=s^{\text{opt}}(p,w,y,A) \end{cases} \tag{7.19}$$

Let $V^{\text{opt}} = U(x^{\text{opt}}, h^{\text{opt}}, \text{s}^{\text{opt}}, A) = V^{\text{opt}}(p, w, y, A)$ be the maximized utility of the individual. Then the method of Lagrange multipliers implies that

$$\left\{\begin{bmatrix} \frac{\partial V^{\text{opt}}}{\partial p} \\ \frac{\partial V^{\text{opt}}}{\partial w} \\ \frac{\partial V^{\text{opt}}}{\partial y} \\ \frac{\partial V^{\text{opt}}}{\partial s} \end{bmatrix}=\lambda\begin{bmatrix} x \\ -h \\ -1 \\ 1 \end{bmatrix}\right. . \tag{7.20}$$

Dividing respectively the first equating cells by the third one and fourth one in Eq. (7.20), dividing the second equating cells by the third and the fourth one, and applying Eq. (7.16) lead to the following result:

Proposition 7.11 The optimal demand x^{opt} for commodities, the optimal labor supply h^{opt}, and the optimal savings x^{opt} are analytically given by the following formulas:

$$\begin{cases} x^{\text{opt}}(p,w,y,A)=-\dfrac{\partial V^{\text{opt}}/\partial p}{\partial V^{\text{opt}}/\partial y}=\dfrac{\partial V^{\text{opt}}/\partial p}{\partial V^{\text{opt}}/\partial s} \\ h^{\text{opt}}(p,w,y,A)=-\dfrac{\partial V^{\text{opt}}/\partial w}{\partial V^{\text{opt}}/\partial s}=\dfrac{\partial V^{\text{opt}}/\partial w}{\partial V^{\text{opt}}/\partial y}. \\ s^{\text{opt}}(p,w,y,A)=wh^{\text{opt}}+y-px^{\text{opt}} \end{cases} \tag{7.21}$$

Example 7.2 For the second scenario considered in the previous sections, where commodity consumption is kept at the minimum for basic survival, while the waged work is enjoyable so that more labor is pleasantly supplied to the work, let us specify individual's utility function be

$$U=2h^{\frac{1}{2}}-\frac{1}{3}x^3+s^2, \tag{7.22}$$

where the first two terms on the right-hand side are the same as those in Eq. (7.12) except that the places of the variables x and h are switched. It is straightforward to check that all the inequalities in Eq. (7.15) are satisfied.

The method of Lagrange multipliers implies that

$$\frac{\partial U}{\partial x} = -x^2 = \lambda p, \quad \frac{\partial U}{\partial h} = h^{-1/2} = -\lambda w, \quad \frac{\partial U}{\partial s} = 2s = \lambda, \tag{7.23}$$

where λ is the Lagrange multiplier. So, we have

$$\frac{x^2}{h^{-1/2}} = \frac{p}{w}. \tag{7.24}$$

To double check Proposition 7.9, we first let $p = w = 1$ and $y = 0$. Then the budget constraint in Eq. (7.16) becomes $x + s = h$. So, Eq. (7.24) can be rewritten as $x^2 = h^{-1/2} = (x + s)^{-1/2}$. Respectively, if we let $p = 1$, $w = 2$ and $y = 0$, then we have $x^2 = h^{-1/2} = [(x + s)/2]^{-1/2}$. Therefore, the following is readily obtained:

$$\left.\frac{\partial U}{\partial x}\right|_{w=1} = \frac{-1}{\sqrt{x+2}} > \frac{-1}{\sqrt{(x+2)/2}} = \left.\frac{\partial U}{\partial x}\right|_{w=2}.$$

This end confirms the conclusion in Proposition 7.9(1). Moroever, similarly, we obtain from Eq. (7.23)

$$\left.\frac{\partial U}{\partial h}\right|_{w=1} = \frac{1}{\sqrt{x+2}} < \frac{1}{\sqrt{(x+2)/2}} = \left.\frac{\partial U}{\partial h}\right|_{w=2},$$

which confirms the conclusion in Proposition 7.9(2). Next, Eq. (7.23) implies that $\partial U/\partial s = -w^{-1}\partial U/\partial h$ and therefore

$$\left.\frac{\partial U}{\partial s}\right|_{w=1} = -\left.\frac{\partial U}{\partial h}\right|_{w=1} > -\left.\frac{\partial U}{\partial h}\right|_{w=2} > \frac{-1}{2}\left.\frac{\partial U}{\partial h}\right|_{w=2} = \left.\frac{\partial U}{\partial s}\right|_{w=2},$$

which confirms the conclusion in Proposition 7.9(3). By letting $p = w = 1$, we obtain

$$\frac{\partial U}{\partial x} = -(h+y-s)^2, \quad \frac{\partial U}{\partial h} = \frac{w}{p}(h+y-s)^2, \quad \frac{\partial U}{\partial s} = \frac{-1}{p}(h+y-s)^2.$$

So, conclusions in Proposition 7.10 are confirmed.

7.4.2 Minimum Consumption and Minimum Labor Output

Regarding scenario (2), as listed at the beginning of this section, that the individual of concern does not enjoy the consumption of commodities and likes to supply as little labor as possible to any waged work, let us additionally assume that the person needs to maintain the minimum level of commodity consumption for basic survival. To this end, he also needs to supply labor, although as little as possible, to a waged work in order to meet the minimum financial requirement to survive. What this scenario describes very well matches the phenomenon of hikikomori in Japan (Bowker et al., 2019). To study this current scenario, let us impose the following conditions on the individual's utility function in Eq. (7.1): There are $x_{\min} > 0$ and $h_{\min} \geq 0$ such that

$$\begin{aligned} &\frac{\partial U}{\partial x} \geq 0, \frac{\partial U}{\partial h} \geq 0, \quad \text{for} \quad 0 \leq x \leq x_{\min}, 0 \leq h \leq h_{\min}, \\ &\frac{\partial U}{\partial x} < 0, \frac{\partial U}{\partial h} < 0, \quad \text{for} \ \ x > x_{\min}, h > h_{\min}, \\ &\frac{\partial^2 U}{\partial x^2} < 0, \frac{\partial^2 U}{\partial h^2} < 0. \end{aligned} \tag{7.25}$$

Such a scenario appears when the individual is addicted to one or several activities he participates in during his leisure time. Assume that the person spends q dollars on his leisure activities. Hence, the budget constraint for this individual is

$$px + q = wh + y. \tag{7.26}$$

Proposition 7.12 The following hold true:

1. The individual's marginal utility of commodity consumption is a non-increasing function in the hourly wage rate w of the waged work.
2. The individual's marginal utility from working extra hours on the waged work is a non-decreasing function in the hourly wage rate w of the waged work.

The proof is similar to those of parts (1) and (2) in Proposition 7.9. All relevant details are omitted.

Proposition 7.13 The following hold true:

1. The individual's marginal utility of commodity consumption drops along with increasing income y that is independent from the waged work.
2. The individual's marginal utility from working extra hours on the waged work increases long with increasing income y.
3. The individual's marginal utility of commodity consumption increases along with increasing unit commodity price p, for when the commodity consumption x is greater than the minimum $x_{\min}$.
4. The individual's marginal utility from working extra hours on the waged work decreases with increasing p, for when the commodity consumption x is greater than the minimum $x_{\min}$.
5. The individual's marginal utility of commodity consumption increases along with increasing expense q on leisure.

6. The individual's marginal utility from working extra hours on the waged work decreases with increasing expense q.

The proof for (1) and (2) is the same as that of Proposition 7.10. For (3), the method of Lagrange multipliers implies that $\partial U/\partial x = \lambda p$; and from Eq. (7.26), it follows that $\partial x/\partial p = -(wh + y - q)/p^2 \le 0$. Hence, we have the following for $x > x_{\min}$

$$\frac{\partial \lambda}{\partial p} = \frac{\partial}{\partial p}\left(\frac{1}{p}\frac{\partial U}{\partial x}\right) = -\frac{1}{p^2}\frac{\partial U}{\partial x} + \frac{1}{p}\frac{\partial^2 U}{\partial x^2}\frac{\partial x}{\partial p} = -\frac{1}{p^2}\frac{\partial U}{\partial x} - \frac{(wh+y-q)}{p^3}\frac{\partial^2 U}{\partial x^2} > 0,$$

because Eq. (7.25) implies that $-p^{-2} \cdot \partial U/\partial x > 0$ for $x > x_{\min}$, while $-(wh + y - q)p^{-3} \cdot \partial^2 U/\partial x^2 \ge 0$, assuming that the individual does not live on borrowed money. That is, for $x > x_{\min}$, λ is an increasing function in p. So, for any p_1 and p_2, satisfying $p_1 < p_2$, we have $\lambda|_{p=p_1} < \lambda|_{p=p_2}$ so that

$$\left.\frac{\partial U}{\partial x}\right|_{p=p_1} = \lambda|_{p=p_1} \cdot p_1 < \lambda|_{p=p_2} \cdot p_2 = \left.\frac{\partial U}{\partial x}\right|_{p=p_2}.$$

This end confirms the conclusion in (3). The proof for (4) follows from $\lambda|_{p=p_1} < \lambda|_{p=p_2}$ and $\partial U/\partial h = -\lambda w$. All details can be filled in as above and are omitted. Similarly, parts (5) and (6) can be shown.

Example 7.3 For the third scenario considered in the previous paragraphs, where the commodity consumption is kept at the minimum for basic survival, and as little labor as possible is supplied to the waged work, let us specify individual's utility function as follows:

$$U = -(x-2)^2 - (h-3)^2, \tag{7.27}$$

so that the inequalities in Eq. (7.25) are satisfied with $x_{\min} = 2$ and $h_{\min} = 3$. This negative utility function means that the individual wants to minimize the adverse impact of labored work and commodity consumption.

By using the method of Lagrange multipliers and budget constraint in Eq. (7.2), we can produce

$$\frac{\partial U}{\partial x} = \frac{2p}{w}\left(\frac{px+q-y}{w} - 3\right) \quad \text{and} \quad \frac{\partial U}{\partial h} = -2\left(\frac{px+q-y}{w} - 3\right). \tag{7.28}$$

So, the conclusions in Propositions 7.12 and 7.13 are confirmed.

7.5 Different Definitions of Maximization

The previous two sections consider three scenarios where the value-belief system A of the individual of concern specifies respectively: (1) more commodity consumption is better, while less labor supply to the waged work is more desirable; (2) commodity consumption is kept at the minimum for basic survival, while the waged work is enjoyable so that more labor is pleasantly supplied to the work; and (3) commodity consumption is kept at the minimum for basic survival, and as little labor as possible is supplied to the waged work. And for each of these cases, the specified scenario can be adequately described as a standard optimization problem with correspondingly varied constraints. Different from the previous discussions, this section looks at such a particular value-belief system A that the output values of the objective function are not ordered as how real numbers are ordered ordinarily.

In particular, let $\mathbb{R}$ be the set of all real numbers and a a positive real number. We define a linear order relation $<_{\mathrm{mod}(a)}$ on $\mathbb{R}$ as follows: For any x and $y \in \mathbb{R}$,

$$x <_{\mathrm{mod}(a)} y \text{ if and only if } x \,\mathrm{mod}(a) < y \,\mathrm{mod}(a), \tag{7.29}$$

where the ordering $<$ is the conventional one defined on $\mathbb{R}$, x mod (a) is the remainder of $x \div a$, and y mod (a) the remainder of $y \div a$, such that $|x \text{ mod } (a)| < a$ and $|y \text{ mod } (a)| < a$. When all the involved numbers a, x, and y are integers, this order relation $<_{\mathrm{mod}(a)}$ degenerates into the one widely studied in number theory (Burton, 2012).

Geometrically, this modular function transforms the real number line $\mathbb{R}$ into a "spring" of infinite length (Fig. 7.2), so that for any positive $r \in \mathbb{R}$, satisfying $0 \le r < a$, the following set of real numbers are classified into one equivalence class:

$$\{x \in \mathbb{R} : \exists q \in \mathbb{Z}(x = aq + r)\}, \tag{7.30}$$

where $\mathbb{Z}$ stands for the set of all whole numbers, that is, $\mathbb{Z} = \{\ldots, -3, -2, -1, 0, +1, +2, +3, \ldots\}$. The arrows in Fig. 7.2 signal the positive direction with the opposite being the negative direction. All such numbers as $0, \pm a, \pm 2a, \pm 3a, \ldots$ are identified as equivalent with 0 serving as the representative of the equivalence class. By doing

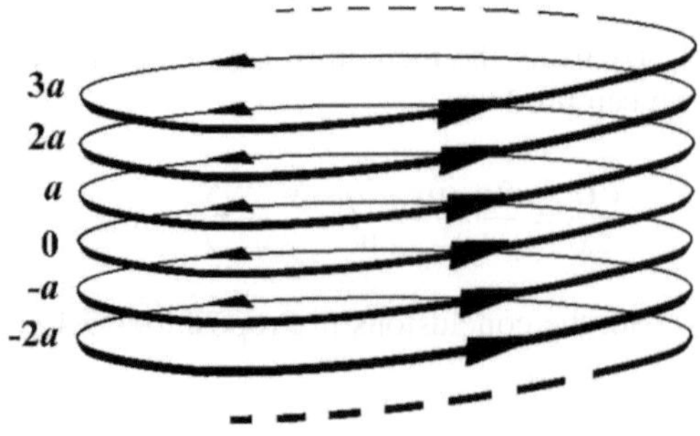

Fig. 7.2 How the mod function turns the real number line into a "spring"

so in general, the class given in Eq. (7.30) can be represented by $r \in [0, a)$. For example, when $a = 2$, because $2.1 = 1 \cdot 2 + 0.1$ and $-2.1 = (-3) \cdot 2 + 0.9$, 2.1 is equivalent to and is represented by 0.1, while -2.1 is equivalent to and is represented by 0.9.

With the geometry of the modular function explained, the linear order relation $<_{\mathrm{mod}(a)}$, as defined in Eq. (7.29), means the following: for any x and $y \in \mathbb{R}$, $x <_{\mathrm{mod}(a)} y$, if and only if $r_x < r_y$, where r_x and $r_y \in [0, a)$ are respectively the representatives of x and y. Next, we look at how this order relation $<_{\mathrm{mod}(a)}$ makes a difference for the case studied in Example 7.1 above.

Example 7.4 First, the maximization problem in Example 7.1, where the budge constraint is specified as $x = h$, provides the following outcomes:

$$\max_{x,h} U = \frac{5}{3} \approx 1.667, \quad x_{\max} = h_{\max} = 1. \tag{7.31}$$

If we consider this maximization problem by respectively introducing mod(2), mod (1.5), and mod(1), then the case of mod(2) provides the same solution as that in Eq. (7.31). However, for the case of mod(1.5), the maximization problem can be rewritten as follows:

$$\max_{x,h}(U \bmod(1.5)) = \left(2x^{1/2} - \frac{1}{3}h^3\right) \bmod(1.5), \text{ subject to } x = h,$$

then the solution becomes

$$\max_{x,h}(U \bmod(1.5)) = 1.5, \quad x_{\max} = h_{\max} \approx 0.62527,$$

where for $x = y = 1$, $U \bmod(1.5) = \frac{5}{3} \bmod(1.5) \approx 0.167$. That is, Eq. (7.31) is no longer the desired solution.

As for the case of mod(1), the maximization problem becomes

$$\max_{x,h}(U \bmod(1)) = \left(2x^{1/2} - \frac{1}{3}h^3\right) \bmod(1), \text{ subject to } x = h.$$

So, the solution to this optimization problem is

$$\max_{x,h}(U \bmod(1)) = \left(\frac{5}{3}\right)^{-} \bmod(1) \approx 0.667, \quad x_{\max} = h_{\max} = 1^{-},$$

where for any real number x, the symbol x^{-} stands for $\lim_{z \to x^{-}} z$. That is, Eq. (7.31) is no longer the desired the solution.

One take-away we can learn from Example 7.4 is that when the set of all possible values of the objective function is ordered in a specific way, the method employed to optimize the objective function must be accordingly adjusted. By combining the conclusions established above, we have

Proposition 7.14 If an individual's decision about the amount of commodity consumption and labor output into a waged work is made by optimizing his corresponding utility subject to the underlying constraints, then both the utility and method of optimization are exclusively defined by the individual's value-belief system.

7.6 A Few Final Words

By setting foot on the four natural human endowments—self-awareness, imagination, conscience, and free will (Forrest & Liu, 2021; Lin & Forrest, 2012)—this chapter innovatively shows how an individual's utility and his method of optimization are fundamentally determined by the person's natural endowments. Therefore, our answer to the question, as posed in the beginning of this chapter, of whether or not an economic man really relies on rationality to make consumption decisions is both yes and no. The yes answer comes from that the endowment of conscience, together with that of imagination, determines what is considered satisfactory (beyond what is morally right or wrong) (Chap. 5). Moreover, the no answer stems from the conclusion implicitly established in this chapter that each utility function is subjectively introduced by the decision-maker, while the consequent optimization of the utility is dictated by criteria formulated within the person's system of values and beliefs. In particular, the literature (Hudik, 2019) tends to have the researcher, whoever he is, define utility functions and determine which method of optimization to use under the implicit assumption that he knows the decision maker well although in real life a person's value-belief system is not known to anybody, including possibly the person himself. That is, the researcher represents the authority who decides which variables to include in a utility function and which specific method of optimization to use, although he has no idea about the underlying value-belief system of the decision-maker. In the contrary, results developed in this chapter clearly demonstrate that both a utility function and consequent method of optimization are determined either consciously or unconsciously by the specific individual involved in a decision situation. That is, when facing a decision situation, different people rely on different utility functions to choose their individually varied courses of actions. That explains in real life why the optimal course of action (or selection) in one person's eyes generally does not seem like optimal at all in another person's eyes.

Beyond the discussion in the previous paragraph, another major contribution this chapter makes to the existent literature is that it relies on pure logical, systemic, and analytical reasonings to derive conclusions without employing any empirically confirmed hypothesis as the basis and starting point of reasoning. Because of this reason, our developed conclusions are more theoretically sound than most of those that are data- or anecdote-based in the literature (Forrest & Liu, 2021).

For possible future research, one can investigate properties of marginal utilities under different circumstances of value-belief systems beyond the ones considered in this chapter. Similarly, additional methods of optimization should be carefully introduced and studied. Another important scenario for future research is the question of what happens when an individual's decision is not derived on the optimization of any underlying objective function. Our expectation is that the same, as what has been obtained in this chapter—the person's utility and his method of optimization are exclusively defined by his value-belief system—will still be the result.

References

Becker, G. S. (1962). Irrational behavior and economic theory. *The Journal of Political Economy, 70*(1), 1–13.

Bowker, J. C., Bowker, M. H., Santo, J. B., Ojo, A. A., Etkin, R. G., & Raja, R. (2019). Severe social withdrawal: Cultural variation in past Hikikomori experiences of university students in Nigeria, Singapore, and the United States. *The Journal of Genetic Psychology, 180*(4–5), 217–230.

Burton, D. M. (2012). *Elementary number theory*. McGraw Hill.

Forrest, J. Y.-L., & Liu, Y. (2021). Value in business—A holistic. In *Systems-based approach to creating and capturing value*. Springer.

Forrest, J. Y. L., Hafezalkotob, A., Ren, L., Liu, Y., & Tallapally, P. (2021). Utility and optimization's dependence on decision-makers' underlying value-belief systems. *Review of Economic and Business Studies, 14*(2), 125–149. https://doi.org/10.47743/rebs-2021-2-0007

Friedman, M. (1953). *Essays in positive economics*. University of Chicago Press.

Gilboa, I. (2010). *Rational choice*. The MIT Press.

Gul, F., & Pesendorfer, W. (2008). The case for mindless economics. In A. Caplin & A. Schotter (Eds.), *The foundations of positive and normative economics: A handbook*. Oxford University Press.

Hill, N. (1928). The law of success. In *Sixteen lessons (reprint of 2007)*. BN Publishing. Retrieved from www.bnpublishing.com

Hudik, M. (2012). Transitivity: A comment on Block and Barnett. *The Quarterly Journal of Austrian Economics, 15*(4), 456–462.

Hudik, M. (2019). Two interpretations of the rational choice theory and the relevance of behavioral critique. *Rationality and Society, 31*(4), 464–489.

Kahneman, D. (2011). *Thinking, fast and slow*. Farrar, Straus and Giroux.

Lin, Y. (2009). *Systemic yoyos: Some impacts of the second dimension*. Auerbach Publications.

Lin, Y., & Forrest, B. (2012). *Systemic structure behind human organizations: From civilizations to individuals*. Springer.

Lovett, F. (2006). Rational choice theory and explanation. *Rationality and Society, 18*(2), 237–272.

Machlup, F. (1946). Marginal analysis and empirical research. *The American Economic Review, 36*(4), 519–554.

Maialeh, R. (2019). Generalization of results and neoclassical rationality: Unresolved controversies of behavioural economics methodology. *Quality & Quantity, 53*, 1743–1761.

Mandler, M. (2001). A difficult choice in preference theory: Rationality implies completeness or transitivity but not both. In E. Milgram (Ed.), *Varieties of practical reasoning* (pp. 373–402). MIT Press.

Maslow, A. H. (1943). A theory of human motivation. *Psychological Review, 50*(4), 370–396.

Maslow, A. H. (1954). *Motivation and personality*. Harper.
McKenzie, R. (2010). Predictably rational? In *Search of defenses for rational behavior in economics*. Springer.
Mullainathan, S., & Thaler, R. H. (2000, October). *Behavioral economics* (NBER Working Paper No. 7948). National Bureau of Economic Research.
Ok, E. A. (2002). Utility representation of an incomplete preference relation. *Journal of Economic Theory, 104*(2), 429–449.
Pencavel, J. (1986). Labor supply of men: A survey. In O. Ashenfelter & R. Layard (Eds.), *Handbook of labor economics* (Vol. 1, pp. 3–102). North-Holland.
Prescott, E. C. (2004). Why do Americans work so much more than Europeans? *Federal Reserve Bank of Minneapolis Quarterly Review, 28*(1), 2–13.
Rubinstein, A. (1998). *Modeling bounded rationality*. The MIT Press.
Samuelson, P. A. (1948). Consumption theory in terms of revealed preference. *Economica, 15*(60), 243–253.
Simon, H. A. (1986). Rationality in psychology and economics. *The Journal of Business, 59*(4), S209–S224.
Thurstone, L. L. (1931). The indifference function. *The Journal of Social Psychology, 2*(2), 139–167.
van Beek, I., Taris, T. W., & Schaufeli, W. B. (2011). Workaholic and work engaged employees: Dead ringers or worlds apart? *Journal of Occupational Health Psychology, 16*(4), 468–482.
Weber, M. (1949). *The methodology of the social sciences*. Free Press.
Weyl, G. E. (2019). Price theory. *Journal of Economic Literature, 57*(2), 329–384.

Chapter 8
Optimal Fit to the Underlying Value-Belief System

Jeffrey Yi-Lin Forrest, Lawrence Shao, Jun Liu, Brian W. Sloboda, and Dale Shao

Abstract Finding the true meaning of the assumption of rationality has attracted the attention of many scholars and brought forward major changes to the discipline of economics. However, the vast amount of literature shows that such attention has not only led to inconsistent interpretations but also contradictory ones. To clear up these inconsistencies and contradictions, this chapter, which is mainly based on Forrest et al. (Pennsylvania Economic Review, 2023), looks at this assumption from a different angle—natural endowments of individuals and business firms, respectively. To do so successfully, this chapter goes far beyond all well-adopted methods of analysis and employs systems methods and such a logical reasoning that is parallel to that widely used in different branches of mathematics, such as plane geometry and topology. Because of the novelty of particularly chosen angle and adopted methodology, this chapter is able to develop the following main conclusion along with other thought-provoking propositions: At either the micro individual level or the macro firm level, the assumed rationality stands for an optimal fit of the decided choice within the underlying natural endowments of the decision-maker.

Keywords Aggregated group decisions · Choice behaviors · Cognitive system · Natural endowments · Self-interests · Tastes

---

Jeffrey Yi-Lin Forrest (Department of Accounting Economics Finance, Slippery Rock University, Slippery Rock, PA, USA; Email: Jeffrey.forrest@sru.edu), Lawrence Shao (College of Business, Slippery Rock University, Slippery Rock, PA, USA; Email: Lawrence.shao@sru.edu), Jun Liu (School of Digital Economics and Management, Wuxi University, Wuxi, China; Email: liujun@nuist.edu.cn), Brian W. Sloboda (University of Phoenix, Phoenix, AZ, USA; Email: bsloboda@email.phoenix.edu), and Dale Shao (Lewis College of Business, Marshall University, Huntington, WV, USA; Email: shaod@marshall.edu) are equally contributed to this chapter.

J. Y.-L. Forrest, *Systemic Principles of Applied Economic Philosophies I*,
Translational Systems Sciences 38, https://doi.org/10.1007/978-981-99-7273-9_8

8.1 Introduction

By rationality, as discussed in the previous chapter, it means that when an economic agent makes decision, the individual maximizes his personal advantage based on relevant cost-and-benefit analysis (e.g., Friedman, 1953; Wu, 2003). It is characterized by self-interested motives that lead the individual to utility maximizing behaviors (Maialeh, 2019). Sen (1991) decomposes such neoclassical rationality into two parts: (1) the involved individual maximizes his self-interest and (2) the individual makes choices consistently. Such rationality, as widely assumed in studies of social science, represents one very important assumption developed to analyze economic and social behaviors (Gilboa, 2010; Gul & Pesendorfer, 2008). At the same time, it has also been widely criticized by behavioral economists; these scholars believe that the assumption rests on realistically untrue assumptions and is empirically confirmed with falsified evidence; and any behavior that deviates from maximizing self-interest is seen by neoclassical economists as irrational (Becker, 1962; Kahneman, 2011; Mullainathan & Thaler, 2000; Sen, 1991). So, how to understand and how to interpret this assumption of rationality have become an important issue in social science, in general, and economics, in particular.

The vast amount of literature on the interpretation of this assumption of rationality provides a very good piece of evidence showing that scholars have all along recognized the inherent uncertainty this assumption embodies. Although all works related to this assumption consider its aim to be about the explanation, prediction, and/or understanding of choice behaviors, major differences exist in these scholarly understandings. For example, Simon (1986) maintains that the assumption of rationality is about accounting for the choice behaviors of individuals instead of differences and variability between groups. Lovett (2006) argues that the assumption does not pinpoint those particular choices (or point predictions) but compares choices at different moments. By seeing each decision-making as a process, Rubinstein (1998) considers the assumption of rationality as a specific choice procedure, through which a decision-maker selects an element that is most preferred among all available alternatives in a given set of choices. Opposite to all these interpretations, Becker (1962) believes that the assumption focuses on aggregated group decisions, because idiosyncratic individual behaviors are believed to dissipate and be averaged out at the aggregate level (Weyl, 2019), although this reasoning does not hold as recently shown (Gabaix, 2011; Wagner, 2012).

By closely comparing these sampled understandings of rationality, one can see at least the following pairs of inconsistencies and/or contradictions, among many others: (1) individual choices vs. aggregated group decisions; (2) behaviors of choice vs. choices (or actions of choosing vs. what are actually chosen); (3) procedures of choice vs. choices (or processes of making choices vs. what are actually chosen); and (4) differences between groups vs. choices at different moments. In short, some people believe that the assumption is about actions or procedures of acts while others regarding specific choices; some involve the concept of time while others do not.

So, the objective of this chapter is to clear up these existent inconsistencies of the literature. To accomplish this end, we establish that no matter whether it is at the micro individual level or the macro firm level, the assumption of rationality stands for an optimal fit of the decided choice within the underlying natural endowments (instead of self-interests) of the decision-maker. In particular, no matter whether the decision-maker is an individual or a business firm, his (or its) natural endowments consist of the economic agent's self-awareness, imagination, conscience, and free will. See Branden (1969) and Lin and Forrest (2012) for discussions for the case of individuals.

As for the contribution, this chapter enriches the literature in two different fronts—methodology and economic theory. In terms of the former, different from what have been commonly applied in relevant studies, this chapter employs systems thinking and the logical reasoning which is parallel to that widely seen in mathematics to establish our main conclusions. Specifically, because each method of reasoning and analysis widely used in economic studies tend to be limited in some aspects (Forrest & Liu, 2022, pp. 11–219), this chapter employs holistic thinking to thread a network model, a systemic yoyo mode, and a market entry model together to establish respective key conclusions. In terms of economic conclusions, current chapter contributes to the literature in several different ways. For example, it supports the claim that the assumed rationality is about the decision behaviors of individuals (Simon, 1986) and demonstrates how the selected option is most preferred among available alternatives (Rubinstein, 1998). However, beyond supporting these claims, this chapter goes much further. What is shown here is not supportive of part (i) of Sen's (1991) decomposition of the neoclassical rationality. Instead of individual's maximization of self-interest in the first part of Sen's decomposition, it is shown that the decision-maker chooses the alternative that best fits his system of values and beliefs, derived out of his natural endowments. This end not only improves Sen's work but also confirms the observation that people give support to options that fit their beliefs and values instead of immediate gains, either financial or not, as shown empirically by Lakoff (1996) and Lakoff and Wehling (1996). In other words, this chapter points out, the first time in the area of economic research, the difference between self-interests and systems of values and beliefs, where the former can be readily influenced by peers and societal pressures (Hu et al., 2021; Mani et al., 2013), while the latter relatively fixed (Lin & Forrest, 2012). That might be one of the reasons why people seem to behave irrationally as claimed by behavioral economists (e.g., Goodwin et al., 2013; Kahneman et al., 1986; Knetsch, 1990; Lee et al., 2009; Mandler, 2001; Robbins, 1932).

Additionally, this chapter does not support that the assumption focuses on aggregated group decisions (Becker, 1962) while confirming the nonexistence of any universally accepted definition of optimum. Instead, what is considered optimal is defined specifically and individually by respective decision-makers. That is, rationality means that when an economic agent makes decision, he chooses the most preferred option among all available alternatives in terms of the individual's underlying natural endowments. That is very different from the well-adopted definition of rationality—maximize the decision-maker's advantage based on relevant cost-and-benefit analysis (e.g., Friedman, 1953; Wu, 2003). For more about this research's contribution, see the final section of this chapter.

The rest of this chapter is organized as follows. Section 8.2 looks at the rationality assumption at the micro individual level through examining how optimum and method of optimization are defined differently and individually. Section 8.3 focuses on similar conclusions for the macro firm level. This section consists of two subsections. The first subsection focuses on the understanding of a firm's goal of efforts and comprehension of market signals; and the second subsection develops similar results shown for micro-level individuals. Section 8.4 concludes and provides final thoughts on the chapter.

8.2 Micro Individual Level Rationality

In terms of literature, one can tell that a man's natural endowments are different from Stigler and Becker's (1977) tastes. In particular, tastes represent a reason for people to act in different ways. Against the conventional view of tastes, which are seen as inscrutable and often capricious, Stigler and Becker (p. 76) believe that "tastes neither change capriciously nor differ importantly between people." In comparison, a man's natural endowments also dictate how an individual would act in specific ways, and do not change easily (Lin & Forrest, 2012), similar to Stigler and Becker's interpretation of tastes. However, from one person to another, their underlying systems of values and beliefs can change drastically, leading to, for example, different orderings of real numbers. For example, driven by their specific systems of values and beliefs, some people take pleasure in their acts of harming others, while some other people would prefer to treating each other with respect. For the former people, they most likely see $3 million as a greater amount than $3K, while the latter would very possibly see $3K as an amount greater than $3 million if these millions are the outcome of successfully robbing a bank.

Similarly, differences in natural endowments are more than differences in relative costs, which represents one of the common variables neoclassical economists prefer to examine. Because different systems of values and beliefs readily lead to different orderings of real numbers, comparisons of costs are no longer the same from one individual to another.

Next, to see why the rationality assumption at the micro individual level stands for an optimal fit of the decided choice as determined by the decision-maker's natural endowments, let pay a revisit to Sect. 6.3. In particular, what Sect.6.3 demonstrated is that differences in individuals' criteria of priority reflect those in individuals' systems of values and beliefs. This end enriches and generalizes what Mises (1949, p. 244) believed when he claimed that "the value judgements a man pronounces about another man's satisfaction do not assert anything about this other man's satisfaction. They only assert what condition of this other man better satisfies the man who pronounces the judgement." That is, what Sect. 6.3 shows is that in neoclassical economics, the rationality assumption means that the economist "asserts this other man's condition that better satisfies the economist," if we rephrase what was concluded in Sect. 6.3 in the language of Mises. That is, in mathematical terms, although the starting point of optimization, such as an objective function, might be the same, the specifically employed criteria or methods of optimization can be different from one person to another.

By carrying the discussion above further, one is able to see why the rationality assumption at the micro individual level represents individual rationality, which changes from one person to another. Specifically, we have

Proposition 8.1 At the micro individual level, the assumption of rationality stands for finding an optimal choice among all available alternatives, where the optimum is determined by the decision-maker's natural endowments.

The correctness of this conclusion comes from the previously established propositions. Specifically, when a set of available alternatives is presented, the decision-maker either consciously or unconsciously studies these alternatives to help reach his ideal state of happiness, as implied by Proposition 5.1. To this end, Proposition 7.1 implies that relevant feelings, judgments, and thoughts in general and the feeling of satisfaction or happier than before, in particular, are classified by mobilizing his endowments. Based on such classifications of how much happiness the individual alternatives can respectively provide, the decision-maker, as implied by Proposition 7.2, selects one of the choices out of all available alternatives that will potentially provide the optimal happiness to the decision-maker. Therefore, the conclusion of this proposition follows.

Proposition 8.2 When confronting a decision-making situation, a person optimizes the potential subject to the given constraints by using his individually specific criteria rooted in the person's system of values and beliefs.

This result collectively follows from Propositions 5.1, 7.2, and 7.5. In particular, to confront a decision-making situation, Proposition 5.1 says that a person aims at getting closer, at least partially, to his imagined state of happiness. Proposition 7.3 implies that from one person to another, individuals have their own different definitions of happiness. So, accordingly, Proposition 7.1 points to the fact that a person decides on how to possibly optimize the potential of the given scenario, subject to the given constraints, by employing his specific set of criteria, derived out of his unique contents of endowments.

Summarizing what has been developed in this section leads us to the following realization: Each person has his own specific and unique system of values and beliefs (Lin & Forrest, 2012). By referencing back to his value-belief system, a person makes the best decisions in reference to his definition of optimization. In particular, the person optimizes a given situation, which might not be expressible in any functional form, by using his underlying structured reservoir of imagination and codes of conduct. What is worth emphasizing at this point is that the optimization is not done by maximizing self-interests or by minimizing costs or level of risk, although for specific circumstances, what is carried out could be so. Moreover, opposite to decisions carefully made, there are frequently seen impulsive purchase decisions made under the influence or pressure of the media or peers. If one of such decisions is later shown to be inconsistent with the underlying values and beliefs of the purchaser, then the purchased product will be returned or it is not used for the originally expected purpose. In either case, the violated values and beliefs are corrected.

In short, the meaning of optimum and the method used to find optimal solutions are different from one individual to another, not as commonly believed and practiced in studies of economics and business. Hence, the discussion in this section indicates that each person, in general, is rational in his own right, as determined by his natural endowments—self-awareness, imagination, conscience, and free will. This end illustrates that a perfect logic in one person's value-belief system can be seen as irrational in other people's value-belief systems. This conclusion literally ends the debates about the meaning of rationality between neoclassical and behavioral economists (Maialeh, 2019).

8.3 Macro Firm Level Rationality

When the decision-maker of concern is a business firm instead of a person, its natural endowments are different from those of individual persons. However, in turn of the literature, the opposite has been commonly assumed. For example, a frequently employed method to study behaviors is the introduction of a fictitious representative agent (or consumer) who faces all the involved constraints. Because of the assumed existence of such an individual, all the real-life behavioral characteristics of individuals, which can be drastically different from one person to another, are "smoothed away" or "averaged out." Moreover, conclusions developed in this fashion are then considered true for macro-level populations or organizations (Hudik, 2012). To avoid this pitfall, this section takes an approach that is more scientifically sound.

8.3.1 A Firm's Goal of Efforts and Understanding of Market Signals

The following result indicates that each viable firm is a system that is oriented towards some definitively defined objective(s), although the objective(s) generally evolve with time and get modified along with the changing market conditions.

Proposition 8.3 The goal of each business firm's effort is to materialize, at least partially or remotely, the firm's clearly stated mission.

Any viable business firm generally has a clearly stated mission that spells out the firm's purpose, including its system of values and beliefs, what it does, and what the targeted market segment it serves (McGrath, 2013), as implied by the firm's endowments of self-awareness and imagination. For example, a firm's mission could be about making as much profit as possible and/or contributing to the wellbeing of the society as much as possible. Because different people have different underlying systems of values and beliefs, as stated in Proposition 7.3, each firm that wishes to excel in the marketplace employs its mission to unify these individually different and most likely diverging systems of values and beliefs. Otherwise, various kinds of managerial inefficiencies appear (Forrest, 2018; Forrest & Orvis, 2016).

To see why Proposition 8.3 holds, let us systemically model such a firm that has a clearly stated mission. First, we identify the firm with the systemic structure of its organizational culture, business model, investment strategy, deployment of human talents, etc. Here, all these listed and unlisted aspects of the firm and its operation have of course been formulated around ultimately materializing the business objectives stated in the mission. Second, we model the specific moment the firm invests its resources in an effort (or operation) by the condition that the firm's underlying yoyo field is about to achieve an upper hand in its interaction(s) with some other systemic field flows in its environment. Then, this systemic model readily implies Proposition 8.3. In particular, the success, either expected or actual, of an effort is measured by comparing the state of the firm when the effort is concluded to the ideal state as described in the firm's mission. Therefore, the goal of each of the firm's efforts is to materialize, at least partially or remotely, the firm's clearly stated mission.

Proposition 8.4 By utilizing a firm's endowment of self-awareness, a firm can examine its understanding of and judgment about a market signal and possible ways to address the market call.

To see why this proposition is true, we note that a firm's self-awareness emerges from relentless interactions between its underlying systemic yoyo structure and those of all other economic agents, such as competitors, upstream suppliers, downstream complementors, and others. In particular, when the yoyo field of a focal firm continuously interacts with other fields in the economy, it engrosses and concurrently gives off things that can take physical, intellectual, tangible, or intangible forms. Therefore, in the market economy, there are constant struggles against each other and attractions that pull various yoyo fields towards one another. The struggles make the focal firm feel that it exists separately from other economic agents, and the attractions create for the firm the recognition of its particular rights and privileges. As time moves forward, the focal firm accumulates the necessary knowledge about how to satisfactorily handle various elements within the economy to harvest desirable outcomes.

Speaking differently, it is through various interactions with the yoyo fields of different economic agents and exchanges of information, knowledge, and ideas that a firm gains an understanding of itself, other economic agents, and various scenarios and challenges. That is, with time, a firm develops its reservoir of increasing magnitude, consisting of information, experience, and knowledge. The firm can employ these elements as freely and as many times as needed.

As for which particular action is considered more profitable than others, it is evaluated by the firm's system of values and beliefs that is derived from the firm's mission. At this stage of evaluation, the firm's endowment "imagination" plays its role. It helps the firm acquire a good command over the elements within the reservoir so that the management can associate the reservoir's elements in various ways imaginable. That is, the firm's imagination can be treated systemically as the place where new product designs, new operational routines, and innovative production procedures are fascinated. Within this place, information, knowledge, experiences, concepts, and facts are associated with each other in different ways, constituting a dynamically living whole that materialistically leads to creative market offers. When necessary, the elements in the reservoir of the firm's imagination are innovatively reconvened and creatively placed into new designs of products, services, managerial routines, and production procedures. In short, by utilizing self-awareness, a firm can examine its understanding of and judgment about a market signal and possible ways to address the market call.

8.3.2 *Facing Market Challenges and Decision-Making Situations*

Proposition 8.5 When a firm encounters a market situation in its pursuit of the stated mission, it utilizes its natural endowment of self-awareness to associate the situation under consideration with relevant elements in the reservoir of the firm's imagination so that an appropriate resolution can be hypothetically formulated based on the firm's conscience.

To see why this result holds, let us continue the analysis of Proposition 8.4. In particular, the yoyo structure of a firm is a complex spinning field, involving many different dimensions. That is, a great number of different variables are needed to describe this systemic structure. These variables and their interactions jointly contribute to the complexity of the systemic structure of the firm. Because each managerial understanding of the firm regarding the market is composed of those understandings of certain individual people, such as the top-level managers, the analysis of Proposition 7.2 shows that a great deal of the yoyo-field structures and systemic interactions that exist in the business world cannot be readily detected by the firm's conscious imagination. Hence, this systemic analysis implies that a firm's imagination is an organized system whose component parts include all the conscious and unconscious records of the interactions between the underlying yoyo field and others. The conscious part will be referred to as the firm's conscious imagination, while the unconscious the firm's unconscious imagination.

When a situation arises in a firm's pursuit of its mission (Proposition 8.3), the firm maps the situation and relevant details onto relevant elements and their particular associations in the structured reservoir of the firm's imagination by using self-awareness. The level of how well the firm's management can mobilize this self-awareness determines how deeply and widely the firm can map into and discover needed associations within this reservoir. This end demonstrates the importance of

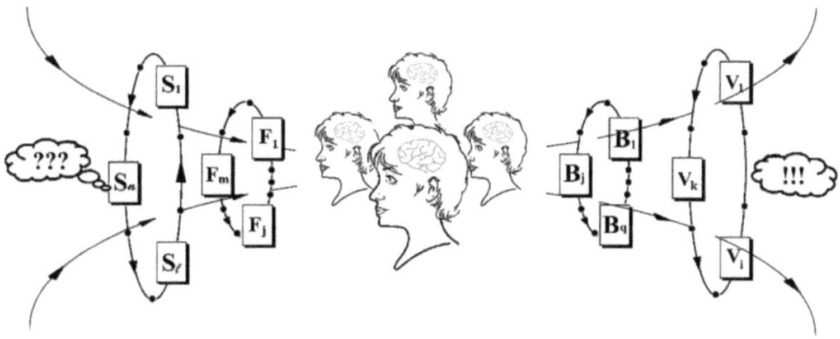

Fig. 8.1 The reflective nature of a firm's understanding of the market

the quality of the decision-making managers. A graphic representation of this mapping from the business world onto a firm's cognitive system is given in Fig. 8.1. In particular, the outwardly immeasurable and perpetual business world is both visually and conceptually seen as a hierarchical network with the firm's internal setting as the bottom layer, the set of the firm's supply-chain ecosystem as the next level, etc. Moroever, the systemic structure of the cognitive system of the firm correspondingly consists of such layers as those labeled by B, V, etc. In particular, B stands for the very basic needs of the firm, consisting of such fundamental elements of the firm's very existence as cash flows, specific design and production of certain products, and relevant market skills, among others. The V layer represents the firm's specific codes of conduct on how the supply-chain ecosystem functions. While the cloud labeled by question marks in the business world represents a situation confronting the firm, the other cloud labeled with exclamation marks in the firm's cognitive system depicts the relevant elements and their associations of the reservoir of the firm's imagination that potentially resolves the challenge of the situation. In this structured cognitive system of a firm, blocks of knowledge, experiences, and information of various kinds interact with each other to form elements of higher levels within the reservoir of the firm's imagination.

Since the cognitive system of a firm is made up of those of relevant people, such as the decision-making managers, Proposition 7.2 indicates that when a firm encounters a market situation in its pursuit of the stated mission, the firm employs its natural endowment of self-awareness to associate the situation with relevant elements in the reservoir of its imagination so that an appropriate resolution can be hypothetically developed based on the firm's conscience. The word "hypothetical" stands for the case that it still needs to confirm whether or not the proposed resolution works.

Proposition 8.6 At the macro firm level, the assumption of rationality stands for finding an optimal choice among all available alternatives with the criteria of optimum determined by the focal firm's management based on the firm's natural endowments.

To validate this conclusion, assume that a set of available alternatives is presented to the management of the focal firm. Then the decision-making management (or manager) compares the alternatives to find which option can provide the best chance for the firm to either materialize or get closer than before to its clearly stated mission as much as possible (Proposition 8.3). To this end, Proposition 8.4 implies that relevant managerial understandings, judgments in general and the feeling that the state of the firm will get closer as much as possible than before to its stated mission, in particular, are classified by mobilizing the firm's endowments. Based on such classification of how much each alternative can assist the firm to materialize or get closer to its mission, the decision-making management, as implied by Proposition 8.5, selects one option out of all available alternatives that will potentially provide the most value to the firm. Therefore, this analysis implies that at the macro firm level, rationality means finding one of the optimal choices among available alternatives with the criteria of optimum determined by the focal firm's management based on the firm's natural endowments.

Proposition 8.7 Each firm has its unique reservoir of imagination and dissimilar value-belief system.

To see the validity of this proposition, let us first look at the concept of value-belief systems. Each firm's value-belief system consists of its understanding of how the business world functions and adopted operational principles with which the firm is known for its particular identity and reputation in the marketplace. As soon as a firm starts to be developed, it begins to interact with various members and elements in the business world. These interactions expand in depth and width over time. It is through these interactions with economic agents, market offers, product designs, and others that the firm's value-belief system begins to sprout and is gradually formulated and solidified. This process is similar to how an individual develops his system of values, beliefs, and codes of conduct. For details, see the argument of Proposition 7.3.

Evidently, from one firm to another, the environment within which a firm develops and grows is different. For example, the founders of one firm are different from those of another firm, as individuals, in terms of their respectively varied backgrounds, how they view the world, and how they manage their businesses and personal lives. Due to all these differences in the business world experienced by individual firms that exist between the interactions with members and elements of the environment, each firm acquires its own set of very specific value-belief system. This system greatly influences and even dictates how a firm makes decisions and how to act out chosen business strategies. Although the differences may be minor compared to the magnificent scale of the interactions that take place in the business world, they surely lead firms to their individually very different systems of values and beliefs. That is why each firm has its unique reservoir of imagination and dissimilar value-belief system.

Proposition 8.8 When a firm faces a decision-making situation, it optimizes the potential subject to the given constraints by using its particular set of criteria formulated consistently with its value-belief system.

This result directly follows Propositions 8.3, 8.4, and 8.7. Specifically, to face a decision-making situation, Proposition 8.3 says that a firm aims at getting closer, at least partially, to its ideal state of business as described in its mission. Proposition 8.7 implies that from one firm to another, firms have either their own different missions or individually varied understandings of the same mission statement (Forrest & Orvis, 2016). Therefore, correspondingly Proposition 8.4 points to that a firm decides on how to possibly optimize the potential of the confronted decision-making situation subject to given constraints by employing its specific set of criteria, derived out of the firm's unique contents of natural endowments.

By combining Propositions 8.2 and 8.8, one can readily see the following conclusion:

Proposition 8.9 At either the micro individual level or the macro firm level, the assumption of rationality stands for an optimal fit of the decided choice within the underlying natural endowments of the decision-maker.

8.4 A Few Final Words

This chapter contributes to and enriches the extensive literature on the interpretation of the assumption of rationality by developing the following result: at both the micro individual level and the macro firm level, the assumption of rationality, as defined by, for example, Friedman (1953) and Wu (2003), represents an optimal fit of the chosen option within the underlying natural endowments (instead of self-interests) of the decision-maker.

The significance of this main conclusion can be seen from different angles. First, although it supports Simon's (1986) claim that the assumed rationality is about accounting for the decision behaviors of individuals, this conclusion specifies that an involved decision-making individual can be either a person or a firm. Second, although the assumption does not pinpoint particular choices (or point predictions) (Lovett, 2006), it does demonstrate that a decision-maker selects the option that is most preferred among available alternatives in any given situation (Rubinstein, 1998). Third, this conclusion does not support Becker's (1962) belief that the assumption focuses on aggregated group decisions. Fourth, this result confirms that there is no universally accepted definition of optimum. Instead, what is considered optimal is defined specifically by respective decision-makers. In other words, what is seen as optimal in one decision-maker's eyes can very well be seen as pessimal by another decision-maker. Fifth, this conclusion and Sect. 6.3 jointly indicate that the method of optimization used in decision-making can and should vary from one decision-maker to another. Six, for each decision-maker, its definition of optimum and method of optimization is defined through its natural endowments—self-awareness, imagination, conscience, and free will. For the case of individuals, see Branden (1969) and Lin and Forrest (2012). Both fifth and sixth contributions provide an explanation for why not all economic agents in real life are maximizers or minimizers, as noted by Taylor (1989), so that some of the main conclusions of economic theories do not hold true in practice. In other words, the system of values and beliefs of a decision-maker directly affects how the decision-maker prioritizes his decision choices and how he practically optimizes his objective (Forrest et al., 2021).

By comparing various interpretations of the assumption of rationality (e.g., Friedman, 1953; Wu, 2003), Hudik (2019) believes that this assumption represents a modeling device and helps predict group behaviors. To this end, the current chapter expands this belief by showing that rationality is needed for scholars to employ readily established mathematical methods to investigate economic topics and issues. In other words, this chapter shows that out of Hudik's two interpretations of this assumption—price-theoretic interpretation (PTI) and decision-theoretic interpretation (DTI)—future works should focus more on DTI. The reason is that PTI generally needs to introduce a fictitious representative into the construction of basic models (Wcyl, 2019).

As for future research along the lines laid out in this chapter, one can pay a revisit to each and every established conclusion of economics or economic theories where the assumption of rationality, no matter whether it is defined in the same was as what is addressed in this chapter or as a complete and transitive preference ordering (Mandler, 2001), is employed as one of the fundamental building blocks. Doing so is expected to reshape the entire landscape of all business-related knowledge, because such basics as the rationality assumption is no longer the same as before and the universally assumed meaning of optimization needs to be localized to individual decision-makers.

References

Becker, G. S. (1962). Irrational behavior and economic theory. *The Journal of Political Economy, 70*(1), 1–13.

Branden, N. (1969). *The psychology of self-esteem*. Nash Publishing Corp.

Forrest, J. Y. L. (2018). *General systems theory; foundation, intuition and applications in business decision making*. Springer.

Forrest, J. Y. L., & Liu, Y. (2022). *Value in business: A holistic, systems-based approach to creating and achieving value*. Springer.

Forrest, J. Y. L., & Orvis, B. (2016). Principles of management efficiency and organizational inefficiency. *Kybernetes, 45*(8), 1308–1322.

Forrest, J. Y. L., Hafezalkotob, A., Ren, L., Liu, Y., & Tallapally, P. (2021). Utility and optimization's dependence on decision-makers' underlying value-belief systems. *Review of Economic & Business Studies, 14*(2), 125–149. https://doi.org/10.47743/rebs-2021-2-0007

Friedman, M. (1953). *Essays in positive economics*. University of Chicago Press.

Gabaix, X. (2011). The granular origins of aggregate fluctuations. *Econometrica, 79*, 733–772.

Gilboa, I. (2010). *Rational choice*. The MIT Press.

Goodwin, N., Harris, J. M., Nelson, J. A., Roach, B., & Torras, M. (2013). *Microeconomics in context*. Routledge.

Gul, F., & Pesendorfer, W. (2008). The case for mindless economics. In A. Caplin & A. Schotter (Eds.), *The foundations of positive and normative economics: A handbook*. Oxford University Press.

Hu, K., Tao, Y., Ma, Y., & Shi, L. (2021). Peer pressure induced punishment resolves social dilemma on interdependent networks. *Scientific Reports, 11*, 15792.

Hudik, M. (2012). Transitivity: A comment on Block and Barnett. *The Quarterly Journal of Austrian Economics, 15*(4), 456–462.

Hudik, M. (2019). Two interpretations of the rational choice theory and the relevance of behavioral critique. *Rationality and Society, 31*(4), 464–489.

Kahneman, D. (2011). *Thinking, fast and slow*. Farrar, Straus and Giroux.

Kahneman, D., Knetsch, J. L., & Thaler, R. H. (1986). Fairness and the assumptions of economics. *Journal of Business, 59*(4), 285–300.

Knetsch, J. L. (1990). *Derived indifference curves*. Working Paper, Simon Fraser University.

Lakoff, G. (1996). *Moral politics: How conservatives and liberals think*. University of Chicago Press.

Lakoff, G., & Wehling, E. (1996). *Your Bain's politics: How the science of mind explains the political divide*. Societas essays in political &cultural criticism, Imprint-Academic.Com.

Lee, L., Amir, O., & Ariely, D. (2009). Search of homo economicus: Cognitive noise and the role of emotion in preference consistency. *Journal of Consumer Research, 36*(2), 173–187.

Lin, Y., & Forrest, B. (2012). *Systemic structure behind human organizations: From civilizations to individuals*. Springer.

Lovett, F. (2006). Rational choice theory and explanation. *Rationality and Society, 18*(2), 237–272.

Maialeh, R. (2019). Generalization of results and neoclassical rationality: Unresolved controversies of behavioural economics methodology. *Quality &Quantity, 53*, 1743–1761.

Mandler, M. (2001). A difficult choice in preference theory: Rationality implies completeness or transitivity but not both. In E. Milgram (Ed.), *Varieties of practical reasoning* (pp. 373–402). Cambridge.

Mani, A., Rahwan, I., & Pentland, A. (2013). Inducing peer pressure to promote cooperation. *Scientific Reports, 3*, 01735.

McGrath, R. G. (2013). *The end of competitive advantage: How to keep your strategy moving as fast as your business*. Harvard Business Review Press.

Mullainathan, S., & Thaler, R. H. (2000). *Behavioral economics*. NBER Working Paper no. 7948, October. National Bureau of Economic Research.

Robbins, L. (1932). *An essay on the nature and significance of economic science*. Macmillan.

Rubinstein, A. (1998). *Modeling bounded rationality*. The MIT Press.

Sen, A. (1991). *On ethics and economics*. Wiley.

Simon, H. A. (1986). Rationality in psychology and economics. *The Journal of Business, 59*(4), S209–S224.

Stigler, G. J., & Becker, G. S. (1977). De Gustibus Non Est Disputandum. *American Economic Review, 67*(2), 76–90.

Taylor, C. R. (1989). Duality, optimization, and microeconomic theory: Pitfalls for the applied researcher. *Western Journal of Agricultural Economics, 14*(2), 200–212.

von Mises, L. (1949). *Human action: A treatise in economics*. Yale University Press.

Wagner, J. (2012). The German manufacturing sector is a granular economy. *Applied Economics Letters, 19*, 1663–1665.

Weyl, G. E. (2019). Price theory. *Journal of Economic Literature, 57*(2), 329–384.

Wu, K. P. (2003). *Advanced microeconomics*. Tsinghua University Press.

Chapter 9
Economy's Properties Emerging Out of Micro Agents of Inconsistent Interests

Jeffrey Yi-Lin Forrest, Zaiwu Gong, Erkan Köse, Diane D. Galbraith, and Oğuzhan A. Arık

Abstract As indicated by the existing literature, computer simulations can reveal how characteristics of micro-level individuals give rise to macro-level phenomena of systemic wholes. This chapter, which is mainly based on Forrest et al. (Naše gospodarstvo/Our Econ 63(3):53–66, 2022), seeks to establish such an important simulation-based observation as a theoretical result on a sound foundation. It develops, by using systems science, a sufficient condition under which characteristics of micro-level agents can naturally lead to the appearance of macro-level properties of a systemic whole, even though the former are heterogeneous and behave in an unintended and uncoordinated manner. Going beyond when holistic phenomena can naturally emerge from micro-level characteristics, this chapter investigates how and why many macro-level entities appear to answer market calls through organically gathering micro-level agents into uniformly oriented operational wholes, even though these agents have inconsistent or even conflicting interests.

Keywords Centralized systems · Complex networks · Computer simulations · Emerged segregation · Keynesian DSGE model · Micro-foundations · Paradigm shift

---

Jeffrey Yi-Lin Forrest (Department of Accounting Economics Finance, Slippery Rock University, Slippery Rock, PA, USA; Email: Jeffrey.forrest@sru.edu), Zaiwu Gong (College of Management Science and Engineering, Nanjing University of Information Science and Technology, Nanjing, China; Email: zwgong26@163.com), Erkan Köse (Industrial Engineering Department, Nuh Naci Yazgan University, Kayseri, Turkey; Email: erkankose93@gmail.com), Diane D. Galbraith (Department of Management and Marketing, Slippery Rock University, Slippery Rock, PA, USA; Email: Diane.galbraith@sru.edu), and Oğuzhan A. Arık (Industrial Engineering Department, Nuh Naci Yazgan University, Kayseri, Turkey; Email: oaarik@nny.edu.tr) are equally contributed to this chapter.

J. Y.-L. Forrest, *Systemic Principles of Applied Economic Philosophies I*, Translational Systems Sciences 38, https://doi.org/10.1007/978-981-99-7273-9_9

9.1 Introduction

Since the time when the Great Recession occurred in 2008, scholars have realized that the currently available economic theories can neither predict the imminent arrival of a crisis nor help understand the underlying mechanism behind the originating imbalances that eventually led to the devastating consequences on unemployment and the real economy. To possibly overcome this recognized deficit in the relevant knowledge, the *Oxford Review of Economic Policy* developed a "Rebuilding Macroeconomic Theory Project" (Vines & Wills, 2018). The project examined a set of six broadly based questions related to the benchmark New Keynesian DSGE (Dynamic Stochastic General Equilibrium) model (Smets & Wouters, 2007). The authors focused on ways to improve or completely replace the benchmark model with another one; and the scholars involved in the project did not believe that a paradigm shift is needed other than enriching and improving the formulas of the model (Vines & Wills, 2018).

In contrast, a team of scholars from Italy proposes to embrace a paradigm shift by employing the theory and methods of the complexity science (Delli Gatti et al., 2010). Specifically, they suggest to apply the concept of complex networks and computer simulations instead of the current reductionist approach at the heart of the mainstream DSGE models. They demonstrate that computational techniques can vividly simulate the natural emergence of macro-level phenomena from unintended and uncoordinated behaviors of micro-level individuals when they follow some simple rules of action, such as financial contagion (Allen & Gale, 2001) and trade-credit relationships (Boissay, 2006; Battiston et al., 2007).

These two strings of efforts reveal a divergence of beliefs and logics of thinking in terms of how the community of economists should work in the coming years or even decades:

- Gradually enrich the benchmark New Keynesian DSGE model so that it can better predict forthcoming economic crises, provide more appropriate policy suggestions, etc.
- Radically adopt a revolutionary new approach so that the consequent theories will be mostly different from the ones currently available and the methods employed will be powerful and effective, both theoretically and practically.

According to Vines and Wills (2018, p. 5), a paradigm shift in an economic theory means drastic changes in both the content of the theory and the method employed to develop the theory. Hence, this chapter supports the Italian team's recognition of a forthcoming paradigm shift in economic theories in general and macroeconomics in particular (Delli Gatti et al., 2011). Specifically, in terms of contents, this chapter suggests to root each and every theoretical result of economics on some of the elementary facts of personal systems of values and beliefs, as suggested by Forrest et al. (2020) and presented earlier in this volume. And, in terms of methods used to develop theoretical results, this chapter expands those of networks and computer simulations, as suggested by the Italian colleagues (Delli

Gatti et al., 2010), to all methods of systems science established for studying organizations, evolutions, and interactions of organizations (Forrest et al., 2013).

Other than the holistic view described in the previous paragraph, in comparison with the literature along the two lines given above, the main contributions of this chapter are outlined below. First, it employs the concept of centralized systems to theoretically explain when macro socioeconomic phenomena emerge out of unintended and uncoordinated actions and interactions of micro economic agents. Such rigorously established conclusions are surely more general and reliable than those observed from computer simulations, such as those respectively observed and recorded by Allen and Gale (2001), Boissay (2006), Battiston et al. (2007), and many others, because each computer simulation-based observation is constrained by particularly chosen models and specified parametric values. Second, other than converting simulation-based observations into theoretical conclusions, this chapter establishes conditions for when macro-level economic entities appear to answer market calls and how micro-level individuals with inconsistent or even conflicting interests can be organically congregated into operational business organizations. The importance of this end cannot be overemphasized in light of the current trend of developing macroeconomic results on micro-foundations, where macro-level conclusions need to be founded on micro-level components (Blanchard, 2018; Lucas, 1976).

The rest of the chapter is organized as follows. Section 9.2 investigates how macro-level holistic phenomena can naturally appear out of the properties of micro-level components. Section 9.3 demonstrates that other than the emergence of macro-level phenomena out of unintended and uncoordinated micro-level properties, the business world consists of many purposively organized macro-level entities by making use of micro-level components, which generally have inconsistent or even conflicting interests. Section 9.4 concludes this chapter with ideas for possible future research.

9.2 Centralizability and Appearance of Holistic Phenomena

This section analyzes the concept of systemic centralizability and ways that it can be employed to explain the emergence of macro socioeconomic phenomena from unintended and uncoordinated actions and interactions of micro economic agents (Delli Gatti et al., 2010; Farmer & Foley, 2009).

9.2.1 Relevant Terminologies of Systems Science

To make this chapter more or less self-contained, this section introduces only concepts of systems relevant to the discussion in this chapter. For slightly more involved introduction, see Chap. 2 of this volume; and for a systematic study of systems science, please consult jointly with Forrest (2018), Forrest et al. (2013), and Klir (2001), each of which emphasizes a different aspect of the particular science.

By system, it means a whole, or an organization, or a structure, where micro-level parts or components are somehow associated with one another to form an organically functional macro-level entity. Historically, this concept can be traced back to the very start of the recorded human history (von Bertalanffy, 1968). To derive useful results and develop scientifically sound theories of systems, various particular specifications of this concept have been introduced by diverse authors for a myriad of purposes (Klir, 2001). Even so, among the most productive is the following specification, as described earlier in Chap. 2:

> *S* is a system, if and only if *S* is equal to an ordered pair (M, R) of sets, where *M* consists of all objects of the system *S* and *R* all relations that associate the component objects in the object set *M*; that is, each element in the relation set *R* is a relation defined on the object set *M*. (Lin, 1987)

Notice that elements in the object set *M* are not specified in this definition; therefore, some of these elements can also be systems themselves. When this happens, this definition of systems can be used to reflect layer structures—the relationship between micro-level economic men (and their individually different characteristics and functionalities) and macro-level business entities (and their holistic interactions).

This very idea of some objects of a system may also be systems themselves is depicted in Fig. 9.1. In particular, the system of the macro-level is $S = (M, R)$, where each object in *M* is shown as a dot, while the relation set *R* consists of four relations r_1, r_2, r_3, and r_4. As depicted, objects $O_i = (m_i, R_i)$ and $O_j = (m_j, R_j)$ in set *M* are also systems themselves. This concept of layered systems and systemic intuition readily reveals the following fact: The macro-level relations r_1, r_2, r_3, and r_4 may or may not be determined or influenced by the micro-level relations in O_i and in O_j. This observation will be shown in Sect. 9.3.

For a given system $S = (M, R)$, it is said to be trivial if $M = R = \varnothing$, that is, the object set is empty. This concept of trivial systems is needed for theoretical reasonings, such as the study of interactions of systems, for the same reason as why the concept of zero is necessary in the study of numbers. For two systems $S_i = (M_i, R_i)$, $i = 1, 2$, they are said to be equal or identical, denoted $S_1 = S_2$, provided that their object sets and relation sets are respectively the same. Symbolically, $S_1 = S_2$, if and only if

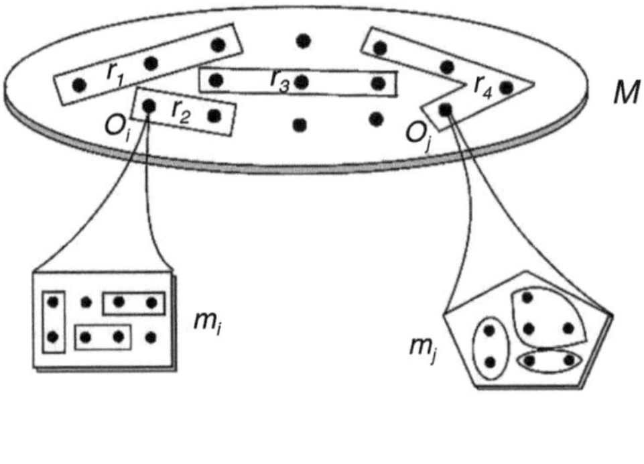

Fig. 9.1 Appearance of object systems

$$M_1 = M_2 \quad \text{and} \quad R_1 = R_2. \tag{9.1}$$

System S_1 is said to be a partial system of the system S_2, if $M_1 \subseteq M_2$, and for each relation $r_1 \in R_1$ there exists a relation $r_2 \in R_2$ such that r_1 is the restriction of r_2 on M_1. Symbolically, $r_1 = r_2 \mid M_1$, where $r_2 \mid M_1$ stands for the restriction of r_2 on M_1, defined by

$$r_2 \mid M_1 = r_2 \cap M_1^{n(r_2)} \tag{9.2}$$

where $M_1^{n(r_2)}$ is the set of all strings of elements from M_1 of length $n(r_2)$. For example, $M_1^3 = \{(m_1, m_2, m_3) : m_i \in M_1, i = 1, 2, 3\}$.

A system $S = (M, R)$ is referred to as a centralized system, provided that (1) each object in M is a system, and (2) there exists a nontrivial system $C = (M_C, R_C)$ such that for any distinct elements $x, y \in M$, say $x = (M_x, R_x)$ and $y = (M_y, R_y)$, the following hold true:

$$M_C = M_x \cap M_y \quad \text{and} \quad R_C \subseteq R_x|M_C \bigcap R_y|M_C, \tag{9.3}$$

where

$$R_x|M_C = \{r|M_C : r \in R_x\} \quad \text{and} \quad R_y|M_C = \{r|M_C : r \in R_y\}. \tag{9.4}$$

The system C is referred to as a center of the centralized system S. The concept of centralized systems was initially introduced by Hall and Fagen (1956) to describe such a system in which one object or a subsystem plays a dominant role in the system's operation. The leading part can be thought of as the center of the system, because when it changes slightly it would affect the entire system, causing considerable alterations. Figure 9.2 shows the structure of a centralized system $S = (M, R)$ with center $C = (M_C, R_C)$, where for any chosen objects $O_i = (M_i, R_i)$, $O_j = (M_j, R_j)$, and $O_k = (M_k, R_k)$ of S, the following hold true: $M_s = m_s \cup M_C$ and $m_s \cap M_C = \varnothing$, for $s = i, j, k$.

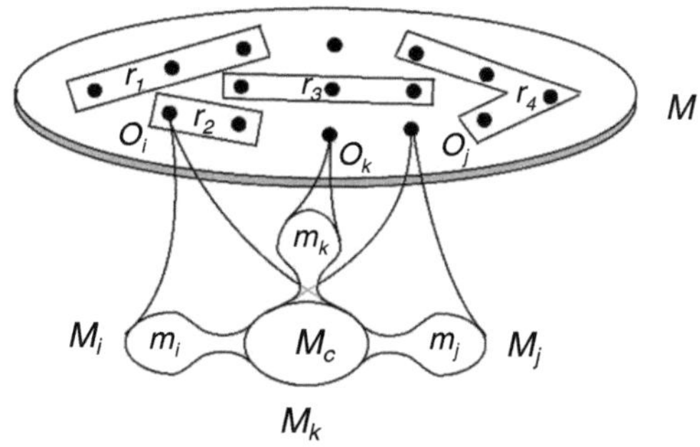

Fig. 9.2 The structure of a centralized system

Assume that κ and θ are two given cardinalities satisfying that θ is regular, and for any $\alpha < \theta$, $|\alpha^{<\kappa}| < \theta$, where $\alpha^{<\kappa} = \{\{f : \lambda \to \alpha\} : \lambda < \kappa\}$ and $|X|$ stands for the cardinality of the set X. For relevant concepts of set theory, see Kuratowski and Mostowski (1976). Assume that $S = (M, R)$ is a given system that satisfies: (1) $|M| \geq \theta$, (2) each object $m = (M_m, R_m) \in M$ is also a system, and (3) for any $m = (M_m, R_m) \in M$, $|M_m| < \kappa$. Then in the language of systems science, the following result holds true:

Theorem 9.1 If at least θ objects in the object set M of the system S contain a common element, then S has a partial system $S^C = (M^C, R^C)$ such that S^C forms a centralized system and $|M^C| \geq \theta$.

This systemic result is initially shown in Lin (1999). For related discussions on applications of this result in business research, see Forrest (2018). For the self-containment of this book, an outline of the proof is given in the appendix below and see Forrest (2018) for related discussions.

In order for us to apply this result to address our concerns here, let us specify this very general conclusion by letting $\theta = c$ and $\kappa = \aleph_0$, where c is the cardinality of the set of all real numbers and $\aleph_0$ the cardinality of the set of all natural numbers. Consequently, the assumption above reduces to the following condition: A given system $S = (M, R)$ satisfies (1) $|M| \geq c$, and (2) each object of S is also a system with a finite number of objects. Then, Theorem 9.1 becomes:

Corollary 9.1 If there is such an element that belongs to at least c objects in M, then system S has a partial system $P = (M_P, R_P)$ satisfying that $|M_P| \geq c$ and P is a centralized system.

This result is initially given by Lin (1988) when he attempted to explain two sociological phenomena systemically.

In the following subsection, we will examine how this corollary can help us explain macro-level phenomena that naturally appear out of micro-level properties of individual component parts. Or, we will look at how a system's holistic properties can emerge out of seemingly unintended and uncoordinated actions and interactions of the system's objects.

9.2.2 Naturally Emerging Macro Phenomena

To see how the previous results of general systems theory can be employed to confirm the appearance of macro-level phenomena, emerging out of unintended and uncoordinated micro-level individual desires, let us detail our analysis of Schelling's (1969) example of racial segregation in cities. In this well-honored work, Schelling shows that when people are allowed to choose which neighborhoods they live in, each person's relatively insignificant preference for neighbors of his own type can, and generally do, lead to macro-level residential segregation through individually and locally repeated housing decisions. In other words, individual's purposive desires of finding neighbors with slightly similar characteristics and relevant behaviors, although they are not coordinated, can indeed lead the emergence of racial segregations in cities. In such a situation, the emerged segregation is a holistic property of the city as a system—the macro level—while individual persons' desires and relevant behaviors are properties of the component micro level. This end reaffirms the adage that "birds" of a feather flock together.

Suppose that A is a set of people and $A^{<\omega}$ is the collection of all finite subsets of people in A. Then for any finite subset, three possibilities exist:

1. There is no relation that associates the people in x in any way.
2. There is exactly one relation that connects the people in the subset x.
3. There is more than one relation that links the people in x.

For situation (1), we construct a system $S_x = (x, \emptyset)$, where the relation set contains no element. For scenario (2), we build a system $S_x = (x, R_x)$ as follows: In the relation set R_x, there is only one element that depicts the relationship among the people in the finite set x. For the case (3), we construct a collection of systems:

$$\left\{S_x^i = \left(x, R_x^i\right) : i \in I_x\right\}, \tag{9.5}$$

where I_x is an index set that depends on the finite subset x, so that I_x and the collection of all relations between the people in subset x are one-to-one correspondent to each other; that is, for any $i \in I_x$, the relation set R_x^i contains only one element that describes an existing relationship between the people in x; and conversely, for any relationship g between the people in x, there is exactly one $i \in I_x$ satisfying that the relation set R_x^i of system $S_x^i = \left(x, R_x^i\right)$ contains exactly one element r_g that describes g. For scenarios (2) and (3), let the set of all existing relations between the people in $x \in A^{<\omega}$ be denoted as C^x. Then, scenario (2) is equivalent to $|C^x| = 1$, and scenario (3) is equivalent to $|C^x| > 1$.

Next, let us consider the particular system $S = (M, \emptyset)$ with an empty relation set so that

$$M = \{S_x : x \in A^{<\omega}(|C^x| \leq 1)\} \cup \left\{S_x^i = \left(x, R_x^i\right) : x \in A^{<\omega}, i \in I_x(|C^x| > 1)\right\}. \tag{9.6}$$

Now, Corollary 9.1 says that if (1) the cardinality $|M| \geq c$, and (2) there exists at least one person from A who belongs to at least c many object systems in M, then there exists a subset $M^C \subseteq M$ such that $S^C = (M^C, \emptyset)$ forms a centralized system and $|M^C| \geq c$.

The construction of the system $S = (M, \emptyset)$ implies that condition (1) means that there exists a complicated network of relationships among the people in A; and condition (2) implies that there exists at least one person in A who is sufficiently associated with the other people in A. When studying the network of relationships among people in an economy, condition (1) can be seen as satisfied without much doubt, while condition (2) surely holds true if we look at a prominent politician. More specifically, when one studies economic issues that involve a set A of people, the sophistication of the network of relationships among the people can be measured by the number of mathematically defined relations (Lin, 1999, p. 97) as follows: If r describes a relation between and among the people in A, then there is an ordinal number $n = n(r)$, a function in r, such that $r \subseteq A^n$, where

$$A^n = \underbrace{A \times A \times \cdots \times A}_{n \text{ times}} = \{f : f \text{ is a mapping } n \to A\}. \tag{9.7}$$

That is, to apply Corollary 9.1 with all necessary rigor, one needs to rewrite each relation between people in the language of set theory. In particular, each relation must be written in such a way that it consists of the following basic blocks only: "x is a set," "$x \in y$," "$x = y$," "and," "or," "if . . . then," and "if and only if." For details see Kuratowski and Mostowski (1976). Because of this requirement, we can generally say based on Corollary 9.1 that as long as a particular human desire appears in the minds of a sufficiently large number of people and these people materially act to realize the desire in real life, then a partial system of sufficient scale of the whole system will reflect the realization of the desire. In other words, for a micro-level desire to blossom into a macro-level phenomenon, even for the case that people with the desire behave uncoordinatedly, the following condition must be met: The people with the particular desire engage in a large number of actions for the purpose of materializing the desire in real life.

In short, a condition for a micro-level desire of the component parts of an economy to eventually lead to the emergence of a macro-level characteristic of the entire economy is the following: A large population of people possess that desire and proactively engage in efforts to materialize the desire, even though they act uncoordinatedly.

Now, let us look at Schelling's (1969) example of racial segregation in cities. In this case, especially in the past in America, the majority of the population felt comfortable to have people of their own type as neighbors, while people were allowed to repeatedly relocate. Evidently, each relocation presented an opportunity for relocators to materialize their desires, which are either spoken or unspoken. Corollary 9.1 implies that such deeply rooted desire in individual minds of the population and opportunities for individuals to make repeated adjustments, although uncoordinated, eventually led to racial segregation in American cities.

Similarly, Thurner et al.'s (2012) example can be systemically revisited and explained. In particular, Thurner et al. show that risk controls at local levels by individual lenders can collectively induce a large instability in prices and involuntarily create more systemic risk. These local lenders, for instance, banks and other financial institutions, rationally adjust their individual leverage exposures of collateralized borrowers in order to avoid unnecessary risks, when the prices of the assets used as collateral are dropping. As a consequence of such uncoordinated adjustments of leverage exposures, margin calls are issued, leading to massive selling of collateralized assets at just the wrong time. Hence, dangerously spiked volatility in price fluctuations appears at the macro-level. Although the emergent property of the economic system as a whole does not seem derivable from the rationales and behaviors of individuals—the lenders—the emergence of the systemic volatility in price fluctuations can be readily seen by using Corollary 9.1. Specifically, although in terms of absolute numbers, there are a few lenders when compared to the entire population, they in reality affect a large segment of the economy through their lending activities. That is, a large portion of the population is adversely disturbed by margin calls so that the resultant massive selling by individual borrowers eventually merges together into a market-wide risk of sufficiently large magnitude. In such a situation, even though the selling of individual borrowers seems to be uncoordinated on the surface, these individuals' actions in reality are unconsciously coordinated by the lenders, due to the overall small number of them.

9.3 Macro-Structures Emergent Out of Micro Economic Agents

This section provides a theoretical explanation for how markets signal for additional competition and innovation. Consequently, this helps various macro organizations, consisting of micro economic men and agents of inconsistent or even conflicting interests, to be organized. In other words, other than many socioeconomic phenomena that naturally emerge at the macro level out of unintended and uncoordinated actions and interactions of micro economic men and agents (Delli Gatti et al., 2010; Farmer & Foley, 2009), as discussed in the previous section, there are many entities (macro-level phenomena) in the business world (the macro-level system) that are organized purposefully to answer calls or invitations of various markets or to satisfy forever-changing consumer demands (Forrest et al., 2017).

9.3.1 The Market Signals Calling for Additional Innovations

First, let us examine how markets within the present business world call for new products and innovation. For this purpose, let us look at such a market that is served by m incumbent firms with their mutually substitutable offerings, $m = 1, 2, \ldots$ Assume that each of these incumbent firms enjoys the backing of loyal customers who only purchase the offering provided by their favorite firm, as long as the price is no more than their reservation value.[1] Within this market, the incumbent firms

[1] In the real business world, loyal-customer bases are formed due to various reasons. One of the key reasons is how the philosophy or the customer value proposition of a particular product fits the value-belief systems of certain groups of customers, as revealed, for example, by studies of marketing scholars (e.g., Li et al., 2022; Payne et al., 2017), by studies of corporate social responsibilities and substainability (e.g., Ashby et al., 2012; Liu et al., 2018) by use values, etc.

compete with each other over those customers, called switchers, who switch from the offering of one firm to that of another depending on whose price is more competitive. The price of a product here does not mean the absolute dollar value of a product. Instead, it stands for the price of per-unit value of a product. For example, the price of a pair of walkie talkies is a lot lower than that of two iPhones. However, other than functioning as equipment for short-distance communications, an iPhone has many other capabilities. So, if one compares their prices of per-unit values, two iPhones are much lower priced than a pair of walkie talkies.

Considering how readily information and knowledge are available due to the rapid development of information and communication technology, assume that the pricing strategies of all interacting firms are known to each other so that the incumbent firms employ their best responses in terms of price by playing the Nash equilibrium through pure self-analysis. Then, the following result holds true:

Theorem 9.2 In the Nash equilibrium of the afore-described market, if the segment of switchers is greater than the minimum loyal-customer base of the incumbent firms, then at least one new firm can gainfully enter into the market by providing its substitute offering, and the total expected profit of all entering firms can be potentially as large as the profit of the incumbent with the smallest base of loyal customers.

The extremely technical proof of this result is given in the appendix below. In terms of the literature, a similar result as Theorem 9.2 is established by Forrest et al. (2017). However, in comparison, the result given here generalizes the previous version in the following sense: The latter result is shown to hold under very strong conditions—the boundary conditions of all the incumbent firms are identical, where the firms' bases of loyal customers have the same magnitude, and they have the same reservation prices, the same cost of production, the same sales price, the same amount of available resources, etc. Differently, Theorem 9.2 holds true without subject to any of these constraints. In a layman's language, Theorem 9.2 states that when there is a sufficient consumer surplus (or a large enough totality of switchers), new competition naturally appears, no matter what entry barriers the incumbent firms attempt to install. That is, it is market characteristics that beget the introduction of new or improved products and innovations that incite the aspiration of new entrants with the promise of potentially making more profits than at least some of the existing firms.

The conclusion in Theorem 9.2 can be applied practically in different ways. First, in the perspective of the incumbent firms in a relatively stable market, their market establishment places them in a state of mutual forbearance. They alleviate rivalry by dividing markets in proportion to their strengths (Bernheim & Whinston, 1990). They discretely allow stronger ones to dominate market segments they are less efficient (Li & Greenwood, 2004). Such codependence of these incumbents helps de-escalate rivalry (Yu & Cannella Jr., 2012) so that interfirm hostility declines (Haveman & Nonnemaker, 2000). To protect their market territory and status, which means steady flows of profits, the incumbent firms need to stay vigilant about the magnitude of the segment of switchers. As soon as this magnitude grows into a sufficiently large scale, new competition will appear; and that will mostly likely disrupt the existing state of mutual forbearance among the incumbent firms. Therefore, these incumbents have to continuously improve their offerings to satisfy consumers' forever-evolving consumption preferences.

Second, in the perspective of firms that attempt to enter in a relatively stable market beyond those they had already established themselves, the large scale of the market segment of switchers indicates that all the available offerings in the marketplace cannot truly satisfy the demands of these particular consumers. Hence, entrepreneurial firms that attempt to enter into this or some other market need to creatively identify the preferences of switchers and determine their optimal entry timing (Zachary et al., 2015), defined as the order of entry into the existing market in various contextual referents. In terms of literature, Lieberman and Montgomery (1988) propose the concept of first-mover advantage. They believe that first (or early) movers enjoy extra time over later ones for them to establish and occupy market territories. That is, entry timing matters in terms of economic performance (Fosfuri et al., 2013). However, studies (e.g., Lieberman & Montgomery, 2013; and references found there) also suggest that time equally benefits later entrants, because delayed entry helps firms avoid costly pitfalls experienced by earlier movers. So, empirical analyses reveal such a logic that it explains why first movers have advantages over later ones and, simultaneously, why later movers enjoy recompenses over earlier ones (Lévesque et al., 2013). To resolve such a predicament, Theorem 9.2 comes to the rescue. In particular, for entrepreneurs who desire to start their own companies, they can purposefully develop their firms to enter such a market based on their innovative understanding of the market signal—the existence of a sufficiently large segment of switchers and their designs and productions of creative solutions. For established business entities that look for a new market to enter, they need to delay their entry into such a market until the market situation clears and settles. Theorem 9.2 states that as long as they can compete with incumbent firms through advanced technology, more efficient management, or other means, they will have a chance to make more profits than some of the established incumbent firms.

Third, when Theorem 9.2 is applied to an emerging market, such as the PC market in the 1970s and 1980s (Sobel, 1999), other than the population of consumers being not well defined, the market segment of switchers expands quickly. It grows in magnitude constantly without any bound in sight. In such a market, first and early movers, if they want to survive and then succeed, have to aggressively reach out to potential consumers, many of whom would be switchers initially at least, in order to establish their corresponding bases of loyal customers while restricting the number of switchers as much as possible. At the same time, it is prudent for established companies in the business world to simply wait until those poorly funded and/or inexperienced start-up firms have steadily developed the width and depth of the market before entering. Other than waiting for the formation of a new market with sufficient depth and width, Theorem 9.2 says that the patience of waiting can provide these companies, as later movers, with the expectation of higher profitability than some of the early movers. This conclusion aligns with Golder and Tellis (1993). In particular, after analyzing 500 products in 50 different product categories, they empirically find that pioneers take approximately 10% of the market share with approximately 50% of them failing outright, while early followers occupy approximately 28% of the market with only approximately 8% failures. Additionally, Theorem 9.2 supports Markides and Geroski (2005) in the conclusion that large, multi-business enterprises exploit slack resources and complementary capabilities to scale up their operation and bypass early entrants.

9.3.2 How Conflicting Micro Agents Can Organically Form Macro-Structures

No matter which case among those discussed in the previous subsection one is reviewed, efforts to succeed in the market that signals for new competition and additional innovation have to start with forming macro-level organizations by employing micro-level individuals and component parts. In particular, for the case of a relatively stable market, one smart incumbent strategy is to uphold their established mutual forbearance with each other so that their corresponding flows of profits can be more or less readily maintained. To accomplish this, these incumbent firms need to organize their business efforts around protecting their market territories and status quos—a macro-level organizational structure—by effectively mobilizing their working units and individual employees, micro-level entities, towards a common goal.

For the case of ambitious start-ups that attempt to launch their operations by entering into a relatively stable market, the entrepreneurs have to first organize intellectual manpower to creatively decipher the meaning of a market signal, second design and produce a brand-new market offer that will potentially satisfy the market demand, and third bring the final product onto the market. All these macro-level efforts require orienting micro-level individuals towards an identified purpose. As for the case of an emerging market, first and early movers have to develop their bases of loyal customers by introducing their innovative market offers, while established companies in the business world only enter when the market has developed its sufficient depth and width. All these macro-level business attempts come to fruition through organized efforts of micro-level individuals.

In short, many macro-level systemic phenomena emerge naturally from micro-level component parts, as discussed in the previous section. At the same time, a lot of macro-level organizations, events, and processes are purposively organized to answer market calls and to meet consumer demands by effectively mobilizing micro-level individuals and component parts. By comparing the two situations—one naturally emergent and the other humanly organized—one can see that the former amplifies micro-level individual properties, no matter how unintended and uncoordinated they might be, onto systemic phenomena. And the latter organically places micro-level individuals and component parts into functional organizations towards the realization of an identified goal. So, a natural question arises: How can micro-level individuals and component parts with inconsistent or even conflicting interests work together to accomplish macro-level common goals?

To answer this question, we examine the following related questions individually: (1) Why do micro-level individuals and component parts mostly possess their individually inconsistent or even conflicting interests? (2) What method do firms effectively employ to orient their employees' otherwise divergent efforts into a unified force? (3) How are micro-level individuals and component parts with individually inconsistent or even conflicting interests practically placed into a cohesive organization?

Regarding question (1), let us focus on how each individual person forms his system of beliefs and values during the person's formative years. As for each component part of a whole, its beliefs and values consist of those shared by the members of the component. In terms of the concept of personal systems of beliefs and values, it means a person's view on how the world functions and how he needs to behave in order to stay within moral boundaries. Because of the existence of such a belief-value system within each person's cognition, a person is recognized with his particular identity and integrity (Forrest, 2018, p. 302).

To help accomplish our goal here, let us borrow the systemic yoyo model of systems; for more details and related discussions, see Chap. 2 of this volume or Lin (2009). Specifically, for each system, it can be intuitively or figuratively imagined as a multidimensional entity as shown in Fig. 9.3. This systemic intuition indicates that each entity, which is naturally a system according to Klir (2001), in the universe, be it physical or intellectual, and be it a tangible or intangible object, a living being, an organization, a market, or an economy, can be intuitively seen as a kind of realization of a certain multidimensional spinning yoyo with an eddy and meridian field around. It stays in a spinning motion. If it stops its spinning, it will no longer exist as an identifiable system. For all detailed discussions on why this abstract yoyo structure behind each and every system exists, please consult with Lin (2009).

This yoyo model implies that each person lives in a large pool of spinning fields, which are the fields of other people, physical things, abstract thoughts, and a myriad of other matters. As soon as a person is born, his yoyo field starts to interact with many different yoyo fields. It is through these interactions with people, with physical

Fig. 9.3 The abstract yoyo model of each system in the three-dimensional space

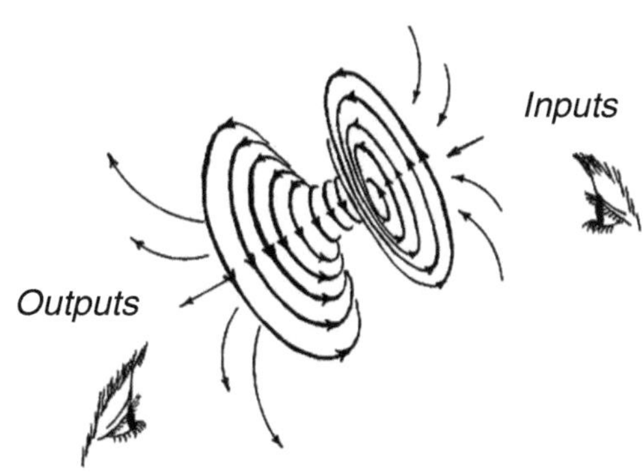

objects, and with abstract thoughts and the various other things and matters that the person develops his system of fundamental beliefs and values through employing the four inherent endowments: self-awareness, imagination, conscience, and free will. This situation of how a person forms his beliefs and values is similar to the way that a civilization formulates its value system (Lin & Forrest, 2011). Within these interactions, there are always inevitable differences. That explains why each person has his own unique system of very specific beliefs and values. It is this specific belief-value system that dictates the person's decision-making for the rest of his life. Although with time the belief-value system evolves with certain components updated while some others replaced, the most fundamental parts stay more or less constant. As for individually inconsistent or even conflicting beliefs and values, they generally stem from the differences in the environments in which people grow up and form their initial beliefs and values. Comparing to the magnificent scale of the entire ocean of spin fields of the world, although differences in environments might be subtle or minor, they are still generally major to individuals involved. These environmental differences lead to important inconsistencies and conflictions in relevant personal belief-value systems. That explains systemically why, for example, children who grow up within the same household possess quite different, even conflicting, personalities, characteristics, and thinking processes (Scott et al., 1991).

In terms of question (2), what method do firms effectively employ to orient their employees' otherwise divergent efforts into a unified force? The answer is that firms, which expect to successfully offer products in the consumer market, clearly state and rigorously commit to their missions. In particular, in its mission, a firm clearly spells out its purpose of existence, including its values and beliefs, what it does, and what the targeted market segment it serves. Because employees tend to have inconsistent or even conflicting beliefs and values, firms employ their missions and serious commitments to the missions to organically unite the otherwise divergent employee efforts towards the practical end of materializing their stated business goals. This approach has been confirmed as effective empirically by McGrath (2013) and theoretically by Forrest et al. (2020).

At this junction, we need to note that although the goal of a firm might be to make as much profit as possible, or contribute to the well-being of the society in a particular way, or others, the maximization of the business objective, as given in the mission statement, has to include the component of staying competitive in the product market. This end is reinforced by Theorem 9.2, because only by maintaining its financial competitiveness in the marketplace, a firm is able to survive economically. And only a financially solvent firm is able to materialize its noneconomic goals of business.

As for question (3), how are micro-level individuals and components with individually inconsistent or even conflicting interests practically placed into a cohesive organization? The answer lies in the systemic yoyo intuition in Fig. 9.4. Specifically, the figure is the bird's-eye view of the yoyo model of a general, market-oriented firm (Fig. 9.3), where the entire dish spins counterclockwise, while each local eddy field models an employee's systemic structure, consisting of all elements in his system of beliefs and values and their associations. The different arrow

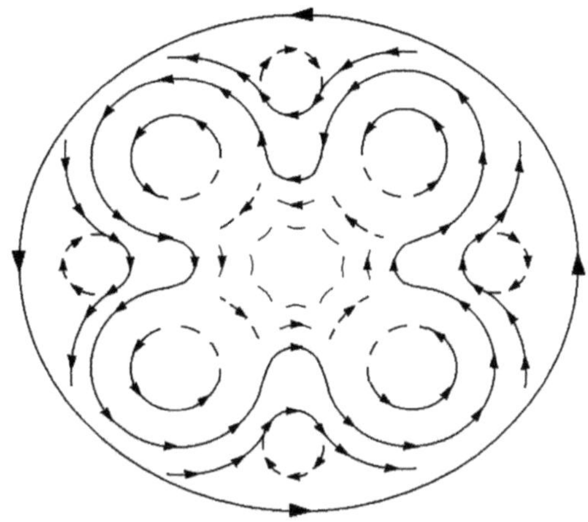

Fig. 9.4 The eddy field of a focal firm

directions model how individual employees display their inconsistent or even conflicting interests with each other.

Because each employee tends to have his own unique system of beliefs and values, one can readily see that for most employees, their personal belief-value systems will more or less disagree with the stated mission of the firm. Therefore, another question that naturally follows the one that is just addressed in the previous paragraph is: When a firm's mission is in conflict with the personal beliefs and values of an employee, can the firm still make use of the talent of the employee while keeping his well-being in mind? For this question, Fig. 9.4 suggests that the answer to this question is: Yes, it is possible. As the conclusion of this section, we use the conventional method of microeconomics to reconfirm this answer.

Assume that other than maximizing its objective, as defined in the written mission statement, the focal firm of our concern constantly examines how well its mission is accomplished. Let the aforementioned employee be i and Y, such a variable that measures a particular aspect of i's personal system of beliefs and values that disagrees with the mission of the firm. In real life, although it is very possible that this variable Y cannot be explicitly measured or even defined clearly, its existence is definitely unquestionable from the assumption that the firm's mission and employee i's personal belief-value system disagree with each other.

Let employee i's utility function be expressed as follows: $U_i = X_i Y$, the degree of accomplishment of the stated mission be measured by the following mission function—mission $= X_C/Y$, where X_i stands for the aggregate consumption of employee i, and X_C the aggregate expenditure of the firm for running its business. Then the objective function of the firm can be particularly given by

$$\text{obj} = \text{obj}(U_i, \text{mission}) = U_i \times \text{mission} = X_i \times X_C, \tag{9.8}$$

in which the particular variable Y disappears. That means that although the firm's mission is in conflict with the personal belief-value system of employee i, in the objective function the firm still cares about employee i as much as if the two does not have any conflict. The key here is that the firm has the freedom to define its objective function in an appropriate functional form. And, from Eq. (9.8), it follows that no matter whether variable Y is measurable or not, the desired conclusion is derived nevertheless. For relevant discussions on managerial efficiency, see Forrest and Orvis (2016).

9.4 A Few Final Words

This chapter examines two diverging efforts that exist in the present literature regarding how to reshape the existing economic theories so that economists will be able to forecast imminent economic crises in a timely fashion and provide policy makers with needed scholarly supports, among others (Delli Gatti et al., 2010; Vines & Wills, 2018). Considering the fact that predicting natural disasters has been an unsettled world-class challenge to the entire world of natural science and mathematics (Lin & OuYang, 2010), the effort of simply modifying the current system of equations in the benchmark New Keynesian DSGE model to forecast imminent economic crises (Vines & Wills, 2018) will be destined to be fruitless. In particular, most large-scale natural events play out through their processes without being disrupted by humans, no matter if their disastrous consequences are predicted or not. However, economic disasters are very different. They are reflexively influenced by human expectations; their courses of evolution are greatly and determinately affected by human participants' estimates and consequent actions (Soros, 2003). This end explains why the attempt of using a few simple DSGE equations (Smets & Wouters, 2007) to forecast disruptively different outcomes of reflexive human processes from any records of the past is practically impossible (Lin & OuYang, 2010). To this end, as a reference, it is necessary for us to note the following effort. For years, there was a well-funded research center for mid-term weather forecasts in Europe. This center developed for its purpose of prediction a system of more than five million equations in over five million variables, while the actual forecasts of weathers had experienced uncertainties (Lorenz, 1993). For similar reason, the effort of providing more adequate scholarly supports for policy making is destined to be unsuccessful if the focus is only on revising the current DSGE model, because adequate policy making is essentially dependent on forecasts of the future (Forrest et al., 2020).

Failures of forecasting the future using the DSGE model or any modified equation-based future version are rooted in the fact that such efforts attempt to extrapolate either the past or the present into the future. Hence, any result of such forecast cannot and will not capture changes that are sudden and disruptively different from the past or the present (Wu & Lin, 2002). That is the reason why this chapter embraces and generalizes the approach of Delli Gatti et al. (2010) from merely employing concepts and methods of complexity and computer simulations to those of systems science.

Because of the novelty of the employed approach—systemic logic of thinking—and methodology that is based on both set theory and game theory, this chapter is able to develop:

- A new way to interpret abstract conclusions of mathematics in terms of when some characteristics of micro-level individuals can give rise to macro-level phenomena of systemic wholes, as revealed by Delli Gatti et al. (2010, 2011) through using computer simulations
- How market sends out its invitations for new products and additional innovations and why new competition appears

And on top of these theoretical conclusions, this chapter theoretically explains:

- When some characteristics of micro-level individuals can give rise to macro-level phenomena of systemic wholes, as revealed by Delli Gatti et al. (2010, 2011) through using computer simulations.
- How racial segregation in American cities appeared (Schelling, 1969) and how risk controls at local levels by individual lenders can collectively induce a large instability in prices and involuntarily create more systemic risk (Thurner et al., 2012).
- Why various macro firms are organized with micro economic men and agents although these micro components have inconsistent or even conflicting interests. That is, not all macro-level phenomena can have direct micro-foundation or micro-founded explanations, as believed by economists since the 1970s (Blanchard, 2018; Lucas, 1976).

Potential future research, building on this chapter, can examine, for example, (1) how individually inconsistent or even conflicting beliefs and values can be smoothly unified under the mission statement of a firm, while the naturally resultant adverse effects or relevant managerial inefficiency (Forrest & Orvis, 2016) is reduced to a minimal level, (2) how an organizational culture inducive to a firm's market success (McGrath, 2013) can be successfully fostered on top of individually inconsistent or even conflicting beliefs and values, and (3) what particular methods of predicting economic crises can be developed on the idea of structural changes (Lin & OuYang, 2010) instead of the current, widely employed extrapolation of the past or present into the future.

Appendix: Proofs of Theorems

The proof of Theorem 9.1: Without loss of generality, let $|M| = \theta$ and assume that there is a common element in each of the object sets of object systems in M. Then $|\cup \{M_x : x = (M_x, R_x) \in M\}| \leq \theta$.

In the general statement of this theorem, the particulars of the objects in each M_x, for each object $x = (M_x, R_x) \in M$, are irrelevant. So, let $\bigcup\{M_x : x = (M_x, R_x) \in M\} \subseteq \theta$. Then, for each $x = (M_x, R_x) \in M$, the object set M_x has some order type $< \kappa$ as a subset of θ. Because θ is a regular cardinality satisfying $\theta > \kappa$, there exists a $\rho < \kappa$ such that $M_1 = \{x \in M: M_x$ has order type $\rho\}$ has cardinality θ. Fix such a ρ and let us deal only with the partial system $S_1 = (M_1, R_1)$ of S, where R_1 is the restriction of the relation set R on M_1.

For each $\alpha < \theta$, $|\alpha^{<\kappa}| < \theta$ implies that less than θ objects of the partial system S_1 have object sets as subsets of α. Thus, $\bigcup\{M_x : x = (M_x, R_x) \in M_1\}$ is cofinal in θ. If $x \in M_1$ and $\xi < \rho$, let $M_x(\xi)$ be the ξth element of M_x. Because θ is regular, there is ξ such that $\{M_x(\xi): x \in M_1\}$ is cofinal in θ. Now fix ξ_0 to be the least such ξ. Then the condition that there exists a common element in each system in M_1 implies that $\xi_0 > 0$. Let $\alpha_0 = \bigcup \{M_x(\eta) + 1 : x \in M_1$ and $\eta < \xi_0\}$. Then $\alpha_0 < \theta$ and $M_x(\eta) < \alpha_0$ for all $x \in M_1$ and all $\eta < \xi_0$.

By transfinite induction on $\mu < \theta$, pick $x_\mu \in M_1$ so that $M_{x_\mu}(\xi_0) > \alpha_0$ and $M_{x_\mu}(\xi_0)$ is above all elements of earlier x_ν; i.e., $M_{x_\mu}(\xi_0) > \max\{\alpha_0, \bigcup\{M_{x_\nu}(\eta) : \eta < \rho \text{ and } \nu < \mu\}\}$.

Let $M_2 = \{x_\mu : \mu < \theta\}$. Then $|M_2| = \theta$ and $M_x \bigcap M_y \subseteq \alpha_0$ whenever $x = (M_x, R_x)$ and $y = (M_y, R_y)$ are distinct objects in M_2. The condition that for each $\alpha < \theta$, $|\alpha^{<\kappa}| < \theta$ implies that there exists an $r \subset \alpha_0$ and a $B \subset M_2$ with $|B| = \theta$ and for each $x \in B$, $M_x \bigcap \alpha_0 = r$, $S^C = (M^C, R^C) = (B, R_B)$ forms a centralized system, where R_B is the restriction of the relation set R on $M^C = B$.

The proof of Theorem 9.2: For incumbent firm i, its selling price P_i satisfies $C_i \le P_i \le M_i$, where C_i is the cost of production and M_i the maximum selling price, which is equal to the reservation price of loyal customers. Hence, there is $\alpha_i \in [0, 1]$ such that $P_i = C_i + \alpha_i(M_i - C_i)$, $i = 1, 2, \ldots, m$. For the rest of the proof, instead of P_i, the incumbent firms compete with each other by adjusting α_i, $i = 1, 2, \ldots, m$. Without confusion, we will use P_i in place of α_i, where all costs of production and maximum selling prices are respectively normalized to 0 and 1.

In terms of performance, each incumbent firm is constrained by its available resources (Harmancioglu et al., 2009; Barney & Arikan, 2001) and how the resources are mobilized (Peteraf & Barney, 2003; Forrest et al., 2020). If the factors involved in business operation include x_1, x_2, x_3, …, then for incumbent firm i (= 1, 2, 3, …, m), the magnitude $N_i(x_1, x_2, x_3, \ldots)$ of its loyal-customer base is bounded in the upper and lower sides: $L_i(x_1, x_2, x_3, \ldots) \le N_i(x_1, x_2, x_3, \ldots) \le U_i(x_1, x_2, x_3, \ldots)$, where L_i is the lower bound and U_i the upper bound. That is, there is a unique number $\beta_i \in [0, 1]$, $i = 1, 2, \ldots, m$, satisfying that $N_i(x_1, x_2, x_3, \ldots) = L_i(x_1, x_2, x_3, \ldots) + \beta_i[U_i(x_1, x_2, x_3, \ldots) - L_i(x_1, x_2, x_3, \ldots)]$. Hence, the magnitude N_i of firm i's loyal-customer base can be normalized to $\beta_i \in [0, 1]$ such that the segment of switchers is of the magnitude β such that $\beta = 1 - \sum_{i=1}^{m} \beta_i$ and $0 \le \beta \le 1$. In the rest of the proof, these normalized parameters are used.

In Nash equilibrium, the given market does not have any pure strategy of pricing for the incumbent firms. In fact, for any portfolio $(x_1, x_2, \ldots, x_m)$ of pure strategies of prices, let i_1, i_2, …, $i_k \in \{1, 2, \ldots, m\}$ such that $1 \le k \le m$ and $x_{i_1} = x_{i_2} = \ldots = x_{i_k} < x_j$, for $j \in \{1, 2, \ldots, m\}$ and $j \ne i_s$, $s = 1, 2, \ldots, n$. If $k = 1$, then firm i_1 has ready won over all switchers and can therefore slightly raise its price x_{i_1} to bring in additional profits as long as the new price is still the lowest. If $1 < k \le m$, then one of the firms i_1, i_2, …, i_k can lower its price slightly to create additional profits by attracting all switchers. Therefore, the portfolio $(x_1, x_2, \ldots, x_m)$ of pure strategies is not a Nash equilibrium.

Let $F_i(P)$ be the price distribution of incumbent firm i with price P. Then, in Nash equilibrium, our market has a unique portfolio $(F_1(P), F_2(P), \ldots, F_m(P))$ of mixed strategies, where for $k = 1, 2, 3, \ldots,$

$$F_k(P) = 1 - \frac{1}{\beta_k}\left(\frac{(1-P)\prod_{i=1}^{m}\beta_i}{\beta P}\right)^{\frac{1}{m-1}}, F_k(1) = 1, F_k\left(\frac{\beta_k}{\beta_k + \beta}\right) = 0. \tag{9.9}$$

In fact, the objective of firm k is to maximize its expected profit from its loyal customers and its share of switchers by selecting an appropriate price distribution $F_k(P)$:

$$\max_{F_k(P)} E(\Pi_k) = \int_{-\infty}^{+\infty}\left\{\beta_k P + \prod_{i=1, i\neq k}^{m}[1 - F_i(P)]\beta P\right\} dF_k(P), \tag{9.10}$$

where Π_k is firm k's profit and $E(\Pi_k)$ its expected profit. Hence, the equilibrium indifference condition for firm k is

$$\beta_k P + \prod_{i=1, i\neq k}^{m}[1 - F_i(P)]\beta P = \beta_k, \quad k = 1, 2, 3, \ldots, \tag{9.11}$$

which implies

$$\prod_{j=1, j\neq i}^{m}[1 - F_j(P)] = \frac{\beta_k(1-P)}{\beta P}, \quad i = 1, 2, \ldots, m. \tag{9.12}$$

Dividing the first equation by the jth in Eq. (9.12) produces

$$1 - F_j(P) = \frac{\beta_1}{\beta_j}[1 - F_1(P)], \quad j = 2, 3, \ldots, m. \tag{9.13}$$

Substituting Eq. (9.13) into Eq. (9.11) leads to the following, and so Eq. (9.9) follows:

$$\beta_1[1 - F_1(P)] = \left(\frac{(1-P)\prod_{i=1}^{m}\beta_i}{\beta P}\right)^{\frac{1}{m-1}}. \tag{9.14}$$

The second part of Eq. (9.9) can be checked directly. For the second part, firm k needs to attract as many switchers as possible to increase its profits from the guaranteed level β_k by charging from its loyal consumers the reservation value 1. So, $\beta_k P + \beta P \geq \beta_k$, which implies $P \geq \beta_k/(\beta_k + \beta)$. Hence, the third part of Eq. (9.9) follows.

When the afore-described market is in the Nash equilibrium, all the normalizations above jointly imply that $\beta_i = \beta_1$, $i = 2, 3, \ldots, m$. In fact, these β_is are not all equal to each other, let $\beta_k = \max\{\beta_1, \beta_2, \ldots \beta_m\}$ and $\beta_k > \beta_{k_0}$, for k and k_0 satisfying $1 \leq k$, $k_0 \leq m$. Then, Eqs. (9.10), (9.11), and (9.9) jointly imply that the expected profit of firm k in the Nash equilibrium is

$$E(\Pi_k) = \int_{-\infty}^{+\infty} \left\{ \beta_k P + \prod_{j=1, j\neq k}^{m} [1 - F_j(P)]\beta P \right\} dF_k(P) = \int_{\frac{\beta_k}{\beta_k+\beta}}^{1} \beta_k dF_k(P) = \beta_k F_k(P)|_{\frac{\beta_k}{\beta_k+\beta}}^{1}$$

$$= \beta_k \left\{ \frac{1}{\beta_k} \left[\frac{\left(1 - \frac{\beta_k}{\beta_k+\beta}\right) \prod_{j=1}^{m} \beta_j}{\frac{\beta\beta_k}{\beta_k+\beta}} \right]^{\frac{1}{m-1}} \right\} = \left(\prod_{j=1, j\neq k}^{m} \beta_j \right)^{\frac{1}{m-1}}.$$

The meaning of loyal customers and the existence of k_0 jointly imply

$$E(\Pi_k) = \left(\prod_{j=1, j\neq k}^{m} \beta_j \right)^{\frac{1}{m-1}} \geq \beta_k = \left(\underbrace{\beta_k \beta_k \ldots \beta_k}_{m-1 \text{ times}} \right)^{\frac{1}{m-1}} > \left(\prod_{j=1, j\neq k}^{m} \beta_j \right)^{\frac{1}{m-1}} = E(\Pi_k),$$

which is a contradiction. Hence, all loyal-customer bases of the incumbent firms must have the same magnitude, which is denoted as α. So, Eq. (9.9) implies that in Nash equilibrium, the afore-described market has a unique symmetric portfolio ($F_1(P)$, $F_2(P)$, ..., $F_m(P)$) of pricing strategies, where $F_k(P) = F(P)$, for $k = 1, 2, 3, \ldots$

To complete the proof of Theorem 9.2, assume without loss of generality that one and only new firm enters the market by uniformly randomizing its price P between the production cost and the expected maximum selling price. The previous discussion indicates that all these variables can be normalized into $P \in [0, 1]$, respectively.

To deal with the market disruption caused by the entrant, each of the m incumbent firms sets its price by considering those of all rivals, including the entrant and other incumbent firms. So, Eqs. (9.9) and (9.11) jointly produce the following equilibrium indifference condition of incumbent firm k:

$$\beta_k P + \beta P(1 - P) \prod_{j=1, j\neq k}^{m} [1 - F_j(P)] = \beta_k. \tag{9.15}$$

From this equation, $\beta_k = \alpha$ and $F_k(P) = F(P)$, $k = 1, 2, 3, \ldots$, we obtain

$$F(P) = 1 - \left(\frac{\alpha}{\beta P}\right)^{\frac{1}{m-1}} \tag{9.16}$$

which is defined when $1 \geq P \geq \alpha/\beta$. Hence, the expected profit of the entrant is

$$E_e(\Pi) = \begin{cases} \frac{-m}{2(m-2)}\frac{\alpha^2}{\beta} + \frac{m-1}{m-2}\frac{\alpha^{\frac{m}{m-1}}}{\beta^{\frac{1}{m-1}}} + \beta\left(\frac{\alpha}{\beta}\right)^{\frac{m}{m-1}}, & \text{if } m \geq 3 \\ \frac{\alpha^2}{2\beta} - \frac{\alpha^2}{\beta} ln \frac{\alpha}{\beta} + \beta\left(\frac{\alpha}{\beta}\right)^{\frac{m}{m-1}}, & \text{if } m = 2 \end{cases} \quad (9.17)$$

And the expected profit of any of the m incumbent firms is

$$\begin{aligned} E_m(\Pi) &= \int_{\alpha/\beta}^{1} \left\{ \alpha \times P + \beta \times P(1-P) \prod_{j \neq i}^{m} [1 - F(P)] \right\} dF(P) + \alpha \times \left(\frac{\alpha}{\beta}\right)^{\frac{1}{m-1}} \\ &= \int_{\alpha/\beta}^{1} \alpha dF(P) + \alpha \left(\frac{\alpha}{\beta}\right)^{\frac{1}{m-1}} = \alpha. \end{aligned} \quad (9.18)$$

Now, it is ready to check that $\frac{\partial}{\partial \alpha}[E_e(\Pi) - E_m(\Pi)] > 0$ and that when $\alpha = 1/(m + 1) = \beta$, $E_e(\Pi) - E_m(\Pi) > 0$. Hence, there is $\alpha^* \in (0, 1/(m + 1))$ such that when $\alpha \geq \alpha^*$, the expected profit $E_e(\Pi)$ of the entering firm is greater than that $E_m(\Pi)$ of any of the incumbent firms. So, the conclusion of Theorem 9.2 follows.

References

Allen, F., & Gale, D. (2001). Financial contagion. *Journal of Political Economy, 108*, 1–33.

Ashby, A., Leat, M., & Hudson-Smith, M. (2012). Making connections: A review of supply chain management and sustainability literature. *Supply Chain Management, 17*(5), 497–516. https://doi.org/10.1108/13598541211258573

Barney, J., & Arikan, A. (2001). The resource-based view: Origins and implications. In M. Hitt, R. Freeman, & J. Harrison (Eds.), *Handbook of strategic management* (pp. 124–185). Blackwell.

Battiston, S., Delli Gatti, D., Gallegati, M., Greenwald, B., & Stiglitz, J. (2007). Credit chains and bankruptcies avalanches in supply networks. *Journal of Economic Dynamics and Control, 31*, 2061–2084.

Bernheim, B. D., & Whinston, M. D. (1990). Multimarket contact and collusive behavior. *RAND Journal of Economics, 21*, 1–26.

Blanchard, O. (2018). On the future of macroeconomic models. *Oxford Review of Economic Policy, 34*(1–2), 43–54.

Boissay, F. (2006). *Credit chains and the propagation of financial distress*. European Central Bank, Working Paper No. 573.

Delli Gatti, D., Gaffeo, E., & Gallegati, M. (2010). Complex agent-based macroeconomics: A manifesto for a new paradigm. *Journal of Economic Interaction and Coordination, 5*, 111–135.

Delli Gatti, D., Desiderio, S., Gaffeo, E., Cirillo, P., & Gallegati, M. (2011). *Macroeconomics from the bottom-up*. Springer.

Farmer, D., & Foley, D. (2009). The economy needs agent-based modelling. *Nature, 460*, 685–686.

Forrest, J. Y. L. (2018). *General systems theory: Foundation, intuition and applications in business decision making*. Springer.

Forrest, J. Y.-L., & Orvis, B. (2016). Principles of management efficiency and organizational inefficiency. *Kybernetes, 45*(8), 1308–1322.
Forrest, J. Y.-L., Duan, X. J., Zhao, C. L., & Xu, L. D. (2013). *Systems science: Methodological approaches*. CRC Press, an imprint of Taylor and Francis.
Forrest, Y. L. J., Buttermore, J., & Wajda, T. A. (2017). At Nash equilibrium when new market competitions appear? *Kybernetes, 46*(2), 256–271.
Forrest, J. Y. L., Nicholls, J., Schimmel, K., & Liu, S. F. (2020). *Managerial decision making: A holistic approach*. Springer.
Forrest, J. Y. L., Gong, A. W., Köse, E., Galbraith, D. D., & Arık, O. A. (2022). An economy's emergent properties and how micro agents with inconsistent or conflicting interests are holistically organized into macro entities. *Naše gospodarstvo/Our Economy, 63*(3), 53–66. https://doi.org/10.2478/ngoe-2021-0017
Fosfuri, A., Lanzolla, G., & Suarez, F. F. (2013). Entry-timing strategies: The road ahead. *Long Range Planning, 46*, 300–311.
Golder, P. N., & Tellis, G. J. (1993). Pioneer advantage: Marketing logic or marketing legend? *Journal of Marketing Research, 30*, 158–170.
Hall, A. D., & Fagen, R. E. (1956). Definitions of systems. *General Systems, 1*, 18–28.
Harmancioglu, N., Droge, C., & Calantone, R. (2009). Strategic fit to resources versus NPD execution proficiencies: What are their roles in determining success? *Journal of the Academy of Marketing Science, 37*(3), 266–282.
Haveman, H. A., & Nonnemaker, L. (2000). Competition in multiple geographic markets: The impact on growth and market entry. *Administrative Science Quarterly, 45*(2), 232–267.
Klir, G. (2001). *Facets of systems science*. Springer.
Kuratowski, K., & Mostowski, A. (1976). *Set theory: With an introduction to descriptive set theory*. North-Holland.
Lévesque, M., Minniti, M., & Shepherd, D. (2013). How late should Johnny-come-lately come? *Long Range Planning, 46*, 369–386.
Li, S. X., & Greenwood, R. (2004). The effect of within industry diversification on firm performance: Synergy creation, multi-market contact and market structuration. *Strategic Management Journal, 25*, 1131–1153.
Li, Z., Choi, S., & Forrest, J. Y. L. (2022). Understanding peer pressure on joint consumption decisions: The role of social capital during emerging adulthood. *Young Consumers*. https://doi.org/10.1108/YC-03-2022-1494
Lieberman, M. B., & Montgomery, D. B. (1988). First-mover advantages. *Strategic Management Journal, 9*, 41–58.
Lieberman, M. B., & Montgomery, D. B. (2013). Conundra and progress: Research on entry order and performance. *Long Range Planning, 44*, 312–324.
Lin, Y. (1987). A model of general systems. *Mathematical Modelling, 9*(2), 95–104.
Lin, Y. (1988). An application of systems analysis in sociology. *Cybernetics and Systems, 19*, 267–278.
Lin, Y. (1999). *General systems theory: A mathematical approach*. Kluwer Academic/Plenum Publishers.
Lin, Y. (2009). *Systemic yoyos: Some impacts of the second dimension*. CRC Press.
Lin, Y., & Forrest, B. (2011). *Systemic structure behind human organizations: From civilizations to individuals*. Springer.
Lin, Y., & OuYang, S. C. (2010). *Irregularities and prediction of major disasters*. CRC Press, an imprint of Taylor and Francis.
Liu, Y., Quan, B. T., Xu, Q., & Forrest, J. Y. L. (2018). Corporate social responsibility and decision analysis in a supply chain through government subsidy. *Journal of Cleaner Production, 208*, 436–447.
Lorenz, E. N. (1993). *The essence of chaos*. Washington University Press.
Lucas, R. (1976). Econometric policy evaluation: A critique. *Carnegie-Rochester Conference Series on Public Policy, 1*, 19–46.

Markides, C. C., & Geroski, P. A. (2005). *Fast second: How smart companies bypass radical innovation to enter and dominate new markets*. Jossey Bass/Wiley.

McGrath, R. G. (2013). *The end of competitive advantage: How to keep your strategy moving as fast as your business*. Harvard Business Review Press.

Payne, A., Frow, P., & Eggert, A. (2017). The customer value proposition: Evolution, development, and application in marketing. *Journal of the Academy of Marketing Science, 45*, 467–489.

Peteraf, M., & Barney, J. (2003). Unraveling the resource-based tangle. *Managerial and Decision Economics, 24*(4), 309–323.

Schelling, T. C. (1969). Models of segregation. *American Economic Review, 59*(2), 488–493.

Scott, W. A., Scott, R., & McCabe, M. (1991). Family relationships and children's personality: A cross-cultural, cross-source comparison. *British Journal of Social Psychology, 30*(1), 1–20.

Smets, F., & Wouters, R. (2007). Shocks and frictions in US business cycles: A Bayesian DSGE approach. *American Economic Review, 97*(3), 586–606.

Sobel, R. (1999). *When giants stumble: Classic business blunders and how to avoid them*. Prentice Hall.

Soros, G. (2003). *The alchemy of finance*. Wiley.

Thurner, S., Farmer, D., & Geanakoplos, J. (2012). Leverage causes fat tails and clustered volatility. *Quantitative Finance, 12*(5), 695–707.

Vines, D., & Wills, S. (2018). The rebuilding macroeconomic theory project: An analytical assessment. *Oxford Review of Economic Policy, 34*(1–2), 1–42.

von Bertalanffy, L. (1968). *General systems theory*. George Braziller.

Wu, Y., & Lin, Y. (2002). *Beyond nonstructural quantitative analysis: Blown-ups, spinning currents and the modern science*. World Scientific.

Yu, T., & Cannella, A. A., Jr. (2012). A comprehensive review of multimarket competition research. *Journal of Management, 39*, 76–109.

Zachary, M. A., Gianiodis, P. T., Payne, G. T., & Markman, G. D. (2015). Entry timing: Enduring lessons and future directions. *Journal of Management, 41*(5), 1388–1415.

Chapter 10
Overcoming the Challenge of the Fallacy of Composition

Jeffrey Yi-Lin Forrest, Joachim Wagner, Jennifer Nightingale, Huan Guo, and Jennifer Roy

Abstract This chapter, which is mainly based on Forrest et al. (The fallacy of composition, its wide-ranging applications in economics/business and why systems science is appropriate for economic and business research, to appear) first looks at how the thinking logic of the well-known fallacy of composition has been widely and erroneously employed in economic and business studies. It then proposes systems science and methodology as an appropriate approach needed for investigating the organizations, evolutions, and interactions of business entities. To demonstrate the theoretical and practical potential of this proposal, the centralizability theorem of general systems is restated here to confirm how unintended and uncoordinated micro-level individual desires can naturally lead to macro-level phenomena, such as racial segregation and major risks of market fluctuations, as discussed in an earlier chapter. In other words, although there are indeed many properties that emerge at the macro level not directly out of the characteristics of micro-level individuals, these systemically emergent properties can indeed be explained by using systems logic. For various reasons, empirical analyses are inevitable for economic and business studies. This chapter proposes a potential way to possibly rewrite statistically confirmed hypotheses into generally true conclusions by referencing to principle of mathematical induction.

Keywords Best practices · Emergent properties · Fallacy of division · Linear thinking · Principle of economic induction · Science of complexity

---

Jeffrey Yi-Lin Forrest (Department of Accounting Economics Finance, Slippery Rock University, Slippery Rock, PA, USA; Email: Jeffrey.forrest@sru.edu), Joachim Wagner (Institute of Economics, Leuphana University, Lueneburg, Germany; Email: wagner@leuphana.de), Jennifer Nightingale (Department of Information Technology and Management, Slippery Rock University, Slippery Rock, PA, USA; Email: Jennifer.nightingale@sru.edu), Huan Guo (School of Mathematics and Computer Science, Jianghan University, Wuhan, China; Email: guohuan@jhun.edu.cn), and Jennifer Roy (Department of Business Administration, Waynesburg University, Waynesburg, PA, USA; Email: jroy@waynesburg.edu) are equally contributed to this chapter.

J. Y.-L. Forrest, *Systemic Principles of Applied Economic Philosophies I*,
Translational Systems Sciences 38, https://doi.org/10.1007/978-981-99-7273-9_10

10.1 Introduction

Although the fallacy of composition is not as heavily studied as some other fallacies, it indeed represents a major erroneous logic of thinking widely employed in many areas of exploration of knowledge (Finocchiaro, 2015). Considering how scholars in natural and social sciences, respectively, apply different methodological approaches to derive their conclusions (Forrest et al., 2020), this chapter examines how the thinking logic of the fallacy of composition is erroneous from the point of view of systems science.

From the angle of commonly employed methods in literature, this chapter demonstrates how widely and deeply the erroneous thinking logic of the fallacy of composition permeates areas of economic and business studies. With such methodological fact convincingly given, our attention turns to finding which methodology is truly appropriate for investigations of economic and business issues. Because most studies of economics and business deal with business organizations, evolutions, and interactions of such organizations, we identify systems science as a truly appropriate and adequate tool and theoretical and methodological foundation for economic and business scholars and practitioners to use in their studies and in their decision-makings. This realization generalizes that of Delli Gatti et al. (2010), who persuasively illustrate how the science of complexity can intuitively produce emergent properties of systems, not shared by constitutive components, because studies of complexity are part of systems science. To confirm the theoretical and practical legitimacy of this generalization, this chapter restates a theorem of systems science, established by using purely logical reasoning without touching on computer simulation or any method from the science of complexity, that is, other than using computational techniques, as suggested by Delli Gatti and his colleagues, how some holistic, emergent properties of systems, such as macro-level racial segregation (Schelling, 1969) and systemically shocking market risks (Thurner et al., 2009), can be quite readily derived by using logically developed conclusions.

Another contribution this chapter makes to the literature is how systems logic of thinking and systems methodology can expectedly help improve a currently helpless situation that faces economists, decision-making managers, and entrepreneurs. Specifically, it can be widely observed that when a business endeavor achieves success, many scholars jump on the opportunity to reveal what had led to the success. They develop theories on what noticeably different the business did from its rivals in the hope that the recognized success can be explained theoretically and duplicated practically in real life. However, such scholarly efforts often produce theories that are inconsistent with or even contradictory to each other; and practical attempts to duplicate the success based on these theories typically are not as successful as had hoped. One example of such helpless situations is the story with the Industrial Revolution (Forrest et al., 2018; Wen, 2016). A second example is the endless number of debates one round after another about the usefulness of industrial policies (Andreoni & Chang, 2019).

Methodologically, the root reason for the helpless situations to appear, as described above, is that the developed theories are mostly empirical and data- or anecdotally driven (i.e., the fallacy of composition is in play). However, a given set of anecdotes (or data) can be generally understood in different ways, many of which can be inconsistent with and even contradictory to each other. Hence, to avoid such scholarly difficulty and the erroneous logic of the fallacy of composition, there is a need for scholars to develop theories on a sound theoretical foundation through employing reliable methodologies, such as systems science. That is exactly where this chapter comes into being. As a matter of fact, this current situation, where business theories are mostly data (or anecdotes) driven, can be seen as parallel to that when Isaac Newton and his contemporaries developed their elementary laws of physics. For example, large amounts of business data are presently collected and made available for analysis in order to find latent profit opportunities. And at the time when Newton and his contemporaries developed their laws, large amounts of data in astronomy and from physics labs were collected. Therefore, history suggests that we can develop sound economic and business theories by using systems science, while referencing to empirically confirmed hypotheses (Lin, 2009). The great successes of physics indicate that this approach can be expectedly successful.

Because empirical studies are inevitable in areas of economics and business, this chapter proposes to develop a principle of economic induction, similar to that of mathematical induction (Forrest, 2013), to potentially rewrite statistically confirmed hypotheses as generally true propositions. The practical significance of this proposal is that if successful, many of the current managerial suggestions of limited validity, given by various scholars, can then become general recommendations for decision-making managers, entrepreneurs, and policy makers.

The rest of this chapter is organized as follows. Section 10.2 reviews the concept and history of the fallacy of composition and how it appears in many areas of knowledge exploration, including mathematics. Section 10.3 reveals how widely the erroneous logic of this fallacy has been applied in studies of economics and business. Section 10.4 demonstrates why comparing to all other widely employed methods and approaches, systems analysis, and methodology is appropriate for economic research. Section 10.5 addresses the issue of how to possibly rewrite empirical conclusions as generally true facts. Finally, Section 10.6 concludes this presentation.

10.2 The Fallacy of Composition and Mathematical Induction

Regarding the definition of this fallacy, there are a number of different versions. For example, Copi (1968, p. 81) provides his definition as follows:

> The fallacy of composition turns on a confusion between the 'distributive' and the 'collective' use of general terms... (It) may be defined as the invalid inference that what may be truly predicated of a term distributively may also be truly predicated of the term collectively.

He then uses an example that illustrates how this fallacy is in the play: From the fact that a bus uses more gasoline than an automobile, one concludes that all buses use more gasoline than all automobiles (Copi, 1968, p. 81). According to the Webster's *Third New International Dictionary* (1976 edition, p. 818), this fallacy is described below:

> (It is) the fallacy of arguing from premises in which a term is used distributively to a conclusion in which it is used collectively or of assuming that what is true of each member of a class or part of a whole will be true of all together.

Halverson (1984, p. 73) gives the following description:

> The fallacy of composition consists in treating a distributed characteristic as if it were collective. It occurs when one makes the mistake of attributing to a group (or a whole) some characteristic that is true only of its individual members (or its parts), and then makes inferences based on that mistake.

For Walton et al. (2008, pp. 112–114), the fallacy is described as follows:

> It goes from the premise that "all the parts of X have property Y" to the conclusion that "X has property Y".

Contemporary scholars treat fallacy of composition with another meaning (Finocchiaro, 2015, p. 27): predicting the whole from its parts, where properties of the parts of a whole are fallaciously imagined as properties of the whole itself. For example, for a particular machine, because each of its parts is light in weight, the machine, as a whole, is light in weight (Kahane, 1973, p. 244).

Historically, the conception of the fallacy of composition can be traced back to Aristotle's writings, although the exact term was not introduced (cf., Hansen & Pinto, 1995, pp. 1–10; Woods, 2012, pp. 521–522). For instance, the Aristotelian *sophistical refutations* contain the "combination" and "division" of words; his theology deals with the relationship between parts and their whole (von Bertalanffy, 1968). The explicit use of the term appears with the *Port Royal Logic* with the original French edition in 1662 (e.g., Arnauld & Nicole, 1965, p. 255; 1685, p. 109; 1996, p. 199), where the fallacy is defined simply as "passing from a divided sense to a composite sense" (Arnauld & Nicole, 1996, p. 199). In 1826, Whately (1826, pp. 174–175) discussed this fallacy in his *Elements of Logic* by saying that "There is no fallacy more common, or more likely to deceive, than the one now before us: the form in which it is usually employed, is, to establish some truth, *separately*, concerning each single member of a certain class, and thence to infer the same of the *whole collectively*." And in the past 50 plus years, this fallacy has been studied in logic and argumentation theory, although mostly as a series of footnotes to Hamblin's (1970) *Fallacies* and of developments culminating with Woods' (2013) *Errors of Reasoning*. For a more systematic historical account, see Finocchiaro (2015).

In terms of applications of this fallacy of composition, it appears in the exploration of many fields of knowledge, ranging from those that are empirically based, where general conclusions are drawn from isolated scenarios, to those that are mostly theoretical, where mathematical induction is employed. As examples of fields that are empirically based, let us first look at environmental research. In particular, the claim of global warming typically involves aggregating individual measures of local temperatures from around the world through grouping and averaging (Haller, 2002, p. 50). Second, in the study of managerial strategies, individual cases of business successes are frequently compared to produce recommendations for general use (McGrath, 2013). Third, for the Great Recession of the recent past, its persistence is believed (Krugman, 2013) to be caused by austerity policies adopted by most developed economies, hoping that the policies would directly work on parts of the economies, such as households and individual firms.

To see why theoretical investigations that employ mathematical induction also suffer from the fallacy of composition, let us take a look at how such principle of induction is phrased. In technical terms, mathematical induction is generally presented in one of the following two versions (Forrest, 2013, p. 192):

Mathematical Induction (version 1): Assume that $\Phi(n)$ is a proposition regarding natural number n. If the following two steps can be shown:

Initial step: $\Phi(k_0)$ holds true for a certain natural number k_0,
Inductive step: If $\Phi(n)$ holds true for $n = k \geq k_0$, then $\Phi(k + 1)$ holds true,

then the proposition $\Phi(n)$ holds true for all natural numbers $n \geq k_0$.

Mathematical Induction (version 2): Assume that $\Phi(n)$ is a proposition regarding natural number n. If the following two steps can be shown:

Initial step: $\Phi(k_0)$ holds true for a certain natural number k_0,
Inductive step: If $\Phi(n)$ holds true for all natural number n satisfying $k_0 \leq n \leq k$, then $\Phi(k + 1)$ holds true,

then the proposition $\Phi(n)$ holds true for all natural numbers $n \geq k_0$.

Intuitively, this mathematical induction can be imagined as follows: Let us abstractly consider the particularly given proposition $\Phi(n)$ as a ladder of infinite length, where the natural number variable n is seen as the nth step of the ladder. Hence, the natural ordering of natural numbers implies that the greater n is, the higher the step is on the ladder. Now, the initial step of the mathematical induction says that a person can actually get on the ladder on step k_0. The inductive step says that if the person can climb the ladder to step k ($\geq k_0$), then he can next climb to step $k + 1$. If these two steps can be confirmed, then the mathematical induction concludes that the person can finish climbing the infinitely long ladder $\Phi(n)$. It is this conclusion that the fallacy of composition comes in, where a jump from individual step n to the collection of all natural numbers takes place. However, it is demonstrated (Forrest, 2013) that such jump cannot really happen; otherwise the foundation of mathematics will collapse. This end of course means that many theorems, such as Debreu's (1959) existence theorem of utility function, in economics, established on mathematical induction either directly or indirectly, will become invalid or need to be reconfirmed.

Note 10.1 This discussion means that the conclusion of mathematical induction needs to be modified as follows: Instead of those given above, the correct conclusion is that the proposition $\Phi(n)$ holds true for *every* natural number $n \geq k_0$.[1] In particular, when the word "all" is replaced by "every", the fallacy of composition no longer occurs.

Note 10.2 On the surface, mathematical induction does not seem to be directly related to the studies of economics and business. However, this feeling cannot be further from the truth. For example, Debreu (1959, pp. 56–59) established the following well-known, fundamental theorem of economics by using mathematical induction: For a consumer, if the set X of his possible consumptions is a connected subset of the ℓth dimensional Euclidean space $\mathbb{R}^\ell$ and his preference relation $\precsim$ is a complete, continuous preorder, then there is a continuous utility function $u : X \to \mathbb{R}$.

The proof of this result consists of four steps:

(a) There is a countable and dense subset D in X, where the case that X is a singleton is ignored, and each point $x \in D \subset \mathbb{R}^\ell$ contains only rational-number components.
(b) An increasing function $u' : D \to [a, b]$ is defined, for any chosen real numbers a and b such that $a < b$.
(c) This function $u' : D \to [a, b]$ is extended to $u : X \to [a, b]$.
(d) Shown is that u is continuous.

In Step (a), Debreu argues for the countability of D based on that one can match *every* rational number with a unique natural number (Kuratowski & Mostowski, 1976). And in Step (b), if D contains either a least element x^α or a greatest element x^β, Debreu defines $u'(x^\alpha) = a$ and $u'(x^\beta) = b$. Next, he orders the other elements of D and all rational numbers in the interval (a, b) as follows, since both sets are countable:

$$\left(x^1, x^2, \ldots, x^p, \ldots\right) \text{ and } \left(r^1, r^2, \ldots, r^q, \ldots\right).$$

Then, in an orderly fashion, he defines $u'(x^p)$, for each $p = 1, 2, 3, \ldots$, so that for every r^q, $q = 1, 2, 3, \ldots$, there is a x^p so that $u'(x^p) = r^q$. That is, the function u' is constructed.

In short, for Steps (a) and (b) in Debreu's proof, the countability of D and the existence of u' are guaranteed by employing mathematical induction.

Opposite to the fallacy of composition is the so-called fallacy of division (Finocchiaro, 2015). It stands for the error in logic one commits when he reasons like: If something is true for a whole, then that something must be true for all or some of the parts of the whole. Speaking differently, the fallacy of division can be phrased as going from the ground that "X has property Y" to the conclusion that "all the parts of X have property Y" (Walton et al., 2008, pp. 316–317).

[1] The vase puzzle (Lin, 1999, pp. 178) explains why "all" and "every" are different when used in the conclusion of mathematical induction. They can lead to completely opposite answers. For more details, please go to the appendix of this chapter.

10.3 The Fallacy in Studies of Economics and Business

To demonstrate the wide-ranging applications of the fallacy of composition in areas of economics and business, we focus on the major methodologies commonly employed by scholars in these areas. In particular, this section examines the construction and development of economic and business theories, language-based analysis and reasoning, calculus-based modeling and analysis, methods of microeconomics, anecdote-based analysis, and statistics-based approaches. Of course, most published works tend to contain two or more of these elements or approaches in one paper.

First, let us look at the construction and development of economic and business theories. A glance of the relevant literature clearly shows that new theories of economics and business are not always consistent with those developed earlier. And in many cases, they are even contradictory to each other. For instance, to address the question of whether or not industrial policies actually work in real life, developmental economists had gone through rounds of debates, even involving emotional debaters, where the conclusion of a later round negated that of the immediate prior round (Andreoni & Chang, 2019). What really happens here methodologically is that claims, empirically developed, are mostly employed as starting foundation for a new theory to appear and take shape. Because the validity of empirically developed claims tends to be limited to the data or anecdotes used, the established theory, however, attempts to reach a whole of all similar situations, the erroneous reasoning of the fallacy of composition is committed. That explains why when a theory, developed in this way, is employed to practically explain a business scenario, scholars tend to speak like, "The (name) theory maintains ……; if this theory could be applied to the current case of concern, then ……. would ……" What is most noticeable in these logical statements is the usage of such words as "believe," "might," "could," "should," "would," and other similar terms or phrases of uncertainty.

Second, let us examine the methodology of ordinary-language-based analysis and reasoning. The advantage of this approach is that developed theories are readily accessible by scholars and practitioners. However, although such analysis and reasoning represent an articulation of logic, inferences are often derived through linear thinking and tend to be inconclusive. Such linearity in reasoning makes ordinary-language-based arguments incapable of revealing simultaneous effects of multiple variables in combination. Derived conclusions in general cannot isolate the most relevant optimal outcome out of several potential choices. Both Rostow (1960) and Wen (2016) are two of many examples that well confirm this end in terms of studies of industrial revolutions. In particular, the same Industrial Revolution of England can be and has been investigated from different angles and perspectives, leading to inconsistent and even contradictory conclusions on what actually underlies the appearance of the Revolution. Additionally, such ordinary-language-based analysis and reasoning have well confused primary determinants of the Revolution with secondary ones by treating them all as being fundamental causes (Wen, 2016). Specifically, secondary determinants are very different from the primary ones, because they naturally emerge when primary causes are in place. Therefore, when ordinary-language-based analysis and reasoning are employed, conclusions are generally influenced by the particular angle or perspective taken. Hence, the erroneous thinking of the fallacy of composition appears with the generation of particular perspective onto all possible perspectives.

Third, let us pay attention to calculus-based modeling and analysis. Such modeling and analysis have achieved great successes in the past several hundred years in natural science one after another. However, when calculus-based approaches are applied to the study of economic and business scenarios, issues start to appear at the stage of modeling where a calculus-based model is developed to describe a specific problem of concern. This modeling stage matches a calculus-based model with a real-life scenario; it is a step way before the step when a conclusion can be potentially derived. In particular, for a calculus-based model to work for analysis, one has to assume some fundamental conditions, such as that each variable involved has to take values on a continuum, that the relationship between variables is in an elementary functional form, and that this relationship between variables is continuous and differentiable. However, when applied to studies of economics and business, the first condition is often violated. For instance, the number of employees of a firm[2] and the collection of all goods considered by a consumer[3] can only take natural numbers as their values. However, to employ methods and results of calculus, scholars often treat such variables as continuous (e.g., Lin, 2009; Melitz, 2003). Additional to this, the functional-form and differentiability conditions, as given above, are simply assumed to hold without providing any justification. In short, when calculus-based methodology is employed in the studies of economics and business, the erroneous thinking of the fallacy of composition is committed. Specifically, conclusions derived under particular assumptions are treated as generally true to the "whole" of all related scenarios.

Fourth, let us scrutinize how the erroneous thinking of the fallacy of composition emerges with applications of the methods of microeconomics. For our illustration, we focus only on those methods of microeconomics that rely on the concept of utilities and utility functions. Before anything else, we must recognize that these methods of microeconomics have assisted economists to develop very important, generally true conclusions. However, when a particular economic situation is

[2]This statement implicitly means that the units of all variables are fixed during this discourse. In particular, by the number of employees of a firm, it does not mean the input of labor in a production function. The former can take only a natural number as its value, while the latter can be treated as a continuous variable because input of labor can be measured in different time units, such as year, month, week, day, hour, second, etc. When one places himself at the unit of year, the unit of second can be seen as infinitesimally small. That is why input of labor can be treated as a continuous variable. Here, the units of "count" and "measure of time" cannot be confused with each other.

[3]Similar to the footnote above, the collection of goods considered for consumption should not be confused with the consumption amount of certain particular good. For example, the amount of coffee consumed, a continuous variable, is different from the number of variously branded coffees to possibly purchase, a discrete variable.

concerned with, these powerful tools become quite inadequate in terms of their use values. In particular, the reason that it turns such otherwise powerful tools inadequate is because the optimization of the appropriately developed model cannot be mathematically carried out. To resolve this challenge, one has to specify all involved functions into particularly specified cases, such as linear cost function for each supplier with constant margin, quadratic utility function for the consumer, and others. To see a good example that well demonstrates what is discussed here, see the appendix of Ye et al. (2012). In short, many methods of microeconomics can be and have been beautifully utilized to show insightful general conclusions. But, when they are employed to examine specific scenarios, constructed models become mathematically unsolvable unless each involved function is specified. Every time when such a situation appears, the validity of the derived conclusions is only limited to cases with the chosen specification. Otherwise, the erroneous thinking of the fallacy of composition is committed.

Fifth, let us see how the fallacy of composition appears with anecdote-based analyses. Each such analysis first draws inferences and then provides managerial suggestions by considering a specific set of events or processes. There are many publications in the area of business and economics that are anecdote-based. Such studies tend to entice managers to impulsively implement the highlighted and identified best practices in their real-life business operations (e.g., Gliva-McConvey et al., 2020; White, 2017) by unconsciously bowing to the fallacy of composition. Although before instigating such so-called best practices, it is necessary to first identify the conditions that are fundamental to the initial business success (Forrest et al., 2020), it does not seem to be the case in general. For instance, after identified a set of best practices underneath the successes of top business organizations from around the world, McGrath (2013) then turns her attention to provide suggestions on how to implement these practices in various different situations.

Lastly, let us analyze how the erroneous thinking of the fallacy of composition appears with statistics-based approaches. In the literature of economics and business, a huge amount of studies employs the format of hypothesis testing, a statistics-based approach. Researchers first develop hypotheses on either prima facie bases or empirically revealed phenomena (e.g., Srivastava et al., 1999). Then, they use particularly collected data to test whether the hypotheses can be confirmed with statistical significance. Once confirmed, the hypotheses will then be treated more or less as established propositions, on which managerial recommendations are provided for practical applications.[4] Such process of hypothesis testing applies the

[4] A good statistics-based study generally uses many different data sets from various settings in terms of time, country, functional forms, and others to test a hypothesis. After a hypothesis survives such repeated confirmations, it is then considered as a stylized fact. However, in reality, such good study hardly exists, because of issues like (1) missing data from the past, from certain countries, and from certain settings (e.g., the studies of the Industrial Revolution (Forrest et al., 2018; Wen, 2016) and those on market entry timing (Zachary et al., 2015)), (2) different measurements of key variables, such as a firm's innovativeness (Becheikh et al., 2006), and (3) the fundamental requirement of functional forms, because a lot of relationships cannot be expressed in functional forms (Liu & Lin, 2010).

erroneous thinking of the fallacy of composition at least three times—once at the development of hypotheses, once at the collection of data, and once at the formulation of managerial suggestions. In particular, hypotheses are generally developed for a wider setting than the bases employed. When data are collected, the consequent hypothesis testing is constrained by the scope of the data beyond the problems of sampling error, missing representation, etc., and the eventual managerial recommendations tend to target managers from business settings different from that where the data were from.

Summarizing what is discussed above, we have demonstrated the wide-ranging applications of the fallacy of composition in studies of economics and business. In terms of the literature, other scholars also note this phenomenon (e.g., Finocchiaro, 2015, p. 36).

10.4 Systems Science: The Methodology and Logic for Economic Research

Continuing the discussions in the previous two sections, this section demonstrates why systems science is truly the adequate methodological tool for studies of economics and business in terms of developing practically useful guidance and theoretically sound theories. In particular, by employing systems science, one will be able to improve the current helpless situation that on a business success established theories are inconsistent and cannot assist decision-makers to reproduce the recognized success in a different geographical location and time, such as in the case of the Industrial Revolution (Forrest et al., 2018).

10.4.1 Reflexive Nature and Systemic Structure of Business Associations

To accomplish our goal, let us first look at numerical variables and related issues. Although the concept of numbers has been widely applied throughout history, it is recognized that there are things, such as organizations, events, and processes, that numbers are incapable of adequately describing (Qu, 1985; Wu & Lin, 2002). Because numbers are introduced to measure and record, they cannot appear before existence. That represents the root cause underneath why modern science has experienced great difficulties in predicting the future and studying the evolution and interaction of organizations (Forrest et al., 2020; Lin & OuYang, 2010), two fundamental issues considered in economics and business. To overcome such limitations of numbers, systems science and methodology emerge, because this science is purposefully developed to deal with organizations and their interactions and evolutions (Klir, 2001). Specifically, a system represents an organization or a structure where components are related somehow to each other to form an organic whole. In this sense, to understand how product market evolves, one has to systemically consider the attributes and structures of the forever-changing economic conditions and their interactions with one another. And, these independent, interacting attributes and structures collectively demonstrate some holistic behaviors that are completely different from the characteristics of the involved individuals (Delli Gatti et al., 2010). Hence, the thinking logic and methodology of analyses that are able to deal with such emerging behaviors have to be different from those developed entirely on numbers and numerical variables.

Although physics has shown the usefulness of quantity-based methods, advanced on quantities' formality and generality, it generally studies lifeless objects without internal structure. That is completely different from what are addressed in economics and business, where every economic agent has its unique internal decision-making mechanism, which is influenced by and in turn alters the evolution of external events. In other words, studies of economics and business will be most effective if they coordinate quantity-based and system-based methodological approaches, depending on whether or not internal organizations can be ignored.

Second, let us examine how the common existence of reflexive relationships in business associations leads to the conclusion that systems science and methodology are truly needed for economic research. To this end, let us look at how a market signal evolves. On one hand, to innovatively decipher a market signal, entrepreneurs generally cannot ignore relevant specifics, although these specifics cannot be handled by using quantitative methods (Chap. 3 in this volume; Bu & Forrest, 2020). On the other hand, entrepreneurs take their individually different actions according to their unique, while varied, understandings of the market signal, which simultaneously alters the market signal. Such reflexive relationship between a market signal and entrepreneurial actions naturally inspires scholars and decision-makers, if they want to develop practically useful and theoretically sound results, to apply concepts and methods of systems science to investigate events and processes. See Soros (2003) for a more general discussion on reflectivity.

In the perspective of systems science, practically meaningful receipts of a market signal need to be acquired in light of the interactional specifics of relevant economic events and agents (Bu & Forrest, 2020; Lin & OuYang, 2010). By being mindful of such specifics of the product market, entrepreneurs will innovatively notice business potentials amid the dynamic evolution of economic structures. These specifics reveal changes occurring in the marketplace before they become quantitatively measurable. To this end, the present push for decision-making based on big data essentially encourages unearthing latent systemic structures in the name of quantities. That represents the fact that knowledge exploration is now in the era of systems thinking of events and processes.

When a market signal appears, it means that the structure of the market has already changed. Hence, the present era of transient competitive advantages (McGrath, 2013) requires managers and entrepreneurs to innovatively comprehend the forever-evolving market by employing the thinking logic and methodology of systems science. By doing so, these decision-makers can walk advantageously out of the realm of quantities and numerical variables and enter into that of organizations and organizational interactions. Additionally, systems thinking helps decision-makers take advantages of the methodologies listed in Sect. 10.3 while avoiding their weaknesses.

Third, let us look at the basics of systems thinking and methodology.

A system, as defined above and discussed in Chap. 2, stands for a whole with components associated to each other (Lin, 1999). And, systems science consists of the studies of all kinds of systems, organizations, and structures (Lin, 1999; Klir, 1985). Hence, studies in economics and business mostly deal with systems in one way or another. Although the concept of systems can be traced as far back as human history goes (von Bertalanffy, 1968), it is in our modern time that scholars recognize the concept's importance in the studies of economics and business, see, e.g., Forrest et al. (2020), Klir (1985), Lin (2009), and Porter (1985).

Different from numbers, one can see systems out of every socially existing object, event, and process. In particular, numbers appear when internal structures are ignored; otherwise, systems dominate the world. For example, when a firm is seen as where values are created, it then consists of a particular organizational culture and philosophical values, human talents, and operational routines, among others. It is the association of these components that the firm exists physically and intellectually. Speaking generally, the firm discussed here can be any economic agent whose behavior is guided by its values and beliefs, a market, an industry, and an economy. Conversely, it is the whole that reflects the interconnection of parts that a firm, or a market, or an industry, or an economy emerges.

Due to their different emphases, one on the systemhood of events, organizations, and processes while the other on the thinghood of lifeless objects, systems science and the traditional science jointly form a two-dimensional spectrum of knowledge (Klir, 2001). With systems science as the new dimension, humans have gained additional capability to more adequately address problems that have been challenging the mankind since the beginning of time (Lin, 2009).

10.4.2 Systemic Emergence and the Reconstruction of Macroeconomics

Fourth, let us conclude this section by examining how emergent properties of systems can help studies of macroeconomics face their current challenges. In particular, the wholeness of a system is vividly reflected in Aristotle's statement that the whole is greater than the sum of its parts (von Bertalanffy, 1968). That is, when component parts are organically associated into a system, the resultant whole possesses some properties the parts do not enjoy individually. That is where the fallacy of division falls apart. Such properties a system possesses while its parts do not are known as the system's emergent properties. One example of emergent properties of systems is the connectedness of a system, which describes how parts are associated to each other (Lin et al., 2013, p. 34). As for challenges macroeconomics faces, they include, among others:

1. The theoretical inability to explain why large-scale financial chaos, such as the one of 2007–2009, appears and what can be done about such chaos (Lindé, 2018; Poole, 2010)
2. The incapability to explain economic systems' holistic structures, emergent unintentionally out of micro agents' inconsistent actions and conflicting interactions (e.g., Farmer & Foley, 2009; Stiglitz, 2009)
3. The development of innovative models and approaches to play similar roles as those played by either the optimization of various functions or the principal-agent frameworks in the mainstream macroeconomic theories (Delli Gatti et al., 2010)

In the following, we will deliberate on these bulleted items one by one in more details. First, there was a recent project on how to rebuild macroeconomic theory in the wake of the 2008 global financial crisis (Vines & Wills, 2018). Aiming at addressing one of the six examination questions of the project, Blanchard (2018) believes that one type of the benchmark model should be able to produce the best forecasts possible. To this end, the fact is that while models of macroeconomics failed to forecast the 2008 financial crisis, other more specialized forecasting models, such as Bayesian vector autoregressions, also did. For the former failures, Vines and Wills (2018) attribute the causes to the following two assumptions: the efficient market hypothesis and rational expectations. However, the latter failures in fact point to a fundamental challenge facing the entire world of learning: No available method in natural science and mathematics can successfully forecast an imminent major *natural* disaster. Methodologically, each such method is at least partially quantity-based and attempts to extrapolate the past or prolong the present state of affairs into the future. So, such methods can, at most, forecast minor deviations from the norm recognized from the past or the present. For details, see Lin and OuYang (2010). Comparing to *natural* events, disasters in the business world are more difficult to forecast, if possible, due to the reflective nature of human participants (Soros, 2003). These participants exert influences on the evolution of business events according to their individually different expectations. Hence, forecasts in the business world generally alter what is expected to occur; and only at places where and moments when no expectation is available, a disastrous crisis appears.

To illustrate item (2) above, let us briefly review that macroeconomics, as a branch of economics, investigates the holistic performance, structure, operation, and decision-making of an economy, either regional or national or international. It deals with the regulation of an economy's growth and stability by closely examining such variables as interest rate, tax, government spending, and monetary policy (O'Sullivan & Sheffrin, 2003). Although this branch of economic studies is rooted in different areas of investigations, its modern form began with Keynes' *General Theory of Employment, Interest and Money*. When the oil shocks of the 1970s appeared, the created stagflation gave rise to the neoclassical revolution in macroeconomics on the assumptions of general equilibrium and rational expectations (Snowdon & Vane, 2005). However, when facing the 2007–2009 global financial turmoil, the then-most updated version of macroeconomics was unable to make desired timely predictions and provide understandings on the turmoil's causes and consequences. That is, the present version of macroeconomics is incapable of appropriately exploring holistic properties and structures of economic systems. This end suggests the need for macroeconomics to adopt a new paradigm, accompanied with appropriate tools and research agendas (Delli Gatti et al., 2010).

Such incapability of macroeconomics is closely related to the fallacy of composition; other than the various erroneous ways of thinking related to the fallacy, as discussed in the previous section, the widely employed starting point of macroeconomic analysis, the equilibrium micro-foundations, cannot naturally lead to the economy-wide emergence of systemic properties and structures. These systemic properties and structures are mostly developed as unintended and unplanned results of the actions and interactions of individual economic agents (Delli Gatti et al., 2010; Farmer & Foley, 2009). However, since the time when Robert Lucas (1976) advanced his critique to econometric policy evaluation, the field of macroeconomics has warmly embraced Locus' proposed solution: Construct macroeconomic models on primitive parameters of microeconomic units so that the aggregate is simply the sum of individual behaviors. Along with such a solution, all macroeconomic explanations must be explainable at the microeconomic level so that Delli Gatti et al. (2010) no longer see the need for macroeconomics to exist as an autonomous field.

For item (3) above, Delli Gatti et al. (2010) advocate the treatment of each market economy as a complex adaptive system so that methods of the science of complexity can be employed to investigate emergent properties of economies. Results, produced out of such a new paradigm, do not seem obtainable from applications of agent-based or multiagent techniques (Farmer & Foley, 2009; Leijonhufvud, 2006). For example, individuals who prefer those with slightly similar characteristics as neighbors can and do organize themselves into highly segregated residential neighborhoods, a systemic phenomenon not shared by all components, through independent, uncoordinated housing decisions (Schelling, 1969). Another good example is how individual risk aversions can collectively and involuntarily create more risk (Thurner et al., 2009). In particular, when a bank adjusts the leverage exposure (in %) of collateralized borrowers while the assets' prices are dropping, margin calls will produce massive number of sales at wrong times. These individual sales most likely increase the volatility in asset prices at the systemic market level even if all traders are value oriented and individually buy assets when prices fall.

As for the recommending appropriate approaches, Delli Gatti et al. (2010) propose to adopt agent-based computational techniques. These techniques are useful for analyzing systemic phenomena at the macro level that emerge from the interactions of self-centered economic agents of the micro level (Judd & Tesfatsion, 2006). In particular, one can falsify propositions at micro, meso, and macro levels by using computer simulations through allowing heterogeneous components of the micro level to follow some simple behavioral rules and local interactions. As interaction nodes and individual rules evolve with time, statistical regularities, unexplainable at the micro level, develop at the meso level. Such emergent regularities feed downward to the micro level to influence how the individual components adjust their behavioral and interaction rules and rise upward to produce aggregate regularities at the macro level. The most noteworthy is that the system at the macro level now possesses properties that cannot be explained by those of the micro-level components.

Although many systemic properties emerge out of unintended and unplanned interactions of the components of a system, such as segregated neighborhoods and risks increased by individual risk aversions, as discussed above, most business activities are goal-oriented and planned. For example, each firm is organized to materialize a specified mission, while each operational routine within a firm is designed to accomplish a particular task in order to answer market invitations for new products and additional innovations (Forrest et al., 2017). Hence, we recommend to expand the pool of these agent-based computational techniques and embrace all methods developed by systems scientists for studying organizations, evolutions, and interactions of organizations (Klir, 2001; Lin et al., 2013). For example, the previous two systemic phenomena—segregated neighborhoods and increased systemic risks—can be seen as direct consequences of the following theorem, which was formally discussed in Chap. 9, where $S = (M, R)$ is a system, satisfying $|M| \geq \theta$, and each object $m = (M_m, R_m) \in M$ is also a system so that $|M_m| < \kappa$, for given cardinality κ and regular cardinality $\theta > \kappa$ such that for $\alpha < \theta$, $|\alpha^{<\kappa}| < \theta$.

Theorem 10.1 If at least θ objects in M contain a common element, then a partial system $S' = (M', R')$ of S exists such that S' forms a centralized system and $|M'| \geq \theta$.

Specifically, this theorem says that as long as a sufficient number of component elements of an economy possess a certain property, such as risk aversion or desire for certain kinds of neighbors, then such property will be manifested in a certain exaggerated way at the economy level. The proof of this theorem and a detailed discussion on risk aversion and desire for certain kinds of neighbors can be found in Chap. 9. For related technical details and discussions, see Lin (1999). For a special case of this result and its application in sociology, see Lin (1988).

10.5 A Potential Path from Empirical Confirmation to General Conclusions

For different reasons, empirical studies in areas of economics and business are inevitable no matter how advanced the relevant theories are. For instance, when a decision-maker needs to know the current state of affairs, empirical investigations will have to be conducted. As a matter of fact, a large portion of the present literature of economics and business consists of empirical studies. At the same time, many authors like to state their empirical conclusions in as general terms as possible, especially in the name of recommendations. This phenomenon surely demonstrates how the fallacy of composition is working in disciplines of economics and business.

So, to prevent the fallacy of composition from entering the development of general economic theories, a natural question arises:

> Is there a methodological means to reliably rewrite the conclusions of individual case studies in general terms without committing to the erroneous logic of the fallacy of composition?

To potentially address this theoretically and practically important question, mathematical induction, as discussed earlier, naturally comes to mind. Evidently, if such a principle of induction can be established for business and economics disciplines, many currently data-based discoveries will have a way to be readily converted into generally true, affirmatively stated conclusions without using such words as "believe," "would," "should," "might," etc. The usage of such words reflects the uncertain nature of relevant theories. If such desired conversion can be accomplished, more reliable recommendations and predictions, instead of suggestions, for decision-making mangers and entrepreneurs can be provided even based on empirical discoveries.

To illustrate the meaning of our proposed principle of induction that can ideally help restate empirical discoveries in business and economics disciplines as generally true conclusions, we first expand the understandings of the proposition $\Phi(n)$ and the natural-number independent variable n; for details, see the previously stated mathematical induction, as follows. First, we treat n as, say, a moment of time, a particular economic state, or a specific political environment, determined by the particular problem of economics and business under consideration. And second, we see $\Phi(n)$ as the conclusion produced out of an empirical study at time moment n, or economic state n, or a political environment n. Such a parallelism illustrates how intuitively and formally the previous stated mathematical induction can be conveniently rephrased for purposes of business and economic studies. To this end, one needs to note that in the principle of mathematical induction, n is definitely a discrete variable, while in the aforementioned new understanding, this independent variable n can potentially be continuous.

For such an induction to actually work out as desired, the field from which the independent variable n takes its values needs to be ordered linearly. For example, if n means time, then any two moments t_1 and t_2 are naturally ordered; that is, one and only one of the following three conditions has to hold true: $t_1 \leq t_2$, or $t_1 = t_2$, or $t_1 \geq t_2$. As for other potential meanings of n, such as an economic state, a specific political environment, etc., a linear order relation needs to be defined in order to compare different states or varied environments. Additionally, when the meaning of the independent variable n is expanded beyond that of natural numbers, or become a continuous variable, the field from which n takes its values can possibly be a continuum, such as a range of time moments. In such a case, the previously stated mathematical induction will not help us achieve what we want to, because n is a discrete variable. Luckily, we have the following mathematical induction recently developed for such an independent various x that takes values from an interval of real numbers (Forrest, 2013, p. 289).

Mathematical Induction over Real Numbers: Let $\Phi(x)$ be a proposition in real-number variable x. If the following steps hold true:

The initial step: There is a real number a so that proposition $\Phi(x)$ holds true for each $x \leq a$;
The inductive step: If for a real number y, $\Phi(x)$ holds true for any $x \leq y$, then there is $z > y$ such that $\Phi(x)$ holds true for each $x < z$,

then $\Phi(x)$ holds true for every real number x.

We now use three simple examples to illustrate how this induction can be practically employed to studies of economic and business scenarios where the proposition $\Phi(x)$ stands for an empirically confirmed hypothesis and x the underlying index determined by the specifics of the focal study. First, assume that the independent variable x means time. Then, to show the general validity of a conjectured proposition $\Phi(x)$ over time from moment a to moment b, one needs to employ a reformulated induction over real numbers so that $a \leq x \leq b$. The validity of $\Phi(a)$ can be a familiar empirical study with data or anecdotes collected at time moment a. To produce the conclusion that proposition $\Phi(x)$ holds true for every time moment (a real number) $x \in [a, b]$, it depends on whether or not one can prove that there is $z \in [a, b]$, satisfying $z > y$, such that $\Phi(x)$ holds true for any $x < z, x \in [a, b]$, based on the assumption that for $y \in [a, b]$, $\Phi(x)$ holds true for any $x \in [a, b]$, satisfying $x < y$. This last step of course is dependent on the time variable $x \in [a, b]$ and the specifics of $\Phi(x)$.

Second, let $\Phi(x)$ be a conjectured proposition on the US politics in variable x that represents a voter's political tilt along the spectrum of the progressive/conservative divide in the United States. The extreme progressivism can be well modeled by the family of a nurturant parent, while the extreme conservatism by the family of a strict father (Lakoff, 1996). Therefore, the independent variable x takes values in the continuum bounded on the left-hand side by the extreme progressivism and on the right-hand side by the extreme conservatism. To show that $\Phi(x)$ is generally true no matter what political value x takes out of its field, the generalized mathematical induction on real numbers implies that one needs to first show the validity of $\Phi(x)$ when $x =$ the extreme progressivism. Next, on the assumption that $\Phi(x)$ holds true for any political x value with no more right-leaning than a political y value ($\neq$ the extreme conservatism), he can prove the existence of a more tight-leaning political z value than y so that $\Phi(x)$ holds true for any political x value that is no more right-leaning than the political z value.

Third, let $\Phi(x)$ be a conjectured proposition in the variable x that describes the degree of individualism that is believed and practiced by a people. Then, the field from which x takes its values will be a continuum bounded on one side by the collectivism of the Far East and the other side by the individualism of the United States (Lin & Forrest, 2011; Marshall, 2016). Therefore, to show that $\Phi(x)$ is generally true no matter what degree of individualism x represents, one needs to first show the validity of $\Phi(x)$ when $x =$ the extreme level of collectivism of the far east. Next, on the assumption that $\Phi(x)$ holds true for any degree x of individualism that is no more than an arbitrarily fixed degree y ($\neq$ the extreme degree of individualism of the United States), he can prove the existence of a higher degree z of individualism than y so that $\Phi(x)$ holds true for any degree x that is less than or equal to the degree z.

At the conclusion of this section, one point needs to be made clear. The arguments in the three examples above are not equivalent to the statistical reconfirmations called for by good statistics-based investigations, as described in footnote 4. The reasoning in the inductive step, as given in the mathematical induction over real numbers, generally cannot be accomplished by conventional statistics-based methods, as vividly shown by the examples listed in the previous paragraphs.

10.6 A Few Final Words

This chapter examines the meaning and history of the fallacy of composition and how it trickles often unnoticeably into the exploration of knowledge. By analyzing the methods commonly employed in the literature, it shows how seriously and permeably the erroneous thinking logic of the fallacy appears in economic and business studies. Riding on this methodological analysis, this chapter demonstrates why systems science and methodology are truly appropriate and adequate for scholars to use in their studies of business organizations, evolutions, and interactions of organizations. This end generalizes that of Delli Gatti et al. (2010), who convincingly illustrate how the science of complexity can intuitively produce emergent properties of systems, not shared by the systems' constitutive components.

To confirm this generalization, displayed is a theorem of systems science that is established on the basis of logical reasoning without using any suggested computer simulation by Delli Gatti et al. This chapter then illustrates how this theorem can help explain the appearance of macro-level racial segregation out of unintended and uncoordinated micro-level slight desires of individuals (Schelling, 1969), and how systemically shocking market risks can emerge out of individual risk aversions (Thurner et al., 2009).

Additionally, this chapter shows how employing systems logic of thinking and systems methodology can help improve the current helpless situation. When a business success appears, scholars often develop various theories on how the success was achieved. However, these theories cannot practically assist decision-making managers and entrepreneurs to reproduce the recognized success in another business settings. And it is often the case that the developed theories are not even consistent with each other, leading to rounds after rounds of so-called debates, some of which had become emotional. One example of repeated failures of inconsistent theories, among many others, is the experience with the Industrial Revolution (Forrest et al., 2018; Wen, 2016). One recent example on endless rounds of debates one after another is about the usefulness of industrial policies (Andreoni & Chang, 2019).

By analyzing the meaning of the fallacy of composition and its wide-ranging, unfortunate permeability in economic and business studies and by considering the practical inevitability of empirical studies, this chapter recommends the development of an economic induction. By utilizing such an induction, many empirically confirmed hypotheses can be expectedly rewritten in general terms so that true recommendations, instead of suggestions of limited validity, can be provided to frontline managers and entrepreneurs.

In terms of future research, this chapter points to several directions. First, each theorem in economics that is either directly or indirectly established by using mathematical induction needs to be reconfirmed in order to prevent any erroneous logic of the fallacy of composition from being applied. Second, real-life scenarios need to be investigated in terms of how to apply the suggested economic induction to rewrite statistically significant hypotheses in general terms. No matter which direction one takes, the consequence is expected to be both theoretically and practically magnificent.

Appendix: The Vase Puzzle

For the purpose of making this chapter as self-contained as possible, let us look at the following vase puzzle.

Suppose (Lin, 1999, p. 178) that a vase and an infinite number of pieces of paper are available. The pieces of paper are labeled by natural numbers 1, 2, 3, . . ., so that each piece has one and only one label on it. Now, the following recursive procedure is performed:

Step 1: Place the pieces of paper, labeled from 1 to 10, into the vase; then remove the piece with label 1 from the vase.

Step n: Place the pieces of paper, labeled from $10n - 9$ through $10n$, into the vase; then remove the piece labeled n, where n is any natural number 1, 2, 3, . . .

Question: After the recursive procedure is finished, how many pieces of paper are left in the vase, assuming the vase is empty before the procedure was started?

Answer 1: By using mathematical induction, one can see readily that when step n is finished, the vase contains $f(n)$ pieces of paper, where

$$f(n) = 9n, n = 1, 2, 3, \ldots.$$

Therefore, if the recursive procedure can be finished, the number of pieces of paper left in the vase should be equal to the limit of $f(n)$ as $n \to \infty$. That is, there are infinite many pieces of paper left in the vase.

Answer 2: There is no piece of paper left in the vase. If, on the contrary, there were pieces of paper left in the vase, let us randomly pick one of these pieces of paper. Assume that the label on the paper is k, which is a natural number. But, this is impossible, because at step k, this particular piece of paper has been removed from the vase. Therefore, the vase is empty.

A careful comparison of these two completely opposite answers, one is 0 and the other ∞, reveals the fact that the difference in the answers comes from whether the recursive procedure can or cannot be finished. If the procedure can be finished, we have the situations described in the versions of mathematical induction in the second section above. However, this IF cannot be carried out in real life. So, it is natural to doubt about the practical usefulness of consequent theories. On the other hand, if the procedure cannot be finished, then the aforementioned versions of mathematical induction need to be modified as suggested in Note 10.1.

In the present state of modern mathematics, these two assumptions about the possibility of completion of the recursive procedure are used widely without clear distinction, depending on what outcome is needed.

References

Andreoni, A., & Chang, H. J. (2019). The political economy of industrial policy: Structural interdependencies, policy alignment and conflict management. *Structural Change and Economic Dynamics, 48*, 136–150.

Arnauld, A., & Nicole, P. (1685). *Logic; or, the art of thinking*. H. Sawbridge.

Arnauld, A., & Nicole, P. (1965). *La Logique ou l'Art de Penser*. Presses Universitaires de France.

Arnauld, A., & Nicole, P. (1996). *Logic or the art of thinking* (J. V. Buroker, Trans.). Cambridge University Press.

Becheikh, N., Landry, R., & Amara, N. (2006). Lessons from innovation empirical studies in the manufacturing sector: A systematic review of the literature from 1993 to 2003. *Technovation, 26*(5), 644–664.

Blanchard, O. J. (2018). On the future of macroeconomic models. *Oxford Review of Economic Policy, 34*(1–2), 43–54.

Bu, Q., & Forrest, J. Y. L. (2020). Comparing sentiment measures in mutual fund performance. *International Journal of Managerial Finance, 17*, 478. https://doi.org/10.1108/IJMF-02-2020-0092

Copi, I. M. (1968). *Introduction to logic* (3rd ed.). Macmillan.

Debreu, G. (1959). *Theory of value: An axiomatic analysis of economic equilibrium*. Yale University Press.

Delli Gatti, D., Gaffeo, E., & Gallegati, M. (2010). Complex agent-based macroeconomics: A manifesto for a new paradigm. *Journal of Economic Interaction and Coordination, 5*, 111–135.

Farmer, D., & Foley, D. (2009). The economy needs agent-based modelling. *Nature, 460*, 685–686.

Finocchiaro, M. A. (2015). The fallacy of composition: Guiding concepts, historical cases, and research problems. *Journal of Applied Logic, 13*(2, Part B), 24–43.

Forrest, J. Y.-L. (2013). *A systemic perspective on cognition and mathematics*. CRC Press.

Forrest, J. Y. L., Buttermore, J., & Wajda, T. A. (2017). At Nash equilibrium when new market competitions appear? *Kybernetes, 46*(2), 256–271.

Forrest, J. Y. L., Zhao, H. C., & Shao, L. (2018). Engineering rapid industrial revolutions for impoverished agrarian nations. *Theoretical Economics Letters, 8*, 2594–2640.

Forrest, J. Y.-L., Nicholls, N., Schimmel, K., & Liu, S. F. (2020). *Managerial decision making: A holistic approach*. Springer.

Forrest, J. Y. L., Wagner, J., Nightingale, J., Guo, H., & Roy, J. (To Appear). *The fallacy of composition, its wide-ranging applications in economics/business and why systems science is appropriate for economic and business research. Pennsylvania Economic Review, 31*. Pennsylvania Economic Review, 31, to appear.

Gliva-McConvey, G., Nicholas, C. F., & Clark, L. (Eds.). (2020). *Comprehensive healthcare simulation: Implementing best practices in standardized patient methodology*. Springer.

Haller, S. A. (2002). *Apocalypse soon? Wagering on warnings of global warming*. McGill-Queens University Press.

Halverson, W. H. (1984). *Concise logic*. Random House.

Hamblin, C. L. (1970). *Fallacies*. Methuen.

Hansen, H. V., & Pinto, R. C. (Eds.). (1995). *Fallacies: Classical and contemporary readings*. Pennsylvania State University Press.

Judd, K., & Tesfatsion, L. (2006). *Handbook of computational economics* (Vol. 2: Agent-based computational economics). North-Holland.

Kahane, H. (1973). *Logic and philosophy* (2nd ed.). Wadsworth.

Klir, G. (1985). *Architecture of systems problem solving*. Plenum Press.

Klir, G. (2001). *Facets of systems science*. Springer.

Krugman, P. (2013, January 8). *Austerity wrought pain, no gain, Las Vegas Sun* (p. 3). Retrieved January 4, 2021, from http://lasvegassun.com/news/2013/jan/08/austerity-wrought-pain-no-gain/#.VHPVyW1c75E.gmail

Kuratowski, K., & Mostowski, A. (1976). *Set theory: With an introduction to descriptive set theory*. North-Holland.

Lakoff, G. (1996). *Moral politics: How conservatives and liberals think*. University of Chicago Press.

Leijonhufvud, A. (2006). Agent-based macro. In K. Judd & L. Tesfatsion (Eds.), *Handbook of computational economics* (Vol. II: Agent-based computational economics). North-Holland.

Lin, Y. (1988). An application of systems analysis in sociology. *Cybernetics and Systems, 19*, 267–278.

Lin, Y. (1999). *General systems theory: A mathematical approach*. Plenum and Kluwer Academic Publishers.

Lin, Y. (2009). *Systemic yoyos: Some impacts of the second dimension*. Auerbach Publication, an imprint of Taylor and Francis.

Lin, Y., & Forrest, B. (2011). *Systemic structure behind human organizations: From civilizations to individuals*. Springer.

Lin, Y., & OuYang, S. C. (2010). *Irregularities and prediction of major disasters*. CRC Press, an imprint of Taylor and Francis.

Lin, Y., Duan, X. J., Zhao, C. L., & Xu, L. D. (2013). *Systems science: Methodological approaches*. CRC Press.

Lindé, J. (2018). DSGE models: Still useful in policy analysis? *Oxford Review of Economic Policy, 34*(1–2), 269–286.

Liu, S. F., & Lin, Y. (2010). *Grey systems: Theory and applications*. Springer.

Lucas, R. (1976). Econometric policy evaluation: A critique. *Carnegie-Rochester Conference Series on Public Policy, 1*, 19–46.

Marshall, T. (2016). *Prisoners of geography: Ten maps that tell you everything you need to know about global politics*. Scribner Book.

McGrath, R. G. (2013). *The end of competitive advantage: How to keep your strategy moving as fast as your business*. Harvard Business Review Press.

Melitz, M. J. (2003). The impact of trade on intra-industry reallocations and aggregate industry productivity. *Econometrica, 71*(6), 1695–1725.

O'Sullivan, A., & Sheffrin, S. M. (2003). *Economics: Principles in action*. Pearson Prentice Hall.

Poole, W. (2010). Causes and consequences of the financial crisis of 2007-2009. *Harvard Journal of Law and Public Policy, 33*, 421–441.

Porter, M. E. (1985). *Competitive advantage: Creating and sustaining superior performance*. Free Press.

Qu, Y. (1985). *The songs of the south: An anthology of ancient Chinese poems by Qu Yuan and other poets* (David Haykes, Trans.). Penguin Classics.

Rostow, W. W. (1960). *The stages of economic growth: A non-communist manifesto*. Cambridge University Press.

Schelling, T. (1969). Models of segregation. *American Economic Review, 59*(2), 488–493.

Snowdon, B., & Vane, H. R. (2005). *Modern macroeconomics: Its origins, development and current state*. Edward Elgar.
Soros, G. (2003). *The alchemy of finance*. Wiley.
Srivastava, R. K., Shervani, T. A., & Fahey, L. (1999). Marketing, business processes, and shareholder value: An organizationally embedded view of marketing activities and the discipline of marketing. *Journal of Marketing, 63*(Special issue), 168–179.
Stiglitz, J. (2009). The current economic crisis and lessons for economic theory. *Eastern Economic Journal, 35*, 281–296.
Thurner, S., Farmer, D., & Geanakoplos, J. (2009). *Leverage causes fat tails clustered volatility*. Santa Fe Institute, Mimeo.
Vines, D., & Wills, S. (2018). The rebuilding macroeconomic theory project: An analytical assessment. *Oxford Review of Economic Policy, 34*(1–2), 1–42.
von Bertalanffy, L. (1968). *General systems theory*. George Braziller.
Walton, D., Reed, C., & Macagno, F. (2008). *Argumentation Schemes*. Cambridge University Press.
Wen, Y. (2016). *The making of an economic superpower: Unlocking China's secret of rapid industrialization*. World Scientific.
Whately, R. (1826). *Elements of logic*. J. Mawman.
White, M. (2017). Keep calm and simulate on: Faculty experiences and insights into implementing best practices in simulation. *Teaching and Learning in Nursing, 12*(1), 43–49.
Woods, J. (2012). A history of the fallacies in Western logic. In D. M. Gabbay, F. J. Pelletier, & J. Woods (Eds.), *Logic: A history of its central concepts* (pp. 513–610). North-Holland.
Woods, J. (2013). *Errors of reasoning: Naturalizing the logic of inference*. College Publications.
Wu, Y., & Lin, Y. (2002). *Beyond nonstructural quantitative analysis: Blown-ups, spinning currents and modern science*. World Scientific.
Ye, G. L., Priem, R. L., & Alshwer, A. A. (2012). Achieving demand-side synergy from strategic diversification: How combining mundane assets can leverage consumer utilities. *Organization Science, 23*(1), 207–224.
Zachary, M. A., Gianiodis, P. T., Payne, G. T., & Markman, G. D. (2015). Entry timing: Enduring lessons and future directions. *Journal of Management, 41*(5), 1388–1415.

Part IV
Producer Firms and an Economy's Aggregated Supply and Demand

Chapter 11
Production, Costs, and Profits of a Producer Firm

Jeffrey Yi-Lin Forrest, Davood Darvishi, Abdou K. Jallow, and Zhen Li

Abstract This chapter, which is mainly based on Forrest et al. (Proceedings of the 2022 conference of Pennsylvania Economic Association, 2022a), looks at how an individual firm's system of values and beliefs, as reflected in the firm's mission statement, influences the firm's decision-making. Based on a minimal level of intuition and common knowledge, four axioms are adopted as the starting points for deriving consequent conclusions. It then explains why other commonly employed assumptions should be abandoned. On the backdrop of a set-theoretic setup, the concepts of production and profit functions are investigated innovatively so that unnecessary assumptions, widely appearing in the current microeconomic theory, can be naturally avoided. Other than generalizing several known results in producer theory, such as Hotelling's lemma, examples are introduced to show that these known results are not universally true when different systems of values and beliefs are considered. This chapter concludes with several suggestions with expected significance for future research.

Keywords Economic crisis · Firm-specific order relation · Hotelling's lemma · Ordering of real numbers · Returns to scale · Uncertainty

11.1 Introduction

The topic of how an economic agent makes decisions has been widely studied by many scholars from different disciplines, such as psychology, economics, management, etc. Although a more or less standardized procedure has been commonly

---

Jeffrey Yi-Lin Forrest (Department of Accounting Economics Finance, Slippery Rock University, Slippery Rock, PA, USA; Email: Jeffrey.forrest@sru.edu), Davood Darvishi (Department of Mathematics, Payame Noor University, Tehran, Iran; Email: darvishidavood@yahoo.com), Abdou K. Jallow (Department of Information Technology and Management, Slippery Rock University, Slippery Rock, PA, USA; Email: Abdou.jallow@sru.edu), and Zhen Li (College of Business, Texas Woman's University, Denton, TX, USA; Email: zli@twu.edu) are equally contributed to this chapter.

J. Y.-L. Forrest, *Systemic Principles of Applied Economic Philosophies I*,
Translational Systems Sciences 38, https://doi.org/10.1007/978-981-99-7273-9_11

developed in such studies (e.g., Forrest & Liu, 2021; Friedman, 1953; Gilboa, 2010; Gul & Pesendorfer, 2008), it has been confirmed again and again many times that this procedure is unable to capture real-life scenarios. For example, after experiencing great losses during the 2008 financial crisis, Paul Krugman provided his point of view regarding why the existing economic theories are incapable of describing, predicting, and providing explanations in a timely manner on what had happened in the past and what would follow next. To this end, he commented in *New York Times* (2009-09-02) that: "... economists, as a group, mistook beauty ... for truth ... as memories of the Depression faded, economists fell back in love with the old, idealized vision of an economy ...." That is, the following question arises naturally at the basic level underneath all investigations of economic decision-making: To avoid the history of repeatedly falling back to treating impressive-looking beauty as truth, what can one do to alter the devastating setup of the existent economic and business theories at the most fundamental level so that all these theories can be rebuilt on a fresh start with the expectation that they will be more practically useful than before?

The importance of this question is evident, as soon as we look at the human sufferings and economic losses experienced during each economic crisis. And, it is also well witnessed by the vast amount of related literature in the name of decision-making with various assumptions closely scrutinized (e.g., Hudik, 2019; Lovett, 2006; Rubinstein, 1998; Weyl, 2019). In other words, both practical and theoretical fronts have loudly called for scholars to reconstruct relevant theories, especially economic theories, so that more practically tangible benefits can be materialized.

This chapoter, which is mainly based on Forrest et al. (2022a), represents one step towards completely addressing the aforementioned question of fundamental importance. It examines a list of common assumptions widely adopted in the producer theory (Debreu, 1959; Levin & Milgrom, 2004; Mas-Collel et al., 1995) by applying the recent development on the natural endowments of a firm—self-awareness, imagination, conscience, and free will (Forrest et al., 2021a). It analyzes which of the assumptions are acceptable and which ones are problematic. After specifying four acceptable assumptions as axioms, the rest of the chapter uses analytical means and systemic logical reasoning to establish conclusions under fewer conditions that generalize some of the well-known results established before under more strict conditions.

Beyond what is described above, one important highlight of this chapter is its emphasis on the existence of a firm-specific order relation of real numbers and that of a firm-specific method of optimization. More specifically, each firm has its own particular means to prioritize the alternatives available in a decision-making situation and very individual way to optimize its objectives. This end is very different from the assumptions widely employed in the literature, where the ordering of real numbers and the method of optimization, although some of the particular details are different, are the same no matter who the decision-maker is.

Because of the novelty of how we look at related issues and concepts, this chapter is able to discover the missing conditions under which some of the very basic properties of a firm's production and profit functions satisfy; and it is able to generalize a few well-known results of the producer theory to stronger versions.

The established conclusions in this chapter reveal the fact that firms with different systems of values and beliefs naturally make different choices when facing the same challenge or opportunity even when they are limited by the same set of constraints. In other words, this chapter contributes to the literature through showing when additional conditions are needed for a desired conclusion to hold, and when a well-known conclusion holds true only under very specific conditions.

The rest of this chapter is organized as follows. Section 11.2 prepares the reader for the following sections by citing results on a firm's natural endowments and decision-making and by setting up the basic notations. Section 11.3 singles out four basic axioms that are intuitively correct in the business world and discusses how and why several other main assumptions adopted in the literature are not generally true. Section 11.4 pays a close visit to the concepts of production and profit functions and their elementary properties. On the basis of these results, Section 11.5 generalizes the well-known Hotelling's lemma and establishes a general conclusion that majorly generalizes a main conclusion of the microeconomic theory. The chapter concludes in Sect. 11.6 with several pointers to some important questions for future research.

11.2 Necessary Basics and Modeling of the Firm's Activities

This section consists of two subsections. The first one cites the key concepts and known conclusions needed for the smooth development of the rest of the chapter. And the second subsection introduces the basics of our modeling of a firm that produces and offers a set of goods to the product market.

11.2.1 A Quick Review of the Firm's Endowments and Decision-Making

As is presented in Chap. 5, each individual person possesses four natural endowments—self-awareness, imagination, conscience, and free will (Lin & Forrest, 2012). As a parallelism, each firm also has its corresponding natural endowments (Forrest et al., 2021b, 2022b). To make this chapter more or less self-contained, let us quickly review the relevant concepts.

For a firm, its self-awareness stands for the firm's cognizance that it exists as an entity of business that is different and separate from other entities with its business strategies and secrets, such as the emphasized value propositions for customers, operational procedures, and protected designs of products, among others. Its imagination defines the firm's facility to acquire and to master newly discovered facts, to originally envision what offer will be appropriate for the market, such as a completely new or an improved product, and to configure the needed method of materially producing the envisioned offer. Its conscience represents the firm's capability to tell which effort would be more advantageous than other efforts within the constraints. For a firm, its free will describes the firm's ability to keep promises, how to keep and to what degree to keep these promises, as reflected in its contracts with the partners within its supply-chain ecosystem.

By employing systems science and its logic of thinking, Forrest et al. (2022b) derive the results below; for relevant details, see Chap. 8, when these scholars investigate the rationality assumption (e.g., Friedman, 1953; Gilboa, 2010; Hudik, 2019):

- A firm's mission clearly states how the firm's efforts should be oriented, at least partially.
- For a firm, the rationality assumption means the selection of a best choice among available options with the so-called best defined by the firm's natural endowments.
- The system of values and beliefs is different from one firm to another.
- To make decision, a firm optimizes its potential within the limit of given constraints, where the optimization is done consistently with the firm's values and beliefs.

The significance of these systemic conclusions is well illustrated by the example given in Sect. 6.3 of Chap. 6. One of the key takeaways of that example is that different systems of values and beliefs dictate their correspondingly varied ways to order real numbers. This end can be illustrated readily with the following real-life scenario of comparing two different incomes—one in the amount of $30 K and the other $3 million. Evidently, without involving systems of values and beliefs, one would naturally order $30K < $3 million. However, if the information behind these amounts is known as follows: the first amount of $30 K is the income from a lawful employment, while the second amount of $3 million is the gain from robbing a bank, and if systems of values and beliefs are considered, a lot of economic agents, be they individual persons or firms, will order $30K > $3 million. Other examples can be easily constructed if one considers, for example, corporate social responsibilities (for a description of this concept, see, e.g., Fahimnia et al., 2015). That is, each system of values and beliefs orders real numbers in its specific way.

That is, different systems of values and beliefs dictate formulations of different priorities, such as different ways to order real numbers; and different definitions of priorities point to different approaches of optimization. That in turn generally leads to different optimal decisions. Underneath all these sets of differences is the fundamental difference in individuals' systems of values and beliefs. In terms of the theory of optimization, the example in Chap. 6 clearly says that even when the objective function of a business situation is the same in the eyes of different decision-makers, the criteria of priority or approaches of optimization can be different from one decision-maker to another. This end supplements the statement (von Mises, 1949, p. 244) that "the value judgements a man pronounces about another man's satisfaction do not assert anything about this other man's satisfaction. They only assert what condition of this other man better satisfies the man who pronounces the judgement." In terms of neoclassical economics, the economist asserts this other man's condition that better satisfies the economist, if we rephrase what the example in Chap. 6 says in the language of Mises. That surely represents one source of uncertainties and risks the economist experiences or takes when he draws conclusions and makes claims, if the other man pursues after his own desires as driven by his values and beliefs, which is mostly the case in real life (Taylor, 1989), instead of what the economist believes and expects.

To accommodate what is observed above, for the rest of this chapter, we assume that for each firm, its system of values and beliefs dictates how real numbers are ordered, especially those real numbers within the domain D of decision-making activities. For a firm's, named F, ordering of real numbers, we use the symbol $\leq_F$ to denote less than or equal to, the symbol $\geq_F$ greater than or equal to, and the symbol $=_F$ for equality.

11.2.2 The Firm's Activities

For the sake of convenience of communication, this chapter focuses on a randomly selected firm, known as the firm. As a form of viable life, the firm does absorb inputs from the outside world, while it gives off outputs into the environment. If it inputs an amount x of a certain commodity by paying a unit price p_x (or simply price), the firm then generates a debit in the amount of xp_x in its account. And in the opposite direction, if the firm peddles one output (or commodity) in the amount of y at price p_y, it produces a credit in the amount of yp_y in its account.

Let us refer to all commodities the firm receives from others as inputs, and offers it provides to others as outputs. Then, the amounts of commodities, both received and given off, can be written as a vector. To distinguish inputs and outputs in such a vector, we use negative numbers to represent the quantities of the former, because debits appear for the firm from these inputs. And, we employ positive numbers to represent the quantities of outputs, because these outputs represent the firm's revenues. To make the following reasoning go smoothly, assume that in the (product) marketplace, all commodities can be exchanged readily. And, assume that all commodities are linearly ordered and respectively labeled as 1, 2, …, ℓ. As commonly done in economic analysis (e.g., Pancs, 2018), assume that the quantity of each input or output commodity is a real number.

Corresponding to the vector convention given above, let $p = (p_1, p_2, \ldots, p_\ell)$ be a price system and $c = (c_1, c_2, \ldots, c_\ell)$ a vector of input and output commodities. Without causing confusion, p_h will stand for the unit price of commodity h, while c_h the amount of the same commodity involved with the firm's operation. Therefore, within the firm's account, there is an overall cash flow $p \cdot c = \sum_{h=1}^{\ell} p_h c_h$, where the dot $\cdot$ means the dot product of vectors p and c. Based on the convention given above, let us assume that each price system $p = (p_1, p_2, \ldots, p_\ell)$ contains only positive components, because when each commodity is market exchanged, the acquisition of any commodity will have to cost money. At the same time, most of the components of the commodity vector c would be zero, because the firm only involves as its inputs and outputs a limited few commodities.

In terms of commodities, they are generally time sensitive and location specific. That is, when the time and location of delivery are different, a same commodity will be seen as different. As what is done in real life, the time axis consists of intervals of equal length, each of which stands for when a delivery takes place so that the time moments within an interval are not distinguishable. Similarly, the land is divided into a finite number of locations, in each of which exchanged commodities are delivered. That is the reason why when a commodity is available at different times and/or exchanged hands at different locations, it is seen in this chapter as different commodities. Additionally, commodity prices are the present values with interests and discounts over time omitted to abridge the analysis in the following sections. And, similarly, the value of money at different locations is ignored.

For our chosen firm, its business operation consists of selecting a plan of production that specifies how much each commodity it either consumes itself or offers to the market. That is, the firm's plan $y = (y_1, y_2, \ldots, y_\ell)$ of action is to select an element from the Euclidean space $\mathbb{R}^\ell$, representing the quantities of commodities the firm either consumes or offers, where $\mathbb{R}$ is the set of all real numbers and the subscripts 1, 2, …, ℓ denote the individual commodities. So, the price of action y is given by $p \cdot y = \sum_{h=1}^{\ell} p_h y_h$, where $p = (p_1, p_2, \ldots, p_\ell)$ is the price system of the commodities and y_h the quantity of commodity h $(= 1, 2, \ldots, \ell)$. Specifically, $y_h = 0$ means that the firm neither consumers nor produces commodity h.

By considering its constraining boundary conditions, the firm picks such a plan of action that optimally fits its unique system of values and beliefs. The idea of maximizing profit, as mostly deliberated in literature, represents the demand of one such particular system of values and beliefs that the ordering of real numbers is identical to the conventional one. In the rest of this chapter, Y stands for the firm's set of all feasible production plans or simply productions. In other words, if $y \in Y$, then y is a production possibility for the firm to technically materialize and meets the firm's moral codes, as defined by its system of values and beliefs.

At this junction, one needs to note that there are two different binary relations, $\leq$ and $\leq_F$, at play here. One is defined on Y such that $x, y \in Y$, $x \leq y$ if and only if for each $h = 1, 2, \ldots, \ell$, $x_h \leq y_h$. And the other is the firm-specific ordering $\leq_F$ of real numbers. Evidently, we cannot assume that $\leq_F$ is rational (i.e., $\leq_F$ is complete, transitive, and reflexive) as assumed by Mas-Collel et al. (1995) for the preference relation of a consumer on his set of all possible consumptions. Since $\leq_F$ represents firm F's specific priorities defined for the real-number domain D of decision-making activities, when no confusion appears, assume that $\leq_F$ satisfies: (1) transitivity (for x, y, $z \in D$, if $x \leq_F y$ and $y \leq_F z$, then $x \leq_F z$), (2) reflexivity (for $x \in D$, $x \leq_F x$), and (3) antisymmetry (for different $x, y \in D$, $x \leq_F y$ and $y \leq_F x$ cannot hold true at the same time). In short, conditions (1)–(3) are not equivalent to assuming that the firm considered in this chapter is rational for the research economist who asserts conditions that satisfy his optimal possibility, as so phrased in the language of von Mises (1949).

11.3 Basic Axioms and Assumptions

This section examines the most fundamental assumptions that have been adopted in the development of microeconomic theory (Mas-Collel et al., 1995). It first formulates some of the most intuitive business experiences into axioms that will be used as the starting points of logical reasoning. And then it discusses why other commonly implemented assumptions should not be employed any further if we desire to develop an economic theory that will be more practically useful than the present one (Forrest & Liu, 2021).

11.3.1 Basic and Necessary Axioms

Without loss of generality, in the rest of this book, the firm of our concern is assumed to satisfy the properties listed in the following Axioms 11.1–11.4 without further explicit declaration unless specifically stated otherwise. And, the names of these axioms are adopted from either Debreu (1959) or Levin and Milgrom (2004).

Axiom 11.1 (The Possibility of Inaction) The firm has the option of not making any production plan and not carrying out any production. Symbolically, what is axiomatized is $0 \in Y$.

This axiom evidently holds true for any existing firm, because when a challenge or an opportunity appears, taking no action for the moment temporarily is surely one strategy the management can adopt. When a firm has no past and does not expect to have any future, then this possibility of inaction axiom simply means that there are no stakeholders that are closely tied to the fortune of the firm. Hence, the firm can simply choose to spend no resources on the production of anything, a state of shutting down (Levin & Milgrom, 2004).

Axiom 11.2 (Free Disposal) Although inputs are increased, the firm can choose to produce less. Symbolically, what is axiomatized here is that if $y \in Y$ and $y' \leq y$, then $y' \in Y$, where $y' \leq y$ means that for each $h = 1, 2, \ldots, \ell$, $y'_h \leq y_h$.

This axiom is rephrased based on Levin and Milgrom (2004). It is similar to the possibility of inaction axiom regarding the freedom the firm has about what it could do in its business operation and its production decisions.

Axiom 11.3 (Impossibility of Free Production) The real-life implementation of any nonzero production plan has to use certain amounts of some inputs, such as labor, work space, etc., and produce certain outputs, such as waste, if nothing useful. Symbolically, what is axiomatized is

$$\forall y \in Y\left(y \neq 0 \rightarrow y_{h_1} < 0 \text{ and } y_{h_2} > 0, \text{for some commodities } 1 \leq h_1, h_2 \leq \ell\right). \quad (11.1)$$

This end can be rewritten equivalently as follows:

$$Y \cap \left(\mathbb{R}^{\ell} - \mathbb{R}_{+}^{\ell}\right) = \{0\} = (-Y) \cap \left(\mathbb{R}^{\ell} - \mathbb{R}_{+}^{\ell}\right), \tag{11.2}$$

where $\mathbb{R}_+$ is the set of all positive real numbers, and $-Y = \{(-y_1, -y_2, \ldots, -y_\ell) : (y_1, y_2, \ldots, y_\ell) \in Y\}$.

This axiom can be generally and readily justified as follows: Even for an output (or goods) that can be produced without applying any physical commodity as input, if such an output exists in the real world, at least some manpower is needed to have the availability of the output known to the participants of the marketplace. That is, human labor, as a commodity input, is still needed for this fictitious case.

Axiom 11.4 (Irreversibility of Production) No production can be reversed, meaning that if a vector c^{in} of inputs leads to the production of a vector c^{out} of outputs, then when c^{out} is applied as inputs, it does not lead to the production of c^{in}. Symbolically, what is axiomatized is

$$Y \cap (-Y) = \{0\}. \tag{11.3}$$

By considering how commodities tend to be dated and how labors and talents can likely be specific, these inputs in real life just cannot be produced by reversing any production process. In particular, to produce output vector c^{out}, the vector c^{in} must contain such inputs as particularly dated commodities, such as labor, talents, and others that are just not possible to produce the inputs in vector c^{in} by using commodities in c^{out}.

At this junction, one should note that Axioms 11.1–11.4 are first introduced by referencing to actual business scenarios that are mostly true in real life and then symbolized by using commonly adopted notations in mathematics. In comparison, the literature tends to take the opposite direction. In particular, the literature first introduces various assumptions so that a certain chosen mathematical theory can be smoothly applied. Some of these assumptions are then given related economic meanings, while the justification for adopting other assumptions is simply omitted with or without such a statement saying that these are needed in order to take advantage of the chosen mathematical theory. By borrowing the metaphor from Lin and OuYang (2010), the comparison between our approach and that of the literature can be described as follows: The former is like the situation of choosing a pair of shoes that fit our feet, while the approach widely appearing in the literature represents the opposite—trim our feet to fit a chosen pair of shoes.

11.3.2 Avoidance of Some Commonly Adopted Assumptions

Conventionally, to derive "beautiful" conclusions, assumptions, additional to the ones listed above, are introduced for the purpose of establishing economic theories that are full of impressive-looking mathematics, as Paul Krugman commented in

New York Times (2009-09-02). For example, (1) the production possibility set Y is assumed to be closed in $\mathbb{R}^\ell$ (Debreu, 1959; Levin & Milgrom, 2004; Mas-Collel et al., 1995), (2) the set Y is convex (Debreu, 1959), and others. In the rest of this subsection, we explain why this chapter and the rest of this book avoids these assumptions unless specific circumstances arise.

First, let us examine the assumption of closedness, meaning that Y is closed in $\mathbb{R}^\ell$. It means that for any sequence $\{y^q\}_{q=1}^{\infty}$ of productions that are feasible for the firm, if the sequence is convergent, then the limit $\lim_{q \to \infty} y^q = y^0$ is also a feasible production of the firm. However, this end is generally untrue in the real-life business world. For example, productions of semiconductor microchips have led to smaller and smaller chips. If we write the corresponding productions as $y^1, y^2, y^3, \ldots$, then $\{y^q\}_{q=1}^{\infty}$ converges to y^0, which would produce microchips of size 0. Evidently, such a chip that will be materially used in various electronic products does not physically exist. So, such an imagined production is not feasible for any firm.

Second, let us look at the assumption of additivity, that is, $(Y + Y) \subset Y$, where $Y + Y = \{y^1 + y^2 : y^1, y^2 \in Y\}$ (Debreu, 1959, p. 41). As above, this assumption is not true in general. One reason for this end is that this assumption implies that the firm cannot produce any profit other than potentially experiencing losses. In particular, assume that for a price system p of commodities, there is a production $y \in Y$ such that

$$p \cdot y = \max_{y^q \in Y} p \cdot y^q > 0,$$

where $>$ represents the conventional ordering relation between real numbers and it is assumed that the firm's system of values and beliefs complies with the conventional ordering of real numbers. If the assumption of additivity holds true, that is, if $(Y + Y) \subset Y$, then for $z = 2y \in Y$, one has the following:

$$p \cdot z = p \cdot 2y > p \cdot y = \max_{y^q \in Y} p \cdot y^q,$$

a contradiction. In other words, the assumption $(Y + Y) \subset Y$ implies that no production $y \in Y$ can lead to a positive profit; otherwise the contradiction, as displayed above, appears. However, if the firm does not have any production plan that can help the firm make a profit, then this firm cannot exist in real life, even for those modern firms, which, other than promises of great futures, have been losing money year after year since their initial launches (Li & Ma, 2015). Another reason for this assumption to fail generally is because when the inputs $y^{1\text{ in}}$ in y^1 and those $y^{2\text{ in}}$ in y^2 are added, some of the summed inputs may very well be beyond the firm's capability to handle. To this end, Forrest and Liu (2021, p. 114) developed the following result:

Proposition 11.1 For two opposing business goals A and B, any interaction between the mutually exclusive sets X and Y of resources, where resources in X lead to the realization of goal A and those in Y help actualize goal B, tends to produce undesirable effects.

For example, when the same amount of labor input, say X, is individually needed for either production y^1 or production y^2, then $X + X = 2X$ can likely be more than the amount of labor available to the firm. That is, although y^1 and y^2 are both feasible to the firm, $y^1 + y^2$ is not. For relevant literature, the study on interacting capabilities related to new product developments, customer management, and supply-chain management suggests that trade-offs may be involved among different resource inputs (Ramaswami et al., 2009). In terms of capabilities purposefully developed for exploiting a set of proven successful competitive advantages, they generally do not work right with those introduced for constantly discovering new competitive advantages (McGrath, 2013). On the other hand, if two productions y^1 and $y^2 \in Y$ require only inputs of various knowledges, then $y^1 + y^2$ might still be a feasible production in Y, depending on whether or not additional manpower is needed and whether or not such additional manpower is available.

Third, we consider the assumption of convexity, meaning that Y is convex; that is, for any y^1 and $y^2 \in Y$ and for any scalar $\alpha \in [0, 1]$, $\alpha y^1 + (1 - \alpha)y^2 \in Y$. Under this assumption, for any $y \in Y$, because $0 \in Y$, it means that $\alpha y + (1 - \alpha)0 = \alpha y \in Y$. So, this assumption implies that the set Y of production possibilities has nonincreasing returns to scale (Mas-Collel et al., 1995). In order to develop an economic theory that can be potentially applied to address real-life problems, such strong holistic, systemic property should not be allowed to hold except for specific cases or some individual productions. In real life, various returns to scale might hold true for one production, but not the entire set of feasible productions. It is because, systemically speaking, returns to scale for one production represent the local characteristics of the production, while those for the entire set of feasible productions are holistic, systemic characteristics of the firm. If the characteristics of one production plan are seen as micro-properties of individual production possibilities, then characteristics of the firm's set of production plans will be correctly treated as macro-features of the firm. As is well-known, some micro-level economic properties do not aggregate into macro-level ones, although some do (Atalay, 2017; Gabaix, 2011; Lucas, 1977). That is, individual characteristics of one production in general cannot be elevated into holistic, systemic properties, although some do (Forrest et al., 2021a). So, a more real-life like scenario should be: The firm's set Y of feasible productions might not have any defined returns to scale; however, there could be some particular production $y^1 \in Y$ that has increasing returns to scale, some other production $y^2 \in Y$ has decreasing returns to scale, etc. In other words, different productions $y^k \in Y, k = 1, 2, 3, \ldots$, may have different kinds of returns to scale or none of them at all. Hence, this convexity assumption should not be adopted in general; otherwise, no production in Y would have increasing returns to scale or constant returns to scale.

Fourth, let us examine the cone assumption, meaning that Y is a cone with vertex 0. It means that for any $y \in Y$ and any scalar $\alpha \in (0, +\infty)$, $\alpha y \in Y$. That is, this assumption implies that the entire set of production possibilities has constant returns to scale. As just discussed in the previous paragraph, such a strong holistic, systemic property should not be assumed to hold true in general in real life, although this property might hold for some individual productions. For instance, after a production process has been implemented for a while, all personnel involved in the process become more efficient over time, leading to increased outputs with the same level of inputs (Forrest et al., 2019). That is, for such a production $y \in Y$, it should have increasing returns to scale.

When these listed assumptions about Y are not assumed, the challenge one can expect to face is to what extent some of the most important results in related economic theory can still be established.

11.4 Production and Profits

As suggested by the title, this section creatively studies both production and profit functions of the firm so that we do not have to focus only on the situation of a single output as the literature commonly does (e.g., Levin & Milgrom, 2004; Mas-Collel et al., 1995; Pancs, 2018).

11.4.1 The Production Function

For each production $y \in Y \subseteq \mathbb{R}^{\ell}$, let

$$y^{\text{in}} = \left(y_{h_1^{\text{in}}}, y_{h_2^{\text{in}}}, \ldots, y_{h_t^{\text{in}}}\right) \in \mathbb{R}_-^t \text{ and } y^{\text{out}} = \left(y_{h_1^{\text{out}}}, y_{h_2^{\text{out}}}, \ldots, y_{h_s^{\text{out}}}\right) \in \mathbb{R}_+^s$$

be respectively the sub-vector of the quantities of all the corresponding commodity inputs h_1^{in}, h_2^{in}, …, h_t^{in}, and that of all commodity outputs h_1^{out}, h_2^{out}, …, h_s^{out}, where $\mathbb{R}_-$ is the set of all negative real numbers. That is, what is implicitly meant is that in both y^{in} and y^{out} no zero components appear so that $h_1^{\text{in}} < h_2^{\text{in}} < \cdots < h_t^{\text{in}}$ and $h_1^{\text{out}} < h_2^{\text{out}} < \cdots < h_s^{\text{out}}$, where

$$y_{h_j^{\text{in}}} < 0 \quad \text{and} \quad y_{h_k^{\text{out}}} > 0, j = 1, 2, \ldots, t; \text{k} = 1, 2, \ldots, s. \tag{11.4}$$

Now, we define the production function f for the firm as follows: For any $y \in Y, f(y^{\text{in}}) = y^{\text{out}}$. Then, the following conclusion holds true:

Proposition 11.2 For the firm, its production function f is well defined. That is, for each $y \in Y, f(y^{\text{in}})$ is uniquely determined.

Proof It suffices to show that for any ${}^1y, {}^2y \in Y$, if ${}^1y^{\text{in}} = {}^2y^{\text{in}}$, then ${}^1y^{\text{out}} = {}^2y^{\text{out}}$. This end follows from the fact that when outputs are different, some of the inputs have to be different, even though all physical commodity inputs can be identical from one production ${}^1y$ to another ${}^2y$. That is, it is the employment of different recourses, such as special talents or additional manpower, in the production that the identical physical inputs are assembled or combined into different outputs.

A mapping $g : U \to W$ from a set U to another set W is said to be a partial function, if the domain of g, denoted by domain(g), is not equal to U; that is, $g(u)$ is defined for some $u \in U$ but not for every $u \in U$. A mapping $g : U \rightarrow W$ is said to be a set-valued function, if for any $u \in \text{domain}(g) \subseteq U$, $g(u)$ is a nonempty subset of W. For the production function f of the firm, the inverse function of f, denoted by f^{-1}, is the following set-valued function: For any production $y \in Y$,

$$f^{-1}(y^{\text{out}}) = \{y^{\text{in}} : y \in Y \text{ and } f(y^{\text{in}}) = y^{\text{out}}\}.$$

Proposition 11.3 For a production $y \in Y$, if $f^{-1}(y^{\text{out}})$ contains more than one element, then at least one commodity input of y has a substitute.

Proof Assume that $u, v \in f^{-1}(y^{\text{out}})$ are two different input vectors, each of which produces the same output vector y^{out}. Without loss of generality, let $u = \left(u_{h_1^{\text{in}}}, u_{h_2^{\text{in}}}, \ldots, u_{h_{t_1}^{\text{in}}}\right)$ and $v = \left(v_{k_1^{\text{in}}}, v_{k_2^{\text{in}}}, \ldots, v_{k_{t_2}^{\text{in}}}\right)$. For convenience of communication, let the involved sets of commodities be $H = \left\{h_1^{\text{in}}, h_2^{\text{in}}, \ldots, h_{t_1}^{\text{in}}\right\}$ and $K = \left\{k_1^{\text{in}}, k_2^{\text{in}}, \ldots, k_{t_2}^{\text{in}}\right\}$, respectively.

Now, we show the conclusion in three cases: (1) There is $h_j^{\text{in}} \in H$ such that $h_j^{\text{in}} \notin K$, (2) there is $k_j^{\text{in}} \in K$ such that $k_j^{\text{in}} \notin H$, and (3) $H = K$.

For case (1), it means that commodity h_j^{in} can be substituted by commodities in K. Similarly, case (2) implies that k_j^{in} can be substituted by commodities in H. As for case (3), because $u \neq v$, there must be $h_j^{\text{in}} \in H = K$ such that $u_{h_j^{\text{in}}} \neq v_{h_j^{\text{in}}}$. Without loss of generality, assume that $u_{h_j^{\text{in}}} < v_{h_j^{\text{in}}}$. Then commodity h_j^{in} can be partially substituted by other commodities in H $(=K)$. This end is generally seen as that more efficient use of other commodities in H can help reduce the demand for h_j^{in}.

Speaking differently, Proposition 11.3 implies that when $f^{-1}(y^{\text{out}})$ contains more than one element, there are several different combinations of commodity inputs that lead to the same specified outputs y^{out}. In other words, some of the inputting commodities can substitute for each other. Evidently, f^{-1} is a set-valued function with domain

$$\text{domain}(f^{-1}) = \{y^{\text{out}} : y \in Y\}$$

and range

$$\text{range}(f^{-1}) = \{y^{\text{in}} : y \in Y\}.$$

A production plan $y \in Y$ is said to have increasing returns to scale, provided that each proportionate increase in inputs leads to increased outputs of a greater proportion. Symbolically, y has increasing returns to scale, if

$$\forall \alpha \in (1, +\infty) \left(f\left(\alpha y^{\text{in}}\right) > \alpha f\left(y^{\text{in}}\right) \right). \tag{11.5}$$

If the inequality sign $>$ in Eq. (11.5) is replaced by $\geq$, then the production y is referred to as having nondecreasing returns to scale.

If a production $y \in Y$ satisfies the following, then y is said to have decreasing returns to scale:

$$\forall \alpha \in (0, 1) \left(f\left(\alpha y^{\text{in}}\right) < \alpha f\left(y^{\text{in}}\right) \right). \tag{11.6}$$

In other words, Eq. (11.6) reflects the following fact: If all inputs of production y are decreased by a scale $\alpha \in (0, 1)$, the corresponding outputs decrease by more than the scale α. When the inequality sign $<$ in Eq. (11.6) is replaced by $\leq$, then y is referred to as having nonincreasing returns to scale.

As for the concept of constant returns to scale, we define similarly as above. In particular, a production $y \in Y$ is said to have constant returns to scale, if the following holds true:

$$\forall \alpha \in (0, +\infty) f\left(\alpha y^{\text{in}}\right) = \alpha y^{\text{out}}. \tag{11.7}$$

In other words, $y \in Y$ implies that for any $\alpha \in (0, +\infty)$, $\alpha y \in Y$. Or, equivalently, y has constant returns to scale if and only if the firm's production function f is homogeneous of degree one with respect to the production inputs y^{in}.

The set Y of production possibilities of the firm is said to have increasing (respectively, nondecreasing, decreasing, nonincreasing, and constant) returns to scale, if every production $y \in Y$ has increasing (respectively, nondecreasing, decreasing, nonincreasing, and constant) returns to scale.

Note that other than the situation of constant returns to scale, for a scalar α and a production $y \in Y$, it is very possible that $\alpha y \notin Y$. That is, our definitions of various returns to scale are different from those given by Levin and Milgrom (2004, p. 5). Additionally, in real life, a scale of increase in a production's inputs generally does not proportionately increase the outputs. For instance, an increased input of labor might very well help make the workplace either less or more efficient, depending on what kinds of new personalities are hired. So, to reflect more adequately the concepts of various returns to scale, as given by Debreu (1959, pp. 40–41) and Gelles and Mitchell (1996), we introduced the concepts above, which are similar in spirit to those seen in Mas-Collel et al. (1995).

11.4.2 The Profit Function

Assume that the firm of our concern is a price taker so that its goal of business is to choose such a production plan that best fits its system of values and beliefs, for any given price system p of commodities. Symbolically, the firm's business goal can be formalized as follows:

$$\max_{y \in Y}^{F} p \cdot y, \text{ for any given } p > 0, \tag{11.8}$$

where the idea of "best fitting the firm's system of values and beliefs" is reflected in the operation of maximization defined specifically by the firm, as reflected by the superscript F. Of course, both theoretically and practically this "best fit" scenario may not exist. In such a case, the firm is forever pursuing after an ideal instead of a definite, tangible target. For this end, we write $\sup_{y \in Y}^{F} p \cdot y$, for any given price system p, in place of the expression in Eq. (11.8).

In Eq. (11.8), the price of production y is maximized in terms of Firm F's specific system of values and beliefs, if the maximum exists. Corresponding to this maximization, in neoclassic economics, there is such a long-standing convention that firms' objective is to maximize their profits (Wu, 2006). In reality, however, there are business firms that do not truly place profit maximization as its primary objective (e.g., Hussain, 2012; Jensen, 2001). Recently, a group of powerful US chief executives abandoned the idea that companies must maximize profits for shareholders above all else (https://opportunity.businessroundtable.org/ourcommitment/, accessed on January 30, 2021). "Americans deserve an economy that allows each person to succeed through hard work and creativity and to lead to a life of meaning and dignity" and "we commit to deliver value to all of them, for the future success of our companies, our communities, and our country," said the statement from the organization (https://s3.amazonaws.com/brt.org/BRT-StatementonthePurposeofaCorporationOctober2020.pdf, accessed on January 30, 2021), chaired by JP Morgan Chase CEO Jamie Dimon. Once again, the reason why many firms don't put profit maximization as the number one priority can be explained by the natural endowments. It is because the conscience of the managers directs them to contribute more to their respective communities. This of course also supports the notion that how a firm behaves is dictated by its system of values and beliefs.

Corresponding to the fact that there are firms that do not solely focus on maximizing their profits as a consequence of their values and beliefs, one might ask the following question: Can these firms financially compete with those that do? Although the answer to this question depends on the particular constraints and circumstances of each specific firm, evidence suggests that generally in a buyer's market, the answer is YES. In fact, in such a market, consumers have shown increasing levels of attention to companies that are socially responsible (Hsueh, 2014), while employees, market competitions and governments pressured downstream companies to distribute and sell socially responsible goods (Letizia & Hendrikse, 2016). In particular, in 1983, American Express's support for the Statue of Liberty encouraged consumers to use their American Express card (Adkins, 1999): Each time the card was used, a 1 cent was donated to the Restoration of the Statue of Liberty fund; and for each new American Express card account approved, a

$1 was donated. This 3-month promotion from September to December 1983 collected over $1.7 million for the fund, while the use of American Express cards rose by 28% in just the first month, compared to the previous year, and new card applications increased by 45%. Cone/Roper research found (Meyer, 1993) that more than 70% of respondents are more likely to choose firms that participate in public service when faced with the same goods in terms of quality and price, and more than half of them are willing to pay a higher premium for their products and/or services.

For the firm, $\pi^F : \mathbb{R}_+^\ell \to \mathbb{R}$, defined below, is referred to as its profit function, assuming that the maximum value on the right-hand side exists according to the firm's system of values and beliefs.

$$\pi^F(p) =_F \max{}^F_{y \in Y} p \cdot y. \tag{11.9}$$

Proposition 11.4 The profit π^F of the firm, as defined above, is a partial function defined on $\mathbb{R}_+^\ell$.

Proof This conclusion follows from the definition of partial functions and the fact that the action of taking maximum in the equation $\pi^F(p) =_F \max{}^F_{y \in Y} p \cdot y$ cannot be guaranteed to be always possible for each price system $p \in \mathbb{R}_+^\ell$.

Proposition 11.5 Assume that the system of values and beliefs of the firm orders real numbers in the same way as the conventional one of real numbers. Then the profit function π^F satisfies $\pi^F(\lambda p) = \lambda \pi^F(p)$, for any scalar $\lambda > 0$ and any $p \in$ domain (π^F). That is, the partial function π^F on $\mathbb{R}_+^\ell$ is homogeneous of degree one on domain (π^F).

Proof This conclusion follows readily from the observation that for any scalar $\lambda > 0$ and any price system $p \in \text{domain}(\pi^F)$, $\pi^F(\lambda p) =_F \lambda \max{}^F_{y \in Y} p \cdot y = \lambda \pi^F(p)$.

Proposition 11.6 In general, when the system of values and beliefs of the firm is not specified, the profit function π^F is not homogeneous of degree one.

To see why this conclusion holds true, we only need to confirm it by constructing a counterexample.

11.4.3 Profit Function's Non-homogeneity of Degree One

This subsection provides a needed example to show that in general, the profit function π^F is not homogeneous of degree one. To this end, we will rely on the generalized modular function; for more details, see Sect. 7.5 or Forrest et al. (2021b).

Example 11.1 The firm operates a specific line of production, into which a unit of each of the following commodities A, A_1, A_2, B, C_1, C_2, and C needs to be imported. Different from others, commodities A_1 and A_2 (and respectively, C_1 and C_2) are

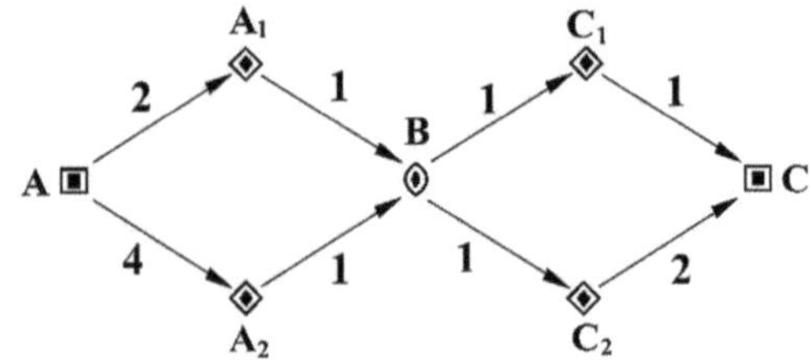

Fig. 11.1 The directed network of a production line

substitutes of each other. The line of production is depicted in Fig. 11.1, where the arrows signal the order these commodities are imported into the line. And, the weights of the arrowed edges indicate the related profits generated by moving from a node to the next.

Assume that the system of the values and beliefs of the firm mandates the manager to find such a path that maximizes the overall profit of the production line.

Case 1: Assume that the firm's system of values and beliefs dictates its order of real numbers the same way as the conventional one. Then, the desired path is $A \to A_2 \to B \to C_2 \to C$ that has a total weight of 8. Other three possible paths have total weights 5, 6, and 7, respectively.

Let the set of all commodities be ordered as follows:

$$A \prec A_1 \prec A_2 \prec B \prec C_1 \prec C_2 \prec C,$$

and the respective paths be:

$$I_1 = A \to A_1 \to B \to C_1 \to C \quad I_2 = A \to A_1 \to B \to C_2 \to C$$
$$I_3 = A \to A_2 \to B \to C_1 \to C \quad I_4 = A \to A_2 \to B \to C_2 \to C$$

Then the corresponding input vectors are respectively ${}^i y = (y_j)_{j \in I_i}$ and the associated output vectors respectively ${}^i Z_{AC}$, for $i = 1, \ldots, 4$. Corresponding to this representation of inputs and outputs, each price vector p will need to be written in the following form:

$$p = \left((p_j)_{j \in I}, \left({}^j Z_{AC}\right)_{j=1}^{4} \right),$$

where I stands for the set of all commodities involved here. Based on this setup, it can be seen that for any production $y \in Y$ of the firm, one can find an index k (= 1, 2, 3, 4), satisfying that after eliminating all zero components from y, we have $y^{\text{in}} = {}^k y$ and $y^{\text{out}} = {}^k Z_{AC}$. Hence, for any price system $p \in \mathbb{R}^\ell$ and any production $y \in Y$, we have $p \cdot y = p^{\text{in}} \cdot y^{\text{in}} + p^{\text{out}} \cdot y^{\text{out}}$, where p^{in} is the price vector of all the commodities in y^{in} and p^{out} price vector of those commodities in y^{out}. So, this analysis indicates the following equation for any scalar $\lambda > 0$:

$$\pi^F(\lambda p) =_F \max{}^F_{y \in Y}\left(\lambda p^{\text{in}} \cdot y^{\text{in}} + \lambda p^{\text{out}} \cdot y^{\text{out}}\right) = \lambda \max{}^F_{y \in Y} p \cdot y = \lambda \pi^F(p) = 8\lambda.$$

In other words, the conclusion in Proposition 11.5 is confirmed.

Case 2: Assume that the firm's system of values and beliefs dictates the ordering of real numbers based on the mod4 function, as described in the example in Chap. 6. In this case, the maximum total profit is equal to 3, which is equal to 7 (mod4), because the respective total profits of the four possible paths are 5 (mod4) = 1, 6 (mod4) = 2, 7 (mod4) = 3, and 8 (mod4) = 0.

Next, we use scalar $\lambda = 3.2$ to multiply each of the local weights, producing respectively the following results: 5×3.2 (mod4) = 0, 6×3.2 (mod4) = 3.2, 7×3.2 (mod4) = 2.4, and 8×3.2 (mod4) = 1.6. Here, the maximum total profit is equal to 3.2=6×3.2 (mod4). That is, we have

$$3.2 \text{ times } 7\ (\text{mod}4) \neq (3.2 \times 6\ (\text{mod}4).$$

That is, we have confirmed the conclusion of Proposition 11.6.

According to Levin and Milgrom (2004), the following partial and set-valued function

$$\eta^F(p) = \left\{y \in Y : p \cdot y =_F \max{}^F_{y^q \in Y} p \cdot y^q\right\} \tag{11.10}$$

is known as the optimal production correspondence of the firm, for any price system $p \in \mathbb{R}^\ell_+$. Intuitively, what the function $\eta^F: \mathbb{R}^\ell_+ \to Y$ does is to map each price vector $p \in \mathbb{R}^\ell_+$ to the subset $\eta^F(p) \subset Y$ of all profit-maximizing productions with this fixed p. Evidently, for some $p \in \mathbb{R}^\ell_+$, $\eta^F(p)$ might be empty.

Proposition 11.7 If the order relation $\leq_F$ that is consistent with the firm's system of values and beliefs satisfies that for any real numbers a_i, b_i, $i = 1, 2$, $a_1 \leq_F b_1$, and $a_2 \leq_F b_2$ imply $a_1 + a_2 \leq_F b_1 + b_2$, then the profit function π^F is convex in p.

Proof For any price systems ${}^1p$, ${}^2p \in \text{domain}(\pi^F)$ and any scalar $\alpha \in [0, 1]$, let ${}^\alpha p = \alpha{}^1p + (1 - \alpha){}^2p$ and pick ${}^\alpha y \in \eta^F({}^\alpha p)$. Then, we have

$$\begin{aligned}\alpha\pi^F({}^1p) + (1-\alpha)\pi^F({}^2p) &\geq_F \alpha{}^1p.{}^\alpha y + (1-\alpha){}^2p.{}^\alpha y \\ &= \left[{}^1p + (1-\alpha){}^2p\right].{}^\alpha y = \pi^F({}^\alpha y).\end{aligned} \tag{11.11}$$

That is, π^F is convex in p.

Evidently, the required property of inequality in Proposition 11.7 is not satisfied by the order relation discussed in case 2 of the example in Chap. 6. In particular, $2 \leq_{\text{mod}(4)} 3$ and $1 \leq_{\text{mod}(4)} 1$ do not lead to $2 + 1 \leq_{\text{mod}(4)} 3 + 1$. Instead, we have

$$2 + 1 \square_{\text{mod}(4)} 3 + 1 =_{\text{mod}(4)} 0.$$

That is, Proposition 11.7 is not guaranteed to be generally true unless the if-condition is held. Specifically, the first line of Eq. (11.11) may very well be violated by various order relations.

Proposition 11.8 For any two price systems $p, p' \in \mathbb{R}_+^\ell$, and productions $y \in \eta^F(p)$, $y' \in \eta^F(p')$, $(p' - p)(y' - y) \geq_F 0$.

Proof Because $p \cdot y =_F \max^F_{y^q \in Y} p \cdot y^q$ and $p' \cdot y' =_F \max^F_{y^q \in Y} p' \cdot y^q$, we have $p \cdot y \geq_F p \cdot y'$ and $p' \cdot y' \geq_F p' \cdot y$. So, $p \cdot (y - y') \geq_F 0 \geq_F p' \cdot (y - y')$, from which $(p' - p)(y' - y) \geq_F 0$ follows.

11.5 The Optimal Production Correspondence

This section assumes that the firm's system of values and beliefs orders real numbers the same way as the conventional one; and that the firm's profit $\pi(p) = \max_{y \in Y} p \cdot y$ exists for an arbitrarily chosen price system $p = (p_1, p_2, \ldots, p_\ell) \in \mathbb{R}^\ell$. Then, the well-known Hotelling's lemma can be generalized as follows:

Proposition 11.9 In a neighborhood of the chosen p, the optimal production correspondence $\eta(p)$ contains only one element, if and only if the partial derivative of the profit function $\pi(\cdot)$ with respect to each p_h exists at p and satisfies the following: for any $y = (y_1, y_2, \ldots, y_\ell) \in \eta(p)$, $h = 1, 2, \ldots, \ell$:

$$\frac{\partial \pi(p)}{\partial p_h} = y_h. \tag{11.12}$$

Proof ($\Rightarrow$) From the assumption that $\eta(p)$ contains only one element in a neighborhood of p, it follows that the envelope theorem applies so that $\partial \pi(p)/\partial p_h = y_h$, for the unique element $y = (y_1, y_2, \ldots, y_\ell) \in \eta(p)$, $h = 1, 2, \ldots, \ell$.

($\Leftarrow$) Assume that $\pi(\cdot)$ is differentiable at p with respect to each p_h, for $h = 1, 2, \ldots, \ell$, Eq. (11.12) holds true. Let us select two arbitrary productions y^1 and $y^2 \in \eta(p)$. Then, the definition of optimal production correspondences implies $\pi(p) = p \cdot y^1 = p \cdot y^2$. So, Eq. (11.12) implies that for any $h = 1, 2, \ldots, \ell$, we have

$$y_h^1 = \frac{\partial \pi(p)}{\partial p_h} = y_h^2.$$

That is, $y^1 = y^2$. From the arbitrariness of y^1 and $y^2 \in \eta(p)$, it follows that $\eta(p)$ is a singleton.

Based on our initial set-theoretical setup, the condition that $\eta(p)$ contains only one element in the previous proposition is different from the statement that the firm produces only one product, as assumed by Levin and Milgrom (2004) and Mas-Collel et al. (1995) in the prevalent producer theory. In particular, according to our setup, a production in $\eta(p)$ can contain a vector of many different products. Because of this reason, Proposition 11.9 is indeed a generalization of the known Hotelling's lemma.

For the set Y of productions, let us define the following real-valued characteristic function: $F: Y \to \mathbb{R}$: $F(y) = 0$, if y is located on the frontier of Y; $F(y) < 0$, if y is located in the interior of Y; and $F(y) > 0$, if y is positioned somewhere outside of Y. By applying this function, we rewrite the following problem of maximization $\max_y p \cdot y$, s. t. $y \in Y$ as $\max_y p \cdot y$, s. t. $F(y) \leq 0$. This problem's Lagrangian is

$$L = p \cdot y - \lambda F(y), \tag{11.13}$$

while its first-order conditions are:

$$p_h = \lambda F_h(y^*), F(y^*) \leq 0, \text{for } y^* \in \eta(p), h = 1, 2, \ldots, \ell. \tag{11.14}$$

Proposition 11.10 Assume that price system $p = (p_1, p_2, \ldots, p_\ell) \in \mathbb{R}^\ell$ satisfies $p_h > 0$, for each $h = 1, 2, \ldots \ell$. Then, the condition of continuous differentiability of $y(p) \in \eta(p)$ implies that $D_p y(p) = D_p^2 \pi(p) = 0$.

Proof First, from Proposition 11.9 we have

$$D_p y(p) = \frac{\partial y(p)}{\partial p} = \left[\frac{\partial y_h}{\partial p_t}\right]_{\ell \times \ell} = \left[\frac{\partial^2 \pi(p)}{\partial p_i \partial p_j}\right]_{\ell \times \ell} = D_p^2 \pi(p)_{\ell \times \ell}, \tag{11.15}$$

where based on Eq. (11.14), the envelope theorem, and the assumption that $p_h > 0$, for $h = 1, 2, \ldots \ell$, the (t, h) cell is equal to:

$$\frac{\partial y_h}{\partial p_t} = \left(\frac{\partial y_h}{\partial p_t} p_h\right) \frac{1}{p_h} = \left(\frac{\partial y_h}{\partial p_t} F_h(y)\right) \frac{\lambda}{p_h} = \frac{\partial F(y)}{\partial p_t} \frac{\lambda}{p_h} = 0 \cdot \frac{\lambda}{p_h} = 0.$$

In this calculation, the reason why $\partial F(y)/\partial p_t = 0$ is that no matter p-value is, we have $y \in \eta(p)$ and $F(y) = 0$. Hence, the derivative of $F(y)$ is always zero. So, $D_p y(p) = D_p^2 \pi(p) = 0$.

In the prevalent producer theory, there is such a theoretical result that Levin and Milgrom (2004) claim to show the advantage of theoretical reasoning over empirical analysis. In particular, this theoretical result states that when the firm produces a single product and that $\eta(p)$ is a singleton, then the matrix $D_p y(p) = D_p^2 \pi(p)$ is symmetric, positive semi-definite. Evidently, in comparison, Proposition 11.10 generalizes this known result greatly.

11.6 A Few Final Words

By employing the four natural endowments of a firm—self-awareness, imagination, conscience, and free will (Forrest et al., 2021a)—this chapter cards through the list of various common assumptions widely adopted in the producer theory (Debreu, 1959; Levin & Milgrom, 2004; Mas-Collel et al., 1995) in order to find out which assumptions are problematic either theoretically or practically or both. As a consequence, we are able to single out four of them as fundamental so that they are emphasized as axioms or starting points from which useful conclusions can be analytically or logically derived.

On the basis of a firm's endowments, this chapter places an emphasis on the existence of a firm-specific order relation for real numbers, and consequently the existence of a firm-specific method of optimization. Because such firm-specific order relations are different from one firm to another, one firm's optimal decision may possibly look ridiculous or stupid in the eyes of another firm. Therefore, our attempt to address the question, as posed in the beginning of this chapter, about how to avoid the history of repeatedly falling back to treating impressive-looking beauty as truth by altering the devastating setup of the existent theories at the most fundamental level, is the recognition of the differences in firm-specific systems of values and beliefs.

Due to such drastically different starting points from the ones widely adopted in the literature, we are able to define a firm's production function innovatively and show, among others, that:

- The firm's profit function in general is not homogeneous of degree one (Proposition 11.6), while it is only for very specific situations.
- For such profit function to be convex in price, the order relation, consistent with the firm's values and beliefs, has to satisfy an additivity property (Proposition 11.7).
- In Hotelling's lemma, a singleton optimal production correspondence is equivalent to the equation that the rate of change of the profit in the price of commodity h is equal to the amount of commodity h either inputted or outputted, for each commodity h (Proposition 11.7).
- When each commodity costs real money, the matrix of rates of changes in commodities with respect to prices is equal to 0 (Proposition 11.10).

In other words, other than the contributions described above, this chapter also greatly generalizes a few very well-known results many steps forward without imposing some of the key conditions as done in the past. Because of the lesser conditions imposed, our conclusions developed in this chapter can be expected to be more practically useful.

For possible future research, one can investigate properties of the production and profit functions, as defined in this chapter, that are specific to different systems of values and beliefs. For example, results established in Sect. 11.5 will not hold true literally for systems of values and beliefs within which the conventional order relation of real numbers is no longer the law of governance. In particular, when the modular function is the rule of game, as shown in the example in Chap. 6 and Example 11.1, an important question is: How would Propositions 11.9 and 11.10 look like?

In terms of the literature, it has been found (Taylor, 1989) that Hotelling's lemma (and other maintained behavioral hypotheses, such as cost minimization and utility maximization) becomes invalid when the firm of concern is not a conventional profit maximizer. In the language of this chapter, the following question is both practically and theoretically important: If a firm, instead of conventionally maximizing its profit, fits its desired business outlook, such as revenue, into its stated mission by involving a different criterion of priority, does a modified version of Hotelling's lemma still hold true? If for a particular system of values and beliefs this lemma does hold true, how will the lemma look like?

Another important question for future research is: What will happen for such a firm when it chooses its most desirable production or business operation without optimizing any foreseeable subjective function?

As the conclusion of this chapter, let us look at the following real challenge that needs to be met by continuing the work presented in this chapter and that will most likely produce additional practical benefits: Because firms in real life are heterogeneous with their individually different systems of values and beliefs, can their interactions be investigated systemically and strategically?

References

Adkins, S. (1999). Cause related marketing: Who cares wins. *Quadrant, 38*(02), 379–388.

Atalay, E. (2017). How important are sectoral shocks? *American Economic Journal: Macroeconomics, 9*(4), 254–280.

Debreu, G. (1959). *Theory of value: An axiomatic analysis of economic equilibrium*. Yale University Press.

Fahimnia, B., Sarkis, J., & Eshragh, A. (2015). A tradeoff model for green supply chain planning: A leanness-versus-greenness analysis. *Omega, 54*(1), 173–190.

Forrest, J. Y. L., & Liu, Y. (2021). *Value in business: A holistic, systems-based approach to creating and achieving value*. Springer.

Forrest, J. Y. L., Galbraith, D. D., Liu, Y., & Pla-Lopez, R. (2019). Interaction between incumbent while entrenched and modern while agile companies at a freezing moment of time. *Advances in Systems Science and Applications, 19*(3), 93–117.

Forrest, J. Y. L., Gong, Z. W., Köse, E., Galbraith, D. D., & Arık, O. A. (2021a). An economy's emergent properties and how micro agents with inconsistent or conflicting interests are holistically organized into macro entities. *Naše gospodarstvo/Our Economy, 63*(3), 53–66.

Forrest, J. Y. L., Hafezalkotob, A., Ren, L., Liu, Y., & Tallapally, P. (2021b). Utility and optimization's dependence on decision-makers' underlying value-belief systems. *Review of Economic & Business Studies*., in final production, *14*, 125.

Forrest, J. Y. L., Darvishi, D., Jallow, A. K., & Li, Z. (2022a). A systemic revisit to the concepts of a firm's production, cost and profit. In *Proceedings of the 2022 Conference of Pennsylvania Economic Association* (pp. 1–15).

Forrest, J. Y. L., Shao, L., Liu, J., & Sloboda, B. W. (2022b). Optimum and method of optimization are individually defined. In *Proceedings of the 2022 Annual Meeting of Pennsylvania Economic Association* (pp. 16–30).

Friedman, M. (1953). *Essays in positive economics*. University of Chicago Press.

Gabaix, X. (2011). The granular origins of aggregate fluctuations. *Econometrica, 79*, 733–772.

Gelles, G. M., & Mitchell, D. W. (1996). Returns to scale and economies of scale: Further observations. *Journal of Economic Education, 27*(3), 259–261.

Gilboa, I. (2010). *Rational choice*. The MIT Press.

Gul, F., & Pesendorfer, W. (2008). The case for mindless economics. In A. Caplin & A. Schotter (Eds.), *The foundations of positive and normative economics: A handbook*. Oxford University Press.

Hsueh, C. F. (2014). Improving corporate social responsibility in a supply chain through a new revenue sharing contract. *International Journal of Production Economics, 151*, 214–222. https://doi.org/10.1016/j.ijpe.2013.10.017

Hudik, M. (2019). Two interpretations of the rational choice theory and the relevance of behavioral critique. *Rationality and Society, 31*(4), 464–489.

Hussain, W. (2012). Corporations, profit maximization and the personal sphere. *Economics and Philosophy, 28*(3), 311–331.

Jensen, M. (2001). Value maximization, stakeholder theory, and the corporate objective function. *European Financial Management, 7*(3), 297–317.

Letizia, P., & Hendrikse, G. (2016). Supply chain structure incentives for corporate social responsibility: An incomplete contracting analysis. *Production and Operations Management, 25*(11), 1919–1941. https://doi.org/10.1111/poms.12585

Levin, J., & Milgrom, P. (2004). *Producer theory*. Retrieved November 5, 2021, from https://web.stanford.edu/~jdlevin/Econ%20202/Producer%20Theory.pdf

Li, T., & Ma, J. H. (2015). Complexity analysis of dual-channel game model with different managers' business objectives. *Communications in Nonlinear Science and Numerical Simulation, 20*, 199–208.

Lin, Y., & Forrest, B. C. (2012). *Systemic structure behind human organizations: From civilizations to individuals*. Springer.

Lin, Y., & OuYang, S. C. (2010). *Irregularities and prediction of major disasters*. CRC Press, an imprint of Taylor and Francis.

Lovett, F. (2006). Rational choice theory and explanation. *Rationality and Society, 18*(2), 237–272.

Lucas, R. E. (1977). Understanding business cycles. *Carnegie-Rochester Conference Series on Public Policy, 5*, 7–29.

Mas-Collel, A., Whinston, M. D., & Green, J. R. (1995). *Microeconomic theory*. Oxford University Press.

McGrath, R. G. (2013). *The end of competitive advantage: How to keep your strategy moving as fast as your business*. Harvard Business Review Press.

Meyer, H. (1993). When the cause is just. *Journal of Business Strategy, 20*(6), 27–31.

Pancs, R. (2018). *Lectures on microeconomics: The big questions approach*. The MIT Press.

Ramaswami, S., Srivastava, R., & Bhargava, M. (2009). Market-based capabilities and financial performance of firms: Insights into marketing's contribution to firm value. *Journal of the Academy of Marketing Science, 37*(2), 97–116.

Rubinstein, A. (1998). *Modeling bounded rationality*. The MIT Press.

Taylor, C. R. (1989). Duality, optimization, and microeconomic theory: Pitfalls for the applied researcher. *Western Journal of Agricultural Economics, 14*(2), 200–212.

von Mises, L. (1949). *Human action: A treatise in economics*. Yale University Press.

Weyl, G. E. (2019). Price theory. *Journal of Economic Literature, 57*(2), 329–384.

Wu, K. P. (2006). *Advanced macroeconomics*. Tsinghua University Press.

Chapter 12
Production Possibilities, Correspondence, and Factor Demand

Jeffrey Yi-Lin Forrest, Kurt Schimmel, Fen Wang, Ashkan Hafezalkotob, and Jian Liu

Abstract Based on the four axioms introduced previously, this chapter, which is mainly based on Forrest et al. (Remarks on production possibilities, optimal production correspondence and conditional factor demand. In Proceedings of the 2022 Annual Conference of the National Association of Business, Economics and Technology, 2022), examines how some of the main results in the producer theory either hold true generally or only conditionally, depending on the firm's particular system of values and beliefs. By using set theory and multidimensional Euclidean space, results are established without imposing as many unnecessary conditions as widely assumed in the literature. In particular, by using counterexamples it is demonstrated that the optimal production correspondence is not generally homogeneous of degree zero. At the same time as reestablishing several known results that hold true under very specific conditions in more general terms, a few important conclusions, such as Shepard's lemma, are also improved to much stronger versions. In the end, several topics of expected significance are suggested for future research.

Keywords Behavioral hypotheses · Conditional factor demand · Decision criteria of priority · Positive multiplicativity · Shepard's lemma

---

Jeffrey Yi-Lin Forrest (Department of Accounting Economics Finance, Slippery Rock University, Slippery Rock, PA, USA; Email: Jeffrey.forrest@sru.edu), Kurt Schimmel (Department of Management and Marketing, Slippery Rock University, Slippery Rock, PA, USA; Email: Kurt.schimmel@sru.edu), Fen Wang (Department of Information Technology and Administrative Management, Central Washington University, WA, USA; E-mail: Fen.Wang@cwu.edu), Ashkan Hafezalkotob (Department of Management and Human Resources, La Trobe University, Melbourne, VIC, Australia; Email: A.HafezAlkotob@latrobe.edu.au), and Jian Liu (School of Economics and Management, Nanjing University of Science and Technology, Nanjing, China; Email: jianlau@njust.edu.cn) are equally contributed to this chapter.

J. Y.-L. Forrest, *Systemic Principles of Applied Economic Philosophies I*, Translational Systems Sciences 38, https://doi.org/10.1007/978-981-99-7273-9_12

12.1 Introduction

Since the time when Debreu (1959) innovatively used the n-dimensional Euclidean space to lay the foundation of microeconomics, many impressive and mathematically beautiful conclusions have been derived (Mas-Collel et al., 1995). Many of these conclusions are then applied to various empirical studies (e.g., Arif & Scott, 1986; Binswanger, 1974; Collins & Taylor, 1983; Kako, 1978; Lau & Yotopoulos, 1972; Trosper, 1978; Young et al., 1987). However, it is found repeatedly (Hammerton, 2020; Lee & Chambers, 1986; Pope, 1980, 1982; Taylor, 1984, 1989; Van Fleet, 2021; Yang & Andersson, 2018) that many maintained behavioral hypotheses, such as cost minimization and utility maximization, and consequent results, such as Shepard's lemma, become invalid when the firm of concern is not a conventional optimizer. Hence, the following natural question arises: If, instead of being a conventional maximizer or minimizer, a firm strives to achieve its desired business outcome, such as revenue, social responsibility, and environmental protection, by materializing its stated mission, will the main results of economics still hold true?

The theoretical and empirical importance of this question is apparent, if we look at how incapable the present theory of economics has been when applied to forecasting economic crises and in terms of critical decision-makings (Forrest & Liu, 2022). That explains why a vast amount of related literature has been devoted to the close scrutinization of various commonly adopted assumptions, such as that of rationality (e.g., Hudik, 2019; Lovett, 2006; Rubinstein, 1998; Weyl, 2019). Speaking differently, empirical studies (e.g., Arif & Scott, 1986; Taylor, 1989) and theoretical investigations (e.g., Mullainathan & Thaler, 2000; Kahneman, 2011) have loudly called for scholars to reconstruct economic theories so that more practically tangible benefits can be materialized. For example, after suffering from great losses during the 2008 financial crisis, Paul Krugman provided his point of view regarding why the existing economic theories are incapable of providing needed practical guidance in a timely manner on what had happened in the past and what would follow next. Specifically, he wrote in *New York Times* (2009-09-02) that: "... economists, as a group, mistook beauty ... for truth ... as memories of the Depression faded, economists fell back in love with the old, idealized vision of an economy ...." That is, by riding on the fresh memory of the 2008 crisis, the present time can be and should be well used to address the question posed above.

To this end, this chapter stands for one dedicated effort towards offering an answer, at least partially, to the previously posed question. Specifically, by adopting only four of the many widely employed assumptions in microeconomics as its starting points, this chapter utilizes the method of Euclidean spaces to investigate a series of important topics. That includes, among others, the structure of production possibilities, the conditional homogeneity of the optimal production correspondence, the uniqueness of the optimal production plan, and various properties of the minimum cost of production and the conditional factor demand. Most of the results in this chapter are established under fewer conditions while, at the same time, generalizing some of the well-known conclusions developed by various scholars before under more strict conditions, such as that the firm of concern produces only one product (Mas-Collel et al., 1995; Levin & Milgrom, 2004).

To make some of our conclusions more general than similar ones in the present theories of microeconomics and more real-life relevant, this chapter emphasizes on the fact that each firm has its own particular order relation of real numbers that is defined on the firm's system of values and beliefs. That firm-specific order relation naturally leads to the existence of the firm's specific method of optimization. In other words, firms respectively have their own particular means to prioritize available alternatives when faced with challenges and opportunities. Therefore, firms apply their very individual ways to optimize their objectives. In comparison, the literature widely assumes that the ordering of real numbers and the method of optimization are the same across the entire business world, although some particular details are different depending on how the objective functions and relevant constraints are different from each other.

Due to our emphasis on a firm-specific system of values and beliefs and firm-specific ordering of real numbers, we are able to establish results not revealed before. At the same time, we are able to generalize some of the previously established results of the producer theory many streets forward. More specifically, the marginal contribution this chapter makes to the literature consists of showing (1) when additional conditions are needed for a desired conclusion to be true and (2) how and when a well-known conclusion holds true only under very specific conditions.

The rest of the chapter is organized as follows. Section 12.2 studies the set-theoretical structure of production possibilities. Section 12.3 investigates the concept and properties of optimal production correspondence. Section 12.4 develops various properties of a firm's minimum cost and conditional factor demand. The chapter concludes in Sect. 12.5 with a few important questions posed for future research.

12.2 Structure of Production Possibilities and Implied Closedness and Convexity

This section consists of two subsections with the first one looking at the particular set-theoretical structure of production possibilities under certain given conditions. In the second subsection, it examines what conventional assumptions are implied by these conditions.

12.2.1 Production Possibilities: Their Set-Theoretical Structure

Given two sets U and W, $f: U \rightarrow W$ is known as a partial function from U into W, if there are $u^1, u^2 \in U$ such that $f(u^1) \in W$ is well-defined while $f(u^2)$ is not defined. In other words, $f\colon U \to W$ is a partial function, if the domain of f, denoted by domain (f), is not equal to U.

For the firm of our concern, its profit function $\pi^F : \mathbb{R}^\ell_+ \to \mathbb{R}$ is given below, as defined by Eq. (11.9):

$$\pi^F(p) =_F \max{}^F_{y \in Y} p \cdot y, \tag{11.9}$$

for any price system $p \in \mathbb{R}^\ell_+$, if the maximum value on the right-hand side of the equation below exists. The superscript F in the expression $\max^F_*$ represents the specific method of optimization employed by the firm.

Implicitly in the rest of this chapter, every time when the expression $\pi^F(p)$ is used, it means that the firm-specific maximum above exists unless stated otherwise. By using this profit function, the following conclusion characterizes the structure of the production possibility set Y under a given condition.

Proposition 12.1 If for any $z \in \mathbb{R}^\ell$, $z \notin Y$ implies that there is a hyperplane L that separates z and Y so that $z \notin L$ based on the order relation $\leq_F$ of the firm, then

$$Y = \left\{ y \in \mathbb{R}^\ell : \forall p \in \mathbb{R}^\ell \left(p \cdot y \leq_F \pi^F(p) \right) \right\} \tag{12.1}$$

$$= \left\{ y \in \mathbb{R}^\ell : \forall p \in \mathbb{R}^\ell_+ \left(p \cdot y \leq_F \pi^F(p) \right) \right\}, \tag{12.2}$$

where if for a particular $p \in \mathbb{R}^\ell_+$, $\pi^F(p)$, as defined in Eq. (11.9), does not exist, then the symbol $\pi^F(p)$ is taken to be $\pi^F(p) =_F \sup^F_{y \in Y} p \cdot y$.

Proof Let the set defined by Eq. (12.1) be $\widehat{Y}$. Then, show $Y = \widehat{Y}$ is equivalent to showing both $Y \subseteq \widehat{Y}$ and $\widehat{Y} \subseteq Y$. The former case is a direct consequence of the definition of $\pi^F(p)$ in Eq. (11.9). Next, let us focus on the argument of the latter case $\widehat{Y} \subseteq Y$.

To this end, let us pick an arbitrary point $z \in \mathbb{R}^\ell$ such that $z \notin Y$. Assume that the guaranteed hyperplane L that separates z and Y, as given in the if condition, be $p \cdot x = \beta$, for some given nonzero $p \in \mathbb{R}^\ell$ and a scalar $\beta \in \mathbb{R}$, so that for any $y \in Y$, $p \cdot y \leq_F \beta <_F p \cdot z$. Hence, taking either maximum or supremum, as seen fit, produces

$$p \cdot z >_F \beta \geq_F \max{}^F_{y \in Y} p \cdot y. \tag{12.3}$$

This end implies $\notin Y \rightarrow z \notin \widehat{Y}$, which establishes the case $\widehat{Y} \subseteq Y$ and consequently Eq. (12.1).

To show Eq. (12.2), let the set defined by Eq. (12.2) be $\check{Y}$. Then the rest of the proof is similar to that given above until the end of Eq. (12.3) by replacing $\widehat{Y}$ with $\check{Y}$. The proof is completed if we can show that the specified p is an element of $\mathbb{R}^\ell_+$. That is, for p to be a price system, p cannot have any zero or negative component. By contradiction, assume that there is an h $(= 1, 2, \ldots, \ell)$ such that $p_h \leq 0$. Then the firm can use as much commodity h as one of its inputs as it wants without any upper limit. Now, the free disposal axiom implies that the right-hand side of Eq. (12.3) is equal to $\max^F_{y \in Y} p \cdot y = \sup^F_{y \in Y} p \cdot y = +\infty$, although the firm's system of values and beliefs might not allow for unnecessary waste of resources, such production plans y are still considered feasible for the firm. A contradiction. So, this argument indicates $p \in \mathbb{R}^\ell_+$. This establishes Eq. (12.2).

12.2.2 Implied Closedness and Convexity

As defined previously in Sect. 11.4.1, the firm's production function f is given below: For each production $y \in Y \subseteq \mathbb{R}^\ell$, $f(y^{\text{in}}) = y^{\text{out}}$, where

$$y^{\text{in}} = \left(y_{h_1^{\text{in}}}, y_{h_2^{\text{in}}}, \ldots, y_{h_t^{\text{in}}}\right) \subseteq \mathbb{R}^t_- \quad \text{and} \quad y^{\text{out}} = \left(y_{h_1^{\text{out}}}, y_{h_2^{\text{out}}}, \ldots, y_{h_s^{\text{out}}}\right) \subseteq \mathbb{R}^s_+$$

are respectively the corresponding input and output sub-vectors of y.

If a production $y \in Y$ satisfies the condition in Eq. (12.4), then y is said to have nonincreasing returns to scale:

$$\forall \alpha \in (0, 1) \left(f\left(\alpha y^{\text{in}}\right) \le \alpha f\left(y^{\text{in}}\right)\right). \tag{12.4}$$

In other words, Eq. (12.4) reflects the following fact: If all inputs of production y are decreased by a scale $\alpha \in (0, 1)$, the corresponding outputs decrease in a scale equal to or less than α. This local property of the firm can be generalized to the following holistic, systemic property: If every production $y \in Y$ satisfies Eq. (12.4), then Y is said to have nonincreasing returns to scale.

The following result shows what the if-condition of the previous proposition implies in terms of the commonly adopted assumptions in the producer theory (Levin & Milgrom, 2004; Mas-Collel et al., 1995), while these assumptions are avoided purposefully in this chapter.

Proposition 12.2 Assume that the firm's order relation $\le_F$ of real numbers is the same as the conventional one $\le$ between these numbers. If for any $z \in \mathbb{R}^\ell$, $z \notin Y$ implies that there is a hyperplane L that separates z and Y so that $z \notin L$, then (1) Y is closed, (2) Y is convex, and (3) Y satisfies that for any $y \in Y$ and any scalar $\alpha \in [0, 1]$, $\alpha y \in Y$; that is, Y has nonincreasing returns to scale.

Proof Let us show (1) by contradiction. Assume that Y is not closed. Then there is at least one $z \in \mathbb{R}^\ell$ such that z is a limit point of Y while $z \notin Y$. However, for this point z, it is impossible for a hyperplane L to exist so that L separates Y and z. A contradiction. Therefore, Y is closed.

We also show (2) by contradiction. Assume that Y is not convex so that there are $y^1, y^2 \in Y$ and $\alpha \in (0, 1)$ such that $z = \alpha y^1 + (1 - \alpha)y^2 \notin Y$. Let L^1 be a hyperplane that separates z and Y, as guaranteed by the given condition, and L^2 the hyperplane $p \cdot x = b$, for some $p \in \mathbb{R}^\ell$ and $b \in \mathbb{R}$, that passes through z and is parallel to L^1. Therefore, $L^2 \cap Y = \varnothing$ and Y is located on one side of L^2. Since z is on the hyperplane, we have $p \cdot z = b$, which is the same as

$$p \cdot \left[\alpha y^1 + (1-\alpha)y^2\right] = b. \tag{12.5}$$

Because no point of Y is on the hyperplane, we have either $p \cdot y^1 < b$ or $p \cdot y^1 > b$. If the former holds true, then from Eq. (12.5), it follows that $\alpha b + (1 - \alpha)(p \cdot y^2) > b$ and then $p \cdot y^2 > b$. That is, y^1 and y^2 are located on different sides of L^2. A contradiction. For the latter case $p \cdot y^1 > b$, the same contradiction follows. So, jointly, what is meant is that the assumption that Y is not convex is incorrect.

Conclusion (3) follows readily from Axiom 11.1 and (2), because for any $y \in Y$ and $\alpha \in [0, 1]$, $\alpha y = \alpha y + (1 - \alpha)0 \in Y$.

In the literature, Eqs. (12.1) and (12.2) hold true under the conditions that (1) the firm's order relation of real numbers coincides with the conventional one between these numbers and (2) the set Y of production possibilities is both closed and convex in $\mathbb{R}^\ell$. Therefore, Proposition 12.2 indicates how Proposition 12.1 significantly carries the corresponding known conclusion to the general case of any system of values and beliefs a firm might have.

12.3 The Production Correspondence

This section contains two subsections. The first one investigates the conditional homogeneity of the optimal production correspondence, while the second subsection examines the uniqueness of elements in the correspondence.

12.3.1 Conditional Homogeneity of Degree Zero

For given sets U and W, a partial function $f : U \to W$ from U to W is said to be set-valued, if for any $u \in \text{domain}(f) \subseteq U$, $f(u)$ is a nonempty subset of W. The following partial, set-valued function $\eta^F: \mathbb{R}^\ell_+ \to Y$, as defined in Eq. (11.10), is referred to as the optimal production correspondence of the firm (Levin & Milgrom, 2004)., where for $p \in \mathbb{R}^\ell_+$, if there is $y \in Y$ satisfying that $p \cdot y =_F \max^F_{y^q \in Y} p \cdot y^q$, then

$$\eta^F(p) = \left\{ y \in Y : p \cdot y =_F \max{}^F_{y^q \in Y} p \cdot y^q \right\}. \tag{11.10}$$

Proposition 12.3 If the firm's order relation $\leq_F$ of real numbers satisfies the condition of positive multiplicativity, that is, for any scalar $\alpha > 0$ and $a, b \in \mathbb{R}$, $a \leq_F b \rightarrow \alpha a \leq_F \alpha b$, then the optimal production correspondence η^F is homogeneous of degree zero. Symbolically, for any scalar $\alpha > 0$, if $a \leq_F b \rightarrow \alpha a \leq_F \alpha b$, for any $a, b \in \mathbb{R}$, then $\eta^F(\alpha p) = \eta^F(p)$.

Proof Let α be a positive scalar. Then, $\eta^F(\alpha p) = \left\{y \in Y : \alpha p \cdot y =_F \max^F_{y^q \in Y} \alpha p \cdot y^q\right\} = \{y \in Y : \alpha p \cdot y \geq_F \alpha p \cdot y^q, \forall y^q \in Y\}$. So, the condition of positive multiplicativity of the order relation $\leq_F$ guarantees that

$$\{y \in Y : \alpha p \cdot y \geq_F \alpha p \cdot y^q, \forall y^q \in Y\} = \{y \in Y : p \cdot y \geq_F p \cdot y^q, \forall y^q \in Y\}.$$

Therefore, $\eta^F(\alpha p) = \eta^F(p)$.

Example 12.1 A scenario is constructed here to show that not all order relations satisfy the condition of positive multiplicativity.

In particular, it can be readily seen that the order relation $\leq_{\text{mod}(4)}$ does not satisfy the condition of positive multiplicativity. In fact, for how positive multiplicativity is violated, we have

$$1 \leq_{\text{mod}(4)} 2 \nrightarrow 2 \cdot 1 \leq_{\text{mod}(4)} 2 \cdot 2$$

where the left-hand side is actually $2 \cdot 1 = 2 \geq_{\text{mod}(4)} 2 \cdot 2 = 0 =$ the right-hand side.

This example suggests that the general homogeneity of the optimal production correspondence may be only conditionally true.

12.3.2 Two General Properties of the Optimal Production Correspondence

The following result confirms the conjecture posed above.

Proposition 12.4 The optimal production correspondence η^F of the firm is generally not homogeneous of degree zero. Symbolically, the equation $\eta^F(\alpha p) = \eta^F(p)$ does not generally hold true, for any scalar $\alpha > 0$ and price system $p \in \mathbb{R}^\ell_+$.

To show this conclusion, it suffices for us to construct a counterexample.

Example 12.2 Assume that the firm has a specific production that involves one unit of each of the commodity inputs A, A_1, A_2, B, C_1, C_2, C, where A_1 and A_2 can substitute for each other and so do C_1 and C_2. A flow chart of the production is shown in Fig. 12.1. The arrows indicate the order with which these commodities are

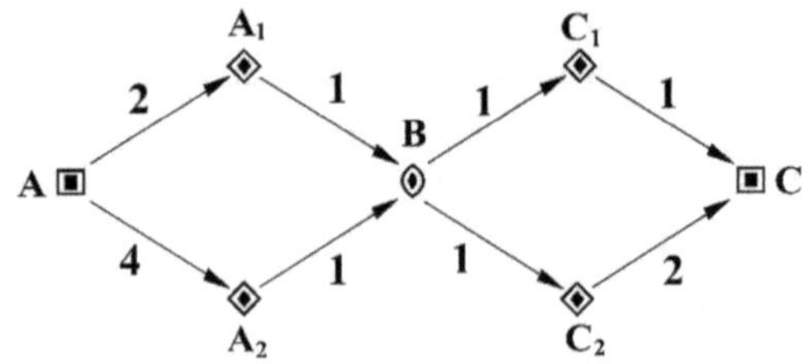

Fig. 12.1 The firm's production line

fed into the assembly line one after another. And, the weights of arrows stand for the relevant profits created by the production sequence from one node to the next. The manager of the firm wants to maximize the total profit, where the order $\leq_F$ of priority is given to be $\leq_{\text{mod}(4)}$ according to the firm's system of values and beliefs. For the sake of convenience of communication, let I be the set of these commodities as ordered above.

The four possible paths and their respective total weights are given as follows:

(a) I_1:A → A_1 → B → C_1 → C with weight 5 mod(4) = 1
(b) I_2:A → A_1 → B → C_2 → C with weight 6 mod(4) = 2
(c) I_3:A → A_2 → B → C_1 → C with weight 7 mod(4) = 3
(d) I_4:A → A_2 → B → C_2 → C with weight 8 mod(4) = 0

Let the corresponding input and associated output vectors are given respectively by ${}^j y = \left(y_j\right)_{j \in I_j}$ and ${}^j Z_{AC}, j = 1, \ldots, 4$. Hence, each price system p can be accordingly written as follows:

$$p = \left(\left(p_j\right)_{j \in I}, {}^1Z_{AC}, {}^2Z_{AC}, {}^3Z_{AC}, {}^4Z_{AC}\right).$$

It can be seen that for any $y \in Y$, there is k (= 1, 2, 3, 4) such that when all zero components are eliminated, we have

$$y^{\text{in}} = {}^k y \text{ and } y^{\text{out}} = {}^k Z_{AC}.$$

For any price system $p \in \mathbb{R}_+^{\ell}$, we have

$$p \cdot y = p^{\text{in}} \cdot y^{\text{in}} + p^{\text{out}} \cdot y^{\text{out}},$$

where p^{in} represents the price vector of the commodities in y^{in} and p^{out} that of the commodities in y^{out}. Therefore, we have

$$\eta^F(p) = I_3 : A \to A_2 \to B \to C_1 \to C. \tag{12.6}$$

Let us choose scalar $\alpha = 3.2$ that is multiplied to each of the individual local values. The corresponding total profits for the four paths are respectively equal to 5 × 3.2

(mod4) = 0, 6 × 3.2 (mod4) = 3.2, 7 × 3.2 (mod4) = 2.4, and 8 × 3.2 (mod4) = 1.6. Therefore, we have

$$\eta^F(\alpha p) = \eta^F(3.2 \cdot p) = I_2 : \mathrm{A} \to \mathrm{A}_1 \to \mathrm{B} \to \mathrm{C}_2 \to \mathrm{C}. \tag{12.7}$$

Hence, Eqs. (12.6) and (12.7) jointly imply that $\eta^F(\alpha p) \neq \eta^F(p)$. That is, the optimal production correspondence η^F is not generally homogeneous of degree zero.

Evidently, for a price system $p \in \mathbb{R}^\ell_+$, if the optimal production correspondence $\eta^F(p)$ is a nonempty set, then it is likely that $\eta^F(p)$ may very well contain more than one element. For practical purposes, the uniqueness of solutions to the maximization problem $\max^F_{y^q \in Y} p \cdot y^q$ is often important. For example, facing a challenge of the marketplace, the firm wants to know whether or not a feasible solution is the best solution for it to implement in order to meet the challenge. If the firm can show that the feasible solution is the only possible one for it to employ, then the management of the firm will focus on how to optimally implement the solution instead of wasting energy on finding alternative solutions. For such a uniqueness problem, the following holds true in general no matter what system of values and beliefs the firm has.

Proposition 12.5 Let p be a nonzero price system satisfying $\eta^F(p) \neq \varnothing$. If for any two different productions $y^1, y^2 \in \eta^F(p)$, there is a scalar $\alpha = \alpha(y^1, y^2) \in (0, 1)$ such that $\alpha y^1 + (1 - \alpha)y^2 \in \text{interior}(Y)$, then $\eta^F(p)$ is a singleton.

Proof First, we show that $\eta^F(p)$ is a convex set. In particular, for any $y^1, y^2 \in \eta^F(p)$ and any scalar $\alpha \in [0, 1]$,

$$\begin{aligned} p \cdot \left[\alpha y^1 + (1-\alpha)y^2\right] &= \alpha\left(p \cdot y^1\right) + (1-\alpha)\left(p \cdot y^2\right) \\ &=_F \alpha \max{}^F_{y^q \in Y} p \cdot y^q + (1-\alpha) \max{}^F_{y^q \in Y} p \cdot y^q \\ &= \max{}^F_{y^q \in Y} p \cdot y^q. \end{aligned}$$

So, $\alpha y^1 + (1 - \alpha)y^2 \in \eta^F(p)$. That is, $\eta^F(p)$ is convex.

Second, by contradiction assume that $\eta^F(p)$ contains more than one element. Pick $y^1, y^2 \in \eta^F(p)$ such that $y^1 \neq y^2$. So, the given condition implies that there is a scalar $\alpha(y^1, y^2) \in (0, 1)$ such that

$$\alpha\left(y^1, y^2\right)y^1 + \left[1 - \alpha\left(y^1, y^2\right)\right]y^2 \in \text{interior}(Y) \cap \eta^F(p)$$

But, this end is impossible, because a nontrivial linear function, where $p \neq 0$, does not have any local maximum.

12.4 Minimum Cost of Production

Let $q = \left(q_{h_1^{\text{out}}}, q_{h_2^{\text{out}}}, \ldots, q_{h_s^{\text{out}}}\right)$ denote the required quantities of production outputs, satisfying that $q_{h_j^{\text{out}}} > 0$, for any $j = 1, 2, \ldots, s$, and $h_1^{\text{out}} < h_2^{\text{out}} < \cdots < h_s^{\text{out}}$. Then, the firm's cost minimization problem can be written as follows, assuming that the firm is a price taker: For a given price system $p \in \mathbb{R}_+^{\ell}$,

$$\begin{aligned} &\min_{y \in Y} p^{\text{in}} \cdot y^{\text{in}}, \\ &\text{s.t. } f\left(y^{\text{in}}\right) \geq q, \end{aligned} \tag{12.8}$$

where p^{in} stands for p's sub-vector of prices of the commodities in y^{in}, and $f(y^{\text{in}}) = y^{\text{out}}$ satisfies that $\left\{h_1^{\text{out}}, h_2^{\text{out}}, \ldots, h_s^{\text{out}}\right\}$ is generally a subset of the set of all commodity subscripts that appear in the components of y^{out}. Without loss of generality, we assume that these two sets are the same, because producing additional products beyond what are listed in q requires at least an increased amount of labor input.

Let $z = z(p, q)$ be a solution of the minimization problem in Eq. (12.8). This solution z is known as a conditional factor demand (Levin & Milgrom, 2004), because of its dependence on the required production outputs q.

The Lagrangian of problem in Eq. (12.8) is

$$L(y, p, q) = -p^{\text{in}} \cdot y^{\text{in}} + \lambda\left[f\left(y^{\text{in}}\right) - q\right] \tag{12.9}$$

where $\lambda = (\lambda_1, \lambda_2, \ldots, \lambda_s) \in \mathbb{R}^s$ is a vector of Lagrange multipliers. So, the Kuhn-Tucker first-order conditions (Wallace, 2004) imply that for any $j = 1, 2, \ldots, t$,

$$\begin{aligned} \frac{\partial L}{\partial y_{h_j^{\text{in}}}} &= -p_{h_j^{\text{in}}} + \lambda_j \frac{\partial f(y^-)}{\partial y_{h_j^{\text{in}}}} \leq 0, \\ &- y_{h_j^{\text{in}}} \geq 0, \text{ and} \\ y_{h_j^{\text{in}}} \frac{\partial L}{\partial y_{h_j^{\text{in}}}} &= 0. \end{aligned}$$

Hence, from our initial setup of this study (Eq. 11.4), it follows that $-y_{h_j^{\text{in}}} > 0$, which in turn means that

$$p_{h_j^{\text{in}}} = \lambda_j \frac{\partial f(y^-)}{\partial y_{h_j^{\text{in}}}}. \tag{12.10}$$

Let $Z = \{z : \exists\, y \in Y(z = y^{\text{in}} \text{ and } f(z) \geq q)\}$ and the optimal value of the objective function in Eq. (12.8) be

$$c^F(p,q) = {}_F \min{}^F_{z \in Z} p^{\text{in}} \cdot z, \text{ for } p \in \mathbb{R}^\ell_+, \tag{12.11}$$

which gives the minimum cost at which the required outputs q can be produced. It can be seen readily from Axiom 11.3 that

$$Z \subseteq \{y^{\text{in}} : y \in Y\} \subseteq \bigcup_{t=1}^{\ell-1} \mathbb{R}^t_-. \tag{12.12}$$

The reason why the union of $\mathbb{R}^t_-$ goes only up to $t = \ell - 1$ from $t = 1$ is because with inputs, at least one output will be produced or expected to be produced even though the firm might choose to produce nothing (Axiom 11.1). For example, if nothing useful is produced, then some of the inputs, for example, those dated labors, could easily become useless wastes, as the outputs of the strategy of taking no action. Additionally, if the firm decides to take no action (Axiom 11.1) after taking in certain amounts of inputs, then for the survival of the firm at least one of the inputs will need to be used as output in order to recapture some of the operational expenses.

In Eq. (12.11), if $\min{}^F_{z \in Z}(p^{\text{in}} \cdot z)$ does not exist, this expression is assumed to be $\inf{}^F_{z \in Z}(p^{\text{in}} \cdot z)$.

12.4.1 Remarks on the Minimum Cost of Production

For given $p \in \mathbb{R}^\ell_+$ and $q \in \mathbb{R}^s$, define the following set-valued function:

$$\xi^F(p,q) = \{z \in Z : p^{\text{in}} \cdot z = {}_F \min{}^F_{z^q \in Z} p^{\text{in}} \cdot z^q\}, \tag{12.13}$$

known as the set of conditional factor demands (i.e., conditional on the desired level of outputs). In other words, ξ^F maps each price system p of commodities to the subset $\xi^F(p,q) \subseteq Z$ of all cost-minimizing commodity inputs of productions, if $\xi^F(p, q) \neq \emptyset$. By combining Eqs. (12.11) and (12.13), it follows readily that

$$c^F(p,q) = p^{\text{in}} \cdot z, \quad \text{for any } z \in \xi^F(p,q). \tag{12.14}$$

Proposition 12.6 The cost $c^F(p,q)$ is a partial function in $p \in \mathbb{R}^\ell_+$. It is homogeneous of degree one in domain(c^F), nondecreasing in q, and concave in p.

Proof The first conclusion comes from the fact that for some $p \in \mathbb{R}^\ell_+$, $\min{}^F_{z \in Z}(p^{\text{in}} \cdot z)$ might not exist. For the homogeneity of $c^F(p,q)$ in p, let $\alpha \in \mathbb{R}$ be a scalar. Then, we have

$$c^F(\alpha p, q) =_F \min{}^F_{z\in Z}\left(\alpha p^{\text{in}} \cdot z\right) = \alpha \min{}^F_{z\in Z}\left(p^{\text{in}} \cdot z\right) =_F \alpha c^F(p, q).$$

For the third conclusion, it suffices to show that for any q_1, $q_2 \in \mathbb{R}^s$, $q_1 \geq q_2$ implies $c^F(p, q_1) \geq_F c^F(p, q_2)$. In fact, this last inequality follows directly from the following:

$$q_1 \geq q_2 \rightarrow \{z \in Z : f(z) \geq q_1\} \subseteq \{z \in Z : f(z) \geq q_2\}.$$

For the concavity of the cost function $c^F(p, q)$ in p, let ${}^1p, {}^2p \in \mathbb{R}_+^\ell$ be two price systems and $\alpha \in [0, 1]$ be a scalar. Define ${}^ap = \alpha{}^1p + (1-\alpha){}^2p$. Then, we have that for $z = z({}^ap, q) \in \xi^F({}^ap, q.)$

$$\begin{aligned} c^F({}^ap, q) = {}^ap^{\text{in}} \cdot z({}^ap, q) &= \alpha{}^1p \cdot z({}^ap, q) + (1-\alpha){}^2p \cdot z({}^ap, q) \\ &\geq \alpha{}^1p \cdot z({}^1p, q) + (1-\alpha){}^2p \cdot z({}^2p, q) \\ &= \alpha c^F({}^ap, q) + (1-\alpha)c^F({}^2p, q) \end{aligned}$$

where the second line follows from the fact that $z({}^ap, q)$ produces outputs q not necessarily in the cost minimizing way at either ${}^1p$ or ${}^2p$.

Proposition 12.7 Assume that each $y \in Y$, when $y^{\text{in}} \in \mathbb{R}_-^t$, while $y^{\text{in}} \notin Z$, for some $t = 1, 2, \ldots, \ell - 1$, there is a t-dimensional hyperplane L: $p^{\text{in}} \cdot x = \beta$, for $x \in \mathbb{R}^t$, some nonzero $p \in \mathbb{R}^\ell$, and a scalar $\beta \in \mathbb{R}$ such that for any $z' \in Z \cap \mathbb{R}_-^t$, $p^{\text{in}} \cdot z' \geq_F \beta$ and $\beta >_F p^{\text{in}} \cdot y^{\text{in}}$. Then, the following equation holds true:

$$Z = \bigcup_{t=1}^{\ell-1} \left\{z \in \mathbb{R}_-^t : \forall p \in \mathbb{R}^\ell \left(p^{\text{in}} \cdot z \geq_F c^F\left(p^{\text{in}}, q\right)\right)\right\}. \tag{12.15}$$

Proof Equation (12.12) implies

$$Z = \bigcup_{t=1}^{\ell-1} Z \cap \mathbb{R}_-^t. \tag{12.16}$$

Hence, because the union in Eq. (12.15) consists of pairwise disjoint terms, we only need to demonstrate that for each $t = 1, 2, \ldots, \ell - 1$,

$$Z \cap \mathbb{R}_-^t = \left\{z \in \mathbb{R}_-^t : \forall p \in \mathbb{R}^\ell \left(p^{in} \cdot z \geq_F c^F\left(p^{in}, q\right)\right)\right\}. \tag{12.17}$$

Let $\tilde{Z}$ be the set defined by the right-hand side of Eq. (12.17). Then, we need to show both $Z \cap \mathbb{R}_-^t \subseteq \tilde{Z}$ and $\tilde{Z} \subseteq Z \cap \mathbb{R}_-^t$.

For the former, it is a direct consequence of how $c^F(p, q)$ is defined in Eq. (12.11). Now, let us focus on examining the second inclusion relationship.

To show $\tilde{Z} \subseteq Z \cap \mathbb{R}_-^t$, for an arbitrary $y \in Y$ satisfying $y^{\text{in}} \in \mathbb{R}_-^t$ and $y^{\text{in}} \notin Z$, a t-dimensional hyperplane L exists with equation given as follows: $p^{\text{in}} \cdot x = \beta$, for $x \in \mathbb{R}^t$, some nonzero $p \in \mathbb{R}^\ell$, and a scalar $\beta \in \mathbb{R}$, satisfying that for any

$z' \in Z \cap \mathbb{R}^t_-$, $p^{\text{in}} \cdot z' \geq_F \beta$ and $\beta >_F p^{\text{in}} \cdot y^{\text{in}}$. So, by taking minimum or infimum, if the former does not exist, we have

$$p^{\text{in}} \cdot y^{\text{in}} <_F \beta \leq_F \min^F_{z \in Z \cap \mathbb{R}^t_-} \left(p^{\text{in}} \cdot z\right) \text{ or } \inf^F_{z \in Z \cap \mathbb{R}^t_-} \left(p^{\text{in}} \cdot z\right). \tag{12.18}$$

Hence, we have

$$\min^F_{z \in Z \cap \mathbb{R}^t_-} \left(p^{\text{in}} \cdot z\right) = c^F\left(p^{\text{in}}, q\right),$$

because for the operation $p^{\text{in}} \cdot z$ to be valid, z has to be from $\mathbb{R}^t_-$. That is, Eq. (12.20) is equivalent to

$$p^{\text{in}} \cdot y^{\text{in}} <_F \beta \leq_F \min^F_{z \in Z} \left(p^{\text{in}} \cdot z\right) \text{ or } \inf^F_{z \in Z} \left(p^{\text{in}} \cdot z\right).$$

In other words, we have shown that if $y^{\text{in}} \in \mathbb{R}^t_-$ and $y^{\text{in}} \notin Z$, then $y^{\text{in}} \notin \tilde{Z}$. This end implies $\tilde{Z} \subseteq Z \cap \mathbb{R}^t_-$. Hence, Eq. (12.16) implies Eq. (12.17) and then Eq. (12.15).

Proposition 12.8 If the same condition as that in Proposition 12.7 holds true, then

$$Z = \bigcup_{t=1}^{\ell-1} \left\{ z \in \mathbb{R}^t_- : \forall p \in \mathbb{R}^t_+ \left(p^{\text{in}} \cdot z \geq_F c^F\left(p^{\text{in}}, q\right)\right)\right\}. \tag{12.19}$$

Proof Define

$$\check{Z} = \left\{ z \in \mathbb{R}^t_- : \forall p \in \mathbb{R}^t_+ \left(p^{\text{in}} \cdot z \geq_F c^F\left(p^{\text{in}}, q\right)\right)\right\}. \tag{12.20}$$

Then the rest of the argument is similar to that of the previous proposition until the end of Eq. (12.18) by replacing $\tilde{Z}$ with $\check{Z}$. This current argument concludes with showing that the specified $p^{\text{in}} \in \mathbb{R}^t$ in the equation of the hyperplane $p^{\text{in}} \cdot x = \beta$ is actually an element of $\mathbb{R}^t_+$. That is, no component of p^{in} can be zero or negative. By contradiction, assume that there is a subscript commodity h (= 1, 2, ..., t) such that the hth component of p^{in} satisfies $p_h \leq 0$. Then the firm can apply as much of commodity h as one of its inputs as it wants to without any upper limit. So, the free disposal axiom (Axiom 11.2) implies that the right-hand side of Eq. (12.18) is equal to $\inf^F_{z \in Z}(p \cdot z) = -\infty$. This end makes Eq. (12.18) invalid. Therefore, it follows that $p^{\text{in}} \in \mathbb{R}^t_+$ so that Eq. (12.20) and then Eq. (12.19) are established.

12.4.2 *The Set of Conditional Factor Demands*

This subsection develops a few important conclusions. The first one demonstrates when a unique solution to the minimization problem in Eq. (12.8) exists. The second result examines how changes in the prices of the input commodities cause changes in the corresponding commodity supplies. The third result generalizes the well-known Shepard's lemma. And the fourth conclusion carries a known result in the producer theory (Levin & Milgrom, 2004; Mas-Collel et al., 1995) much forward.

Proposition 12.9 For any fixed $q = \left(q_{h_1^{\text{out}}}, q_{h_2^{\text{out}}}, \ldots, q_{h_s^{\text{out}}}\right) \in \mathbb{R}_+^s$ and any $p \in \mathbb{R}_+^\ell$, satisfying $\xi^F(p,q) \neq \emptyset$, if for any $z^1 \neq z^2 \in \xi^F(p,q)$, there is a scalar $\alpha = \alpha(z^1, z^2) \in (0, 1)$ such that $\alpha z^1 + (1 - \alpha)z^2 \in \text{interior}(Z)$, then $\xi^F(p,q)$ is a singleton.

Proof First, $\xi^F(p,q)$ is a convex set. Specifically, for any z^1, $z^2 \in \xi^F(p,q)$ and $\alpha \in [0, 1]$, we have

$$\begin{aligned} p^{\text{in}} \cdot \left[\alpha z^1 + (1-\alpha)z^2\right] &= \alpha\left(p^{\text{in}} \cdot z^1\right) + (1-\alpha)\left(p^{\text{in}} \cdot z^2\right) \\ &= {}_F\alpha \min{}_{z\in Z}^F p^{\text{in}} \cdot z + (1-\alpha) \min{}_{z\in Z}^F p^{\text{in}} \cdot z \\ &= \min{}_{z\in Z}^F p^{\text{in}} \cdot z \end{aligned}$$

So, $\alpha z^1 + (1 - \alpha)z^2 \in \xi^F(p,q)$. That is, $\xi^F(p,q)$ is a convex set.

Second, we show that $\xi^F(p,q)$ is a singleton by contradiction. Assume that $\xi^F(p,q)$ contains more than one element. Pick z^1, $z^2 \in \xi^F(p,q)$ such that $z^1 \neq z^2$. Then, for some $\alpha = \alpha(z^1, z^2) \in (0, 1)$, we have

$$\alpha z^1 + (1-\alpha)z^2 \in \text{interior}(Z) \cap \xi^F(p,q).$$

But, this end is impossible, because a nontrivial linear function, where $p \neq 0$, does not have any local minimum.

Proposition 12.10 For any two price systems ${}^1p$, ${}^2p \in \mathbb{R}_+^\ell$, and commodity inputs ${}^1z \in \xi^F({}^1p,q)$, ${}^2z \in \xi^F({}^2p,q)$, $({}^2p^{\text{in}} - {}^1p^{\text{in}})({}^2z - {}^1z) \leq 0$, assuming that the dimensions of ${}^1z$ and ${}^2z$ do match up perfectly, otherwise, necessary zero components are used to make them match.

Proof Because ${}^1p^{\text{in}}.{}^1z = \min{}_{z^q\in Z}^F {}^1p^{\text{in}} \cdot z^q$ and ${}^2p^{\text{in}}.{}^2z = \min{}_{z^q\in Z}^F p' \cdot z^q$, we have ${}^1p^{\text{in}}.{}^1z \leq {}^1p^{\text{in}}.{}^2z$ and ${}^2p^{\text{in}}.{}^2z \leq {}^2p^{\text{in}}.{}^1z$. So, ${}^1p^{\text{in}} \cdot ({}^1z - {}^2z) \leq 0 \leq {}^2p^{\text{in}} \cdot ({}^1z - {}^2z)$, from which $({}^2p^{\text{in}} - {}^1p^{\text{in}})({}^2z - {}^1z) \leq 0$ follows.

What Proposition 12.10 says is that to maintain minimum cost, when the prices of commodity inputs change, the corresponding changes in the required amounts of these input commodities also change but in the opposite direction. In particular, when the prices of commodity inputs increase, Proposition 12.10 indicates that the amounts of the required input commodities will be reduced. Therefore, this conclusion can be seen as the property of supplier shortage.

The following result generalizes the well-known Shepard's lemma, where it is assumed that for a given price system $p \in \mathbb{R}_+^\ell$, $p^{\text{in}} = \left(p_{h_1^{\text{in}}}, p_{h_2^{\text{in}}}, \ldots, p_{h_t^{\text{in}}}\right) \in \mathbb{R}_+^t$, for some $t = 1, 2, \ldots, \ell - 1$, the firm minimizes its cost of production by using the conventional Lagrangian approach.

Proposition 12.11 The set $\xi^F(p, q)$ of conditional factor demands contains only one element $z(p, q)$ in a neighborhood of p^{in}, if and only if the partial derivative of $c(\cdot, q)$ with respect to each $p_{h_j^{\text{in}}}$ exists at p^{in} and satisfies the following:

$$\frac{\partial c(p,q)}{\partial p_{h_j^{\text{in}}}} = z_{h_j^{\text{in}}}(p,q), \text{ for } j = 1, 2, \ldots, t. \tag{12.21}$$

Proof (⇒) As assumed, the set $\xi^F(p, q)$ of conditional factor demands contains only one element $z(p, q)$in a neighborhood of p, while the firm minimizes its cost by using the conventional Lagrangian approach. Hence, from the envelope theorem, it follows that for $j = 1, 2, \ldots, t$, we have

$$\frac{\partial c(p,q)}{\partial p_{h_j^{\text{in}}}} = \frac{\partial}{\partial p_{h_j^{\text{in}}}}\left[p^{\text{in}} \cdot z(p,q)\right] = \frac{\partial p}{\partial p_{h_j^{\text{in}}}} \cdot z(p,q) = z_{h_j^{\text{in}}}(p,q).$$

(⇐) Pick two arbitrary conditional factor demands $z^1, z^2 \in \xi^F(p, q)$. Without loss of generality, assume that $z^1 = \left(z^1_{h_1^{\text{in}}}, z^1_{h_2^{\text{in}}}, \ldots, z^1_{h_t^{\text{in}}}\right)$ and $z^2 = \left(z^2_{h_1^{\text{in}}}, z^2_{h_2^{\text{in}}}, \ldots, z^2_{h_t^{\text{in}}}\right)$. That is, both z^1 and z^2 are of the same dimensionality, which can be readily satisfied by filling unmatching components with zeros. From the definition of $\xi^F(p, q)$, it follows that $c(p, q) = p \cdot z^1 = p \cdot z^2$. So, from Eq. (12.21), we have the following, for each $j = 1, 2, \ldots, t$:

$$z^1_{h_j^{\text{in}}} = \frac{\partial c(p,q)}{\partial p_{h_j^{\text{in}}}} = z^2_{h_j^{\text{in}}},$$

which means $z^1 = z^2$. So, the arbitrariness of the chosen conditional factor demands z^1, z^2 implies that $\xi^F(p, q)$ contains only one element.

For the rest of this subsection, we assume that the firm's order relation $\leq_F$ of real numbers is the same as the conventional one $\leq$, that a particular price system $p \in \mathbb{R}^\ell_+$ makes the set $\xi^F(p, q)$ of conditional factor demands contain only one element in a neighborhood of p^{in}, and that this element $z(p, q)$ is continuously differentiable with respect to each $p_{h_j^{\text{in}}}$, for $j = 1, 2, \ldots, t$, where $p^{\text{in}} = \left(p_{h_1^{\text{in}}}, p_{h_2^{\text{in}}}, \ldots, p_{h_t^{\text{in}}}\right) \in \mathbb{R}^t_+$.

Proposition 12.12 The matrix $D_p z(p, q)$ is identical to $D_p^2 c(p, q)$ and is equal to $0_{t \times t}$. That is, the following holds true:

$$D_p z(p,q) = \frac{\partial z(p,q)}{\partial p} = \left[\frac{\partial^2 c(p,q)}{\partial p_{h_i^{\text{in}}} \partial p_{h_j^{\text{in}}}}\right]_{t \times t} = D_p^2 c(p,q) = 0_{t \times t}.$$

Proof First, from Proposition 12.11 we have:

$$\begin{aligned} D_p z(p,q) &= \left[\frac{\partial z_{h_1^{\text{in}}}(p)}{\partial p}, \frac{\partial z_{h_2^{\text{in}}}(p)}{\partial p}, \ldots, \frac{\partial z_{h_t^{\text{in}}}(p)}{\partial p}\right] \\ &= \left[\frac{\partial^2 c(p,q)}{\partial p \partial p_{h_1^{\text{in}}}}, \frac{\partial^2 c(p,q)}{\partial p \partial p_{h_2^{\text{in}}}}, \ldots, \frac{\partial^2 c(p,q)}{\partial p \partial p_{h_t^{\text{in}}}}\right] \\ &= D_p^2 c(p,q) \end{aligned} \tag{12.22}$$

To show $D_p^2 c(p,q) = 0_{t \times t}$, define the characteristic function F of Z as follows: $F(z) = 0$, if z is on the frontier or boundary of Z; $F(z) < 0$, if z is in the interior of Z; and $F(z) > 0$, if z is located somewhere outside of Z. Then, the following problem, $\min_z p \cdot z$, s. t. $z \in Z$, is equivalent to $\min_z p \cdot z$, s. t. $F(z) \leq 0$ with the Lagrangian being

$$L = p \cdot z - \lambda F(z) \tag{12.23}$$

from which the first-order conditions are obtained as follows. For any $z^* \in \xi^F(p,q)$ and $j = 1, 2, \ldots, t$

$$p_{h_j^{\text{in}}} = \lambda F_{h_j^{\text{in}}}(z^*), F(x^*) \leq 0. \tag{12.24}$$

For $z(p,q) = \left(z_{h_1^{\text{in}}}, z_{h_2^{\text{in}}}, \ldots, z_{h_t^{\text{in}}}\right) \in \xi^F(p,q)$, because $z \in \xi^F(p,q)$, we have $F(z) = 0$, no matter how p changes. Hence, we obtain $\partial F(z)/\partial p_{h_i^{\text{in}}} = 0$. By riding on this conclusion, Eqs. (12.22)–(12.24) jointly imply

$$\begin{aligned} D_p^2 c(p,q) &= \left[\frac{\partial z_{h_j^{\text{in}}}}{\partial p_{h_i^{\text{in}}}} \cdot \frac{p_{h_j^{\text{in}}}}{p_{h_j^{\text{in}}}}\right]_{t \times t} = \left[\frac{\lambda}{p_{h_j^{\text{in}}}} \cdot \frac{\partial z_{h_j^{\text{in}}}}{\partial p_{h_i^{\text{in}}}} \cdot F_{h_j^{\text{in}}}(z)\right]_{t \times t} \\ &= \left[\frac{\lambda}{p_{h_j^{\text{in}}}} \frac{\partial F(z)}{\partial p_{h_i^{\text{in}}}}\right]_{t \times t} = \left[\frac{\lambda}{p_{h_j^{\text{in}}}} \cdot 0\right]_{t \times t} = 0_{t \times t}. \end{aligned}$$

That is, $D_p z(p,q) = D_p^2 c(p,q) = 0_{t \times t}$.

Regarding the literature, Levin and Milgrom (2004) and Mas-Collel et al. (1995) recorded that the matrix $D_p z(p,q) = D_p^2 c(p,q)$ satisfies the following properties: (1) It is symmetric, (2) it is negative semidefinite according to a general theorem of multi-variable calculus, and (3) for the price system p as given in Proposition 12.12, the equation $D_p z(p,q) p^{\text{in}} = 0$ holds true. Therefore, in comparison, the last proposition, derived above, represents a much-improved version of this well-known result from before.

12.5 A Few Final Words

By starting with a firm's four natural endowments (Forrest et al., 2021, 2023), this chapter employs a set-theoretical approach to establish a series of 12 propositions, most of which hold true no matter what system of values and beliefs a firm embraces. Because of the novel application of firms' natural endowments, this chapter convincingly demonstrates the existence of firm-specific order relations of real numbers, reflecting differences in the decision criteria of priority from one firm to another, and consequently the existence of firm-specific methods of optimization. For related discussions, see, for example, Hammerton (2020), Van Fleet (2021), and Yang and Andersson (2018). This end represents a major contribution this chapter makes to the literature, beyond that of establishing the formal set-theoretic conclusions.

By accentuating firms' different decision criteria of priority, this chapter is able to address, although only partially, the question about how some of the main results of the producer theory (Levin & Milgrom, 2004; Mas-Collel et al., 1995) still hold true, when each firm strives to achieve its desired business outcome through materializing its stated mission. Because of our innovative starting points adopted for the subsequent reasoning and logical analysis, which is drastically different from those widely adopted in the literature, we are able to redefine a firm's optimal production correspondence and minimum cost production and develop, among others, the following main results:

- In general, a firm's optimal production correspondence is generally not homogeneous of degree zero (Proposition 12.4), unless the firm's order relation of real numbers satisfies the condition of positive multiplicativity (Proposition 12.3).
- It is generally true that the minimum cost of a firm is homogeneous of degree one, no matter what system of values and beliefs the firm holds (Proposition 12.6).
- The set of all conditional factor demands is equal to the union of the subsets of those conditional factor demands from the Euclidean spaces of dimension 1 to the number of commodities minus one (Propositions 12.7 and 12.8).
- If each firm minimizes its business cost no matter how the minimization is defined, changes in the prices of commodity inputs bring forward changes in the demand of these commodities in the opposite direction (Proposition 12.10).
- In Shepard's lemma, the condition of a single conditional factor demand is equivalent to the equation that the rate of change of the cost in the price of commodity h is equal to the demand of commodity h, for each input commodity h (Proposition 12.11).
- When no commodity can be inputted for free, the matrix of rates of change of the unique conditional factor demand in input commodities with respect to prices is equal to 0 (Proposition 12.12).

To summarize, in addition to demonstrating the existence of firm-specific order relations of real numbers and firm-specific methods of optimization, this chapter also reestablishes a few very well-known results to the general case of whichever system of values and beliefs a firm might embrace. At the same time, because we impose fewer conditions than earlier works in the literature, our results, although developed set-theoretically in this chapter, are expected to be more practically relevant than the corresponding results derived previously.

Many important aspects of this chapter call for continued further research. For example, only two different order relations of real numbers—the conventional one and the one defined by the modular function—are considered here. However, definitely in real life, as indicated by the literature, do other means of prioritizing available decision alternatives exist (Hammerton, 2020; Lee & Chambers, 1986; Pope, 1980, 1982; Taylor, 1984, 1989; Van Fleet, 2021; Yang & Andersson, 2018)? Hence, to make the imagined, reestablished theory of economics more relevant to real-life applications, there is strong need for scholars to discover how the results, developed in either this chapter or the ones from the literature, remain valid for firms with varied systems of values and beliefs or different criteria of priority.

As for research topics for the immediate future, one can pay a revisit to Propositions 12.2, 12.3, 12.11, and 12.12, developed above, and see how they would look like for systems of values and beliefs that order real numbers by employing the modular function. Another important topic is to study how firms with dissimilar systems of values and beliefs interact with each other systemically and strategically.

References

Arif, S., & Scott, J. T. (1986). Economic-efficiency in integrated pest-management decisions of Illinois corn farmers. *American Journal of Agricultural Economics, 68*(5), 1385–1385.

Binswanger, H. P. (1974). A cost function approach to the measurement of elasticities of factor demand and elasticities of substitution. *American Journal of Agricultural Economics, 56*(1974), 377–386.

Collins, G. S., & Taylor, C. R. (1983). TECHSIM: A regional field crop and national livestock econometric simulation model. *Agricultural Economic Research, 35*(2), 1–18.

Debreu, G. (1959). *Theory of value: An axiomatic analysis of economic equilibrium*. Yale University Press.

Forrest, J. Y. L., & Liu, Y. (2022). *Value in business: A holistic, systems-based approach to creating and achieving value*. Springer.

Forrest, J. Y. L., Hafezalkotob, A., Ren, L., Liu, Y., & Tallapally, P. (2021). Utility and optimization's dependence on decision-makers' underlying value-belief systems. *Review of Economic & Business Studies, 14*, 125.

Forrest, J. Y. L., Schimmel, K., Wang, F., Hafezalkotob, A., & Liu, J. (2022). Remarks on production possibilities, optimal production correspondence and conditional factor demand. In *Proceedings of the 2022 Annual Conference of the National Association of Business, Economics and Technology*.

Forrest, J. Y. L., Shao, L., Liu, J., Sloboda, B. W., & Shao, D. (2023). The meaning of optimum and chosen method of optimization are individually defined. *Pennsylvania Economic Review*. Accepted for publication.

Hammerton, M. (2020). Deontic constraints are maximizing rules. *Journal of Value Inquiry, 54*(4), 571–588. https://doi.org/10.1007/s10790-020-09731-8

Hudik, M. (2019). Two interpretations of the rational choice theory and the relevance of behavioral critique. *Rationality and Society, 31*(4), 464–489.

Kahneman, D. (2011). *Thinking, fast and slow*. Farrar, Straus and Giroux.

Kako, T. (1978). Decomposition analysis of derived demand for factor inputs: The case of rice production in Japan. *American Journal of Agricultural Economics, 60*(4), 628–635.

Lau, L. J., & Yotopoulos, P. A. (1972). Profit, supply, and factor demand functions. *American Journal of Agricultural Economics, 54*(1), 11–18.

Lee, H., & Chambers, R. G. (1986). Expenditure constraints and profit maximization in U.-S. agriculture. *American Journal of Agricultural Economics, 68*(4), 857–865.

Levin, J., & Milgrom, P. (2004). *Producer theory*. Retrieved November 5, 2021, from https://web.stanford.edu/~jdlevin/Econ%20202/Producer%20Theory.pdf

Lovett, F. (2006). Rational choice theory and explanation. *Rationality and Society, 18*(2), 237–272.

Mas-Collel, A., Whinston, M. D., & Green, J. R. (1995). *Microeconomic theory*. Oxford University Press.

Mullainathan, S., & Thaler, R. H. (2000, October). *Behavioral economics*. NBER Working Paper no. 7948. National Bureau of Economic Research.

Pope, R. D. (1980). The generalized envelope theorem and price uncertainty. *International Economic Review, 21*(1), 75–85.

Pope, R. D. (1982). Expected profit, price change, and risk aversion. *American Journal of Agricultural Economics, 64*(3), 581–584.

Rubinstein, A. (1998). *Modeling bounded rationality*. The MIT Press.

Taylor, C. R. (1984). Stochastic dynamic duality: Theory and empirical applicability. *American Journal of Agricultural Economics, 66*(3), 351–357.

Taylor, C. R. (1989). Duality, optimization, and microeconomic theory: Pitfalls for the applied researcher. *Western Journal of Agricultural Economics, 14*(2), 200–212.

Trosper, R. L. (1978). American Indian relative ranching efficiency. *American Economic Review, 68*(4), 503–516.

Van Fleet, D. D. (2021). Utility, maximizing, and the satisficing concept: A historical approach at reconciliation. *Journal of Behavioral and Applied Management, 21*(2). https://doi.org/10.21818/001c.29691

Wallace, B. (2004). *Constrained optimization: Kuhn-Tucker conditions*. Retrieved November 24, 2021, from http://amber.feld.cvut.cz/bio/konopka/file/5.pdf

Weyl, G. E. (2019). Price theory. *Journal of Economic Literature, 57*(2), 329–384.

Yang, X., & Andersson, D. E. (2018). Spatial aspects of entrepreneurship and innovation. *The Annals of Regional Science, 61*, 457–462. https://doi.org/10.1007/s00168-018-0888-z

Young, D.L., Mittelhammer, R.C., Rostamizadeah, A., & Holland, D.W. (1987). *Duality theory and applied production economics research: A pedagogical treatises*. Washington State University Bulletin 0962.

Chapter 13
Optimal Production Correspondence and Aggregated Supply/Demand

Jeffrey Yi-Lin Forrest, Zaiwu Gong, Rhonda S. Clark, and Reneta Barneva

Abstract Many theoretically beautiful conclusions of the prevalent producer theory were derived on the common assumption that every firm attempts to maximize its profit and minimize its cost, while all firms employ the same methodology in their optimization efforts. By losing up these two behavioral assumptions and by introducing the concept of value-belief systems for individual firms, this chapter, which is mainly based on Forrest et al. (Math Appl 12:27–47, 2023), reestablishes a few well-known results of the producer theory for the general case of not specifying what criteria of priority a firm holds. At the same time, this chapter shows by using counterexamples, among others, that generally, even when individuals act in their own best self-interests, they may not collectively produce unintended greater social benefits and public goods. In the last section, several topics of expected significance are suggested for future research.

Keywords Invisible hand · Mission optimization · Shadow prices · Supply-chain ecosystems · Total production · Total supply

13.1 Introduction

Raiffa (1982) points out the fact that because results of the classical game theory hold true mostly on the ground of strict assumptions, that makes it difficult for practitioners to apply these results to real-life situations. For other criticisms of game theory, see, e.g., Abedian et al. (2022) and Nishino and Tjahjono (2018). Although

Jeffrey Yi-Lin Forrest (Department of Accounting Economics Finance, Slippery Rock University, Slippery Rock, PA, USA; Email: Jeffrey.forrest@sru.edu), Zaiwu Gong (College of Management Science and Engineering, Nanjing University of Information Science and Technology, Nanjing, China; Email: zwgong26@163.com), Rhonda S. Clark (Department of Management and Marketing, Slippery Rock University, Slippery Rock, PA, USA; Email: Rhonda.clark@sru.edu), and Reneta Barneva (School of Business, The State University of New York at Fredonia, Fredonia, NY, USA; Email: reneta.barneva@fredonia.edu) are equally contributed to this chapter.

J. Y.-L. Forrest, *Systemic Principles of Applied Economic Philosophies I*,
Translational Systems Sciences 38, https://doi.org/10.1007/978-981-99-7273-9_13

Raiffa only talks about game theory here and how results developed on such a theory suffer from difficulties in practice, this phenomenon in fact appears in the entire spectrum of business studies in general and economics in particular (e.g., Taylor, 1989). For example, Forrest and Liu (2022) carefully analyze how various methodologies widely employed in the studies of value creation and capture suffer from deficits of one kind or another so that the truthfulness of consequently established conclusions is subject to the constraint of these deficits. Parallel to such methodological deficits in terms of producing practically useful results, crucially criticized are various commonly imposed behavioral hypotheses in social science and economics (e.g., Mullainathan & Thaler, 2000; Kahneman, 2011). Such hypotheses include, in particular, that (1) all decision-makers prioritize their available alternatives in the same way in terms of how real numbers are ordered and (2) all economic agents aim at maximizing their profits.

It is evident that in real life, these two behavioral hypotheses are simply not generally true. Firms with different systems of values and beliefs order real numbers differently and employ respectively firm-specific methods to optimize their individual objective functions (Forrest et al., 2021; Hammerton, 2020; Van Fleet, 2021; Yang & Andersson, 2018). For example, there are firms that do not place profit maximization as their primary objective (e.g., Hussain, 2012; Jensen, 2001). Instead of maximizing profits for shareholders above all else, an increasing number of firms have also focused their operations on various other purposes, such as:

- Providing opportunities for citizens to succeed through hard work and creativity while enjoying a life of meaning and dignity (https://s3.amazonaws.com/brt.org/BRT-StatementonthePurposeofaCorporationOctober2020.pdf, accessed on January 30, 2021)
- Taking corporate social responsibilities (e.g., Fahimnia et al., 2015)
- Protecting the environment through designing and producing green products (e.g., Hong & Guo, 2019)

In short, not all economic agents in real life are maximizers or minimizers, as defined conventionally in the literature. Hence, some of the established theoretical results of economics may not apply to such agents (Taylor, 1989). In other words, a firm's system of values and beliefs directly affects how the firm prioritizes its decision choices and how it practically optimizes its objective function (Forrest et al., 2021). Based on this realization, this chapter studies how some of the well-known properties of a firm's factor demands, optimal production correspondence, and an economy's aggregated supply/demand can be extended to the general case of no matter what a system of values and beliefs a firm may embrace, while how some other known results are only true under specific conditions.

Specifically, this chapter employs the method of Euclidean spaces to investigate whether or not we can generalize a series of well-known conclusions of the producer theory. The considered known conclusions include, among others, the monotonicity of a firm's conditional factor demands, the homogeneity of a firm's optimal production correspondence, the aggregated supply and aggregated demand of an economy, and the maximization of total productions in an economy.

The contribution this chapter makes to the literature is that this chapter emphasizes the fact that each firm employs its own particular order relation of real numbers, which is defined on the firm's system of values and beliefs. Such a firm-specific order relation naturally forces the firm to adopt its specific method of optimization that reflects how well the stated mission is at least partially materialized. Speaking differently, firms respectively have their particular ways to prioritize their available decision alternatives, when faced with challenges and opportunities. Therefore, they accordingly apply their very individual ways to optimize their objectives. Contrary to this more realistic setting, the literature widely assumes that the ordering of real numbers and the method of optimization are the same across the entire business world, although certain particular details are different from one firm to another depending on the specifics of the objective functions and relevant constraints.

Because of our emphasis on firm-specific systems of values and beliefs, firm-specific orderings of real numbers, and firm-specific methods of mission optimization, this chapter is able to establish results not discovered before. At the same time, it is able to generalize some of the previously established results of the producer theory. More specifically, the marginal contribution this chapter makes to the literature consists of showing:

1. When additional conditions are needed for a desired conclusion to be true
2. How and when a well-known conclusion holds true only under very specific conditions

The rest of this chapter is organized as follows. Section 13.2 studies the monotonicity of a firm's conditional factor demands and the prices of the firm's products. Section 13.3 turns attention to the homogeneity of the optimal production correspondence. Section 13.4 investigates the monotonicity of factor demands in prices of input commodities. Section 13.5 considers both the aggregated supply and aggregated demand and the maximization problem of total productions of an economy. Then, this chapter is concluded in Sect. 13.6 with several important open questions listed for future research.

13.2 Conditional Factor Demands and the Firm Price of Its Product

To help smoothly present the rest of the chapter, let us restate the following conventions as introduced earlier. There are two binary relations $\leq$ and $\leq_F$ that we will look at. The first one is defined on $Y \subseteq \mathbb{R}^{\ell}$, the set of all feasible production plans of the firm, such that $x, y \in Y$, $x \leq y$ if and only if $x_h \leq y_h$, for each $h = 1, 2, \ldots, \ell$, where ℓ stands for the total number of commodities; for details, see Sect. 11.2.2. The second is the firm-specific ordering $\leq_F$ of real numbers. Evidently, we do not assume that each firm is rational; that is, $\leq$ is not assumed to satisfy the conditions of completeness, transitivity and reflexivity, as in Mas-Collel et al. (1995) for the preference relation of a consumer on his set of all possible consumptions.

Since $\leq_F$ represents firm F's specific criteria of priorities defined on the real-number domain D of decision-making activities, when no confusion appears, assume that $\leq_F$ satisfies: (1) transitivity (for $x, y, z \in D$, if $x \leq_F y$ and $y \leq_F z$, then $x \leq_F z$), (2) reflexivity (for $x \in D$, $x \leq_F x$), and (3) antisymmetry (for different $x, y \in D$, $x \leq_F y$ and $y \leq_F x$ cannot hold true at the same time). In short, conditions (1)–(3) are not equivalent to the assumption that the firm considered in this chapter is rational for the research economist who asserts conditions that achieve his optimal possibility, as so phrased in the language of von Mises (1949).

Given two sets U and W, $f: U \to W$ is known as a partial function from U into W, if there are $u^1, u^2 \in U$ such that $f(u^1) \in W$ is a well-defined element, while $f(u^2)$ is not defined. In this case, the domain of f, denoted by domain(f), is not equal to U. Without causing confusion, f will be simply known as a function from U into W. If for each $u \in$ domain(f), $f(u)$ is a nonempty subset of W, then f is known as a set-valued function from U into W.

For each production $y \in Y \subseteq \mathbb{R}^\ell$, let $\mathbb{R}_-$ bet the set of all negative real numbers, $\mathbb{R}_+$ the set of all positive real numbers, and

$$y^{\text{in}} = \left(y_{h_1^{\text{in}}}, y_{h_2^{\text{in}}}, \ldots, y_{h_t^{\text{in}}}\right) \in \mathbb{R}_-^t \quad \text{and} \quad y^{\text{out}} = \left(y_{h_1^{\text{out}}}, y_{h_2^{\text{out}}}, \ldots, y_{h_s^{\text{out}}}\right) \in \mathbb{R}_+^s$$

be respectively the sub-vector of the quantities of all the corresponding commodity inputs $h_1^{\text{in}}, h_2^{\text{in}}, \ldots, h_t^{\text{in}}$, and that of all commodity outputs $h_1^{\text{out}}, h_2^{\text{out}}, \ldots, h_s^{\text{out}}$. That is, what is implicitly meant is that in both y^{in} and y^{out} no zero components appear so that $h_1^{\text{in}} < h_2^{\text{in}} < \cdots < h_t^{\text{in}}$ and $h_1^{\text{out}} < h_2^{\text{out}} < \cdots < h_s^{\text{out}}$, and

$$y_{h_j^{\text{in}}} < 0 \quad \text{and} \quad y_{h_k^{\text{out}}} > 0, j = 1, 2, \ldots, t; k = 1, 2, \ldots, s. \tag{13.1}$$

Correspondingly, to distinguish prices of commodity inputs and outputs, for any given price system $p \in \mathbb{R}_+^\ell$, we write $p^{\text{in}} \in \mathbb{R}^t$ for the price system of all inputs in y^{in} and $p^{\text{out}} \in \mathbb{R}^s$ for the corresponding price system of the outputs in y^{out}. Hence, the production function f for the firm is defined as follows: For any $y \in Y$, $f(y^{\text{in}}) = y^{\text{out}}$. And the firm's cost minimization problem can be written as follows, assuming that the firm is a price taker. For a given price system $p \in \mathbb{R}_+^\ell$,

$$\begin{aligned} &\min{}_{y \in Y}^{F} p^{\text{in}} \cdot y^{\text{in}}, \\ &s.t.\ f\left(y^{\text{in}}\right) \geq q, \end{aligned} \tag{13.2}$$

where q is a given vector of some commodity quantities, representing the market demand for these commodities. The constraint in Eq. (13.2) implies that the set of all commodities $\left\{h_1^{\text{out}}, h_2^{\text{out}}, \ldots, h_{s_1}^{\text{out}}\right\}$ contained in q is a subset of the set of all the commodities $\left\{k_1^{\text{out}}, k_2^{\text{out}}, \ldots, k_{s_2}^{\text{out}}\right\}$ that appear in $f(y^{\text{in}}) = y^{\text{out}}$. Without loss of generality, we assume that these two sets are the same, that is,

$$\left\{h_1^{\mathrm{out}}, h_2^{\mathrm{out}}, \ldots, h_{s_1}^{\mathrm{out}}\right\} = \left\{k_1^{\mathrm{out}}, k_2^{\mathrm{out}}, \ldots, k_{s_2}^{\mathrm{out}}\right\}, \tag{13.3}$$

because producing additional products beyond what are listed in q requires at least an increased amount of labor input.

In Eq. (13.2), the total cost of production y is minimized in terms of Firm F's specific system of values and beliefs. Corresponding to this minimization, in neoclassic economics, there is such a long-standing convention that one of a firm' objectives is to minimize its cost (Wu, 2006). In reality, however, there are business firms that do not truly place cost minimization as one of their primary objectives. The executives of these firms run their businesses to best fit their values and beliefs, as defined by their systems of values and beliefs. For more detailed discussions regarding this end, see Sect. 11.4.2.

Let $Z = \{z :$ there is $y \in Y$ such that $z = y^{\mathrm{in}}$ and $f(z) \geq q\}$. Assume that the objective function in Eq. (13.2) has the following solution:

$$c^F(p, q) =_F \min{}_{z\in Z}^{F} p^{\mathrm{in}} \cdot z, \text{ for } p \in \mathbb{R}_+^{\ell}, \tag{13.4}$$

which stands for the minimum cost that is needed for producing the demanded outputs q. As for other symbols, the components of p^{in} are determined accordingly by those of $z \in Z$. In other words, for any $z, z' \in Z$, if $z = \left(z_{h_1^{\mathrm{in}}}, z_{h_2^{\mathrm{in}}}, \ldots, z_{h_{t_1}^{\mathrm{in}}}\right)$ and $z' = \left(z'_{h_1'^{\mathrm{in}}}, z'_{h_2'^{\mathrm{in}}}, \ldots, z'_{h_{t_2}'^{\mathrm{in}}}\right)$, in the expressions $p^{\mathrm{in}} \cdot z$ and $p^{\mathrm{in}} \cdot z'$, the corresponding p^{in}'s are given respectively as follows:

$$\left(p_{h_1^{\mathrm{in}}}, p_{h_2^{\mathrm{in}}}, \ldots, p_{h_{t_1}^{\mathrm{in}}}\right) \quad \text{and} \quad \left(p_{h_1'^{\mathrm{in}}}, p_{h_2'^{\mathrm{in}}}, \ldots, p_{h_{t_2}'^{\mathrm{in}}}\right).$$

For a given price system $p \in \mathbb{R}_+^{\ell}$ and a market demand vector $q \in \mathbb{R}_+^{s}$, for some $s < \ell$, define the set of conditional factor demands as follows:

$$\xi^F(p, q) = \left\{z \in Z : p^{\mathrm{in}} \cdot z =_F \min{}_{z'\in Z}^{F} p^{\mathrm{in}} \cdot z'\right\}, \tag{13.5}$$

Each element of this set is conditional on the desired level of outputs q, as reflected in the definition of Z. In other words, ξ^F maps each price system p of commodities to the subset $\xi^F(p, q) \subseteq Z$ of all cost-minimizing commodity inputs of productions, if $\xi^F(p, q) \neq \varnothing$.

Proposition 13.1 For each conditional factor demand $z(p^{\mathrm{in}}, q) \in \xi^F(p, q)$, $z(p^{\mathrm{in}}, q)$ is nonincreasing in $p \in \mathbb{R}_+^{\ell}$.

Proof For any price systems ${}^1p, {}^2p \in \mathbb{R}_+^{\ell}$ such that ${}^1p \geq {}^2p$, let ${}^1z \in \xi^F({}^1p, q)$ and ${}^2z \in \xi^F({}^2p, q)$ be two conditional factor demands. Without loss of generality, as reasoned for Eq. (13.3), assume that the set of commodities that appear in ${}^1z$ is the same as those in ${}^2z$. Then, we have

$$ {}^1p^{\text{in}}\cdot{}^1z\leq_F{}^1p^{\text{in}}\cdot{}^2z \quad \text{and}{}^2p^{\text{in}}\cdot{}^2z\leq_F{}^2p^{\text{in}}\cdot{}^1z. $$

Hence, ${}^1p^{\text{in}}\cdot({}^1z-{}^2z)\leq_F 0\leq_F{}^2p^{\text{in}}\cdot({}^1z-{}^2z)$. From this inequality, it follows that $({}^1p^{\text{in}}-{}^2p^{\text{in}})\cdot({}^1z-{}^2z)\leq_F 0$. Therefore, when ${}^1p\geq{}^2p$, which implies ${}^1p^{\text{in}}-{}^2p^{\text{in}}\geq 0$, ${}^1z-{}^2z\leq_F 0$. That is, $z(p^{\text{in}},q)$ is nonincreasing in $p\in\mathbb{R}^{\ell}_{+}$.

Proposition 13.2 If the firm's order relation $\leq_F$ of real numbers is the same as the conventional one $\leq$, then the price of the firm's product h_j^{out} is equal to the marginal cost of producing this product. Symbolically,

$$ p^{\text{out}}_{h_j^{\text{out}}}=\frac{\partial c(p,q)}{\partial q_{h_j^{\text{out}}}}, \quad \text{for } j=1,2,\ldots,s. \tag{13.6} $$

Proof According to Forrest et al. (2022), the firm has a clearly stated mission, which is formulated consistently with the firm's underlying system of values and beliefs; and its business goal in general is to optimally materialize, at least partially or remotely, the mission. So, in particular to the firm, its goal is to solve the following profit maximization problem for the purpose of materializing its stated mission. For any fixed price system $p\in\mathbb{R}^{\ell}_{+}$ and chosen output commodities h_1^{out}, h_2^{out}, …, h_s^{out}, satisfying $h_1^{\text{out}}<h_2^{\text{out}}<\cdots<h_s^{\text{out}}$,

$$ \max{}^{F}_{q\in\mathbb{R}^s_+} p^{\text{out}}\cdot q-c\left(p^{\text{in}},q\right), \tag{13.7} $$

where p^{out} stands for the price system of the commodities in $q=\left(q_{h_1^{\text{out}}},q_{h_2^{\text{out}}},\ldots,q_{h_s^{\text{out}}}\right)$, and $c(p^{\text{in}},q)$ the minimum cost given in Eq. (13.4). In this symbolic setup, it is assumed that for every possible q-value, the firm has solved its cost minimization problem so that the cost function $c(p^{\text{in}},q)$ is well defined and known.

Since the firm's order relation $\leq_F$ of real numbers is the same as the conventional one $\leq$, the first-order condition of the maximization problem in Eq. (13.1) holds true. That is, Eq. (13.6) holds true.

Speaking differently, what Proposition 13.2 says is that when the firm's order relation of real numbers is the same as the conventional one, and the firm is able to maximize its profit conventionally, then the shadow prices of its products $h_1^{\text{out}},h_2^{\text{out}},\ldots,h_s^{\text{out}}$ are respectively the same as the market prices of these products.

13.3 When Optimal Production Correspondence Is Homogeneous of Degree Zero

Let us define the optimal production correspondence of the firm (Levin & Milgrom, 2004) as the following partial, set-valued function η^F: $\mathbb{R}_+^\ell \to Y$: For $p \in \mathbb{R}_+^\ell$, if there is $y \in Y$ satisfying that $p \cdot y =_F \max_{y^q \in Y}^F p \cdot y^q$, then

$$\eta^F(p) = \left\{ y \in Y : p \cdot y =_F \max{}_{y^q \in Y}^F p \cdot y^q \right\}. \tag{13.8}$$

Intuitively speaking, for each price system p, $\eta^F(p)$ is the subset of Y that contains all mission-maximizing productions, if this subset exists and is not empty.

This setting generalizes the conventional one where scholars automatically assume that each firm maximizes its profit, although this end is not true in real life (Li & Ma, 2015). By employing this general mission maximization problem, we will be expectedly able to resolve the difficulty that some well-established conclusions in microeconomics cannot be empirically applied (Taylor, 1989) when the decision-maker of concern is not an optimizer (e.g., neither a maximizer nor a minimizer) as in the conventional sense.

Evidently, there are three possibilities for the mission maximization problem in Eq. (13.6) or (13.7): the problem has multiple solutions, or a unique solution or no solution. Different from Proposition 12.4, the following result shows that under the condition of positive multiplicativity, the optimal production correspondence η^F is of the homogeneity of degree zero.

Proposition 13.3 If the firm's order relation $\leq_F$ of real numbers satisfies the condition of positive multiplicativity, that is, for any scalar $\alpha > 0$ and $a, b \in \mathbb{R}$, $a \leq_F b \to \alpha a \leq_F \alpha b$, then the optimal production correspondence η^F is homogeneous of degree zero. Symbolically, for any scalar $\alpha > 0$, if $a \leq_F b \to \alpha a \leq_F \alpha b$, for any $a, b \in \mathbb{R}$, then $\eta^F(\alpha p) = \eta^F(p)$.

Proof Let α be a positive scalar. Then, $\eta^F(\alpha p) = \left\{ y \in Y : \alpha p \cdot y =_F \max_{y^q \in Y}^F \alpha p \cdot y^q \right\} = \{ y \in Y : \alpha p \cdot y \geq_F \alpha p \cdot y^q, \forall y^q \in Y \}$. So, the condition of positive multiplicativity of the order relation $\leq_F$ guarantees that

$$\{ y \in Y : \alpha p \cdot y \geq_F \alpha p \cdot y^q, \forall y^q \in Y \} = \{ y \in Y : p \cdot y \geq_F p \cdot y^q, \forall y^q \in Y \}.$$

Therefore, $\eta^F(\alpha p) = \eta^F(p)$.

Example 13.1 Constructed here is another scenario, slightly different from Example 12.2, where the set-valued function η^F is not homogeneous of degree zero. In particular, assume that a specific production of the firm, as shown in Fig. 13.1, involves one unit of each of the commodity inputs A, $A_?$, B, $C_?$, C, where $A_?$ can be either A_1 or A_2, but not both, and similarly, $C_?$ can be either C_1 or

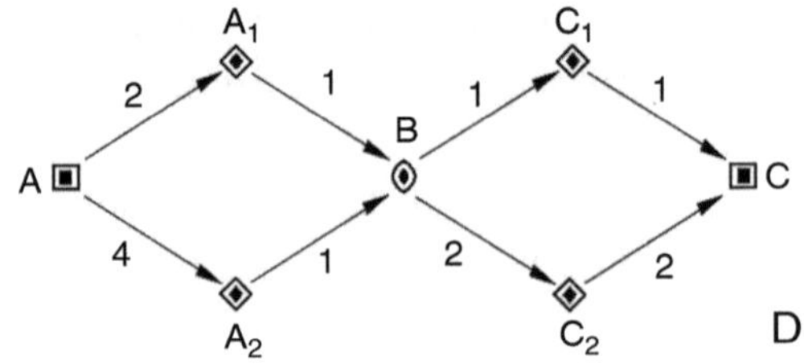

Fig. 13.1 How product D can be produced

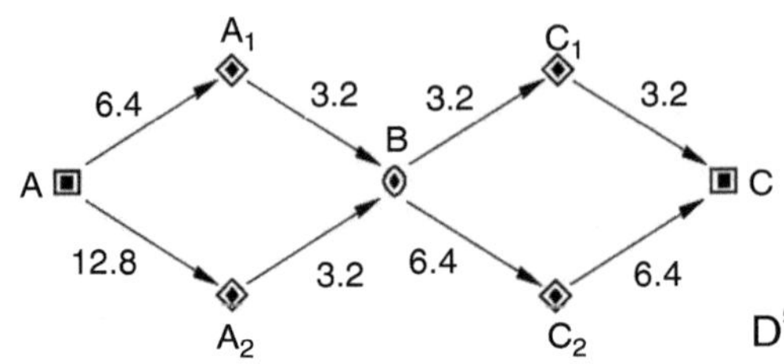

Fig. 13.2 The price system is enlarged 3.2 times

C_2, but not both. That is, commodities A_1 and A_2 can substitute for each other and the same holds true for commodities C_1 and C_2. In Fig. 13.1, the arrows stand for the sequence the corresponding commodities are fed into the production line one after another, while the weights the relevant dollar values created by the production sequence from one node to the next.

Without loss of generality, assume that each of these specific commodities costs \$1.00 a unit. The production produces only one output, named D, which can be sold at the market price that is equal to the sum of the path that leads to D.

The goal of the firm is to maximize the total profit of this production, while the firm orders real numbers by referring to the mod4 function. In particular, for any two real numbers x and y, $x < y$ if and only if $x(\text{mod}4) < y(\text{mod}4)$. In this case, there are four possible ways to produce D with their respective profits being given as follows:

(a) $A \to A_1 \to B \to C_1 \to C$ with profit $5 - 5 = 0\ (\text{mod}4) = 0$.
(b) $A \to A_1 \to B \to C_2 \to C$ with profit $7 - 5 = 2\ (\text{mod}4) = 2$.
(c) $A \to A_2 \to B \to C_1 \to C$ with profit $7 - 5 = 2\ (\text{mod}4) = 2$.
(d) $A \to A_2 \to B \to C_2 \to C$ with profit $9 - 5 = 4\ (\text{mod}4) = 0$.

Therefore, the maximum profit is equal to 2, as produced out of either the production $A \to A_1 \to B \to C_2 \to C$ or $A \to A_2 \to B \to C_1 \to C$.

If we choose scalar $\lambda = 3.2$ to multiply to each of the individual local values, then the corresponding productions are depicted in Fig. 13.2; and the corresponding profits for the four productions are respectively equal to $0 \times 3.2\ (\text{mod}4) = 0$, $2 \times 3.2\ (\text{mod}4) = 1.6$, $2 \times 3.2\ (\text{mod}4) = 1.6$, and $4 \times 3.2\ (\text{mod}4) = 3.2$. That is, the maximum profit is equal to 3.2, as produced out of the production $A \to A_2 \to B \to C_2 \to C$.

What has been shown here is that $\eta^F(3.2p)$ is the singleton $A \to A_2 \to B \to C_2 \to C$, while $\eta^F(p)$ is equal to the set that contains the following two elements:

(1) $A \to A_1 \to B \to C_2 \to C$ and (2) $A \to A_2 \to B \to C_1 \to C$. Hence, what is shown is that $\eta^F(3.2p) \neq_F \eta^F(p)$.

This example implies once again Proposition 12.4, which is restated below.

Proposition 13.4 The optimal production correspondence η^F in general is not homogeneous of degree zero on domain(η^F).

13.4 Factor Demands in Terms of Input Commodities' Prices

For a price system $p \in \mathbb{R}_+^\ell$, if $\eta^F(p) \neq \varnothing$, then Eq. (13.8) implies that each $z = z(p) \in \eta^F(p)$, referred to as a factor demand at price p (Levin & Milgrom, 2004), solves

$$\max{}_{y\in Y}^F p \cdot y = \max{}_{y\in Y}^F \left(p^{\text{out}} \cdot f\left(y^{\text{in}}\right) + p^{\text{in}} \cdot y^{\text{in}}\right).$$

Proposition 13.5 Assume that the firm's order relation $\leq_F$ of real numbers satisfies the condition of positive multiplicativity, that is, for any scalar $\alpha > 0$ and $a, b \in \mathbb{R}$, $a \leq_F b \to \alpha a \leq_F \alpha b$. Let $p \in \mathbb{R}_+^\ell$ be a price system, satisfying $\eta^F(p) \neq \varnothing$. If $z = z(p) \in \eta^F(p)$, then for each input commodity h_j^{in}, $z_{h_j^{\text{in}}}(p)$ is nondecreasing in $p_{h_j^{\text{in}}}$.

Proof Let us pick two price systems $p, p' \in \mathbb{R}_+^\ell$ and two factor demands $z \in \eta^F(p)$, $z' \in \eta^F(p')$. Then the definition of the optimal production correspondence implies that

$$p \cdot z =_F \max{}_{y\in Y}^F p \cdot y \quad \text{and} \quad p' \cdot z' =_F \max{}_{y\in Y}^F p' \cdot y.$$

Hence, we have $p \cdot z \geq_F p \cdot z'$ and $p' \cdot z' \geq_F p' \cdot z$. So, $p \cdot (z - z') \geq_F 0 \geq_F p' \cdot (z - z')$ follows. By combining the two ends of this inequality, we produce $(p' - p) \cdot (z' - z) \geq_F 0$. This inequality of vectors implies that for any input commodity h_j^{in}

$$\left(p'_{h_j^{\text{in}}} - p_{h_j^{\text{in}}}\right) \cdot \left(z'_{h_j^{\text{in}}} - z_{h_j^{\text{in}}}\right) \geq_F 0.$$

So, the assumed condition of positive multiplicativity implies that if $p'_{h_j^{\text{in}}} - p_{h_j^{\text{out}}} >_F 0$, then $z'_{h_j^{\text{in}}} - z_{h_j^{\text{in}}} \geq_F 0$.

Example 13.2 Constructed here is a scenario where for a particular order relation $\leq_F$ the firm has for real numbers, $z_{h_j^{\text{in}}}(p)$ is not nondecreasing in $p_{h_j^{\text{in}}}$. To this end, assume that $\leq_F = \leq_{\text{mod}(4)}$, where for real numbers x and $y \in \mathbb{R}$,

$$x <_{\mathrm{mod}(4)} y \text{ if and only if } x \bmod(4) < y \bmod(4), \tag{13.9}$$

where the order $<$ is the conventional one defined on $\mathbb{R}$, x mod (4) is the remainder of $x \div 4$, and y mod (4) is the remainder of $y \div 4$, such that $0 \leq x \bmod (4) < 4$ and $0 \leq y \bmod (4) < 4$.

Let $p'_{h_j^{\mathrm{in}}} - p_{h_j^{\mathrm{out}}} =_{\mathrm{mod}(4)} 2 >_{\mathrm{mod}(4)} 0$ and $z'_{h_j^{\mathrm{in}}} - z_{h_j^{\mathrm{in}}} =_{\mathrm{mod}(4)} -2$. Then, we have

$$\left(p'_{h_j^{\mathrm{in}}} - p_{h_j^{\mathrm{in}}}\right) \cdot \left(z'_{h_j^{\mathrm{in}}} - z_{h_j^{\mathrm{in}}}\right) \geq_{\mathrm{mod}(4)} 0.$$

However, $z'_{h_j^{\mathrm{in}}} - z_{h_j^{\mathrm{in}}} <_{\mathrm{mod}(4)} 0$. In other words, for Proposition 13.5 to hold true, the assumed positive multiplicativity is also a sufficient condition.

13.5 Economy's Overall Supply/Demand and Maximization of Total Productions

In this section, instead of looking at the firm as an individual, independent business entity, we examine the economy as a whole that consists of a collection of many interacting agents, such as producers and consumers. In particular, Sect. 6.1 focuses on the aggregated supply and aggregated demand in an economy; and Sect. 6.1 addresses the problem of maximization of total productions in an economy.

13.5.1 Economy's Total Supply and Demand

Each agent in the economy, be it an individual person, or a firm or an organization, chooses a plan $A = (a_1, a_2, \ldots, a_\ell) \in \mathbb{R}^\ell$ of action for the purpose of first staying alive and then thriving. Interactions exist in the fashion of input and output connections, forming various kinds of supply-chain ecosystems (Adner, 2017; Hendrikse et al., 2015; Nohria & Garcia-Pont, 1991). In particular, an agent's inputs are the outputs of some other agents and vice versa unless the agent is an ultimate consumer in the consumer product market.

Assume that the economy of our concern has n producers. Producer j $(= 1, 2, \ldots, n)$ makes and carries out a production plan, which specifies the quantities of all input and output commodities. That is, the production plan (or simply production) of producer j is an element $y_j = (y_{j1}, y_{j2}, \ldots, y_{j\ell}) \in \mathbb{R}^\ell$ with outputs written as positive numbers and inputs negative numbers, as assumed before. If producer j chooses its production plan $y_j \in \mathbb{R}^\ell$, $j = 1, 2, \ldots, n$, then

$$y = y_1 + y_2 + \ldots + y_n = \sum_{j=1}^{n} y_j = \left(\sum_{j=1}^{n} y_{j1}, \sum_{j=1}^{n} y_{j2}, \ldots, \sum_{j=1}^{n} y_{j\ell} \right)$$

stands for the total production or total supply to the consumer market, where supplies to producers are counted twice, once as outputs and once as inputs so that they cancel each other in this summation.

Let Y_j be the set of all feasible production plans of producer j, meaning that each $y_j \in Y_j$ is technically materializable for producer j within its boundary conditions meeting the moral codes of its system of values and beliefs. Then, the set

$$Y = Y_1 + Y_2 + \cdots + Y_n = \sum_{j=1}^{n} Y_j = \left\{ \sum_{j=1}^{n} y_j : y_j \in Y_j, j = 1, 2, \ldots, n \right\}$$

represents the set of total productions of the producers or the production possibilities of the entire economy.

Proposition 13.6 For each aggregated production $y = y_1 + y_2 + \cdots + y_n \in Y = Y_1 + Y_2 + \cdots + Y_n$ such that $y_j \in Y_j$, for $j = 1, 2, \ldots, n$, and each physical commodity h, the aggregated supply of h is greater than or equal to the aggregated demand of h. Symbolically,

$$y_h \geq 0 \quad \text{or} \quad \sum\nolimits_{j=1}^{n} y_{jh} \geq 0.$$

Proof If there is a physical commodity h such that for some y_j, $y_{jh} < 0$, then this commodity h has to be produced by at least one other producer. So, in general, there are two sets $\left\{ y_{j_p} \right\}_{j_p \in I_p}$ and $\left\{ y_{j_q} \right\}_{j_q \in I_q}$ of producers, for some index sets I_p and $I_q \subseteq \{1, 2, \ldots, n\}$, such that the former ones input commodity h in their productions, while the latter ones produce h as outputs of their productions. Note that in real life, these two index sets I_p and I_q do not have to be disjoint. That is, $y_{j_p h} < 0$ and $y_{j_q h} > 0$ for each j_p and j_q such that

$$\sum_{j_q} y_{j_q h} + \sum_{j_p} y_{j_p h} \geq 0.$$

That is, the total input of commodity h by all producers is sufficiently covered by the total output of commodity h from all the producers.

The importance of Proposition 13.6 is demonstrated by the following conclusion: The assumption $Y \supset \left(-\mathbb{R}_{-}^{\ell} \right)$, as introduced by Debreu (1959, p. 42), cannot hold true in general. In particular, what Gerard Debreu intended to mean by introducing this assumption is that it is possible for a total production to notify all of its outputs or for all producers to dispose of all commodities. However, Proposition 13.6 says that any commodity input of a producer has to come from at least one producer who produces the very commodity.

13.5.2 Maximization of Total Productions

In this subsection, assume that each producer is a price taker, that it maximizes the realization of its mission by choosing a production y_j, and that it uses its unique system of values and beliefs to define the meaning of maxima and to construct the method of maximization. Because in this chapter every commodity and its price are time and location specific, each producer is required to choose a production so that its inputs and outputs are optimally distributed over both time and space. Such a desired production is known as one of producer j's equilibrium productions (Debreu, 1959) with respect to the price system p.

Let $p \in \mathbb{R}_+^\ell$ be a price system and $y_j \in Y_j$ a production. The profit π_j of producer j is $p \cdot y_j$ and the total profit π of all the producers is

$$\pi = \sum_{j=1}^{n} p \cdot y_j = p \cdot \sum_{j=1}^{n} y_j = p \cdot y.$$

Assume that producer j's order of real numbers is $\leq_j$, when the firm solves for optimal decisions, while the conventional order between real numbers is $\leq$. For the entire economy, let us define the collective order $\leq_E$ of real numbers as follows: For any u and $v \in \mathbb{R}$,

$$u \leq_E v \text{ if and only if } u \leq_j v, \text{ for each } j = 1, 2, \ldots, n \tag{13.10}$$

where the society is assumed to be democratic.

For the following proposition, we assume that each producer j's order of real numbers is the same as the conventional one.

Proposition 13.7 For a given price system $p \in \mathbb{R}_+^\ell$, and a total production $y = \sum_{i=1}^{n} y_i \in \sum_{i=1}^{n} Y_i$, satisfying $y_j \in Y_j$, for each $j = 1, 2, \ldots, n$, the following statements are equivalent:

(a) $p \cdot y =_E \max^E_{y^q \in Y} p \cdot y^q$;
(b) $p \cdot y_j =_j \max^j_{y_j^q \in Y_j} p \cdot y_j^q$, for $j = 1, 2, \ldots, n$.

Proof (a) $\Rightarrow$ (b) By contradiction, let us assume that for $y_j \in Y_j$, for $j = 1, 2, \ldots, n$,

$$p \cdot y = p \cdot y_1 + p \cdot y_2 + \cdots + p \cdot y_n =_E \max{}^E_{y^q \in Y} p \cdot y^q;$$

however, there is a producer j, for some $1 \leq j \leq n$, such that

$$p \cdot y_j <_j \max{}^{j}_{y_j^q \in Y_j} p \cdot y_j^q.$$

Hence, we have

$$\max{}^{E}_{y^q \in Y} p \cdot y^q =_E p \cdot y_1 + p \cdot y_2 + \cdots + p \cdot y_n <_E p \cdot y_1 + \cdots$$
$$+ p \cdot y_{j-1} + \max{}^{j}_{y_j^q \in Y_j} p \cdot y_j^q + p \cdot y_{j+1} + \cdots + p \cdot y_n,$$

a contradiction. That means $p \cdot y =_E \max{}^{E}_{y^q \in Y} p \cdot y^q$.

(b) $\Leftarrow$ (a) Once again, we prove this conclusion by contradiction. To this end, we assume

$$p \cdot y_j =_j \max{}^{j}_{y_j^q \in Y_j} p \cdot y_j^q, \quad \text{for } j = 1, 2, \ldots, n,$$

while

$$p \cdot y =_E p \cdot y_1 + p \cdot y_2 + \cdots + p \cdot y_n <_E \max{}^{E}_{y^q \in Y} p \cdot y^q.$$

Hence, there are $y_j^* \in Y_j$, for $j = 1, 2, \ldots, n$, such that

$$p \cdot y_1 + p \cdot y_2 + \cdots + p \cdot y_n <_E p \cdot y_1^* + p \cdot y_2^* + \cdots + p \cdot y_n^*.$$

So, for some j, $1 \le j \le n$, we have

$$p \cdot y_j =_j \max{}^{j}_{y_j^q \in Y_j} p \cdot y_j^q <_j p \cdot y_j^*,$$

a contradiction. Therefore, the assumption $p \cdot y <_E \max{}^{E}_{y^q \in Y} p \cdot y^q$ does not hold true.

Speaking differently, the equivalent statements in Proposition 13.7 imply

$$\max{}^{E}_{y^q \in Y} p \cdot y^q =_E \max{}^{1}_{y_1^q \in Y_1} p \cdot y_1^q + \max{}^{2}_{y_2^q \in Y_2} p \cdot y_2^q + \cdots + \max{}^{n}_{y_n^q \in Y_n} p \cdot y_n^q. \tag{13.11}$$

However, the following example shows that this equation is not generally true when the producers are allowed to individually order real numbers differently from the conventional one and from each other.

Example 13.3 To simplify our discussion, let us consider an economy that consists only of two producers, named 1 and 2, and that these producers order real numbers by using mod4 function, that is, $\le_{\text{mod}(4)}$. As in the previous examples, we assume that one unit of each commodity is imported into the production line and is produced out of the line, where the production lines of producer 1 and 2 are respectively given in Figs. 13.3 and 13.4. In particular, the arrows stand for the sequence for the

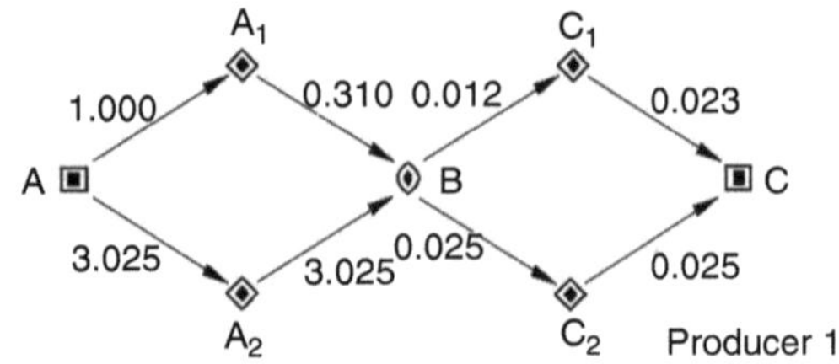

Fig. 13.3 Flow chart of producer 1's productions

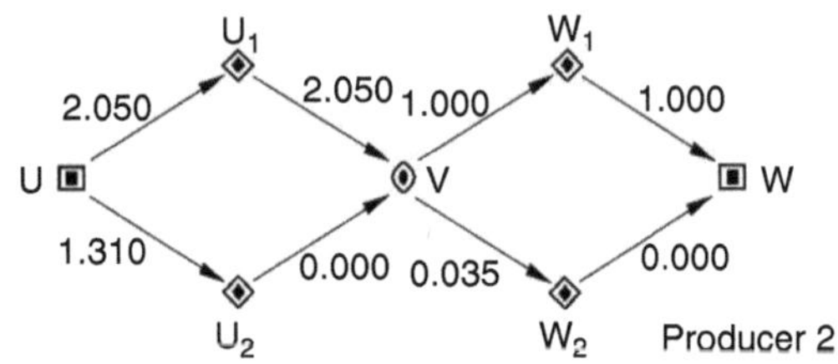

Fig. 13.4 Flow chart of producer 2's productions

commodities to be fed into the production line; and, the weights of the edges represent the relevant profits generated by the production sequence.

For producer 1, its potential commodity inputs are A, $A_?$, B, $C_?$, C, where $A_?$ can be either A_1 or A_2, but not both, and similarly, $C_?$ can be either C_1 or C_2, but not both. That is, commodities A_1 and A_2 (respectively, C_1 and C_2) are substitutes of each other. Hence, the set Y_1 of all production possibilities of producer 1 contains the following elements (or paths) and the corresponding profits are 1.345, 1.36, 6.085 mod(4) = 2.085, and 6.1 mod(4) = 2.1, respectively:

I_{11}: A → A_1 → B → C_1 → C
I_{12}: A → A_1 → B → C_2 → C
I_{21}: A → A_2 → B → C_1 → C
I_{22}: A → A_2 → B → C_2 → C

Therefore, we have

$$\max{}^{1}_{y\in Y_1} p \cdot y = {}_1 2.1. \tag{13.12}$$

Similarly for producer 2, its commodity inputs are U, $U_?$, V, $W_?$, W, where $U_?$ (respectively, $W_?$) can be either U_1 or U_2 (respectively, either W_1 or W_2), but not both.

The set Y_1 of production possibilities of producer 2 contains the following elements (or paths) and the corresponding profits are 6.1 mod(4) = 2.1, 4.135 mod (4) = 0.135, 3.31, and 1.315, respectively.

J_{11}: U → U_1 → V → W_1 → W
J_{12}: U → U_1 → V → W_2 → W
J_{21}: U → U_2 → V → W_1 → W
J_{22}: U → U_2 → V → W_2 → W

Table 13.1 Computation of $p \cdot y_1 + p \cdot y_2$ mod(4)

P2				
P1	2.100	0.135	3.310	1.345
1.345	3.445	1.480	0.655	2.690
1.360	3.460	1.495	0.670	2.705
2.085	0.185	2.220	1.395	3.430
2.100	0.200	2.235	1.410	3.445

P1 producer 1, *P2* producer 2

That is, we have

$$\max{}^{2}_{y \in Y_2} p \cdot y =_2 3.31. \tag{13.13}$$

Therefore, from Eqs. (13.12) and (13.13), we have

$$\max{}^{1}_{y \in Y_1} p \cdot y + \max{}^{2}_{y \in Y_2} p \cdot y =_{\text{mod}(4)} 2.1 + 3.31 \text{ mod}(4) =_{\text{mod}(4)} 1.41. \tag{13.14}$$

To compute $\max{}^{E}_{y \in Y} p \cdot y$, we first find the set $Y = \{y_1 + y_2 : y_1 \in Y_1, y_2 \in Y_2\}$ of total productions of the economy. The economy's order of real numbers is equal to $\leq_E = \leq_{\text{mod}(4)}$. The computational results of $p \cdot y = p \cdot y_1 + p \cdot y_2$ mod(4) are shown in Table 13.1.

Therefore, we obtain $\max{}^{E}_{y \in Y} p \cdot y = 3.46$. So, by referencing back to Eq. (13.14), we have

$$\max{}^{E}_{y \in Y} p \cdot y >_E \max{}^{1}_{y_1^q \in Y_1} p \cdot y_1^q + \max{}^{2}_{y_2^q \in Y_2} p \cdot y_2^q + \cdots + \max{}^{n}_{y_n^q \in Y_n} p \cdot y_n^q. \tag{13.15}$$

That end implies that Eq. (13.11) does not generally hold in terms of systems of values and beliefs.

In terms of real life, economies in general do not have such a linear order $\leq_E$ of real numbers that is consistent with that of each individual producer. That is, Eq. (13.10) generally does not hold true. For instance, if in Example 13.3, producer 1's order of real numbers is $\leq_{\text{mod}(3)}$, and producer 2's is $\leq_{\text{mod}(4)}$, then real numbers 1 and 3.2 cannot be ordered in the economy, because these producers have inconsistent order relations:

$$3.2 \leq_{\text{mod}(3)} 1 \quad \text{and} \quad 1 \leq_{\text{mod}(4)} 3.2.$$

That is, in this case, the economy's order $\leq_E$ of real numbers is not linear.

Closely relevant to this end is Adam Smith's "invisible hand," as initially introduced in 1759 in Part IV and Chap. 1 of his work *The Theory of Moral Sentiments*. In particular, the imagined "invisible hand" pronounces that although individuals are selfish, their self-interest centered actions collectively produce unintended greater social benefits and public goods (Sen, 2010). Here, what does the word "greater" mean? According to the discussion above, the greater community of selfish individuals mostly likely does not have any order of real numbers that is consistent with that of every producer, as long as the producers order real numbers differently. Speaking differently, in general, there is not an unanimously acknowledged method to decipher the meaning of "greater social benefits and public good." It is because in any economy of more than two economic agents there are different systems of values and beliefs (Forrest, 2018), and these differences define an inconsistent economy-wide order $\leq_E$ of real numbers. In terms of the literature, based on Greenwald and Stiglitz (1986), Joseph E. Stiglitz (Altman, 2006) believes that the invisible hand is often not there. In comparison, what we achieved here definitively confirms analytically that Stiglitz's belief is correct.

13.6 A Few Final Words

This chapter establishes a series of seven propositions by employing the methodology of Euclidean spaces on the bases of the four natural endowments of firms. These conclusions extend some of the well-known results from the prevalent producer theory (Levin & Milgrom, 2004; Mas-Collel et al., 1995) to the general case of no matter what system of values and beliefs a firm may possibly embrace. At the same time, we construct four counterexamples to confirm the fact that some of the fundamental results in the prevalent producer theory only hold true under very specific conditions.

By highlighting the real-life fact that firms generally employ different decision criteria of priority and employ their specific means to optimize the realization of their missions (Hammerton, 2020; Van Fleet, 2021; Yang & Andersson, 2018), this chapter is able to partially actualize the goal of research outlined in the introduction section earlier. Because this chapter starts its analytical reasoning on the concept of firms' natural endowments, it opens up a large area of research, where most, if not all, of the established results in economics need to be checked to see whether or not they still hold true when the order of real numbers is not the same as the conventional one.

Specific to this chapter, due to its novel methodological approach, which was initially adopted by Debreu (1959), and its emphasis on firms' natural endowments (Forrest et al., 2021; Forrest et al., 2022), it establishes, among others, the following main results:

- Each conditional factor demand is a nonincreasing function of prices (Proposition 13.1).
- A firm's optimal production correspondence in general is not homogeneous of degree zero (Proposition 13.4), which is different from what is known before (Levin & Milgrom, 2004).

- In a functional economy, the aggregated supply of a commodity is more than or equal to the aggregated demand of the commodity (Proposition 13.6), when the time factor is ignored.
- Micro players' actions on their self-interests do not generally lead to unintended greater macro-level social benefits and public good (Example 13.3), as commonly believed and known as the "invisible hand" (Sen, 2010).

To summarize, it is indeed true that this chapter is 100% based on the set theory of Euclidean spaces. However, because this chapter considers how a firm prioritizes its decision alternatives on the basis of its system of values and beliefs, which has been totally ignored in the literature, results established herein are expected to be more practically relevant than the corresponding results derived previously.

As for potential future research along the lines drawn in the previous sections, there are many topics one can look at closely. More specifically, among all potentials for future research, one can formalize additional ways on how decision-making managers and entrepreneurs prioritize their available alternatives in real life. Only by doing so, we can hopefully answer the loud calls for the desperate need to reconstruct the existent economic theories (e.g., Arif & Scott, 1986; Hammerton, 2020; Kahneman, 2011; Mullainathan & Thaler, 2000; Taylor, 1989; Van Fleet, 2021; Yang & Andersson, 2018).

References

Abedian, M., Amindoust, A., Maddahi, R., & Jouzdani, J. (2022). A game theory approach to selecting marketing-mix strategies. *Journal of Advances in Management Research, 19*(1), 139–158.

Adner, R. (2017). Ecosystem as structure: An actionable construct for strategy. *Journal of Management, 43*(1), 39–58.

Altman, D. (2006). Managing globalization. In *Q & A with Joseph E. Stiglitz, Columbia University and The International Herald Tribune*, October 11, 2006 05:03AM. Retrieved February 3, 2022, from https://web.archive.org/web/20090122214457/, http://blogs.iht.com/tribtalk/business/globalization/?p=177

Arif, S., & Scott, J. T. (1986). Economic-efficiency in integrated pest-management decisions of Illinois corn farmers. *American Journal of Agricultural Economics, 68*(5), 1385–1385.

Debreu, G. (1959). *Theory of value: An axiomatic analysis of economic equilibrium*. Yale University Press.

Fahimnia, B., Sarkis, J., & Eshragh, A. (2015). A tradeoff model for green supply chain planning: A leanness-versus-greenness analysis. *Omega, 54*(1), 173–190.

Forrest, J. Y. L. (2018). *General systems theory: Foundation, intuition and applications in business decision making*. Springer.

Forrest, J. Y. L., & Liu, Y. (2022). *Value in business: A holistic, systems-based approach to creating and achieving value*. Springer.

Forrest, J. Y. L., Hafezalkotob, A., Ren, L., Liu, Y., & Tallapally, P. (2021). Utility and optimization's dependence on decision-makers' underlying value-belief systems. *Review of Economic & Business Studies, 14*(2), 125–149. https://doi.org/10.47743/rebs-2021-2-0007

Forrest, J. Y. L., Shao, L., Liu, J., & Sloboda, B. W. (2022). Optimum and method of optimization are individually defined. In *Proceedings of the 2022 Annual Conference of Pennsylvania Economic Association* (pp. 16–30).

Forrest, J. Y. L., Gong, Z. W., Clark, R. S., & Barneva, B. (2023). Properties of a firm's factor demands, optimal production correspondence, and an economy's aggregated supply/demand. *Mathematics for Applications, 12*, 27–47.

Greenwald, B. C., & Stiglitz, J. E. (1986). Externalities in economies with imperfect information and incomplete markets. *Quarterly Journal of Economics, 101*(2), 229–264.

Hammerton, M. (2020). Deontic constraints are maximizing rules. *Journal of Value Inquiry, 54*(4), 571–588. https://doi.org/10.1007/s10790-020-09731-8

Hendrikse, G., Hippmann, P., & Windsperger, J. (2015). Trust, transaction costs and contractual incompleteness in franchising. *Small Business Economics, 44*(4), 867–888.

Hong, Z. F., & Guo, X. L. (2019). Green product supply chain contracts considering environmental responsibilities. *Omega, 83*(1), 155–166.

Hussain, W. (2012). Corporations, profit maximization and the personal sphere. *Economics and Philosophy, 28*(3), 311–331.

Jensen, M. (2001). Value maximization, stakeholder theory, and the corporate objective function. *European Financial Management, 7*(3), 297–317.

Kahneman, D. (2011). *Thinking, fast and slow*. Farrar, Straus and Giroux.

Levin, J., & Milgrom, P. (2004). *Producer theory*. Retrieved November 5, 2021, from, https://web.stanford.edu/~jdlevin/Econ%20202/Producer%20Theory.pdf

Li, T., & Ma, J. H. (2015). Complexity analysis of dual-channel game model with different managers' business objectives. *Communications in Nonlinear Science and Numerical Simulation, 20*, 199–208.

Mas-Collel, A., Whinston, M. D., & Green, J. R. (1995). *Microeconomic theory*. Oxford University Press.

Mullainathan, S., & Thaler, R. H. (2000). *Behavioral economics*. NBER Working Paper no. 7948. National Bureau of Economic Research.

Nishino, N., & Tjahjono, B. (2018). Game theory approach to product service systems. *Procedia CIRP, 73*, 304–309.

Nohria, N., & Garcia-Pont, C. (1991). Global strategic linkages and industry structure. *Strategic Management Journal, 12*(Special Issue), 105–124.

Raiffa, H. (1982). *The art and science of negotiation*. Harvard University Press. https://doi.org/10.2307/2232420

Sen, A. (2010). Introduction. In A. Smith (Ed.), *(1790): The theory of moral sentiments* (6th ed., pp. vii–xxix). Penguin.

Taylor, C. R. (1989). Duality, optimization, and microeconomic theory: Pitfalls for the applied researcher. *Western Journal of Agricultural Economics, 14*(2), 200–212.

Van Fleet, D. D. (2021). Utility, maximizing, and the satisficing concept: A historical approach at reconciliation. *Journal of Behavioral and Applied Management, 21*(2). https://doi.org/10.21818/001c.29691

von Mises, L. (1949). *Human action: A treatise in economics*. Yale University Press.

Wu, K. P. (2006). *Advanced macroeconomics*. Tsinghua University Press.

Yang, X., & Andersson, D. E. (2018). Spatial aspects of entrepreneurship and innovation. *The Annals of Regional Science, 61*, 457–462. https://doi.org/10.1007/s00168-018-0888-z

Part V
Consumers

Chapter 14
Consumption Preferences and Utilities

Jeffrey Yi-Lin Forrest, Davood Darvishi, Rhonda S. Clark, Mojtaba Seyedian, Jun Liu, Lawrence Shao, Shynara Sarkambayeva (Jumadilova), Dale Shao, and Sunita Mondal

Abstract Many well-known conclusions about consumer preferences and utility representations of consumptions are developed on the assumption that possible consumptions are completely ordered. This chapter, which is mainly based on Forrest et al. (South Bus Econ J, 2023), looks at what could happen when such an unrealistic assumption is removed, hoping that the consequent theory will be more relevant to real life than before. Different from some of the known hypotheses and/or conclusions in the literature, this chapter shows, among other results, that for an individual no matter how he prefers one consumption over another, (1) there are incomparable consumptions, (2) his consumption preferences may not be transitive, and (3) his indifference relation of consumptions *in practice* may not be transitive. Although these results have been confirmed by different authors with varied settings, our confirmations are based purely on analytical analysis without making use of any auxiliary concepts. More importantly, this chapter generalizes the classical conclusion of Debreu (Theory of value: An axiomatic analysis of economic equilibrium, Yale University Press, New Haven and London, 1959) on when a continuous utility representation exists in a very different way from these published recently by Efe Ok and his colleagues. In the end, several topics of expected significance are suggested for future research.

Jeffrey Yi-Lin Forrest (Department of Accounting Economics Finance, Slippery Rock University, Slippery Rock, PA, USA; Email: Jeffrey.forrest@sru.edu), Davood Darvishi (Department of Mathematics, Payame Noor University, Tehran, Iran; Email: darvishidavood@yahoo.com), Rhonda S. Clark (Department of Management and Marketing, Slippery Rock University, Slippery Rock, PA, USA; Email: Rhonda.clark@sru.edu), Mojtaba Seyedian (School of Business, The State University of New York at Fredonia, Fredonia, NY, USA; Email: Mojtaba.Seyedian@fredonia.edu), Jun Liu (School of Digital Economics and Management, Wuxi University, Wuxi, China; Email: liujun@nuist.edu.cn), Lawrence Shao (College of Business, Slippery Rock University, Slippery Rock, PA, USA; Email: Lawrence.shao@sru.edu), Shynara Sarkambayeva (Jumadilova) (Department of Management and Mathematical Economics, Satbayev University, Almaty, Kazakhstan; Email: shynara.jumadilova@gmail.com), Dale Shao (Lewis College of Business, Marshall University, Huntington, WV, USA; Email: shaod@marshall.edu), and Sunita Mondal (Department of Accounting Economics Finance, Slippery Rock University, Slippery Rock, PA, USA; Email: Sunita.mondal@sru.edu) are equally contributed to this chapter.

J. Y.-L. Forrest, *Systemic Principles of Applied Economic Philosophies I*, Translational Systems Sciences 38, https://doi.org/10.1007/978-981-99-7273-9_14

Keywords Measurement of utility · Non-optimizing consumptions · Perception difficulties · Preference representations · Property of reflexivity · Use values

14.1 Introduction

Central to economics is the behavioral hypothesis of rationality that individual decision-makers optimize their subjective functions (Sobel, 2005). However, among many existing problems with this hypothesis, such as those raised by behavioral economists (e.g., Kahneman, 2011; Mullainathan & Thaler, 2000), are the following two problems that this chapter attempts to address:

- How can one alter the hypothesis that a consumer's set of consumption possibilities is completely ordered by his preferences (Dubra & Ok, 2002; Hervés-Beloso & Cruces, 2019) in order to reflect the fact that the opposite should be generally true?
- When a consumer's satisfaction from consumption is not measurable by the conventional concept of continuous utility functions (Estevez-Toranzo & Herves-Beloso, 1995; Ok, 2002), what can one do to reflect the levels of satisfactions?

These are very important problems if we want to make consequent theories practically relevant. For example, Jacob et al. (2018) find that most US college students value living amenities, such as spending on student activities, sports, and dormitories, over academic quality that is only a concern of the small number of high-achieving students. By looking at cosmopolitan cultural consumption—consumer's openness for cultural products from foreign countries—Rössel and Schroedter (2015) maintain that cosmopolitan consumption is a class-based practice, determined by different forms of cultural capitals. Similarly, many other researches point to the same fact that as a human being, each consumer's physiological needs are of multidimensional. When two consumption choices belong to two different dimensions, respectively, these choices will not be comparable in terms of consumption preferences.

Although the assumption that consumer's preference can order all available consumption choices (Hervés-Beloso & Cruces, 2019) does not reflect the relevant reality, it does play the role of starting points of countlessly many theoretical reasonings and practical applications of economic theories. Hence, to make relevant theories practically relevant, it is important both theoretically and practically to address the previously posed problems so that adopted assumptions are closer to real life than the ones widely adopted currently.

In terms of methodology, similar to the previous chapter in Part III on producer firms, this chapter also employs Euclidean spaces to investigate whether or not some of the well-known conclusions of the consumer theory still hold true when consumptions are not assumed to be completely comparable in terms of individual preferences (the first problem above) and how potentially another set of indicators instead of that of real numbers can be employed to measure utilities (the second problem above). Different from some of the known hypotheses and/or conclusions in the literature, this chapter shows, among other results, that for an individual consumer, (1) there are incomparable consumptions, (2) his consumption preferences may not be transitive, (3) his indifference relation of consumptions *in practice* may not be transitive, and (4) the classical conclusion of Debreu (1959) on when a continuous utility representation exists is generalized.

As for the contribution this chapter makes to the literature, it can be examined in both theoretical and practical perspectives. In the former case, this chapter is the first in four different fronts. (1) It *analytically* shows the fact that for each consumer, there are possible consumptions that are not comparable in terms of his preferences. (2) It officially embraces the fact that each consumer or decision-maker orders real numbers differently based on his system of values and beliefs. (3) Due to measurement uncertainties in real life, a constructed example shows that for an economic theory to be practically useful, the theory has to allow some of the involved variables to assume interval values instead of exact numerical ones. (4) In terms of utility representations of a preference relation, this chapter takes a different approach from the one taken by Efe Ok and his colleagues. In comparison, our conclusion can be more easily fathomed behaviorally than the ones derived by Ok's team (e.g., Dubra & Ok, 2002; Evren & Ok, 2011; Nishimura & Ok, 2016; Ok, 2002; Ok & Masatlioglu, 2007).

In practical perspective, because consumers are allowed to order real numbers differently, conclusions derived in this chapter can be practically applied to situations that involve irrational behaviors and non-optimizing consumptions (Taylor, 1989).

The rest of this chapter is organized as follows. Section 14.2 provides a brief literature review and lays the basic conventions for the development of the following reasonings. Section 14.3 shows the existence of incomparable consumptions and intransitive preferences. Section 14.4 looks at the set-theoretical structural properties of consumption preferences and in which form a subset of consumptions has a real-number valued utility representation. Section 14.5 concludes this presentation. The Appendix to this chapter examines how each preference relation can be extended into a complete binary relation that is reflexive.

14.2 Background Setting and the Basic Model

This section lays down the basics needed for the rest of the chapter to develop smoothly. It consists of two subsections. The first one provides a quick literature review and how conclusions derived here enrich the existing knowledge. The second subsection constructs an individual's set of possible consumptions and introduces the axiom of lower boundedness.

14.2.1 The Relevant Literature

In the economic literature, the word utility commonly means the satisfaction a consumer acquires from consuming a good or service. It has been in use since at least the time of Aristotle (Gordon, 1964; Kauder, 1953). Even so, its current meaning was only crystallized in the twentieth century. With such a long history and importance in economic studies, actual measurement of utility has never been established, although various scholars have devoted time and efforts on this task throughout the history (Stigler, 1950).

To avoid the problem of not being able to observe pleasure acquired from consuming a good or service, economists turned their attention and efforts to observable aspects of decisions in terms of which commodity is selected for consumption in the name of preferences (Varian, 2010). Such shift of attention enabled economists to study concrete, observable phenomena, making economic theories, to a degree, similar to physics where the movement of bodies is addressed (Pareto, 1906).

Before the twentieth century, it was assumed that one could always assign a real number to every consumption bundle available to a consumer to represent the order in which he prefers them. That is, it was believed that a preference relation could always be measured numerically. In the effort to make such belief more scientific, Fisher (1892), Pareto (1906), and others realized that in terms of utility, focusing on the ranking of consumption alternatives, instead of on how much these alternatives differ from each other, can very well address the problems to which utility theory was conventionally applied. By adopting this new approach, utility no longer needed to be numerically measurable (Strotz, 1953).

This approach of ranking consumption alternatives, known as ordinalism, has paved the way for the development of modern microeconomics. And, Slutsky (1915), Hicks and Allen (1934), Samuelson (1938), and others contributed to make this approach the dominant one in consumer theory and opened up new theoretical possibilities through the study of preferences. In particular, a consumer's preference is assumed to completely order all available consumption alternatives and satisfies the property of transitivity (Hervés-Beloso & Cruces, 2019). To this end, this chapter shows, by using an example, that in general for each consumer there are consumption alternatives that are not comparable with each other in terms of his preferences. That is, in the studies of preferences, this chapter is expected to open up new possibilities for the consequent economic theories to be closer to situations of real life.

Let $\precsim$ be a consumer's preference relation defined on the set X of his consumption alternatives. It is said to possess a utility representation, if there is a function $u : X \to \mathbb{R}$, where $\mathbb{R}$ represents the set of all real numbers, such that for any $x, y \in X$, $x \precsim y$, if and only if $u(x) \leq u(y)$ (Hervés-Beloso & Cruces, 2019). Here, the function u is known as a utility function. Different from the earlier times, Wold (1943) was the first to investigate the conditions under which a utility function could represent some ranking of a consumer's preferences.

Following Wold, Debreu (1959) and many others over the following years and up to the present time (Mehta, 1998) have been trying to refine and generalize the established results on when representable consumer preferences exist. Because of the continued efforts to bring economics into scientific grounds, various mathematical methods and approaches were critically introduced to hopefully reshape the discipline (e.g., Debreu, 1959; Mas-Collel et al., 1995). And with the increasing level of scientification of economics, it is confirmed (Estevez-Toranzo & Herves-Beloso, 1995; Hervés-Beloso & Cruces, 2019) that there are indeed preference relations that do not have any utility representation. For a very nice historical account of this area of literature, see Hervés-Beloso and Cruces (2019).

Contributing to this branch of the literature, this chapter generalizes Debreu's (1959) existence theorem of representable preference relations. Here, a particular condition is imposed based on the most recent development in mathematics.

To make the rest of this chapter more reader friendly, let us introduce the order relation $\leq$ on $\mathbb{R}^\ell$ as follows, as in the previous part of this book, where ℓ is a natural number. For any $x^1 = \left(x_1^1, x_2^1, \ldots, x_\ell^1\right)$ and $x^2 = \left(x_1^2, x_2^2, \ldots, x_\ell^2\right) \in \mathbb{R}^\ell$,

$$x^1 \leq x^2 \quad \text{if and only if} \quad x_h^1 \leq x_h^2, \quad \text{for each} \quad h = 1, 2, \ldots, \ell.$$

Evidently, there are elements x^1 and $x^2 \in \mathbb{R}^\ell$ such that x^1 and x^2 are not comparable in terms of this order relation $\leq$. And, a subset $X \subseteq \mathbb{R}^\ell$ is known as connected, if X cannot be partitioned into two nonempty open subsets in the relative topology induced on X.

14.2.2 Consumptions and the Consumption Set of a Consumer

By a consumer, it means an individual person, a household, or a group of people organized either purposefully or naturally together around a common purpose or reason, such as an extended family. For the sake of communication convenience, we will treat a consumer as "he."

Assume that what a consumer does is to choose and to carry out a consumption plan, or simply a consumption, selected now for the present moment and the entire future, as what has been done in the literature (Debreu, 1959; Levin & Milgrom, 2004a; Mas-Collel et al., 1995). In other words, he specifies the quantities of all his input commodities and all his output commodities subject to a set of constraints, assuming that he does not have a single or a particularly preferred consumption. The constraints consist of those that are of, for example, physiological nature, such as those needed to sustain survival and basic living, and that the total value of his consumption must not be greater than his level of wealth.

Without loss of generality, assume that there are m consumers, for some $m \in N$ (= the set of all natural numbers). For consumer i (= 1, 2, ..., m), to distinguish inputs (i.e., those goods and services consumed by *i*) and outputs (= what *i* offers to the world), the quantities of his commodity inputs are written as positive numbers, while the quantities of his commodity outputs negative numbers. Assume that there is a total of ℓ commodities, which are ordered and named as h=1, 2, ..., ℓ. As commonly done in economic analysis (e.g., Pancs, 2018), assume that the quantity of each commodity, as shown in a consumption plan, is a real number.

In this model setup, assumed include (1) perfect information, where each consumer knows each commodity perfectly without any uncertainty, (2) each consumer is a price taker, and (3) prices are linear without quantity discount.

Let x_i ($\in \mathbb{R}^\ell$) represent a consumption of consumer *i* and X_i be the set of all consumptions possible for consumer *i*, known as his consumption set or his demand. Then, this set X_i is completely determined by consumer *i*'s constraints. Based on this convention, it can be seen that each consumption $x_i \in X_i$ generally contains a relatively small number of nonzero components.

For each individual, his typical inputs of a consumption consist of various dated and location-specific goods and services, while the only outputs are various dated and located labors provided. What is assumed here is that goods, services, or labors that become available and/or are delivered at different times and/or different locations are seen as different commodities. To separate a consumer from a producer, assume that each consumer plays two roles:

- A provider of services that facilitate the transactions of purchase and sale of products, such as a house, a car, etc.
- A consumer of services and products from others

Let $x_i \in \mathbb{R}^\ell$ be a consumption of consumer *i* (=1, 2, ..., *m*). Then

$$x = \sum_{i=1}^{m} x_i \text{ and } X = \sum_{i=1}^{m} X_i \tag{14.1}$$

are, respectively, known as a total consumption and the total consumption set.

When commodity *h* is an input for a consumer, the consumed quantity of *h* must have a lower bound, such as zero. On the other hand, when commodity *h* is an output of a consumer, then the quantity of this commodity must be bounded from above, because the individual can only produce a limited amount of output at a specified time-interval, no matter what other commodities he might input and output. For instance, if for consumer *i*', commodity output *h* is a type of labor offered to the market, then the amount of such labor has to be limited with an upper cap. Because the quantity of output commodity *h* is written as a negative number, it means that the quantity of *h* has a lower bound. Based on this understanding, we adopt the following axiom:

Axiom 14.1 (Lower boundedness): For each consumer *i* (= 1, 2, ..., *m*), his consumption set X_i has a lower bound for the order relation $\leqq$ defined on $\mathbb{R}^\ell$.

Without causing confusion, once an axiom is introduced, this axiom will be assumed to hold true in the following reasonings unless it is stated otherwise. Hence, the following result naturally flows:

Proposition 14.1 The total consumption set X of all consumers has a lower bound in terms of the order relation $\leq$ defined on $\mathbb{R}^{\ell}$.

In fact, if $\chi_i \in \mathbb{R}^{\ell}$ is a lower bound of the consumption set X_i, for $i = 1, 2, \ldots, m$, then Eq. (14.1) implies that $\chi = \sum_{i=1}^{m} \chi_i$ is a lower bound of X.

Among many commonly adopted assumptions about consumption sets X_i, $i = 1, 2, \ldots, m$, is the assumption of continuity. That is, for each $i = 1, 2, \ldots, m$, X_i is assumed to be closed. This end means that for any infinite sequence $(x_i^q)_{q=1}^{\infty}$ of consumptions possible for consumer i, if $x_i^q \in X_i$, $q = 1, 2, \ldots$, and $x_i^q \to x_i^0$, as $q \to \infty$, then $x_i^0 \in X_i$.

Evidently, in real life, this assumption of continuity cannot be true in general. For instance, assume that consumer i is a person with a very strong conceit and a comparing heart and that $x_1^1 \in X_i$ is i's current consumption. Then driven by his natural desire to satisfy his vanity, especially when there are stimulating comparisons with others (Blanchflower et al., 2009; Esposito & Villaseñor, 2019; Schneider & Day, 2018), i would prefer a better consumption $x_1^2 \in X_i$. As the living quality of the competing members of the community rises, comparisons with each other within the community further encourage i to pursue another preferred consumption $x_1^3 \in X_i$ above x_1^2. Over time, a sequence $(x_i^q)_{q=1}^{\infty}$ of consumptions are obtained. If such a sequence is convergent to x_i^0, most likely, $x_i^0 \notin X_i$, because such consumption x_i^0 of the limit state will be most likely not materializable, although imaginable, within the constraints of consumer i.

14.3 Incomparable Consumptions and Intransitivity Preferences

This section investigates the preference relation of a consumer's consumption. It consists of three subsections. The first subsection demonstrates by using an example that the preference of one consumption over another might not be applied to compare some consumptions. The second subsection shows also by using an example that the preference relation that naturally exists in the set X_i of consumptions in general cannot be seen as a preorder, because in real life the property of transitivity may not hold true. The third subsection shows how the indifference relation of consumptions can help partition X_i into disjoint equivalence classes, while showing that in real life, the indifference relation does not necessarily satisfy the property of transitivity.

Speaking differently, the significance of this section is the discovery that the widely adopted assumptions in the studies of consumers regarding consumer preferences (Debreu, 1959; Levin & Milgrom, 2004a; Mas-Collel et al., 1995) need to be modified. Consequently, that means some of the main conclusions in such studies need to be generalized to capture additional real-life scenarios.

14.3.1 Consumptions Can Be Incomparable in Terms of Preferences

When two consumptions $x_i^1, x_i^2 \in X_i$ are available but only one of them can be chosen, then in real life it is very likely that one is more preferred than the other. In such a case, we say that consumptions x_i^1, x_i^2 are comparable with each other in terms of consumer i's preferences.

Axiom 14.2 (Comparability). If two consumptions $x_i^1, x_i^2 \in X_i$ are comparable in terms of the preference of consumer i, as determined by his system of values and beliefs, then one and only one of the following alternatives holds true:

1. x_i^1 is preferred to x_i^2.
2. x_i^1 is indifferent to x_i^2.
3. x_i^2 is preferred to x_i^1.

The following example shows that in real life, there is such a potential consumer that some of his consumption possibilities are simply not comparable in terms of his preferences.

Example 14.1 Assume that we look at a consumer who drinks coffee, although he has no particular preference of one coffee type over another. Let X be the set of consumption possibilities of this consumer, h_1 represent a coffee made from Arabic beans, and h_2 another coffee made from Robusta beans. Assume that h_1 and h_2 are, respectively, priced at p_{h_1} and p_{h_2}. For the convenience of presentation, we also use the same symbols h_1 and h_2 to represent the quantities of these coffees available to this consumer.

Let $x^1, x^2 \in X \subseteq \mathbb{R}^\ell$ be two such consumption possibilities that they satisfy

$$x_h^1 = x_h^2, h = 1, 2, \ldots, \ell, h \neq h_1, h_2,$$

$$x_{h_1}^1 = 0, x_{h_1}^2 \neq 0, x_{h_2}^1 \neq 0, x_{h_2}^2 = 0,$$

and

$$p_{h_1} x_{h_1}^2 = p_{h_2} x_{h_2}^1.$$

That is, these consumptions x^1 and x^2 are identical except their h_1th and h_2th components. Then, for this particular non-coffee drinker, x^1 and x^2 are not comparable consumption possibilities in terms of his preferences. It is because no matter which coffee is served, the cost is the same while he does not care or even enjoy which coffee is provided.

More generally, each consumer is a physiological being with multidimensional needs for basic survival. Hence, his set of consumption possibilities cannot be completely comparable in terms of his preferences. In other words, when two commodities from two different dimensions of human survival are presented, no consumer can really say which commodity is preferred over the other. In terms of literature, several scholars had also noticed this issue of incomplete preferences. For example, Dubra and Ok (2002) introduce a risky choice model in which an individual naturally possesses an incomplete preference relation. Ok (2002) considers the problem of how to represent an incomplete preference relation by means of a vector-valued utility function. Based on these works, Alonso et al. (2010) present a web-based consensus support system that involves decision-makers with incomplete preference relations; Meng and Chen (2015) develop a group-decision-making method to cope with incomplete preference information; and Cettolin and Riedl (2019) conduct experiments to test for either complete or incomplete preferences.

14.3.2 Preference Relations Are Generally Nontransitive

For any two consumptions $x_i^1, x_i^2 \in X_i$, if they are comparable and x_i^1 is at most as preferred as x_i^2, then we write $x_i^1 \precsim_{\mathrm{i}} x_i^2$. In other words, the inequality $x_i^1 \precsim_{\mathrm{i}} x_i^2$ means that x_i^1 is less preferable than or indifferent from x_i^2. Symbolically, we have

$$\precsim_{\mathrm{i}} \leftrightarrow (\prec_i \text{or} \sim_i). \tag{14.2}$$

It can be seen that this preference relation $\precsim_i$ satisfies the following property of reflexivity: For any $x_i \in X_i$,

$$x_i \precsim_{\mathrm{i}} x_i.$$

If for any $x_i^1, x_i^2, x_i^3 \in X_i$,

$$x_i^1 \precsim_{\mathrm{i}} x_i^2 \quad \text{and} \quad x_i^2 \precsim_{\mathrm{i}} x_i^3 \quad \text{imply} \quad x_i^1 \precsim_{\mathrm{i}} x_i^3,$$

then $\precsim_i$ is said to be a transitive preference. For consumer i, if his preference relation $\precsim_i$ satisfies both reflexivity and transitivity, then $\precsim_i$ is known as a preorder. If, additionally, for any consumption possibilities $x_i^1, x_i^2 \in X_i$, one of the conditions (1)–(3) in Axiom 14.2 holds true, then $\precsim_i$ is said to be a complete preorder (relation).

In order to make the research in this chapter relevant to real life, one needs to be cautioned that consumer i's preference relation $\precsim_i$ might not be transitive in some cases of practical applications. To demonstrate this end, let us look at such a consumer whose particular system of values and beliefs makes the outputs of the objective function not ordered as how real numbers are ordered ordinarily. In particular, let $a \in \mathbb{R}$ be a positive real number. We define a preorder $<_{\mathrm{mod}(a)}$ on $\mathbb{R}$

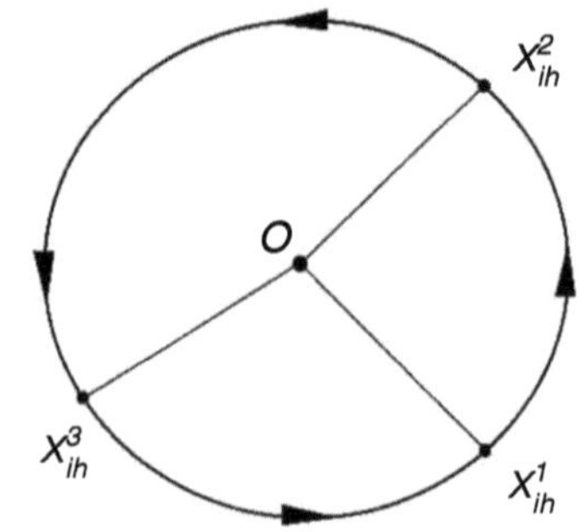

Fig. 14.1 How the real-number line looks like after applying a modular operation

as follows (Forrest et al., 2021), where a is a positive real number: For any x and $y \in \mathbb{R}$,

$$x <_{\text{mod}(a)} y \quad \text{if and only if} \quad x\text{mod}(a) < y\text{mod}(a). \tag{14.3}$$

Example 14.2 Let r be a fixed positive real number and the set $\mathbb{R}$ of all real numbers be partitioned into the following equivalence classes (Kuratowski & Mostowski, 1976) by using the modular operation mod(r). Let us still use $s \in [0, r)$ to represent the equivalence class below:

$$s = \{x \in \mathbb{R} : s = \text{remainder of } x \div r\} = \{x \in \mathbb{R} : x\ mod(r) = s\}.$$

In other words, these equivalence classes, when represented by numbers in the interval $[0, r)$, can be arranged in a circle with r being the circumference length, Fig. 14.1, where the arrows stand for the direction of order from small magnitudes to large ones.

For a consumption $x_i \in X_i$, let h (= 1, 2, ..., ℓ) be such a particular commodity that the demanded quantity of h satisfies the following preference relation: For two demanded quantities x^1_{ih} and x^2_{ih} of commodity h, $x^1_{ih} \prec_{\text{mod}(r)} x^2_{ih}$ if and only if on the shorter arc between x^1_{ih} mod(r) and x^2_{ih} mod(r), the arrow points from x^1_{ih} mod(r) to x^2_{ih} mod(r). In real life, this particular commodity could be a specific kind of carbohydrate consumer i can physically intake in a day and r the maximum amount of this food required for a day. So, for any real number $x > 0$, x mod (r) stands for the amount left over after the consumption of the food within a number of days.

Hence, the given points $x^1_{ih}, x^2_{ih}, x^3_{ih}$ on the circle in Fig. 14.1 satisfy

$$x^1_{ih} \prec_{\text{mod}(r)} x^2_{ih} \quad \text{and} \quad x^2_{ih} \prec_{\text{mod}(r)} x^3_{ih}.$$

Define three consumptions $x^a_i, x^b_i, x^c_i \in X_i$ such that

$$x_{ik}^{j} = x_{ik}, \quad j = a, b, c, \quad k = 1, \ldots, h-1, h+1, \ldots, \ell,$$

and

$$x_{ih}^{a} = x_{ih}^{1}, \ x_{ih}^{b} = x_{ih}^{2}, \ x_{ih}^{c} = x_{ih}^{3}. \tag{14.4}$$

That is, the consumptions x_i^a, x_i^b, and x_i^c are identical except their components of commodity h, which satisfy Eq. (14.4). Then we can conclude that

$$x_i^a \prec_i x_i^b \quad \text{and} \quad x_i^b \prec_i x_i^c.$$

But, $x_i^c \prec_{\text{mod}} x_i^a$ holds true instead of $x_i^a \prec_{mod} x_i^c$ as expected as the consequence of transitivity.

One real-life example of such a commodity h that possesses a non-transitive preference relation often appears in the fashion industry, such as that of women's clothing. In particular, what was in fashion a while ago might be in fashion again many years later.

In terms of the literature, Tversky (1969) reports that consumer preferences don't generally satisfy the condition of transitivity. And, by using a new statistical technique and by revisiting the same gambles Tversky studied earlier, Birnbaum and Gutierrez (2007) conclude that there are indeed a few individual consumers who repeat intransitive preference patterns. More recently, the rationality assumption means (Mandler, 2001) that consumers can rank any pair of possible consumptions and the rankings satisfy the property of transitivity. Hence, either Example 14.1 or Example 14.2 or both of them demonstrate that the widely assumed rationality in economic theories does not hold true in real life.

By combining Examples 14.1 and 14.2, the result below follows naturally:

Proposition 14.2 For consumer i, his preference relation $\precsim_i$ cannot compare every pair of possible consumptions. And, although $\precsim_i$ is reflexive, it is not generally transitive.

Speaking differently, $\precsim_i$ might be neither a complete preorder nor a preorder.

14.3.3 Indifference Relations Can Also Be Nontransitive

For two consumptions x_i^1 and x_i^2 of consumer i, if $x_i^1 \succsim_i x_i^2$ and not $x_i^2 \succsim_i x_i^1$, then x_i^1 is said to be preferred to x_i^2, denoted by $x_i^1 \succ_i x_i^2$. If $x_i^1 \precsim_i x_i^2$ and $x_i^2 \precsim_i x_i^1$, then x_i^1 is said to be indifferent of x_i^2, denoted by $x_i^1 \sim_i x_i^2$. The relation $\sim_i$, defined on X_i, will be referred to as the indifference relation of consumer i. Notice that this indifference relation $\sim_i$ is only defined for comparable consumptions. When two consumptions x_i^1 and x_i^2 are not comparable, they are evidently also indifferent because none of them is preferred over the other. For our purpose in this chapter, incomparable consumptions x_i^1 and x_i^2 will not be seen as indifferent of each other.

For any $x_i \in X_i$, define the indifference class of x_i as follows:

$$[x_i] = \{x_i' \in X_i : x_i' \precsim_i x_i \text{ and } x_i \precsim_i x_i' \}.$$

That is, the indifference class $[x_i]$ contains only those consumptions that are comparable with x_i and indifferent from x_i in terms of the preference relation $\precsim_i$.

Proposition 14.3 For consumer i, assume that his preference relation $\precsim_i$ constitutes a preorder. Then, for any consumptions $x_i^1, x_i^2 \in X_i$, if $[x_i^1] \neq [x_i^2]$, then $[x_i^1] \cap [x_i^2] = \varnothing$.

Proof By contradiction, assume that there are $x_i^1, x_i^2 \in X_i$ such that $[x_i^1] \neq [x_i^2]$ and $[x_i^1] \cap [x_i^2] \neq \varnothing$. Then, each $z_i^* \in [x_i^1] \cap [x_i^2]$ satisfies $x_i^1 \sim_i z_i^* \sim_i x_i^2$. That is, we have

$$x_i^1 \precsim_i z_i^*, x_i^1 \succsim_i z_i^*, \text{and } z_i^* \precsim_i x_i^2, z_i^* \succsim_i x_i^2.$$

Therefore, the assumed transitivity implies that $x_i^1 \precsim_i x_i^2$ and $x_i^1 \succsim_i x_i^2$ or $x_i^1 \sim_i x_i^2$. That is, the indifference relation $\sim_i$ is transitive, which implies that for any $z_i \in [x_i^1]$, $z_i \sim_i x_i^1 \sim_i x_i^2$. Hence, $z_i \in [x_i^2]$. That is, $[x_i^1] \subseteq [x_i^2]$. Similarly, we can show that $[x_i^1] \supseteq [x_i^2]$. Therefore, we can conclude $[x_i^1] = [x_i^2]$. A contradiction. That means $[x_i^1] \cap [x_i^2] = \varnothing$.

The following example shows that in general the indifference relation, as defined by incomparability, of an individual consumer is not transitive. For convenience, this indifference relation is also denoted by $\sim_i$ but in this example only.

Example 14.3 Continue using the setup in Fig. 14.1, as produced by employing the modular operation mod(r) on $\mathbb{R}$ in Example 14.2. Without loss of generality, let us identify consumptions $x_i^1, x_i^2 \in X_i$ that satisfy

$$x_{ik}^1 = x_{ik}^2, \quad k = 1, \ldots, h-1, h+1, \ldots, \ell,$$

and

$$x_{ih}^1 \neq x_{ih}^2,$$

with points x_{ih}^1 and x_{ih}^2 on the circle. To this end, instead of the locations of x_{ih}^1 and x_{ih}^2 in Fig. 14.1, let these points be given in Fig. 14.2. That is, in this case, x_{ih}^1 and x_{ih}^2 (or x_i^1 and x_i^2) are located on the opposite sides of a diameter of the circle. Therefore, consumptionsx_i^1 and x_i^2 are incomparable and so indifferent consumptions for consumer i.

Due to measurement uncertainty and other factors in real life, for more detailed discussions, please consult with the concepts of gray numbers and systems in Liu and Lin (2010); the quantity of the demanded commodity h can never be provided in

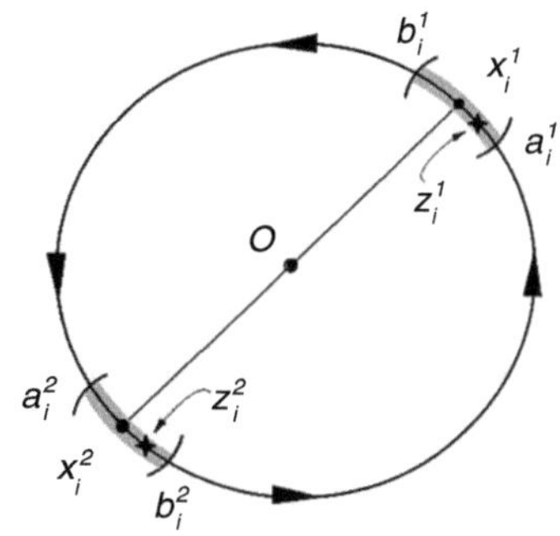

Fig. 14.2 Arc intervals of indifferent quantities of demands

any exact amount. For example, a box of breakfast cereal is planned to contain 14 ounces of contents. However, in real life, hardly any such cereal box truly contains this exact amount as specified. Instead, the exact amount of the contents in a box of this special cereal is equal to a number very close to 14 ounces.

So, there are arc intervals, one of which is centered around x_i^1 and the other around x_i^2. Assume that the former arc interval is $\left(a_i^1, b_i^1\right)$ and the latter is $\left(a_i^2, b_i^2\right)$, Fig. 14.2. Symbolically, for consumer i, for any $z_i^1 \in arc\left(a_i^1 b_i^1\right)$ and any $z_i^2 \in arc\left(a_i^2 b_i^2\right)$, we have

$$z_i^1 \sim_i x_i^1 \quad \text{and} \quad z_i^2 \sim_i x_i^2. \tag{14.5}$$

However, if $z_i^1 \in arc\left(a_i^1 x_i^1\right)$ and $z_i^2 \in arc\left(x_i^2 b_i^2\right)$, then z_i^1 and z_i^2 are not indifferent. In fact, in this case, we have

$$z_i^1 \succ_i z_i^2. \tag{14.6}$$

Hence, Eqs. (14.5) and (14.6) jointly imply that

$$z_i^1 \sim_i x_i^1, \quad x_i^1 \sim_i x_i^2, \quad \text{and} \quad x_i^2 \sim_i z_i^2 \nrightarrow z_i^1 \sim_i z_i^2.$$

That is, the indifference relation $\sim_i$ is not transitive.

In terms of the literature, the topics of nontransitive indifferences have been noticed and investigated by various authors. For example, such intransitivity can arise from perception difficulties, as noted by Luce (1956), or procedural decision-making, when similarities are compared or regrets are considered (e.g., Loomes & Sugden, 1982; Rubinstein, 1988), or time inconsistencies caused by relative time discounting (e.g., Ok & Masatlioglu, 2007; Roelofsma & Read, 2000).

One consumption $x_i \in X_i$ is said to be a satiation consumption of consumer i if there is not any other $y_i \in X_i$ such that consumer i prefers y_i to x_i. Evidently, if consumer i has incomparable consumptions, then he may very well have several incomparable satiation consumptions simultaneously.

In this research, preferences considered do not take the resale value of commodities into account. Each consumer is only interested in their personal use values. Because our convention on commodities are specific in terms of date or location or both, consumers' interests in certain commodities are date and/or location specific. Considering the seemingly never-ending human desires for better living, let us adopt the following axiom from Debreu (1959)).

Axiom 14.3 (Insatiability of preferences). For any chosen consumer, he does not have any satiation consumption.

Speaking differently, this axiom means that no matter what consumption $x_i \in X_i$ is concerned with, there is another consumption $y_i \in X_i$ such that $x_i \prec_i y_i$. That is, consumer i prefers y_i to x_i.

14.4 Set-Theoretical Structures and Representations of Preferences

As the title suggests, this section studies the structure of the preference set X_i. Specifically, this section consists of two subsections, the first of which looks at how the preference relation of individual consumptions can be elevated to the level of indifference classes. Thc second subsection generalizes the conventional concept of utility functions with real-number ranges to that of more general ranges of indicative elements.

14.4.1 Consumption Sets Partitioned by Preference Relations

This subsection studies the following question that when the consumption set X_i is partitioned into equivalence classes by the indifference relation $\sim_i$, how can the preference relation $\precsim_i$ be employed to order these equivalence classes of X_i?

Proposition 14.4 Assume the same as in Proposition 14.3. Then i's set X_i of consumption possibilities can be partitioned into indifference classes such that for any $x_i^1, x_i^2 \in X_i$, if $x_i^1 \prec_i x_i^2$, then that any $z_i^1 \in [x_i^1]$ and any $z_i^2 \in [x_i^2]$, $z_i^1 \prec_i z_i^2$.

Proof The possibility to partition X_i into equivalence classes follows from Proposition 14.3. The condition that $x_i^1 \prec_i x_i^2$ implies that $[x_i^1] \neq [x_i^2]$. Let $z_i^1 \in [x_i^1]$ and $z_i^2 \in [x_i^2]$ be arbitrary. Hence, the definition of the indifference relation $\sim_i$ implies that

$$z_i^1 \precsim_i x_i^1 \text{ and } x_i^2 \precsim_i z_i^2.$$

So, the transitivity of $\precsim_i$ and the condition that $x_i^1 \prec_i x_i^2$ jointly imply that $z_i^1 \prec_i z_i^2$.

Proposition 14.5 Assume the same as in Proposition 14.3. Then, if x_i^1 and $x_i^2 \in X_i$ are not comparable in terms of $\precsim_i$, then $[x_i^1] \cap [x_i^2] = \varnothing$; and for any $z_i^1 \in [x_i^1]$, $z_i^2 \in [x_i^2]$, z_i^1 and z_i^2 are also not comparable.

Proof We show $[x_i^1] \cap [x_i^2] = \varnothing$ by contradiction. Assume that there is at least one $z_i \in [x_i^1] \cap [x_i^2]$. Then $x_i^1 \sim_i z_i \sim_i x_i^2$. So, the transitivity of $\precsim_i$ implies that x_i^1 and x_i^2 are comparable. A contradiction. Hence, $[x_i^1] \cap [x_i^2] = \varnothing$.

For the second conclusion, we also argue for it by contradiction. Without loss of generality, assume that there are $z_i^1 \in [x_i^1]$ and $z_i^2 \in [x_i^2]$ such that $z_i^1 \precsim_i z_i^2$. Then the definition of the indifference relation $\sim_i$ implies that

$$x_i^1 \precsim_i z_i^1 \text{ and } z_i^2 \precsim_i x_i^2.$$

These inequalities, the assumption that $z_i^1 \precsim_i z_i^2$, and the transitivity of $\precsim_i$ jointly imply that $x_i^1 \precsim_i x_i^2$. This end contradicts the assumption that x_i^1 and x_i^2 are not comparable. Therefore, for any $z_i^1 \in [x_i^1]$ and $z_i^2 \in [x_i^2]$, z_i^1 and z_i^2 are also not comparable.

Propositions 14.3 and 14.4 collectively indicate that there is a subset $X_i^* \subseteq X_i$ such that for any x_i^1 and $x_i^2 \in X_i^*$, $x_i^1 \neq x_i^2$ implies that $[x_i^1] \neq [x_i^2]$ and $X_i = \cap_{x_i \in X_i^*} [x_i]$. This subset X_i^* is referred to as a set of (consumer i's) preference representations. Evidently, in general the existence of X_i^* is not unique. As a corollary of Propositions 14.3 and 14.4, we have

Proposition 14.6 If X_i^* ($\subseteq X_i$) is a set of i's preference representations, then $\precsim_i$ is a complete preorder on X_i, if and only if $\precsim_i$ is a complete preorder on X_i^*.

14.4.2 A Generalization of the Concept of Utility

Define a function $u_i : X_i \to X_i^*$ as follows: For any consumption $x_i \in X_i$,

$$u_i(x_i) = x_i^* \in X_i^*, \text{if } x_i \in [x_i^*].$$

We treat u_i as a utility function of consumer i; and Propositions 14.3 and 14.4 jointly imply that for any $x_i^1, x_i^2 \in X_i$, $x_i^1 \precsim_i x_i^2$ if and only if $u_i(x_i^1) \precsim_i u_i(x_i^2)$.

Because the existence of the set X_i^* of preference representations is not unique, in real-life applications, one can readily employ a convenient set of preferred commodities from different areas of life as basic marks of measurement for preferences. In other words, in terms of practical applications, a certain more practically indicative set U_i that is order-isomorphic to X_i^* can be used in the place of X_i^*, where U_i does not have to involve any real numbers at all. That is, this method of using such a

U_i to evaluate whether or not a particular consumption is preferred is more natural than that of using the conventional real-number valued functions of utilities.

On the other hand, the previous paragraph indicates that although the choice of X_i^* is generally not unique, the utility function u_i exists uniquely up to an order isomorphism. For example, if consumer i's preference $\precsim_i$ is a complete preorder, then one can easily use a subset of $\mathbb{R}$ to be the range of u_i such that u_i is an increasing function. That is, in this case, X_i^* can be replaced by a set of some real numbers; and u_i is seen as an increasing function from completely preordered X_i into the set $\mathbb{R}$ of real numbers.

Let $X_i' \subseteq X_i^*$ be a subset satisfying that any two consumptions $x_i^1, x_i^2 \in X_i'$ are comparable in terms of the preference relation $\precsim_i$. Then X_i' is known as a chain in X_i^*. A subset X_i' of X_i^* is referred to as a maximal chain, provided that for any $x_i \in X_i$, if x_i is comparable with each element in X_i', then $x_i \in X_i'$. For more details on ordered sets, please consult with Kuratowski and Mostowski (1976).

For a chosen maximal chain $X_i^{\max}$ in X_i^*, the u_i-preimage of the chain $X_i^{\max}$ is equal to

$$u_i^{-1}\left(X_i^{\max}\right) = \cup\left\{\left[x_i^*\right] : x_i^* \in X_i^{\max}\right\}.$$

Assume that for each $x_i' \in u_i^{-1}\left(X_i^{\max}\right)$, the following sets are closed in $u_i^{-1}\left(X_i^{\max}\right)$
:

$$\left\{x_i \in u_i^{-1}\left(X_i^{\max}\right) : x_i \precsim_i x_i'\right\} \quad \text{and} \quad \left\{x_i \in u_i^{-1}\left(X_i^{\max}\right) : x_i \succsim_i x_i'\right\}. \tag{14.7}$$

Then the well-known and classic conclusion (Debreu, 1959) on when a continuous real-number valued utility function exists can be generalized as follows.

Proposition 14.7 If the following hold true, then there is a continuous utility function $u_i^* : u_i^{-1}\left(X_i^{\max}\right) \to [a, b] \subset \mathbb{R}$, where a, b are two arbitrary real numbers such that $a < b$.

- Each infinity can be actually (not potentially) achieved.[1]
- Subset $u_i^{-1}\left(X_i^{\max}\right)$ is connected in $\mathbb{R}^\ell$.
- For each $x_i' \in u_i^{-1}\left(X_i^{\max}\right)$, the sets, as defined in Eq. (14.7), are closed in $u_i^{-1}\left(X_i^{\max}\right)$.

Proof In Debreu (Debreu, 1959, p. 56–59), the set X_i of consumer i's consumptions is assumed to be completely preordered with the preference relation $\precsim_i$. Hence, by identifying $u_i^{-1}\left(X_i^{\max}\right)$ with the set X_i in Debreu (1959, p. 56–59), the original argument for the existence of the desired utility function u_i^* will go through in its

[1]The concepts of both actual and potential infinities have been considered by various scholars throughout the history since at least the time of Aristotle. However, it is only a recent event that they are found to lead to contradictory outcomes. For relevant details, see Appendix 1 to Chap. 14.

entirety, except that both Steps 1 and 2 (Debreu, 1959, p. 57–58) cannot be successfully completed without the assumption that each infinity can be actually (not potentially) achieved.

In particular, Debreu's argument consists of four parts:

(a) There is a countable and dense subset D in $u_i^{-1}\left(X_i^{\max}\right)$, where the case that $X_i^{\max}$ is a singleton is ignored, and each point $x \in D \subset \mathbb{R}^\ell$ contains only rational-number components.
(b) An increasing function $u_i' : D \to [a, b]$ is defined, for any chosen real numbers a and b such that $a < b$.
(c) This function $u_i' : D \to [a, b]$ is extended to $u_i^* : u_i^{-1}\left(X_i^{\max}\right) \to [a, b]$.
(d) Shown is that u_i^* is continuous.

For our purpose, let us focus on the first two steps. According to the set theory accepted as true until 2008, Debreu's original argument is perfectly fine. However, according to Lin (2008), potential infinities and actual infinities are fundamental different concepts; and they can lead to and have indeed led to completely inconsistent outcomes (Forrest, 2013), while both the existence of D in Step (a) and the construction of $u_i' : D \to [a, b]$ in Step (b) mistakenly treated potential infinities as actual ones.

To understand this statement, we first look at the concept of infinities. It deals with two kinds of infinities—actual infinities and potential infinities (Lin, 2008). Specifically, each potential infinity means a present progressive tense or a forever, ongoing, and never-ending process; and every actual infinity represents a present or past perfect tense or a process that actually ends or had ended.

In Step (a) of Debreu's original proof, the underlying argument for the countability of D is based on that one can match *every* rational number with a unique natural number (Kuratowski & Mostowski, 1976). Such process of matching stands for a present progressive tense, which is forever ongoing—a potential infinity. However, to derive the needed conclusion, the set of rational numbers is countable, and this forever ongoing—a potential infinity—is forced to end so that what is imposed is the potential infinity = an actual infinity. According to Lin (2008) and Forrest (2013), this is a mistake and can lead to inconsistent conclusions.

In Step (b) of Debreu's original proof, if D contains either a least element x^α and/or a greatest element x^β, define $u_i'(x^\alpha) = a$ and $u_i'\left(x^\beta\right) = b$. (Note: The assumption that consumer i does not have any satiation consumption means that such a greatest element x^β cannot exist.) Next, order the other elements of D and all rational numbers in (a, b) as follows, since both sets are countable:

$$\left(x^1, x^2, \ldots, x^p, \ldots\right) \text{ and } \left(r^1, r^2, \ldots, r^q, \ldots\right). \tag{14.8}$$

Then, in an orderly fashion, define $u_i'(x^p)$, for each $p = 1, 2, 3, \ldots$, so that for every r^q, $q = 1, 2, 3, \ldots$, there is a x^p so that $u_i'(x^p) = r^q$. That is, the function u_i' is constructed in a forever ongoing process—a potential infinity. So, the eventual

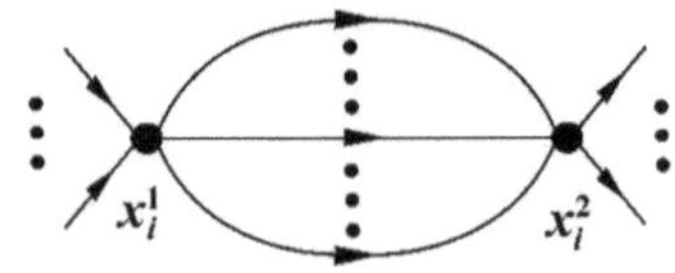

Fig. 14.3 The chain structure of consumption set

existence of this function u_i' can only be guaranteed under the assumption that this particular potential infinity is equal to an actual infinity.

In short, for Steps (a) and (b) of Debreu's original proof to hold true, we must assume that each infinity can be actually achieved.

All established propositions above lead to the chain structure of the consumption set X_i, as shown in Fig. 14.3. In particular, for two consumptions x_i^1 and $x_i^2 \in X_i$, satisfying $x_i^1 \precsim_I x_i^2$, there might be several chains that connect into x_i^1, going from x_i^1 to x_i^2, and leaving x_i^2. Even so, when each maximal chain is concerned with, Proposition 14.7 says that there is a continuous and increasing function from this chain into the set $\mathbb{R}$ of all real numbers.

In terms of the literature, Eilenberg (1941) considered cases for a continuous strict total order in connected and separable spaces. Wold (1943) listed a number of conditions under which a preference order possesses a real-number valued utility representation although he did not explicitly assume continuity. And, Debreu (1959) represents such a piece of work that has been seen as classical (Hervés-Beloso & Cruces, 2019). By using the same terms and symbolism as in Proposition 14.7, Monteiro's (1987) and Candeal et al.'s (1998) theorems for the existence of a continuous utility representation of a preference order can be accordingly generalized. All relevant details are omitted because in spirit, they are similar to those given in the proof of Proposition 14.7. On the other hand, in terms of utility representations of an incomplete preference relation, Proposition 14.7 represents a totally different conclusion than the ones in Ok (2002).

14.5 A Few Final Words

By employing the methodology of Euclidean spaces, this chapter makes important strides towards answering the questions posed in the introduction section earlier. First, several counterexamples on the analytical basis are constructed to demonstrate that:

- In real life, there is such a potential consumer that some of his consumption possibilities are simply not comparable with each other in terms of his preferences.
- In real life, a consumer's preferences are not generally transitive.
- Generally, a consumer's indifferent preferences in reality, as defined by incomparability, are not transitive.

Although these results have been confirmed by different authors in varied perspectives (for related references, see the discussions above), our confirmations are based purely on analytical analysis without making use of any auxiliary concepts. As is well-known in the research of paradoxes (Forrest, 2013, Chap. 11), when seemingly minor concepts are involved, unexpected outcomes can be produced. In other words, the literature includes various supports on how these results could be true in different settings; however, the specified scenarios in each case could not potentially help develop the desired results. In comparison, our counterexamples do not suffer from such potential issues so that the developed observations are analytically more reliable than those observed within any specified scenarios.

Second, instead of a real-number valued utility representation, there is indeed a set of preference representations for the preferences of a consumer that can be employed as the range of a utility function. Beyond that, the existence of such a set is unique up to an order isomorphism. The importance of this discovery is that when authors forced themselves to uncover real-number valued utility representations for preferences that are incomplete and nontransitive (e.g., Nishimura & Ok, 2016), the produced outcomes are quite remote from being intuitively clear and more difficult for even theorists to understand behaviorally. That is, such efforts, at least for the present time, loses their practical significance.

Third, although a consumer's satisfaction from consuming a good or service may not be generally measurable by the conventional concept of continuous utility functions (Estevez-Toranzo & Herves-Beloso, 1995), each maximal chain of transitively comparable consumptions is shown in this chapter to still enjoy a conventional utility representation.

What needs to be emphasized here is our focus on developing an economic theory that is practically applicable in terms of producing tangible economic benefits, instead of another repeat of the history of taking beauty for truth. That end is exactly what Paul Krugman commented in *The New York Times* (2009-09-02), as outlined below:

> The economic profession went astray because economists, as a group, mistook beauty, clad in impressive-looking mathematics, for truth ... As memories of the Depression faded, economists fell back in love with the old, idealized vision of an economy in which rational individuals interact in perfect markets ... Unfortunately, this romanticized and sanitized vision of the economy led most economists to ignore ... things that can go wrong. They turned a blind eye to the limitations of human rationality that often leads to bubbles and burst; to the problem of institutions that run amok; to the imperfection of markets ... that can cause the economy ... to undergo sudden, unpredictable crashes; and to the dangers created when regulators don't believe in regulation.

As for potential future research, one can readily compare what are derived in this chapter with the known existence and nonexistence theorems of utility representations (Candeal et al., 1998; Eilenberg, 1941; Estevez-Toranzo & Herves-Beloso, 1995; Monteiro, 1987; Herves-Beloso & Monteiro, 2010). In particular, these known theorems are derived on the assumption that preferences of consumptions are complete. So, that opens up the opportunity for one to consider how these theorems would look like when the preferences of consumptions under concern are not complete and not transitive by referencing to the recent works, such as Bosi and Herden (2012), Cettolin and Riedl (2019), Evren and Ok (2011), Nishimura and Ok (2016), and Ok (2002). Once again, the emphasis of our suggested future works needs to be placed on how the consequently derived results can be employed to produce tangible economic outcomes, instead of their theoretical beauties.

Appendix 1: Actual and Potential Infinities

Abstract This appendix discusses the concepts of actual and potential infinities and shows how they are different from each other. It firstly looks at an example that these concepts can and do lead to different answers, and secondly examines the impacts of assuming either that they are the same or that they are different. Thirdly, the appendix turns its attention to checking how modern mathematics unconsciously applies both of these two assumptions simultaneously depending on which one is needed to produce desired conclusions. For more detailed discussions, see Forrest (2013, 2021).

Keywords Infinity • Mathematical induction • Vase puzzle

The Vase Puzzle

By potential infinity, it means a present progressive tense or a forever, ongoing and never-ending process. And, by actual infinity, it stands for a present or past perfect tense or a process that actually ends or had ended. Now, let us examine the following vase puzzle (Lin, 1999) and see how these two concepts of infinity can lead to different consequences.

Consider a vase and pieces of paper. Assume that there are infinitely many of pieces of paper, each of which is labelled by one and only one natural number starting from 1, 2, 3, ... Let us now do the following step after step, assuming that the vase is initially empty:

Step 1: Place the pieces of paper with labels 1 to 10 into the vase and then take out the piece with label 1.

Step *n*: Place the pieces of paper with labels $10n$–9 through $10n$ into the vase and then take out the piece with label n, for any natural number n.

Now, the question is: when this process is completed, how many pieces of paper will be left in the vase?

Solution 1: Assume that the aforementioned process is ongoing and never-ending—a potential infinity. Then, right after step n, there are $f(n) = 9n$ pieces of paper left in the vase. Therefore, the statement "when this process is completed" means the limit state when $n \to \infty$ so that there will be $\lim_{n \to \infty} f(n) = \lim_{n \to \infty}(9n) = \infty$ pieces of paper left in the vase.

Solution 2: Assume that the aforementioned process is able to complete—an actual infinity. In this case, the statement "when this process is completed" literally means the completion of the aforementioned recursive process so that one can look backward at the completed process.

Now, the answer to the previous question is zero, because if not, let us pick one piece of paper out of the vase. According to the pre-described procedure, let the label of the paper be k, a natural number. However, that is impossible, because this kth piece of paper had been taken out of the vase at step k.

In short, to the previous question, potential infinity implies the answer ∞, while actual infinity leads to 0. This end implies that actual and potential infinities are not the same and do lead to different consequences. Therefore, actual infinity is not the same as potential infinity.

As shown by Lin (1999), the size of the vase and the total area of the pieces of paper can be any predetermined values. And, of course, in theoretical discussions, the terms "vase" and "pieces of paper" are symbolic and imaginary so that there is no need to think about size and area.

How Mathematical Induction Needs to be Correctly Stated

The vase puzzle above suggests that the concept of actual infinity $\neq$ as that of potential infinity or that the conclusion "the proposition $\Phi(n)$ holds true for all (or for every) natural number n" of mathematical induction, for details, see Sect. 10.2, should be limited to the use of "for every." In particular, the phrases "for all" and "for every" are different from each other with the former representing a finished process while the latter an ongoing and never-ending process. The previous section shows that quantitatively, these different phrases do lead to different answers.

The one-word adjustment from "for all" to the restrictive use of "for every" affects economics in particular and mathematics in general a great deal. It is because, for example, most constructive proofs of existence, such as the utility representation theorem in Debreu (1959), tend to be mathematical-induction based so that they need to be re-established. In particular, each such proof first demonstrates the possibility to construct an ongoing process—a potential infinity, and then claims that the process can be materialistically completed—an actual infinity.

What is more amazing is that in the development of mathematics, the assumption:

$$\text{the concept of actual infinity} \neq \text{as that of potential infinity}$$

and that

the concept of actual infinity = as that of potential infinity

are assumed simultaneously and applied conditionally, depending what result is desired and expected. For details on this end, see Forrest (2013).

Appendix 2: Complete Extensions of Consumption Preferences

Abstract As recently pointed out by different scholars that consumer's consumption preferences can only be assumed to satisfy reflexivity, this abstract, which is mainly based on Forrest et al. (to appear), examines whether or not a preference relation that is not necessarily complete and transitive can be extended to a complete binary relation that is not necessarily transitive. The affirmative conclusion obtained here is similar to Szpilrajn extension theorem for partial orders and Hansson theorem for preorders. As consequences of our conclusion, we show that the order dimension of each incomplete partial order or incomplete preference relation is equal to 2; and that each countable, incomplete and partially ordered set $(X, \succsim)$ is representable by a function $u : X \rightarrow \mathbb{R}^2$. All of these results majorly improve a series of conclusions derived in the recent past.

Keywords Multidimensionality • Order dimensions of posets • Physiological needs • Representable preference relation • Sensual extension • Suzumura-consistency

Introduction

The fact that a consumer's consumption preferences, in general, are neither a partial order nor a preorder has been well established from different angles and in various perspectives (e.g., Aumann, 1962; Birnbaum & Gutierrez, 2007; Bosi & Herden, 2012; Cettolin & Riedl, 2019; Dubra & Ok, 2002; Evren & Ok, 2011; Hansson, 1968; Mandler, 1999; Nishimura & Ok, 2016; Ok, 2002; Tversky, 1969). However, for the established consumer theory (Levin & Milgrom, 2004b; Mas-Collel et al., 1995; Miller, 2006) and choice theory (e.g., Glasser, 1999; Levin & Milgrom, 2004b), many important conclusions are developed on such preference relations that are assumed to be either partial orders or preorders. So, it is both theoretically and practically important to see how these conclusions would look like when the preference relation of concern is merely reflexive without transitivity and completeness. To help possibly accomplish this end, this appendix investigates how some of the fundamental results regarding partial orders or preorders can be established for preference relations that are reflexive without definitely satisfying the conditions of transitivity and completeness.

Specifically, this appendix looks at the question of whether or not a result similar to Szpilrajn extension theorem for partial orders and Hansson extension theorem for preorders can also hold true for preference relations without transitivity and completeness. Based on our affirmative answer to this question, we are able to show, among others, that (1) each such preference relation is equal to the intersection of all sensually completed consumption preferences; (2) each such relation $\succsim$ has two sensually completed extensions L_1 and L_2 so that for each pair of $\succsim$-incomparable $x, y \in X$, either (xL_1y and yL_2x) or (yL_1x and xL_2y), but not both, holds true; and (3) the order dimension of every such relation (and that of each incomplete partial order) is equal to 2. And each of the developed results in this appendix greatly improves corresponding results established in the past by different authors.

The rest of the appendix is organized as follows. Section "Terminology Related to Consumption Preferences" familiars the reader with the basic terminology used in the rest of this presentation. Section "Completed Extensions of Consumption Preference" derives the result that each preference relation can be completely extended so that originally incomparable consumptions can now be compared. Section "A Preference Relation's Order Dimension" looks at the order dimension of preference relations. Section "A Partial Order's Linear Extensions" pays a revisit to linear extensions of partial orders. Then, this appendix concludes in section "A Few Final Words".

Terminology Related to Consumption Preferences

Let X be the set of the focal consumer's possible consumptions. As in Debreu (1959), let X contain all possible consumptions of the consumer in his entire lifetime without discounting the future. So, X will be seen as an infinite set. For $x, y \in X$, if the consumer can choose only one of them, then in real life he would likely choose the one that is more preferred than the other. In such a case, x, y are said to be comparable consumptions in terms of the consumer's preferences.

Axiom 14.4 (Comparability). If consumptions $x, y \in X$ are comparable in terms of the consumption preferences of a consumer, then one and only one of the following alternatives holds true:

1. x is preferred to y;
2. x is indifferent of y;
3. y is preferred to x.

Let $\succ$ denote the focal consumer's preference relation (or simply preference) of the consumptions in X. Then, $\succ$ is a binary relation defined on X. That is, $\succ$ is a subset of $X \times X$. If $(x, y) \in X \times X$ belongs to $\succ$, we use $x \succ y$ to mean that x is preferred to y, and $x \succsim y$ to mean that x is at least as preferred as to y. Two possible consumptions $x, y \in X$ are $\succsim$-comparable, if either x $\succsim$ y or y $\succsim$ x holds; otherwise x and y are said to be $\succsim$-incomparable. Such a $\succsim$ is said to be complete binary relation if any possible consumptions x and y in X are $\succsim$-comparable, otherwise incomplete. The strict or asymmetric part of the binary relation $\succsim$ is denoted as $\succ$, representing a relation on X defined as $x \succ y$ iff $x \succsim y$ and $\neg(y \succsim x)$, for $x, y \in X$. The symmetric part of the relation $\succsim$ represents the relationship of indifferences, denoted as $\sim$, and is defined as follows: for $x, y \in X$, $x \sim y$ iff $x \succsim y$ and $y \succsim x$. Symbolically, $\sim \equiv \succsim \setminus \succ$. In other words, $x \sim y$ means that consumptions x and y are indifferent in terms of the consumer's consumption preferences.

This preference relation $\succsim$ on X is said to be a preorder (or a quasiorder), provided that $\succsim$ is reflexive and transitive; that is, for any consumptions $x, y, z \in X$, $x \succsim x$ and $(x \succsim y) \wedge (y \succsim z) \rightarrow (x \succsim z)$. It is a partial order, provided that other than reflexivity and transitivity, $\succsim$ also satisfies antisymmetry; that is, for any $x, y \in X$, $x \succsim y$ and $y \succsim x$ imply $x = y$. It is a linear order, provided that $\succsim$ is a complete partial order; that is, $\succsim$ is a partial order and for any $x, y \in X$, x, y are $\succsim$-comparable.

With these terms in place, Axiom 14.4 implies that the focal consumer's preference of consumptions can be at most a preorder, as the situation in real life. First, because of the existence of indifferent consumptions, antisymmetry required for a partial order cannot hold for consumption preferences in real life. As for transitivity, Aumann (1962) and Mandler (1999) find that due to wide range appearances of indecisiveness, consumer preferences tend to be intransitive, while Tversky (1969) reports that consumer preferences don't generally satisfy the condition of transitivity. And, by using a new statistical technique and by revisiting the same gambles Tversky studied earlier, Birnbaum and Gutierrez (2007) conclude that there are indeed individual consumers who repeat intransitive preference patterns. So, in the rest of this appendix, consumption preferences are not assumed to be preorders; and according to Axiom 14.4, without being particularly specified, each consumption preference is only assumed to be reflective. That is, when a binary relation R on a set X is said to be a consumption preference (or simply preference), it means that R is reflexive. For related, but dissimilar works, see, for example, Nishimura and Ok (2016) and references found there.

Because each individual consumer is a physiological being and each business consumer stands for a form of life (Lin & Forrest, 2011), the person's or firm's needs for basic survival and for better living conditions have to be multi-dimensional. That is, possible consumptions of any consumer, be it an individual or a firm, cannot be assumed to be completely comparable in terms of his preferences, as so commonly done in studies of economics (e.g., Debreu, 1959; Levin & Milgrom, 2004b; Mas-Collel et al., 1995). Speaking differently, when faced with two commodities from two different dimensions of survival, such as the dimension of shelter, that of foods, that of drinks, that of medicine, etc., no matter who is concerned with, he, as a consumer, cannot really say which commodity is preferred to the other. In terms of literature, several scholars had also noticed this issue of incompleteness in consumption preferences. For example, Dubra and Ok (2002) introduce a risky-choice model in which an individual naturally possesses an incomplete preference relation. Ok (2002), Nishimura and Ok (2016), and Bosi and Herden (2012) consider the problem of how to represent an incomplete preference relation by means of a collection of real-number valued functions. Based on such a quickly expending literature, Alonso et al. (2010) present a web-based consensus support system that involves decisions makers with incomplete preference relations; Meng and Chen (2015) develop a group-decision-making method to cope with incomplete preference information; and Cettolin and Riedl (2019) conduct experiments to test whether a preference is either complete or incomplete.

In the rest of this appendix, without any particular emphasis, each preference relation is assumed to be merely reflexive without necessarily satisfying transitivity and completeness.

Completed Extensions of Consumption Preference

Let R and S be two binary relations on a set X, satisfying reflexivity. The former relation R is said to be contained in the latter relation S, if $R \subset S$. That is, for any $x, y \in X$, xRy implies xSy, while there are $a, b \in X$ such that aSb and $\neg(aRb)$. In this case, S is seen as an extension of R. Corresponding to Szpilrajn extension theorem for partial orders (Szpilrajn, 1930) and Hansson extension theorem for preorders (Hansson, 1968), one would naturally inquire the possibility to extend any given preference relation $\succsim$. Indeed, in pure symbolic terms, the answer to this inquiry is YES, because $\succsim$ can be trivially extended to $\succsim^*$ by treating all $\succsim$-incomparable pairs of possible consumptions as indifferent in $\succsim^*$. That is, $\succsim^* = \succsim \cup \{(x, y) \in X^2 : \neg\, x \succsim y \text{ and } \neg\, y \succsim x\}$.

The reason why we say that $\succsim^*$ exists in pure symbolic terms is because $\succsim$ is assumed to be a preference relation on the set X of all possible consumptions of our focal consumer. That is, other than being a reflexive binary relation on an abstract set $\succsim$ also embodies other meanings of life, such as the multidimensionality of a life's physiological needs. In particular, when x, y are two possible consumptions in X and incomparable in terms of the preference $\succsim$, it means that the focal consumer can in some way consume either x or y, while the incomparability between x and y indirectly implies that these consumptions potentially come from different physiological dimensions so that they are both needed for survival. Therefore, to make our established results practically useful instead of some additional symbolic statements irrelevant to real life, such possible consumptions x and y cannot be and should not be simply treated as indifferent. Instead, they are different, very different from each other. However, they are indispensable for the survival and livelihood of the focal consumer. Due to this reason, any extension of the preference relation $\succsim$ that makes a pair of originally incomparable consumptions indifferent, such as the previous extension $\succsim^*$, will be referred to as a non-sensual extension and denoted as $\succsim^{nonsense}$. Therefore, the natural inquiry about the possibility to extend a preference relation becomes that of finding a sensual extension, denoted as $\succsim^{sense}$, in terms of the physiological needs of a life form.

Theorem 14.1 Assume the Axiom of Choice and that each infinity can be actually (not potentially) achieved. Let $\succsim$ be the preference relation on the set X of all possible consumptions of the focal consumer. Then $\succsim$ can be extended to a sensual binary relation $\succsim^{\text{sense}}$ such that for any $x, y \in X$, x and y are $\succsim^{\text{sense}}$-comparable.

Although the proof of this result, which is given in the appendix, is very technical, the idea underneath the argument is quite straightforward. First, by using the axiom of choice, well order X into $\{x^\alpha : \alpha \in I\}$, where I is the set of ordinal numbers in $|X|$—the cardinality of X^2, as an index set, so that any nonempty subset of X has a unique element with the least index α. Define a subset N^0 of X by

$$N^0 = \{x \in X : \exists y \in X\, [\neg(x \succsim y) \wedge \neg(y \succsim x)]\}. \tag{14.9}$$

If x^{β_0} is the element in N^0 with the least index β_0, then we extend the preference relation $\succsim$ to

$$\succsim^0 = \succsim \cup \{(x^{\beta_0}, y) : y \in X\, [\neg(x^{\beta_0} \succsim y) \wedge \neg(y \succsim x^{\beta_0})]\},$$

where $(x^{\beta_0}, y) \in \succsim^0$ mean that x^{β_0} is preferred over y in terms of the extended preference $\succsim^0$.

Next, repeat this process by looking at

$$N^1 = N^0 - \{x^{\beta_0}\}$$

and extend $\succsim^0$ to $\succsim^1 = \succsim^0 \cup \{(x^{\beta_1}, y) : y \in X\, [\neg(x^{\beta_1} \succsim y) \wedge \neg(y \succsim x^{\beta_1})]\}$, where x^{β_1} is the element in N^1 with the least index β_1 and $(x^{\beta_1}, y) \in \succsim^1$ mean that x^{β_1} is preferred over y in terms of the extended preference $\succsim^1$. When this process is completed, which is guaranteed by the transfinite induction applied on $\alpha \in I$ and the assumption that each infinity can be actually (not potentially) achieved, by checking through all the elements in $X = \{x^\alpha : \alpha \in I\}$, the desired sensual extension of $\succsim$ is then given by $\succsim^* = \succsim \cup \succsim^0 \cup \succsim^1 \cup \ldots$ In the following, let dive into the details of the proof.

Proof By using the axiom of choice, let us well order X as follows:

$$x^0, x^1, x^2, \ldots, x^\alpha, \ldots \tag{14.10}$$

where α is an ordinal-number index from the index set $I = |X|$, so that each nonempty subset $Y \subseteq X$ contains such an element that its ordinal index, as it appears in the list in Eq. (14.10), is the smallest compared to those of other elements in Y.

In the rest of this argument, we apply transfinite induction on $\alpha \in I$.

[2]The symbol $|X|$ stands for the cardinality of set X. In axiomatic set theory (Kunen, 1980), each ordinal number α is equal to the set of all ordinals $< \alpha$. For instance, $1 = \{0\}$, $2 = \{0, 1\}$, ..., $\alpha = \{\rho : \rho\ (<\alpha)$ is an ordinal number$\}$. Within this framework, $|X|$ is simply the least element in $\{\rho : \rho$ is an ordinal number and equipollent to $X\}$. That is why we can employ $|X|$ as an index set.

Step 1. Check α values from 0, 1, ..., until such least index β_0 in Eq. (14.10) that there is $y = x^{\beta} \in X$ satisfying that x^{β_0} and y are $\precsim$-incomparable and $\beta_0 < \beta$. Let us then sensually extend $\precsim$ to $\precsim^0$ by adding all these $\precsim$-incomparable pairs (x^{β_0}, y). Symbolically, we have

$$\precsim^0 = \precsim \cup \{(x^{\beta_0}, y) : y \in X \text{ and} \neg(x^{\beta_0} \precsim y) \wedge \neg(y \precsim x^{\beta_0})\}.$$

Step 2. Continue checking α, starting from $\beta_0 + 1$, until we find consumption x^{β_1} with the least index $\beta_1 > \beta_0$ in Eq. (14.10) so that there is $y = x^{\beta} \in X$ such that x^{β_1} and y are $\precsim^0$-incomparable and $\beta_1 < \beta$. We now sensually extend $\precsim^0$ to $\precsim^1$ by adding all such $\precsim^0$-incomparable pairs (x^{β_1}, y). Symbolically, we have

$$\precsim^1 = \precsim^0 \cup \{(x^{\beta_1}, y) : y \in X \text{ and} \neg(x^{\beta_1} \precsim y) \wedge \neg(y \precsim x^{\beta_1})\}.$$

Step $\kappa \in I$. Assume that for any ordinal $\tau < \kappa$, three sequences $\{\beta_\rho : \rho \in I_\tau\}$, $\{x^{\beta_\rho} : \rho \in I_\tau\}$ and $\{\precsim^\rho : \rho \in I_\tau\}$ have been constructed, for some ordinal $I_\tau \subset \kappa$, so that for any $\rho, \sigma \in I_\tau$, $\rho < \sigma$ implies $\beta_\rho < \beta_\sigma$, the index of x^{β_σ} is the least satisfying $\beta_\sigma > \beta_\rho$ in Eq. (14.10) so that there is $y = x^{\beta} \in X$ such that x^{β_σ} and y are $\precsim^\rho$-incomparable and $\beta_\sigma < \beta$, and

$$\precsim^\sigma = \bigcup_{\varsigma < \sigma} \precsim^\varsigma \cup \{(x^{\beta_\sigma}, y) : y \in X \quad \text{and} \quad \neg(x^{\beta_\sigma} \precsim y) \wedge \neg(y \precsim x^{\beta_\sigma})\}.$$

Find $x^{\beta_{I_\tau+1}}$ with the least index $\beta_{I_\tau+1} > \beta_\tau$, if such a consumption $x^{\beta_{I_\tau+1}}$ still exists, for any $\tau < \kappa$, in Eq. (14.10) so that there is $y = x^{\beta} \in X$ such that $x^{\beta_{I_\tau+1}}$ and y are $\precsim^\tau$-incomparable and $\beta_{I_\tau+1} < \beta$. Let us sensually extend $\{\precsim^\tau : \tau \in I_\tau\}$ to $\precsim^{I_\tau+1}$, where

$$\precsim^{I_\tau+1} = \bigcup_{\tau \in I_\tau+1} \precsim^\tau \cup \{(x^{\beta_{I_\tau+1}}, y) : y \in X \quad \text{and} \quad \neg(x^{\beta_{I_\tau+1}} \precsim y) \wedge \neg(y \precsim x^{\beta_{I_\tau+1}})\}.$$

If the aforementioned consumption $x^{\beta_{I_\tau+1}}$ no longer exists, then the desired sensual extension of $\precsim$ is simply given by $\precsim^* = \bigcup_{\tau \in I_\tau} \precsim^\tau$.

By using transfinite induction, this constructive process can be completed by checking through all α in I. Let I^* denote the index set $\{\beta_0, \beta_1, \ldots, \beta_\kappa, \ldots\}$, then the desired sensual extension of the preference relation $\precsim$ is equal to

$$\precsim^* = \bigcup_{\kappa \in I^*} \precsim^\kappa. \tag{14.11}$$

The consumption set X can be either finite or infinite (for the most likely case of an infinite X, see discussion given earlier and Debreu, 1959). If X is infinite, the construction of $\precsim^*$ in general involves an infinite process. That is when the assumption that each infinity can be actually (not potentially) achieved is needed to successfully exhaust the list in Eq. (14.10) of the consumptions in X and to complete the construction of $\succsim^*$.

Due to the reason that a preference relation considered in this appendix does not require transitivity, the so-called Suzumura-consistency (Suzumura, 1976) is not needed for Theorem 14.1 to hold true. Here, a binary relation $\succsim$ is Suzumura-consistent if there are no such consumption choices x_i, $i = 0, 1, 2, \ldots, n - 1$, for some natural number n, such that $x_i \succsim x_{i+1}$, for $i = 0, 1, \ldots$, mod (n), and $\neg x_{j+1} \succsim x_j$, for some $j = 0, 1, \ldots$, mod (n). And without causing confusion, in the rest of this appendix, it is always assumed that that each infinity can be actually (not potentially) achieved.

A Preference Relation's Order Dimension

Related to Theorem 14.1, Dushnik and Miller (1941) prove that any strict partial order is the intersection of strict linear orders; and Donaldson and Weymark (1998) confirm that each preorder is equal to the intersection of complete preorders. Accordingly, in terms of consumption preferences, we have the following result, where each binary relation $\succsim^+$, which sensually extends the consumption preference $\succsim$ so that for any $x, y \in X$, x and y are $\succsim^+$-comparable, is referred to as a sensually completed consumption preference or sensually completed extension.

Theorem 14.2 The preference relation $\succsim$ defined on the consumption set X of the focal consumer is equal to the intersection of all sensually completed consumption preferences of $\succsim$.

Proof Let $\mathcal{L}(X, \succsim)$ be the set of all sensually completed extensions of $\succsim$. Then, Theorem 14.1 implies that for the focal consumer, $\mathcal{L}(X, \succsim) \neq \emptyset$. Now, it suffices to show

$$\succsim = \bigcap_{R \in \mathcal{L}(X, \succsim)} R. \tag{14.12}$$

Let $\succsim^\dagger$ denote the right-hand side of Eq. (14.12). Then, the definition $R \in \mathcal{L}(X, \succsim)$ indicates that $\succsim \subseteq \succsim^\dagger$. As for the opposite direction $\succsim \supseteq \succsim^\dagger$, let $\succsim^\# \in \mathcal{L}(X, \succsim)$ be defined as follows:

$$\succsim^\# = \succsim \cup \{(x, y) \in X \times X : (y, x) \in (\succsim^* - \succsim)\}, \tag{14.13}$$

where $\succsim^*$ is the sensually completed consumption preference constructed in the proof of Theorem 14.1. Hence, for any $x, y \in X$, if x and y are $\succsim$-incomparable, it must be that either $x \succsim^* y$ or $x \succsim^\# y$, but not both. That is, x and y are $(\succsim^* \cap \succsim^\#)$-incomparable. So, $\succsim^* \cap \succsim^\# \supseteq \succsim^\dagger$ implies that x and y are $\succsim^\dagger$- incomparable. This concludes the proof of $\succsim \supseteq \succsim^\dagger$.

Theorem 14.3 For the focal consumer's preference relation $\precsim$ on the set X of all possible consumptions, there are two sensually completed extensions L_1 and L_2 such that for each pair $x, y \in X$ of $\precsim$-incomparable consumptions, one and only one of the following statements holds true:

- xL_1y and yL_2x;
- yL_1x and xL_2y.

Proof The conclusion follows for $L_1 = \precsim^*$ in Eq. (14.11) and $L_2 = \precsim^\#$ in Eq. (14.13).

By borrowing the concept of order dimensions of posets—partially ordered sets (Dushnik & Miller, 1941), let us similarly define the order dimension of a preference relation $\precsim$ defined on a set X of possible consumptions, denoted dim(X, $\precsim$), as the minimum number of sensually completed extensions of $\precsim$ so that their intersection is equal to $\precsim$, if this number is finite, and ∞, otherwise. Symbolically, if dim(X, $\precsim$) $\in \mathcal{N}$ (= the set of all natural numbers), then

$$\dim(X, \precsim) = \min\left\{ k \in \mathbb{N} : R_i \in \mathcal{L}(X, \precsim), \quad i = 1, \ldots, k, \quad \text{and} \quad \precsim = \bigcap_{i=1}^{k} R_i \right\}.$$

Corollary 14.1 For each preference relation $\precsim$ on a set X of all consumptions possible for the focal consumer, dim(X, $\precsim$) = 2.

Proof This result follows readily from Theorem A2-14.3, where $\precsim = \precsim^* \cap \precsim^\#$.

A Partial Order's Linear Extensions

By slightly modifying the proof of Theorem 14.1, the following result can be shown.

Theorem 14.4 Let $\precsim$ be an incomplete partial order defined on a nonempty set X. Then, $\precsim$ can be extended to two linear orders $\precsim^*$ and $\precsim^\dagger$ such that for any pair of $\precsim$-incomparable elements a and b in X, either $(a\precsim^* b) \wedge (b\precsim^\dagger a)$ or $(b\precsim^* a) \wedge (a\precsim^\dagger b)$, but not both, holds true.

The idea behind the argument for Theorem 14.4 is similar to that of the proof of Theorem 14.1. In particular, after well ordering X into $\{x^\alpha : \alpha \in I\}$ with $I = |X|$, let x^{β_0} and x^{γ_0} be the elements from N^0, as defined in Eq. (14.9), with the least and the second least indexes β_0 and γ_0. Then, we extend $\precsim$ into two partial orders R^0 and S^0 by, respectively, adding $\left(x^{\beta_0}, x^{\gamma_0}\right)$ and $(x^{\gamma_0}, x^{\beta_0})$, and then taking their individual transitive closures.

Next, repeat this process by singling out x^{β_1} and x^{γ_1} from N^1 the least and the second least indexes β_1 and γ_1 from $N^1 = N^0 - \left\{x^{\beta_0}, x^{\gamma_0}\right\}$. Then, extend R^0 and S^0 to R^1 and S^1 by, respectively, adding $\left(x^{\beta_1}, x^{\gamma_1}\right)$ and $(x^{\gamma_1}, x^{\beta_1})$, and then taking their individual transitive closures. By applying the transfinite induction on $\alpha \in I$, this process can be completed; and so, the desired linear extensions $\succsim^*$ and $\succsim^\dagger$ of $\succsim$ can be produced as $\succsim^* = \cup R^\varsigma$ and $\succsim^\dagger = \cup S^\varsigma$. Let us now check out the technical details of the proof.

Proof Similar to Eq. (14.10), we well order X as follows:

$$x^0, x^1, x^2, \ldots, x^\alpha, \ldots \tag{14.14}$$

where $\alpha \in I = |X|$ is an ordinal-number index from the index set I. Next, we apply transfinite induction on $\alpha \in I$.

Step 1. Check α values from 0, 1, …, until such least index β_0 in Eq. (14.14) that there is $y = x^{\gamma_0} \in X$ with the least index $\gamma_0 > \beta_0$ so that x^{β_0} and y are $\succsim$-incomparable. Let us then extend $\succsim$ into R^0 and S^0, respectively, by adding this $\succsim$-incomparable pair $\left(x^{\beta_0}, y\right)$ and then taking transitive closure and by adding pair $\left(y, x^{\beta_0}\right)$ and then taking transitive closure. Symbolically, R^0 and S^0 are given as follows (Szpilrajn, 1930):

$$R^0 = \succsim \cup \left\{\left(x^{\beta_0}, x^{\gamma_0}\right)\right\} \cup \left\{(p, q) \in X^2 : p \succsim x^{\beta_0} \wedge x^{\gamma_0} \succsim q\right\}$$

and

$$S^0 = \succsim \cup \left\{\left(x^{\gamma_0}, x^{\beta_0}\right)\right\} \cup \left\{(q, p) \in X^2 : q \succsim x^{\gamma_0} \wedge x^{\beta_0} \succsim p\right\}$$

so that both $R^0$and S^0 are individually partial orders, $R^0 \cap S^0 = \succsim$ and x^{β_0} and x^{γ_0} are both R^0- and S^0-comparable.

Step $\kappa < |X|$. Assume that for any ordinal $\tau < \kappa$, four sequences $\left\{x^{\beta_\rho} : \rho \in I_\tau\right\}$, $\left\{x^{\gamma_\rho} : \rho \in I_\tau\right\}$, $\{R^\rho : \rho \in I_\tau\}$ and $\{S^\rho : \rho \in I_\tau\}$ have been constructed, for some ordinal $I_\tau \subset \kappa$, so that for any $\rho, \sigma \in I_\tau$,

- $\beta_\rho < \gamma_\rho$,
- $\rho < \sigma$ implies $\beta_\rho < \beta_\sigma$ and $\gamma_\rho < \gamma_\sigma$,
- the index of x^{β_σ} is the least satisfying $\beta_\sigma > \beta_\rho$ in Eq. (14.14) so that there is $y = x^{\gamma_\sigma} \in X$ with the least index such that $\gamma_\sigma > \gamma_\rho$ and x^{β_σ} and y are R^ρ- and S^ρ-incomparable, for $\rho < \sigma$, and

$$R^\sigma = \bigcup_{\varsigma < \sigma} R^\varsigma \cup \left\{\left(x^{\beta_\sigma}, x^{\gamma_\sigma}\right)\right\} \cup \left\{(p, q) \in X^2 : p \succsim x^{\beta_\sigma} \wedge x^{\gamma_\sigma} \succsim q\right\}.$$

and

$$S^\sigma = \bigcup_{\varsigma < \sigma} S^\varsigma \cup \left\{\left(x^{\gamma_\sigma}, x^{\beta_\sigma}\right)\right\} \cup \left\{(q, p) \in X^2 : q \succsim x^{\gamma_\sigma} \wedge x^{\beta_\sigma} \succsim q\right\}$$

satisfying that both R^{σ} and S^{σ} are partial orders, $R^{\sigma} \cap S^{\sigma} = \succsim$ and x^{β_σ} and x^{γ_σ} are both R^{σ}- and S^{σ}-comparable.

Find $x^{\beta_{I_\tau+1}}$ with the least index $\beta_{I_\tau+1} > \beta_\tau$, if such a consumption $x^{\beta_{I_\tau+1}}$ still exists, for each $\tau < I_\tau + 1$, in Eq. (14.14) so that there is $y = x^{\gamma_{I_\tau+1}} \in X$ with the least index $\gamma_{I_\tau+1}$ such that $x^{\beta_{I_\tau+1}}$ and y are R^{τ}- and S^{τ}-incomparable and $\beta_{I_\tau+1} < \gamma_{I_\tau+1}$. Let us extend $\cup\{R^{\tau} : \tau \in I_\tau\}$ and $\cup\{S^{\tau} : \tau \in I_\tau\}$ to $R^{I_\tau+1}$ and $S^{I_\tau+1}$, where

$$R^{I_\tau+1} = \underset{\tau \in I_\tau}{\cup} R^{\tau} \cup \left\{ \left(x^{\beta_{I_\tau+1}}, x^{\gamma_{I_\tau+1}} \right) \right\} \cup \left\{ (p,q) \in X^2 : p \succsim x^{\beta_{I_\tau+1}} \wedge x^{\gamma_{I_\tau+1}} \succsim q \right\}. \quad (14.15)$$

and

$$S^{I_\tau+1} = \underset{\tau \in I_\tau}{\cup} S^{\tau} \cup \left\{ \left(x^{\gamma_{I_\tau+1}}, x^{\beta_{I_\tau+1}} \right) \right\} \cup \left\{ (q,p) \in X^2 : q \succsim x^{\gamma_{I_\tau+1}} \wedge x^{\beta_{I_\tau+1}} \succsim p \right\} \quad (14.16)$$

where the third parts of the union expressions in Eqs. (14.15) and (14.16) represent, respectively, the transitive closures. So, from Szpilrajn (1930), it follows that $R^{I_\tau+1}$ and $S^{I_\tau+1}$ are partial orders. And the constructions given above indicate that $R^{I_\tau+1} \cap S^{I_\tau+1} = \succsim$ and $x^{\beta_{I_\tau+1}}$ and $x^{\gamma_{I_\tau+1}}$ are both R^{κ}- and S^{κ}-comparable.

If the aforementioned consumption $x^{\beta_{I_\tau+1}}$ no longer exists in the list in Eq. (14.14), then the desired extensions of $\succsim$ are simply given by $\succsim^* = R^* = \bigcup_{\tau \in I_\tau} R^{\tau}$ and $\succsim^{\dagger} = S^* = \bigcup_{\tau \in I_\tau} S^{\tau}$.

By using transfinite induction, this constructive process can be completed by checking through all α in I or all the listed elements in Eq. (14.14) for least indexed incomparable consumptions $x^{\beta_{I_\tau+1}}$ and $x^{\gamma_{I_\tau+1}}$. Let I^* denote the index set of $\{\beta_0, \beta_1, \ldots, \beta_\kappa, \ldots\}$ or that of $\{\gamma_0, \gamma_1, \ldots, \gamma_\kappa, \ldots\}$, then the desired linear extensions $\succsim^*$ and $\succsim^{\dagger}$ of the partial order $\succsim$ are equal to R^* and S^*, respectively, where

$$R^* = \underset{\kappa \in I^*}{\cup} R^{\kappa} \quad \text{and} \quad S^* = \underset{\kappa \in J^*}{\cup} S^{\kappa} \quad (14.17)$$

such that both R^* and S^* are linear orders, $R^* \cap S^* = \succsim$ and every $\succsim$-incomparable pair x and $y \in X$ are both R^*- and S^*-comparable.

A related result of Szpilrajn (1930) states that for every partial order $\succsim$ on a set S, if a and b are two $\succsim$-incomparable elements of S, there then exist two extensions L_1 and L_2 such that $a\ L_1 b$ and $b\ L_2 a$. In comparison, these extensions L_1 and L_2 are generally a- and b-dependent, while the extensions R^* and S^* in Theorem 14.4 exist for each given partial order.

A partial order $\succsim$, defined on a nonempty set X, is said to be a representable partial order (Ok, 2002), if there are $n \in \mathbb{N}$ (= the set of all natural numbers) and $u : X \to \mathbb{R}^n$, where $\mathbb{R}$ is the set of all real numbers, such that

$$x \succsim y \quad \text{iff} \quad u(x) \geqq u(y), \quad \text{for any} \quad x, y \in X. \quad (14.18)$$

To emphasize the n-dimensional Euclidean space $\mathbb{R}^n$, we will say that $\succsim$ is an n-dimensional representable partial order. So, as a consequence of Theorem 14.4, we have the following.

Theorem 14.5 Let $\succsim$ be an incomplete partial order defined on a nonempty set X. If X is countable, then $\succsim$ is 2-dimensional representable.

Proof From Theorem 14.4 or Eq. (14.17), it follows that $\succsim$ has two linear extensions $\succsim^*$ and $\succsim^\dagger$ such that $\succsim = \succsim^* \cap \succsim^\dagger$. Because both $(X, \succsim^*)$ and $(X, \succsim^\dagger)$ are countable and linearly ordered sets, there are numerical representations $u_i : X \to \mathbb{R}$ such that for any $x, y \in X$, $x \succsim y$ iff $u_i(x) \succsim u_i(y)$, for $i = *, \dagger$. Therefore, $u = (u_*, u_\dagger) : X \to \mathbb{R}^2$ is a 2-dimensional representation of $(X, \succsim)$.

This theorem generalizes a conclusion established by Ok (2002), where Ok proves that if X is countable, $\succsim$ is a partial order on X and $\dim(X, \succsim) < \infty$, then $\succsim$ is n-dimensional representable, for some $n \in \mathcal{N}$. In comparison, Theorem 14.5 avoids the condition of $\dim(X, \succsim) < \infty$, while the uncertain $n \in \mathcal{N}$ is specified to be 2.

Because Theorem 14.5 deals with the representation of binary relations, this is a good place for us to quickly survey some of the excellent works to round up our presentation here. Evidently, due to the lack of transitivity, a preference relation is generally neither representable nor multi-utility representable, as, respectively, noted by Ok (2002), Evren and Ok (2011), and Bosi and Herden (2012). As for the question of how to represent a general preference relation that is incomplete and nontransitive, Nishimura and Ok (2016) provide an excellent solution.

A Few Final Words

In this appendix, we examine whether or not a preference relation that is possibly incomplete and nontransitive can be extended to a sensually complete and possibly nontransitive binary relation, similar to the case of the extension theorem for partial orders (Szpilrajn, 1930) and that for preorders (Hansson, 1968).

After affirmatively answered this question, we strengthen a result developed by Szpilrajn (1930) greatly through showing that the order dimension of each incomplete partial order and each preference relation is equal to 2. And then, a result by Ok (2002) is refined to that each countable, incomplete and partially ordered set $(X, \succsim)$ is representable by a function $u : X \to \mathbb{R}^2$.

Beyond what are mentioned above, this appendix establishes the conclusion that each preference relation is equal to the intersection of all sensually completed preference extensions. That generalizes the result of Dushnik and Miller (1941) for partial orders and that of Donaldson and Weymark (1998) for preorders.

The key for us to successfully develop our conclusions with technical arguments lies on the employment of well-ordering of any nonempty set, while the previous works used different techniques, such as the Zorn's lemma. Although these techniques are different, they are all equivalent to the Axiom of Choice. Although this axiom is employed indirectly and differently by each of these involved authors, our application enables us to derive stronger results.

References

Alonso, S., Herrera-Viedma, E., Chiclana, F., & Herrera, F. (2010). A web-based consensus support system for group decision making problems and incomplete preferences. *Information Sciences, 180*(23), 4477–4495.

Aumann, R. (1962). Utility theory without the completeness axiom. *Econometrica, 30*, 445–462.

Birnbaum, M. H., & Gutierrez, R. J. (2007). Testing for intransitivity of preferences predicted by a lexicographic semi-order. *Organizational Behavior and Human Decision Processes, 104*, 96–112. https://doi.org/10.1016/j.obhdp.2007.02.001

Blanchflower, D. G., Landeghem, B. V., & Oswald, A. J. (2009). Imitative obesity and relative utility. *Journal of the European Economic Association, 7*(2–3), 528–538.

Bosi, G., & Herden, G. (2012). Continuous multi-utility representations of preorders. *Journal of Mathematical Economics, 48*, 212–218.

Candeal, J. C., Herves-Beloso, C., & Indurain, E. (1998). Some results on representation and extension of preferences. *Journal of Mathematical Economics, 29*(1), 75–81.

Cettolin, E., & Riedl, A. (2019). Revealed preferences under uncertainty: Incomplete preferences and preferences for randomization. *Journal of Economic Theory, 181*(May), 547–585.

Debreu, G. (1959). *Theory of value: An axiomatic analysis of economic equilibrium*. Yale University Press.

Donaldson, D., & Weymark, J. A. (1998). A quasiordering is the intersection of orderings. *Journal of Economic Theory, 78*, 382–397.

Dubra, J., & Ok, E. A. (2002). A model of procedural decision making in the presence of risk. *International Economic Review, 43*(4), 1053–1080.

Dushnik, B., & Miller, E. W. (1941). Partially ordered sets. *American Journal of Mathematics, 63*, 600–610.

Eilenberg, S. (1941). Ordered topological spaces. *American Journal of Mathematics, 63*(1), 39–45.

Esposito, L., & Villaseñor, A. (2019). Relative deprivation and school enrollment: Evidence from Mexico. *The Review of Income and Wealth, 65*(1), 166–186.

Estevez-Toranzo, M., & Herves-Beloso, C. (1995). On the existence of continuous preference orderings without utility representations. *Journal of Mathematical Economics, 24*(4), 305–309.

Evren, O., & Ok, E. A. (2011). On the multi-utility representation of preference relations. *Journal of Mathematical Economics, 47*, 554–563.

Fisher, I. (1892). Mathematical investigations in the theory of value and prices. *Transactions of the Connecticut Academy of Arts and Sciences, 9*(1), 1–124.

Forrest, J. Y. L. (2013). *A systemic perspective on cognition and mathematics*. CRC Press, an Imprint of Taylor and Francis.

Forrest, J. Y. L. (2021). Infinity, where some of the key concepts of analysis start to fall apart. *Pure Mathematics and Applied Mathematics, 37*(4), 379–393. https://doi.org/10.3969/j.issn.1008-5513.2021.04.001

Forrest, J. Y. L., Hafezalkotob, A., Ren, L., Liu, Y., & Tallapally, P. (2021). Utility and optimization's dependence on decision-makers' underlying value-belief systems. *Review of Economic and Business Studies, 14*(2), 125–149. https://doi.org/10.47743/rebs-2021-2-0007

Forrest, J. Y. L., Darvishi, D., Clark, R. S., Seyedian, M., & Jun Liu, J. (2021). Consumption preferences and generalized utility functions. *Southern Business and Economics Journal*, 44(2), 29–65.

Forrest, J. Y. L., Shao, L., Sarkambayeva, S., Shaw, D., & Sunita Mondal, S. (to appear). *Completed extensions and set-theoretical structures of an individual's consumption preferences.* Submitted for possible publications. New York Economic Review, vol. 53, no. Fall, 5–18

Glasser, W. (1999). *Choice theory: A new psychology of personal freedom.* Harper Perennial.

Gordon, B. J. (1964). Aristotle and the development of value theory. *The Quarterly Journal of Economics, 78*(1), 115–128.

Hansson, B. (1968). Choice structures and preference relations. *Synthese, 18*, 443–458.

Hervés-Beloso, C., & Cruces, H. V. (2019). Continuous preference orderings representable by utility functions. *Journal of Economic Surveys, 33*(1), 179–194.

Herves-Beloso, C., & Monteiro, P. K. (2010). Strictly monotonic preferences on continuum of goods commodity spaces. *Journal of Mathematical Economics, 46*(5), 725–727.

Hicks, J., & Allen, R. G. D. (1934). A reconsideration of the theory of value (parts 1 & 2). *Economica NS, 1*(1 & 2), 52–76. 196-219.

Jacob, B., McCall, B., & Stange, K. (2018). College as country club: Do colleges cater to students' preferences for consumption? *Journal of Labor Economics, 36*(2), 309–348.

Kahneman, D. (2011). *Thinking, fast and slow.* Farrar, Straus and Giroux.

Kauder, E. (1953). Genesis of the marginal utility theory: From Aristotle to the end of the eighteenth century. *The Economic Journal, 63*(251), 638–650.

Kunen, K. (1980). *Set theory: An introduction to independence proofs.* North-Holland.

Kuratowski, K., & Mostowski, A. (1976). *Set theory: With an introduction to descriptive set theory.* North-Holland.

Levin, J., & Milgrom, P. (2004a). *Consumer theory.* Retrieved February 7, 2022, from https://web.stanford.edu/~jdlevin/Econ%20202/Consumer%20Theory.pdf.

Levin, J., & Milgrom, P. (2004b). *Introduction to choice theory.* Retrieved September 29, 2022, from https://web.stanford.edu/~jdlevin/Econ%20202/Choice%20Theory.pdf.

Lin, Y. (1999). *General systems theory: A mathematical approach.* Plenum and Kluwer Academic.

Lin, Y. (2008). Systematic studies: The infinity problem in modern mathematics. *Kybernetes: The International Journal of Cybernetics, Systems and Management Sciences, 37*(3–4), 385–542.

Lin, Y., & Forrest, B. (2011). *Systemic structure behind human organizations: From civilizations to individuals.* Springer.

Liu, S. F., & Lin, Y. (2010). *Grey systems: Theory and applications.* Springer.

Loomes, G., & Sugden, R. (1982). Regret theory: An alternative theory of rational choice under uncertainty. *The Economic Journal, 92*, 805–824.

Luce, D. (1956). Semiorders and a theory of utility discrimination. *Econometrica, 24*, 178–191.

Mandler, M. (1999). Incomplete preferences and rational intransitivity of choice. *mimeo*. Harvard University.

Mandler, M. (2001). A difficult choice in preference theory: Rationality implies completeness or transitivity but not both. In E. Milgram (Ed.), *Varieties of practical reasoning* (pp. 373–402). Cambridge.

Mas-Collel, A., Whinston, M. D., & Green, J. R. (1995). *Microeconomic theory.* Oxford University Press.

Mehta, G. B. (1998). Preference and utility. In S. Barbera, P. J. Hammond, & C. Seidl (Eds.), *Handbook of utility theory. Chapter 1* (pp. 1–47). Kluwer Academic.

Meng, F. Y., & Chen, X. H. (2015). A new method for group decision making with incomplete fuzzy preference relations. *Knowledge-Based Systems, 73*(January), 111–123.

Miller, N. H. (2006). *Notes on microeconomic theory.* Retrieved July 11, 2022, from https://nmiller.web.illinois.edu/notes.html.

Monteiro, P. K. (1987). Some results on the existence of utility functions on path connected spaces. *Journal of Mathematical Economics, 16*(2), 147–156.

Mullainathan, S., & Thaler, R. H. (2000). Behavioral economics. *NBER working paper no. 7948*. National Bureau of Economic Research.
Nishimura, H., & Ok, E. A. (2016). Utility representation of an incomplete and nontransitive preference relation. *Journal of Economic Theory, 166*(November), 164–185.
Ok, E. A. (2002). Utility representation of an incomplete preference relation. *Journal of Economic Theory, 104*(2), 429–449.
Ok, E. A., & Masatlioglu, Y. (2007). A theory of (relative) discounting. *Journal of Economic Theory, 137*, 214–245.
Pancs, R. (2018). *Lectures on microeconomics: The big questions approach*. The MIT Press.
Pareto, V. (1906). *Manuale di Economia Politica*. Societa Editrice Libraria. Reprinted as *manual of political economy*. Augustus M. Kelley.
Roelofsma, P., & Read, D. (2000). Intransitive intertemporal choice. *Journal of Behavioral Decision Making, 13*, 161–177.
Rössel, J., & Schroedter, J. H. (2015). Cosmopolitan cultural consumption: Preferences and practices in a heterogenous, urban population in Switzerland. *Poetics, 50*(June), 80–95.
Rubinstein, A. (1988). Similarity and decision-making under risk. *Journal of Economic Theory, 46*, 145–153.
Samuelson, P. A. (1938). A note on the pure theory of consumer's behaviour. *Economica NS, 5*(17), 61–71.
Schneider, M., & Day, R. (2018). Target-adjusted utility functions and expected-utility paradoxes. *Management Science, 64*(1), 271. https://doi.org/10.1287/mnsc.2016.2588
Slutsky, E. (1915). Sulla Teoria def Bilancio def Consumatore. *Giornale Degli Economisti, 51*(1), 1–26.
Sobel, J. (2005). Interdependent preferences and reciprocity. *Journal of Economic Literature, 43*(June), 392–436.
Stigler, G. J. (1950). The development of utility theory I. *Journal of Political Economy, 58*(4), 307–327.
Strotz, R. H. (1953). Cardinal utility. *The American Economic Review, 43*(2), 384–397.
Suzumura, K. (1976). Remarks on the theory of collective choice. *Economica, 43*, 381–390.
Szpilrajn, E. (1930). Sur l'Extension de l'Orde Partiel. *Fundamenta Mathematicae, 16*, 386–389.
Taylor, C. R. (1989). Duality, optimization, and microeconomic theory: Pitfalls for the applied researcher. *Western Journal of Agricultural Economics, 14*(2), 200–212.
Tversky, A. (1969). Intransitivity of preferences. *Psychological Review, 76*(1), 31–48.
Varian, H. R. (2010). *Intermediate microeconomics: A modern approach*. WW Norton.
Wold, H. (1943). A synthesis of pure demand analysis I, II and ill. *Scandinavian Actuarial Journal, 26*, 85–118. 220–263, 69–120.

Chapter 15
Convexities of Consumption Preferences

Jeffrey Yi-Lin Forrest, Tufan Tiglioglu, Yong Liu, Donald Mong, and Marta Cardin

Abstract The concept of convexity plays an important role in the studies of economics in general and consumer theory in particular. By removing the unrealistic assumption that consumer preferences are complete on the set X of consumption choices, this chapter, which is mainly based on Forrest et al. (Studia Universitatis "Vasile Goldis" Arad—Economics Series, 2023), examines how the various concepts of convex preferences and relevant properties can be reestablished. Different from the literature, this chapter derives a series of formal propositions and constructs counterexamples. Among others, it shows the following: (1) The weighted combination of two possible consumptions is not necessarily comparable with any of the possibilities; (2) not every convergent sequence of a consumer's preferable consumptions asymptotically preserves his preference preordering; (3) not all preferences satisfy either positive multiplicativity or additive conservation; (4) all three types of preference convexities—weak convexity, convexity, and strong convexity—can be introduced to general convex spaces. In the conclusion section, some research topics of expected significance are suggested for future works.

Keywords Additive conservation · Balanced bundles · Balanced diversification · Bounded rationality · Convex space · Vector-valued utility function

---

Jeffrey Yi-Lin Forrest (Department of Accounting Economics Finance, Slippery Rock University, Slippery Rock, PA, USA; Email: Jeffrey.forrest@sru.edu), Tufan Tiglioglu (Department of Leadership Studies, Alvernia University, Reading, PA, USA; Email: tufan.tiglioglu@alvernia.edu), Yong Liu (School of Business, Jiangnan University, Wuxi, Jiangsu, China; Email: clly1985528@163.com), Donald Mong (Department of Accounting Economics Finance, Slippery Rock University, Slippery Rock, PA, USA; Email: Donald.mong@sru.edu), and Marta Cardin (Department of Economics, Ca' Foscari University of Venice, Venezia, Italy; Email: mcardin@unive.it) are equally contributed to this chapter.

J. Y.-L. Forrest, *Systemic Principles of Applied Economic Philosophies I*,
Translational Systems Sciences 38, https://doi.org/10.1007/978-981-99-7273-9_15

15.1 Introduction

As a physiological being or a form of life, each consumer, either an individual person or a business firm, has to first satisfy his basic needs of survival before considering the consumption of other more luxurious products, goods, and services. At the level of basic survival, it is evident that each living being's need has to be multidimensionally met, such as the dimension of shelter or office domain, that of various nutrition intakes or business inputs, etc. Examples of such multidimensionality also appear frequently in other levels of real-life living. For instance, tickets to different world series games, soft drink choices, or alternatives of hotels represent examples of consumptions from three different dimensions; they cannot be directly compared by using a consumer's preferences. In other words, consumer preferences come into play only when two consumption alternatives belong to the same dimension, such as food choice 1 and food choice 2.

Such multidimensionality makes a consumer's preferences not able to compare one consumption possibility from one dimension to another one from a different dimension. That is, in real life there are consumption possibilities, none of which is preferred over the others due to the reason that different dimensions are involved. In other words, the set of a consumer's possible consumptions is not completely ordered by his preferences. Although such incompleteness of consumer preferences is also noticed by Ok (2002), he only considers it from the angle of bounded rationality and consumers' indecisiveness by citing Aumann (1962), Bewley (1986), and Mandler (1999) without noticing the multidimensionality of a living being's physiological needs.

Riding on the recognition of the aforementioned multidimensionality, this chapter studies the following problems: (1) Under what conditions will some of the most basic properties of consumer preferences, derived on the assumption of complete preferences, still hold true when preferences are incomplete? And, (2) how will the three concepts of convexities of consumer preferences—weak convexity, convexity, and strong convexity—look like for this new scenario?

These problems are undoubtedly very important. Specifically, in the theoretical front, in investigations of consumer behaviors and consumer decision-making, the completeness of consumer preferences represents one of the most fundamental assumptions (e.g., Debreu, 1959; Hervés-Beloso & Cruces, 2019; Mas-Collel et al., 1995). On top of such key assumption, various concepts of preference convexity have been subsequently introduced to capture different aspects of consumer characteristics (e.g., Brandl & Brandt, 2020; Debreu, 1959; Mas-Collel et al., 1995). Additionally, in other fields of studies, similar concepts have also been considered canonical (e.g., Chateauneuf & Tallon, 2002). In particular, in one way or another, various convex preferences have been employed to express how each consumer may be inclined for diversification and how consumers tend to prefer more balanced bundles of products, goods, and services than extreme ones. When the aforementioned completeness assumption is altered, all the previously established conclusions need to be reexamined for their validity. In other words, the earlier assumed completeness of consumer preferences indeed lays a foundation for various economic theories to appear. Hence, when this completeness is replaced by incompleteness, all relevant conclusions of economics will most likely take their correspondingly different forms.

Practically speaking, it has been widely noted that the existing economic theories become useless when they are employed to provide guidelines for practical purposes or make predictions about what drastic changes might occur in the economy; for relevant details, see Paul Krugman (*New York Times*, 2009-09-02) and Paul De Grauwe (*Financial Times*, 2009-07-21). So, by replacing an unrealistic assumption with one that is more relevant to life, one can expect that the consequent theories will be more likely to be useful in practice than the prevalent theories.

Through reexamining some of the major results known in the prevalent consumer theory, this chapter, which is mainly based on Forrest et al. (2023), is able to enrich the literature by showing, among other conclusions, the following unorthodox conclusions: (1) The weighted combination of two possible consumptions is generally not comparable with any of the possibilities; (2) not every convergent sequence of preferable consumptions of a consumer asymptotically preserves his preference preordering; (3) not all preferences satisfy either positive multiplicativity or additive conservation; and, (4) all three types of preference convexities can be introduced to general convex spaces.

The rest of this chapter is organized as follows. After providing a literature review in Sect. 15.2, Sect. 15.3 looks at various types of convex preferences and introduces the concept of asymptotically preserving preferences and conditions of positive multiplicativity and additive conservation. This section ends with a study on how to develop the concepts of weak convex, convex, and strong convex preferences on a general convex space. This chapter concludes in Sect. 15.4.

15.2 Literature Review

Relevant to the content of this chapter, the literature consists of two parts: studies on incomplete preference relation and those on convex preferences.

Regarding the incompleteness of a consumer's preferences, Dubra and Ok (2002) and Ok (2002) are the first people who recognize the importance of imposing the condition of incompleteness on a consumer's set X of possible consumptions. In particular, X is said to be incomplete, if there are possible consumptions $x, y \in X$ such that x is not preferred over y, and y is not preferred over x, either. More specifically, Dubra and Ok (2002) develop a risky choice model, where the considered consumer naturally has such a preference relation that cannot compare each and every pair of possible consumptions. Ok (2002) looks at how to represent an incomplete preference relation by means of a vector-valued utility function, where the conventional idea of a real-number valued utility representation is no longer possible.

Based on these pioneering works, a good number of scholars look at many related but different issues addressed in the prevalent consumer theory. For example,

Alonso et al. (2010) develop a !!web-based consensus support system for decision-makers who possess incomplete preference relations. Meng and Chen (2015) introduce a group-decision-making method to deal with incomplete preference information. And, Cettolin and Riedl (2019) test for complete and/or incomplete preferences by designing and conducting particular experiments. For our purpose here, we only cite a few related studies among many to demonstrate the rise of an important research area.

To enriching this literature, we have gone beyond the known justification for studying incomplete preference relations. For example, Ok (2002) only considers it in terms of bounded rationality and consumers' indecisiveness, as noticed by Aumann (1962), Bewley (1986), and Mandler (1999). On the contrary, we point to the fact that the root of all human consumptions drills down to the physiological needs or business needs for survival; and only when survival is no longer any concern, consumers will look further into the consumption of more luxurious products, goods, and services. However, at the level of survival, the needs of a living being are multidimensional, including such dimensions as need for shelter, need for foods, need for drinks, need for medicine, etc. Speaking differently, when two commodities from two different dimensions of a living being's survival are presented, no consumer can really say which commodity is preferred over the other, because they are both needed for basic survival.

Regarding convex consumer preferences, our literature search reveals a very huge volume of research works involving either the studies of the concepts of various convexities or applications of such concepts in the investigations of innumerable topics. In short, convexity represents one of the canonical concepts in economic theories (Jehle & Reny, 2000; Mas-Collel et al., 1995; Silberger, 2000; Simon & Blume, 1994). Other than being a convenience for analytical reasoning, it is also an intuitive property for the preferences of a consumer to possess. The idea this concept attempts to reflect is such an algebraic characteristic of consumption preferences that consumers exhibit—individuals incline more towards a balanced diversification of commodity consumptions than any extreme composition.

The contribution of this chapter to the existent literature is that we reexamine some of the key properties of the three types of convex preferences—weak convexity, convexity, and strong convexity. By doing so, we are able to provide their corresponding general forms for the case that a consumer's set of possible consumptions is not completely ordered by his preference relation.

For the reader to go through the following reasoning smoothly, let us define the order relation $\leq$ on $\mathbb{R}^\ell$ as follows, where $\mathbb{R}$ represents the set of all real numbers and $\ell \in N$ (= the set of all natural numbers). For $x^1 = (x_1^1, x_2^1, \ldots, x_\ell^1)$ and $x^2 = (x_1^2, x_2^2, \ldots, x_\ell^2) \in \mathbb{R}^\ell$,

$$x^1 \leq x^2 \text{ if and only if } x_h^1 \leq x_h^2, \quad \text{for each} \quad h = 1, 2, \ldots, \ell.$$

Other than using his system of values and beliefs to determine his consumption preferences, a consumer also employs this system to order real numbers in a particular way. For instance, an income in the amount of \$30 K is mostly seen as less than that of \$3 million. However, when value-and-belief systems are involved, such order as \$30 K < \$3 million can be easily reversed. For example, assume that the former income is produced out of lawful works, while the latter the outcome of robbing a bank. Then, people with certain types of value-and-belief systems will easily order \$30 K as greater than \$3 million. If we let $\leq_i$ (respectively, $<_i$, $>_i$, $\geq_i$, $=_i$) be consumer i's particular order of real numbers, there then are three order relations:

- $\leq$ (respectively, $<$, $>$, $\geq$, $=$), defined on $\mathbb{R}^\ell$, as given above
- $\precsim_i$ (respectively, $\prec_i$, $\succ_i$, $\succsim_i$, $=_i$) (defined on X_i)
- $\leq_i$ (defined on $\mathbb{R}$ by the system of values and beliefs of consumer i)

One needs to note that different from both $\leq$ and $\leq_i$, consumer i's consumption preferences $\precsim_i$ in real life are generally influenceable and often influenced by peers and frequently altered temporarily by peer pressures, especially for emerging adults, as documented in Hu et al. (2021) and Mani et al. (2013). Because the concept of time is ignored in this chapter, or what is considered here represents only a freezing moment in time, the relation $\precsim_i$ becomes fixed and not influenceable by peers.

The preference relation $\precsim_i$ is said to be a preorder, if it satisfies (i) the property of reflexivity, for any $x_i \in X_i$, $x_i \precsim_i x_i$, and (ii) the property of transitivity, for any $x_i^1, x_i^2, x_i^3 \in X_i$, $x_i^1 \precsim_i x_i^2$ and $x_i^2 \precsim_i x_i^3$ imply $x_i^1 \precsim_i x_i^3$. It is said to be complete, if each pair $x_i^1, x_i^2 \in X_i$ can be compared by $\precsim_i$.

15.3 Various Convex Preferences

This section consists of six subsections by focusing on three types of convex preferences—weak convexity, convexity, and strong convexity—as well investigated by Debreu (1959) and many others (e.g., Mas-Collel et al., 1995). In particular, Sect. 15.3.1 looks at the concept of weak convexity and the possibility that when the preference relation is not complete, a weighted combination of two possible consumptions may not be comparable with any of the consumptions in terms of the preference relation. Section 15.3.2 examines the concept of convex preferences and its relation with that of weak convexity. Section 15.3.3 looks at asymptotically preserving preferences. Section 15.3.4 studies such preference relations that satisfy the conditions of either additive conservation or positive multiplicativity. After investigating the concept of strong convexity in Sect. 15.3.5, the attention is turned to the development of these three types of convex preferences on the general convex spaces in Sect. 15.3.6.

15.3.1 Weakly Convex Preferences

Assume that in this section X_i is convex, that is, for any x^1 and $x^2 \in X_i$ and for any scalar $\alpha \in [0, 1]$, $\alpha x^1 + (1 - \alpha)yx^2 \in X_i$. If X_i additionally satisfies that for distinct $x_i^1, x_i^2 \in X_i$ and arbitrary $\alpha \in (0, 1)$,

$$x_i^1 \precsim_i x_i^2 \rightarrow x_i^1 \precsim_i \alpha x_i^2 + (1-\alpha)x_i^1, \tag{15.1}$$

then X_i is said to be weakly convex with respect to $\precsim_i$ (Debreu, 1959, p. 59). When no confusion is caused, the phrase "with respect to $\precsim_i$" will be omitted.

Proposition 15.1 If X_i is convex and the preference relation $\precsim_i$ is complete, then the set X_i of all possible consumptions is weakly convex if and only if

$$\forall x_i' \in X_i, \left\{x_i \in X_i : x_i' \precsim_i x_i\right\} \text{ is convex.} \tag{15.2}$$

Proof ($\rightarrow$). For any $x_i' \in X_i$, let $x_i^1, x_i^2 \in Z = \left\{x_i \in X_i : x_i' \precsim_i x_i\right\}$ and $\alpha \in (0, 1)$. Without loss of generality, assume $x_i^1 \precsim_i x_i^2$. We need to show $\alpha x_i^2 + (1-\alpha)x_i^1 \in Z$.

To this end, we have $x_i' = \alpha x_i' + (1-\alpha)x_i' \precsim_i x_i^1 = \alpha x_i^1 + (1-\alpha)x_i^1$. Since $\precsim_i$ is assumed to be complete, x_i^1 and $\alpha x_i^2 + (1-\alpha)x_i^1$ are comparable with respect to $\precsim_i$. And,

$$x_i' \precsim_i x_i^1 = \alpha x_i^1 + (1-\alpha)x_i^1 \precsim_i \alpha x_i^2 + (1-\alpha)x_i^1. \tag{15.3}$$

Hence, $\alpha x_i^2 + (1-\alpha)x_i^1 \in Z$. That is, Z is convex.

($\leftarrow$). For any distinct $x_i^1, x_i^2 \in X_i$ and arbitrary $\alpha \in (0, 1)$, satisfying $x_i^1 \precsim_i x_i^2$, we want to show $x_i^1 \precsim_i \alpha x_i^2 + (1-\alpha)x_i^1$ by assuming Eq. (15.2). Because $Z = \left\{x_i \in X_i : x_i^1 \precsim_i x_i\right\}$ is convex, from $x_i^2 \in Z$, it follows that $\alpha x_i^2 + (1-\alpha)x_i^1 \in Z$, for any $\alpha \in (0, 1)$. That is, $x_i^1 \precsim_i \alpha x_i^2 + (1-\alpha)x_i^1$. So, Eq. (15.1) holds true.

The following example shows that if the preference relation $\precsim_i$ is not complete, there might be $x_i^1, x_i^2 \in X_i$ and a scalar $\alpha \in (0, 1)$ such that x_i^1 and $\alpha x_i^2 + (1-\alpha)x_i^1$ are not comparable with respect to the preference relation $\precsim_i$ on X_i.

Example 15.1 Assume that consumer i's system of values and beliefs defines the order relation $\leq_i$ of real numbers by referring to the mod4 function and the arc length between the comparing quantities. In particular, for two demanded quantities x_{ih}^1 and x_{ih}^2 of commodity h, $\leq_i = \leq_{\text{mod}(4)}$ such that $x_{ih}^1 <_{\text{mod}(4)} x_{ih}^2$ if and only if on the shorter arc between $x_{ih}^1 \bmod(4)$ and $x_{ih}^2 \bmod(4)$, the arrow points from $x_{ih}^1 \bmod(4)$ to $x_{ih}^2 \bmod(4)$, Fig. 15.1.

Define the preference relation $\precsim_i = \precsim_{\text{mod}(4)}$ as follows: For any $x_i^1, x_i^2 \in X_i \subseteq \mathbb{R}^\ell$,

$$x_i^1 \precsim_{\text{mod}(4)} x_i^2 \quad \text{if and only if} \quad \forall h \left(x_{ih}^1 \leq_{\text{mod}(4)} x_{ih}^2\right).$$

Let $x_i^1, x_i^2 \in X_i$ be two consumptions such that

Fig. 15.1 How the particular order $\leq_{\text{mod}(4)}$ is defined

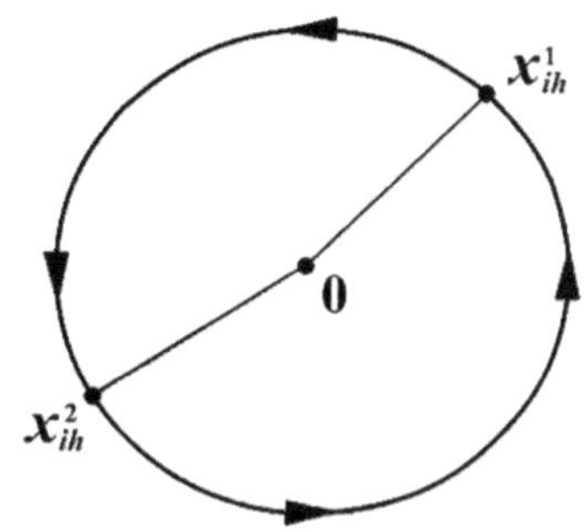

$$x_{ik}^1 = x_{ik}^2, \quad k = 1, 2, \ldots, \ell, \quad k \neq h,$$

and

$$x_{ih}^1 = 1, \quad \text{and} \quad x_{ih}^2 = 3.5.$$

Then, for $\alpha = 2/2.5 \in (0, 1)$, x_i^1 and $\alpha x_i^2 + (1-\alpha)x_i^1$ are not comparable with respect to $\precsim_{\text{mod}(4)}$. In particular, because $x_{ik}^1 = \alpha x_{ik}^2 + (1-\alpha)x_{ik}^1$, for $k = 1, 2, \ldots, \ell$, $k \neq h$. The comparability of x_i^1 and $\alpha x_i^2 + (1-\alpha)x_i^1$ with respect to $\precsim_{\text{mod}(4)}$ becomes that of x_{ih}^1 and $\alpha x_{ih}^2 + (1-\alpha)x_{ih}^1$ with respect to $\leq_{\text{mod}(4)}$. And since $x_{ih}^1 = 1$ and $\alpha x_{ih}^2 + (1-\alpha)x_{ih}^1 = \left(\frac{2}{2.5}\right) \cdot 3.5 + \left(\frac{0.5}{2.5}\right) \cdot 1 = 3$, it follows that x_{ih}^1 and $\alpha x_{ih}^2 + (1-\alpha)x_{ih}^1$ are not comparable with respect to $\leq_{\text{mod}(4)}$. Hence, x_i^1 and $\alpha x_i^2 + (1-\alpha)x_i^1$ are not comparable with respect to $\precsim_{\text{mod}(4)}$.

Not only so, it can be seen that $x_i^2 \precsim_i x_i^1$, because $x_{ih}^2 = 3.5 \leq_{\text{mod}(4)} x_{ih}^1 = 1$. Therefore, this example shows that Proposition 15.1 does not hold true, if the preference relation $\precsim_i$ is not complete.

Regarding this example, one natural question arises as follows. When does a mod function (also known as modular operation) actually appear in real life? To this end, we in fact see such operations often in different walks of life, such as 12-h clocks, 7-day weeks, months of various numbers of days, and durations of projects that follow one after another. In each of these cases, when a cycle is fully traversed, a new round of counting or measurement begins again from the starting mark 0. In terms of foods, a person's consumption of any particular food is not the more the better. In fact, the opposite is generally true: The one-time consumption of any food has to be limited within a certain upper bound; otherwise, the food will become something the consumer avoids completely in the future.

In terms of the literature, the concept of weakly convex preferences is the same as that of convex preferences given in Mas-Collel et al. (1995, p. 44). To this end, Example 15.1 shows the importance of this chapter: To make the consequent economic theory more real-life relevant, there is a need to revisit the prevalent consumer theory. The purpose of the revisit is to see what developed conclusions are really true or how they would look like, if preferences are neither complete nor transitive or if they are not rational as presently known (Mas-Collel et al., 1995; Miller, 2006).

15.3.2 Convex Preferences

Slightly different from the concept of weak convexity, if X_i is convex and the following condition holds true, then X_i is said to be convex with respect to $\precsim_i$ (Debreu, 1959, p. 60). For any distinct consumptions $x_i^1, x_i^2 \in X_i$ and arbitrary scalar $\alpha \in (0, 1)$,

$$x_i^1 \prec_i x_i^2 \rightarrow x_i^1 \prec_i \alpha x_i^2 + (1-\alpha)x_i^1. \qquad (15.4)$$

As before, when no confusion is caused, the phrase "with respect to $\precsim_i$" will be omitted.

Proposition 15.2 If X_i is convex and the preference relation $\precsim_i$ on X_i is a complete preorder, then X_i is convex with respect to $\precsim_i$ if and only if

$$\forall x_i' \in X_i, \left\{x_i \in X_i : x_i' \prec_i x_i\right\} \text{ is convex.} \qquad (15.5)$$

Proof ($\rightarrow$) To show Eq. (15.5), for any $x_i' \in X_i$, let $Z = \left\{x_i \in X_i : x_i' \prec_i x_i\right\}$. Pick arbitrary $x_i^1, x_i^2 \in Z$ and let $\alpha \in (0, 1)$ be an arbitrary scalar. Without loss of generality, assume that $x_i^1 \precsim_i x_i^2$. Then we have

$$x_i' \prec_i x_i^1 = \alpha x_i^1 + (1-\alpha)x_i^1.$$

Since $\precsim_i$ is assumed to be complete, x_i^1 and $\alpha x_i^2 + (1-\alpha)x_i^1$ are comparable. So, from $x_i^1 \precsim_i x_i^2$, it follows that

$$x_i' \prec_i x_i^1 = \alpha x_i^1 + (1-\alpha)x_i^1 \precsim \alpha x_i^2 + (1-\alpha)x_i^1.$$

So, $\alpha x_i^2 + (1-\alpha)x_i^1 \in Z$. Hence, Z is convex.

($\leftarrow$) Assume that for any $x_i' \in X_i$, $\left\{x_i \in X_i : x_i' \prec_i x_i\right\}$ is convex. Pick two arbitrary consumptions $x_i^1, x_i^2 \in X_i$ and an arbitrary scalar $\alpha \in (0, 1)$, satisfying $x_i^1 \prec_i x_i^2$. Then the convexity of $Z = \left\{x_i \in X_i : x_i^1 \prec_i x_i\right\}$ implies that

$$x_i^1 = \alpha x_i^1 + (1-\alpha)x_i^1 \prec_i \alpha x_i^2 + (1-\alpha)x_i^1,$$

where the comparability of x_i^1 and $\alpha x_i^2 + (1-\alpha)x_i^1$ comes from the assumption that $\precsim_i$ is complete.

In terms of the literature, the concept of convex preferences, as seen above, is the same as that of strict convex preferences given in Mas-Collel et al. (1995, p. 44). And, Example 15.1 shows why the condition that the completeness of the preference preorder $\precsim_i$ is necessary for Proposition 15.2 to hold true.

For any consumption $x_i \in X_i$, define the indifference class (or indifference curve) of x_i as follows (Debreu, 1959; Miller, 2006):

$$[x_i] = \{x_i' \in X_i : x_i' \precsim_i x_i \text{ and } x_i \precsim_i x_i' \}.$$

Let X_i^* be a subset of X_i, known as a set of (consumer i's) preference representations, such that for any x_i^1 and $x_i^2 \in X_i^*$, $x_i^1 \neq x_i^2$ implies $[x_i^1] \neq [x_i^2]$ and $X_i = \bigcup_{x_i \in X_i^*} [x_i]$. If a subset $X_i' \subseteq X_i^*$ satisfies that any consumptions x_i^1, $x_i^2 \in X_i'$ are comparable in terms of the preference relation $\precsim_i$, then X_i' is known as a chain in X_i^*. A chain X_i' in X_i^* is referred to as a maximal chain, provided that for any $x_i \in X_i$, if x_i is comparable with each element in X_i', then $x_i \in X_i'$. For more details on ordered sets, please consult with Kuratowski and Mostowski (1976).

Define a function $u_i : X_i \to X_i^*$ as follows: For any $x_i \in X_i$, $u_i(x_i) = x_i^* \in X_i^*$, if $x_i \in [x_i^*]$. Then, we treat u_i as the canonical utility function of consumer i, satisfying that for any x_i^1, $x_i^2 \in X_i$, $x_i^1 \precsim_i x_i^2$ if and only if $u_i(x_i^1) \precsim_i u_i(x_i^2)$. For any chosen maximal chain $X_i^{\max}$ in X_i^*, the preimage of u_i of the chain $X_i^{\max}$ is equal to

$$u_i^{-1}(X_i^{\max}) = \cup \{ [x_i^*] : x_i^* \in X_i^{\max} \}.$$

The relation $\precsim_i$ is said to be a continuous preference relation, if for any maximal chain $X_i^{\max}$ in X_i^* and any $x_i' \in u_i^{-1}(X_i^{\max})$, the following sets are closed in $u_i^{-1}(X_i^{\max})$:

$$\{x_i \in u_i^{-1}(X_i^{\max}) : x_i \precsim_i x_i'\} \quad \text{and} \quad \{x_i \in u_i^{-1}(X_i^{\max}) : x_i \succsim_i x_i'\}. \tag{15.6}$$

In other words, the closedness of the first set in Eq. (15.6) means that for any sequence $\{x_i^q\}_{q=1}^{\infty}$ of consumptions possible for consumer i, if each x_i^q is at most as desired as x_i' and $x_i^q \to x_i^*$ (a consumption in X_i), then x_i^* is also at most as desired as x_i'. And similarly, the closedness of the second set in Eq. (15.6) is defined.

Proposition 15.3 If the preference relation $\precsim_i$ on X_i is a complete and continuous preorder, then X_i's convexity with respect to $\precsim_i$ implies X_i's weak convexity with respect to $\precsim_i$.

Proof For any consumptions $x_i^1, x_i^2 \in X_i$ and any scalar $\alpha \in (0, 1)$, assume that $x_i^1 \precsim_i x_i^2$. We want to show Eq. (15.1). To this end, let

$$[x_i^1, \to) = \{x_i \in X_i : x_i^1 \precsim_i x_i\}.$$

Since X_i is assumed to be convex, for any scalar $\alpha \in (0, 1)$, $\alpha x_i^2 + (1 - \alpha) x_i^1 \in X_i$. Because $\precsim_i$ is complete, it means that x_i^1 and $\alpha x_i^2 + (1 - \alpha) x_i^1$ are comparable. The continuity of the preference relation $\precsim_i$ implies that $[x_i^1, \to)$ is closed in X_i. We need to prove $\alpha x_i^2 + (1-\alpha)x_i^1 \in [x_i^1, \rightarrow)$. By contradiction, assume the opposite holds true. That is, we assume that

$$\alpha x_i^2 + (1-\alpha)x_i^1 \in Z = \{x_i \in [x_i^1, \rightarrow) : x_i^1 \succ_i x_i\}. \tag{15.7}$$

In the rest of this proof, we show that Z is in fact an empty set. Assume that $Z \neq \emptyset$. Let us pick an element $x_i' \in Z$. From the fact that $[x_i^1, \rightarrow)$ is closed in X_i and that $(\leftarrow, x_i'] = \{x_i \in X_i : x_i \precsim_i x_i'\}$ is also closed (since $\precsim_i$ is continuous), satisfying that $(\leftarrow, x_i'] \cap [x_i^1, \rightarrow) = \emptyset$, the assumption that X_i is convex implies that there is another point $x_i'' \in X_i$ such that $x_i' \prec_i x_i'' \prec_i x_i^1$. Hence, the convexity of X_i implies that for any scalar $\alpha \in (0, 1)$

$$\begin{aligned} x_i'' &\prec_i \alpha x_i^1 + (1-\alpha)x_i'' \\ &\prec_i \alpha x_i' + (1-\alpha)x_i' \\ &= x_i', \end{aligned}$$

where the second line is from the fact that $x_i' \in Z$ and so $x_i' \in [x_i^1, \rightarrow)$. That contradicts with $x_i' \prec_i x_i''$. That is, $Z = \emptyset$ so that Eq. (15.7) is impossible. That is, $\alpha x_i^2 + (1-\alpha)x_i^1 \in [x_i^1, \rightarrow)$, which confirms that X_i is weakly convex.

15.3.3 Asymptotically Preserving Preferences

If for each sequence $\{x_i^q\}_{q=1}^{\infty}$ of consumptions in X_i, satisfying $x_i^q \succsim_i x_i^0$ (respectively, $x_i^q \precsim_i x_i^0$), for every q and some $x_i^0 \in X_i$, $\lim_{q\rightarrow\infty} x_i^q \succsim_i x_i^0$ (respectively, $\lim_{q\rightarrow\infty} x_i^q \precsim_i x_i^0$), whenever the limit exists, then we say that consumer i's consumptions asymptotically preserve preference preordering $\precsim_i$.

Proposition 15.4 If consumer i's preferable consumptions asymptotically preserve preference preordering $\precsim_i$ and X_i is convex with respect to $\precsim_i$, then for any $x_i' \in X_i$, x_i' is a limit point of $\{x_i \in X_i : x_i \succ_i x_i'\}$.

Proof The convexity of X_i with respect to $\precsim_i$ implies that for any $z_i \in \{x_i \in X_i : x_i \succ_i x_i'\}$,

$$x_i' \prec_i \alpha z_i + (1-\alpha)x_i', \quad \text{for any} \quad \alpha \in (0, 1), \tag{15.8}$$

where the existence of consumption z_i comes from Axiom 14.3 that no satiation consumption exists for consumer i.

Therefore, for $q = 1/n$, $n = 2, 3, \ldots$, the sequence $\{x_i^q\}_{q=1}^{\infty}$, where $x_i^q = qz_i + (1-q)x_i'$, converges to x_i'. So, Eq. (15.8) indicates that x_i' is a limit point of $\{x_i \in X_i : x_i \succ_i x_i'\}$.

An indifference class is said to be thick (Debreu, 1959), if its interior in X_i is not empty. What Proposition 15.4 says is that the indifference class of each consumption of consumer i is not thick, when his set X_i of possible consumptions is convex with respect to $\precsim_i$ and asymptotically preserves preference preordering.

The following example demonstrates that, generally, not every convergent sequence of preferable consumptions of a consumer asymptotically preserves his preference preordering.

Example 15.2 Assume that the system of values and beliefs of consumer i ranks the quantity of a specific commodity h as follows: For any two real numbers x and y, $x \prec_i y$ if and only if $x(\mathrm{mod}4) < y(\mathrm{mod}4)$. Let $x_i^1, x_i^2, \ldots, x_i^q, \ldots \in X_i$ be a sequence of possible consumptions for consumer i such that

$$x_{ik}^q = x_{ik}^1, \quad k = 1, 2, \ldots, \ell, \quad k \neq h, \quad q = 1, 2, \ldots \tag{15.9}$$

and

$$x_{ih}^q = 3 + \frac{q}{q+1}, \quad q = 1, 2, \ldots \tag{15.10}$$

Then, it is clear to see that $x_i^q \to x_i^0$, as $q \to \infty$, where $x_{ik}^0 = x_{ik}^1, k = 1, 2, \ldots, \ell, k \neq h$, and $x_{ih}^0 = 0$, which is equal to 4 (mod4).

Define x_i^{low} as follows: $x_{ik}^{\mathrm{low}} = x_{ik}^1, k = 1, 2, \ldots, \ell, k \neq h$, and $x_{ih}^{\mathrm{low}} = 3$. Then, Eqs. (15.9) and (15.10) imply that

$$x_i^q \succsim_i x_i^{\mathrm{low}} \quad \text{and} \quad \lim_{q \to \infty} x_i^q = x_i^0 \prec_i x_i^{\mathrm{low}}.$$

The significance of Example 15.2 is that it confirms the fact that $\{x_i \in X_i : x_i \succ_i x_i'\}$ is generally different from $\{x_i \in X_i : x_i \succsim_i x_i'\}$. That disproves an equivalence relation in Debreu (1959, p. 59).

15.3.4 *Additively Conserved and Positively Multiplicative Preferences*

A preference relation $\precsim_i$ on X_i is said to satisfy the condition of additive conservation, if for any consumptions $a_i^j, b_i^j \in X_i, j = 1, 2$,

$$a_i^1 \precsim_i b_i^1 \quad \text{and} \quad a_i^2 \precsim_i b_i^2 \to a_i^1 + a_i^2 \precsim_i b_i^1 + b_i^2, \tag{15.11}$$

where the sign $\precsim_i$ will become $\prec_i$ in the consequence, if $\prec_i$ appears in at least one of the two antecedents.

The preference relation $\precsim_i$ is said to satisfy the condition of positive multiplicativity, if for any consumptions $x_i^1, x_i^2 \in X_i$ and any scalar $\alpha > 0$,

$$x_i^1 \precsim_i x_i^2 \rightarrow \alpha x_i^1 \precsim_i \alpha x_i^2,$$

where the sign $\precsim_i$ will become $\prec_i$ in the consequence, if $\prec_i$ appears in the antecedent.

Proposition 15.5 If the preference relation $\precsim_i$ on a connected X_i satisfies the conditions of both positive multiplicativity and additive conservation, then X_i is both weakly convex and convex with respect to $\precsim_i$.

Proof For any consumptions $x_i^1, x_i^2 \in X_i$ and arbitrary scalar $\alpha \in (0, 1)$, if $x_i^1 \precsim_i x_i^2$, then the condition of positive multiplicativity implies

$$\alpha x_i^1 \precsim_i \alpha x_i^2 \quad \text{and} \quad (1-\alpha)x_i^1 \precsim_i (1-\alpha)x_i^1.$$

Now, the condition of additive conservation guarantees that

$$x_i^1 = \alpha x_i^1 + (1-\alpha)x_i^1 \precsim_i \alpha x_i^2 + (1-\alpha)x_i^1.$$

Since X_i is connected, we have $\alpha x_i^2 + (1-\alpha)x_i^1 \in X_i$. That is, X_i is weakly convex. And similarly, we can show the convexity of X_i.

The following example shows that not all preorders satisfy the condition of additive conservation.

Example 15.3 Assume that consumer i's system of values and beliefs preorders the quantities of a particular commodity h by referring to the mod4 function so that for any two real numbers x and y, $x \prec_i y$ if and only if $x(\text{mod}4) < y(\text{mod}4)$. Let $x_i^1, x_i^2, x_i^3 \in X_i$ be three consumptions such that

$$x_{ik}^1 = x_{ik}^2 = x_{ik}^3, \quad k = 1, 2, \ldots, \ell, \quad k \neq h,$$

and

$$x_{ih}^1 = 2, \; x_{ih}^2 = 3 \quad \text{and} \quad x_{ih}^2 = 1.$$

Then, we have $x_i^1 \precsim_i x_i^2$ and $x_i^3 \precsim_i x_i^3$. However, instead of $x_i^1 + x_i^3 \precsim_i x_i^2 + x_i^3$, we have

$$x_i^1 + x_i^3 \succsim_i x_i^2 + x_i^3,$$

because

$$x_{ik}^1 + x_{ik}^3 = x_{ik}^2 + x_{ik}^3, \quad k = 1, 2, \ldots, \ell, \quad k \neq h,$$

and

$$x_{ih}^1 + x_{ih}^3 = 3 \succsim_i x_{ih}^2 + x_{ih}^3 = 3 + 1 \ =_{\text{mod}4} 0.$$

That is, Proposition 15.5 is not guaranteed to be generally true without assuming that the preference relation $\precsim_i$ on X_i satisfies the condition of additive conservation. Specifically, the implication in Eq. (15.11) cannot be successfully guaranteed without assuming additive conservation.

Similar to the previous example, the following one demonstrates that not all preference relations satisfy the condition of positive multiplicativity.

Example 15.4 Continuing from Example 15.3, it is clear to see that the preference relation $\precsim_i$ $(= \leq_{\text{mod}(4)})$ of commodity h does not satisfy the condition of positive multiplicativity. In fact, for how positive multiplicativity is violated, we have

$$1 \precsim_i \left(\text{or} \leq_{\text{mod}(4)}\right) 2 \nrightarrow 2 \cdot 1 \precsim_i \left(\text{or} \leq_{\text{mod}(4)}\right) 2 \cdot 2$$

where the left-hand side is actually $2 \cdot 1 = 2 \succsim_i (\text{or} \geq_{\text{mod}(4)}) 2 \cdot 2 = 0 =$ the right-hand side. In other words, let $x_i^1, x_i^2 \in X_i$ be two consumptions such that

$$x_{ik}^1 = x_{ik}^2, \quad k = 1, 2, \ldots, \ell, \quad k \neq h,$$

and

$$x_{ih}^1 = 1, x_{ih}^2 = 2.$$

Then we have $x_i^1 \precsim_i x_i^2$ and $2x_i^1 \succsim_i 2x_i^2$. That is, the condition of positive multiplicativity does not hold true for consumer i's $\precsim_i$.

15.3.5 Strongly Convex Preferences

If for any two indifferent consumptions x_i^1 and x_i^2, their weighted average with an arbitrary positive weight is preferred to both of them, then X_i is said to be strongly convex with respect to $\precsim_i$ (Debreu, 1959, p. 61). Symbolically, X_i is strongly convex with respect to $\precsim_i$, if for any consumptions $x_i^1, x_i^2 \in X_i$ and arbitrary scalar $\alpha \in (0, 1)$,

$$x_i^1 \sim_i x_i^2 \rightarrow x_i^1 \prec_i \alpha x_i^2 + (1-\alpha)x_i^1. \tag{15.12}$$

As before, when no confusion is caused, the phrase "with respect to $\precsim_i$" will be omitted.

Proposition 15.6 Assume that each infinity can be actually (not potentially) achieved. If for each maximal chain $X_i^{\max} \subseteq X_i$, $u_i^{-1}(X_i^{\max})$ is a connected subset of $\mathbb{R}^\ell$ and X_i is convex, where $u_i : X_i \rightarrow X_i^*$ is the canonical utility function, and the preference relation $\precsim_i$ is a continuous preorder, then X_i's strong convexity with respect to $\precsim_i$ implies X_i's convexity with respect to $\precsim_i$.

Proof Assume that X_i is strongly convex with respect to $\precsim_i$ so that for any consumptions $x_i^1, x_i^2 \in X_i$ and arbitrary scalar $\alpha \in (0, 1)$, Eq. (15.12) holds true, where the conclusion $\alpha x_i^2 + (1-\alpha)x_i^1 \in X_i$ comes from the convexity of X_i. We need to show if these consumptions x_i^1, x_i^2 satisfy $x_i^1 \prec_i x_i^2$, then

$$x_i^1 \prec_i \alpha x_i^2 + (1-\alpha)x_i^1 \tag{15.13}$$

holds. To this end, let $X_i^{\max}$ be a maximal chain in X_i such that $u_i^{-1}(X_i^{\max})$ contains both x_i^1 and x_i^2. Then the connectedness of $u_i^{-1}(X_i^{\max})$ implies that $\alpha x_i^2 + (1-\alpha)x_i^1 \in u_i^{-1}(X_i^{\max})$. That is, $\alpha x_i^2 + (1-\alpha)x_i^1$ is comparable with each of x_i^1 and x_i^2.

Let u_i^r be a real-number valued utility function on $u_i^{-1}(X_i^{\max})$. Under the assumption that each infinity can be actually (not potentially) achieved, the connectivity of $u_i^{-1}(X_i^{\max})$ and the continuity of $\precsim_i$ jointly imply that this utility function u_i^r exists according to the famous Debreu's (1959) existence theorem. In particular, the original argument for the existence of the desired utility function u_i^r will go through in its entirety, except that both Steps 1 and 2 (Debreu, 1959, p. 57–58) cannot be successfully completed without the assumption that each infinity can be actually (not potentially) achieved.

To make this last statement understandable, let us briefly examine the concept of infinities. Roughly, this concept deals with two kinds of infinities. One is known as actual infinities and the other potential infinities (Forrest, 2013; Lin, 2008). Each so-called potential infinity stands for such a process that is forever, ongoing, and never-ending; and every so-called actual infinity denotes such a process that truly completes or had been completed. Relating to Debreu's (1959) existence theorem, its constructive process cannot be completed, unless one assumes that each infinity can be actually (not potentially) achieved.

Since u_i^r is an increasing function on $u_i^{-1}(X_i^{\max})$, we have $u_i^r(x_i^1) < u_i^r(x_i^2)$. And because for any scalar $\alpha \in (0, 1)$, $x_i = \alpha x_i^2 + (1-\alpha)x_i^1$ is located between x_i^1 and x_i^2, we obtain $u_i^r(x_i^1) < u_i^r(x_i^\prime) < u_i^r(x_i^2)$. Therefore, from the definition of real-number valued utility functions, it follows that Eq. (15.13) holds true. That is, X_i is convex with respect to $\precsim_i$.

Proposition 15.7 If the following conditions hold true, then for any indifferent consumptions $x_i^1, x_i^2 \in X_i$, the weighted average $\alpha x_i^2 + (1-\alpha)x_i^1$ is also indifferent from x_i^1 and x_i^2, for any scalar $\alpha \in (0, 1)$:

(i) Each infinity can be actually (not potentially) achieved.
(ii) For each maximal chain $X_i^{\max} \subseteq X_i$, $u_i^{-1}\left(X_i^{\max}\right)$ is a connected subset of $\mathbb{R}^\ell$ and X_i is convex, where $u_i : X_i \to X_i^*$ is the canonical utility function.
(iii) The preference relation $\precsim_i$ on X_i is a complete and continuous preorder.
(iv) X_i is strongly convex with respect to $\precsim_i$.

Proof From Proposition 15.3, it follows that X_i is weakly convex. Hence, for any indifferent consumptions $x_i^1, x_i^2 \in X_i$, we have $x_i^1 \precsim_i x_i^2$ and $x_i^2 \precsim_i x_i^1$. So, the weak convexity of X_i implies that $x_i^1, x_i^2 \precsim_i \alpha x_i^2 + (1-\alpha)x_i^1$, for any scalar $\alpha \in (0, 1)$. Then a similar argument as the one in the proof of Proposition 15.6 produces $\alpha x_i^2 + (1-\alpha)x_i^1 \precsim_i x_i^1, x_i^2$. Therefore, the desired conclusion follows.

Proposition 15.8 If the set X_i of consumption possibilities is strongly convex and the preference relation $\precsim_i$ is a preorder, then for any $x_i \in X_i$ and any maximal chain $X_i^{\max} \subseteq X_i$ such that $x_i \in u_i^{-1}\left(X_i^{\max}\right)$, where $u_i : X_i \to X_i^*$ is the canonical utility function, then the indifference class $[x_i]$ does not contain any non-degenerate closed segment of $u_i^{-1}\left(X_i^{\max}\right)$.

Proof By contradiction, assume that the given conditions are satisfied while there are (i) a particular consumption $x_i \in X_i$, (ii) a maximal chain $X_i^{\max} \subseteq X_i$ such that $u_i^{-1}\left(X_i^{\max}\right)$ contains x_i, and (iii) two distinct consumptions $x_i^1, x_i^2 \in u_i^{-1}\left(X_i^{\max}\right)$ such that the closed segment $\left[x_i^1, x_i^2\right] \subseteq [x_i] \subseteq u_i^{-1}\left(X_i^{\max}\right)$, where $[x_i]$ is the indifference class of x_i.

The assumption that $\precsim_i$ is a preorder implies that for any $z_i \in \left[x_i^1, x_i^2\right]$, $z_i \sim_i x_i$. However, the assumed strong convexity of X_i implies that $x_i^1 \prec_i z_i = \alpha x_i^2 + (1-\alpha)x_i^1$, for any $\alpha \in (0, 1)$. This end contradicts the previous statement, since $z_i = \alpha x_i^2 + (1-\alpha)x_i^1$ belongs to the segment $\left[x_i^1, x_i^2\right]$. That is, for any $x_i \in X_i$ and any maximal chain $X_i^{\max}$ such that $u_i^{-1}\left(X_i^{\max}\right)$ contains x_i, the indifference class $[x_i]$ does not contain any non-degenerate closed segment of $u_i^{-1}\left(X_i^{\max}\right)$.

15.3.6 Abstract Convex Structures

The technique used to establish the previous model of consumption sets is the employment of the quantities of commodities a consumer desires to consume. Hence, it is natural for us to think about how to directly examine the entire collection of various bundles of commodities without first identifying it with a subset in the Euclidean space $\mathbb{R}^\ell$. To this end, the abstract convex structures come to mind.

Let X be a nonempty set and $\mathbb{C}$ a family of subsets of X. The family $\mathbb{C}$ is known as a convexity on X (Kubis, 1999; van de Vel, 1993), if the following conditions hold true:

(a) $\varnothing, X \in \mathbb{C}$.
(b) For any subfamily $\mathbb{C}' \subseteq \mathbb{C}$, $\bigcap\{Z : Z \in \mathbb{C}'\} \in \mathbb{C}$ (or $\mathbb{C}$ is closed under arbitrary intersections).
(c) For any subfamily $\{Z_i : i \in I\} \subseteq \mathbb{C}$, where I is an index set, if $\{Z_i : i \in I\}$ is a chain in terms of the inclusion relation $\subseteq$ between sets, then $\bigcup\{Z_i : i \in I\} \in \mathbb{C}$ (or $\mathbb{C}$ is closed under unions of chains).

In this case, each element in $\mathbb{C}$ is known as a convex (sub)set of X, and the ordered pair $(X, \mathbb{C})$ a convex space. For $Z \in \mathbb{C}$, if its complement $Z^C = X - Z$ also belongs to $\mathbb{C}$, then Z is known as a half-space. Let $\mathcal{H}$ denote the set of all half-spaces in $\mathbb{C}$.

Given a convex space $(X, \mathbb{C})$ and a subset $A \subseteq X$, the convex hull of A, denoted by $co(A)$, is defined as follows: $co(A) = \cap \{Z \in \mathbb{C} : A \subseteq Z\}$. It can be seen readily that $Z \in \mathbb{C}$ if and only if $co(Z) = Z$. For n ($\in \mathbb{N}$) many arbitrary elements $x^i \in \mathbb{C}$, $i = 1, 2, \ldots, n$, where $\mathbb{N}$ is the set of all natural numbers, $co\left(\{x^i\}_{i=1}^n\right)$ is known as the n-polytope of the elements, while the 2-polytope $co(\{x^1, x^2\}) = co(x^1, x^2)$ is known as the segment joining x^1 and x^2.

A convex space $(X, \mathbb{C})$ (or convexity $\mathbb{C}$) is known as N-ary, for some fixed $N \in \mathbb{N}$, if for any $A \subseteq X$, $co(F) \subseteq A$, whenever $F \subseteq A$ contains at most N elements, then $A \in \mathbb{C}$. A 2-ary convexity is also known as an interval convexity.

Example 15.5 Show that the ordered pair $(\mathbb{R}^\ell, \mathbb{C})$, where $\mathbb{C}$ is the collection of all convex subsets in $\mathbb{R}^\ell$, is an interval (or 2-ary) convex space.

To this end, it is clear to see that conditions (a) and (b) are satisfied. To show condition (c), let $\{Z_i : i \in I\} \subseteq \mathbb{C}$ be an arbitrary chain in terms of $\subseteq$, x^1, $x^2 \in \bigcup \{Z_i : i \in I\}$ two arbitrary elements, and $\alpha \in (0, 1)$ an arbitrary scalar. There then are $i_1, i_2 \in I$ such that $x^1 \in Z_{i_1}$ and $x^2 \in Z_{i_2}$. Because $\{Z_i : i \in I\}$ is a chain in terms of $\subseteq$, it follows that either $Z_{i_1} \subseteq Z_{i_2}$ or $Z_{i_2} \subseteq Z_{i_1}$. That is, we have either $x^1, x^2 \in Z_{i_2}$ or $x^1, x^2 \in Z_{i_1}$. No matter which is the case, it follows that $\alpha x^1 + (1 - \alpha)x^2 \in Z_{i_1}$ or $Z_{i_2} \subseteq \bigcup \{Z_i : i \in I\}$. Therefore, $\bigcup\{Z_i : i \in I\} \in \mathbb{C}$.

To show that $(\mathbb{R}^\ell, \mathbb{C})$ is a 2-ary convex space, let $A \subseteq \mathbb{R}^\ell$ be a subset and $x^1, x^2 \in A$ be arbitrary such that $co(x^1, x^2) \subseteq A$; we need to show that A is a convex subset. That is equivalent to demonstrate that $co(x^1, x^2) = \{\alpha x^1 + (1 - \alpha)x^2 : \alpha \in [0, 1]\}$. To this end, let $z^1, z^2 \in co(x^1, x^2)$ and $\alpha \in (0, 1)$ be arbitrary. So, there are $\alpha^1, \alpha^2 \in [0, 1]$ such that

$$z^1 = \alpha^1 x^1 + \left(1 - \alpha^1\right)x^2 \text{ and } z^2 = \alpha^2 x^1 + \left(1 - \alpha^2\right)x^2.$$

Therefore,

$$\alpha z^1 + (1 - \alpha)z^2 = \beta x^1 + [1 - \beta]x^2$$

where $\beta = \alpha\alpha^1 + (1 - \alpha)\alpha^2 \in [\alpha^1, \alpha^2] \subseteq [0, 1]$. That is, what is shown is that $\{\alpha x^1 + (1 - \alpha)x^2 : \alpha \in [0, 1]\}$ is convex so that $co(x^1, x^2) = \{\alpha x^1 + (1 - \alpha) x^2 : \alpha \in [0, 1]\}$. QED

For a convex space $(X, \mathbb{C})$, a preference relation $\precsim$ defined on X is said to be weak convex, if for any x^1, $x^2 \in X$, $x^1 \precsim x^2$ implies that for any $x \in co(\{x^1, x^2\})$, $x^1 \precsim x$. This concept extends that of weak convex preferences proposed in Sect. 15.3.1 for the convex space $(\mathbb{R}^\ell, \mathbb{C})$, where $\mathbb{C}$ is the collection of all convex sets in $\mathbb{R}^\ell$. Because of Proposition 15.9, we can see that in a 2-ary convex space a weak convex preference, as defined here, is the same as convex preference, as so defined in Cardin (2019, 2022).

Proposition 15.9 If $(X, \mathbb{C})$ is a 2-ary convex space and $\precsim$ a complete preorder on X, then $\precsim$ is weak convex if and only if for every $z \in X$, the set $\{x \in X : z \precsim x\}$ is convex.

Evidently, this proposition generalizes Proposition 15.1 from the Euclidean space $\mathbb{R}^\ell$ to the case of any convex space $(X, \mathbb{C})$, where X can be any general set of elements.

Proof ($\Rightarrow$) Let $x^1, x^2, x' \in X$ such that $x^1, x^2 \in \{x \in X : z \precsim x\}$ and $x' \in co(\{x^1, x^2\})$. If $x^1 \precsim x^2$, then from the assumption that $\precsim$ is weak convex, it follows that $z \precsim x^1 \precsim x'$. So, $x' \in \{x \in X : z \precsim x\}$. Since $(X, \mathbb{C})$ is a 2-ary convex space, we conclude that $\{x \in X : z \precsim x\}$ is convex.

($\Leftarrow$) Assume that for any $z \in X$, $\{x \in X : z \precsim x\}$ is convex. Hence, if $x^1, x^2 \in X$ satisfy $x^1 \precsim x^2$, then x^1, $x^2 \in \{x \in X : x^1 \precsim x\}$ and if $z \in co(\{x^1, x^2\})$, then $z \in \{x \in X : x^1 \precsim x\}$.

Proposition 15.10 Let $(X, \mathbb{C})$ be a convex space and $\precsim$ a complete preorder on X. Then, for every $z \in X$, the set $\{x \in X : z \precsim x\}$ is convex, if and only if for any x^1, x^2, ..., $x^n \in X$, for any $n \in \mathbb{N}$,

$$z \precsim x^i, \forall i, 1 \le i \le n, \rightarrow \forall x \in co\left(\{x^1, x^2, \ldots, x^n\}\right), z \precsim x. \tag{15.14}$$

Proof ($\Rightarrow$) If $\{x \in X : z \precsim x\}$ is convex, then for each i, $1 \le i \le n$, $z \precsim x^i$ implies $co(\{x^1, x^2, \ldots, x^n\}) \subseteq \{x \in X : z \precsim x\}$.

($\Leftarrow$) If for every finite subset F of $Z = \{x \in X : z \precsim x\}$ we have $co(F) \subseteq Z$, then by Proposition 2.1 of van de Vel (1993), we can prove that $co(Z) = Z$. Moreover, it is straightforward to show that if $\{x \in X : x^1 \precsim x\}$ is convex and $x^1 \precsim x^2$, then $co(\{x^1, x^2\}) \subseteq \{x \in X : x^1 \precsim x\}$.

Example 15.6 For a given convex space $(X, \mathbb{C})$, let us define a preference relation $\precsim$ on X as follows: For any x, $y \in X$, $y \precsim x$, if

$$\{H \in \mathcal{H} : x \in H\} \supseteq \{H \in \mathcal{H} : y \in H\}.$$

Then, $\precsim$ is reflexive, because for any $x \in X$, $\{H \in \mathcal{H} : x \in H\} \supseteq \{H \in \mathcal{H} : x \in H\}$. The relation $\precsim$ is transitive, because for any x, y, $z \in X$, if $y \precsim x$ and $z \precsim y$, then by definition we have

$$\{H \in \mathcal{H} : x \in H\} \supseteq \{H \in \mathcal{H} : y \in H\} \supseteq \{H \in \mathcal{H} : z \in H\}.$$

Evidently, for each half-space $H \in \mathcal{H}$, if $x \in H$ and $y \notin H$, then x and y are not comparable in terms of the afore-defined relation $\precsim$. That is, $\precsim$ is a preorder defined on X; but, it is not complete.

For any $z \in X$, it can be seen that

$$\{x \in X : z \precsim \mathrm{x}\} = \cap \{H \in \mathcal{H} : z \in H\},$$

so that condition (b) of convex spaces implies that $\{x \in X : z \precsim x\}$ is convex. Hence, the preorder $\precsim$ is a weak convex preference.

By combining Propositions 15.9 and 15.10, it can be readily seen that when $\precsim$ satisfies the condition in Eq. (15.14), $\precsim$ is weak convex.

As for the concept of convex preferences, as proposed in Sect. 15.3.2, we can generalize it to the framework of abstract convex structures. In particular, for a convex space $(X, \mathbb{C})$, a preference relation $\precsim$ defined on X is said to be convex, if for any $x^1, x^2 \in X$, $x^1 \prec x^2$ implies that for each $x \in co(\{x^1, x^2\})$, if $x \square x^1$, then $x^1 \prec x$. For convex preferences, we have the following result:

Proposition 15.11 If $(X, \mathbb{C})$ is a 2-ary convex space and $\precsim$ a complete preorder, then $\precsim$ is convex if and only if for each $z \in X$, the set $\{x \in X : z \prec x\}$ is convex.

If a complete preference is considered, the following can also be shown.

Proposition 15.12 Let $\precsim$ be a complete preorder in a convex space $(X, \mathbb{C})$ such that for every $z \in X$, the set $\{x \in X : z \prec x\}$ is convex. Then, for each $z \in X$, the set $\{x \in X : z \precsim x\}$ is convex.

Proof Since $\precsim$ is a complete preorder, we have

$$\{x \in X : z \precsim \mathrm{x}\} = \bigcap_{y \prec z} \{x \in X : y \prec x\}$$

for every $z \in X$. Because each $\{x \in X : y \prec x\}$ belongs to $\mathbb{C}$, we can conclude that $\{x \in X : z \precsim x\}$ is a convex set.

Hence, as a corollary of Proposition 15.12, the result below follows readily.

Proposition 15.13 If $(X, \mathbb{C})$ is a 2-ary convex space and $\precsim$ a convex complete preorder, then $\precsim$ is weak convex.

Similar to the concepts of weak convex and convex preferences, that of strongly convex preferences can be defined for the general convex space $(X, \mathbb{C})$. Specifically, a preference relation $\precsim$ defined on the convex space $(X, \mathbb{C})$ is said to be strongly convex, if for any $x, y, z \in X$, $x \sim y$ and $B]x, z, y[$ imply $x \prec z$, where $B \subseteq X^3$ is the betweenness relation defined (Cardin, 2019) as follows: $(x, z, y) \in B$ if and only if $\forall\, C \in \mathbb{C}, x, y \in C \rightarrow z \in C$. For convenience, $(x, z, y) \in B$ is written also as $B[x, z, y]$ and is understood as z is located between x and y with the possibility that $z \sim x$ or $z \sim y$. To emphasize the fact that z is between x and y but neither $z \sim x$ nor $z \sim y$, the symbol $B]x, z, y[$ is used.

15.4 Some Final Words

We employ the methods of Euclidean and general convex spaces to address the two theoretically and practically questions posted at the beginning of this chapter. By constructing six examples, we are able to show that:

- The condition that the preference relation of a consumer needs to be complete in order to derive some of the most basic results of the consumer theory.
- Not all consumers have asymptotically preserving preferences.
- The conditions of additive conservation and positive multiplicativity do not generally hold true for the consumption preferences of each and every consumer.
- On a general convex space, a weakly convex preference preorder can be naturally induced by the collection of half-spaces.

And by recognizing the multidimensionality of each consumer's physiological needs, we naturally remove the completeness assumption imposed on each consumer's set of consumption possibilities, as mostly done in the literature (e.g., Hervés-Beloso & Cruces, 2019; Mas-Collel et al., 1995). Doing so enables us to reintroduce the concepts of weak convexity, convexity, and strong convexity for consumer preferences and to reexamine the validity of some of the basic properties of these preferences. Other than confirming the necessity of a few key conditions in order for some known properties to hold, we are able to study issues not faced before so that brand new results are developed.

Beyond its theoretical significance, this chapter also assists in the effort of developing a new consumer theory that will be more practically applicable than the prevalent one, as so called for loudly by Paul Krugman (*New York Times*, 2009-09-02), Paul De Grauwe (*Financial Times*, 2009-07-21), and others.

Due to the length limitation of this presentation, many important questions are left open for future consideration. For example, under the condition that a consumer's set of consumption possibilities is not completely ordered by his preferences, it will be important to uncover the key properties of non-convex preferences (Halevy et al., 2017). And riding on the various concepts of convex preferences established in Sect. 15.3.6, it will be theoretically important to generalize Propositions 15.3–15.8 to the case of general convex spaces (Kubis, 1999; van de Vel, 1993).

References

Alonso, S., Herrera-Viedma, E., Chiclana, F., & Herrera, F. (2010). A web-based consensus support system for group decision making problems and incomplete preferences. *Information Sciences, 180*(23), 4477–4495.

Aumann, R. (1962). Utility theory without the completeness axiom. *Econometrica, 30*, 445–462.

Bewley, T. (1986). *Knightian uncertainty theory: Part I.* Cowles Foundation Discussion Paper No. 807.

Brandl, F., & Brandt, F. (2020). Arrovian aggregation of convex preferences. *Econometrica, 88*(2), 799–844.

Cardin, M. (2019). Convex preferences as aggregation of orderings. In *Proceedings of the 11th conference of the European Society for Fuzzy Logic and Technology* (Vol. 1, pp. 792–796).

Cardin, M. (2022). Convex preferences: An abstract approach. *Fuzzy Sets and Systems, 446*, 233–242.

Cettolin, E., & Riedl, A. (2019). Revealed preferences under uncertainty: Incomplete preferences and preferences for randomization. *Journal of Economic Theory, 181*(May), 547–585.

Chateauneuf, A., & Tallon, J. M. (2002). Diversification, convex preferences, and non-empty core in the Choquet expected utility model. *Economic Theory, 19*(3), 509–523.

Debreu, G. (1959). *Theory of value: An axiomatic analysis of economic equilibrium*. Yale University Press.

Dubra, J., & Ok, E. A. (2002). A model of procedural decision making in the presence of risk. *International Economic Review, 43*(4), 1053–1080.

Forrest, J. Y. L. (2013). *A systemic perspective on cognition and mathematics*. CRC Press, an Imprint of Taylor and Francis.

Forrest, J. Y. L., Tiglioglu, T., Liu, Y., Mong, D., & Cardin, M. (2023). Various convexities and some relevant properties of consumer preference relations. *Studia Universitatis "Vasile Goldis" Arad—Economics Series, 33*(4), 145–168. https://doi.org/10.2478/sues-2023-0021.

Halevy, Y., Persitz, D., & Zrill, L. (2017). Non-parametric bounds for non-convex preferences. *Journal of Economic Behavior & Organization, 137*(May), 105–112.

Hervés-Beloso, C., & Cruces, H. V. (2019). Continuous preference orderings representable by utility functions. *Journal of Economic Surveys, 33*(1), 179–194.

Hu, K., Tao, Y., Ma, Y., & Shi, L. (2021). Peer pressure induced punishment resolves social dilemma on interdependent networks. *Scientific Reports, 11*, 15792.

Jehle, G., & Reny, P. (2000). *Advanced microeconomic theory* (3rd ed.). Pearson.

Kubis, W. (1999). *Abstract convex structures in topology and set theory*. PhD thesis, University of Silesia.

Kuratowski, K., & Mostowski, A. (1976). *Set theory: With an introduction to descriptive set theory*. North-Holland.

Lin, Y. (2008). Systematic studies: The infinity problem in modern mathematics. *Kybernetes: The International Journal of Cybernetics, Systems and Management Sciences, 37*(3–4), 385–542.

Mandler, M. (1999). Incomplete preferences and rational intransitivity of choice. *Mimeo*. Harvard University.

Mani, A., Rahwan, I., & Pentland, A. (2013). Inducing peer pressure to promote cooperation. *Scientific Reports, 3*, 01735.

Mas-Collel, A., Whinston, M. D., & Green, J. R. (1995). *Microeconomic theory*. Oxford University Press.

Meng, F. Y., & Chen, X. H. (2015). A new method for group decision making with incomplete fuzzy preference relations. *Knowledge-Based Systems, 73*(January), 111–123.

Miller, N. H. (2006). *Notes on microeconomic theory*. Retrieved July 11, 2022, from https://nmiller.web.illinois.edu/notes.html.

Ok, E. A. (2002). Utility representation of an incomplete preference relation. *Journal of Economic Theory, 104*(2), 429–449.

Silberger, E. (2000). *The structure of economics: A mathematical analysis* (3rd ed.). Irwin McGraw Hill.

Simon, C. P., & Blume, L. E. (1994). *Mathematics for economists*. W.W. Norton.

van de Vel, M. L. J. (1993). *Theory of convex structures. North-Holland mathematical library* (Vol. 50). Elsevier.

Chapter 16
Budget and Demand Correspondence

Jeffrey Yi-Lin Forrest, Zaiwu Gong, Zhen Li, Shynara Sarkambayeva (Jumadilova), and John Golden

Abstract By clearly distinguishing three binary relations, the first one $\leqq$ defined on the Euclidean space $\mathbb{R}^\ell$, the second one $\precsim_i$ on a consumer's set of all possible consumptions, and the third one $\leq_i$ on real numbers, this chapter, which is mainly based on Forrest et al. (to appear), pays a revisit to some of the elementary properties of budget sets, demand correspondences, and the relationship between an individual's preferences and his specific order $\leq_i$ of real numbers. Other than finding that these visited properties are not generally true without assuming that $\leq_i$ is equal to the conventional order $\leq$ of real numbers and/or without letting the preference relation $\precsim_i$ be complete, reflexive, and transitive on the set X_i of all consumption choices and other than successfully developing results that are parallel to the known ones without imposing unnecessary conditions, this chapter constructs four counterexamples to demonstrate that (1) when $\leq_i \neq \leq$, the continuity of the budget set is in doubt; (2) generally, an individual consumer's demand correspondence is not homogeneous of degree zero; (3) the preference relation $\precsim_i$ is generally not additively conservative or positively multiplicative; and (4) not every preference relation $\precsim_i$ is asymptotically preserving. In the final section, this chapter provides a few topics with expected significance for future research.

Keywords Asymptotically preserving preference · Budget function · Demand correspondence · Price-wealth pair · Semicontinuity

Jeffrey Yi-Lin Forrest (Department of Accounting Economics Finance, Slippery Rock University, Slippery Rock, PA, USA; Email: Jeffrey.forrest@sru.edu), Zaiwu Gong (College of Management Science and Engineering, Nanjing University of Information Science and Technology, Nanjing, China; Email: zwgong26@163.com), Zhen Li (College of Business, Texas Woman's University, Denton, TX, USA; Email: zli@twu.edu), Shynara Sarkambayeva (Jumadilova) (Department of Management and Mathematical Economics, Satbayev University, Almaty, Kazakhstan; Email: shynara.jumadilova@gmail.com), and John Golden (Department of Accounting Economics Finance, Slippery Rock University, Slippery Rock, PA, USA; Email: john.golden@sru.edu) are equally contributed to this chapter.

J. Y.-L. Forrest, *Systemic Principles of Applied Economic Philosophies I*, Translational Systems Sciences 38, https://doi.org/10.1007/978-981-99-7273-9_16

16.1 Introduction

Each consumer, be it an individual person or a business firm, either is a physiological being or takes the form of life that goes through such stages as birth, growth, maturing, and death. To maintain his or its basic survival before consuming any luxurious products, goods, and services, no matter whether it is an individual person or a business firm, it has to first satisfy its basic, physiological/business needs. These needs are generally multidimensional in nature. For example, it needs a shelter or an office domain to house its physical and/or virtual existence and various nutritional intakes or business inputs to satisfy his physiological needs or to maintain its operational demands. When two consumption choices from different dimensions are presented, the consumer cannot truly tell which alternative is preferred to the other. For example, for an individual person, tickets to different world series games and soft drink choices represent examples of consumption alternatives from two different dimensions; for a business firm, personnel needed for maintaining regular operational routines and talents required for innovative R&D purposes are also examples of consumption choices from different dimensions. In either of these two scenarios, the consumption alternatives cannot be directly compared by using the individual consumer's or the business firm's preferences. Speaking differently, only when two consumption alternatives come from the same dimension, a consumer *might* be able to make a pick based on what he prefers. This recognition of incompleteness is different from that as noticed before from the angle of bounded rationality and consumers' indecisiveness (Aumann, 1962; Bewley, 1986; Mandler, 1999; Ok, 2002).

Because of the existence of such multidimensionality with consumption choices, one can readily see that a consumer's set of all possible consumptions cannot be completely ordered by his/its preferences. Hence, to make the relevant economic theory, such as the consumer theory, practically useful in real life, we cannot continue to assume that consumer preferences can compare any two consumption alternatives, as conventionally done as in widely used textbooks and lecture notes (Levin & Milgrom, 2004; Mas-Collel et al., 1995). The existence and maintenance of this convention, to a large extent, are due to the desire for the community of economists to develop a theory that is mathematically beautiful and satisfactory; for more details about this end, see von Neumann and Morgenstern (1944, p. 29) and Paul Krugman's comment (*New York Times*, 2009-09-02). Therefore, the following question naturally arises at this junction. Can we reestablish the key conclusions of the prevalent consumer theory regarding a consumer's budget set and demand correspondence without assuming the completeness of consumption preferences?

As expected, this chapter, which is mainly based on Forrest et al. (to appear), demonstrates that when the assumed completeness is replaced by incompleteness, all related conclusions regarding a consumer's budget set and demand correspondence mostly take their correspondingly different forms or only hold true conditionally. And, because the incompleteness assumption is much closer to real life, one can expect the consequent conclusions to be more useful than the conventional ones in terms of their explanation abilities. Compared to what we attempt to do here, there are also parallel efforts in the literature. For example, when it is recognized that preference relations generally only satisfy reflexivity without completeness and transitivity, Ok (2002), Bosi and Herden (2012), and Nishimura and Ok (2016) consider the problem of how to represent an incomplete preference relation by means of a collection of real-number valued functions. This end is parallel to the classical conclusion that a complete preference relation can be possibly represented by a real-number valued utility function.

The rest of this chapter is organized as follows. Section 16.2 studies the continuity of a consumer's budget set and consists of two subsections, one about when a consumer's budget function is continuous and the other on the necessity of assuming $\leq_i = \leq$. Section 16.3 looks at the demand correspondence of an individual, while Sect. 16.4 looks at some properties of the total demand correspondence. Section 16.5 explores the relationship between consumption preferences and the order of real numbers. It is made up of two subsections with one on the consistency between preference relations and orders of real numbers, and the other a few properties on feasible price-wealth pairs. The chapter is concluded in Sect. 16.6 with several suggestions for future research topics.

16.2 Is a Consumer's Budget Function Continuous?

This section examines the continuity of a consumer's budget set, while a counter-example is constructed to show that without assuming consumer-specific order of real number is the same as the conventional one, a consumer's budget set cannot be shown to be continuous with the argument given here.

To make this chapter as self-contained as possible, let us quickly review some of the key terminologies introduced earlier.

Assume that $\leq_i$ (respectively, $<_i$, $>_i$, $\geq_i$, $=_i$) represents consumer i's order of real numbers. There are then three order relations involved here:

- $\leqq$ (respectively, $<$, $>$, $\geqq$, $=$) defined on $\mathbb{R}^\ell$, where $\mathbb{R}$ is the set of all real numbers (in the rest of this paper, $\mathbb{R}_+$ stands for the set of all positive real numbers), as in Eq. (16.1). For any $x^1, x^2 \in \mathbb{R}^\ell$,

$$x^1 \leqq x^2 \quad \text{if and only if} \quad x_h^1 \leq x_h^2, \quad \text{for} \quad h = 1, 2, \ldots, \ell. \tag{16.1}$$

- $\precsim_i$ (respectively, $\prec_i$, $\succ_i$, $\succsim_i$, $=_i$) defined on X_i.
- $\leq_i$ (defined on $\mathbb{R}$).

The binary relation $\precsim_i$ is said to be a preorder, if it satisfies (i) reflexivity (for any $x_i \in X_i$, $x_i \precsim_i x_i$) and (ii) transitivity (for any $x_i^1, x_i^2, x_i^3 \in X_i$, $x_i^1 \precsim_i x_i^2$ and $x_i^2 \precsim_i x_i^3$ imply $x_i^1 \precsim_i x_i^3$). It is said to be complete, if each pair $x_i^1, x_i^2 \in X_i$ can be compared by $\precsim_i$. To make our conclusions closer to real-life situations, the preference relation $\precsim_i$

considered in this chapter is not generally assumed to be a complete preorder unless it is specifically mentioned so.

Without loss of generality, we assume that $\leq_i$ is reflexive, transitive, and anti-symmetric (for any a, b, $c \in \mathbb{R}$, $a \leq_i b$ and $b \leq_i c$ imply $a \leq_i c$). Please note that this assumption does not mean that $\precsim_i$ is rational or that $\precsim_i$ is reflexive, transitive, and complete (Mas-Collel et al., 1995).

16.2.1 Condition Under Which a Consumer's Budget Function Is Continuous

For consumer i, assume that he has accumulated a certain amount of wealth, denoted as a real number w_i. So, he chooses his consumption $x_i \in X_i$ subject to the constraint $p \cdot x_i \leq_i w_i$, for any given price system $p \in \mathbb{R}_+^\ell$ of commodities, where $p = (p_1, p_2, \ldots, p_\ell)$ stands for the price vector of the commodities $h = 1, 2, \ldots, \ell$. As noted above, consumer i's order $\leq_i$ of real numbers is defined specifically by consumer i's system of values and beliefs. In terms of the literature, the consumer-specific order $\leq_i$ of real numbers has been assumed to be the same as the conventional one $\leq$ (Levin & Milgrom, 2004; Mas-Collel et al., 1995). Evidently, this commonly adopted order $\leq$ of real numbers reflects a certain category of systems of values and beliefs. However, there are such value-belief systems that dictate the ordering of real numbers differently. For example, corresponding to the concept of corporate social responsibilities (Liu et al., 2018; Poist, 1989), consumer i pledges to give back to the society by donating a portion of his wealth to his favorite charity organizations, following the following scheme: As soon as the accumulation of his wealth reaches the level of, say, 30 units, he will donate away that entire 30 units of wealth. In other words, consumer i's consumption $x_i \in X_i$ is subject to the constraint $p \cdot x_i \leq w_i \bmod (30)$.

Assume that there are m consumers in the population of concern so that the wealth vector $w = (w_1, w_2, \ldots, w_m) \in \mathbb{R}^\ell$ expresses the wealth distribution of the population. The vector $(p, w) \in \mathbb{R}^{\ell + m}$ is referred to as the price-wealth pair (Debreu, 1959) of the population. Define the set of feasible price-wealth pairs of consumer i, for each $i = 1, 2, \ldots, m$,

$$S_i = \left\{(p, w) \in \mathbb{R}^{\ell+m} : \exists x_i \in X_i \text{ such that } p \cdot x_i \leq_i w_i\right\},$$

and a set-valued budget function $\gamma_i : S_i \to X_i$: For any $(p, w) \in S_i$,

$$\gamma_i(p, w) = \{x_i \in X_i : p \cdot x_i \leq_i w_i\}, \tag{16.2}$$

where $\gamma_i(p, w)$ is referred to as the budget set of consumer i (Levin & Milgrom, 2004), when the price system is p and the wealth level is w.

A set-valued function $f: A \to B$, for A and $B \subseteq \mathbb{R}^{\ell}$, is said to be continuous at a point $a^0 \in A$ (Kuratowski & Mostowski, 1976), if f satisfies both

- (Upper semicontinuity at a^0) For any $\{a^q\}_{q=1}^{\infty} \subseteq A$ such that $a^q \to a^0 \in A$, if $b^q \to b^0 \in B$, for any $\{b^q\}_{q=1}^{\infty} \subseteq B$ with $b^q \in f(a^q)$, then $b^0 \in f(a^0)$.
- (Lower semicontinuity at a^0) If $a^q \to a^0$ and $b^0 \in f(a^0)$, then there is $\{b^q\}_{q=1}^{\infty} \subseteq B$ with $b^q \in f(a^q)$ such that $b^q \to b^0$.

Proposition 16.1 Assume that each infinity can be actually (not potentially) achieved and that $\leq_i$ is the same as $\leq$. If a price-wealth pair $(p^0, w^0) \in S_i$ satisfies $w_i^0 \neq \min_{x_i \in X_i} p^0 \cdot x_i$, then γ_i is continuous at (p^0, w^0).

Proof First, we show the upper semicontinuity. Assume that $\{(p^q, w^q)\}_{q=1}^{\infty} \subseteq S_i$ is a convergent sequence of price-wealth pairs such that $(p^q, w^q) \to (p^0, w^0) \in S_i$. Then,

$$\gamma_i(p^q, w^q) = \{x_i \in X_i : p^q \cdot x_i \leq w_i^q\}, \quad q = 0, 1, 2, \ldots$$

For any convergent sequence $\{x^q\}_{q=1}^{\infty}, x_i^q \in \gamma_i(p^q, w^q), q = 1, 2, \ldots$, if $x_i^q \to x_i^0 \in X_i$, as $q \to \infty$, we need to show $x_i^0 \in \gamma_i(p^0, w^0)$. This end follows from the facts that $x_i^q \in X_i$ satisfies

$$p^q \cdot x_i^q \leq w_i^q \tag{16.3}$$

and that in Euclidean space $\mathbb{R}^{\ell + m}$, $(p^q, w^q) \to (p^0, w^0)$ is equivalent to $p^q \to p^0$ and $w^q \to w^0$. Hence, Eq. (16.3) implies that as $q \to \infty$, we have $p^0 \cdot x_i^0 \leq w_i^0$. That is, $x_i^0 \in \gamma_i(p^0, w^0)$.

Second, we show the lower semicontinuity. Assume that $\{(p^q, w^q)\}_{q=1}^{\infty} \subseteq S_i$ is a convergent sequence of price-wealth pairs such that $(p^q, w^q) \to (p^0, w^0) \in S_i$, and that $x_i^0 \in \gamma_i(p^0, w^0)$ so that $p^0 \cdot x_i^0 \leq w_i^0$. To conclude the rest of the argument, it needs to show the existence of an infinite sequence $\{x_i^q\}_{q=1}^{\infty} \subseteq X_i$ such that $p^q \cdot x_i^q \leq w_i^q$, for $q = 1, 2, \ldots$, and $x_i^q \to x_i^0$, as $q \to \infty$. This is where the assumption that each infinity can be actually (not potentially) achieved comes into play. In particular, Lin (2008) documents that potential infinities and actual infinities are fundamental different concepts; and they can lead to and have indeed led to completely inconsistent outcomes (Forrest, 2013), while the existence of the desired sequence $\{x_i^q\}_{q=1}^{\infty} \subseteq X_i$ mistakenly treated potential infinities as actual ones.

To understand the previous paragraph, let us briefly examine the concept of infinities. It involves two different types of infinities with one known as actual infinities and the other potential infinities (Lin, 2008). Specifically, a potential infinity represents a forever-ongoing and never-ending process or procedure; and every actual infinity characterizes a process that actually ends or had ended. To see how this concept of infinities applied to our current situation, let us construct the desired sequence in two different cases: (i) $p^0 \cdot x_i^0 < w_i^0$ and (ii) $p^0 \cdot x_i^0 = w_i^0$.

For case (i), because $(p^q, w^q) \longrightarrow (p^0, w^0)$, there is a subsequence $\{(p^q, w^q)\}_{q=q^*}^{\infty}$, for some large integer q^*, such that $p^q \cdot x_i^0 < w_i^q$, for $q = q^*, q^* + 1, q^* + 2, \ldots$ Now, each term x_i^q of the desired sequence $\{x_i^q\}_{q=1}^{\infty} \subseteq X_i$ can be constructed as follows:

$$x_i^q = \begin{cases} \text{an element in } \gamma_i(p^q, w^q), & \text{if } q \leq q^* \\ x_i^0, & \text{if } q > q^* \end{cases}$$

That is, for each chosen q, the term x_i^q is defined, representing a potential process, while the existence of the entire sequence $\{x_i^q\}_{q=1}^{\infty}$ stands for an actual infinity, where a forever-ongoing process is assumed to be finished. That is, potentials are actual infinities seen as the same.

For case (ii). where $p^0 \cdot x_i^0 = w_i^0$, the assumption $w_i^0 \neq \min_{x_i \in X_i} p^0 \cdot x_i$ implies that there is $z_i \in X_i$ such that $p^0 \cdot z_i < w_i^0$. So, the assumed limit $(p^q, w^q) \longrightarrow (p^0, w^0)$ implies that there is an integer q^*, such that for $q = q^*, q^* + 1, q^* + 2, \ldots,$

$$p^q \cdot z_i < w_i^q \text{ and } p^q \cdot z_i < p^q \cdot x_i^0. \tag{16.4}$$

For each q (=1, 2, ...), let us respectively consider the following hyperplane determined by (p^q, w^q) and the line that passes through z_i and x_i^0:

$$p^q \cdot x_i = w_i^q \text{ and } x_i = x_i^0 + t\left(z_i - x_i^0\right),$$

for $x_i \in \mathbb{R}^\ell$ and $t \in \mathbb{R}$. It can be seen that the intersection a_i^q of this hyperplane and the line is determined by $a_i^q = x_i^0 + t^*\left(z_i - x_i^0\right)$, where

$$t^* = \frac{w_i^q - p^q \cdot x_i^0}{p^q \cdot (z_i - x_i^0)}.$$

So, the second inequality in Eq. (16.4) implies $p^q \cdot \left(z_i - x_i^0\right) \neq 0$, for $q \geq q^*$. That means that for large q ($\geq q^*$), a_i^q is well defined uniquely and satisfies $\lim_{q \to \infty} a_i^q = x_i^0$. So, the qth term of the imagined sequence $\{x_i^q\}_{q=1}^{\infty}$ can be defined as follows:

$$x_i^q = \begin{cases} \text{an element in } \gamma_i(p^q, w^q), & \text{if } q \leq q^+ \\ a_i^q, & \text{if } q > q^+ \end{cases},$$

where $a_i^q \in \gamma_i(p^q, w^q)$. Once again, the existence of the sequence $\{x_i^q\}_{q=1}^{\infty}$ is only possible under the assumption that potential and actual infinities are the same.

16.2.2 The Necessity of the Assumed $\leq_i = \leq$

In terms of the literature, Proposition 16.1 generalizes relevant results (e.g., Debreu, 1959, p. 63) by removing unnecessary conditions imposed on the range of the set-valued function γ_i, such as the assumptions of compactness and convexity of X_i.

There are two assumptions in Proposition 16.1. The reason why the first one on infinities is needed is explained within the proof; and, without it, the conclusion cannot be established, because potential and actual infinities are generally different (Forrest, 2013). As for the second assumption $\leq_i = \leq$, the following Example 16.1 shows that in general, the conclusion in Proposition 16.1 does not follow without this assumption.

Example 16.1 Assume that an economy has only one consumer, such as the economic situation of an individual consumer that he does not have any financial responsibilities for anybody except himself. Assume that his system of values and beliefs demands him to order real numbers by using modular r function, for $r \in \mathbb{R}_+$. That is, this consumer orders real numbers by using $\leq_{\text{mod}(r)}$ so that for any $a, b \in \mathbb{R}$, $a \leq_{\text{mod}(r)} b$ if and only if the positive remainder of $a \div r \leq$ that of $b \div r$. For example, $4.1 \leq_{\text{mod}(4)} 1.2$, because $4.1 \div 4 = 0.1$, while $0.1 \leq 1.2$; and $-1.2 \leq_{\text{mod}(4)} -4.1$, because $2.8 \leq 3.9$, where $-1.2 \div 4 = (-4 + 2.8) \div 4 = -1 + 2.8 \div 4$ and $-4.1 \div 4 = (-8 + 3.9) \div 4 = -2 + 3.9 \div 4$.

Consider the following sequence $\{(p^q, w^q)\}_{q=1}^{\infty} \subseteq \mathbb{R}_+^{\ell+1}$ of price-wealth pairs defined by $p^q = p^0$, for a fixed price system $p^0 = (1, 1, \ldots, 1) \in \mathbb{R}_+^{\ell}$, and $w^q = r - 1/q$, for a fixed price system $p^0 \in \mathbb{R}^{\ell}$, and $q = 1, 2, \ldots$ It is ready to see that $(p^q, w^q) \to (p^0, r)$, when $q \to \infty$.

Next, let us construct a sequence $\{x^q\}_{q=1}^{\infty}$ of possible consumptions from the consumer's set X as follows: For any $q \in \mathbb{N}$,

$$x^q = \left(x_1^q, x_2^q, \ldots, x_\ell^q\right) \in \gamma(p^q, w^q) = \left\{x \in X : p^q \cdot x \leq_{\text{mod}(r)} w^q\right\}$$

such that $x_i^q = (r - 1/q)/\ell$, for $i = 1, 2, \ldots, \ell$. Then it can be readily seen that $x^q \to x^0 = \left(x_1^0, x_2^0, \ldots, x_\ell^0\right)$ so that $x_i^0 = r/\ell$, for $i = 1, 2, \ldots, \ell$. However, we have

$$\left(x_1^0, x_2^0, \ldots, x_\ell^0\right) = \left(\frac{r}{\ell}, \frac{r}{\ell}, \ldots, \frac{r}{\ell}\right) \notin \gamma(p^0, w^0)$$

because $\gamma(p^0, w^0) = \{x \in X : p^0 \cdot x \leq_{\text{mod}(r)} w^0\} = \{x \in X : (1, 1, \ldots, 1) \cdot x = 0\} = \{(0, 0, \ldots, 0)\}$.

That is, what is shown is that for this particular single consumer economy, when the consumer orders real numbers based on his system of values and beliefs by using $\leq_{\text{mod}(r)}$, for any $r \in \mathbb{R}_+$, the set-valued function $\gamma(p, w)$ is not upper semicontinuous from the feasible price-wealth set into the budget set.

16.3 A Consumer's Demand Correspondence

As the title suggests, this section studies a consumer's demand correspondence and establishes four propositions regarding the relevant concepts. In particular, for any given price-wealth pair $(p, w) \in S_i$, consumer i chooses such a consumption $x_i' \in \gamma_i(p, w)$ that $x_i' \succsim_i z_i$, for any $\precsim_i$-comparable $z_i \in \gamma_i(p, w)$. If such consumption x_i' exists, it is known as an i's equilibrium consumption relative to (p, w), denoted by $x_i^{\max}(p, w)$. For consumer i to select $x_i^{\max} \in \gamma_i(p, w)$, it means that:

(a) He selects the quantities of the commodities he will consume.
(b) He decides on the quantities of the kinds of labor he will provide to the market.
(c) The chosen quantities of commodities and labor jointly form an optimal consumption within his limited wealth.

Because consumptions in X_i are generally not completely comparable by the preference relation $\precsim_i$, if there is such an equilibrium consumption $x_i^{\max}$, its existence is not generally unique. Hence, for $(p, w) \in S_i$, there are three possibilities: No equilibrium consumption $x_i^{\max}(p, w) \in \gamma_i(p, w)$ exists, a unique $x_i^{\max}(p, w) \in \gamma_i(p, w)$ exists, and multiple $x_i^{\max}(p, w) \in \gamma_i(p, w)$ exist. Define the following subset of S_i

$$S_i^{\max} = \{(p, w) \in S_i : \exists x_i^{\max}(p, w) \in \gamma_i(p, w) \; w.r.t. \precsim_i\}, \tag{16.5}$$

and a set-valued function $\xi_i : S_i^{\max} \to X_i$, known as consumer i's demand correspondence (Debreu, 1959), such that for any $(p, w) \in S_i^{\max}$,

$$\xi_i(p, w) = \{x_i \in X_i : x_i \in \max_{\precsim_i} \{z_i \in X_i : p \cdot z_i \leq_i w_i\}\}, \tag{16.6}$$

where $\max_{\precsim_i}$ stands for the maximal or maximum operation with respect to the preference relation $\precsim_i$. Hence, the conclusion below comes naturally from these definitions above:

Proposition 16.2 For any consumptions x_i^1, $x_i^2 \in \xi_i(p, w)$, one of the following holds true:

(i) $x_i^1 \sim_i x_i^2$;
(ii) x_i^1 and x_i^2 are not comparable with respect to the preference relation $\precsim_i$.

As for the case when the preference relation $\precsim_i$ is complete, such as the case that $\precsim_i$ becomes complete on a subset A of X_i, although the original $\precsim_i$ is incomplete, the following holds true.

Proposition 16.3 If the preference relation $\precsim_i$ is a complete preorder and for $(p^1, w^1), (p^2, w^2) \in S_i^{\max}$, there are $x_i^{10} \in \xi_i(p^1, w^1)$ and $x_i^{20} \in \xi_i(p^2, w^2)$ such that $x_i^{20} \prec_i x_i^{10}$, then for any $x_i^1 \in \xi_i(p^1, w^1)$ and $x_i^2 \in \xi_i(p^2, w^2)$, neither $x_i^1 \prec_i x_i^2$ nor $x_i^1 \sim_i x_i^2$ holds true.

Proof By contradiction, assume that there are certain $x_i^k \in \xi_i(p^k, w^k)$, for $k = 1$, 2, such that either (i) $x_i^1 \prec_i x_i^2$ or (ii) $x_i^1 \sim_i x_i^2$. From $x_i^{k0}, x_i^k \in \xi_i(p^k, w^k)$, for $k = 1, 2$, it follows that $x_i^{10} \sim_i x_i^1$ and $x_i^{20} \sim_i x_i^2$, because $\precsim_i$ is complete.

If case (i) is true, then we have

$$x_i^{10} \sim_i x_i^1 \prec_i x_i^2 \sim_i x_i^{20},$$

which contradicts to the assumption of $x_i^{20} \prec_i x_i^{10}$. So, case (i) cannot be true.

If case (ii) holds true, then we have

$$x_i^{20} \prec_i x_i^{10} \sim_i x_i^1 \sim_i x_i^2 \sim_i x_i^{20},$$

which means $x_i^{20} \prec_i x_i^{20}$ because of the transitivity of $\precsim_i$, an impossible scenario for complete preorder $\precsim_i$. Hence, case (ii) is an incorrect assumption.

Combining what are argued above, we conclude that neither (i) nor (ii) can be true.

Similar to Proposition 16.3, the following result can be shown:

Proposition 16.4 If the preference relation $\precsim_i$ is a complete preorder, and for $(p^1, w^1), (p^2, w^2) \in S_i^{\max}$, there are $x_i^{10} \in \xi_i(p^1, w^1)$ and $x_i^{20} \in \xi_i(p^2, w^2)$ such that $x_i^{20} \sim_i x_i^{10}$, then for any $x_i^1 \in \xi_i(p^1, w^1)$ and $x_i^2 \in \xi_i(p^2, w^2)$, the indifference relation $x_i^2 \sim_i x_i^1$ holds true.

Proof By contradiction. Assume that there are $x_i^1 \in \xi_i(p^1, w^1)$ and $x_i^2 \in \xi_i(p^2, w^2)$ such that $x_i^1 \not\sim_i x_i^2$. Then there are two possibilities: (i) $x_i^1 \succ_i x_i^2$ or (ii) $x_i^1 \prec_i x_i^2$. However, according to Proposition 16.3, if either (i) or (ii) holds true, then $x_i^{20} \sim_i x_i^{10}$ cannot hold true. This end contradicts the given conditions. Hence, the assumption that $x_i^1 \not\sim_i x_i^2$, for some $x_i^k \in \xi_i(p^k, w^k)$, for $k = 1$, 2, cannot hold true.

For $(p^1, w^1), (p^2, w^2) \in S_i^{\max}$, consumer i prefers the price-wealth pair (p^1, w^1) to the pair (p^2, w^2), if there are $x_i^1 \in \xi_i(p^1, w^1)$ and $x_i^2 \in \xi_i(p^2, w^2)$ such that $x_i^2 \prec_i x_i^1$. If, instead, there are such consumptions $x_i^k \in \xi_i(p^k, w^k)$, $k = 1$, 2, that $x_i^1 \sim_i x_i^2$, then the price-wealth pairs (p^1, w^1) and (p^2, w^2) are said to be indifferent.

Proposition 16.5 If the preference relation $\precsim_i$ is a complete preorder, then the preference relation, as just defined above on $S_i^{\max}$, is also a complete preorder.

This conclusion follows directly from Propositions 16.3 and 16.4. And without causing confusion, in this case, the preference relation defined on $S_i^{\max}$ will also be written as $\precsim_i$.

The following reasoning illustrates that when the preference relation $\precsim_i$ is not a complete preorder, then the preference relation defined above on $S_i^{\max}$ might not be well defined. Specifically, there might be price-wealth pairs (p^1, w^1) and $(p^2, w^2) \in S_i^{\max}$ such that there are $x_i^1, x_i^{10} \in \xi_i(p^1, w^1)$ and $x_i^2, x_i^{20} \in \xi_i(p^2, w^2)$ such that

$$x_i^1 \prec_i x_i^2 \quad \text{and} \quad x_i^{20} \prec_i x_i^{10}.$$

For this end to hold, we only need to make sure to select $x_i^1, x_i^{10} \in \xi_i(p^1, w^1)$ and $x_i^2, x_i^{20} \in \xi_i(p^2, w^2)$ so that x_i^1 and x_i^{10} are $\precsim_i$ incomparable, and so are x_i^2 and x_i^{20}.

16.4 Homogeneity of the Total Demand Correspondence

Expanding the scope of attention in the previous sections, this section examines the total demand correspondence of all consumers.

If for the preference relation $\precsim_i$ there is such a subset $X_i^* \subseteq X_i$ that for any x_i^1 and $x_i^2 \in X_i^*$, $x_i^1 \neq x_i^2$ implies that $\left[x_i^1\right] \neq \left[x_i^2\right]$ and $X_i = \cap_{x_i \in X_i^*} [x_i]$, then this subset X_i^* is referred to as a set of (consumer i's) preference representations. The idea behind such a set X_i^* is that when the preference relation $\precsim_i$ is only reflexive without being complete and transitive, it cannot generally be utility representable. For the incompleteness of some $\precsim_i$, see, for example, Bosi and Herden (2012) and Nishimura and Ok (2016), and for the nontransitivity of certain $\precsim_i$, see, for example, Birnbaum and Gutierrez (2007), Forrest et al. (2023a), and Tversky (1969). Therefore, in real-life applications of relevant economic theories, an appropriate X_i^* can be chosen to play the role as that a real-number valued utility function has conventionally played (Mas-Collel et al., 1995).

For a chosen set $X_i^* \subseteq X_i$ of consumer i's preference representations, let $u_i : X_i \to X_i^*$ be the canonical utility function of consumer i such that for any consumption $x_i \in X_i$, $u_i(x_i) = x_i^* \in X_i^*$, if $x_i \in \left[x_i^*\right]$. It is shown (Forrest et al., 2023a) that if $\precsim_i$ is a complete preorder on X_i, the aforementioned subset $X_i^* \subseteq X_i$ exists.

For each maximal chain $X_i^{\max}$ in X_i^*, the u_i-preimage of the chain $X_i^{\max}$ is equal to

$$u_i^{-1}\left(X_i^{\max}\right) = \cup\left\{\left[x_i^*\right] : x_i^* \in X_i^{\max}\right\}.$$

In the rest of this chapter, assume that a set X_i^* of (consumer i's) preference representations exists and is chosen, and for any maximal chain $X_i^{\max}$ in X_i^* a utility function $u_i^{\max} : u_i^{-1}\left(X_i^{\max}\right) \to \mathbb{R}$ also exists and is fixed.

Proposition 16.6 If consumer i's ordering $\leq_i$ of real numbers satisfies the condition of positive multiplicativity, that is, for any scalar $\alpha > 0$ and $a, b \in \mathbb{R}$, $a \leq_i b \to \alpha a \leq_i \alpha b$, then for any $t \in \mathbb{R}_+$, $\xi_i(tp, tw) = \xi_i(p, w)$.

Proof From Eq. (16.6), it follows that

$$\xi_i(tp, tw) = \left\{x_i \in X_i : x_i \in \max_{\precsim_i}\{z_i \in X_i : tp \cdot z_i \leq_i tw_i\}\right\}.$$

Because the ordering $\leq_i$ satisfies the condition of positive multiplicativity, $tp \cdot z_i \leq_i tw_i$ is equivalent to $p \cdot z_i \leq_i w_i$. Hence, the previous expression is equal to

$$\left\{x_i \in X_i : x_i \in \max_{\precsim_i}\{z_i \in X_i : p \cdot z_i \leq_i w_i\}\right\} = \xi_i(p, w).$$

That is, we have shown $\xi_i(tp, tw) = \xi_i(p, w)$, for any $t \in \mathbb{R}_+$.

The condition of positive multiplicity evidently holds true for the conventional ordering of real numbers. However, the following example shows that it does not hold true generally for a randomly chosen ordering of real numbers.

Example 16.2 Here a situation is constructed to show that positive multiplicativity is not generally satisfied by any ordering of real numbers. In particular, the condition of positive multiplicativity is not satisfied by the order relation $\leq_{\mathrm{mod}(4)}$. In fact, we have

$$1 \leq_{\mathrm{mod}(4)} 2 \nrightarrow 2 \cdot 1 \leq_{\mathrm{mod}(4)} 2 \cdot 2$$

where the left-hand side is actually $2 \cdot 1 = 2 \geq_{\mathrm{mod}(4)} 2 \cdot 2 = 0 =$ the right-hand side.

For a price-wealth pair $(p, w) \in \mathbb{R}^{\ell + m}$, if $(p, w) \in \cup_{i=1}^{m} S_i^{\max}$, meaning that for each $i = 1, 2, \ldots, m$, there is at least one maximal consumption $x_i^{\max} \in \gamma_i(p, w)$, define the following set-valued, partial function $\xi : \mathbb{R}^{\ell+m} \to \sum_{i=1}^{m} X_i = \{x = x_1 + x_2 + \ldots + x_m : x_i \in X_i, i = 1, 2, \ldots, m\}$:

$$\xi(p, w) = \sum_{i=1}^{m} \xi_i(p, w), \tag{16.7}$$

such that the domain of ξ is $\cap_{i=1}^{m} S_i^{\max}$ and that for each $x = x_1 + x_2 + \ldots + x_m \in \xi(p, w)$, $x_i = x_i^{\max} \in \xi_i(p, w)$ is a maximal consumption of consumer i. This function ξ is referred to as the total demand correspondence (Debreu, 1959). Both Proposition 16.6 and Eq. (16.7) jointly imply that

Proposition 16.7 For any $(p, w) \in \cap_{i=1}^{m} S_i^{\max}$ and any scalar $t \in (0, +\infty)$, $\xi(tp, tw) = \xi(p, w)$.

Proposition 16.8 For a given price-wealth pair $(p, w) \in S_i$, x_i^* is a maximal element in $\gamma_i(p, w)$ with respect to the preference relation $\precsim_i$, if and only if x_i^* minimizes the expenditure $p \cdot x_i$ on the set $\left\{x_i \in X_i : x_i \succsim_i x_i^*\right\}$.

Proof $(\Rightarrow)$ Assume that $x_i^* \in \max_{\precsim_i} \gamma_i(p, w)$. From Eq. (16.2), it follows that:

$$\begin{aligned} x_i^* \quad &\in \max_{\precsim_i}\{x_i \in X_i : p \cdot x_i \leq_i w_i\} \\ &= \min_{\precsim_i}\{x_i \in X_i : p \cdot x_i \geq_i w_i\} \\ &= \min_{x_i \in X_i, p \cdot x_i \geq_i w_i}\left\{x_i \in X_i : x_i \succsim_i x_i^*\right\}. \end{aligned}$$

That is, x_i^* minimizes the expenditure $p \cdot x_i$ on the set $\left\{x_i \in X_i : x_i \succsim_i x_i^*\right\}$.

(⇐) The argument for this part is similar to the reasoning above except that we move forward in the opposite direction.

16.5 Individually Defined Preferences and Orders of Real Numbers

This section scrutinizes the relationship between preferences and orders of real numbers. It constructs two counterexamples to demonstrate the necessity for the preference relation to satisfy the conditions of additive conservation and positive multiplicativity.

16.5.1 Consistency Between Preference Relations and Orders of Real Numbers

One can readily see that both $\precsim_i$ and $\leq_i$ are defined on consumer i's system of values and beliefs, although the preference relation $\precsim_i$ can be temporarily influenced by peers and altered slightly by peer pressures (Hu et al., 2021; Li et al., 2022; Mani et al., 2013). In other words, because of their common roots, in some measures $\precsim_i$ and $\leq_i$ cannot be inconsistent with each other. One way to describe such consistency between these orders is for us to adopt the following axioms from Debreu (1959).

Axiom 16.1 For any price-wealth pair $(p. w) \in S_i$, any consumption $x_i \in X_i$, and a chosen $x_i^* \in X_i$, $p \cdot x_i \leq_i w_i$ implies $x_i \precsim_i x_i^*$.

Axiom 16.2 For any price-wealth pair $(p. w) \in S_i$, any consumption $x_i \in X_i$, and a chosen $x_i^* \in X_i$, $x_i \succsim_i x_i^*$ implies $p \cdot x_i \geq_i w_i$.

Preference relation $\precsim_i$ is said to be continuous (Forrest et al., 2023a), if for any maximal chain $X_i^{\max}$ in X_i^*, and for each $x_i' \in u_i^{-1}(X_i^{\max})$, the following sets are closed in $u_i^{-1}(X_i^{\max})$:

$$\left\{x_i \in u_i^{-1}\left(X_i^{\max}\right) : x_i \precsim_i x_i'\right\} \quad \text{and} \quad \left\{x_i \in u_i^{-1}\left(X_i^{\max}\right) : x_i \succsim_i x_i'\right\}. \tag{16.8}$$

The relation $\precsim_i$ is said to be an additively conserved preference, if for any consumptions $a_i^j, b_i^j \in X_i, j = 1, 2,$

$$a_i^1 \precsim_i b_i^1 \text{ and } a_i^2 \precsim_i b_i^2 \rightarrow a_i^1 + a_i^2 \precsim_i b_i^1 + b_i^2, \tag{16.9}$$

where the sign $\precsim_i$ becomes $\prec_i$ in the consequence, if $\prec_i$ appears in at least one of the two antecedents. Accordingly, the relation $\precsim_i$ is said to be a positively multiplicative preference, if for any consumptions $x_i^1, x_i^2 \in X_i$ and any scalar $\alpha > 0$,

$$x_i^1 \precsim_i x_i^2 \rightarrow a x_i^1 \precsim_i a x_i^2,$$

where the sign $\precsim_i$ will become $\prec_i$ in the consequence, if $\prec_i$ appears in the antecedent. And, $\precsim_i$ is said to be an asymptotically preserving preference, if for each sequence $\{x_i^q\}_{q=1}^{\infty} \subseteq X_i$, satisfying $x_i^q \succsim_i x_i^0$ (respectively, $x_i^q \precsim_i x_i^0$), for each $q \in \mathbb{N}$ and some $x_i^0 \in X_i$, $\lim_{q\rightarrow\infty} x_i^q \succsim_i x_i^0$ (respectively, $\lim_{q\rightarrow\infty} x_i^q \precsim_i x_i^0$), whenever the limit exists.

Proposition 16.9 If the following conditions hold true, then Axiom 16.2 implies Axiom 16.1.

(i) $w_i \neq_i \min_{z_i \in X_i} p \cdot z_i$.
(ii) Preference relation $\precsim_i$ satisfies the conditions of additive conservation and positive multiplicativity.
(iii) Consumer i's consumptions asymptotically preserve preference relation $\precsim_i$.

Proof For any price-wealth pair $(p. w) \in S_i$, any consumption $x_i \in X_i$, and a fixed $x_i^* \in X_i$, assume that $x_i \succsim_i x_i^*$ implies $p \cdot x_i \geq_i w_i$. Equivalently, $p \cdot x_i <_i w_i$ implies $x_i^* \succ_i x_i$. We need to show that for any consumption $x_i \in X_i$, if $p \cdot x_i \leq_i w_i$, then $x_i \precsim_i x_i^*$.

Axiom 16.2 implies that for any consumption $x_i \in X_i$, $p \cdot x_i <_i w_i$ implies $x_i \prec_i x_i^*$. For the rest of this proof, we focus on showing that for any consumption $x_i \in X_i$, $p \cdot x_i =_i w_i$ implies $x_i \precsim_i x_i^*$. To this end, because $w_i \neq_i \min_{z_i \in X_i} p \cdot z_i$, there is a consumption $x_i^1 \in X_i$ such that $x_i^1 \neq x_i$, and $p \cdot x_i^1 <_i w_i$.

For any scalar $\alpha \in (0, 1)$, define $z_i(\alpha) = \alpha x_i^1 + (1-\alpha)x_i$. From $p \cdot x_i^1 <_i w_i$ and $p \cdot x_i =_i w_i$, the condition of positive multiplicativity guarantees that $p \cdot \left(\alpha x_i^1\right) <_i \alpha w_i$ and $p \cdot (1-\alpha)x_i =_i (1-\alpha)w_i$. So, the condition of additive conservation implies

$$p \cdot z_i(\alpha) = p \cdot \alpha x_i^1 + p \cdot (1-\alpha)x_i <_i \alpha w_i + (1-\alpha)w_i = w_i.$$

So, Axiom 16.2 implies that $z_i(\alpha) \prec_i x_i^*$ and that for any natural number q, $z_i(q^{-1}) = q^{-1}x_i^1 + (1-q^{-1})x_i \rightarrow x_i$. So, the asymptotical preservation of consumer i's preference implies that $x_i = \lim_{q\rightarrow\infty} z_i(q^{-1}) \precsim_i x_i^*$.

In terms of the literature, the conclusion that Axiom 16.2 implies Axiom 16.1 was established under a different set of conditions. In particular, instead of conditions (ii) and (iii) in Proposition 16.9, Debreu (1959) requires that X_i is convex, and $\precsim_i$ is a continuous and complete preorder. Therefore, what is established here is a generalization of Debreu's work, because in this chapter the preference $\precsim_i$ is not generally assumed to be a complete preorder.

As for condition (ii) in Proposition 16.9, Example 16.3 demonstrates that in general, the preference relation $\precsim_i$ does not necessarily satisfy the condition of additive conservation. And similar to Example 16.2, one can readily see that not all preorders satisfy the condition of positive multiplicativity.

Example 16.3 Assume that consumer i's system of values and beliefs preorders the quantities of a particular commodity h by referring to the mod4 function so that for any two real numbers x and y, $x \prec_i y$ if and only if $x(\text{mod}4) < y(\text{mod}4)$. Let $x_i^1, x_i^2, x_i^3 \in X_i$ be three consumptions such that

$$x_{ik}^1 = x_{ik}^2 = x_{ik}^3, k = 1, 2, \ldots, \ell, k \neq h,$$

and

$$x_{ih}^1 = 2, x_{ih}^2 = 3 \text{ and } x_{ih}^2 = 1.$$

Then, we have $x_i^1 \precsim_i x_i^2$ and $x_i^3 \precsim_i x_i^3$. However, instead of $x_i^1 + x_i^3 \precsim_i x_i^2 + x_i^3$, we have

$$x_i^1 + x_i^3 \succsim_i x_i^2 + x_i^3,$$

because

$$x_{ik}^1 + x_{ik}^3 = x_{ik}^2 + x_{ik}^3, k = 1, 2, \ldots, \ell, k \neq h,$$

and

$$x_{ih}^1 + x_{ih}^3 = 3 \succsim_i x_{ih}^2 + x_{ih}^3 = 3 + 1 =_{\text{mod}4} 0.$$

That is, the specifically defined $\precsim_i$ is not additively conserved.

16.5.2 Feasible Price-Wealth Pairs

As for condition (iii) in Proposition 16.9, Example 16.4 shows that not every preference relation $\precsim_i$ is asymptotically preserving.

Example 16.4 Let us continue to employ the preference relation $\precsim_i$, defined in the previous example. And, define a sequence $x_i^1, x_i^2, \ldots, x_i^q, \ldots \in X_i$ of possible consumptions for consumer i such that

$$x_{ik}^q = x_{ik}^1, k = 1, 2, \ldots, \ell, k \neq h, q = 1, 2, \ldots \tag{16.10}$$

and

$$x_{ih}^q = 3 + \frac{q}{q+1}, q = 1, 2, \ldots \tag{16.11}$$

Then, it is ready to see that $x_i^q \to x_i^0$, as $q \to \infty$, where $x_{ik}^0 = x_{ik}^1, k = 1, 2, \ldots, \ell, k \neq h$, and $x_{ih}^0 = 0$, which is equal to 4 (mod4).

Define x_i^{low} as follows: $x_{ik}^{\text{low}} = x_{ik}^1, k = 1, 2, \ldots, \ell, k \neq h$, and $x_{ih}^{\text{low}} = 3$. Then, Eqs. (16.10) and (16.11) imply that

$$x_i^q \succsim_i x_i^{\text{low}} \quad \text{and} \quad \lim_{q \to \infty} x_i^q = x_i^0 \prec_i x_i^{\text{low}}.$$

That is, the specifically defined preference relation $\precsim_i$ is not asymptotically conserved.

The set X_i of consumer i's possible consumptions is said to be convex with respect to $\precsim_i$ (Debreu, 1959, p. 60; Forrest et al., 2023b) or $\precsim_i$ is said to be convex, if X_i is convex, as a subset of $\mathbb{R}^\ell$, and for any distinct consumptions $x_i^1, x_i^2 \in X_i$ and arbitrary scalar $\alpha \in (0, 1)$,

$$x_i^1 \prec_i x_i^2 \to x_i^1 \prec_i \alpha x_i^2 + (1 - \alpha) x_i^1. \tag{16.12}$$

One consumption $x_i \in X_i$ is said to be satiation for consumer i (Mas-Collel et al., 1995), if for any $y_i \in X_i$, $y_i \precsim_i x_i$. It is ready to see that if consumer i has incomparable consumptions, then there might be several incomparable satiation consumptions in X_i simultaneously.

Proposition 16.10 If both X_i and $\precsim_i$ are convex, $x_i^* \in X_i$ is not a satiation consumption, and consumer i's consumptions asymptotically preserve preference relation $\precsim_i$, then Axiom 16.1 implies Axiom 16.2.

Proof For any price-wealth pair $(p. w) \in S_i$, any consumption $x_i \in X_i$, and a chosen $x_i^* \in X_i$, Axiom 16.1 is equivalent to $x_i \succ_i x_i^* \to p \cdot x_i >_i w_i$. Let $x_i \in X_i$ satisfy $x_i \succsim_i x_i^*$, which can be split into two cases: $x_i \succ_i x_i^*$ and $x_i \sim_i x_i^*$. Axiom 16.1 guarantees that the former case leads to the desired conclusion $p \cdot x_i >_i w_i$ or $p \cdot x_i \geq_i w_i$.

For the second case $x_i \sim_i x_i^*$, because $x_i^* \in X_i$ is not a satiation consumption, there is a consumption $x_i^1 \in X_i$ such that $x_i^1 \succ_i x_i^*$. So, for any scalar $\alpha \in (0, 1)$, the convexity of X_i implies that $\alpha x_i^1 + (1 - \alpha) x_i \in X_i$; and the convexity of $\precsim_i$ guarantees that $\alpha x_i^1 + (1 - \alpha) x_i$ and x_i are comparable in terms of $\precsim_i$ such that $x_i^* \sim_i x_i \prec_i z_i(\alpha) = \alpha x_i^1 + (1 - \alpha) x_i$. So, Axiom 16.1 implies that

$$p \cdot z_i\left(\frac{1}{n}\right) >_i w_i, \quad \text{for} \quad n = 2, 3, 4, \ldots \tag{16.13}$$

From $z_i\left(\frac{1}{n}\right) \to x_i$, the asymptotic preservation of the preference relation $\precsim_i$ and Eq. (16.13) guarantee that $p \cdot x_i \geq_i w_i$.

Comparing to what has been established in the literature (e.g., Levin & Milgrom, 2004; Mas-Collel et al., 1995), when the preference relation $\precsim_i$ is no longer assumed to be a complete preorder, the convenient fact that $p \cdot x_i$ is a continuous function in x_i cannot be readily employed (e.g., Dubra & Ok, 2002; Ok, 2002; Nishimura & Ok, 2016; Bosi & Herden, 2012) in the proof of Proposition 16.10, as Example 16.4 demonstrates.

Proposition 16.11 For given $(p, w) \in S_i^{\max}$ and $x_i^* \in \xi_i(p, w)$, if the following hold true, then $p \cdot x_i^* = w_i$:

- X_i is convex, as a subset of $\mathbb{R}^\ell$, and is convex with respect to $\precsim_i$.
- x_i^* is not a satiation consumption.
- Consumer i's consumptions asymptotically preserve the preference relation $\precsim_i$.

Proof From $x_i^* \in \xi_i(p, w)$, it follows that $p \cdot x_i^* \leq_i w_i$. To establish the desired equality, it suffices to show that $p \cdot x_i^* \geq_i w_i$. To this end, let $X_i^* \subseteq X_i$ be a chosen subset of consumer i's preference representations, $u_i : X_i \to X_i^*$ the canonical utility function, and $X_i^{\max}$ a maximal chain in X_i^* such that $x_i^* \in u_i^{-1}(X_i^{\max})$.

Hence, for any $x_i \in u_i^{-1}(X_i^{\max})$, if $p \cdot x_i \leq_i w_i$, then $x_i \in \gamma_i(p, w)$ and therefore $x_i \precsim_i x_i^*$. That is, Axiom 16.1 holds true on $u_i^{-1}(X_i^{\max})$, which, from Proposition 16.10, implies that Axiom 16.2 holds true. That is, $p \cdot x_i^* \geq_i w_i$.

Proposition 16.12 Assume that each infinity can be actually (not potentially) achieved. If $u_i^{-1}(X_i^{\max})$ is a connected subset of $\mathbb{R}^\ell$, for each maximal antichain $X_i^{\max} \subseteq X_i^*$, and the preference relation $\precsim_i$ is continuous on X_i, then $S_i^{\max} = S_i$.

Proof For each maximal antichain $X_i^{\max} \subseteq X_i^*$, let us choose a continuous utility function $u_i^{\max} : u_i^{-1}(X_i^{\max}) \to \mathbb{R}$. The existence of $u_i^{\max}$ is confirmed by the famous Debreu (1959), where the original proof is valid only with the assumption that each infinity can be actually (not potentially) achieved (for details, see the proof of Proposition 16.9).

For each price-wealth pair $(p, w) \in S_i$, consumer i chooses a maximum in $u_i^{-1}(X_i^{\max}) \cap \gamma_i(p, w)$ in terms of $\precsim_i$, which reflects the principles held in his system of values and beliefs. That is, he maximizes $u_i^{\max}$ on $u_i^{-1}(X_i^{\max}) \cap \gamma_i(p, w)$, which is nonempty and compact, because of the lower boundedness axiom (Axiom 14.1) and the definition of γ_i. Therefore, the real-number valued utility function $u_i^{\max}$ actually reaches its maximum on $u_i^{-1}(X_i^{\max}) \cap \gamma_i(p, w)$. In other words, there is a nonempty subset of maximal consumptions in $\gamma_i(p, w)$. That is, $(p, w) \in S_i^{\max}$. Hence, the equality $S_i^{\max} = S_i$ has been shown.

Comparing to the literature, this result generalizes the corresponding result (Debreu, 1959, p. 72) by removing the one imposed condition: The set X_i of consumption is a compact subset in $\mathbb{R}^\ell$.

16.6 A Few Final Words

This chapter embeds a consumer's set X_i of all possible consumptions in a Euclidean space $\mathbb{R}^\ell$ while removing the unrealistic assumption that a consumer's consumption preferences are complete (e.g., Hervés-Beloso & Cruces, 2019; Levin & Milgrom, 2004; Mas-Collel et al., 1995). On such bases, this research pays a revisit to the part of the prevalent consumer theory regarding a consumer's budget set and demand correspondence and show, among other conclusions, that:

- Only when a consumer's order of real numbers is the same as the conventional one, the budget set function γ_i is continuous at the price-wealth pair $(p^0, w^0) \in S_i$ satisfying $w_i^0 \neq \min_{x_i \in X_i} p^0 \cdot x_i$ (Proposition 16.1 and Example 16.1).
- If consumer i's ordering $\leq_i$ of real numbers satisfies the condition of positive multiplicativity, then this consumer i's demand correspondence is homogenous of degree zero in price and in wealth. That is, for any $t \in \mathbb{R}_{+}$, $\xi_i(tp, tw) = \xi_i(p, w)$ (Proposition 16.6).
- The conditions of additive conservation and asymptotic preservation are not generally satisfied by preference relations (Examples 16.3 and 16.4).
- If each maximal chain $U \subseteq X_i$ is connected in $\mathbb{R}^\ell$ and preference relation $\precsim_i$ is continuous on X_i, then for each feasible price-wealth pair (p, w) there is at least one equilibrium consumption $x_i^{\max}(p, w)$ (Proposition 16.12).

As highlighted by these results, this chapter necessarily introduces several unconventional concepts, such as consumer-specific order of real numbers, positive multiplicativity, additive conservation, and asymptotic preservation. And, then it confirms when some of the previously known properties continue to hold true. At the same time, this chapter is able to investigate issues not faced before so that brand new conclusions are established.

Other than its theoretical contribution, as outlined above, this chapter can also be seen as a small part of a much larger effort of developing a new consumer theory for the purpose of producing more tangible economic values than the prevalent theory can. Such need has been loudly called for by Paul Krugman (*New York Times*, 2009-09-02), Paul De Grauwe (*Financial Times*, 2009-07-21), and others.

As for future research, there are evidently many important questions still left open. For example, if a preference relation $\precsim_i$ is not a complete preorder, under what conditions will the relation $\precsim_i$ on $S_i^{\max}$, as given in Sect. 16.3, be well defined? What will be the form of Proposition 16.1 if $\leq_i$ is not the same as $\leq$? Under what conditions does the preference relation $\precsim_i$ have a set X_i^* $(\subseteq X_i)$ of preference representations, when $\precsim_i$ is not a complete preorder, as mentioned at the start of Sect. 16.4? In some measure the binary relations $\precsim_i$ and $\leq_i$ cannot be inconsistent with each other, as stated in Sect. 16.5. Can such an unspecified measure be identified for each given system of values and beliefs?

References

Aumann, R. (1962). Utility theory without the completeness axiom. *Econometrica, 30*, 445–462.

Bewley, T. (1986). *Knightian uncertainty theory: Part I.* Cowles Foundation Discussion Paper No. 807.

Birnbaum, M. H., & Gutierrez, R. J. (2007). Testing for intransitivity of preferences predicted by a lexicographic semi-order. *Organizational Behavior and Human Decision Processes, 104*, 96–112. https://doi.org/10.1016/j.obhdp.2007.02.001

Bosi, G., & Herden, G. (2012). Continuous multi-utility representations of preorders. *Journal of Mathematical Economics, 48*, 212–218.

Debreu, G. (1959). *Theory of value: An axiomatic analysis of economic equilibrium*. Yale University Press.

Dubra, J., & Ok, E. A. (2002). A model of procedural decision making in the presence of risk. *International Economic Review, 43*(4), 1053–1080.

Forrest, J. Y. L. (2013). *A systemic perspective on cognition and mathematics*. CRC Press, an Imprint of Taylor and Francis.

Forrest, J. Y. L., Darvishi, D., Clark, R. S., Seyedian, M., & Liu, J. (2023a). Consumption preferences and generalized utility functions. *Southern Business & Economic Journal, 44*, 29.

Forrest, J. Y. L., Tiglioglu, T., Liu, Y., Mong, D., & Cardin, M. (2023b). Various convexities and some relevant properties of consumer preference relations. *Studia Universitatis "Vasile Goldis" Arad—Economics Series, 33*(4), 145–168. https://doi.org/10.2478/sues-2023-0021

Forrest, J. Y. L., Gong, Z. W., Li, Z., Sarkambayeva, S., & Golden, J. (to appear). How consumer value-belief system affects his budget set and demand correspondence. In *The Proceedings of the 2023 Annual Conference of National Association of Business, Economics and Technology, State College, PA*, November 2–3, 2023.

Hervés-Beloso, C., & Cruces, H. V. (2019). Continuous preference orderings representable by utility functions. *Journal of Economic Surveys, 33*(1), 179–194.

Hu, K., Tao, Y., Ma, Y., & Shi, L. (2021). Peer pressure induced punishment resolves social dilemma on interdependent networks. *Scientific Reports, 11*, 15792.

Kuratowski, K., & Mostowski, A. (1976). *Set theory: With an introduction to descriptive set theory*. North-Holland.

Levin, J., & Milgrom, P. (2004). *Consumer theory*. Retrieved February 7, 2022, from https://web.stanford.edu/~jdlevin/Econ%20202/Consumer%20Theory.pdf.

Li, Z., Choi, S., & Forrest, J. Y. L. (2022). Understanding peer pressure on joint consumption decisions: The role of social capital during emerging adulthood. *Young Consumers, 24*(1). https://doi.org/10.1108/YC-03-2022-1494

Lin, Y. (2008). Systematic studies: The infinity problem in modern mathematics. *Kybernetes: The International Journal of Cybernetics, Systems and Management Sciences, 37*(3–4), 385–542.

Liu, Y., Quan, B. T., Xu, Q., & Forrest, J. Y. L. (2018). Corporate social responsibility and decision analysis in a supply chain through government subsidy. *Journal of Cleaner Production, 208*, 436–447.

Mandler, M. (1999). Incomplete preferences and rational intransitivity of choice. *mimeo*. Harvard University.

Mani, A., Rahwan, I., & Pentland, A. (2013). Inducing peer pressure to promote cooperation. *Scientific Reports, 3*, 01735.

Mas-Collel, A., Whinston, M. D., & Green, J. R. (1995). *Microeconomic theory*. Oxford University Press.

Nishimura, H., & Ok, E. A. (2016). Utility representation of an incomplete and nontransitive preference relation. *Journal of Economic Theory, 166*(November), 164–185.

Ok, E. A. (2002). Utility representation of an incomplete preference relation. *Journal of Economic Theory, 104*(2), 429–449.

Poist, R. F. (1989). Evolution of conceptual approaches to the design of logistics systems: A sequel. *Transportation Journal, 28*(3), 35–39.

Tversky, A. (1969). Intransitivity of preferences. *Psychological Review, 76*(1), 31–48.

von Neumann, J., & Morgenstern, O. (1944). *Theory of games and economic behavior*. Princeton University Press.

Part VI
Value-Belief Systems and Firms' Efficiencies

Chapter 17
Management Efficiency and Organizational Inefficiency

Jeffrey Yi-Lin Forrest, Dillon S. Forrest, and Bruce Orvis

Abstract Shown in this chapter, which is mainly based Lin and Forrest (Kybernetes 37(1):149–165, 2008) and Forrest and Orvis (Kybernetes 45(8):1308–1322, 2016), among other results, are the never-perfect value theorem and two important principles of efficiency. One principle is on business management and the other on the structure of employees' efforts and devotion towards realizing the mission of their organization. What is presented includes how each firm's system of values and beliefs can never be perfect and needs to evolve with market conditions, how management can become efficient through managerial flexibility in terms of allowing individual employees to have conflicting personal values, and no matter how a business entity is set up, certain organizational inefficiency always exists. By understanding and practicing these results, managers and entrepreneurs could simply devote more of their time and effort on continuously improving their firms' organizational cultures, codes of conduct, and flexibility in terms of management styles and focusing on the big picture of the corporation and its supply-chain ecosystem instead of dwelling on how to improve employees' efficiencies.

Keywords Data envelopment analysis · Information entropy principle · Never-perfect value systems · Samaritan dilemma · Self-organization · Selfish employee theorem

---

Jeffrey Yi-Lin Forrest (Department of Accounting Economics Finance, Slippery Rock University, Slippery Rock, PA, USA; Email: Jeffrey.forrest@sru.edu), Dillon S. Forrest (Steady Capital, LLC., USA; Email: dillon@steady.capital), and Bruce Orvis (School of Business, Slippery Rock University, Slippery Rock, PA, USA; Email: bruce.orvis@sru.edu) are equally contributed to this chapter.

J. Y.-L. Forrest, *Systemic Principles of Applied Economic Philosophies I*,
Translational Systems Sciences 38, https://doi.org/10.1007/978-981-99-7273-9_17

17.1 Introduction

No matter which business entity a person works for, he tends to find inefficiencies in the management, in the business operation, and in employees' efforts and devotions. And many people always seem to have ideas about how things could improve if this or that is introduced and/or implemented.

One reason why a person can easily discover abundant inefficiencies is because each person, as a living being that is severely limited by its sensing organs, looks at the world with a pair of colored eyes. The word "color" here is also known in the literature by the term of personal values and philosophical assumptions (or beliefs) about the world (Lin & Forrest, 2011; Villalobos & Vargas, 2015; Terán et al., 2015). In other words, because philosophical assumptions and value-belief systems vary from one person to another, from one people to another, from one culture to another, etc., the same physical world becomes extremely beautiful and multi-colored when people individually try to describe what they see and what the world is really about.

The concept of beliefs has different connotations. For example, some beliefs are involved with faith, while others with emotions (Jervis, 2006). In real life, grasping the system of a person's values and beliefs is often difficult. According to Rokeach (1968), beliefs that are as global as those that transcendentally guide actions and judgments across specific objects and situations constitute values. When beliefs are confined to the social world, they are seen as social axioms (Leung et al., 2007). When the belief about reality is joined with that about order, formed is a basis for values (Narasimhan et al., 2010).

As for values, the relevant research is extensive; and topics on values and value systems have interested researchers from different disciplines, such as sociology, psychology, philosophy, and political science. For instance, the concepts of values and value systems are shown to be useful in understanding subjective well-being (Diener, 1984, 2000), psychological well-being (Ryff, 1989), and individual psychology (Taylor, 1988, 1989). They have enhanced the understanding of work values (Hofstede, 1980; Ros et al., 1999; Schwartz, 1999), organization behaviors (Meglino & Ravlin, 1998), and organization culture (Schein, 1985).

This chapter, which is mainly based on Lin and Forrest (2008) and Forrest and Orvis (2016), attempts to address the situation just described above by investigating the following questions: How management efficiency could be potentially achieved? And, why achieving organizational efficiency could only be a conceptual dream?

To accomplish these objectives, this chapter first develops the never-perfect value theorem for firms and studies when managers could possibly play favors to certain employees among his subordinates. Secondly, it turns its attention to the concept of organizational efficiency and addresses whether or not an organization could ever be efficient by looking at examples that are rigorously constructed.

Through strenuous reasoning based on the intuition of the systemic yoyo model, this chapter reveals the fact that inconsistencies between employees' personal value-belief systems and those between these systems and the organization's mission unavoidably lead to organizational inefficiencies. At the same time, the relevant analyses suggest that management efficiency can be potentially achieved by being managerially flexible in terms of management styles.

The concepts of organizational and management efficiency have been investigated by different authors from various angles. For example, Pawłowski et al. (2012) look at modern management as a series of decision-makings and creations of conditions for effective realization of the decisions. Ren and Xiong (2010) investigate the measurement of management efficiency from the angle of systems involving many mutual-coupling and unknown or uncertain factors by using the information entropy principle. Considering the fact that the management increases the functionality and competitiveness of its company and impacts the organization's efficiency and efficacy, Laura-Georgeta (2011) studies the performance management by using an approach that joins both organization efficiency and efficacy and the grounds for achieving organization's competitiveness. Burton et al. (1991) research the relationship between organizational size and performance. Cummins et al. (1999) introduce the technique of cross-frontier analysis for estimating the relative efficiency of alternative organizational forms in an industry. Ismail et al. (2011) provide an empirical study on the relationship between efficiency and organizational structure for takaful operators of the dual financial system in Malaysia by using a sample of 19 firms chosen over the time period of 2004–2009. Alvesson (1989) surveys some of the common conceptualizations of organizational culture as a building block in organizational design, as the outcome of symbolic management, as a diagnostic instrument, and as a paradigmatic concept. By recognizing the fact that benchmarking for decision-making units (DMUs) is more than a purely monitoring process and includes a component of future planning, Stewart (2010) extends the standard data envelopment analysis model to include longer-term top management goals. By identifying the manager of an organization as a systems designer who plays the role of self-organization both within and outside the organization of concern, Kasianiuk (2016) presents identification models useful for understanding self-organization processes within and outside the organizations facilitated by leaders.

So, our present work formulates the concepts of management and organizational efficiency at the theoretical height of abstraction and carries the existing literature on these concepts steps forward with a much wider range of applicability.

The rest of this chapter is organized as follows: Section 17.2 examines why for economic viability a firm has to grow its system of values and beliefs unremittingly over time. Section 17.3 investigates when and how a manager could potentially play favors to certain subordinates. Section 17.4 demonstrates the nonexistence of organizational efficiency. Section 17.5 provides one approach for decision-making managers to become efficient in his managerial works, while the following Section 17.6 introduces the principle of organizational inefficiency. This chapter is concluded in Section 17.7 with suggestions for future research.

17.2 The Need for a Firm to Grow Its Value-Belief System Unremittingly

To make the situation convenient to analyze, let us look at a focal firm F and a selfish employee E. In this case, the interactions between the organizational yoyo of the firm and that of the employee can be depicted in Fig. 17.1. Specifically, because the firm transfers financial and other benefits to the employee, the firm is represented as a divergent whirlpool, while the selfishness of the employee as a convergent whirlpool.

If both transfers b_1 and b_2 stand for contractual and/or voluntary monetary and benefit transfers from F, the spin field of employee E in Fig. 17.1 will accept b_1 happily and the transfer b_2 unwillingly (Fig. 17.1b) or even likely reject such a transfer (Fig. 17.1a). Here, b_1 is transferred to the selfish employee E without violating his preference of consumption, while b_2 is forced on E against his will or personal consumption preferences. In particular, although unwillingly, the employee accepts transfer b_2 (Fig. 17.1b). However, for the situation in Fig. 17.1a, transfer b_2 is rejected by the employee. Hence, the theorem of never-perfect value system (Lin & Forrest, 2008), established for the family (Becker, 1991), can be generalized to the case of a business firm as follows, where the same name for the theorem is used.

Theorem 17.1 (The Theorem of Never-Perfect Value Systems). In a firm of at least two employees, one of them, named h, is the manager who evaluates each employee's performance against the system of values and beliefs of the firm. If a selfish employee measures up well against the value-belief system, the manager h will positively award the employee. Unfortunately, the more effort an employee E puts in to measure up to the value system, the more he or she will be punished by the award system.

Before symbolically proving this theorem, let us explain the backdrop on which this result is formulated. First of all, the setting of a firm and its employees suggests that monetary and benefit transfers stand for a periodic, ongoing process without a definite end in sight. The role the firm's system of values and beliefs plays is that the manager confirms with the employees at some time moment(s) along the timeline that starting at a certain pay period, each employee's behavior and performance will affect how much he will receive from the company at the end of that period. And the

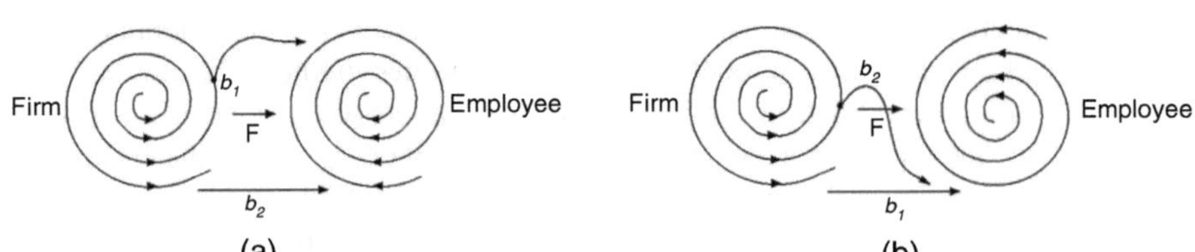

Fig. 17.1 Interactions between the focal firm and a selfish employee

manager will design his responses to employees' behaviors and levels of performance in such a way as to maximize his own utility (or measure of performance). Speaking differently, Theorem 17.1 portraits a progressive behavioral change and reflection over time between the manager and the employees of the firm.

Proof Let Y_E be an index, satisfying $0 < Y_E < 1$, established to check how well employee E measures up to the firm's system of values and beliefs, predetermined by the firm and communicated by the manager h. This index satisfies the condition that the greater Y_E is, the better employee E measures up to the value-belief system. The reason why the index Y_E is specified to the individual employee E is because although the firm might have a common set of detailed codes of conduct applicable to all employees, each application of the codes has to be tailored to the specifics of each particular employee, as what actually happens in real life.

Because E has to put in extra effort to increase the value of Y_E, this employee's utility function $U_E = U_E\ (X_E, Y_E)$ satisfies

$$\frac{\partial U_E}{\partial X_E} > 0 \quad \text{and} \quad \frac{\partial U_E}{\partial Y_E} < 0, \tag{17.1}$$

where X_E stands for employee E's total consumption of numeraire good. The reason why $\partial U_E/\partial Y_E < 0$ is because all people are lazy to a certain degree.

Let the manager h's utility function be

$$U_h = U_h(X_h, U_{E_1}, U_{E_2}, \ldots, U_{E_n})$$

where it is assumed that other than the manager h, the firm contains n other employees who are all selfish, X_h represents the manager's own consumption, and U_{E_i} is the utility function of employee member E_i, $i = 1, 2, \ldots, n$.

Assume that the award that applied to employee E is determined by

$$h_E = h_E(Y_E)$$

such that $\partial h_E/\partial Y_e > 0$. Now, the total consumption of employee E is given by

$$X_E = I_E + h_E = I_E + h_E(Y_E),$$

where I_E is employee E's own income, such as the base pay and incomes from other opportunities beyond the employment with the focal firm, that is unrelated to Y_E. To reflect the fact that the index Y_E represents E's performance, as evaluated by the manager according to how he interprets the codes of conduct (or the value-belief system of the firm), and how the manager assumes it will make employee E better off, this end explains why Y_E does not explicitly appear as an independent variable in the manager's utility function. Instead, Y_E shows up in the total consumption $X_E = I_E + h_E(Y_E)$ of E. That is, an increase in the value of Y_E has a complex effect on employee E, both positively and negatively. Being positive is in the short term because the manager h will help to bring E's monetary and benefit transfer from the company to a higher level, and it could be negative because employee E has to put in more effort to raise the value of Y_E. So, to make our model more plausible, we can add the assumption that

$$\left|\frac{\partial U_E}{\partial X_E}\cdot\frac{\partial X_E}{\partial Y_E}\right| > \left|\frac{\partial U_E}{\partial Y_E}\right|.$$

That is, the increased utility of E, brought forward by the higher-level consumption $X_E = I_E + h_E(Y_E)$, is more than enough to offset the decreased utility of E when he has to put in additional effort to incrementally raise the value of Y_E.

To the manager h, his distribution plan of the company's resources to all other employees has to maximize his utility function subject to the following budgetary constraint:

$$X_h + \sum_{i=1}^{n} X_{E_i} = X_h + \sum_{i=1}^{n} (I_{E_i} + h_{E_i}) = I_h + \sum_{i=1}^{n} I_{E_i}.$$

By ignoring all employees except the manager h and employee E, then the first-order condition for the manager's optimization problem is given by

$$\begin{bmatrix}\frac{\partial U_h}{\partial X_h}\\ \frac{\partial U_h}{\partial X_E}\\ \frac{\partial U_h}{\partial Y_E}\end{bmatrix} = \begin{bmatrix}\frac{\partial U_h}{\partial X_h}\\ \frac{\partial U_h}{\partial U_E}\cdot\frac{\partial U_E}{\partial X_E}\\ \frac{\partial U_h}{\partial U_E}\cdot\frac{\partial U_E}{\partial Y_E}\end{bmatrix} = \lambda\begin{bmatrix}1\\ 1\\ \frac{\partial h_E}{\partial Y_E}\end{bmatrix}$$

And employee E chooses such a Y_E-value Y_E^* to satisfy his first-order condition

$$\frac{\partial U_E}{\partial Y_E} = \frac{\partial U_E}{\partial Y_E} + \frac{\partial U_E}{\partial X_E}\cdot\frac{\partial h_E(Y_E)}{\partial Y_E} = 0$$

so that he maximizes his utility.

Now, the third equation in the manager's first-order condition implies that when the manager's expected Y_E-value is greater than Y_E^*, employee E award $h_E(Y_E)$ would have a negative rate of increase. That is, what is shown is that the more effort employee E puts in to measure up to the value-belief system of the firm, the more he will be punished by the award system.

Example 17.1 To see how the result in Theorem 17.1 materially acts out, let us look at a firm with two employees: one manager h and one selfish employee E. Let Y_E be the index outlined in the proof of Theorem 17.1. Assume that employee E's utility function be given as follows:

$$U_E = U_E(X_E, Y_E) = X_E(1 - Y_E) \tag{17.2}$$

where X_E is employee E's total goods consumption and $(1 - Y_E)$ stands for his degree of laziness, and let the manager's utility function be

$$U_h = U_h(X_h, U_E) = X_h + \sqrt{U_E} = X_h + \sqrt{X_E(1 - Y_E)}. \tag{17.3}$$

Assume that the award from the firm, as determined by the manager h, to employee E is determined by

$$h_E = wY_E \tag{17.4}$$

where w is a fixed constant >0. Then the total consumption of E is

$$X_E = I_E + h_E = I_E + wY_E, \tag{17.5}$$

where I_E is the total of employee E's income unrelated to Y_E.

To the manager, he needs to maximize his utility function subject to the budgetary constraint:

$$X_h + X_E = X_h + (I_E + h_E) = I_E + I_E. \tag{17.6}$$

The first-order condition for this optimization problem is given by

$$\begin{bmatrix} \frac{\partial U_h}{\partial X_h} \\ \frac{\partial U_h}{\partial X_E} \\ \frac{\partial U_h}{\partial Y_E} \end{bmatrix} = \begin{bmatrix} 1 \\ \frac{1 - Y_E}{2\sqrt{X_E(1 - Y_E)}} \\ \frac{w(1 - Y_E) - X_E}{2\sqrt{X_E(1 - Y_E)}} \end{bmatrix} = \lambda \begin{bmatrix} 1 \\ 1 \\ -w \end{bmatrix} \tag{17.7}$$

where $\lambda = 1$ is the Lagrange multiplier. So, from Eq. (17.7), it follows that

$$\sqrt{\frac{1 - Y_E}{X_E}} = 2 \quad \text{and} \quad \frac{X_E - w(1 - Y_E)}{\sqrt{X_E(1 - Y_E)}} = 2w. \tag{17.8}$$

So, $w = 1/8$ and the employee E chooses $Y_E^* = 1/2 - 4I_E$ to maximize his utility, and when $Y_E \neq Y_E^*$, we have

$$X_E = \frac{1}{4}(1 - Y_E). \tag{17.9}$$

Substituting Eq. (17.9) into Eq. (17.6) and solving for h_E leads to

$$h_E = \frac{1}{4}(1 - Y_E) - I_E.$$

This equation implies that employee E's award h_E from the company, as evaluated by the manager h, is a decreasing function of Y_E, an index that measures how well E is doing in terms of the established system of values and beliefs of the firm.

17.3 The Manager Who Plays Favors

Because no value system is perfect, as concluded by Theorem 17.1, there naturally appears a large gray area for managers to either consciously or unconsciously misinterpret the adopted systems of values and beliefs. To support this end, this section introduces one example and proves one theorem to demonstrate how a manager could misuse company asset to benefit himself and how selfish employees could take advantage out of a particular managerial style of the manager.

Example 17.2 Suppose that the firm of concern has a manager and two other employees, named respectively h, 1 and 2. The manager will be provided with an amount of money at the end of the time period by the firm to award the employees except himself for their hard works for the firm. The question that the manager likes to address is how to divide up the unknown amount of the money that will become available in the future so that his personal utility can be maximized.

To help resolve his problem, the manager defines the utilities of the employees as follows as his subjective functions:

$$U_i = m_i, i = 1, 2, \tag{17.10}$$

where m_i stands for the amount of employee i's awards the manager determines to offer beyond i's basic pays. The reason why U_i does not involve employee i's spending of his other income, such as his basic salary and those earned from various other endeavors, is because the manager purposely ignores the effect of those incomes so that he could focus more on how to motivate the employees so that they will help to maximize his utility function. That is why the manager subjectively defines the employees' utility functions as in Eq. (17.10).

Let the manager's utility function be

$$U_h = U_1 U_2 \tag{17.11}$$

with the budget constraint

$$I_h = m_1 + m_2, \tag{17.12}$$

where I_h represents the amount of available funds in the future the manager is able to distribute to his subordinates except himself.

Maximizing the manager's utility U_h subject to the constraint in Eq. (17.12) implies that the manager will distribute the available funds I_h to his subordinates evenly. That is, $U_i = 0.5I_h$, for $i = 1, 2$.

To make comparisons, let us now assume that the manager also thinks about how the employees enjoy their leisure beyond working for the company and possibly other endeavors for additional income. Hence, the manager's subjective utility functions of the employees are

$$U_i = m_i + L_i(Y_i), \quad i = 1, 2, \tag{17.13}$$

where m_i is employee i's award offered by the manager and $L_i(Y_i)$ his spending on leisure, with Y_i being his effort invested in his work and other possible endeavors to earn his additional income $I_i(Y_i)$. Assume that in this model setup, $L_i(Y_i)$ is not a function in m_i, where the award m_i is paid at the end of time of concern while $L_i(Y_i)$ is cumulative throughout the time.

Assume that the manager's utility function is still given in Eq. (17.11). So, the total income of the firm's employees, except the manager, is $I_h + I_1(Y_1) + I_2(Y_2)$. From Eq. (17.13), it follows that to maximize U_h in Eq. (17.11) subject to the constraint

$$U_1 + U_2 = I_h + I_1(Y_1) + I_2(Y_2), \tag{17.14}$$

one of the first-order conditions is $\partial U_h / \partial m_1 = 0$, which can be rewritten as follows:

0=	$\frac{\partial U_h}{\partial m_1} = \frac{\partial U_h}{\partial U_1} \cdot \frac{\partial U_1}{\partial m_1}$	
=	$\frac{\partial U_h}{\partial U_1} \cdot 1$	Equation (17.13)
=	$\frac{\partial}{\partial U_1}(U_1 U_2)$	Equation (17.11)
=	$\frac{\partial}{\partial U_1}\{U_1[I_h + I_1(Y_1) + I_2(Y_2) - U_1]\}$	Equation (17.14)
=	$[I_h + I_1(Y_1) + I_2(Y_2) - U_1] - U_1$	

so that the manager will distribute available funds in such a way that

$$U_i = 0.5[I_h + I_1(Y_1) + I_2(Y_2)] \tag{17.15}$$

Now, the manager faces two possible scenarios: Y_i is not observable and Y_i is observable. For the former case, because $L_i(Y_i)$ is a decreasing function of Y_i, the more effort employee i puts into his work and/or other endeavors, the less opportunity he has for leisure, a lazy and selfish employee will not have enough incentive to work to generate his income $I_i(Y_i)$. Therefore, the manager runs into the problem of incentives with each lazy and selfish employee. For the latter case, where Y_i is observable, let us consider the following extreme situation: Employee 1 works extremely hard on his various endeavors except his waged work within the focal firm so that he has no time for activities of leisure, while employee 2 enjoys leisure to the fullest extent without putting in any effort in any kind of work. Symbolically, what is assumed is $L_1(Y_1) = 0$, $I_1(Y_1) > 0$ and $L_2(Y_2) > 0$, $I_2(Y_2) = 0$, so that Eqs. (17.13) and (17.15) jointly lead to:

$$m_1 = 0.5I_h + 0.5I_1(Y_1) \quad \text{and} \quad m_2 = 0.5I_h + 0.5I_1(Y_1) - L_2(Y_2), \tag{17.16}$$

where $I_1(Y_1)$ stands for the total income employee 1 makes from endeavors outside the focal firm.

Behaviorally, the expression for m_1 in Eq. (17.16) contradicts the assumptions that the manager purposefully uses awards (m_i, $i = 1, 2$) to stimulate the employees to devote more efforts on their works within the firm. Jointly, Eqs. (17.12) and (17.16) produce

$$m_1 + m_2 = I_h = I_h + I_1(Y_1) - L_2(Y_2)$$

Therefore, $L_2(Y_2) = I_1(Y_1)$, which contradicts the assumption that employee 2 enjoys leisure to the fullest extent, because this equation implies that employee 2 can only spend as much as the amount employee 1 makes from various endeavors outside the focal firm.

The expression for m_1 in Eq. (17.16) provides a lot of room for interpretation, since the manager uses the company money to award an employee who devotes 100% his efforts and time on endeavors beyond the firm's works. One such interpretation is that the manager plays favor towards that particular employee, while that employee spends some of his income $I_1(Y_1)$ to "bribe" the manager. The justification for this interpretation is that the values of $I_i(Y_i)$, $L_i(Y_i)$, $i = 1, 2$, are really unknown to the manager, unless they are purposely revealed by the employees.

The earlier understanding of Fig. 17.1 is that the firm makes transfers of b_1 and/or b_2 to employee E. However, in a real-life situation, as often seen in various work places, Fig. 17.1 can also suggest the possibility that the spin field of the selfish employee *E* may very well take its initiative and proactively grab as much of the potential total amount of the fund, although the exact amount might not be known until a future date, allocated for awarding employees for their hard works. Such possibilities have been well described in studies of the Samaritan dilemma (Buchanan, 1975; Lagerlof, 2004). To this end, the following result can be established.

Theorem 17.2 (Selfish Employee Theorem) If the manager of the focal firm cares about all employees of the firm so that he distributes the funds of the firm, allocated for awarding employees for their good performance, to them as long as they need to satisfy their own desires of consumption, then the selfish employees will devote as little effort to their works as possible while maximizing their amounts of transfers from the firm.

Proof Assume that the firm hires a manager, named *H*, and *n* selfish employees, named respectively, 1, 2, …, *n*. Because the employees are selfish and only care about satisfying their own consumption desires, their utility functions can be written as

$$U_i = U_i(m_i, Y_i), i = 1, 2, \ldots, n, \tag{17.17}$$

where m_i is employee i's commodity consumption in the marketplace and Y_i his effort invested in his work to earn his income $I_i(Y_i)$ satisfying

$$\frac{\partial U_i}{\partial m_i} > 0 \text{ and } \frac{\partial U_i}{\partial Y_i} < 0, i = 1, 2, \ldots, n, \tag{17.18}$$

and

$$\frac{\partial I_i}{\partial Y_i} > 0, i = 1, 2, \ldots, n. \tag{17.19}$$

Because the manager H cares about all employees of the firm, his utility can be written as

$$U_H = U_H(m_H, U_1, U_2, \ldots, U_n), \tag{17.20}$$

where m_H represents the manager's own consumption of numeraire good. The firm's total income is

$$I_H + I_1(Y_1) + I_2(Y_2) + \ldots + I_n(Y_m) = m_H + m_1 + m_2 + \ldots + m_n, \tag{17.21}$$

assuming, without loss of generality, that everybody involved here spends every penny he makes from the job of the firm.

To make all the selfish employees as happy as he could help, the manager distributes the funds that will become available at the end of the time period to maximize his utility. So, from Eqs. (17.20) and (17.21), the following condition emerges:

$$\begin{bmatrix} \frac{\partial U_H}{\partial m_i} \\ \frac{\partial U_H}{\partial Y_i} \end{bmatrix} = \begin{bmatrix} \frac{\partial U_H}{\partial U_i} \cdot \frac{\partial U_i}{\partial m_i} \\ \frac{\partial U_H}{\partial U_i} \cdot \frac{\partial U_i}{\partial Y_i} \end{bmatrix} = \lambda \begin{bmatrix} 1 \\ -\frac{\partial I_i(Y_i)}{\partial Y_i} \end{bmatrix}, \tag{17.22}$$

for $i = 1, 2, \ldots, n$, where λ is the Lagrange multiplier. The reason for the bottom cells in the matrix equation in Eq. (17.22) to equal one another is because the manager has to do his job by awarding the employees based on their individual performances. What is assumed here is that the more effort leads to better performance.

Dividing the second-row entry equation by that of the first-row entry equation in Eq. (17.22) and simplifying the result lead to

$$\frac{\partial m_i}{\partial Y_i} = -\frac{\partial I_i(Y_i)}{\partial Y_i} < 0, i = 1, 2, \ldots, n, \tag{17.23}$$

where the inequality comes from Eq. (17.19).

Now, Eq. (17.23) implies that the more effort is devoted to his job, the less commodity consumption each selfish employee will enjoy, although more effort means more income. This end means, based on Eqs. (17.23) and (17.18), that as long as the selfish employees could obtain financial care from the manager, the employees would devote as little effort to their work as possible.

In terms of the literature, the conclusion, given in Theorem 17.2, is empirically supported by countless real-life evidences documented by Stanley and Danko (1996) in their over 20 years of research on financially successful Americans.

17.4 Organizational Efficiency

The conclusions, presented in the previous sections, naturally lead to the question of how or under what conditions a firm can be organizationally efficient. In particular, by organization, it means an economic entity, where people are connected by some purpose, and it is economically viable through its members' efforts. That is, any organization considered in this chapter has to be a nontrivial system (Lin, 1999) that is made up of people, and has to produce some kind of products or services to sustain its existence. What is implied here is that each organization has a mission, by which all employees produce their products or services to sustain the economic viability of the organization.

For any organization, its organizational efficiency is defined as how well its employees help reach the defined mission. An organization is said to be efficient, if all employees work towards the common goal and help materialize the mission; otherwise, the organization is said to be inefficient. In this section, we look at the question of whether or not an organization could ever be efficient. First let us see two examples.

Example 17.3 This example is based on the reading nightlight example (Becker, 1974; Bergstrom, 1989; Lin, 2009).

Assume an organization has two such employees i and j in which a particular effort of i potentially strengthens the viability of the organization and helps increase i's income, but bothers j, while for some reason, j cannot simply leave the organization. In order to calm j down and hopefully make j become supportive of i's effort, i will compensate for j's frustration by transferring monetary contribution to j from his increased income, a result of his particular effort. Now, if the organization is efficient for this scenario, then how much and how long will both i and j be better off without selfish j starting to interfere with i's effort, which will make the organization inefficient?

Assume that the production function of the organization is

$$P_c = P(U_i(X_i, X_j, Y), U_j(X_j Y), \ldots) = U_i U_j^a \Pi, 0 < a < 1, \tag{17.24}$$

satisfying

$$\frac{\partial U_i}{\partial X_k} > 0, k = i, j; \frac{\partial U_i}{\partial Y} > 0, \frac{\partial U_j}{\partial X_j} > 0, \text{ and } \frac{\partial U_j}{\partial Y} < 0,$$

where the condition $0 < a < 1$ reflects the assumption that i's effort is potentially beneficial to the organization in several ways while it really bothers j, because $a < 1$ is the root reason, the dots represent an abbreviation of the utilities of all employees other than i and j, and Π is the product of all other employees' utilities and U_k the utility of employee k $(= i, j)$, defined as follows:

$$U_i = X_i X_j (Y + 1) \tag{17.25}$$

and

$$U_j = X_j e^{-Y}, \tag{17.26}$$

where X_k is the total consumption of goods of employee k $(= i, j)$ and Y an index that measures the effort i puts into his work. Here, we assume that while j is so selfish that he does not care about the well-being of any other co-workers, i is so altruistic that he includes j's utility in his utility function while knowing that his effort bothers j. In Eq. (17.25), the factor $(Y + 1)$ indicates that other than receiving a portion of utility from the joint consumptions of both i and j, i also enjoys additional utility that is proportional to how much effort i puts into his work. In Eq. (17.26), the factor e^{-Y} models the fact that j is really bothered by i's effort Y exponentially.

Substituting Eqs. (17.25) and (17.26) into Eq. (17.24) produces

$$P_c = U_i U_j^a = X_i X_j^{1+a} (Y + 1) e^{-1Y}. \tag{17.27}$$

Now, the organization wants to maximize P_c subject to:

$$\sum_{k=1}^{n} X_k = I_1 + I_2 + \ldots + I_n = \sum_{k=1}^{n} I_k \tag{17.28}$$

where n is the total number of employees and I_k the personal income of k, $k = 1, 2, \ldots, n$. The first-order condition for this optimization problem is

$$\begin{bmatrix} \frac{\partial P_c}{\partial X_i} \\ \frac{\partial P_c}{\partial X_j} \\ \frac{\partial P_c}{\partial Y} \end{bmatrix} = \begin{bmatrix} X_j^{1+a}(Y+1)e^{-aY} \\ (1+a)X_j^a X_i(Y+1)e^{-aY} \\ X_i X_j^{1+a} e^{-aY}[1-a(Y+1)] \end{bmatrix} = \lambda \begin{bmatrix} 1 \\ 1 \\ -\frac{dI_i}{dY} \end{bmatrix}, \tag{17.29}$$

where $\lambda > 0$ is the Lagrange multiplier. The (3.1)-entries in Eq. (17.29) show that only when

$$Y > \frac{1}{a} - 1, \tag{17.30}$$

i's income I_i has an up-trend with Y. Dividing the (1.1)-entries in Eq. (17.29) by the corresponding (2.1)-entries produces

$$X_j = (1+a)X_i.$$

Solving this equation for X_i and inserting into Eq. (17.28) produce j's consumption:

$$X_j = \frac{1+a}{2+a}\left(\sum_{k=1}^{n} I_k - \sum_{\substack{k=1 \\ k \neq i,j}}^{n} X_k\right) \tag{17.31}$$

Because a value in Eq. (17.30) is really not known to either i or j, and because j's consumption in Eq. (17.31) does not have a clear connection with Y, in a real-life setting i will be in a very inauspicious position to truly strike any deal regarding how much he should devote himself to the particular effort while j continues to be bothered. It is because Eq. (17.30) implies that Y could potentially take a very large value, if a is close to 0, which, to j, is not realistic in terms of getting compensated for his frustration, since no one knows when i will get any additional pay for his particular effort.

In terms of organizational efficiency, the difficulty in this scenario becomes obvious: To have the desired organizational efficiency, a negotiation between i and j (not between the organization and employee j, because the organization has done its part by including j's utility within its production function) needs to take place. At the same time, the analysis above indicates that j might give in temporarily when he imagines a foreseeable a-value, which means when j foresees when he might get compensated for his frustration. However, if such an imagined a-value were not materialized in a timely fashion, then a frustrated j will sooner or later start to interfere with i's effort, making the organization inefficient.

Example 17.4 This example is based on Lindbeck and Weibull (1988) and Bergstrom (1989) to show that organizational efficiency cannot be generally achieved or maintained.

Consider an organization with n different departments. Each department receives a lump sum of money as its budget at the start of each time period for all operational expenses of the department throughout the period. Look at one department, named k, and non-overlapping time periods 1 and 2. In period 1, k has a budget to operate on. It has the option to spend it all now or to spend some now and save the rest for future. In period 2, k knows that it will receive a new budget from the parent organization, assuming the organization cannot make any pre-commitment to punish k for any of its profligate period 1 behavior. Suppose the production functions P_k and P_o of k and the organization are

$$P_k\left(c_k^1, c_k^2\right) = \ln c_k^1 + \ln c_k^2 \tag{17.32}$$

and

$$P_o\left(c_o^1, c_o^2, c_k^1, c_k^2\right) = \ln c_o^1 + \ln c_o^2 + \alpha U_k = \ln c_o^1 + \ln c_o^2 + \alpha \ln c_k^1 + \alpha \ln c_k^2 \tag{17.33}$$

where c_k^i and c_o^i are respectively k's and the organization's direct expenses in period $i\,(=1, 2)$ and $\alpha > 0$ a constant. If in period 2, the organization allocates its available budget to k to maximize its production P_o subject to

$$c_o^2 + c_k^2 = w_o^2 + w_k^2, \tag{17.34}$$

where w_j^2 represents the available money in j's budget in period 2, $j = o$, k, then the first-order condition of this optimization problem is:

$$\begin{bmatrix} \dfrac{\partial P_o}{\partial c_o^2} \\ \dfrac{\partial P_o}{\partial c_k^2} \end{bmatrix} = \begin{bmatrix} \dfrac{1}{c_o^2} \\ \dfrac{\alpha}{c_k^2} \end{bmatrix} = \lambda \begin{bmatrix} 1 \\ 1 \end{bmatrix}, \tag{17.35}$$

where λ is the Language multiplier. Dividing the first entry equation in Eq. (17.35) by the second gives

$$c_k^2 = \alpha c_o^2. \tag{17.36}$$

So, Eq. (17.34) implies that

$$c_o^2 = \frac{1}{1+\alpha}\left(w_o^2 + w_k^2\right) \quad \text{and} \quad c_k^2 = \frac{\alpha}{1+\alpha}\left(w_o^2 + w_k^2\right). \tag{17.37}$$

That is, to maximize its production in period 2, the organization will divide the organization's total budget $\left(w_o^2 + w_k^2\right)$ so that the fraction $1/(1 + \alpha)$ of the total will go to the organization's budget for its direct expenses, and the fraction $\alpha/(1 + \alpha)$ will go to k.

This end implies that if department k controls its expenses in period 1, then it will have a greater sum of money available for period 2. That is, to obtain more money from the parent organization in period 2, k should have spent all or more than its period 1 allotment during period 1. In terms of Pareto efficiency, it will be wise for k to squander as much as it can during period 1 so that its parent organization will provide more during period 2. If the organization's mission can only be further materialized with budgetary support, then this end implies that with the organization's budgetary arrangement no department will be automatically motivated to maximize the overall monetary asset of the organization. In other words, the organization is not efficient.

The reason why organizational inefficiency appears here can be further seen as follows: Firstly, the budget of the organization is not the sum of all the available money supplies of the departments. Secondly, if k saves money in period 1, k would naturally not want this money to affect its budget of period 2. Since in Eq. (17.34) k's budget w_k^2 is used against k's will, there appears an inconsistency in the desires of departments and the organization, the root cause for departments to be not motivated to further achieving the organization's mission.

Although Examples 17.3 and 17.4 have only shown that under particular circumstances organizational inefficiency is unavoidable, we in fact have the following general result.

Theorem 17.3 Inefficiency always exists in any organizational system that has at least one full-time employee whose personal value is not in total agreement with the organization's mission.

Proof By contradiction, assume that there is a fully efficient organization that satisfies the conditions of the theorem, while the organization's mission is not in total agreement with the personal value of full-time employee k. Let Y be a variable measuring one aspect of employee k's personal value such that the utility of k increases with Y while the work efficiency of k in terms of helping to realize the mission of the organization decreases with Y. Symbolically, we have

$$U_k = U_k(X_k, Y), \quad \text{satisfying} \quad \frac{\partial U_k}{\partial X_k} > 0 \quad \text{and} \quad \frac{\partial U_k}{\partial Y} > 0 \tag{17.38}$$

where U_k is the utility of k, X_k is the total consumption of k, and the production function of the organization is

$$P = P(X_c, U_k, \ldots), \quad \text{satisfying} \quad \frac{\partial P}{\partial X_c} > 0, \ \frac{\partial P}{\partial U_k} > 0, \ \ldots \tag{17.39}$$

where X_c represents the expenditure of the organization, including the monetary expenses on all employees except k, and the dots the abbreviation of all the utilities of all other employees. The fact that employees' utilities enter into the organization's production function means that the organization keeps its employees' welfare as part of its objectives of operation. Now, the monetary bonus that measures the work efficiency of k is expressed by

$$h_k = h_k(Y), \quad \text{satisfying} \quad \frac{dh_k}{dY} < 0. \tag{17.40}$$

Note: In real life, such a variable Y might only exist implicitly and cannot be measured readily. However, its negative effect on the quality and efficiency generally can be clearly seen. So, we simply assume without loss of generality that Y can be measured in determining the monetary bonus.

To the organization, its resources are distributed to its employees to maximize its production function P in Eq. (17.39) subject to the following constraint:

$$X_c + X_k = X_c + (I_k + h_k), \tag{17.41}$$

where I_k is k's income from his work at the organization. Maximizing the production function in Eq. (17.39) subject to the constraint in Eq. (17.41) leads to the contradiction:

$$\frac{\partial X_k}{\partial Y} > 0 \quad \text{and} \quad \frac{\partial X_k}{\partial Y} = \frac{dh_k}{dY} < 0.$$

That implies that the assumption that the organization that satisfies the conditions of the theorem is fully efficient is incorrect.

17.5 The Principle of Management Efficiency

To materialize its purpose, an organization generally has to hire employees with desired talents. So, a natural question arises: If two employees i and j have conflicting personal values, can the organization still operate smoothly while keeping the best interests of these employees in mind at the same time? The answer is: YES, it is possible. To this end, let us look at the following example.

Example 17.5 Assume that the utilities of *i* and *j* are given by

$$U_i = X_i - Y \text{ and } U_j = X_j + Y, \tag{17.42}$$

where X_k is the consumption of k (= i, j) and Y the conflicting personal value.

Then, the organization's production function could be defined by

$$P_c = X_c(U_i + U_j) = X_c(X_i + X_j), \tag{17.43}$$

where X_c represents the expenditure of the organization. That is, in the face of conflict in personal values between *i* and *j*, the organization can still be completely neutral.

A second natural question is that when the organization's mission is in conflict with the personal value of an employee *i*, can the organization still function smoothly while keeping *i*'s well-being in mind? The answer is: YES, it is possible. To this end, let us look at the following example.

Example 17.6 Let *Y* represent an aspect of *i*'s personal value that disagrees with the organization's mission. Let the utility of *i* be given by

$$U_i = X_i Y \tag{17.44}$$

and the utility of the organization

$$U_c = \frac{X_c}{Y}, \tag{17.45}$$

where X_i stands for the consumption of *i* and X_c the expenditure of the organization. If the product function of the organization is

$$P_c = P_c(U_c, U_i) = U_i \cdot U_c = X_i \cdot X_c, \tag{17.46}$$

which implies that although the organization is in conflict with *i*'s personal value, in the production function, the organization still cares about *i* as much as if they did not have any conflict.

These examples imply that no matter whether there exists a conflict between employees' personal values or between some employees' personal values and the mission of the organization, the organization can still operate smoothly. So, if we define efficiency of management as keeping all employees' well-being in mind while materializing the mission of the organization, then we can suggest the following:

Principle of Management Efficiency Management flexibility in terms of managerial style is the key for maintaining management efficiency.

Examples 17.5 and 17.6 suggest that flexibility in defining the organization's production function is the key for eliminating any potential effect of existing conflicts between personal values and the mission of the organization. Here, different ways of formulating the product function is seen as different approaches of management. Speaking differently, if an organization's management has a fixated method to measure success, then it will have difficulties to handle varied personalities; and crucial talents, badly needed for the organization's success, will be forced out of the organization.

17.6 Principle of Organizational Inefficiency

From Sect. 17.4, it follows that if an organization has two employees with conflicting personal values, then the organization will have to suffer from organizational inefficiency, because one of the conflicting personal values will not be in total agreement with the organization's mission. In order to increase the efficiency of the organization, why can't a firm hire only people whose personal values are in complete agreement with the organization's mission?

Firstly, from Chap. 5 about consumers' natural endowments and how systems of values and beliefs are formed, it follows that finding such employees with identical personal values are practically impossible. Secondly, personal values evolve with time and changes of the environment. So, initially similar personal values tend to diverge over time. Thirdly, suppose we can find all the employees who have the desirable identical personal value, then what is observed in the dishpan experiment (Hide, 1953; Fultz et al., 1959) suggests that differences among the personal values will inevitably appear within the smooth operation of the organization.

In particular, when we look at one of the spinning fields of the yoyo model in Chap. 1 from a distance, although everything is set up perfectly symmetric about the axis of rotation, both flow patterns in Fig. 17.2 appear alternatively, where the speed of alteration depends on the rotational speed.

Within our current context, we can naturally imagine that the entire pan represents the mission of our organization, the spin of the organization's operation, and individual employees' personal values drops of the fluid. So, this experiment indicates that although the organization could find employees of identical personal value, this initial uniformity will be destroyed by the smooth operation of the

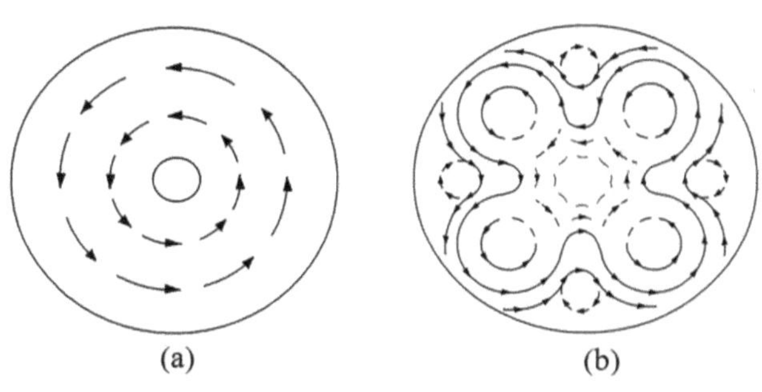

Fig. 17.2 Patterns observed in Fultz's dishpan experiment

organization. That is, uniformity in personal values is materialistically destroyed by employees' interactions and conflicts of interests. Therefore, the previous discussions imply that organizational inefficiency appears. So, we have the following general result.

Principle of Organizational Inefficiency Inefficiency always exists in any organization.

Here, the concept of efficiency includes all aspects of running the organization beyond from what is specified earlier. It could include, but not limited to, efficiencies of communication (both internal and external), management efficiency, public relations, employee satisfactions, etc. For example, communication efficiency consists of the efficiencies of the media, the receivers, and the senders of information, where the media could be somehow deficient, defective, or even dysfunctional, while due to diverse perceptions involved, receivers and senders of information could misunderstand each other in many different ways. Management efficiency is very delicate, because any push from the management could easily upset some employees, leading to purposefully delayed work progress or unconscious slowdown.

Suppose inefficiencies of all kinds do not exist; this proposed principle of organizational inefficiency still holds true no matter if the organization has full-time employees or not. To this end, we only need to address the situation where the organization has only part-time employee(s) and none of them has a conflicting personal value with the organization's mission. Let us consider:

1. The organization has only one part-time employee who is the founder.
2. The organization hires at least one employee who is not the founder.

For scenario 1, we could reasonably imagine that the founder employee would formulate his organization's mission in reference to his personal value system. Now, there are three systems involved here: the founder himself, his organization, and the environment. When the founder interacts with the environment, inevitable consequences appear. In Fig. 17.3 N represents the founder and M the environment. As an input-output system, N has to interact with M so that some unexpected subeddies appear. That means that the stated mission becomes inadequate. So, from the definition of organizational efficiency, it follows that this organization experiences inefficiency.

For scenario 2, assume that the organization hires only one employee, who is not the founder. Then, in this case, we have four systems that interact with each other: the founder himself, the hired employee, the organization, and the environment, with the former three being input-output systems. Similar to what is analyzed above, by being input-output systems, the founder and the employee have to interact with the environment, creating unexpected consequences, as indicated by the subeddies in the relevant interacting yoyo fields. So, similar organizational inefficiencies appear as in the analysis of scenario 1.

Let us now look at a case study to illustrate how widely useful the established principles are in real life. To this end, let us imagine a university, whose mission is to produce as many graduates who are assets to the society as possible.

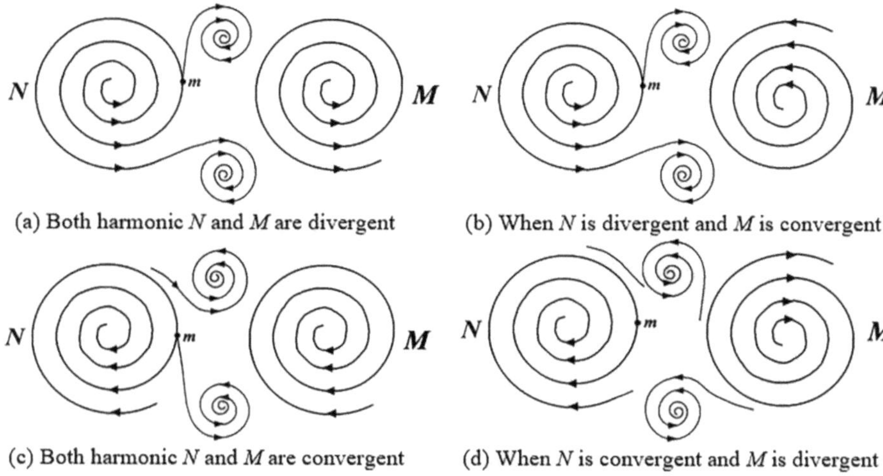

Fig. 17.3 How consequences appear when two systems interact. (**a**) Both harmonic N and M are divergent. (**b**) When N is divergent and M is convergent. (**c**) Both harmonic N and M are convergent. (**d**) When N is convergent and M is divergent

First, around this mission statement, organizational inefficiencies will naturally appear. Specifically, professors, who believe in passing on book knowledge is of the ultimate importance than anything else, will focus on doing so, while those professors, who believe in cultivating the spirit and desire to succeed in life in the students, would beyond passing on book knowledge place an additional emphasis on motivating students to work hard and smart in order to achieve personal and career successes. When students have these professors for their classes, the professors' different professional orientations and emphases will surely create chaos in at least some of the students. That leads to an organizational inefficiency for the university.

Second, suppose that the head of one particular department is a faithful believer of that education only means passing on book knowledge to students. Due to various reasons at the university level, such as recruitment, third-party university ranking, etc., the faculty of the department also consists of some believers of that it is more important to inspire students than simply passing on book knowledge to students. Now, in order to manage the department efficiently, the department head has to be flexible in his style of management; otherwise the department will be dysfunctional in no time.

17.7 A Few Final Words

By employing the intuition and thinking logic of the systemic yoyo model, this chapter first presents, among other important conclusions, the never-perfect value theorem and the selfish employee theorem. On the basis of these results, it then looks at the concept of organizational efficiency and whether or not an organization could ever be efficient. As a consequence of this effort, it is found that inconsistencies between employees' personal values and between personal values and the organization's mission always lead to organizational inefficiencies. Based on this realization and the underlying analyses, the principle of management efficiency and the principle of organizational inefficiency are introduced.

What remains unsettled here is that in practical situations, how can one actually become efficient in terms of management styles? And, how can organizational inefficiencies be improved?

References

Alvesson, M. (1989). Concepts of organizational culture and presumed links to efficiency. *Omega, 17*(4), 323–333.

Becker, G. (1974). A theory of social interactions. *Journal of Political Economy, 82*(6), 1063–1093.

Becker, G. (1991). *A treatise of the family*. Harvard University Press.

Bergstrom, T. (1989). A fresh look at the rotten kid theorem and other household mysteries. *Journal of Political Economy, 97*(5), 1138–1159.

Buchanan, J. (1975). The Samaritan's dilemma. In E. S. Phelps (Ed.), *Altruism, morality and economic theory* (pp. 71–85). Russell Sage Foundation.

Burton, R. M., Minton, J. W., & Obel, B. (1991). Organizational size and efficiency: An information processing view. *Scandinavian Journal of Management, 7*(2), 79–93.

Cummins, J. D., Weiss, M. A., & Zi, H. M. (1999). Organizational form and efficiency: The coexistence of stock and mutual property-liability insurers. *Management Science, 45*(9), 1254–1269.

Diener, E. (1984). Subjective well-being. *Psychological Bulletin, 95*, 542–575.

Diener, E. (2000). Subjective well-being: The science of happiness, and a proposal for a national index. *American Psychologist, 55*, 34–43.

Forrest, J. Y.-L., & Orvis, B. (2016). Principles of management efficiency and organizational inefficiency. *Kybernetes: The International Journal of Cybernetics, Systems and Management Sciences, 45*(8), 1308–1322.

Fultz, D., Long, R. R., Owens, G. V., Bohan, W., Kaylor, R., & Weil, J. (1959). *Studies of thermal convection in a rotating cylinder with some implications for large-scale atmospheric motion. Meteorological monographs* (Vol. 21). American Meteorological Society.

Hide, R. (1953). Some experiments on thermal convection in a rotating liquid. *Quarterly Journal of the Royal Meteorological Society, 79*, 161.

Hofstede, G. (1980). *Culture's consequences: International differences in work related values*. Sage.

Ismail, N., Alhabshi, D. S. O., & Bacha, O. (2011). Organizational form and efficiency: The coexistence of family takaful and life insurance in Malaysia. *Journal of Global Business and Economics (Global Research Agency), 3*(1), 122–137.

Jervis, R. (2006). Understanding beliefs. *Political Psychology, 27*(5), 641–663.

Kasianiuk, K. (2016). White box, black box and self-organization: A system-to-environment approach to leadership. *Kybernetes, 45*(1), 126–140.

Lagerlof, J. (2004). Efficiency-enhancing signalling in the Samaritan's dilemma. *The Economic Journal, 114*(492), 55–68.

Laura-Georgeta, T. (2011). Organizational management, efficiency, efficacy and competitiveness. *Ovidius University Annals, Economic Sciences Series, 11*(2), 1261–1264.

Leung, K., Au, A., Huang, X., Kurman, J., Niit, J., & Niit, K. (2007). Social axioms and values: A cross-cultural examination. *European Journal of Personality, 21*, 910–111.

Lin, Y. (1999). *General systems theory: A mathematical approach*. Plenum and Kluwer Academic.

Lin, Y. (2009). *Systemic yoyos: Some impacts of the second dimension*. Auerbach Publication, an imprint of Taylor and Francis.

Lin, Y., & Forrest, D. (2008). Economic yoyos and never-perfect value system. *Kybernetes: The International Journal of Systems and Cybernetics, 37*(1), 149–165.

Lin, Y., & Forrest, B. (2011). *Systemic structure behind human organizations: From civilizations to individuals*. Springer.

Lindbeck, A., & Weibull, J. (1988). Altruism and time consistency: The economics of fair accompli. *Journal of Political Economy, 96*, 1165–1182.

Meglino, B. M., & Ravlin, E. C. (1998). Individual values in organizations: Concepts, controversies, and research. *Journal of Management, 24*(3), 351–389.

Narasimhan, N., Bhaskar, K., & Prakhya, S. (2010). Existential beliefs and values. *Journal of Business Ethics, 96*, 369–382.

Pawłowski, M., Piątkowski, Z., & Żebrowski, W. (2012). Management efficiency. *Foundations of Management, 1*(1), 95–110.

Ren, J., & Xiong, Y. J. (2010). Measurement of enterprise management efficiency based upon information entropy and evidence theory. *International Journal of Applied Management Science, 2*(1), 93–106.

Rokeach, M. (1968). *Beliefs, attitudes, and values*. Jossey-Bass.

Ros, M., Schwartz, S. H., & Surkis, S. (1999). Basic individual values, work values, and the meaning of work. *Applied Psychology. An International Review, 48*(1), 49–71.

Ryff, C. D. (1989). Happiness is everything or is it? Explorations on the meaning of psychological well-being. *Journal of Personality and Social Psychology, 57*, 1069–1081.

Schein, E. H. (1985). *Organizational culture and leadership*. Jossey-Bass.

Schwartz, S. H. (1999). A theory of cultural values and some implications for work. *Applied Psychology. An International Review, 48*(1), 23–47.

Stanley, T., & Danko, W. (1996). *The millionaire next door: The surprising secrets of America's wealthy*. Simon and Schuster.

Stewart, T. J. (2010). Goal directed benchmarking for organizational efficiency. *Omega, 38*(6), 534–539.

Taylor, C. (1988). The moral topography of the self. In S. B. Messer, L. A. Saas, & R. A. Woolfolk (Eds.), *Hermeneutics and psychological theory: Interpretive perspectives on personality, psychotherapy and psychopathology* (pp. 288–320). Rutgers University Press.

Taylor, C. (1989). *Sources of the self: The making of the modern identity*. Harvard University Press.

Terán, O., Sibertin-Blanc, C., & Gaudou, B. (2015). The influence of moral sensitivity on organizational cooperation. *Kybernetes, 44*(6/7), 1067–1081.

Villalobos, J., & Vargas, M. (2015). Towards a simple dynamical model of citizens' perception. *Kybernetes, 44*(6/7), 1134–1145.

Index

J. Y.-L. Forrest, *Systemic Principles of Applied Economic Philosophies I*,
Translational Systems Sciences 38, https://doi.org/10.1007/978-981-99-7273-9

MIX
Papier aus verantwortungsvollen Quellen
Paper from responsible sources
FSC® C105338

If you have any concerns about our products,
you can contact us on
ProductSafety@springernature.com

In case Publisher is established outside the EU,
the EU authorized representative is:
Springer Nature Customer Service Center GmbH
Europaplatz 3, 69115 Heidelberg, Germany

Printed by Libri Plureos GmbH
in Hamburg, Germany